The Process of Economic Development
3rd Edition

KU-247-469

James M. Cypher and James L. Dietz

Routledge
Taylor & Francis Group

LONDON AND NEW YORK

First edition published 1997

Second edition published 2004

Third edition published 2009 by Routledge
2 Park Square, Milton Park, Abingdon, Oxon OX14 4RN

Simultaneously published in the USA and Canada
by Routledge
270 Madison Ave, New York, NY 10016

Routledge is an imprint of the Taylor & Francis Group, an informa business

© 1997, 2004, 2009 James M. Cypher and James L. Dietz

Typeset in Times New Roman by
Bookcraft Ltd, Stroud, Gloucestershire
Printed and bound in Great Britain by
The Cromwell Press, Trowbridge, Wiltshire

British Library Cataloguing in Publication Data
A catalogue record for this book is available from the British Library

Library of Congress Cataloging in Publication Data
Cypher, James M.
The process of economic development / James M. Cypher and
James L. Dietz. – 3rd ed.
    p. cm.
    Includes bibliographical references and index.
    1. Economic development. I. Dietz, James L., 1947– II. Title.
HD82.C96 2008
338.9–dc22   2007051285

ISBN13: 978-0-415-77103-0 (hbk)
ISBN13: 978-0-415-77104-7 (pbk)
ISBN13: 978-0-203-89506-1 (ebk)

ISBN10: 0-415-77103-X (hbk)
ISBN10: 0-415-77104-8 (pbk)
ISBN10: 0-203-89506-1 (ebk)

The Process of Economic Development

The third edition of *The Process of Economic Development* offers a thorough and up-to-date presentation of development economics. This landmark text will continue to be an invaluable resource for students, teachers and researchers in the fields of development economics and development studies.

Each subject area in this vast, inter-disciplinary field has been thoroughly re-analyzed in light of current published material in specialized journals, books, and United Nations, World Bank and International Monetary Fund publications. Much has happened in the developing world since the appearance of the second edition in 2002. The period has seen remarkable growth rates in countries such as China and India, the accession of a number of post-communist economies to the European Union, the financial crisis in Argentina and continuing desperate poverty in many African countries. This third edition reflects these developments and includes new material on the following:

- national systems of innovation, including information technology in India
- the ongoing impact of globalization
- the continuing programs of foreign aid across all developing countries.

Cypher and Dietz's text is the development economics text *par excellence*, as it takes a much more practical, hands-on approach to the issues facing developing countries than its overly mathematical rivals. It will appeal to all those studying this important subject area.

James M. Cypher is Research Professor, Doctoral Program in Development Studies, Universidad Autónoma de Zacatecas, Mexico.

James L. Dietz is Professor in the Department of Economics at California State University, Fullerton, USA.

Contents

3   Development in historical perspective   73

PART 2
Theories of development and underdevelopment   107

4   Classical and neoclassical theories   109

8 Endogenous growth theories and new strategies for development

9 The initial structural transformation: initiating the industrialization process

Figures

Tables

Focuses

Preface to the third edition

This third edition of *The Process of Economic Development* offers an up-to-date and comprehensive presentation of development economics. Each subject area in this vast, inter-disciplinary field has been thoroughly re-analyzed in light of current published material in specialized journals, books, and United Nations, World Bank and International Monetary Fund publications. Limitations of space have led us to condense material in many instances. All data presented are the most recent available. The revisions have been thorough, comprehensive, and painstaking, even as the basic format of the book has remained much the same.

The current state of economic development is distinct in many ways from that in which the initial chapters of the first edition of this book were written in 1993. Practitioners and observers in the field were then growing acclimatized to the so-called "Washington Consensus". Briefly put, this was the encapsulation of mainstream development thinking in the early 1990s. What poor nations needed, it was argued, was not more capital or technological capacity or infrastructure or land redistribution, all ideas that had played a prominent role in development economics since the inception of the field in the aftermath of the Second World War. Rather than resources, particularly physical capital, poor nations essentially needed better organization. Better organization was something of a code word that meant, primarily, shifting resources away from the state sector into areas assumed to be of much higher value in the private sector.

According to the Washington Consensus – a set of ideas held in common by the power triad in Washington D.C. composed of the International Monetary Fund, the World Bank, and the US Government, assisted by privately funded think tanks such as the American Enterprise Institute – developing nations should sell off their state-owned assets in mines, manufacturing plants, and most infrastructure. And they were urged to reduce all tariffs and quotas, and to minimize domestic content laws and restrictions on foreign ownership. In other words, the more *laissez-faire* the better. An unfettered market system was capable of taking less-developed nations from poverty to development. Too much government was the problem in too many economies.

Deregulation of prices and the elimination of subsidies would also help set developing nations on an upward path. In short, developing nations were told they would be better off if they dispensed with many of the policies that had been utilized in the past by the economies that are now considered to be developed. Of course, it was argued, developing nations, guided by market forces rather than ill-advised state direction, could benefit from some resource supplement in the form of foreign direct investment. Transnational corporations, the Washington Consensus argued, would bring not only needed capital, but also learning and technological capacity.

This perspective shaped new policies in many economies around the world beginning in the 1980s, especially in Latin America, but also in Eastern Europe and Asia. The result? Many developing nations experienced what came to be called a "lost decade," with economic growth rates sagging and, far too often, per capita income levels falling.

Not all economies suffered this fate, because not all economies followed the Washington Consensus recommendations. Some nations, at first concentrated in East Asia, but since spreading to other economies, took another path. Much of this book is designed around understanding how that "process" of economic development took place and how other economies might follow suit. Development does not take place in a vacuum. Both the state and the private sector have essential, and complementary, roles to play. They always have, and they always will.

We never accepted the Washington Consensus as a valid approach to development economics, even though there might have been elements of truth to parts of the analysis offered. Our original attempt to write a different development text beginning with the first edition was not based simply on dissent from the prevailing policy orthodoxy. Rather, we were more concerned about the great themes in development economics that were generally absent from or inadequately portrayed in the existing books on development economics.

There was insufficient material on several matters that we have addressed here as completely as space would permit, such as: (1) endogenous growth theory; (2) technology; (3) income distribution; (4) agriculture; (5) the colonial legacy and its (mis)shaping of institutions; (6) the underlying importance of heterodox economic ideas as expressed by Hans Singer, Raúl Prebisch, Gunnar Myrdal, and numerous others; (7) the often defining role played by the IMF, the World Bank, and aid programs in poor nations; (8) the role of multinational corporations; and (9) the centrality of fundamental structural change via properly orchestrated industrialization.

We also felt that, particularly beginning in the early 1990s, when a polemic arose over the interpretation of East Asia's rapid economic ascent, the at times divisive issue of "state versus market" needed to be recast. Too much ideology too often clouded the facts. The state needed to be brought back into the center of development economics as the facilitator of progress it has been in the past. The lessons of Asia's development needed clearer contrast to development policies attempted in Latin America from the 1930s through the 1970s. You will see that these themes appear frequently throughout the text.

Finally, we felt that many books on development economics failed to present a comprehensive, interlocking, understanding of the various issues, concepts, and theories that needed presentation. As a consequence, not only are all of the above topics given a chapter-length treatment in this book, they and other more standard topics are continually cross-referenced with the objective of providing a comprehensive view on development economics that is much greater than the sum of the parts of this book. This text is different, too, from many development books in which the chapters seem to be different "boxes" on distinct themes. We think there is an integrated "story" of how development takes place that is comprehensible and connected.

Nearly two decades after first beginning this project, it is an encouraging sign that: (1) the Washington Consensus is crumbling (sometimes disguised now, but far from gone); (2) it is widely accepted that the colonial legacy was crucial in terms of imposing lasting distortions on many nations; (3) endogenous growth theory has been given its due (if not more so); (4) agriculture is once again a major theme, including being the subject of the *World Development Report 2007*; (5) a renewed interest in Schumpeter has brought with it a focus on the crucial importance of technology and innovation; (6) employing a broader-based institutional analysis became increasingly acceptable in the late 1990s; (7) questions of income distribution and poverty have again more directly found their way into development economics; and (8) the international community has committed, at least on paper in the Millennium Development Goals, to dramatically reduce the debilitating poverty that still afflicts one-third of humanity.

More important for us, however, than seeing these themes we dealt with from the beginning become almost mainstream is the fact that the underlying conditions for developing nations have dramatically changed for the better. And change has come from a totally unexpected, but welcome, quarter, and that is from growing trade. From 2003 through 2007, according to the UN's data and projections in the *World Economic Situation and Prospect, 2007*, developing nations have enjoyed five years of rapid growth of output, as measured by gross domestic product (GDP). Less-developed economies have been growing, on average, at the rate of 6.2 percent per year. Nothing like this has been experienced since the 1970s.

Population growth rates also have been falling. This means that, on a per capita basis, income growth is all that much greater. This satisfying turn-around from the dismal 1980s and dragging 1990s has been due to a *global commodities boom*. Only a few countries have been left out: those that have historically specialized in the few primary commodities that are sinking, such as coffee, and those that have specialized in labor-intensive, low-technology manufactured goods for export.

When scanning the newspapers or watching the evening news or reading the headlines on Yahoo, it is common to find wrenching photographic evidence of poverty and despair, often in Africa. It is, therefore, worth noting that Africa is in the midst of an economic revival, the first good news on economic growth the continent as a whole has had in more than twenty years. From 2003 to 2007, the average rate of economic growth was 5.2 percent, and it was slightly higher, 5.5 percent, in Sub-Saharan Africa, where growth has been nil or negative for far too long.

The potential for lasting transformation in the developing world is present, even in regions that have commonly been thought to be desperate. Economic progress is not only possible, it is happening. More needs to be done, of course, much more in some places, but the direction of change since 2000 has been promising. Perhaps, just perhaps, the Millennium Development Goals discussed in Chapter 1 will be met by their target date of 2015. There is hope, and building on hope and moving forward is what this book is all about.

Acknowledgements

As is always the case, this book could not have been written without the help of many individuals. As is also the case, none should be held responsible in any way for the result.

To begin, we sincerely thank the reviewers of the first edition and the five anonymous reviewers who labored over the second edition and offered us detailed and well thought-out suggestions for further revision.

Next we thank our students. We have had the good fortune of teaching from this book at both the undergraduate and graduate levels to students of economics and to those of other fields in Mexico and the US. Nothing could be more immediate than the give-and-take of the classroom, along with the pleasant surprises and sometimes painful awareness that arises from reading exams. These activities with quite varied students have given us new insight into how we should best present the material in this book.

Many colleagues played a role in the years of research that have gone into the preparation of various editions of this book. We thank the following individuals: M. Shahid Alam, Paul Bowles, Paul Dale Bush, Jun Borras, Al Campbell, Juan Castaings Teillery, Ha-Joon Chang, Eugenia Correa, Willy Cortez, Raúl Delgado Wise, Enrique Dussel Peters, David Fairris, Sasan Fayazmanesh, Raúl Fernandez, Guillermo Foladori, Kevin Gallagher, Ross Gandy, Rodolfo Garcia Zamora, Alicia Gíron, Arturo Guillén, Martin Hart-Landsberg, Peter Ho, Barney Hope, Marc Humbert, Noela Invernizzi, Cristóbal Kay, Kathy Kopinak, Fred Lee, Yan Liang, Oscar Muñoz, Gerardo Otero, Robert Pollin, Skye Stephenson, Carolina Stefoni, Miguel Ángel Rivera, Cesar Ross, Howard Stein, Osvaldo Sunkel, Linda Shaffer, Janet Tanski, Marc Tool, Mayo Toruño, Henry Veltmeyer, Gregorio Vidal, and Eduardo Zepeda.

At Routledge we have experienced the best of all possible worlds. Editors Terry Clague and Robert Langham ably facilitated the second edition. Alan Jarvis, who first accepted our outline and provisional chapters for the original manuscript, along with Alison Kirk and Kate Stone, who edited the first edition, are not to be forgotten. For the third edition Robert Langham has pitched in at every turn, even editing several chapters with a careful eye and kind words. Sarah Hastings has shepherded the manuscript of the third edition through the intricate production process without a hitch. Unlike so many in the corporatized world of publishing, Routledge has given us wide latitude to present our ideas, while providing sensible editing and clear, crisp communication. What else could be asked?

For institutional support we thank the Doctoral Program in Development Studies at the Universidad Autónoma de Zacatecas, Mexico, and California State University, Fullerton. In addition special thanks are due to the Latin America Studies Program at Simon Fraser University for electronic access to that university's remarkable library.

Finally, we thank our families for their steadfast support and understanding over the years.

JMC
JLD

Part 1

An overview of economic development

1 The development imperative

No society can surely be flourishing and happy, of which the far greater part of the members are poor and miserable.

Adam Smith, *The Wealth of Nations*

Working for a World Free of Poverty

Heading on the World Bank website

After reading and studying this chapter, you should better understand:
- trends in poverty rates and some of its human and social costs;
- differences in income levels amongst regions;
- trends in economic growth in different regions;
- the extent of inequality in the distribution of income and in participation in economic and social life by the world's poor;
- the obstacles to development, both internal and external, that tend to thwart economic, social, and human development;
- the significance of fundamental structural change and of technological and institutional innovation to more rapid progress in the future.

Why study economic development?

On September 11, 2001, the Twin Towers of the World Trade Center in New York City collapsed after being struck by two commercial airliners commandeered by suicide terrorists. Another aircraft stuck the Pentagon in Washington, D.C., and a fourth crashed into an open field in Pennsylvania after the passengers overcame the hijackers, who may have had the White House, the home of the US President, as their target. All told, nearly 3,000 perished in the attacks. The world community responded to this aggression with outrage and support, both material and moral.

On December 26, 2004, the second-most powerful earthquake ever recorded struck in the Indian Ocean, setting off a series of tsunamis that struck coastal areas of Indonesia, Thailand, Sri Lanka, India, Somalia, and other countries on the east coast of Africa. Some 187,000 died from these devastating walls of water and rising tides, with another 43,000 listed as missing. Again, the world's nations and people reacted rapidly to this tragedy, seen over and over again on television and via the internet, with an outpouring of financial aid and direct assistance.

What do these two events have to do with economic development? Wasn't 9/11 a tragic political attack, while the tsunami was an unpredictable natural catastrophe? What does either have to do with economics and the subject of this book? The answer, in both cases, is: a lot.

Many of those killed by the tsunamis were the very poor who lived in low-lying areas prone to flooding from the yearly monsoons. They lived on marginal lands that should not have been occupied at all or, if they were to be occupied, should have been protected from the ravages of natural disasters that are common and expected occurrences. A tsunami of the size that stuck in 2004 is, thankfully, a very rare occurrence, but low-quality housing construction and the absence of man-made barriers to flooding contributed to the deadly outcome. With greater economic progress in the affected countries, human devastation from future natural disasters could be reduced dramatically.

What about the attack on the World Trade Center? Surely that cannot be linked to issues of economic development? Read what economist Jeffrey Sachs (2005: 215) has to say:

> terrorism has complex and varying causes. ... To fight terrorism, we will need to fight poverty and deprivation as well ... we need to address the underlying weaknesses of the societies in which terrorism lurks – extreme poverty; mass unmet needs for jobs, incomes, and dignity; and the political and economic instability that results from degrading human conditions.

So, economic development *is* about life-and-death issues. Literally. And consider this fact. As tragic and horrific as the 9/11 attack was, some 35,000 children under the age of five die *daily* in the less-developed world – the equivalent of more than ten 9/11s every single day, day after day, year after year! This adds up to more than 12 million children who perish every year from largely *preventable illnesses* (UNDP 2001: 9; World Bank 1993a: 1; WHO 1994). Let us repeat that: millions of young children die each year in the less-developed world from treatable illnesses, not natural disasters or political conflict that seem to attract the world's attention.

This works out to roughly 1,400 preventable deaths every hour of every day of every week and of every month of the year, children whose lives end before they really have an opportunity to begin. More than half of these deaths are due to respiratory illnesses or to diarrhoea and the severe dehydration that can ensue, though of course the children's weakened condition is exacerbated by malnutrition that results in a vicious circle of hunger and disease (see Focus 1.1 Saving lives: ORT).[1] These are sobering numbers and may be difficult to grasp as aggregate abstractions. Think of this: in the roughly ten seconds it has taken you to read this paragraph, five more children in the less-developed world will have died, and they will have perished unnecessarily.[2]

Adults also die in pointless numbers in the less-developed world: more than seven million each year from illnesses such as tuberculosis and malaria and other diseases that could be prevented or cured at a relatively small cost to society, illnesses that are almost unknown in most developed nations. Most of these deaths are rooted in extreme poverty and deprivation, including famine and sometimes civil war. They are human losses that, in our modern and affluent times, are not the result of any lack of human knowledge about how to prevent them.[3] The means to prevent this waste of human life is at hand; what is lacking seems to be the will.

If all this were not bad enough, since the 1980s the HIV/AIDS epidemic in many African countries has decimated and even reversed what limited progress there had been on the health and poverty fronts, with some nations, such as Botswana and Zimbabwe, especially hard hit. In confronting these and other problems, many of the barriers to progress in the less-developed countries seem to continue to be found in obstinate economic, political, and social structures that remain resistant to the changes that could make extreme poverty and

FOCUS 1.1   SAVING LIVES: ORT

Imagine yourself for a moment as a rural villager in a less-developed nation with a young child in your care who develops diarrhoea. How did this child become sick? Was it from drinking water fetched from a river? From a well? An irrigation ditch? What would you do to prevent the illness from becoming life threatening, regardless of the cause?

Here's the threat. Diarrhoea causes the body to throw off more water than can be reabsorbed. Death can result if more than 15 percent of the body's fluid is lost. What does this child need? What can you do to prevent dehydration and death? Clinics, phone calls, medicine, and a visit to a pharmacy are not options! You must come up with a home remedy. And fast! Think carefully about what you would do to save this child's life before reading on.

Did you decide to give the child water? That seems to make sense to replace the water being lost. If so, will that be sufficient to stop the diarrhoea and prevent the plunge into fatal dehydration?

It is important to remember that along with the loss of water due to the diarrhoea, sodium (salt) is also washed away. There is a fairly precise concentration of sodium in the human blood supply required for the body to function properly. With diarrhoea, this balance is upset as the kidneys, which normally regulate the salt level in the blood supply, are unable to maintain the proper balance. What the sick body needs is both sodium *and* more liquid, but the illness disturbs this delicate equilibrium and threatens survival. If you thought more liquid alone was the solution, you may have contributed to the death of the child under your care!

The necessary remedy is called "oral rehydration therapy" or ORT. Simply providing the sick child with water to drink – which may have been the immediate cause of the diarrhoea in the first instance – is not enough. Nor, interestingly, is water mixed with salt. Because of the diarrhoea, the body cannot absorb the salt properly, with the result that excess salt gets stored in the intestinal tract and causes more water to pass into the intestine, actually worsening the diarrhoea. However, a mixture of water, salt and sugar (glucose) *will* work, allowing the salt to be properly processed by the body and for water retention to be increased and the dehydration process halted.

A mixture of glucose (20 grams), sodium chloride (salt, 3.5 grams), sodium citrate (citric salt, 2.5 grams) and potassium chloride (1.5 grams) in one litre of clean water provides the ideal mixture for ORT. However, mixing salt and sugar in water in roughly the right proportions will also work fine. ORT must be initiated quickly, before the dehydration becomes too severe. If it is not, intravenous rehydration may be the only alternative.

Why do so many children die each year if the means to halt the dehydration is seemingly so simple? Lack of knowledge about what must be done, and that for children that action must be swift, is part of the problem. Simple hands-on exercises in primary school classes could help to spread the knowledge at a very low cost. Instead of abstract adding and subtraction in mathematics lessons, the measuring and combining of clean water, salt, and sugar in the recommended proportions could transmit information to millions of children who could then educate their families about how to respond when someone falls ill with diarrhoea.

Source: Foster 1992: 197–8

privation – and millions of deaths from poverty-related illnesses each year – the relics of history they deserve to be (World Bank 1993a: 116; 2000: 4–5).

Not all of the blame for this on-going tragedy of death and poverty can be placed on the affected countries. The developed nations have failed to carry through on their oft-professed promises and responsibilities to assist the poorest of the poor nations in escaping from the trap of deprivation in which so many millions continue to live. On this, we shall have more to say later in this chapter.

Poverty in the less-developed world

Table 1.1 provides an overview of the extent of poverty facing the less-developed nations. In 1985, one out of every three persons, some 1,116 million men, women, and children, were "extremely poor" by the World Bank's classification of having less than the equivalent of about $1 a day per person to meet their needs. By 2002, this number had fallen slightly to 1,015 million persons in poverty. Former World Bank president Robert McNamara called these people the "absolute poor," human beings who suffer "a condition of life so degraded by disease, illiteracy, malnutrition, and squalor as to deny its victims basic human

Table 1.1 Extent of world poverty and the poverty gap

Part I. 1985

Region	Extremely poor (%)	Poor (%)	Millions of poor	Poverty gap[a]
East Asia	9	20	280	1
China	8	20	210	3
Latin America and Caribbean	12	19	70	1
Middle East and North Africa	21	31	60	2
South Asia	29	51	520	10
India	33	55	420	12
Sub-Saharan Africa	30	47	180	11
All less-developed countries	18	33	1,116	3

Part II. 1981–2004 *Percentage of population living on less than $1 per day*

	1981	1984	1987	1990	1993	1996	1999	2004	Poverty gap (2004)
East Asia and Pacific	57.7	38.9	28.0	29.6	24.9	16.6	15.7	9.0	
China	63.8	41.0	28.5	33.0	28.4	17.4	17.8	12.5	2.1
Latin America and Caribbean	9.7	11.8	10.9	11.3	11.3	10.7	10.5	8.6	
Middle East and North Africa	5.1	3.8	3.2	2.3	1.6	2.0	2.6	1.5	
South Asia	51.5	46.8	45.0	41.3	40.1	36.6	32.2	30.8	
India									7.9
Sub-Saharan Africa	41.6	46.3	46.8	44.6	44.0	45.6	45.7	41.1	
Total	40.4	32.8	28.4	27.9	26.3	22.8	21.8	18.1	

Source: World Bank 1990: Table 2.1, p. 29; 2000: Table A.1, p. 13; data from World Bank website. The $1 a day (actually now $1.08) standard is based on a fixed, real 1993 price base, that is, it is adjusted for inflation.

Note
a   The "poverty gap" is the percentage by which the aggregate income of the poor falls short of the poverty line.

necessities. ... [It] is life at the very margin of physical existence." As McNamara suggested, the wretched condition of life of the absolute poor is almost beyond the power of understanding of those who live in developed countries (McNamara 1976: 5).

If the cut-off line for poverty is extended to $2 a day, some 2.6 billion individuals fell below that standard in 2002, just a bit less than half the world's population. This is a larger number of poor than in 1985 (World Bank data).

Part II of Table 1.1 shows the evolution of extreme poverty (< $1 a day) for all the less-developed regions. Overall, the incidence of extreme poverty by 2004 had fallen by more than half compared to 1981. That is good news. Of course, world population has grown too, so the number of persons in extreme poverty had declined by less than 50 percent, from 1.5 billion in 1981 to about 968 million in 2004.

What is disheartening is the relatively small decrease in poverty in some of the regions shown in Part II of Table 1.1, not to mention the increase in the incidence of poverty in Africa in the early 1990s. The decline in the share of the population in poverty in East Asia from 20 percent of the region's population in 1985 (Part I of Table 1.1) to 9.0 percent in 2004 (and even lower when China is excluded) is one of the success stories of the past two decades, one that will be highlighted throughout this text. Still, poverty levels remain agonizingly high, reducing opportunities for the poor and their children over the future in a vicious circle. Quoting the World Bank from more than a decade ago: "more than 1 billion people, one-fifth of the world's population, live on less than one dollar a day – a standard that Western Europe and the United States attained two hundred years ago" (World Bank 1991: 1). This is still true today. It is also important to recognize that the incidence of poverty is not gender-neutral, something the aggregate figures in the table obscure: "Poverty has a woman's face – of 1.3 billion people in poverty 70% are women [female]" (UNDP 1995: 4).

With the exception of the last column of both Part I and Part II, the numbers in Table 1.1 provide what is called a "headcount" of the numbers of poor falling below the poverty line. Such a measure does not distinguish between those whose incomes are far below the poverty line and who hence need more assistance to reach the poverty threshold and those whose incomes already have brought them closer to the income level needed to escape official poverty. The headcount measure of poverty simply counts all persons below some income level as poor. The headcount measure is thus not at all sensitive to the *severity* of the poverty situation of those counted as poor; it treats all poor as if they were somehow the same simply because all have income less than $1 or $2 per day.

The condition of being poor, however, is not the same for all those who are so classified. Imagine, for example, one country with half its population below the poverty line, but each is only 10 percent per day away from the poverty level of income. That is poverty of quite a different magnitude from another country which also has half its population below the poverty line, but each is 25 percent per day away from escaping poverty. The headcount measure of poverty, by simply adding up how many people fall below the poverty line, fails to capture this distinction and both countries will be counted as having 50 percent of their citizens in poverty by the headcount measure. Obviously, however, the *severity* of poverty in the first country is substantially less than in the second. There is another way to measure poverty that considers this issue.

The last columns of Table 1.1 provide this alternative perspective on measuring poverty. The concept of the "poverty gap" captures the severity of the poor's plight. It is the additional amount of consumption (or income) that must be generated by a country to bring all the poor above the poverty line. The poverty gap is measured as a percentage of a region's (or a country's) total current consumption (or it could be measured as a percentage of income) that must be created and received by the poor in the right amounts to bring each family's income above the poverty line. For some regions of the world and for some countries the poverty gap was as low as 1–2 percent of current consumption in 1985; in other regions, the poverty gap was as high as 10–12 percent of total consumption. Part II of Table 1.1 shows the poverty gap for China and India in 2004. More recent data is available on the poverty gap for individual economies, not regions, as the note to this paragraph shows, but it is not uniform by years and thus is not so easily displayed for comparison.[4]

For all the less-developed nations, an increase in income equivalent to about 3–4 percent of current consumption received in the right amounts by each family or individual in poverty would have been sufficient to shift all the poor above the World Bank's $2 per day poverty line in 1985. Though we do not have access to regional data in 2004, both China's and India's poverty gaps were smaller than they were in 1985. Thus it might be reasonable to assume that there has been some decrease in the *aggregate* poverty gap between 1985 and 2004, so that it perhaps is in the 2–3 percent range.

Obviously, to accomplish the long-term goal of a world without poverty, a simple transfer of income from better-off citizens to the poor is not the ultimate means or goal. Reducing poverty is not about transfers of income, except in the short run to alleviate the worst kinds of suffering. Rather, a *permanent reduction* in poverty requires a sufficient increase in production, jobs, and incomes for the now poor such that they are no longer poverty-stricken and remain non-poor through their own efforts, not handouts.

This objective of a permanent increase in income and output that reaches the poor in the magnitudes shown in Table 1.1 would not seem to be an overwhelmingly large technical barrier. For example, India could resolve to generate sufficient extra income and output in the economy over a generation to contribute to an increase in the income of the poor in the amount equal to 8 percent of total consumption. Over ten or fifteen or certainly twenty-five years, this does not seem to be a technically unattainable goal, amounting to an increase in total consumption on the order of less than 1 percent per year.

The possibility of fully eradicating poverty would seem to be within reach. It is not an impossible aspiration requiring super-human efforts beyond current resource capabilities. Greater productivity of labor and a better distribution of the world's productive resources, both human and physical, are what are needed to effect a long-term decrease in the poverty profile. It is a reasonable and humane objective for all the less-developed nations to target the elimination of absolute poverty from within their borders. It is a goal that the World Bank has embraced, with the target of cutting poverty in half by 2015 (World Bank 2000: 5–6; also see UNDP 2001: 22–5). Even for the poorest nations, the magnitude of the increase in output and income required to reduce poverty is within their grasp over a medium-range period of time with the right policies, the right decisions, and the requisite political will (see Focus 1.2).

The relatively modest size of the poverty gap compared to current incomes in the less-developed world strongly suggests that poverty is a problem of distribution, and not only of income, but especially of access to society's productive resources, particularly human capital-enhancing assets like education and other training. The existence of world poverty does not appear to be the consequence of a fundamental shortfall in aggregate productive capacity given the fairly small size of the poverty gap in most regions. Eradication of absolute poverty is a political–economic problem, not a technical matter. Ending absolute poverty is a challenge of political will and to existing political and economic power structures.

Poverty is not just measured by a shortfall in income, of course. Low incomes have real consequences. For example, of the approximately 4.6 billion people in the less-developed countries 968 million persons lacked access to "improved water sources"; 2.4 million were

FOCUS 1.2   THE MILLENNIUM DEVELOPMENT GOALS

On September 8, 2000, the United Nations General Assembly adopted the Millennium Declaration. The Millennium Development Goals (MDGs) emerged as a means to meet some of the aspirations of the Millennium Declaration. The Secretary-General of the UN issues an annual report on progress toward meeting these goals (see the World Bank website for more details: http://www.worldbank.org, "Topics"). Throughout this and following chapters, we will look at how specific MDGs are being met.

The MDGs comprise eight broad goals and fifteen more specific "target" policies to reach those goals. The success of reaching these targets is measured by fifty-three individual quantitative indicators.

The MDGs represent concrete objectives of the entire international community for reducing the ravages of poverty by 2015. Yes, 2015. The approval of these goals by all the members of the UN demonstrates the importance the international community, including the World Bank, places upon reducing poverty, improving health care, expanding educational opportunities, and promoting sustainability for hundreds of millions of poor people around the world. This unified effort of the world community recognizes that all economies are connected and that severe poverty affects us all, directly or indirectly.

Goal 1 Eradicate extreme poverty and hunger

Target 1: Halve, between 1990 and 2015, the proportion of people whose income is less than $1 a day

Target 2: Halve, between 1990 and 2015, the proportion of people who suffer from hunger

Goal 2 Achieve universal primary education

Target 3: Ensure that, by 2015, children everywhere, boys and girls alike, will be able to complete a full course of primary schooling

Goal 3 Promote gender equality and empower women

Target 4: Eliminate gender disparity in primary and secondary education preferably by 2005 and in all levels of education no later than 2015

Goal 4 Reduce child mortality

Target 5: Reduce by two-thirds, between 1990 and 2015, the under-five mortality rate

Goal 5 Improve maternal health

Target 6: Reduce by three-quarters, between 1990 and 2015, the maternal mortality ratio

Goal 6 Combat HIV/AIDS, malaria, and other diseases

Target 7: Have halted by 2015 and begun to reverse the spread of HIV/AIDS

Target 8: Have halted by 2015 and begun to reverse the incidence of malaria and other major diseases

Goal 7 Ensure environmental sustainability

Target 9: Integrate the principles of sustainable development into country policies and programs and reverse the loss of environmental resources

Target 10: Halve, by 2015, the proportion of people without sustainable access to safe drinking water and basic sanitation

Target 11: Have achieved, by 2020, a significant improvement in the lives of at least 100 million slum dwellers

Continued

Goal 8 Develop a global partnership for development

Target 12: Develop further an open, rule-based, predictable, non-discriminatory trading and financial system (includes a commitment to good governance, development, and poverty reduction – both nationally and internationally)

Target 13: Address the special needs of the least developed countries (includes tariff- and quota-free access for exports, enhanced program of debt relief for HIPCs and cancellation of official bilateral debt, and more generous ODA for countries committed to poverty reduction)

Target 14: Address the special needs of landlocked countries and small island developing states

Target 15: Deal comprehensively with the debt problems of developing countries through national and international measures in order to make debt sustainable in the long term

Target 16: In cooperation with developing countries, develop and implement strategies for decent and productive work for youth

Target 17: In cooperation with pharmaceutical companies, provide access to affordable essential drugs in developing countries

Target 18: In cooperation with the private sector, make available the benefits of new technologies, especially information and communications

---

FOCUS 1.3   MDG GOAL 1: ERADICATE EXTREME POVERTY AND HUNGER

Meeting MDG Targets 1 and 2 would reduce by half the share of the population with incomes of less than $1 per day and of those suffering from hunger. A glance back at Table 1.1 shows that there has been substantial progress toward achieving Target 1. In 1990, 27.9 percent of the less-developed world's population received less than $1 per day; by 2004, the proportion of the population in the LDCs with incomes below the $1 per day standard had dropped to 18.1 percent. This represents substantial progress in the incidence of extreme poverty, though more obviously remains to be done if the 50 percent reduction by 2015 is to be reached.

One region (East Asia and the Pacific) has already met MDG Target 1; China's progress in reducing poverty in that region has been extraordinary. The Middle East and North Africa are close to meeting Target 1. There was an increase in the incidence of poverty after 1990 in Europe and Central Asia, primarily due to the collapse of the former Soviet bloc; the trend now seems to be downward. Progress in South Asia (with India and its large population) has been below average, with the share of the population receiving less than $1 a day falling by less than 25 percent. Clearly, to reach the goal of a 50 percent reduction, progress needs to be more rapid in this region.

Sub-Saharan Africa, unfortunately, has seen almost no movement toward reducing extreme poverty. If the MDG goals are going to be reached in any meaningful way, the international community needs to find ways to kick-start development in Sub-Saharan Africa. In future chapters we shall see that it is this region where progress toward development has been the weakest, with tragic consequences.

In 2002, despite the more than 30 percent decline in the incidence of overall poverty since the MDGs were announced, 1,015 million persons still fell below the $1 per day poverty line, compared to 1,218 million in 1990, a decrease in the *absolute* number of poor of only 16.7 percent. The number of extremely poor in Sub-Saharan Africa actually increased by more than a third (from 227 million to 303 million) because of the lack of progress in reducing the incidence of poverty.

without proper sanitation; 854 million adults were illiterate (64 percent of whom were women); 34 million were infected with HIV/AIDS, the great majority of these in Africa; and 2.2 million persons were dying annually from indoor air pollution from, particularly, exposure to toxic fumes from wood-burning cooking (the data is for the late 1990s and 2000; UNDP 2001: 9, 13).

The good news, despite these sobering statistics on poverty, is that there have been undeniable improvements in living standards in the less-developed world since 1970. Life expectancy at birth rose absolutely and relatively compared to the developed world, from forty-six years in 1960, when it was equal to 67 percent of life expectancy in the developed nations, to sixty-five years in 2005, which is equal to 82 percent of the level achieved in the developed countries. Infant mortality between birth and age one fell from 149 per 1,000 live births in 1960 to 56 in 2005. Adult literacy rose from 46 percent to nearly 80 percent over the same period to 2005, though in the least-developed nations 70 percent of all adults and only half

FOCUS 1.4 PROGRESS AND REGRESS, WINNERS AND LOSERS

We have relied above on some statistical data to get a "snap-shot" of the situation of poverty in the less-developed world. It is important and instructive to collect and try to understand some of this data yourself.

To get you started in that direction, and if you have access to the internet, go to the website of the World Bank, http://www.worldbank.org (alternatively, look for a recent issue of the World Bank's *World Development Report*, which will have similar data, though what is now available is substantially less in the print edition than was available in the past). Click on "Data & Research" in the "Key Statistics" column and then "Data by Country". You are going to use the "Country Profiles" drop-down menu in the middle of that page to find the following information.

Find data for Brazil, China, Costa Rica, Kenya, Korea (Rep.), Mexico, Pakistan, Sri Lanka, and Zimbabwe for the following social and economic variables for the most recent year available: mortality rate, infant; malnutrition prevalence; life expectancy at birth; improved water source; school enrolment, primary; and the population growth rate.

What "picture" does this data give you about each of these countries? What general conclusions can you draw about these countries just using this data as your source of information? Which country do you think is "best off"? Which is "worst off"? Rank these countries from best to worst using these indicators alone as your guide. You will have to decide which indicators are more important to your ranking and which are less important.

Now, record the income per person (GNI per capita) for each of the countries from the same tables. Rank the countries again from best to worst using only the GNI per capita data. Is this ranking of countries substantially different from the first ranking you did using the social and economic variables? If there is a difference in your ranking of countries, what is the significance of that?

What about poverty levels in these countries? Does the country you rank first have the lowest level of poverty? Does the country you rank last have the highest rate of poverty? Let's see.

Go back to the main World Bank website link above. Click again on "Data & Research." In the "Key Statistics" column, choose "Data by Topic" from the drop-down menu. Choose the "Poverty" link and then record the data for each of the above countries for "poverty gap at $1 a day" and the "poverty headcount ratio." Does the incidence of poverty in the countries match what you thought it would be, given your previous rankings of the countries? Did the "poorest" country have the highest incidence of poverty? The "richest" have the lowest incidence of poverty? If there are discrepancies, can you explain them?

of adult females could be classified as literate (see Focus 1.4 Progress and Regress, Winners and Losers).

Except for the last figures, all of the above are average values. In general, women do not fare as well as men on these social indicators. Rural areas suffer relative to urban areas, and ethnic groups and different social classes often have widely diverging outcomes as well. One can find nations that have made, at best, only modest progress on the path toward fuller economic and social development. But there are reasons to be hopeful in many nations.

There remains much to be done to bring as many persons as possible out of poverty and the deprivation it produces and that is one reason why understanding how economic development takes place is so important.

The development enigma

It was the disturbing reality of world poverty, of a sharp division between rich nations and poor nations and within nations, and of so much human suffering in far too many countries that first brought us, in the late 1960s and early 1970s, to be keenly interested in development economics and the problems of what was then called the "Third World."[5] Why, we asked ourselves, when crossing the international border between the United States and Mexico from San Diego to Tijuana, did we witness such a dramatic and obvious change in incomes, living standards, and levels of human development? After all, the boundary between these two nations is an artificial political division. The geography on one side of the frontier is much like that on the other; in fact, until the mid-1800s, these lands still were all part of one nation, Mexico.

Why, then, does one enter after only a few steps or a short drive across the boundary into Mexico, not only a different world culturally and linguistically, but also one so unquestionably poorer and with fewer possibilities for individuals to realize their full potential when compared to the United States?

Other similar enigmas come easily to mind. Why is so much of Africa substantially less developed and poorer than Latin America (see Table 1.2 below), though both regions

Table 1.2 Average income per capita and growth rates of per capita output

	Income per capita[a]				*Annual % change in real output*[b]		
	1970	*1980*	*2000*	*2005*	*1980–1990*	*1990–2000*	*2000–2005*
Less-developed economies	222	702	1,155	1,742	1.03	2.14	3.89
East Asia and Pacific	122	294	907	1,628	5.38	7.08	7.32
Latin America and Caribbean	579	2,053	3,770	4,157	−0.87	1.62	1.13
Middle East and North Africa	256	1,266	1,662	2,223	−0.05	1.76	2.07
South Asia	117	264	444	693	3.37	3.21	4.71
Sub-Saharan Africa	207	662	485	743	−1.04	−0.34	2.05
Developed economies	2,918	10,456	26,305	34,962	2.62	1.87	1.40

Source: World Bank, *World Development Indicators Online.*

Notes
a   Gross National Income (GNI) per capita, in US dollars
b   Of per capita Gross Domestic Product (GDP) in 2000 dollars

are considered part of the less-developed world? What accounts for the recent economic success of some East Asian countries, like South Korea and Taiwan, or, taking a slightly longer time span, of Japan, such that they seem to have passed over the threshold from underdevelopment to development? Why does India, with its large number of highly educated citizens and its immense potential market, remain one of the most impoverished nations, while other countries – again, South Korea is an illustration – with a skilled and educated labor force have been able to make the transition toward higher and more equitable levels of economic development? How has China, the most populated nation on earth, been able to make such remarkable progress that it went from being poorer than India to having nearly three times the income per person?

These are the sorts of incongruities and conundrums – and the list could be extended quite easily – that both vex and excite those interested in the problems of economic development. Trying to formulate reasonable explanations for such observed disparities, and, by extension, suggesting what might be done to overcome the barriers that retard economic, social, and human development is what development economics is all about.

It is on this adventure into theory and reality that we are about to embark. There are no easy answers that apply always and everywhere. There is no magic, one-stop, cure-all solution that can be offered that applies to every country in all parts of the world. Becoming more developed is a challenge that requires vision and hard work from both the leaders of nations and their citizens. Nonetheless, there are patterns and lessons to be learned from successful as well as unsuccessful development experiences that can help those with the power and the will to move their economies and nations forward.

It is to these patterns and regularities based upon the concrete historical experiences of successful and failed development episodes that we shall turn repeatedly. We are looking for the critical signposts that mark the "process" of development, such that it will be possible to determine what, broadly speaking, needs to be done and what should be avoided if progress is to be made.

Many abstract theories about how to develop have been advanced by economists, and some of these will be considered in later chapters. Such theories are an integral part of development economics and provide an important historical window on how economists have thought and continue to think about development.

Also of importance for less-developed nations are the concrete, positive, historical experiences of successful developers. We shall be looking to the lessons that can be gleaned from the rapid growth of Japan, South Korea, Taiwan, and Hong Kong, as well as other nations of that region that the World Bank calls the "High-Performing Asian Economies" (HPAEs).[6] China's amazing rates of growth over more than two decades provide lessons too, though in many ways what is happening there affirms what others have done before them. The analysis and recommendations for action in subsequent chapters often are based upon the lessons of the HPAEs and the now-developed nations, as well as contrasts with less productive cases of transformation, such as the Latin American economies, where the growth process slowed dramatically after initial successes.

Underlying our interest in development there exists a definite moral dimension. For us, development is about realizing very fundamental human values and finding the means to extend the fruits of these values to the greatest majority of the world's population. These human values include, but are not limited to:

- the opportunity for meaningful employment and the possibility to provide for one's self and family;

- sufficient food, shelter, and other amenities for a decent and meaningful life above the poverty line;
- the opportunity to pursue education and the increased quality of life it promises;
- a reasonable level of health care;
- social security for old age;
- democracy and political participation in the life of the community and society;
- equal treatment under the law and in the economy, regardless of race, gender, class, ethnicity, religion, nationality, or other differences; and
- respect for individual dignity.

This listing of development goals is not meant to be all-inclusive. It is intended simply to touch upon at least some of the primary ingredients toward which development, and not just economic development, is directed. We will have more to say on this in the following chapter.

For us, and we hope for you too, economic development is of the utmost interest and of the gravest consequence. It touches our shared humanity. The great economists of the eighteenth, nineteenth, and early twentieth centuries – Adam Smith, David Ricardo, John Stuart Mill, Karl Marx, Alfred Marshall – were inspired by a profound concern for understanding the roots of economic wealth and the reasons for poverty, as well as for discovering the mechanisms through which economic and social gains might best be increased and shared amongst the members of society. These matters have captured the attention and hearts as well as the minds of many brilliant thinkers. They are noble questions that often lead students to wish to study economics in the first instance.

This book is an inquiry into what those in the less-developed nations must do if they are to improve their economic and social lot. As well, there is reflection on how the developed world, including concerned citizens of those countries, might understand their role and responsibilities in our increasingly interdependent world of rich and poor. The MDGs are an important recognition of the global obligation of all nations to end extreme poverty, wherever it is found. Everyone's economic interests are joined in a global economic system, sometimes positively, other times negatively, no matter how remotely connected we at times may seem to be. It is one world, albeit unequal, but our destinies are increasingly intertwined via markets, communication networks, the environment, and politics. Achieving the MDGs and making progress toward fundamental structural reforms of the sorts discussed throughout this book is a win–win outcome for all nations.

Recent trends in economic growth

The 1980s and early 1990s were not particularly propitious for either economic growth or development (the differences between the "growth" and "development" are spelled out in greater detail in Chapter 2). Even the developed world suffered a slowdown in its rate of economic expansion from the 3 percent per person growth rates of the 1960s and 1970s to the slower growth of GDP per person shown in Table 1.2. Some developed countries experienced a sharp decline in living standards after years of prosperity following the Second World War. Unemployment rose in the European Union (EU) to levels that proved difficult to reduce.

The greatest number of jobs being created in the developed nations were concentrated heavily in segments of relatively lower-paying, lower-productivity service sectors that offered meagre benefits and other perquisites – from sick leave to health care to retirement packages – that had become integral to the rising living standards of the developed economies after the Great Depression of the 1930s.

In the United States, real wages have decreased for a broad spectrum of the workforce since 1973. Family incomes barely have edged upward, and when they did it was due primarily to the fact that more family members, particularly women, entered the labor force in record numbers in an effort to maintain a family standard of living. For increasing numbers who do find work, it is often irregular and part-time, as permanent workforces were replaced by *contingent workers* with fewer rights, lower incomes, and futures that have become ever more precarious. So even the already-developed economies can experience problems of long-term progress during some periods, and these problems are often more complex today given the impact of global competition amongst nations and firms.[7]

The less-developed world, on average, fared even worse than the developed economies during the 1980s. However, average growth rates of output for the less-developed economies have exceeded those of the developed world since 1990. But, as can be seen from Table 1.2, much of this success is due to rapid growth of production in South Asia and in East Asia and the Pacific. Not all regions have done as well as the average might suggest.

Table 1.2 provides summary data on the levels of income since 1970 and growth rates of output per person since 1980 in different regions. Although, as we shall learn in Chapter 2, output and income growth are not the whole of what development is about, these numbers, along with the data on poverty in Table 1.1 above, do shed some initial light on the wide disparities in living standards which continue to plague many regions and peoples of the world.

South Asia ranks as the poorest region by income per person in the world, but if the trends shown in the table continue that will soon change.[8] Annual income per capita in South Asia in 2005 averaged less than 2 percent of what was received in the developed world. Comparing regions within the less-developed world, South Asia received 42.6 percent of the average income received in East Asia and the Pacific and just 16.7 percent of what was received in Latin America and the Caribbean, the region in the less-developed world with the highest income per person.

Sub-Saharan Africa fared only slightly better than South Asia; it is the second-poorest region in the world.[9] Income per person was actually lower in 2000 than in 1980, and the growth rate of real output per capita over the same period was nil.

Among the less-developed regions of the world, the Middle East and North Africa and Latin America and the Caribbean are, on average, relatively better-off. Still, compared to the developed world, their average incomes were, respectively, only 6.4 percent and 11.9 percent of what was received in the developed economies in 2005.

Clearly there remains a substantial gap in average incomes between the less-developed and the developed worlds, a gap that has widened on average from 1970, when income in the less-developed world was 7.6 percent of that in the developed, to 2000, when average income in the less-developed economies had fallen to but 4.4 percent of the average in developed economies. By 2005, there had been a change in direction, but average income in the less-developed economies in 2005 as a share of that in the developed world was still below what it had been in 1970.

Of course, as can be confirmed from the data in Table 1.2, East Asia's average income gap compared to the developed economies has shrunk over time, but even there, much remains to be done in terms of absolute income levels.

Low- and middle-income less-developed nations

In our study of economic development, we shall be mostly concerned with the so-called low- and middle-income economies. By the World Bank's categorization, 149 economies fell into these two groupings in 2007 out of a total of 209 nations and territories. Of these, fifty-three nations were included in the World Bank's "low-income" subgroup, eleven fewer than in 1999; another fifty-five fell into the "lower-middle" income range, the same number as had been in this grouping in 1999.

Incomes ranged from the poorest nation in the world, Burundi, with a meagre $100 per capita yearly income in 2006, to Argentina, with $5,150 per person, to $17,690 for South Korea (which has "graduated" from its former "upper-middle-income" status in the less-developed world to now being including among the "high income" economies of the developed world). The world's two most populous economies, India ($820 per capita income) and China ($2,010) now share different fates. India remains in 2006 classified among the low-income economies, while China, as a result of two decades of unprecedented economic expansion, has been "promoted" to "lower-middle-income" status among the less-developed economies.

The average annual income of the low-income subgrouping of the less-developed nations in 2005 was $584 per person. For the middle-income less-developed economies, the average income was $2,636, with the "upper-middle-income" group averaging $5,053 (more complete data for other nations and analysis of the meaning of these data are presented in the next chapter).

The last columns of Table 1.2 show what was happening to the growth of real, inflation-adjusted output (= income) per person since the 1980s. For all regions except East Asia and the Pacific and South Asia, income per person declined over the 1980s, as output contracted or as output growth relative to population growth was inadequate to prevent declines in income per person. For these regions, the income gap with the high-income nations, which experienced positive economic growth, widened in both absolute and relative terms over that decade.[10]

Over the 1990s, all the regions of the less-developed world returned to positive per capita income growth rates, with the exception of Sub-Saharan Africa, which suffered two consecutive decades of declining income per person. Since 2000, growth rates have improved everywhere except in Latin America; what is critical is to keep this momentum of positive growth rates going, as it must, if the MDGs have any hope of being reached.

While Table 1.2 highlights the enormous divergence in incomes separating the less-developed nations from the developed, and among the less-developed regions of the world themselves, even that data fails to fully convey the magnitude of this disparity. Table 1.3 provides a more global and yet extraordinarily dramatic portrayal of the distance that continues to separate the developed "have" nations from the less-developed "have-not" economies.

The less-developed world, with more than four-fifths of the world's population, received slightly more than one-fifth of total world income in 2005. In a cruel symmetry, the developed world nations, with well less than one-fifth of the world's population, received nearly four-fifths of total world income in 2005, precisely the same share as in 1985, though with a smaller proportion of total world population in 2005. Looked at slightly differently, the developed world received about five times its "equality share" of total world income (78.1 percent of world income divided by 15.9 percent of world population).[11] The less-developed world received 26 percent of what its equality share of world income would have been.

Or consider this fact: in the mid-1990s, the richest 1 percent of the world's population received as much total income as the poorest 57 percent of the world's population (UNDP 2001: 19).

Examining particular regions within the less-developed world, inequality was even more extreme and income more meagre. South Asia, with nearly 23 percent of total world population, received but slightly more than 2 percent of world income in 2005. This meant that

Table 1.3 World income, world population, and their distribution, 2001

	Share of world's income (%)			Share of world's population (%)		
	1985	*1995*	*2005*	*1985*	*1995*	*2005*
Less-developed economies	22.0	17.5	22.0	81.7	83.2	84.1
East Asia and Pacific	4.1	4.4	6.8	30.5	30.2	29.2
Latin America and Caribbean	5.8	5.8	5.5	8.2	8.4	8.5
Middle East and North Africa	2.5	1.2	1.6	4.1	4.5	4.7
South Asia	2.4	1.6	2.3	20.8	21.8	22.8
Sub-Saharan Africa	1.6	1.0	1.3	9.3	10.4	11.7
Developed economies	78.1	82.5	78.1	18.3	16.8	15.9

Source: World Bank, *World Development Indicators Online.*

Note
Missing data for the Europe and Central Asia mean that subtotals do not add to totals for the less-developed economies. The income shares are computed as a percentage of total world Gross Domestic Income.

South Asia received only 10.1 percent of its equality share of income (2.3 percent of total income/22.8 percent of total population).

The relatively better-off Latin America and the Caribbean region, by comparison, received about 65 percent of what its hypothetical equality share of world income would have provided in 2005 (5.5 percent of total income/8.5 percent of total population). From 1985 to 1995, Sub-Saharan Africa's share of total world income fell slightly, even as its share of the world's population rose, which is why average income fell in the region over that period. Since 1995, Sub-Saharan Africa's share of world income has recovered slightly, but the region's share of total world population has grown. As a consequence, Sub-Saharan Africa's average income declined from 17.2 percent of its equality share in 1985 to slightly more than 11 percent in 2005.

East Asia and the Pacific increased its share of total world income since 1985. At the same time, the region's share of total population declined. This meant rising average income levels.

The disparities between the less-developed nations *vis-à-vis* the developed nations shown in Tables 1.2 and 1.3 are not of recent origin. Worse, differences *within* the less-developed world itself have been growing, both between regions and within countries themselves. Many of the poorest countries have suffered a relative decline, and in some instances, an absolute deterioration in their position on many significant measures of productivity and in their contribution to world output.

Between 1960 and 1990, for example, the share of total world output received by the poorest 20 percent of the world's population fell from 2.3 percent to 1.3 percent. Their share of world trade decreased from 1.3 percent to 0.9 percent, and their contribution to global domestic investment fell from 3.5 percent to 1.1 percent (UNDP 1993: 27, Table 2.1). The contributions of the poorest to production, to trade, and their share of world income declined relative to those of other groups in society, including better-off nations within the less-developed world.

It is a cliché, perhaps, to say that "the rich get rich and the poor get poorer." But in the 1980s and 1990s, cliché or not, that is what took place in some regions of the world, particularly in South Asia and Sub-Saharan Africa. Since 1995 or so, some improvement in incomes can be noted from the tables. But not enough.

Nonetheless, there are gains that have been made in the less-developed world *despite* a sometimes weak and uneven record of economic growth and production since the 1980s that provide reason for continued hope that positive and reasonably equitable progress remains possible if societies make the right choices. Advances in the human condition continue to be made, often in the direst circumstances. Continued progress toward the amelioration of poverty and further improvements in the standard of living of a greater part of the world's population must be one of the highest goals, and the Millennium Development Goals are a constant reminder of what remains to be done.

Why development, and why now?

Nations like Great Britain, the United States, Germany, Japan, Australia, France, and the Scandinavian countries that today can be considered developed did not attain that status over-night.[12] In fact, development in all its economic, political, and social dimensions took place quite slowly and proceeded unevenly over a very long period of time, centuries in fact.

The great majority of the countries now considered to be less developed have had significantly less time to become developed, at least as independent political entities. It is important to recall how many of the nations of Africa, Asia, and the Caribbean achieved political independence only since the end of the Second World War in 1945, when the drive to de-colonize as a result of pressure from the newly created United Nations began in earnest. Since then, well over 120 newly independent countries have been established from the former colonial empires and later the collapse of the former Soviet bloc. It is in these new nations that the problematic of becoming developed and of making progress toward authentic human well-being and of achieving the MDGs is most pressing.

It is essential to keep this time dimension in mind, without finding in it an ultimate excuse for slow progress in some economies. Most of the less-developed nations have had, at best, only a few decades to work on the fundamental twin goals of post-colonial construction: nation-building and progress on the path toward higher levels of economic and social development. One can argue that it takes time to undo the ingrained patterns of production, social class, and power inherited from the past. What we will call adverse *path dependence* in Chapter 3 often weighs heavily on the present in many poor nations.

On the other hand, the means to realize development goals are closer to hand than at any time in history.[13] The range of available and potentially applicable knowledge would seem to make the diffusion of technological progress, of advances in medicine, of techniques of efficient business and government administration, and so on easier to attain for today's less-developed nations than it was for earlier developers who had to painstakingly create that knowledge. If only this vast array of knowledge could be effectively transferred, harnessed, and applied in the less-developed nations, the current state of poverty in most parts of the world could be overcome.

It is thus necessary to try to balance the short time-frame that most countries have had in which to try to become more developed with the fact that the "know-how" for achieving development is available now as never before. Does that then mean that the less-developed nations are on the brink of becoming developed? Not necessarily. Whether the knowledge about *how* to increase economic growth and about *how* to become more developed can be applied in ways that succeed in taking the less-developed nations across the threshold to developed-world status depends upon how stubborn the barriers to development continue to be in each of those nations. Possibility still needs to be transformed into actuality, and the means to effect that transformation is central to the subject matter of development economics.

Economic growth and development require structural change

Economics is often defined as the study of "how societies can best allocate scarce resources among alternative uses" so as to maximize something – usually the level of each individual's or household's satisfaction or utility – the presumption being that maximizing individual satisfaction also will maximize society's total well-being simultaneously. The allocation of society's resources is assumed to take place within a *given* institutional and organizational setting that is taken to be exogenous to the analysis done by the economist.

This operating framework of orthodox, or neoclassical, economics in which the allocation of existing resources occurs within a given and presumably immutable or slowly changing social and institutional structure has been the key to the robust analysis and the predictive capability of modern economic models. These are the theories studied in most introductory and intermediate economic theory courses. The presumption of *given* institutions and of *marginal* adjustments by economic agents to their environment is at the heart of neoclassical economics as taught around the world. So basic are these underlying presumptions of marginalism and nearly fixed institutions that the great English economist Alfred Marshall was able to write on the title page of his *Principles of Economics*, first published in 1890, "*Natura non facit saltum*": nature makes no leaps.

The real-world process of a country becoming more developed, of getting on the path to development, and shedding the ways of the past that resulted in low growth rates and limited progress, is not, however, simply about the efficient allocation of existing resources within a given institutional regime. It is not simply about maximizing utility or profits within the constraints of what is currently available to that society and inherited from the past. Rather, development is fundamentally about *regime change* and about the search for an optimal growth path, or at least one that is superior to the existing allocation of resources and current efficiency levels. Further, fomenting development typically requires substantially new institutional patterns and organizational structures necessary to support such a dynamic process of change.

To get a country on the road to development very often requires a "leap" – often a quite substantial one – away from the past structures. Marginal modifications of the economy and society simply may be insufficient to initiate the forward momentum needed to propel the system in the requisite new direction and on to a higher path of progress for the future. For the less-developed nations, development compels them to undertake substantial *qualitative* structural change. The future cannot be just an extension of the past, of doing more of what is now being done. Change must be dramatic. The past and its weight on the present are precisely what have made these nations poor and are what need to be transcended.

There are a number of major *structural changes* and patterns identified by development economists and economic historians that are believed to be characteristic of any successful development process. We shall be examining these in detail in later chapters. In fact, much of this book is about the importance of these structural changes and what can be done to foment change in the desired direction. Here these structural changes are briefly introduced to suggest the nature of *qualitative* change required and to point out the direction we shall be taking in the chapters that follow.

1   **Increase in industrialization.** Economic growth and development are strongly associated with an increasing share of a nation's output and labor force involved in industrial, especially manufacturing, activities, at least initially, as we will see in Chapter 9. Over time, services become increasingly important too as an economy matures even further.

Wages tend to be higher in the industrial sector than in agriculture, because the level and use of technology is greater. This leads to both higher levels of production and worker productivity, and the resulting higher income that is created is shared by workers and owners of enterprises. Production methods also become relatively intensive in the use of knowledge – human capital – and of physical capital. As part of this unfolding process, the urban population tends to grow both relatively and absolutely compared to the rural population, as rural workers migrate to the cities in search of the higher income promised by urban and industrial pursuits.

2   **A decrease in agriculture.** Parallel to the expansion of the industrial sector of the economy is a decline in the share of agricultural output in total output. This also means a reduction in the share of the total labor force employed in agriculture and a decrease in the share of the rural population within the total population.

The increase in industrialization and the decrease in agriculture are intimately related. "Surplus labor" (i.e. low-productivity labor) in agriculture migrates to urban areas in search of the promise of better-paid and higher productivity industrial employment. It is this shift of workers from low-productivity agricultural employment to higher-productivity industrial employment that contributes to a sharp increase in total national output when this process of internal labor migration is initiated. Technological progress and labor productivity is typically lower in the primary (agriculture, mining, and fishing) sector, but over time, output per person approaches the level reached in the industrial, or secondary, sector as the fewer workers in agriculture produce more output per worker.

One leading development expert has written that "economic development is a process of moving from a set of assets based on primary products, exploited by unskilled labor, to a set of assets based on knowledge, exploited by skilled labor" (Amsden 2001: 2). This description captures the nature of these first two fundamental structural changes required for long-term development progress.

3   **Changing trade patterns.** Successful development is almost always marked by a maturation in the structure of trade, as a limited range of primary exports – agriculture and fishing products, unprocessed mining and other extractive minerals, and forestry products – is replaced by both a greater diversity of export products and by an evolving export mix toward manufactured goods and services.

Successful developers shift from a dependence on the traditional, primary export products that marked their colonial past toward, first, simpler manufactured and non-traditional primary exports, and ultimately toward more complex commodity exports, from motor cars to computers to biotechnology products to information technology and other types of high value-added production.

As a result of this evolutionary transformation, manufacturing exports typically come to dominate the export profile of more developed nations as the share of primary exports in total exports shrinks within the export profile.

4   **Increased application of human capital and knowledge to production.** Economic growth and development require increases in the productivity of labor in all sectors of the economy if incomes and the standard of living of the population are to rise. This is achieved partly, but quite importantly, through improvements in the training and education of the existing and future labor force by means of increases in what economists call *human capital accumulation*. This takes place not only through the formal schooling process but also via "learning-by-doing" at the workplace.

Increased productivity of labor is also a consequence of an expansion in the use of more physical capital, that is, more machines and tools which typically embody more advanced technology and knowledge that can help to make a properly trained labor force even more efficient.

Human capital accumulation, physical capital accumulation, and technology thus all contribute in a synergistic process to increase the productivity of the labor force. Greater productivity means the possibility of higher wages for labor and an easier workplace environment, both of which contribute to the potential well-being of the population.

We shall stress again and again the essential *complementarity* of human and physical capital accumulation and the urgency for less-developed nations not only to tap into the existing pool of knowledge available at the world level but also developed over time an autonomous technological capacity based on indigenous labor skills (this is discussed in Chapters 8 and 13).

5   **Undertaking essential institutional change.** Economic growth and development require fundamental institutional change. New organizations such as banks, stock and bond exchanges, and insurance companies gain added importance as an economy modernizes. The role of the central government – the *state* – must change to facilitate and not thwart private initiatives. Physical infrastructure such as roads, ports, communications, the provision of electricity, water, and other essential services must be improved, and the state typically must play a central role in these areas, particularly during early stages of structural transformation.

The specific nature of the legal system and of property rights; the rules and regulations governing the emerging financial system of banks, stock and bond markets and other financial intermediaries; the creation and operation of a civil service system; determining what will be taught in the schools and how success will be measured and so on all must be worked out and codified by government.

Without fundamental changes in the rules of the game, without the specifics defining how new institutions will work and provide improved outcomes compared to existing institutions, many of the "big-picture" structural changes suggested in this text will not have their full desired effects. The state thus has a challenge in clearly defining and enforcing the rule of law, including the defense of property rights, as one of its fundamental tasks. This means that the central government, which is itself an institution inherited from the past, must be modified and made more efficient and streamlined if economic growth and development are to be advanced effectively.

It is thus not only physical infrastructure that must be built, maintained, and improved, but also these "soft" infrastructural institutions of the state, like the law and property rights, that must be created and put into place if a more modern, productive, and equitable outcome is to be attained.

Needed institutional change runs deep into basic values and motivations too. Businesses must increasingly be operated with more attention to efficiency and profitability in a more competitive and open environment. Old ways of thinking and doing will undoubtedly be threatened by what often will appear to be unsettling attention paid to profit maximization by "new" entrepreneurs in industry, agriculture, and services, like retail sales. Even the family is often redefined during the process of development and structural transformation, as the extended family of the past is replaced by the nuclear family of modern society, as individualism becomes more ingrained in behavior patterns, and as maximization behavior replaces the satisficing mode of operating in the past.

These institutional changes and others will be considered in the following chapters. Economic growth and development, however, definitely require a break with the past.

Some of the most cherished institutions of many societies today, such as close family structures and interpersonal relations, religious traditions and the general pace of life, will be altered over time, becoming more and more like those institutions and patterns of behavior in other societies on the path to development and more like those institutions and values already in place in developed nations. There is no doubt that these changes can be conflictual and often wrenching.

Barriers to development

Throughout our study of economic development, we will confront repeatedly the perplexing problem as to why some countries are more developed than others are. Why is Great Britain more developed than Angola, or the United States than Colombia? The very simple answer, since it is basically a truism, is that the level and pace of economic development are lower the greater are the barriers to economic progress and transformation in a country, and more rapid the fewer and less intractable are those obstacles.

The challenge for the development analyst is thus to attempt to identify the most significant barriers to development in each country and to formulate effective measures, including public policy, that can begin to undo, remove, or at least minimize the effects of these obstacles to progress that slow or thwart the development process.

Potential internal barriers to development: Some examples of possible internal barriers that may block fundamental structural change and thus thwart economic growth and development are:

a   inequalities in the existing distributions of income and wealth, including the distribution of land ownership. For most countries, the wealth distribution is intimately related to the nature and power of class relations in society and to control over economic resources and the political sphere;

b   the level and efficiency of physical infrastructure (roads, electricity, water, communication services, port facilities, and so on);

c   the role and level of development of organized banking and lending activities and of equity (stock) and other financial markets and financial intermediaries;

d   an ineffective or underdeveloped educational system, including low levels of general literacy and an imbalance between allocations of financing to primary, secondary, and higher education;

e   prevailing ideological concepts and their impact on thinking and behavior, including the influence of religious thinking, the accepted role of women and ethnic or religious minorities, the prevailing economic orthodoxy, and so on;

f   the initial endowment of natural resources of a nation;

g   the role of the state, that is, the power and nature of the influence of the central government, including the degree of political freedom and the strength of democratic processes (included here is the macroeconomic environment that government at least partially controls, including the nature and definition of property rights and the functioning of the legal system);

h   the extent and importance of political corruption and patronage and the impact of these on public policies and on economic behavior of those governed;

i   the existence of substantial "market failures" such that market signals are not fully, completely, or accurately transmitted to economic agents, thus distorting resource allocation, production decisions and spending patterns;

j   geographic characteristics, for example, land-locked nations, mountainous terrain, extensive
     deserts, and even small country size;
k   diseases specific to certain locations;
l   civil war, and so on.

Potential external barriers to development: Examples of possible external barriers to
development include:

a   multinational corporations that control national resources;
b   the international division of labor and the prevailing patterns of international trade (e.g.
     primary commodity exporting countries versus manufactured-good exporting countries),
     including the operation of the organized institutional structure of the international trade
     system, the effects of the World Trade Organization's negotiations and of regional trade
     blocs, such as the European Union (EU) or the North American Free Trade Agreement
     (NAFTA);
c   the functioning of international financial institutions, including not only the interna-
     tional private commercial banks but also the World Bank and the International Monetary
     Fund (IMF);
d   the influence of the geopolitical and strategic interests of larger economic powers *vis-à-vis*
     smaller and weaker economic entities;
e   the economic policies of more developed nations on interest rates, for example, or on
     tariffs or non-tariff barriers on the global economic system;
f   external debt;
g   the availability of foreign aid and investment, and so on.

This very broad listing of internal and external barriers is meant only to be suggestive in a
general way of the types of barriers to progress that can confront individual countries; it could
be extended and refined almost indefinitely. Throughout the book we shall be considering
and analyzing these and other specific barriers to progress that many less-developed nations
confront.

For any specific nation, be it India or Thailand, Côte d'Ivoire or Somalia, Bolivia or
Guyana, the list of possible internal and external obstacles can only be a guide toward the
identification and detailed specification of the unique particulars of the barriers actually operating to thwart progress in that country. For every nation, the barriers to change, and then the
specifics of how each obstacle acts as a restraint on progress, need to be clearly and analyti-
cally defined so that the nature of the remedy is also made more apparent.

The relative weight of external versus internal barriers should not be considered a constant
in any particular situation.[14] The influence of internal and external barriers can and will alter
in importance over time and because of unique situations particular to specific countries. The
relative influence of internal and external barriers cannot be presumed a priori but must be
understood in each specific and changing circumstance.

What we can state with confidence is that where barriers to change, be they internal or
external, are not terribly powerful, progress tends to be more rapid. On the other hand, development will be less vigorous where the barriers to change exert a more powerful adverse
influence.

All countries, including developed nations, always face both internal and external barriers
that act as possible obstacles to continued progress. What is central in any particular nation,
then, is not whether there are obstacles to progress – for there *always are* – but rather how

these existing barriers are to be overcome by that society so that positive change can follow. New obstacles to continued progress inevitably will arise as growth and development proceeds, often as a consequence of overcoming an earlier barrier, and solutions to these new obstacles must be devised. All countries thus confront forces – some active, others simply a consequence of lethargy – that tend to slow the pace of change and block the path of development unless they are overcome.

The issue, then, is not why some countries face obstacles and others do not, since all nations constantly encounter barriers to further progress. The challenge is to try to discover how those nations that have been successful at fostering and sustaining economic growth and development have been able to do so by overcoming successive barriers to change and what might be learned from their experiences.

Resources for student use and suggestions for further reading

With every passing day, there are more resources available containing data and other information on the situation of nearly every country in the world. Of course, the internet has opened up possibilities for research and data collection and analysis beyond what could have been imaged even a decade ago. Every year the data become somewhat more comprehensive and reliable. It is possible to find information on everything from income to levels of education of women, to kilometers of roads, to the number of doctors and nurses, to the percentage of dwellings with indoor plumbing. Most college and university library collections are likely to have one or more of the publications listed below and those with access to the internet have a world of information at their fingertips – for free!

The statistical data included in this text are but an insignificant fraction of the data to be obtained from the available sources. You are encouraged to peruse the sources listed here and others in your library. We already encouraged you to begin to do that in Focus 1.2 at the beginning of this chapter. Learning how to "read" statistics, that is, attempting to determine the meaning and implications of data presented in statistical tables without reading the text accompanying such data, will vastly improve your powers of economic and social analysis.

The following sources should be of great help in studying the problems of economic development.

- World Bank, *World Development Report*, by year. Issued annually, this is an invaluable resource tool. Besides the statistical tables at the end of every volume, which, unfortunately, have been reduced in recent years, each report has a "theme" that is explored in detail. For 2007, the focus was on youth and their prospects; the 2006 report returned to the theme of equity and development; in 2003, the focus was on "transforming institutions, growth, and quality of life"; for 2002, it was institution-building for development; in 2001 the theme was poverty, and in 1999, it was knowledge. In previous years, the focus had been on workers (1995), health (1993), poverty (1990), the environment (1992), and development strategies (1991). Every major university library should have copies of at least some of these volumes.

    Some of the data in the current *World Development Report* is available on-line at http://www.worldbank.org. Look in the Data category. This site has a large and varied quantity of data available for use. Many of the problems at the end of the chapters in this text ask you to access the World Bank data.
- United Nations Development Programme, *Human Development Report*, by year. Also issued annually, this report is complementary to the *World Development Report* in that it

covers a broader range of development indicators and issues (available on-line at http:// www.undp.org). The focus is more on people and the changes in economies that impact on "human development," as opposed to focusing on the economic side of the ledger. This is an important, evolving source of information, having been published only since 1990. We will examine in more detail in the next chapter some specific information on human development published in the *Human Development Report*. Larger university libraries are also likely to have this publication in hard copy in their international documentation section, but the full report is available electronically.

- The United Nations also publishes various kinds of data, mostly economic in nature, via its several regional Economic Commissions. One can find statistical and interpretive data published by: the UN Economic Commission for Asia and the Pacific; the UN Economic Commission for Africa and the Middle East; the UN Economic Commission for Latin America and the Caribbean; and the UN Economic Commission for Europe. If you can locate these volumes, interesting and often quite detailed statistical data may be discovered, though it may be more difficult to work with than data from either of the above two sources, since different assumptions or definitions may be used in assembling the data.
- There are a number of scholarly journals related to the study of economic development that often have recent empirical research, as well as more "cutting-edge" theoretical articles. The most widely distributed are *World Development* (monthly), *Economic Development and Cultural Change* (quarterly), *Journal of Development Economics* (quarterly), and the *Journal of Development Studies* (quarterly). Also worth reading are the *World Bank Economic Review* (thrice annually) and the papers of the *Annual Bank Conference on Development Economics* available on the World Bank website.
- If you have not visited or lived in a less-developed country, it is often difficult to fully comprehend what it means to be extremely poor. To convey a sense of the deprivation which absolute poverty entails, Robert Heilbroner in *The Great Ascent*, Chapter 2, transforms a middle-class family in a developed country into an impoverished family in a "typical" less-developed nation. For gaining a sense of empathy short of travelling to a less-developed nation, this is an excellent resource.

  As an alternative, there also are short vignettes scattered throughout Jeffrey Sachs' powerful *The End of Poverty* that drive home the reality of living poverty daily. His book can usefully be read alongside this text.

Questions and exercises

1   List five key characteristics that you think are shared by most less-developed economies (not just "low income," which is obvious, but things like "low level of education," etc.).

2   How does the "headcount" measure of poverty differ from the "poverty gap" measure? Do these two measures provide different information about the extent of poverty in a country? Explain in what sense they tell us different things about the extent of poverty.

3   Development tends to be slower the stronger are a nation's barriers to the fundamental structural changes enumerated near the end of the chapter.

   a   For your own country, or for a less-developed nation about which you know something, list three specific obstacles that you think may be acting to slow the pace of economic development. Indicate whether each is an internal or an external barrier.

   b   Briefly explain how each obstacle acts to retard economic progress.

4   Foreign multinational corporations (MNCs) often are the target of criticism for their alleged detrimental impact on the economic welfare of less-developed nations. Their operations in the less-developed world are often controversial and evoke strong emotional responses. In actuality, the operations of MNCs, discussed in more detail in Chapter 14 as transnational corporations (TNCs), can be either positive or negative in their consequences.

List and explain (a) two possible advantages that MNCs might provide to the less-developed nations where they operate *and* (b) two possible disadvantages that might result in those nations from the operations of MNCs within their borders. (In Chapter 14, we consider how a country might go about attempting to maximize the *net* benefits from the location of foreign MNCs within its economy; here you are being asked only to speculate about the effects of MNCs on the less-developed nations based upon your existing level of knowledge.)

5   Why might former colonies that are only recently independent be more likely to be less-developed than long-independent nations? Can you think of any former colonies of European powers that have become developed? Of long-independent nations that remain less developed?

6   The deadline for attaining the Millennium Development Goals (MDGs) outlined in Focus 1.2 is approaching. In Focus 1.3, we looked at the success of meeting Goal 1 on poverty reduction by mid-2007 or so. What progress have the major regions made in attaining Goal 1? You can find the data at the World Bank website in the Data section.

7

a   How does the technology of agricultural production in use differ in, say, the Sudan from that used in a developed nation, like the United States? Why do such differences exist?

b   Could Sudan use the same kinds of technology – tractors, harvesters, combines, fertilizers, irrigation, and the know-how to effectively utilize these tools – on its lands? Why, or why not? (Hint: If you have learned about isoquants and isocost curves in one of your economics courses, draw two graphs with capital measured on one axis and labor on the other. Make one of the graphs for the Sudan and the other for the US. Consider how the different prices of capital and labor in the two countries might affect the most efficient combination of machines and labor in use.)

8   Many countries in Sub-Saharan Africa suffer from a high level of HIV/AIDS infection, in some cases above 20 percent of the population. What are some of the direct and indirect (opportunity) costs to an economy of a high incidence of HIV/AIDS?

9   Just to help cement the concepts in your head, list here the fundamental structural changes that countries must undertake if they are to make progress over the future. Discuss briefly the ways in which these changes are interrelated.

Notes

1 Another way of looking at these statistics is to realize that if children in the less-developed world faced the same mortality rates as children in the already-developed nations, the number of deaths would be reduced by more than 90 percent. That would have meant 1.1 million under-five deaths, rather than the 12.4 million actually recorded.

2 Most often diarrhoea is the result of a lack of access to safe drinking water and inadequate sanitation. Young girls or women often collect the water for their families from irrigation ditches, rivers and streams, or dirty well sources. If this water is not properly handled – boiled, for example – and even when it is, intestinal problems that can lead to diarrhoea can easily develop.

3 This is not to suggest that no progress has been made. Since 1945, the death rate of children under

the age of five has dropped by half, but the growth in population since that time means the total number dying from poverty remains unacceptably high.

4 See Blackwood and Lynch (1994) for formal definitions of poverty, including alternative definitions, such as the Sen Index, which attempts to combine a headcount of the numbers in poverty, the poverty gap, and the distribution of income into one measure of poverty. Their article is an excellent primer on the differences in, and the variety of, poverty measures.

For more recent measures of the poverty gap, but for different years for most countries, see the World Bank's Global Poverty Monitoring site at http://www.worldbank.org/research/povmonitor. There they provide poverty gap measures for the $1 and $2 per day poverty thresholds. The poverty gap in Table 1.1 is for the $1 per day poverty line. For some Sub-Saharan African countries, such as Gambia, Lesotho, Mali, and Niger, the poverty gap now exceeds 20 percent and in some cases, 30 percent for the $1 per day poverty line and is even higher for the $2 per day gap as the poverty situation in Africa worsened over the 1990s.

5 The term "Third World" was used to describe those nations and regions that were neither developed capitalist (i.e. "First World") nations and regions, like the United States, Canada, Europe, and Japan, for example, nor part of the socialist (i.e. "Second World") bloc of China, the former Soviet Union, and Eastern Europe. There was some blurring around the edges (was Cuba part of the Third or Second World?), but in general, the Third World nations were considered to be the less-developed, poorer nations of Asia, Africa, and Latin America and the Caribbean. In gross numbers, some 140 countries might still be considered as coming within such a Third World classification.

With the collapse and fragmentation of the Soviet bloc after 1989, the continued usefulness of the First, Second, and Third World categories has been called into question. The People's Republic of China remains the sole major Second World nation, and many would have classified China as part of the Third World, not the Second. Also in vogue for a time was the "North–South" terminology, with "North" being a shorthand for the already developed capitalist nations and the "South" denoting the less-developed countries. We have elected, for simplicity's sake, to use the terms "developed" and "less-developed" (or sometimes "underdeveloped" or "developing") to describe those nations which were considered part of, respectively, the First and Third Worlds.

6 The publication of a World Bank (1993c) study and responses to it by Asian economic specialists provides a growing body of knowledge that may be applicable to those nations that continue to be less-developed.

7 In fact, the emergence of the so-called new, or endogenous, economic growth theories in the 1980s can at least partly be traced to a concern with the stagnation of economic growth and the rise in unemployment rates in Europe and the United States. These theories and their important implications for economic development in the less-developed world are discussed in detail in Chapter 8.

8 Included in South Asia are Afghanistan, Bangladesh, Bhutan, India, Maldives, Nepal, Pakistan, and Sri Lanka.

9 Included in Sub-Saharan Africa are Angola, Botswana, Burundi, Comoros, Democratic Republic of the Congo, Eritrea, Ethiopia, Kenya, Lesotho, Madagascar, Malawi, Mauritius, Mayotte, Mozambique, Namibia, Rwanda, Seychelles, Somalia, South Africa, Sudan, Swaziland, Tanzania, Uganda, Zambia, and Zimbabwe in East and Southern Africa; and Benin, Burkina Faso, Cameroon, Cape Verde, Central African Republic, Chad, Republic of Congo, Côte d'Ivoire, Equatorial Guinea, The Gambia, Gabon, Ghana, Guinea, Guinea-Bissau, Liberia, Mali, Mauritania, Niger, Nigeria, São Tomé and Príncipe, Senegal, Sierra Leone, and Togo in West Africa.

10 What was the cost of that economic slowdown? The World Bank (1993a: 41–2) estimated that if economic growth rates had been as rapid in the 1980s as in the period 1960–80 the number of infant deaths in the less-developed world would have been reduced by 6 percent (350,000 fewer deaths). In Latin America, which especially suffered from the slowdown in economic growth in the 1980s, infant deaths would have been 12 percent lower if there had been an economic growth rate more similar to the historical trend.

11 With 15.9 percent of world population, the equality share of world income for the developed world also would be 15.9 percent. Since, however, world income was not distributed equally, the developed world actually received 78.1 percent of total world income, or roughly five times its hypothetical equality share.

12 Of course, there are some who would argue that the crime, violence, drugs, lack of community, unemployment, pollution and environmental degradation, growing relative poverty, and homelessness in many of the developed nations, especially in their crowded urban areas, make them unworthy

of the name "developed." If "development" is the goal, some would argue, there is much about the already-developed economies that it is not particularly desirable to emulate. An economist might suggest that these are, perhaps, trade-offs that are the "price" of economic progress, that economic growth and development are not "costless," and that what each nation must do is to evaluate both the benefits and the costs associated in achieving a higher level of economic growth and development.

One must also question as well to what extent the problems of the developed nations are perhaps the result of particular patterns of unequally shared growth and development, rather than being necessarily inherent problems that accompany progress per se. Is it possible to achieve a higher level of economic growth and a higher level of development without incurring the problems mentioned above? That, too, is a challenge for the future.

13 See Gerschenkron (1962) for a fascinating study of so-called "late developers." Gerschenkron believed that late-developing economies had advantages in attempting to accelerate their pace of development by having access to the most recent technological advances, but that this was always a latent possibility. There was no guarantee that late-developing economies actually would utilize that knowledge to the best advantage. In other words, progress toward higher levels of economic and social development, though possible, was not predetermined simply by the availability of higher levels of world technological knowledge and know-how. It was still up to individual economies to find the means to effectively make use of such possibilities and to create the institutional structures capable of effecting such a transition. This theme, well captured by the endogenous growth theories and theories of technological progress we will be discussing in later chapters, forms a large part of this book's understanding of the development process.

14 For example, it was common in the dependency literature on development in the 1960s and 1970s (see Chapter 6) to assume that the less-developed nations were poor primarily because of external forces. Whether these external barriers were the International Monetary Fund, the multinational corporations, or simply "imperialism," the presumption was that it was the external barriers that kept the less-developed nations poor, and that internal barriers, while perhaps not insignificant, were largely secondary to broader external forces.

We make no such a priori presumption about what the barriers to development are or of their relative weight in any particular country. Nor do we presume anything about the relative importance of internal versus external obstacles to future progress. Each nation's situation is somewhat sui generis and must be analyzed with as few preconceptions as possible.

References

Amsden, Alice H. 2001. *The Rise of "the Rest": Challenges to the West from Late-Industrializing Countries*. Oxford: Oxford University Press.

Blackwood, D.L. and R.G. Lynch. 1994. "The Measurement of Inequality and Poverty: A Policy-Maker's Guide to the Literature," *World Development* 22 (April): 567–78.

Foster, Phillips Wayne. 1992. *The World Food Problem: Tackling the Causes of Undernutrition in the Third World*. Boulder, CO: Lynne Rienner Pubs.

Gerschenkron, Alexander. 1962. *Economic Backwardness in Historical Perspective*. Cambridge, MA: Harvard University Press.

Heilbroner, Robert. 1963. *The Great Ascent*. New York: Harper & Row.

Kuznets, Simon. 1971. *Economic Growth of Nations*. Cambridge, MA: Harvard University Press.

McNamara, Robert S. 1976. *Address to the Board of Governors of the World Bank*, Manila, Philippines, 4 October. Washington, D.C.: World Bank.

Sachs, Jeffrey. 2005. *The End of Poverty: Economic Possibilities for Our Time*. New York: Penguin Books.

UNDP (United Nations Development Programme). 1993. *Human Development Report 1993*. Oxford: Oxford University Press.

——. 2001. *Human Development Report 2001*. Oxford: Oxford University Press.

——. 1995. *Human Development Report 1995*. Oxford: Oxford University Press.

World Bank. 1990. *World Development Report 1990*. Oxford: Oxford University Press.

——. 1991. *World Development Report 1991*. Oxford: Oxford University Press.

——. 1993a. *World Development Report 1993*. Oxford: Oxford University Press.

——. 1993b. *Development Brief* 20 (July): 1–2.

——. 1993c. *The East Asian Miracle: Economic Growth and Public Policy*. New York: Oxford University Press.

——. 1994. *World Development Report 1994*. Oxford: Oxford University Press.

——. 1995. *World Development Report 1995*. Oxford: Oxford University Press.

——. 2000. *World Development Report 2000/2001*. Oxford: Oxford University Press.

——. 2003. *World Development Report 2003*. Oxford: Oxford University Press.

World Development. 1994. Special section reviewing *The East Asian Miracle*, vol. 22 (April).

WHO (World Health Organization). 1994. *The State of the World's Children 1994*. Geneva: WHO.

2 Measuring economic growth and development

After reading and studying this chapter, you should better understand:
- the difference between economic growth and development;
- why GNI and GDP can differ, how to calculate each, and the adjustments to these so they can be used as more reliable measures of the level and rate of development of economies;
- how the purchasing power parity (PPP) definition of income differs from the usual GNI or GDP measure and why it may be a better indicator for comparing nations;
- the importance of knowing something about income distribution, the Lorenz curve, and the Gini coefficient when evaluating the level of development of a country;
- the Human Development Index (HDI) and how it can be used as an alternative or complementary measure of development;
- the importance of sustainable development;
- the significance of the Kuznets inverted-U hypothesis.

Introduction

What is meant by development? The answer to this deceptively simple question shapes how one judges the respective levels of development of different economies. It affects what factors we consider as contributing to progress, and our answer to what development is will influence the public policies aimed at achieving a society's development goals. Knowing what is meant and what is not meant by development is thus a necessary first step if, as the British economist Joan Robinson once insisted, we are to ask the right questions.

We begin by considering how economists typically measure the level of development of a nation. There are two broad methodologies. One, the income per person, or *economic growth* criterion, suggests that income levels are reasonably good approximate measures for comparing economies. In this view, income per person can serve as a surrogate for gauging overall progress.

The competing perspective argues that development is such a complex, multi-faceted notion that it should be conceived from the outset as considerably broader than income and hence can only be measured by entirely different standards. Let us turn to a discussion of these two viewpoints and methodologies.

The economic growth/income criterion of development

Economists often use the level of a nation's per capita income as a proxy measure for evaluating the overall level of national development and welfare. The rate of growth of income per person can be used to judge the progress of economies over time.

Those who use income per person to evaluate progress are quite aware that the development of a nation encompasses much more than the level of average income and the growth rate of that income. Development incorporates the diverse and broad aspirations of what might be called the "good life" in all its economic, social, and political dimensions that each society sets, if only implicitly, for itself.

Societies may value, each perhaps differently, goals as diverse as:

a   equality of opportunity;
b   a rising income and standard of living, including a wider array of consumable goods and services over time;
c   equity in the distributions of income and wealth;
d   political democracy and widespread participation in society's decision-making;
e   an expanded role for women, minorities, and all social classes in economic, political, and social life;
f   increased opportunities for education and self-improvement irrespective of class, race, ethnicity, religion, or gender;
g   the expanded availability of, and improvements in, health care;
h   public and private safety nets to protect the most vulnerable – particularly the young, the old, the infirm and the poorer – from extreme hardship;
i   a reasonably clean and healthy environment;
j   an efficient, competent, transparent, and fairly administered public sector;
k   a reasonable degree of competition in the private sector; and so on.

Each of us could add to or subtract from this list of goals (see Alkire 2002 for an overview of the issues involved in defining what encompasses human development). But there is no doubt that development encompasses a wide range of social and human goals that, while including the level of income and economic growth, go well beyond these as well (see Focus 2.1 on high-quality growth).

Development, being broader than income alone, typically requires fundamental structural change in the economy and society, as discussed at the end of Chapter 1. To attain a higher level of development does not mean that a poor economy simply needs to do more of what it already has been doing. Less-developed countries are less developed precisely because they produce, sell, and export a sub-optimal array of goods and services in inefficient ways. Development requires that these nations make changes that will result in a radically transformed future in which new values and ways of doing things, new institutions, and better functioning markets emerge. It is not small marginal change that is required, though that can help. Ultimately, however, wholesale social and economy-wide transformations are essential.

The process of becoming more developed by undertaking the necessary fundamental structural reforms is without doubt often a process of wrenching social change. The full range of development goals of any nation goes far beyond any simple concern with the level of income per person. *All* economists recognize this, including those who use a nation's income per person as an index for the broader development ambitions listed above.

FOCUS 2.1   HIGH-QUALITY GROWTH

The International Monetary Fund (IMF) has often been taken to task for the "condition-ality" it puts on borrowing countries, conditions that often have contributed to increases in poverty and lower average incomes (Chapter 17 considers this issue in depth). Over the 1990s, the IMF seemed slowly to be learning from the criticisms of its policies and from its own evaluations of past lending policies and their impact on economic growth.

Now, the IMF sees itself as promoting so-called "high-quality growth," defined as:

> growth that is sustainable, brings lasting gains in employment and living stand-ards and reduces poverty. High-quality growth should promote greater equity and equality of opportunity. It should respect human freedom and protect the envi-ronment. Obviously, growth cannot be high quality ... if it does not benefit fully, tangibly, and equitably a group that constitutes more than one half the population of the world and still bears the primary responsibility for the care, nutrition, and education of the world's children. Achieving high-quality growth depends, there-fore, not only on pursuing sound economic policies, but also on implementing a broad range of social policies.

Economic development is not just about economic growth, then, but about a *particular kind* of economic growth: high-quality growth in the IMF's terminology. And you will notice how many of the broader development goals we listed above are touched upon in the IMF's definition.

Source: "Gender Issues in Economic Adjustment Discussed at UN Conference on Women," *IMF Survey* (September 25, 1995): 286–8

Nonetheless, it is often convenient and simpler to use income per person as a substitute gauge for the broader goals of development. Imagine how difficult it would be to not only collect data on a wide range of development goals such as those listed above but then, with so many variables, trying to compare these for several countries to rank them in terms of which were "better off." The complexity of comparing across many variables with different values and interpretations is simply too daunting, even if each goal can be measured. (You'll remember that we asked you to try to do precisely this in Focus 1.4 in Chapter 1.) Our brains, as complex as they are, still need some degree of simplification when many dimensions are being compared.

Fortunately, there is empirical evidence, some of which we shall examine below, to at least partially support the claim that income per person is highly correlated with key measures of the broader aspirations of economic, social, and political progress. Thus many economists, acknowledging that it would be wrong-headed to suggest that higher income and economic growth are the same as development, firmly believe that it is reasonable to focus on a nation's economic growth and level of income as the measure of development. This is because it is believed that improvements in the specific dimensions of development, such as those listed earlier, are more easily achieved at higher income levels. It is precisely from such higher income over time that the means for reaching the broader goals of development can be obtained.[1]

For most economists, then, it is reasonable as a first approximation to rank nations from highest to lowest by per capita income levels as a measure of their relative development achievement. Focus 2.1 on "high-quality growth" illuminates this view of the process of economic growth and its relation with the broader concept of development.

Part of the attractiveness of using the per capita economic growth criterion is its very simplicity. All countries collect data on their level of economic activity, though with varying degrees of accuracy, despite efforts by international institutions to unify the methods of data collection and to strive, to the degree feasible, for the comparability of the information collected.[2] The data for comparing income among countries, or for any particular country over time, are thus reasonably readily available and roughly comparable. We make use here of the annual data published by the World Bank in its *World Development Report* and in its World Development Indicators, a source which provides a consistent and reliable series of data available to researchers around the world.

Measuring economic growth

The level of economic development and economic growth can be measured either by the growth of total output or of total income. The two most common measures used for international income and output comparisons, and hence for measuring economic growth, are *gross national income* (GNI) and *gross domestic product* (GDP).

GNI is the total value of all income *accruing to* residents of a country, regardless of the source of that income, that is, irrespective of whether such income is derived from sources within or outside the country.[3] **GDP** is the total value of all income (= value of final output) *created within* the borders of a country, regardless of whether the ultimate recipient of that income resides within or outside the country.

How and why do the GNI and GDP measures of income differ? There will be no difference if an economy is completely "closed" to the rest of the world. Closed in this sense means that there is no migration of workers and no flows of investment between a country and the rest of the world. Exports and imports of goods, however, do *not* affect the measurement of GNI or GDP since trade flows do not have anything to do with differences in the values of the two income measures. It is simply that can be no labor or investment flows between economies if GNI is to equal GDP and an economy is to be considered "closed."

If an economy is closed in this sense, then the only income that would be received by residents of a country would be derived from new productive activity taking place within the borders of that country. There would be no income received by residents inside the country originating from sources outside the country and no flows of income created within the borders of the country going to income recipients in other nations. In this case, GDP – the income produced within the borders of the country – would equal GNI – the income received by residents of that country.

Income flows between economies and GNI and GDP

However, in a world with multinational corporate investment moving across national boundaries and with a myriad of financial flows between nations, an economy's GNI will typically diverge from its GDP.

Take the case of the United States, which has many of its corporations and banks operating in other economies. As a result of these multinational investments, as well as US bank loans to other countries and other financial investments, the US economy received an inflow of profit, dividend, and interest income from the rest of the world equal to $350.9 billion in 2000 and $474.6 billion in 2005.

This income inflow *from outside the US* became part of the *GNI* of the United States. It was not part of the US GDP, however, since it did not from income created within the borders of the US. In fact, the value of this flow of profits, dividends, and interest to the US was included as part of the GDP of the *other* nations from which it originated. These income flows from other countries added to US GNI, tending to make the income available to US residents greater than the income created within the borders of the US, that is, greater than US GDP.

Of course, just as US firms, banks, and individuals had investments in other countries, so too do foreign firms, banks and individuals have investments in the US. These investments created income and output within the US borders that were included as part of US GDP. However, not all that income remained in the US to become part of US GNI. Profit, interest, and dividend income equal to $329.9 billion in 2000 and $463.4 billion in 2005 flowed to countries like the United Kingdom, Germany, Mexico, and Japan that had made investments in the United States in the past. This income was created in the US (that is, it was part of US GDP), but it belonged to and flowed to income recipients outside the US, thus tending to reduce US GNI below the level of US GDP.

The *net* effect of the inflow of profits, interest and dividends to the US from other nations *minus* the outflow of profits, interest, and dividends from the US to the rest of the world was equal to $21.1 billion in 2000 and $11.3 billion in 2005. This made US GNI > US GDP, everything else was the same, since more income payments flowed into the United States as returns on US investments and loans abroad than was paid to foreigners who had invested in or made loans to the United States. The same sorts of flows can create a divergence between GDP and GNI in other economies as well, as a result of the flows of investments that take place between nations.

A second type of income flow between nations that can result in a divergence between GDP and GNI is due to worker remittances. As workers migrate from their home country to another in search of work, it is not uncommon that they leave some members of their families and other relatives behind. Often these workers send a portion of their income home. Such remittances by workers in one country to their families in their home country have the effect of tending to make GNI < GDP in the sending country where the migrating worker is located and GNI > GDP in the receiver nation where the family and relatives of the worker reside, all else being the same.

For example, many workers from the Philippines work in Asia and Europe. Some of their income is sent home to family still living in the Philippines, which adds to the GNI in the Philippines above the GDP created in the Philippines. In 2000, workers' remittances sent to the Philippines totaled $5.2 billion; by 2005, this inward flow of income from the rest of the world had reached $10.7 billion (World Development Indicators Online). These inflows of income tended to make the Philippines' GNI > GDP, as there was more income to be spent by residents of the Philippines than there was income created within the Philippines.

In general, then, whether a country's GDP < GNI or its GDP > GNI depends on the sum of all the income inflows into the country from the rest of the world (ROW) less the sum of the income leakages leaving the country and flowing to the ROW. Again, remember that the only transactions between nations that create a difference between GNI and GDP are *income* flows; the level of exports and imports do not create any difference between the measured values of GNI and GDP.

When the income inflows received by a country from the ROW exceed the income outflows to the ROW, then that country's GNI > GDP. When the income inflows from the ROW are smaller than the income outflows to the ROW, then GDP > GNI for that country.

Table 2.1 provides some summary data on the two income measures for a number of economies for 1990 and 2006.

This table provides information on total GDP, total GNI, and the GDP/GNI gap, that is, the difference between GDP and GNI. When the GDP/GNI gap is positive (i.e. GDP − GNI > 0),

Table 2.1 GDP and GNI comparisons, selected nations, 1990 and 2006

	Population (millions)		Total GDP[a]		Total GNI[a]		GDP/GNI gap[b]	GNI per capita ($)	
	1990	*2006*	*1990*	*2006*	*1990*	*2006*	*2006*	*1990*	*2006*
Algeria	25.3	33.3	62.0	114.7	60.0	107.3	7.4	2,371	3,218
Argentina	32.6	39.1	141.4	214.1	135.2	208.6	5.4	4,148	5,333
Bangladesh	104.0	144.3	30.1	62.0	30.8	65.4	−3.5	296	453
Bolivia	6.7	9.3	4.9	11.2	4.6	10.8	0.4	694	1,156
Botswana	1.4	1.8	3.8	10.3	3.7	9.7	0.7	2,580	5,498
Brazil	149.4	188.7	462.0	1,068.0	449.7	1,038.4	29.5	3,010	5,503
Cambodia	9.7	14.4	1.1	7.2	1.1	6.9	0.3	114	481
Chile	13.2	16.5	31.6	145.8	29.8	129.8	16.0	2,261	7,892
China	1,135.2	1,311.8	354.6	2,668.1	355.7	2,694.8	−26.8	313	2,054
Côte d'Ivoire	12.7	18.5	10.8	17.5	9.2	16.0	1.5	728	865
Costa Rica	3.1	4.4	7.4	22.1	7.2	21.4	0.8	2,325	4,870
Egypt	55.7	75.4	43.1	107.5	42.0	108.0	−0.5	755	1,433
Ethiopia	51.2	72.7	12.1	13.3	12.0	13.3	0.0	235	183
Ghana	15.5	22.5	5.9	12.9	5.8	12.8	0.1	373	569
Guatemala	8.9	12.9	7.7	35.3	7.5	35.3	0.0	843	2,735
Haiti	6.9	8.6	2.9	5.0	2.8	4.3	0.6	413	501
India	849.5	1,109.8	316.9	906.3	312.7	900.9	5.3	368	812
Indonesia	178.2	223.0	114.4	364.5	109.2	348.7	15.7	613	1,563
Jamaica	2.4	2.7	4.6	10.5	4.2	9.4	1.1	1,740	3,525
Kenya	23.4	35.1	8.6	21.2	8.2	20.9	0.3	351	596
Korea (Rep.)	42.9	48.4	263.8	888.0	263.6	888.0	0.0	6,149	18,340
Malaysia	17.8	25.8	44.0	148.9	42.2	144.2	4.7	2,362	5,596
Mexico	83.2	104.2	262.7	839.2	254.1	830.7	8.5	3,053	7,970
Mozambique	13.4	20.1	2.5	7.6	2.3	6.9	0.7	173	344
Nigeria	94.5	144.7	28.5	114.7	25.6	103.3	11.4	271	713
Pakistan	108.0	159.0	40.0	128.8	41.7	126.2	2.7	387	793
Philippines	61.1	84.6	44.3	116.9	44.1	127.8	−10.9	721	1,511
Rwanda	7.1	9.2	2.6	2.5	2.6	2.5	0.0	362	268
Sri Lanka	17.0	19.8	8.0	27.0	7.9	26.6	0.4	462	1,344
Sudan	26.1	37.0	13.2	37.6	12.4	34.2	3.4	476	925
Thailand	54.6	64.7	85.3	206.2	84.3	202.1	4.1	1,542	3,122
Venezuela	19.8	27.0	47.0	181.9	46.3	180.4	1.5	2,342	6,676
Vietnam	66.2	84.1	6.5	60.9	6.1	59.4	1.5	92	706

Source: World Bank, *World Development Indicators Online.*

Notes
a Billions of US dollars.
b GDP/GNI gap = GDP − GNI, in billions of US dollars. A positive value means that GDP > GNI; a negative value indicates that GNI > GDP.

a country had outflows of income to the ROW that exceeded inflows into the economy from the ROW, and thus its GDP > GNI. When the GDP/GNI gap is negative (GDP − GNI < 0), the economy had inflows of income from the ROW that exceeded outflows to the ROW, and thus its GNI > GDP.

For example, China's total GDP was $2,668.1 billion in 2006 while its total GNI equaled $2,694.8 billion; thus China's GDP/GNI gap was −$26.8 billion. More income was received by residents of China (GNI) than was created within the borders of China (GDP) due to a net inflow of income from the rest of the world. In Brazil, on the other hand, there was more income created within the borders of the country (GDP) than was received by residents of Brazil, and the positive GDP/GNI gap of $29.5 billion is the amount of income created within Brazil that did not remain for the use of Brazilians but rather belonged to residents of other economies.

Which of the two measures of an economy's income is preferred when using an economy's income as a proxy measure of its overall level of development: GDP – all income created within a country regardless of who received it – or GNI – all income received by residents of a country and available for use? You may already have a good idea of which is a better indicator of total welfare, but before we answer that question directly, it is necessary to look a little deeper into the two measures of income and refine them a bit.

Necessary adjustments to the GDP and GNI measures

The values for both total GDP and total GNI for 1990 and 2006 shown in Table 2.1 are total **nominal** figures, that is, they are the *total current US dollar value* of the two alternative measures of total income. There are a number of adjustments to these total nominal values that are desirable if income is to be used in a reliable manner as a surrogate measure suitable for ranking economies as to their level of development.

1 Adjusting for population size

A first necessary correction to the total GNI and total GDP figures in Table 2.1 is to adjust them for population size. Dividing GNI (or GDP) by the total population provides a measure of per person income, or, simply, average income. Nominal per capita GNI figures are shown in the last columns of Table 2.1 for 1990 and 2006. If you wish, you can calculate per capita GDP from the data provided, but these are not shown in the table.

This population adjustment is essential for two reasons. First, *using total* GNI (or GDP) to compare different countries makes little sense. From Table 2.1, China had the highest total GNI, followed very closely by India. But these two economies also had the largest populations. To be able to compare countries in terms of their *relative* level of development, it is essential to use average income, as in the last columns of the table, to account for differences in the size of economies. Otherwise, we would be trying to compare essentially non-comparable values. Total GNI or total GDP tells us nothing about the average standard of living; average GNI, or average GDP, gets us a little closer.

In 1990, South Korea, Argentina and Mexico had the highest average incomes of the countries listed in the table; Mozambique, Cambodia, and Vietnam had the lowest per capita income levels. In 2006, South Korea remained first in per capita income by a substantial margin, followed by Chile and Venezuela. The three poorest economies were now Mozambique, Rwanda, and Ethiopia, with the last two economies experiencing *declining* income per person between the two years.

We can thus use per capita income as a means to rank countries from richest to poorest, with differences in incomes reflecting presumed differences in the quality of life, which is the rationale behind using income per person as a proxy for overall welfare.

A second reason for using per capita income is to determine if, over time, changes in the level of aggregate income of any particular economy (a) are just sufficient to keep up with population growth, so that per capita GNI (or GDP) remains constant over time; (b) are more than sufficient to keep up with population growth, so that per capita GNI is rising over time; or (c) are insufficient to keep pace with population growth, such that per capita GNI is falling over time. Using per person income figures allows us to measure, for any particular economy, whether average income – and hence the average standard of living – is growing or not.

Since GNI per capita is simply total GNI ÷ population, the percentage change in GNI per capita can be determined as in equation 2.1. This tells us whether an economy's total income is growing fast enough to provide for an increase in the income available per person.

% change GNI per capita = % Δ (total GNI/total population)
$$= \% \, \Delta \text{ total GNI} - \% \, \Delta \text{ population} \qquad (2.1)$$

The rate of growth of GNI per capita thus can easily be approximated as the difference between the rate of growth of total GNI and the rate of population expansion. GDP can be substituted for GNI in equation 2.1 to determine the rate of change of GDP per capita.

Equation 2.1 makes it clear why countries with high rates of population growth need to generate higher rates of growth in total income just to keep the level of per capita income constant compared to countries with lower population growth. If one country's population is growing at 2 percent per year, total GNI must increase by 2 percent per annum just to maintain a constant level of income per capita; from equation 2.1, this results in a zero percent change in per capita income. Another economy with 1 percent growth in population and the same 2 percent growth in total GNI would experience an increase in per capita GNI of 1 percent.

It would not be correct, however, to infer from equation 2.1 that slow population growth *causes* a faster rate of growth of income per person or that rapid population growth causes slower growth in income per person. Equation 2.1 is true by definition; it is a mathematical identity. It does not uncover the underlying reasons that result in rapid or slow per capita income growth. Equation 2.1 only indicates the *consequences* of specific rates of change of both total population and total income. This important issue of population growth and its precise relation to economic growth is examined in more detail in Chapter 12.

Having made this population adjustment to total income, countries with higher levels of income per capita may be said to be more developed than countries with lower levels of income per capita by the income criterion of development. Similarly, countries with faster growth rates of average income as indicated by larger percentage increases in income per person may be said to be developing faster than countries with lower growth rates of per capita income.

2 Adjusting nominal income (GNI or GDP) for price changes over time

The total and per capita GNI and GDP measures in Table 2.1 are what are called nominal values. To judge how any economy is performing over time, that is, to really be able to compare 1990 and 2006 per capita income figures, it is necessary to convert *nominal or current price* GNI (or GDP) to *real or constant price* GNI (or GDP).

For example, the total GDP figures shown in Table 2.1 were calculated at their nominal values, that is, they were estimated by multiplying the *current*, or nominal, market price of each newly produced good and service by the number of units of new production of each of these goods and services and then summing across all goods and services. Prices act as a common unit of measure that allows us to add together physical quantities of different goods and services that otherwise would not be able to be totaled.

The economic wealth of society that economists wish to measure is composed of what is produced in actual physical terms, for it is that material production which is potentially available for use in consumption and investment and which can contribute to individual and social welfare. The available output is thus the "income" of an economy. The nominal GDP measure of output (*which is equal to total income created in an economy*) permits us to compute the total value of dissimilar physical outputs and services by measuring them with a comparable yardstick: first by using prices stated in a nation's own currency and then converting this to US dollars at the official exchange rate for each economy to allow comparisons among countries in a common currency, the US dollar.

The problem of using current prices is that when comparing different years, unless prices have remained constant, the current price measure of each year's GDP will be a mix not only of changes in physical production (the Qs below) but also of the variations in the prices of the goods and services produced (the Ps below).

Equation 2.2 shows how total nominal GDP is determined as the sum of all newly produced final goods and services with: n being the number of goods and services produced; P_i being the price of good or service i in each country's own currency; and Q_i representing the quantity of good or service i produced.

$$\text{Total GDP} = \sum_{i=1}^{n} P_i Q_i \tag{2.2}$$

From this simple statement, it is clear that in different years the prices of goods and services – the P_is – may vary and that different prices can affect the nominal value of total GDP even if total physical output – the Q_is – have not changed at all.

For example, imagine in equation 2.2 that from one year to the next all the P_i values double, so that all prices are twice what they were in the previous year. Even with the same level of production in both years, that is, even if the Q_is are the same in both years, *total nominal* GDP will be twice as large in the second year as in the first. However, such an economy would be no better off with twice the level of nominal GDP, since all the increase was due to price increases. There is no additional real output or income available, as the Q values did not change. So, if prices change over time, as they do, nominal GDP and nominal GNI values are distorted by the price changes when what interests us is the "real" amount of stuff available to be consumed or invested.

In comparing GDP in different years, then, what we want to measure is how much real physical output, the Q_is, have changed, independent of any price changes that may have taken place between the years. To calculate real, or constant, price GDP, economists simply value the output in different years by using the same prices, P_i, for all years compared. Once the base year vector of prices is chosen, these constant P_is can be used in equation 2.2 to value the current Q_is. Thus we can write, for example,

$$2008 \text{ GDP}_{1992} = \sum_{i=1}^{n} P_{i,1992} Q_{i,2008} \tag{2.3}$$

Equation 2.3 shows how real GDP for 2008, calculated at 1992 prices (1992 is the *base year* for prices in this case), would be determined. Using the prices prevailing for each good and service in 1992 ($P_{i,1992}$), this price vector is multiplied by the physical quantities of all newly produced final goods and services produced in 2008 ($Q_{i,2008}$). The resulting sum is the *real value* of 2008 total GDP stated in 1992 prices. Comparing 1992 GDP and 2008 GDP, prices would be the same and any differences in total GDP values between the two years would be due to differences in the quantity of goods and services produced and not price changes.

In practice, an equivalent approach for calculating 2008 GDP in 1992 prices is to deflate nominal 2008 GDP by an appropriate price index, such as the GDP deflator. For example, if the total nominal GDP of the fictional country of Luanda in 2008 was US$3,337 million, and the price index for 2008 was 331.7 (with 1992, the base year = 100, as is always the case for the base year), then real 2008 GDP for Luanda, calculated in constant 1992 US dollars, would be equal to US$1,006 million, as shown in equation 2.4.

$$\frac{\text{2008 total GDP}}{\text{2008 Price Index}} \times 100 = \frac{\text{US\$3,337 million}}{331.7} \times 100$$
$$= \text{US\$1,006 million} \tag{2.4}$$

This calculation adjusts Luanda's 2008 GDP for the change in prices that occurred between 1992, the base year, and 2008. This operation is equivalent to the calculation in equation 2.3, where 1992 prices are multiplied by 2008 quantities.[4] After making this correction, which is absolutely necessary when comparing income between years, then real GDP per capita can be calculated by making the population adjustment discussed above, if it was not done prior to the price adjustment.

A similar correction also must be done to total nominal GNI to find *real* GNI per person by deflating total GNI by the appropriate price index. Table 2.2 shows the real GNI per person and the nominal GNI per person for 1990 and 2006 for a sample of the economies shown in Table 2.1 to give an idea of why it so important to make this adjustment for price changes if we are to compare income between years.

The real average GNI figures in the first two columns are calculated in constant real 2000 US dollars. Effects of price changes between 1990 and 2006 have been corrected by deflating (dividing) each year's nominal GNI per person by the corresponding price index (in this case, the Consumer Price Index).[5] The percent change in real GNI per capita between 1990 and 2006 is shown in the third column.

For the sake of comparison, the nominal GNI per capita values for each of the countries is also shown (taken from Table 2.1) and the percentage change in nominal income per person has been calculated in the last column of Table 2.2.

Table 2.2 Real GNI per person versus nominal GNI per person, 1990 and 2006

	Real GNI per person[a]			*Nominal GNI per person*		
	1990	*2006*	*% Change*	*1990*	*2006*	*% Change*
Argentina	$16,681	$3,093	−81.5	$4,148	$5,333	28.6
Botswana	6,989	3,376	−51.7	2,580	5,498	113.1
Chile	5,555	6,717	20.9	2,261	7,892	249.0
China	627	1,896	202.6	313	2,054	556.2
India	872	631	−27.6	368	812	120.7
Indonesia	2,132	886	−58.4	613	1,563	155.0
Kenya	1,542	357	−76.8	351	596	69.8
Korea	10,092	15,224	50.9	6,148	18,340	198.3
Malaysia	3,348	4,956	48.0	2,362	5,596	136.9
Mexico	16,445	6,049	−63.2	3,053	7,970	161.1
Pakistan	932	572	−38.6	387	793	104.9

Sources: World Bank, *World Development Indicators Online* and Table 2.1.

Note
a In constant 2000 US prices.

First, the change in *real* income per capita is lower in all economies than the change in *nominal* income per person. Some of the differences are quite dramatic. For example, Botswana's nominal income per person increased by 113 percent; however, once price changes are taken into account, real average income actually fell by more than 50 percent! In 2006, on average, less than half as many goods and services were available per person than in 1990.

In Kenya and Mexico, the deterioration in real income was even more extreme. However, if we had looked only at nominal income per person in Table 2.1, it would have appeared that Botswana, Kenya and Mexico were making substantial progress because of the large increases in average nominal income recorded. We now know from equations 2.3 and 2.4 that increases in nominal income are a mix of price and quantity changes, and that it is necessary to remove the price variations so as to get a better idea of what is actually available for consumption and investment. Clearly in these countries, price increases were much larger than the increases in nominal GDP, so that real GDP per person was shrinking.

China's real income growth stands out, having more than tripled, per person, since 1990. This is remarkable progress in average income growth, which if sustained, could bring China out of its less-developed status very soon, much as has happened in South Korea, which joined the ranks of the high-income economies in the space of a half-century (see Focus 2.5 later in the chapter on China's economic successes in recent decades).

3 Accounting for income distribution

Income per capita values, as shown in Tables 2.1 or 2.2, are at best an imprecise measure of the *actual income* received by any particular person, since they are only a simple average derived by dividing total GNI or GDP by total population. The per capita income measure does not provide any information about the *dispersion* of actual incomes around this mean.

It is thus helpful to also know something about the distribution of income in an economy if one is to make reasonable sense of the average income figures. Table 2.3 provides income distribution information on most of the countries in Table 2.1.

The first two columns show the shares of total income (or consumption) received by the poorest 20 percent of the population (the lowest fifth or quintile of income earners) and for the richest 20 percent (the highest quintile). The number of persons or families in each quintile is the same in any nation, representing exactly one-fifth of all income recipients in that economy.

Also shown in the table in the third column is the ratio of the share of total income received by the richest 20 percent of the population divided by the share of total income received by the poorest 20 percent for each country. This tells us how many times larger the average income of the richest 20 percent of the population is as a multiple of the average income of the poorest 20 percent of the population. The closer this number is to 1, the greater the degree of equality between the lowest and highest income receivers, and the further away is the ratio from 1, the greater the degree of relative inequality. In no country is this ratio very close to 1.

In only a few economies – Bangladesh, Ethiopia, Pakistan, and Korea – is the degree of inequality between the richest and the poorest a multiple of 5 or less. In all countries, the richest 20 percent of income recipients receive more of the total income than do the poorest 20 percent, since no economy, not even ostensibly communist China, where the income distribution is worse than in the US, has anything approaching complete equality of income. Thus, the average income of the richest 20 percent in all countries is higher, sometimes significantly so, than that of the poorest fifth of the population.

Of the countries shown in Table 2.3, the richest 20 percent of the population in Botswana, Brazil, and Guatemala receive at least 20 times the average income received by the poorest

Table 2.3 Income distribution, selected economies

Country	Poorest 20%	Richest 20%	Richest 20%[a] Poorest20%	Gini coefficent
Algeria (1995)	7.0	42.6	6.1	35.3
Argentina (2004)	3.1	55.4	7.9	51.3
Bangladesh (2000)	8.6	42.7	5.0	33.4
Botswana (1993)	3.2	65.1	20.3	60.5
Brazil (2004)	2.8	61.1	21.8	57.0
Chile (2003)	3.8	60.0	15.8	54.9
China (2004)	4.3	51.9	12.1	46.9
Côte d'Ivoire (2002)	5.2	50.7	9.8	44.6
Egypt (1999–2000)	8.6	43.6	5.1	29.5
Ethiopia (1999–2000)	9.1	39.4	4.3	25.5
Ghana (1998–99)	5.6	46.6	8.3	40.8
Guatemala (2002)	2.9	59.5	20.5	55.1
India (2004–05)	8.1	45.3	5.6	36.8
Indonesia (2002)	8.4	45.3	5.4	34.3
Jamaica (2004)	5.3	51.6	9.7	45.5
Kenya (1997)	6.0	49.1	8.2	42.5
Korea (1998)	7.9	37.5	4.7	31.6
Malaysia (1997)	4.4	54.3	12.3	49.2
Mexico (2004)	4.3	55.1	12.8	46.1
Morocco (1998–9)	6.5	46.6	7.2	39.5
Mozambique (2002–3)	5.4	53.6	9.9	47.3
Pakistan (2002)	9.3	40.3	4.3	30.6
Philippines (2003)	5.4	50.6	9.4	44.5
Rwanda (2000)	5.3	53.0	10.0	46.8
Thailand (2002)	6.3	49.0	7.8	42.0
Venezuela (2003)	3.3	52.1	15.8	48.2
Vietnam (2004)	4.2	44.3	10.5	34.4
Japan (1993)	10.6	35.7	3.4	24.9
US (2000)	5.4	45.8	8.5	40.8

Source: World Bank, *World Development Indicators 2007*: 66–8, Table 2.7.

Note

a Share of total income (or, for some economies, consumption) received by the richest 20 percent of the population divided by the share of total income (or consumption) received by the poorest 20 percent of the population.

20 percent. This is a substantial degree of inequality, which, as we shall see later in the chapter, can have dramatic effects on economic growth.

We can go a little deeper into the relation of income equality to average income. It is actually possible to estimate the per person income of the poorest and richest income groups separately using the data in Tables 2.1 and 2.3, as follows.

Applying Brazil's income distribution figures to its 2006 total GNI of $1,038.4 billion (from Table 2.1), the richest 20 percent of the population (equal to 0.2 × 188.7 million total population = 37.74 million persons) received $634.5 billion (= 0.611 × $1,038.4 billion total GNI) of the economy's total GNI, for a per capita income for the richest 20 percent equal to roughly $16,811 ($634.5 billion ÷ 37.74 million persons). The poorest 20 percent of the Brazilian population (also 37.74 million persons) received $29.1 billion of the total income in 2006 (0.028 × $1,038.4 billion total GNI), for an estimated annual average per capita income for the poorest 20 percent of Brazilians of about $770 ($29.1 billion ÷ 37.74

million persons).[6] You will note that the $16,811 average annual income of the richest quintile in Brazil is 21.8 times larger than the $770 annual income of the poorest quintile of the population, as Table 2.3 indicated.

Compare these two average income values with Brazil's average per capita GNI of $5,503 shown in the last column of Table 2.1. The richest 20 percent of income earners received an average income more than three times the level of average GNI per capita reported in Table 2.1, while the poorest 20 percent of the Brazilian population received incomes that on average were equal to about 14 percent of average GNI for the country as a whole. This clearly illustrates the importance of at least having some rough idea of the income distribution in a country if the per capita income figures such as those in Tables 2.1 and 2.2 are to be used to gauge the level of development of an economy. When the gap between the richest and poorest is quite wide, as is the case in Brazil, the average GNI value should be interpreted with some caution. This is especially true when we are using GNI per person as a measure of the well-being of a population.

Other countries have substantial deviations between the richest income recipients and the poorest, though none are so wide as those found in Brazil. For any country, the percent of income received by the richest 20 percent divided by the percent of income received by the poorest 20 percent tells us by how many times the *average* income of the richest 20 percent of the population in a country exceeds the average income received by the poorest quintile of income earners in that economy. The larger this ratio in the penultimate column, the less meaningful is the average GNI per capita figure shown in Table 2.1 as a measure of the actual average income received and as a measure of the degree of average development of an economy.

Interestingly, the lowest such ratio shown in Table 2.3 is for Japan, which has the smallest gap – 3.4 times – between the average income of the richest and poorest. Why do you think there is so little inequality in Japan? Has this relatively low level of inequality been harmful or helpful to the Japanese growth and development experience?

Also shown in Table 2.3 are estimates of Gini coefficients for each economy. The *Gini coefficient* is another method for attempting to capture in a simple form – as does the ratio of income of the richest 20 percent of income earners to the income of the poorest 20 percent – the degree of income inequality in a country, though the Gini coefficient is often a superior measure of the overall distribution of income.

The value of the Gini coefficient can vary between 0 and 100. The closer the Gini coefficient is to 100, the greater the degree of income inequality; the closer it is to 0, the lesser the degree of inequality. Similarly, over time, a rising Gini coefficient within an economy would indicate a worsening of the income distribution, while a falling Gini coefficient suggests an improvement in the overall distribution of income.[7]

With some caution, it would be possible to say that Bangladesh with a Gini coefficient of 33.4 has a more equal distribution of income (or consumption) than did Chile with a Gini coefficient of 54.9. More interesting and revealing, however, is to compare the evolution of an individual country's Gini coefficient over time. This would be an excellent class assignment.

4 Other considerations when using the GNI or GDP measure

Both GNI and GDP fail to include some new production and income that adds to the level of well-being of individuals, while at the same time they count some production as income that does not contribute to human welfare.

One of the most significant omissions from the GNI and GDP measures is an estimate for the value of home production. In particular, the value of the output derived from the labor of women and children, who cook and clean and tend children, who make and mend clothing, who toil in home gardens and subsistence farms and who perform a variety of other unpaid tasks in the production of non-traded goods and services for their families' own consumption, are not included in the traditional GNI or GDP estimates. And to the extent that men and boys do work on subsistence farms, in gardens, and in workshops at home resulting in the production of goods or services consumed solely by the family, the value of their production to an economy's total production also is underestimated and ignored.

The value of this home production, including food produced on subsistence farms, is excluded because such goods and services are not valued by or exchanged in the market. GDP and hence GNI include only goods and services which are bought and sold on the market. Home and subsistence production, by definition destined for the use of the household producing them, do not get counted in total GDP or GNI. Without doubt, these productive activities contribute to the well-being and to the social reproduction of these families by putting food on the table, providing clothing, making tools, and so on (see Focus 2.2 on Women's Work). In fact, for poor families, such non-market activities are likely to make a larger contribution to their total income and consumption than is true for better-off families who receive more of their income from paid pursuits and who purchase a larger proportion of their consumption goods in the marketplace.

FOCUS 2.2   VALUING WOMEN'S WORK

A part of the work that women do is not counted as contributing to an economy's GNI or GDP. That is because the great bulk of work done by women in poor economies is often done in and for the home – caring for and instructing children, preparing meals, drawing drinking and cooking water from wells, washing dishes, cleaning, and so on – and is not paid employment. The system of national accounts used to calculate the value of an economy's total income excludes such unpaid, non-market production from the total, whether it is done by men or women, or boys or girls. However, since it is women who more likely to be involved in unpaid household production, much of women's work is said to be "invisible."

What is especially interesting is that women and girls everywhere put in more total hours per week at paid *and* unpaid work than do men or boys. Women in less-developed countries accounted for 53 percent of total work hours to men's 47 percent share. Rural women tended to carry an even larger burden of all work performed. For example, in rural Kenya, women were found to labour an average of 1.35 times more hours than men; in Bangladesh, the ratio was 1.1 times more.

However, though women work more in total than men in less-developed economies, more of women's effort is carried out in non-paid activities (66 percent) than in paid work, which accounted for 34 percent of women's total contribution of hours worked. For men, on the other hand, 76 percent of their labor contribution was in paid pursuits, while only 24 percent of men's total effort was performed in non-paid, non-market activities such as home food production, child care, cooking, tool repairs, or other unpaid activities within the home or on the farm.

For example, more than fifteen hours per week were expended by women in Mozambique just to fetch water. Women in rural Kenya labored an average of fourteen hours per week more than men and did ten times as much housework, none of which has a "value" in terms of adding to total income. Obviously, though, such unpaid labor is essential to the living standard of poor families and may often spell the difference between survival and perishing.

One estimate of the total contribution of women's unpaid, "invisible" activities was put at $11 trillion in 1993. Given that total global GDP was estimated at $23 trillion in that year, an adjusted measure of all production, both that which is exchanged in the market and that which is produced for own-consumption, might result in a value for total global GDP that is as much as 50 percent higher than the standard measure of GDP. It's certainly something to think about!

Source: UNDP 1995: Chapter 4

Thus, social or actual per capita income – from paid and unpaid sources – of poorer families are likely to be underestimated compared to the income for families with higher incomes. Poorer families may have less income from paid sources to use to purchase goods and services on the market, but that paid income underestimates the purchasing power and actual level of consumption of poorer families by not valuing those goods and services produced at home or on a farm that are part of total consumption for that family.

On the other hand, the production of military goods, logging operations that cause environmental destruction of forests, and production processes that spew toxic wastes into the air and water and then force society to pay for their clean-up or which create health problems requiring remediation via higher health costs are counted as positive contributions to the measured level of GNI and GDP. Such activities do not add to the level of development or to society's welfare to the degree that their market-valued contributions would suggest, since social costs and private costs of such goods diverge, often dramatically, as a result of the negative externalities created by their production (see Focus 2.3 on Sustainable Development).

Economists have devised alternative methods to measure an economy's "true" output and income that go beyond the traditional GDP and GNI values, such as the Measure of Economic Welfare (MEW) and the Genuine Progress Indicator (GPI). These alternatives adjust the GNI and GDP measures both for the omissions that contribute to human welfare not included in the traditional methodology for determining GNI or GDP, as well as for those included values that adversely impact human welfare. While the specifics of making such adjustments are not examined here,[8] it is important to keep in mind that some of the goods and services included in the GNI and GDP measures may contribute negatively to a nation's development goals, while others, such as so-called "women's work" and much of home production in general, represent activities that contribute positively to a nation's total production and to its potential for full human development.

FOCUS 2.3   SUSTAINABLE DEVELOPMENT: BALANCING ECONOMIC GROWTH AND THE ENVIRONMENT

Since the 1970s, there has been a growing concern about the impact of economic growth on the natural environment. In 1971, a United Nations conference on the Environment and Development was held in Switzerland, followed in 1972 by the UN conference on the Human Environment in Sweden. These and other gatherings of academics, politicians, activists, and NGOs (non-governmental organizations) culminated in the UN conference on Environment and Development – the so-called "Earth Summit" – held in Rio de Janeiro, Brazil, in 1992. And, of course, concern over global warming and its relationship to how and what economies produce has become front-page news since the late 1990s.

The outcome of these various forums and of a growing body of scientific research has been an increasing awareness of and interest in the issue of the *sustainability* of economic growth. Sustainable development was defined by the Brundtland Commission as "development that meets the needs of the present without compromising the ability of future generations to meet their own needs." Simple, but quite a powerful concept.

While there is still debate over precisely what this definition means, efforts to operationalize it to account for the impact of current economic activities on natural resource use and the carrying capacity of the environment to absorb changes are evident in the creation of the Genuine Progress Indicator (GPI) and in other measures, such as the Environmentally-adjusted net Domestic Product (EDP), as well as other efforts to "green" the national accounts countries traditionally use to measure their economic progress.

The motivating conviction of sustainable development is that economic growth need not be in conflict with the natural environment if attention is paid in economic and public policy decisions to the goal of conserving and enhancing the natural resource base and in using technology in ways that value not only higher levels of output but also consider the impact of such economic expansion on the environment.

Part of the new way of looking at sustainability rests on the critical observation that there is pollution due to poverty, as well as the perhaps more familiar pollution arising from affluence. Pollution due to poverty exists in less-developed nations as a result of the degradation of marginal farm lands by landless farmers, leading to the erosion of top-soil and desertification, and from the clear-cutting of forests, both of which lead to poorer water quality after rains and run-off exacerbated by the lack of sanitation facilities. Toxic fumes enter the atmosphere, generated by using wood as a cooking fuel and the burning of trash by many small farms.

Pollution due to poverty extends to the cities of less-developed countries, in the slums and shanty towns where unclean water and a lack of sanitation create environmental hazards for the poor urban dwellers who crowd into areas that are too small and lacking in necessary services.

But whatever the specific problem that generates "pollution of poverty," it is the consequence of a lack of overall economic growth and of national systems of income and wealth distribution that lead desperately poor people to abuse their environment and their nation's stock of natural resources in their effort to simply survive. The effects of such pollution are intensely local, of course, but often they have global consequences, too.

Pollution arising from affluence is the environmental damage due to increased industrial production and from higher-income consumption patterns, such as the proliferation of private motor vehicles and of non-recyclable waste and refuse that contribute to air, land, and water degradation. This type of pollution tends to increase with economic growth, while pollution from poverty tends to decrease, and it is not clear that they cancel out over time with world-wide economic expansion.

Both pollution arising from poverty and pollution due to affluence can have local and global effects. Pollution has been blamed for global warming, the depletion of the ozone layer, desertification, and species extinction (estimated in excess of 5,000 annually). The danger is that degradation of the water, air, and land has set in motion potentially irreversible processes, the effects of which, if unchecked, could have devastating consequences for future generations. Goal 7 of the Millennium Development Goals introduced in Chapter 1 is focused precisely on this sustainability and irreversibility issue.

There thus is a compelling need to find the means and the will to balance the pressing need for continued economic growth and a better distribution of income and wealth in the poorest nations against the effects this can have on the natural environment. Equally important, then, is the necessity to *value* the world's natural and environmental resources more rationally, from a social point of view, so that the increased mass consumption that accompanies higher levels of GDP is not automatically counted as having value, while the environmental costs of increased production and consumption are ignored, as if the environment essentially was valued at a zero price. This neglect of environmental costs has resulted in excesses in the pollution of affluence attributable to the richer nations and in the urban areas of many less-developed countries.

In discussions over the sustainability of economic growth, however, views often become polarized. The so-called "deep ecology" perspective tends to be virulently anti-growth, valuing all of nature and all species and natural habitat equally. Humans, in this perspective, have no special rights *vis-à-vis* other species or the environment. The deep ecology perspective exalts relatively simple living with limited material wants as a desirable objective.

Continued

Opposed to this viewpoint is that of those who promote economic growth as the means to best improve human development. In this traditional perspective, nature is there for the use of human beings. Not all species have equal value, and the expansion of consumption is one of the chief ends of economic life. The environment and its resources are a means to the end of increasing average incomes. The environment is just another input to production that can help to increase individual income. Relatively little attention had been afforded to environmental concerns until quite recently for those holding to this perspective.

The truth no doubt lies somewhere between these two extreme perspectives. The effort to define "sustainability" has been devoted to finding a middle ground between the view that all of nature is equally valuable and should be preserved as much as possible and the alternative view that nature is to be conquered for the benefit of human beings. Just as we shall find that development economists are taking a closer look at human capital inputs as being critical to progress, concern over sustainability can be seen as part of an effort to view environmental and resource capital as key inputs to potential national and global prosperity. In this vein, environmental and resource capital is now beginning to be valued, measured, and thought about as a non-zero price input to production at least as important as the more traditional inputs of labor and capital.

Increasingly, then, development economists are cognizant of the "*eco*-nomics" involved in the connection between ecology and development. This requires going beyond the attention to the potential "negative externalities" of particular behavior, such as the dumping of toxic wastes in landfills, which has been the traditional way economics has incorporated environmental and resource concerns into its purview. New ways of measuring and valuing environmental and resource capital are called for, as are new institutions that can operationalize and internalize such calculations, including the nature of property rights to resources, land, and water. Increasingly, these have become not just local issues, but global concerns, requiring coordinated action and responses.

The concept of the sustainability of economic growth and development need not be limited to considerations about the natural environment alone. It is also possible to conceive of the sustainability of an economy's social structures. The pace, level, and distribution of economic growth can be extended to quality of life issues, such as the impact of economic change on urban crime and violence, on illegal drug addiction, on racial and ethnic tensions, on religious conflict, on gender issues, and so on.

Goal 7 of the Millennium Development Goals focuses on the environment, including the issue of sustainability. The World Bank (www.worldbank.org) includes updated data on progress toward meeting this MDG's three targets that is worth examining to see how individual countries, as well as the world, are doing in meeting the goals set for 2015.

Sources: Bartelmus (1994: Chapter 2); Elliott (1994); Redclift (1987); WCED (1987: 43)

GNI or GDP: is one income measure better than the other?

Which income measure of economic growth should one use: real GNI per capita or real GDP per capita? Does it make a difference?

The GNI measure provides some notion of what the residents of a nation have available to them for consumption and investment, including government spending. GNI thus furnishes a measure of the sum total of new final goods and services available to the residents of a country for their final use. In economic terms, the level of output and income measured by GNI is a proximate gauge of the aggregate material welfare or well-being of the residents of a nation. If one is going to use income and the economic growth criterion as a substitute measure for the broader goals of development for a nation, it probably makes sense to use real GNI per capita as the standard, since it measures what is actually available for contributing to the standard of living of the population, both now, for current consumption, and, in the future, as investment.

GDP, on the other hand, measures all the output and income produced within the borders of a country, even though not all of that income will necessarily be received by residents of the country. GDP is more purely an index of the value of all new goods and services and total income produced within the frontiers of a nation rather than of the income and output available for use to the nation. Real GDP per capita is a less desirable measure to use if one is interested in a surrogate welfare measure for the broad range of development goals of nations. Real GDP per capita does give information on how output is changing in an economy, but it does so irrespective of who ultimately receives the income earned from such production. The GDP per capita measure, then, is not as closely connected to what remains in the hands of the residents of the nation for current and future consumption as the GNI per capita measure, and thus GDP per person is a more imperfect measure of a nation's overall well-being.

Which measure is employed will be determined by the use to which the income criterion is to be put. If one is solely interested in the pace of economic growth and total production for a country, then the real GDP per capita measure will serve quite nicely. If, however, one wishes to use the income proxy that best measures what is available for use by a country's residents and which can concretely contribute to their level of well-being, it makes more sense to use the real GNI per capita measure as the surrogate yardstick.

Having said all this, a glance back at Table 2.1 shows that for most of the economies shown in the table, the GDP/GNI gap is not that large. Thus in most cases, using GDP or GNI per capita will make little substantive difference in evaluating the level of development using the income criterion. There are, however, exceptions, not shown in the table, such as Angola, Brunei, Puerto Rico, Republic of the Congo, and Gabon, where the gap is such that GNI is anywhere from 20 percent to 40 percent smaller than the value of GDP (based on data in the Penn World Tables). For such countries, using real GDP per capita will be a less reliable measure for approximating the level of development of those countries than the GNI per capita measure.

International comparisons of income: purchasing power parity (PPP) income

There is a further issue to consider when using income levels as a basis of comparison and as proxy measures of the level of development of different economies. What exactly does a comparison of Cambodia's 2006 GNI per capita of $481 with Chile's average income of $7,892 mean? Of Malaysia's GNI per capita of $5,596 with Mexico's $7,970 per capita income? Is it legitimate to infer from comparing these figures that one dollar of income in each economy is worth the same? Does the local equivalent of one US dollar purchase an equivalent quantity of goods in every single country, so that one could say that the equivalent of US$1,500 of income would provide the same standard of living in Chile, Malaysia, Mexico, and Cambodia?

The simple answer is, no, it is not the case that the equivalent of one US dollar purchases the same quantity of goods regardless of the economy. A little introspection perhaps suggests why this is the case. Would you expect the price of housing, for example, to be the same in Cambodia with a lower level of income per person than the US? Of a haircut? Of medical and dental services? Of public transportation?

What is likely is that economies with lower per capita GNI will have lower prices for some items when these values are converted from the local currency to US dollars than will a country with a higher average GNI. In other words, the equivalent of US$1,500 will buy different quantities of goods and services in different economies since the prices of some – *but not all* – goods and services will vary with the level of average income of an economy.

The GNI and GDP and the GNI per capita measures shown in Tables 2.1 and 2.2 are shown in US dollar units, but these values are not precisely comparable among economies, for reasons we just hinted at. These values were calculated by taking each economy's own GNI and GDP values, calculated by each country's statistical agencies in their own currency units (pesos for Mexico, rupees for India, for example) and converting these values to US dollars. How is this conversion to US dollars done? Very simply, the average *official exchange rate* between each country's currency and the US dollar is used as the means to arrive at the US dollar values shown in Table 2.1 (and the real values in Table 2.2).

Let's imagine that the average exchange rate over a year between the Indian rupee and the US dollar is 1 US dollar = 39.45 rupees. If India's GDP is determined to be 41,525,000,000 rupees, when that is converted to dollars using the official exchange rate, it would be equal to $1,052,598,226. What such a conversion from rupees to dollars implies is that 1 US dollar in the US can buy exactly the same bundle of goods and services as can 39.45 rupees in India. That is, the buying power of 1 dollar is the same as the buying power of 39.45 rupees.

But you already know that this is not likely to be true. This official exchange rate conversion only makes comparable the prices of *traded goods*, that is, goods that are traded internationally, such as computers, motor cars, shoes, oranges, and wine. The presumption is that the prices of traded goods will be quite similar between countries because of the forces of international competition and the potential for *arbitrage* that large differences in prices would offer.[9]

However, for *non-traded goods and non-traded services*, which by definition do not enter into international trade between nations, prices between countries can vary quite substantially. These differences will depend upon conditions internal to each country, particularly the average level of income, but also local customs, regulations, the degree of competition, and so on. For non-traded goods and services, like housing, transportation, personal services, and prepared foods that are location-specific, there are no international forces of competition or the possibility of arbitrage to bring prices into line *between* economies. Significant price differentials for these goods and services between economies can make international GNI and GDP comparisons like those shown in Table 2.1 based on simply converting domestic currency measures to a common US dollar measure somewhat deceiving, since a US dollar does not have the same buying power everywhere. In poor countries, a US dollar, converted into the local currency, can buy more than a dollar can in the US, since the prices of non-traded goods and services tend to be lower.

There, is however, another way to compare income between countries that attempts to overcome the shortcoming of the traditional exchange rate-converted GNI or GDP values. This is known as the *purchasing power parity*, or PPP, income measure.

Table 2.4 provides a comparison between the values of GNI per capita calculated at the official exchange rate (the same as those shown in Table 2.1) and GNI per capita calculated at PPP values, both in US dollars. The PPP measure makes an adjustment to GNI between countries similar to the adjustment made to determine real GNI discussed earlier. The prices of one country, in this case the United States, become the base prices for determining the purchasing power parity value of GNI per capita in other countries. Thus, Mozambique's PPP GNI ("purchasing power parity GNI") per capita is determined as

Table 2.4 Purchasing power parity (PPP) measure of GNI per capita

	GNI per capita at official exchange rate, 2005	PPP GNI per capita, 2005
Algeria	2,730	6,770
Argentina	4,470	13,920
Bangladesh	470	2,090
Botswana	5,590	10,250
Brazil	3,550	8,230
Chile	5,870	11,470
China	1,740	6,600
Côte d'Ivoire	870	1,490
Egypt	1,260	4,440
Ethiopia	160	1,000
Ghana	450	2,370
Guatemala	2,400	4,410
Haiti	450	1,840
India	730	3,460
Indonesia	1,280	3,720
Jamaica	3,390	4,110
Kenya	540	1,170
Korea	15,840	21,850
Malaysia	4,970	10,320
Mexico	7,310	10,030
Morocco	1,740	4,360
Mozambique	310	1,270
Pakistan	690	2,350
Philippines	1,320	5,300
Thailand	2,720	8,440
Rwanda	230	1,320
Venezuela	4,820	6,440
Vietnam	620	3,010
Ireland	41,140	34,720
Japan	38,950	31,410

Source: World Bank, *World Development Indicators 2007*: 14–16, Table 1.1.

$$\text{PPP GNI per capita} \quad = \quad \frac{\sum_{i=1}^{n} P_{i,\,US} \times Q_{i,M}}{\text{Population}} \tag{2.5}$$

$Q_{i,M}$ is the output vector of all newly produced final goods and services, i, available for use by residents of Mozambique and $P_{i,US}$ is the price vector for these goods and services, i, in US prices. Effectively, then, what the PPP GNI measure provides is the estimated value of Mozambique's available output valued at the prices for such goods and services prevailing in the United States. There is no need to use the exchange rate between the two countries to find the value of Mozambique's GNI per person. Mozambique's output is valued directly by multiplying that production by US prices.

Obviously, large differences not only in the prices of non-traded goods and services between the two countries but of the mix of traded to non-traded goods in total national output will affect the PPP measure of GNI per capita compared to the value obtained from the official exchange rate conversion. From Table 2.4, for example, the 2005 per capita PPP value of income in Mozambique was estimated as $1,270, which is more than three times greater than the exchange rate-converted GNI per capita value of $310. This PPP per capita income figure is more meaningful when comparing incomes among economies at any point in time. The PPP value of Mozambique's income can be interpreted as follows: $1,270 of income would be required in the US to buy what the equivalent of $310 is able to purchase in Mozambique with its lower prices for non-traded goods and services compared to the US. In other words, the equivalent of $310 in Mozambique can buy, roughly, what it would take $1,270 to buy in the US.

For the less-developed countries in the top part of Table 2.4, all have PPP GNI per capita > the exchange rate determined value of GNI per capita. For example, Rwanda had a PPP GNI per capita nearly six times as large as the exchange rate GNI per capita value. Rwanda is undoubtedly a poor country, but the $230 income per person figure makes the economy seem poorer than it is. That income buys more in Rwanda than it would in the US or other more developed economies, and there is also more home production not counted as income, as you read about in Focus 2.2, that adds to the standard of living but does not appear as income. For all the less-developed countries shown in Table 2.4, PPP GNI per capita exceeds the exchange rate GNI value by at least a third and most often by significantly more. The PPP measure of income gets us a little closer to understanding the levels of income among diverse economies.

On the other hand, look at the comparison between Japan's PPP GNI per capita and the value of GNI per person found by simply converting per capita GNI in yen to US dollars using the exchange rate. PPP GNI per capita is substantially less. Why do you think that is? What does this say about the prices of non-traded goods and services in Japan compared to those prices in the US (again, we expect the prices of traded goods to be very similar in all economies)?

Typically, then, the actual purchasing power of income in lower-income countries tends to be *understated* by simply converting local GDP or GNI per capita to US dollars using the official exchange rates as a result of the lower prices of non-traded goods and services, such as housing, retail services, local food products, and local transportation in poorer nations. These prices are lower because the lower income of these countries keeps the prices of these non-traded goods below what they are in more developed nations. The more developed economies tend to have PPP GNI per capita values closer to that calculated at the official exchange rate because of the greater openness to world trade, a mix of production with more traded goods relative to non-traded goods, and because of their more modern structures of production, which result in greater efficiency in production in both traded and non-traded goods and service sectors.

There is an increasing tendency to prefer the PPP measure of income in making comparisons among countries over the exchange rate-converted GNI or GDP values. In future, income comparisons used as a basis of determining relative levels of development will more and more use the PPP income measure and that will improve the quality of such comparisons and the meaning we attach to them.

The indicators criterion of development: the *Human Development Index*

In the 1960s, there emerged from the International Labour Organization, from the World Bank, and from independent researchers a growing backlash against the use of per capita income and the rate of economic growth criterion as the exclusive measures of development. Whether what was proposed as an alternative to the GNI, GDP, or PPP GNI per capita measures was the basic needs approach or the physical quality of life index (PQLI), or some other composite measure, the objection to the use of the economic growth and income standard was the same: it was far too aggregate and did not capture the distributional inequalities all too common in many of the poor nations of the world.

The income per capita criterion gave a biased view, it was argued, of the level of progress achieved by many countries. Income per capita was, in and of itself, an insufficient target for ultimately achieving society's broader development goals listed earlier in this chapter. The link between the level of income per capita and the full range of development objectives was considered much too tenuous and unreliable, particularly in the poorest nations that needed to make the most progress.

Neither the basic needs nor PQLI methodologies took hold, however; the former perhaps because of some undeniable theoretical and empirical ambiguity and the latter possibly for lack of a powerful institutional champion.[10] Since 1990, when it was first proposed, a new measure of development has gained credibility. The *Human Development Index*, or simply the HDI, has been calculated and published each year by the United Nations Development Programme in its annual *Human Development Report*.

The HDI is a composite index using "longevity, knowledge, and a decent standard of living," as the representative indicators for development. The actual index uses estimates of life expectancy at birth, the adult literacy rate, school enrolment ratios, and PPP GDP per capita to calculate an HDI value for each economy.[11] The HDI measure of development is thus broader than the simple income per person yardstick, though income does enter into the calculation of the HDI. At the same time, the HDI gives direct value to those factors, particularly education, which help create opportunities for individuals to reach a higher and more fulfilling standard of living that may not be captured by the income measure alone. As the UN Development Programme described the issue:

> Human development is about much more than the rise and fall of national incomes. It is about creating an environment in which people can develop their full potential and lead productive, creative lives in accord with their needs and interests. People are the real wealth of nations.
>
> (UNDP 2001: 9)

That last sentence is extremely important. Read it again. It is a nation's people that comprise the wealth of any society, and meeting the needs and desires of those people is the ultimate purpose of economic growth and development.

The HDI simplifies the comparison among countries by combining the achievement on a number of different variables into a single number. The value of the HDI index can vary between 0 and 1, with an HDI score closer to 0 indicating greater distance from the maximum to be achieved on the aggregate of the factors entering the HDI. An HDI value closer to 1 indicates greater achievement relative to the maximum attainable on the variables that comprise the index and thus a higher level of human development.

The HDI may be said to be measuring "relative deprivation," that is, it is a gauge as to how far a country is from reaching, on average, the maximum value of the components that make up the HDI. Roughly, since this is a deprivation index, one can interpret an HDI = 0.660 to mean that an economy has, on average, attained 66 percent of what is possible.

The HDI measure was created with the purpose of attempting to take into account the fact that countries, meaning both governments and individuals, make choices on their spending and use of resources among alternative uses. The use of these resources affects the range of choices open to people and their level of well-being, with effects that may not always be captured in the income per person ranking of nations.

For example, among the less-developed nations, the UNDP found that though one-quarter of national income was spent via government, less than 10 percent of this share, on average, was dedicated to identifiable human development expenditures, such as education, health care, and social security. The largest area of government spending was on the military, the contribution of which to human development is, at best, controversial (UNDP 1993: 10). Of course, different nations will allocate their public expenditures in different ways, both to achieve particular development goals, as well as to accomplish other priorities, such as defense, that are deemed significant. The impact of these choices, at least partly, will be captured by the variables included in the HDI, and thus, it is argued, provide a more robust view of the average level of development of an economy than is possible by simply looking at income per person.

Table 2.5 shows the value of the HDI for 1990 and 2004 and the HDI ranking for 2004 for an even broader range of countries than was listed in Table 2.1. What do the numbers show?

Consider, for example, Mexico in the top part of the table for economies with "high human development" in 2004. In 1990, Mexico's HDI value had been 0.766, which meant that the country was then still ranked among the "medium human development" economies. By 2004, with an HDI of 0.821, Mexico had joined the "high human development" economies, being fifty-third among the 177 countries. Remember, too, that an HDI = 0.821 means that, on average, Mexico has attained 82.1 percent of the maximum values possible on the individual components of the HDI – life expectancy, school enrolments, adult literacy, and PPP GDP per capita. Chile, Costa Rica, and Malaysia also made the jump from medium to high human development between 1990 and 2004.

By comparison, Niger, the lowest ranked economy in 2004, had an HDI = 0.246, indicating that only about 25 percent of what could be achieved was attained, or, looking at it from the other side, Niger had an average 75 percent shortfall from the maximum values on the HDI components.

Two countries – Kenya and Rwanda – dropped from the medium human development ranking in 1990 to the low human development grouping in 2004. In the case of Zimbabwe, the deterioration in its HDI value from 0.639 to 0.491 was substantial. It will be noted that all the low human development economies in Table 2.5 – and the great majority of the thirty-one economies with low human development in 2004 – are Sub-Saharan African countries for which the difficulties of sustaining economic growth and development has been most critical. In some cases this has been due to civil war or other conflicts; in others, the HIV/AIDS crisis has had devastating consequences on human development. Much more attention needs to be given to Sub-Saharan Africa's particular problems if the MDGs are to have any chance of being attained.

Table 2.5 also provides information in the penultimate column on the difference between the PPP GDP per capita ranking and the HDI ranking for each country for 2004. What is the significance of these numbers?

A positive value in that column indicates by how much a country's HDI ranking exceeded its PPP GDP per capita, or income, ranking among all economies. That value is determined by taking a country's PPP GDP ranking minus the country's HDI ranking. Countries with a positive value in the PPP GDP ranking − HDI ranking column thus were ranked higher among all economies in the HDI ranking of countries than they were in the PPP GDP income ranking of economies. For such countries, their PPP GDP per capita ranking *understated* the country's overall level of development, as more broadly defined by the HDI. Looking

Table 2.5 Human development index (HDI) and GDI, selected countries, 1990 and 2004

	HDI value		HDI rank[a]	PPP GDP ranking − HDI Ranking[b]	GDI[c]
	1990	2004	2004	2004	
High Human Development (HDI > 0.800 in 2004)					
Australia	0.893	0.957	3	11	0.956
Japan	0.914	0.949	7	11	0.942
United States	0.917	0.948	8	−6	0.946
United Kingdom	0.889	0.940	18	−5	0.938
Singapore	0.823	0.916	25	−4	–
Korea	0.823	0.912	26	5	0.905
Argentina	0.813	0.863	36	10	0.859
Chile	0.787	0.859	38	18	0.850
Costa Rica	0.793	0.841	48	13	0.831
United Arab Emirates	0.810	0.839	49	−25	0.829
Mexico	0.766	0.821	53	7	0.812
Malaysia	0.723	0.805	61	−44	0.795
Medium Human Development (0.500 < HD < 0.799 in 2004)					
Brazil	0.720	0.792	69	−5	0.789
Venezuela	0.760	0.784	72	17	0.780
Thailand	0.717	0.784	74	−9	0.781
Saudi Arabia	0.708	0.774	76	−31	0.744
China	0.628	0.768	81	9	0.765
Philippines	0.722	0.763	84	19	0.761
Turkey	0.682	0.757	92	−22	0.745
Sri Lanka	0.706	0.755	93	13	0.749
Jamaica	0.719	0.724	104	6	0.721
Indonesia	0.626	0.711	108	8	0.704
Vietnam	0.618	0.709	109	12	0.708
South Africa	0.735	0.653	121	−66	0.646
Morocco	0.549	0.640	123	−15	0.615
India	0.515	0.611	126	−9	0.591
Botswana	0.680	0.570	131	−73	0.555
Pakistan	0.463	0.539	134	−6	0.513
Bangladesh	0.422	0.530	137	7	0.524
Congo	0.528	0.520	140	25	0.519
Low Human Development (HDI < 0.500 in 2004)					
Zimbabwe	0.639	0.491	151	−18	0.483
Kenya	0.548	0.491	152	7	0.487
Rwanda	0.339	0.450	158	−5	0.449
Nigeria	0.407	0.448	159	−1	0.443
Côte d'Ivoire	0.443	0.421	164	−15	0.401
Mozambique	0.316	0.390	168	−14	0.387
Ethiopia	0.314	0.371	170	1	–
Niger	0.246	0.311	177	−7	0.292
High Income Economies		0.942			
Middle Income Economies		0.768			
Low Income Economies		0.556			

Source: UNDP 2006: 283–91, Tables 1 and 2, 210–13, Table 21.

Notes

a The highest, or best, ranking was 1 (Norway) in 2004; the lowest, or worst, ranking, was 177 (Niger).

b If positive, the ranking for the country on the HDI is higher than the country's ranking on per capita PPP GDP (PPP GDP rank − HDI rank > 0); if negative, the HDI ranking for the country is lower than the per capita PPP GDP ranking (PPP GDP rank − HDI rank < 0).

c Gender-related Development Index; adjusts HDI for differences in achievement on the HDI variables between males and females.

at income alone, these economies seemed worse off compared to other economies than they really were when a broader definition of development, the HDI, was used.

For example, the Philippines (HDI = 0.763) had an HDI ranking that exceeded its per capita PPP GDP ranking by nineteen places, since its PPP GDP ranking − HDI ranking difference was a positive 19. (What, then, was the Philippine's per capita PPP GDP ranking? We can infer its value from the table. Since the PPP GDP ranking − HDI ranking = x − 84 = 19, then the Philippines PPP GDP ranking must have been 103 in 2004, since 103 − 84 = 19.) In other words, the Philippines did substantially better on the HDI measure, ranking, at eighty-fourth, nineteen countries higher among the 177 countries than it had ranked on its PPP GDP, being one-hundred-and-third among the 177 countries. This was a better showing on the broader range of development indicators captured in the HDI than would have been expected from its per capita income ranking alone.

On the other hand, a negative value in the penultimate column of Table 2.5 indicates by how many positions a country's HDI ranking *fell* among all countries compared to where the country ranked when using its PPP GDP per capita only. The value of "PPP GDP ranking − HDI ranking" can only be less than 0 if the PPP GDP ranking < HDI ranking. For those nations with a negative gap, their income ranking tends to overstate the broader level of development as measured by the HDI.

For example, South Africa's HDI ranking was 66 places below its income ranking (PPP GDP ranking − HDI ranking = x − 121 = −66, which means that the PPP GDP ranking had to be 55 since 55 − 121 = −66). This strongly suggests that had we looked at income alone, it would have been reasonable to believe that South Africa's population had a higher level of development, ranking fifty-fifth among the 177 countries, than it actually does, at least as measured by the additional development indicators included in the HDI, where South Africa ranked significantly lower, one-hundred-and-twenty-first among the 177 countries. That is quite a significant drop in ranking, reflecting the fact that average income in South Africa fails to provide a reasonable proxy measure of the level of development.

Looking down the column of values in the PPP GDP − HDI column, they do not seem to vary systematically in any immediately obvious way, underscoring the point of those who have argued that the GNI (or GDP) per person measure alone is an incomplete index of development and that there is no automatic link between the level of income per capita and the level of development (at least as measured by the HDI).[12]

Adjustments to the HDI

Just as it is useful to adjust the GDP or GNI income figures so that they provide a more reliable standard for evaluating the level of development if one is to use that measure, so too are there some modifications that can be made to the HDI that refine the information it provides.

The Gender-related Development Index (GDI)

The UNDP also calculates a gender-adjusted HDI, called the "gender-related development index" or GDI, which takes into account differences in the level of attainment of women and men on the values of the indicators that enter the HDI. The GDI values are shown in the last column of Table 2.5. In making such a correction for gender differences in life expectancy, education, and income, every country suffers a deterioration in the value of its gender-adjusted HDI, meaning in no country do women, on average, score higher than or equal to men on the HDI components (though some are very close). Thus, the GDI, which is simply a gender-adjusted HDI value, is less than the average HDI reflecting the lower average level of attainment of women compared to men on the variables entering the HDI.

Some countries do better than others on gender equality, however, so that the GDI ranking of all countries is different from the HDI ranking, rising for those nations for which the average achievement of women is closer to that of men and falling for those nations where the achievement of women is more distant from that of men as a group. That can be seen, for example in looking at Saudi Arabia and China in the table. Saudi Arabia has a higher HDI value than does China and thus ranks higher, seventy-sixth versus China, which is ranked eighty-first on the HDI. However, looking at the GDI values of each country, we see that China scores higher than Saudi Arabia and thus China ranks higher on the GDI, sixty-fourth versus seventy-second for Saudi Arabia (the GDI rankings are not shown in Table 2.5). Still, no country had a GDI equal to or greater than its HDI. Closing the gaps in education, health, income, and political participation between men and women is essential for full development of a nation, and the GDI gives us some indication of the success of countries in achieving gender equity.

The Human Poverty Index

Another weakness of the HDI is that it does not indicate what is happening to the poorest members of society, except to the extent that this is reflected in the overall HDI value via, say, the impact of poverty on average life expectancy. To attempt to capture the conditions of living of the poor more directly, the UNDP introduced in 1997 a Human Poverty Index (HPI) that utilizes slightly different variables from either the HDI or the GDI and hence is not directly comparable. Instead of life expectancy as a variable, the HPI includes the probability at birth that a child will *not* survive to age 40; for education, adult *illiteracy* is included as a variable; and in place of an income variable, the HPI includes the "percentage of people without sustainable access to an improved water source" and the "percentage of children under five who are underweight" as variables entering the index. All of these variables are stated in percentages, and lower values for each is better than higher values since each variable is actually a "deprivation" indicator rather than an achievement indicator, as is the case of the HDI or GDI variables (for a sample calculation, see UNDP 2001: 241).

In 2005, for example, Costa Rica had an HPI of 4.4 percent, which means the combined probability of not living to age 40, of the incidence of illiteracy, of lack of access to improved water sources, and of underweight children is quite low. Pakistan's HPI was equal to 36.3 percent, meaning a worse performance on these deprivation indicators. Of the 102 less-developed countries with calculated HPI values, Mali was last, with an HPI = 60.2 percent, the result of having a 37.3 percent chance at birth of not living to age 40; of having 81.0 percent adult illiteracy; of 50 percent of the population lacking access to improved water sources; and of having a third of all children below age 5 being underweight (UNDP 2006: 293–4). While this index is not as easy to use as the HDI, it does give some useful information about the levels of relative deprivation of different countries that can be used in conjunction with the HDI value.

The HDI is thus an imperfect measure of the well-being of a nation, just as is the income criterion. Neither measure is capable of capturing *all* the critical dimensions of development that might be thought important, but the HDI is broader in some important respects than is a simple income per person indicator.

For the future, it might be desirable to have an HDI that included some measure capable of quantifying environmental and sustainability issues that are a part of the Millennium

Development Goals. Such environmental matters are left out of the HDI, except to the extent they might indirectly affect life expectancy. With the growing awareness of the pressing need to understand the interrelation between biological and economic systems and the concern that an environmental threshold may be being reached with continued global economic expansion, this is a glaring deficiency of the HDI, as it is in the GNI and GDP measures. So, too, is the absence of any weight in the gross HDI given to the degree of political democracy and participation. Other considerations and variables may also be important to include in an adjusted HDI, as has been the case with the GDI.

Comparing the income per capita and HDI measures

Is the effort to construct an HDI for each country worth the effort? Does the HDI provide information about the level of development of a country that is different from that which can be obtained from GDP or GNI per capita figures? Is it reasonable to use real GNI or GDP per capita as a proxy for the level of development, rather than the admittedly more-difficult-to-estimate HDI? As the UNDP writes (2001: 13):

> Rankings by HDI and by GDP per capita can be quite different, showing that countries do not have to wait for economic prosperity to make progress in human development. ...
> Costa Rica and Korea have both made impressive human development gains, reflected in HDIs of more than 0.800, but Costa Rica has achieved this human outcome with only half the income of Korea. Pakistan and Viet Nam have similar incomes, but Viet Nam has done much more in translating that income into human development. ... So, with the right policies, countries can advance faster in human development than in economic growth.

In a statistical study comparing GNI per capita and the HDI as means for ranking nations as to level of development, the question of a divergence between the HDI and income rankings was considered. It was found that there was a high correlation between the GNI per person ranking and the HDI ranking when the entire sample of countries was considered (Dietz and Gibson 1994; in that study there were 143 economies). This tends to support the view of those who argue that per capita income is a reasonable proxy for ranking nations as to their relative and absolute level of development. However, when the sample was examined in more detail, this conclusion could be supported only weakly.

Using income per capita as a surrogate for development is most reliable both for the highest-income nations and for the lowest-income, least-developed nations, with some notable exceptions, like Sri Lanka, China, Guyana, and Indonesia in the latter category. For the seventy-two lower-middle and upper-middle income countries in the study, however, the level of income per capita turned out to be an unreliable indicator for the level of human development and an unreliable ranking methodology for relative human development among those nations.

The results of this study strongly suggest that considering both the level and relative position of a country using GNI per capita or GDP per capita (particularly if the PPP values are used) *and* the HDI score is, perhaps, the more prudent way to evaluate the level of development. Since the link between economic growth and development is neither direct nor consistent for all countries, tracking progress over time using both the HDI and income provides more robust information than either per capita income or the HDI value alone. Given that both income and HDI values now are readily available annually, there is a strong argument for making use of both, perhaps especially so for the middle-income, less-developed nations.

The HDI thus provides an alternative measure to the income per person, economic growth criterion for evaluating the progress of a country in terms of achieving broadly accepted development goals. The HDI reminds us that though increased income is vital for the expanded choices it provides individuals and families, it is not the whole of what development is about. The unadjusted HDI partly captures the extent to which the spread effects of growing incomes are filtered through education, health, social security, and other areas of the economy and how incomes are distributed to expenditures that are both means to, and ends of, higher levels of development.

The search for any single indicator that will provide all the information that is important and relevant to evaluating development is perhaps elusive. Any single indicator is likely to be at best an imperfect measure. Awareness of the weaknesses of whatever measure is used and an effort by the observer of the development process of any nation to "fill in the gaps" of coverage inevitable to any single index remains, nonetheless, an essential and somewhat subjective ingredient to the evaluation of progress and to making recommendations for change.

Economic growth and equity: goals at odds?

If a country places an emphasis on development and the targeting of objectives such as increased education and better health care that contribute to improvements on the HDI measure or to a reduction in the numbers of the poor, will this adversely affect economic growth? Conversely, if a country takes steps aimed at accelerating economic growth, what effect will this have on the goals of development, as measured by the HDI or by poverty reduction? In other words, are economic growth and development at odds or are they broadly complementary?

Underlying the insistence of some economists on measuring development by income per capita and of targeting this as a proximate goal for development is a concern that if policy-makers place too much emphasis on achieving other, more specific development goals this may slow the pace of economic growth by taking scarce resources away from investment and other uses. A slower pace of economic growth may actually make the achievement of these desired development goals all that more difficult by reducing the material resources available to improve the level of human welfare. Is there, in fact, such a conflict between pursuing economic growth and pursuing development, more broadly defined?

An influential study published in 1955 by the late Nobel Prize-winning economist Simon Kuznets examined the historical relationship between income per capita and income distribution, one broad indicator of equity. While trends in a country's income inequality are an imperfect indicator of what is happening to the broader goals of development, rising and high levels of income inequality, if persistent, may be a signal of underlying weaknesses in an economy's structure in being able to broadly deliver a higher level of development. The research by Kuznets and others following in his footsteps has had a great influence on how many analysts think about the relation between economic growth, as measured by rising per capita income, and the achievement of the broader goals of development.

Kuznets's analysis suggested that at low income levels economic growth and rising average income tended to create more income inequality as measured by the Gini coefficient. As income per capita continues to increase, however, a critical threshold level of income was reached, and further economic growth and even higher average income tended to reduce a nation's overall income inequality. This relationship between the level of per capita income and income inequality is referred to as the Kuznets inverted-U hypothesis, from the shape of the curve shown in Figure 2.1

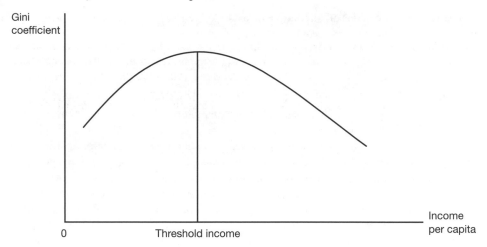

Figure 2.1 The Kuznets curve.

The Kuznets hypothesis is often interpreted to mean that there is a minimum level of income that a country must achieve before greater equity and higher levels of development can be attained. Once that threshold level of income is reached, further increases in income contribute to greater equity, as shown by the falling value of the Gini coefficient after the peak of the curve is reached at the threshold income level of approximately $1,000 per person in this graph.

Prior to reaching the threshold level of income in Figure 2.1, however, rising income is associated with increasing inequality, as shown by the rising Gini coefficient value associated with higher income on the upward sloping portion of the curve. What the Kuznets curve suggests is that greater income inequality is the "cost" of rising income per capita prior to reaching the threshold level of income, a cost that is necessary if the threshold level of income is ever to be reached. After passing the threshold level of income per person, income inequality will begin to fall as there is additional economic growth and higher levels of per capita income are reached.

In other words, the Kuznets curve can be interpreted to mean that poorer countries at an early stage of their economic development can expect a deterioration in income inequality until the threshold level of income is reached. "Things must get worse before they can get better and a higher level of development can be attained" is one way to summarize this interpretation of what is called the Kuznets hypothesis.

This Kuznets inverted-U hypothesis sometimes has been interpreted as something of a law of economic growth and development. Nations wishing to promote equity and human development in the wider sense can best do so by increasing income per capita. Initially, at income levels below the threshold level, rising income per capita makes income inequality worse, but that is the price that must be paid both to attain higher average income and to eventually reduce inequality.

There is no apparent necessity to target development goals or poverty reduction per se if one accepts this view. The short-term loss in equity that accompanies economic growth before the threshold level of income is reached is the necessary price of progress over the longer haul. From this interpretation of the Kuznets curve, growth and development are not rival goals. Economic growth promotes development and equity in income over the longer term, even if there would seem to be a short-term trade-off (see Focus 2.4 for more on the possible trade-off between inequality and growth).[13]

FOCUS 2.4   INEQUALITY AS A CONSTRAINT ON GROWTH

The conventional wisdom as expressed in the Kuznets curve is that there is a trade-off between economic growth and reducing inequality. Thus an unequal distribution of income is sometimes believed necessary for rapid economic growth, at least at low income levels prior to reaching the threshold income level shown in Figure 2.1. If this is so, however, why do we find in Latin America relatively low rates of economic growth and high inequality, and in East Asia low inequality and rapid growth?

Differences in the political economy and the policies of the two regions may be part of the explanation. In the period after 1945, governing elites in East Asia had their legitimacy threatened by domestic communist insurgents. They thus sought to widen their base of political support via policies such as land reform, public housing, investment in rural infrastructure, and, most commonly, widespread high-quality education. In Latin America, governing elites acted as if they believed they could thrive irrespective of what happened to those with the lowest income as reflected in the tax, expenditure, and trade policies that the political elites legislated and that benefited the poor relatively little.

The association of slow economic growth and high inequality in Latin America may in part be because too much income inequality may act as a constraint on growth by limiting demand and the size of the market. Gini coefficients in Table 2.3 are higher for Argentina, Brazil, Chile, and Mexico than they are for Korea or Thailand. By contrast, East Asia's lower level of income inequality as a result of different policies may have provided significant stimulus to economic growth by increasing domestic demand and spending, as more people had more income to spend.

If this was the case, there is a strong argument that East Asia's investment in education has been a key difference from Latin America, as increases in the average level of schooling had a leveling effect on the income distribution. Rising average levels of education in East Asia, of course, contributed to increasing economic growth directly through the positive effect on productivity. But higher levels of education spread among the population also resulted in a larger core of better-educated workers who all earned more, and this reduced income inequality at the same time.

How significant a constraint on economic growth is "too much" income inequality? It appears to be quite substantial. Research suggest that, *ceteris paribus*, after twenty-five years, GDP per capita could be 8.2 percent higher in a country with low inequality than in a country with income inequality one standard deviation higher.

Simulation results suggest that if, in 1960, Brazil had had Korea's lower level of income inequality, Brazil's growth rate over the following twenty-five years would have been 0.66 percentage points higher each year. This implies that after a quarter-century, GDP per capita in Brazil would have been 17.2 percent higher than it was with the higher degree of inequality in that economy, a substantial difference that could have contributed not only to a higher average standard of living but, perhaps, to the broader goals of development as well.

Source: Birdsall and Sabot 1994

The debate over the Kuznets inverted-U hypothesis and whether it represents the "true" relation between rising average income and income inequality has generated a vast and often complicated literature. The relation Kuznets discovered between income and equity is not, in fact, a law of economics but rather a statistical relation that does not show causality.[14] What seems to happen is that once nations pass the threshold level of income, government expenditures on health, education, social security, and other social and human capital areas tend to rise relative to total expenditures in the economy as public revenues rise. Thus, improvement in equity and on the HDI measure would be expected, as governments are able to focus on broader development goals, which leads to more economic growth in the future.[15]

More importantly, the Kuznets hypothesis – which was found by looking at cross-section data for a number of countries at one point in time – cannot be sustained as a "law" once the experience of individual nations is singled out and examined over time rather than at just one point in time. Some countries have experienced worsening equity along with economic growth, even after what might reasonably be thought to be the threshold level of income has been reached (Brazil is an example), while other nations have been able to improve equity and score higher on the HDI measure at income levels well below Kuznets's threshold level of income (Sri Lanka, for example). The reason? Specific government policies on, for example, education, land and wealth distribution, and other social policies can be focused on the broader development goals early on (Sri Lanka) or taken away from such goals (Brazil), somewhat independently of the level of current income. There is no hard and fast law that says that a country cannot have both rising income and more development at low income levels – or vice versa.

What the Kuznets inverted-U demonstrates, then, is historically what on average did happen for a group of nations at one point in time. It does not imply that all countries, especially late developers, must necessarily tolerate or even promote increasing inequality to achieve economic growth over time. The particular path which any nation follows in terms of the relation between its economic growth rate and its success in reaching the broader goals of development is at least partly a consequence of conscious public policy. Such policy can be geared toward high economic growth and greater equity and development, or high growth and slow development. Even slow economic growth paths can generate increasing or decreasing inequality, depending on government policies aimed at confronting the sources of inequality and the commitment to achieving important development objectives.

The particular mix of economic growth and development that results is at least partly a public policy choice that a nation's leaders determine, with or without popular consent. This is not to say economic growth does not matter for equity or development objectives; it does. Over time, more economic growth and a higher average income level should contribute to greater development by providing the resources needed to achieve those broader goals. The reverse is also true, since increased human development can importantly contribute to higher levels of labor productivity, particularly via increased education and better health care, which lead to higher economic growth and income, thus creating a virtuous circle as more economic growth contributes to improvements in development and vice versa.

Countries cannot ignore one side of the development equation – either economic growth or development – for very long without suffering the consequences of a lop-sided policy. As we shall see in later chapters, some East Asian countries were able to achieve quite substantial progress on both the economic development and equity ledgers simultaneously, and that would seem to be a path worth emulating (see Focus 2.5 on China).

The differences in the GDP and HDI rankings of economies shown in Table 2.5 suggested the importance of policy decisions by government and society in achieving development goals, as measured by the HDI, at different levels of income, especially for the middle-income, less-developed nations. The divergence in the rankings of countries on their income per person and on their HDI values also confirms that the Kuznets curve is not strictly a law governing the relation between equity and development and the level of per capita income, or there would be no, or fewer, non-zero values for the PPP GDP–HDI rankings.

Depending on a nation's policies, greater equity and progress on development goals can be achieved even at relatively low levels of income. It is not necessary for countries to await the threshold level of per capita income shown in Figure 2.1 before progress toward greater

FOCUS 2.5 CHINA: A NEW TIGER?

Is the Chinese economy another example of an East Asian economy that is on a path that will bring it to developed country status sooner rather than later?

There certainly is ample evidence of rapid progress. From 1986–96, GDP per person rose by 8.6 percent per year; from 1996–2006, income per person grew by 8.2 percent annually. It is predicted to grow even faster, nearly 10 percent per year until at least 2010 (World Bank data). What does such rapid growth mean in concrete terms? With compounding, income per person increased nearly fivefold over the twenty-year period from 1986 to 2006. A glance back at Table 2.1 shows that GNI per capita grew even faster, since GNI > GDP in China.

If we look at income distribution, there has been a trend toward greater inequality over this period of rapid growth. In 1998, the richest 20 percent earned 7.9 times what the poorest 20 percent earned, compared to 12.1 times more income in 2004, as shown in Table 2.3. The Gini coefficient rose between the two years from 40.3 to 46.9, suggesting that economic growth has not been equally shared among income groups. This perhaps reflects the transition China is making from a socialist to a mixed economy, where capitalism and markets play a larger role, and where greater inequality may be both more likely and more functional than it was in a socialist setting. Or this relationship may simply reflect the movement along a traditionally interpreted Kuznets curve prior to reaching the threshold level of income, as discussed in this section, when income distribution worsens before it gets better. Only time will tell.

China's HDI has increased over time, reaching 0.768 in 2004, not far from the 0.800 threshold that would advance the country into the high human development category. That is quite an accomplishment. On individual indicators, life expectancy is seventy-two years; more than 90 percent of the population aged fifteen or more is literate; there is universal primary school enrolment; and PPP income is about $6,000 per person. On many indicators, then, China has made remarkable progress. For a country that is still relatively poor, it has achieved a population growth rate that is more like that in developed economies than in less-developed nations, as we shall see in Chapter 12.

There are concerns about the sustainability of China's growth path and the issue of the use of prison labor and a grossly undervalued exchange rate that help to make the economy internationally competitive. There is little doubt that exports of manufactured goods to world markets have helped to fuel these rapid growth rates. In fact, China's consumption as a proportion of total GDP fell from more than 60 percent in 2000 to about 50 percent in 2006, as exports grew rapidly. This is where things get tricky.

China's exports and the profits of its large industrial corporations have been a driving force for rapid economic growth over the recent past. It is this external dynamic, not the internal economy, that is providing the motor force for much of China's rapid economic growth. If there is an interruption in trade or a world slowdown in economic expansion, this could have a severe impact on China's income and growth. This is why concern about the balance between internal demand, especially for consumption spending, and the external demand from exports is of such concern. Too much of a good thing could turn into too much of a bad thing.

Source: Anderson 2007

equity and development can be accomplished. It is a matter of policy decisions, and even after attaining the threshold level of income there still is no guarantee of progress toward greater equity if governments are not partners to positive change. Meeting development objectives depends on the nature of state and social policy aimed at attaining greater equity and a higher level of human development. Development and equity are not mechanically determined by the level of income per person.

An innovative use of the Kuznets curve is to consider the relation of income levels and income growth and the level of pollution (see Focus 2.6).

FOCUS 2.6   AN ENVIRONMENTAL KUZNETS CURVE?

Some researchers have suggested there may be an environmental Kuznets curve, similar to Figure 2.1, but with pollution levels measured on the vertical axis rather than income inequality. At relatively low income levels, increases in economic growth result in increased pollution and environmental destruction. However, after a threshold level of income per person is reached, pollution and adverse environmental effects will be reduced. Why might such a relationship be expected?

At low income levels, societies typically place a relatively low value on a clean environment compared to the value of increasing economic growth; thus little attention will be paid to environmental conditions. Increases in agricultural output might be expected to expand the volume of toxic wastes created, and if industrialization is just beginning it is quite likely that air and water pollution will accompany the growth of new factories. Clean and safe technologies for production may not be available to poor countries at a reasonable cost. The alternative to paying for cleaner technologies is to absorb the damage caused by pollution and other environmental degradation as one of the "costs" of improvements in average living conditions.

A clean environment is often assumed to be a "luxury good" in the sense that its income elasticity is greater than one. If this is the case, only at higher income levels will a clean environment have a value worth preserving. If this is correct, then one would expect to see an environmental Kuznets curve, at least for some kinds of pollution and environmental damage (e.g. sulphur dioxide, particulate matter) that accompany industrialization. Other types of environmental damages increase with higher income levels, e.g. carbon dioxide emissions from vehicles, groundwater contamination, and municipal waste and garbage, as the discussion of the pollution of affluence earlier in the chapter in Focus 2.3 suggested.

However, much like the traditional Kuznets curve for income growth, the observation of an environmental Kuznets curve has been based on what has occurred in the past. Now, there is better information, better environmental accounting methods, and greater awareness of the global significance of promoting a kind of economic growth that takes into consideration environmental effects, in poor and rich countries alike. There is increasing awareness that progress over time needs to be economically, politically, and environmentally sustainable. In other words, it is recognized that steps need to be take to flatten out or even induce a downturn of the environmental Kuznets curve. The real issue is whether it is also politically feasible to do so. As the World Bank noted:

> The principles of sound environmental policy … are well understood. But they are difficult for national governments to introduce and are even more difficult to translate into international agreements. National governments may be reluctant to challenge those who cause environmental damage; they are likely to be rich and influential, while those who suffer most are often the poor and powerless.

In other words, it is not wise to leave the environment to chance and to purely market decisions. In many poor countries, it is not possible to simply wait until incomes rise and hope that the environment will be valued more. Environmental degradation is now a global problem and though its causes are often local, the international community needs to work to see that the age of an environmental Kuznets curve is increasingly in the past. This reality is recognized in the Millennium Development Goals discussed in Chapter 1, especially Goal 7.

Sources: Dasgupta and Mäler 1995: 2384–8;
World Bank 1992: 10–13, 18, 38–41, 43

Summary and conclusions

We have considered in this chapter how to measure development among diverse economies. One way is to use income per person as a proxy measure for the long list of objectives enumerated at the beginning of the chapter that actually comprise "becoming" developed. It is necessary, however, to make several adjustments to the total income (GDP or GNI) values calculated by each country so as to improve the usefulness of income as a simple measure of the level of development of economies.

1   Each economy's income needs to be converted to a common currency to make comparison among economies possible.
2   Total nominal income needs to be converted to income per capita values by dividing total income in the common currency by total population to make comparison among economies meaningful.
3   To compare economies over time, it is necessary to calculate real income per person by deflating nominal income values by an appropriate price deflator.
4   The best measure of income per capita for comparing economies over time is purchasing power parity (PPP) GDP or GNI.

The following chart summarizes the various income measures for GDP, clearly showing how they differ, as well as how they are similar. The 'i's are the different goods and services produced.

Calculating GDP for Botswana

Measure	Price vector	×	Output vector	Text reference
Nominal GDP =	$P_{i,\ \text{current year, Botswana}}$	×	$Q_{i,\ \text{current year, Botswana}}$	Equation 2.2
Real GDP, base year 1992 =	$P_{i,\ 1992,\ \text{Botswana}}$	×	$Q_{i,\ \text{current year, Botswana}}$	Equation 2.3
PPP GDP =	$P_{i,\ \text{current year, US}}$	×	$Q_{i,\ \text{current year, Botswana}}$	Equation 2.5

In calculating the different measures of GDP (or GNI), the Q_is used in each calculation are the same; what differs are the prices used to value each country's current output levels.

As an alternative, or as complement to using income as a means to rank economies as to their level and rate of economic development, the human development index, the HDI, has gained support. The HDI includes education, life expectancy, and income to capture more dimensions of development. It still is not used to the extent that income per person is, but it serves as a reminder that development is not just about income but a broader range of goals that societies set for themselves, if only implicitly at times.

Questions and exercises

1   In the discussion as to why GNI and GDP may diverge, the focus was on inflows and outflows of profits and dividends as a result of foreign investments and on workers' remittances. What other inflows of income to and outflows of income from a country can cause the GNI measure of income to differ from the GDP measure of income?
2   This problem will give you some practice examining the relationship between economic growth and population growth.

a   Over the period 1970–80, Tanzania's total GDP grew at 3.0 percent per annum and by 3.6 percent from 1980–93, while population expanded at 3.1 percent over the earlier period and by 3.2 percent, 1980–93. What was the rate of growth of GDP per capita over both periods?

b   Botswana's population grew by 3.5 percent per year, 1970–80, and by 3.4 percent, 1980–93, while total GDP grew by 14.5 percent per year, 1970–80, and by 9.6 percent per annum, 1980–93. What was happening to Botswana's GDP per person over each period?

c   Does population growth "cause" slow or fast growth in GDP? What is the connection between population growth and the increase in income per person suggested by these two examples?

3   Determine the estimated *average* income of the poorest 20 percent and of the richest 20 percent of income earners in Rwanda, Malaysia, Korea, Botswana, and Kenya by applying the income distribution shares in Table 2.3 to GNI per capita in Table 2.1. Compare these estimated average incomes for the richest and poorest 20 percent with the per capita GNI values shown in Table 2.1. For which of these economies does the average income shown in Table 2.1 give a good idea of actual living standards of the poorest and richest?

4   You are going to draw a scatter diagram, with 2006 GNI per capita (from Table 2.1) on the horizontal axis and the ratio of income received by the richest 20 percent to the share received by the poorest 20 percent (from Table 2.3) on the vertical axis.

a   Plot the data for ten of the countries in the tables.

b   Is there any systematic relation between GNI per capita and the degree of income inequality? Do countries with low levels of GNI per capita have more or less inequality than economies with higher levels of GNI per capita? (If you have access to Excel or a simple statistical analysis package, you could run a simple regression between the two variables to look for a relation.)

5   In 1990, Pakistan's total nominal GDP was $34,050 million. In 2000, total nominal GDP had increased to $51,920 million.

a   What was the *total* percentage change in nominal GDP between 1990 and 2000?

b   What was the percent change, on average, per year of nominal GDP over the decade?

c   Now determine real (constant price) GDP in 2000 calculated at 1990 prices, given that the price index in 1990 = 100 and in 2000 = 215.9.

d   What was the percent change in real GDP between 1990 and 2000, both in total and the per year average?

6   What explains the fact that Japan's purchasing power parity (PPP) level of GNI per capita is so much lower than its GNI per capita calculated at the official exchange rate (Table 2.4)? What does that difference indicate about the prices of *non-traded* goods in Japan relative to US prices?

7   Explain why using the purchasing power parity measure of GNI per capita is considered a better measure for comparing development levels between nations than the exchange rate-converted GNI per person level.

8   Using the methodology for determining the value of the HDI shown in the UNDP *Human Development Report* and summarized in Appendix 2B, calculate the value of the HDI

for a country that interests you and that is not listed in Table 2.5. Does that country's level of GDP per capita provide a reasonable proxy for the country's level of development as measured by the HDI? Are there other countries with a similar level of income to that of the country you have selected that have substantially different HDI values? How might you account for those differences?

9 Focus 2.6 discusses the environmental Kuznets curve and suggests that avoiding such an outcome is more of a political problem than one of know-how. What does the World Bank mean in the quotation in Focus 2.6 that it tends to be the "rich and powerful" that cause much of the pollution and the poor who suffer from the effects? In what specific ways do the "rich and powerful" cause environmental damage? In what ways do the poor bear such costs? Can you identify instances where it is the poor who contribute to environmental damage? (Hint: think of clear-cutting of forests for wood for charcoal or for grazing of animals, as one instance; also, reread Focus 2.3, which considers the "pollution of poverty.")

10 In the exercise below, you will be calculating the GDP for two countries, the US and India. To simplify, each country produces only one good and one service, copper and retail sales. Fill in the blanks to determine the total nominal GDP for each country in its *own* currency for 2001. Don't worry about the units in the problem below. Just do the calculations using the numbers without attaching units. Remember equation 2.2 above for doing the calculations! Can the GDP values you calculated be compared?

	United States			India		
	Quantity	Price ($)	Value of output ($)	Quantity	Price	Value of output (rupees)
Copper (million tons)	160	$210/ton	_____	20	R 2,625	_____
Retail sales (millions of workers)	4.68	$5,200/ worker	_____	16	R 22,280	_____
Total GDP in local currency (total *nominal* GDP)			_____			_____

11 Now calculate total nominal GDP for each country valued not in its own currency, but in US dollars. If the average exchange rate in 2001 was 12.5 rupees = $1, India's total nominal GDP valued in US$ at the official exchange rates is equal to _____? Can US and India GDP be compared now to say which country is "better off"? Explain.

12 This problem will give you practice in understanding how *real GDP* is determined. In 2000 in India (the figures in problem 10 above are for 2001), the price of copper was R 2,500/ton, while the value of retail sales per worker was R 20,200. What is the value of India's real GDP in 2001, assuming the 2000 prices are the base year prices for comparison? Remember, real GDP measures only changes in actual physical output, holding prices constant between years; if you need to, look back at Equation 2.3. (We could then convert this value to US dollars using the exchange rate as we did in problem 11 and then divide by population to get real GDP per person.)

13   Now, calculate India's 2001 purchasing power parity GDP valuing India's 2001 output using 2001 US prices (Equation 2.5 from the text). Is this value larger or smaller than India's total nominal GDP you calculated in problem 11 using the official exchange rate conversion rate? What does the PPP GDP value you have calculated mean compared to the value you calculated in problem 11?

14   If income were perfectly equally distributed, the poorest 20 per cent of individuals or families would receive 20 percent of the economy's total income, the second poorest 20 percent of individuals or families would receive 20 percent of the economy's total income, and so on, and the richest 20 percent of individuals or families would receive 20 percent of the economy's total income. In such a case of *perfect equality*, each individual's or family's income would be equal to per capita income. Everyone would receive the same income. However, in the real world income is distributed unequally so that a country's per capita income is not necessarily telling us much about the living standard of all the population. This problem highlights how the average income measure may not give a full picture of the living standards of an economy if income distribution is highly skewed.

   In Uganda, the poorest 20 percent of the population received 6.2 percent of total income while the richest 20 percent received 63.5 percent of total income of the country. Given that income per capita for Uganda was $310 in 2004, what was the *average income per capita* of the poorest 20 percent and of the richest 20 percent of the population? What was the average income of the remainder of the population?

15   Let's consider what the Kuznets curve looks like for an individual country. The data may not be easy to find, but look for Gini coefficient values, or as an alternative, the ratio of the income of the richest 20 percent of the population to the income of the poorest 20 percent as a proxy measure of inequality, for a number of years. The World Bank website has such data. Then plot the data you find against income per person for the same years on the vertical axis of a graph. Does it look like the Kuznets curve in Figure 2.1? If not, what does the curve you have found tell you about the relation between income inequality and growth in that country? Does the data you plot show a threshold level of income as in Figure 2.1?

16   Focus 2.5 considered the viability of China's continued economic growth given the heavy dependence on exports for growth and the relatively small proportion of impetus to growth from consumption. Find some recent data on China's economic growth and its exports. Has there been a slowdown in economic expansion? Have exports continued to grow as rapidly as in the past? You should be able to find some data at the World Bank website.

Notes

1   Further, it is a strongly held belief of many economists that economic growth in capitalist societies occurs via a trickle-down process. With economic growth and an expansion of society's total income, there is assumed to exist a more or less automatic dispersion of the benefits of this growth to all income classes of society. While it is admitted that the incomes of the wealthiest in society perhaps grow most rapidly, those at lower income levels are presumed to benefit also from economic expansion as income "trickles down" the income pyramid. This may occur via the provision of new and better jobs that result from the increased investment undertaken by higher-income individuals who finance such ventures, given their higher disposable incomes.

Thus, one view is that income inequality has a functional purpose in capitalist economies in that it is higher-income individuals who are likely to save a larger portion of their incomes relative to lower-income recipients. It is from this pool of savings that the loanable funds for investment arise. Much like a boat, all of whose passengers are lifted together on a rising tide, it is suggested that greater economic growth benefits all, or certainly the great majority, of the members of society via the automatic mechanism of trickle-down growth. This, of course, is only a theory; the important question is whether this process works as described in each economy.

2 Poorer nations tend to have less dependable estimates of their national income for one obvious reason: collecting data is expensive, and for economies already facing the constraint of limited financial and human resources, the gathering and evaluation of economic data is likely to be done in a manner that is less than desirable and certainly less than would be optimal. To develop strategies that contribute to development, however, there is a compelling need for reliable and timely statistical data concerning the objective reality in less-developed nations. In fact, one is tempted to state that the effort put into collecting dependable and timely statistics, making such information available to the public, and in analyzing such data is one measure of a country's commitment to doing something positive about its future development.

3 Gross national income (GNI) is the same concept as the former gross national product (GNP) terminology. The use of the term GNI, however, is an improvement as it more accurately conveys what is being measured, i.e. national income available foe use.

4 There are some further caveats worth mentioning when calculating real GNI or real GDP and using these values to judge an economy's progress over time. The farther apart in time the comparisons of income are, the less meaningful they are likely to be. For example, some goods and services may no longer be produced in later years, while new goods and services can enter the production stream. Thus, price indices and the deflating technique become less reliable for comparing real output over long periods.

The issue of the quality of the Q_is is not captured by the price index adjustment either. Prices may rise with quality improvements over time (some couture clothing) or they may fall (as with computers and HDTVs), so some price changes reflect not inflation or deflation but rather differences in product quality. These differences will be lost in adjusting for real income with a price deflator and such improvements in quality, when they occur, must be reintroduced via other methods.

Still, while always being cognizant of these weaknesses in calculating real GDP or GNI figures, if the years being compared are not too far apart in time, calculations as in equations 2.3 and 2.4 can be taken as reasonable approximations for estimating changes in real output and income over time.

5 Other deflators might be used, for example, the GDP price deflator. In the case of Mexico, for example, using the GDP deflator would have resulted in a very slightly greater drop in income per person.

6 An equivalent and perhaps easier method for calculating the average income of the lowest and highest quintiles is to remember that the $5,503 GNI per capita figure for Brazil shown in Table 2.1 would be the actual income of all individuals in Brazil only if income were perfectly equally distributed. However, the richest 20 percent actually received 3.055 times their equality share of total GNI (their 61.1 percent actual share of total income ÷ their 20 percent equality share). Thus the per capita income of the richest 20 percent in Brazil can be calculated as 3.055 × $5,503 = $16,812, very close to the figure in the text, the difference being due solely to rounding. For the poorest 20 percent, their per capita income is but 0.14 their equality share (the actual 2.8 percent of total income received ÷ a 20 percent equality share), for a per capita income of 0.14 × $5,503 = $770 for the poorest fifth of the population.

7 A Gini coefficient of 0 would indicate perfect equality of income. A Gini coefficient of 100 would indicate perfect inequality in the distribution of income, i.e. one person or family receiving 100 percent of the economy's total income and everyone else receiving nothing.

8 Any good macroeconomics book will have the details on this problem. On the GPI, for which calculations have been made for the United States, see Cobb and Halstead (1994).

9 Arbitrage is the process in which goods are purchased in one market to be resold in another at a higher price and with a known and certain profit. For example, if the price of a bar of Nestlé's chocolate in India sells for the equivalent of $1.50, while it sells for the equivalent of $2.50 in the

Philippines, it would be to the advantage of profit-maximizing traders to purchase Nestlé bars in India and resell them in the Philippines, as long as the transaction costs of doing so – transportation, tariffs, etc. – are less than $1 per bar of chocolate, since there would be profit to be made on such a transaction.

This process of arbitrage tends to bring the prices of the traded goods in line between countries. How does this happen? In our example, the price of Nestlé's bars in India would tend to rise with the increased demand as traders bought in that market in pursuit of the profits of arbitrage, while the price of chocolate bars would tend to fall in the Philippines as a result of the increased supply as chocolate bars would be introduced to that market.

Ultimately, an equilibrium price would exist in both countries at which all the opportunities for arbitrage and the making of a sure profit from trade would have been exhausted. For this reason, the prices of traded goods are expected to be very similar across economies.

10 See Streeten (1979) and Streeten *et al.* (1981) on the basic needs approach and Morris (1979) for the original contribution to the creation of the PQLI measure.

11 The actual calculation of the HDI value for any country is based on that country's deviation from the maximum values for each component of the index: a maximum life expectancy of eighty-five years at birth; 100 percent literacy and 100 percent combined (primary and secondary) school enrolment; and a maximum PPP GDP per capita income of $40,000.

The HDI thus measures the relative position of an economy compared to the maximum (and minimum) levels of achievement. In other words, the HDI is a measure of how far away a country is from the current maximum achievable values on the selected variables that enter the HDI (see any recent edition of the UNDP *Human Development Report* for the methodology and an example of how the HDI is determined; Appendix 2B illustrates such a calculation).

12 Until 1994, the HDI was calculated and compared with GNI per capita evaluated at official exchange rates. Beginning in 1995, however, the HDI has been calculated using a PPP measure of GDP per capita within the index. It is thus not strictly correct to compare the HDI values calculated for years after 1992 (the HDI values in the 1995 *Human Development Report*), with the HDI values calculated for 1987–91. Further changes in the methodology for calculating the HDI are possible in future.

13 It is perhaps worth remembering an important axiom of economic theory which states that there are an infinite number of efficient, i.e. Pareto optimal, outcomes for both the production and distribution of goods and services among the members of any society. No single distribution of income or resources is "better" than another. As can easily be demonstrated with an Edgeworth-Bowley box diagram, any initial distribution of wealth will, under conditions of perfect competition and free exchange, generate a locally efficient level of production and distribution of society's goods and services, with trade resulting in the contract curve being attained.

Thus the distribution of wealth and income amongst society's members is a choice variable open to economies, since the distribution issue is independent of the issue of efficiency. *Any* initial distribution can be efficient. For an excellent exposition of this issue, see Bator's (1957) classic article.

14 See Anand and Kanbur (1993) for a review of the literature. These authors argue that the best empirical relation between income growth and equity or development is actually the opposite of the Kuznets hypothesis! This contradictory result illustrates one of the problems in studying economics. There often are competing models that purport to explain some particular phenomenon, frequently based on extremely complicated mathematical and statistical analyses, done by equally competent and respected investigators, that nonetheless come to diametrically opposed and often irreconcilable conclusions. How does one choose between such competing theories when compelling empirical evidence can be mustered supporting alternative theories? This is an excellent question for class discussion!

15 It is not just governments that today can affect the level of inequality and reduce poverty, even at lower income levels than in the past. There are also a growing number of non-governmental organizations, or NGOs, which operate in the less-developed nations and which often have as their primary objective the alleviation of poverty. These range from large and relatively well-financed groups like Oxfam, the International Red Cross and Crescent, CARE, Caritas, World Vision to small, region- and often country-specific groups, such as the Voluntary Action Network India.

References

Alkire, Sabrina. 2002. "Dimension of Human Development," *World Development* 20: 181–205.

Anand, S. and Kanbur, S.M. 1993. "Inequality and Development: A Critique," *Journal of Development Economics* 41: 19–43.

Anderson, Jonathan. 2007. "Solving China's Rebalancing Puzzle," *Finance & Development* 44 (September): 32–5.

Bartelmus, Peter. 1994. *Environment, Growth and Development*. London: Routledge.

Bator, Francis. 1957. "The Simple Analytics of Welfare Maximization," *American Economic Review* (March): 22–59.

Birdsall, Nancy and Richard Sabot. 1994. "Inequality as a Constraint on Growth in Latin America," *Development Policy*, Newsletter on Policy Research by the Inter-American Development Bank (September): 1–5.

Cobb, Clifford and Ted Halstead. 1994. *The Genuine Progress Indicator*. San Francisco, CA: Redefining Progress (September).

Dasgupta, Partha and Karl-Göran Mäler. 1995. "Poverty, Institutions, and the Environmental Resource-Base," Chapter 39 in Jere Behrman and T.N. Srinivasan (eds.), *Handbook of Development Economics*, vol. IIIA. Amsterdam: Elsevier Science.

Dietz, James L. and Louise Gibson. 1994. "What is Development? The Human Development Index, a New Measure of Progress?," mimeo, California State University, Fullerton.

Elliott, Jennifer A. 1994. *An Introduction to Sustainable Development*. London: Routledge.

Morley, Samuel A. 1995. *Poverty and Inequality in Latin America*. Baltimore, MD: The Johns Hopkins University Press.

Morris, Morris D. 1979. *Measuring the Condition of the World's Poor: The Physical Quality of Life Index*. New York: Pergamon Press.

Redclift, Michael. 1987. *Sustainable Development: Exploring the Contradictions*. London: Routledge.

Stewart, Frances. 1995. *Adjustment and Poverty*. London: Routledge.

Streeten, Paul. 1979. "From Growth to Basic Needs," *Finance and Development* 16 (September): 5–8.

—— *et al.* (eds.). 1981. *First Things First*. Oxford: Oxford University Press.

UNDP (United Nations Development Programme). 1993. *Human Development Report 1993*. Oxford: Oxford University Press.

——. 1995. *Human Development Report 1995*. Oxford: Oxford University Press.

——. 2001. *Human Development Report 2001*. Oxford: Oxford University Press.

——. 2006. *Human Development Report 2006*. Oxford: Oxford University Press.

US Department of Commerce. 1994. *Survey of Current Business* 74 (July).

——. 1995. *Survey of Current Business* 75 (August).

WCED (World Commission on Environment and Development). 1987. *Our Common Future*. Oxford: Oxford University Press.

World Bank. 1992. *World Development Report 1992*. Oxford: Oxford University Press.

——. 1995. *World Development Report 1995*. Oxford: Oxford University Press.

——. 2000. *World Development Report 2000/2001*. Oxford: Oxford University Press.

——. 2001. *World Development Indicators*. On-line.

——. 2007 *World Development Indicators*. On-line.

Appendix 2A: Calculating the Gini coefficient

To understand how the Gini coefficient is calculated, it is helpful to look at a Lorenz curve which provides a graphical representation of a nation's income distribution. Figure 2.1A shows a simple Lorenz curve drawn from the following hypothetical income distribution figures.

Income distribution, by quintiles

	Share of total income	*Cumulative percent of total income*
Poorest 20% of families	4% of total GNI	4%
Second 20% of families	8% of total GNI	12% (= 4% + 8%)
Third 20% of families	11% of total GNI	23% (= 4% + 8% +11%)
Fourth 20% of families	18% of total GNI	41%
Richest 20% of families	59% of total GNI	100%
	100% of total GNI	

In Figure 2.1, the box measures the percent of population on the horizontal axis and the percent of total income received by each percent of the population on the vertical axis. The diagonal in Figure 2.1 is a reference "line of equality." Any point along it would mean that X percent of the population received exactly X percent of total income (where X could be any number between 1 and 100). Along the "line of equality," for example, ten percent of the population would be receiving 10 percent of society's total income; 40 percent of the population would be receiving 40 percent of total income; and so on. The diagonal provides a referent for visually comparing and precisely measuring the dispersion of the *actual* income distribution of a nation with what would be a perfectly equal distribution of income among all members of society.

By plotting the "actual" aggregate values of income received against the quintiles of population for our hypothetical example, the bowed Lorenz curve in Figure 2.1A can been drawn. Very roughly, the further away the Lorenz curve is from the line of equality, the greater the degree of income inequality.

From the Lorenz curve diagram, the Gini coefficient can be calculated. It is equal to the area A (the area between the Lorenz curve and the diagonal "line of equality") divided by the total area (A + B) of the triangle below the "line of equality." Thus the Gini coefficient is equal to A/(A + B).

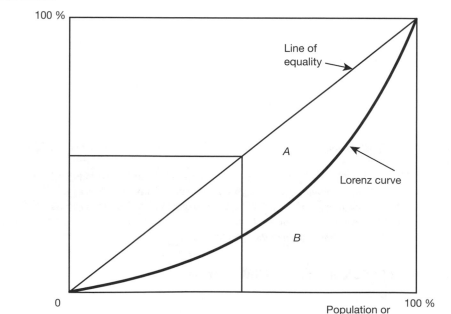

Figure 2.1A A Lorenz curve of income distribution.

Appendix 2B: Calculating the HDI index

With the 1995 issue of the *Human Development Report*, the HDI is calculated as a weighted average of educational attainment, life expectancy at birth, and income. All components of the index measure the relative distance between a country's achievement and what is possible. Thus,

$$\text{index value} = \frac{\text{actual value of } x_i - \text{minimum value of } x_i}{\text{maximum value of } x_i - \text{minimum value of } x_i}$$

Educational attainment (E) is measured as a combination of two indices, one for adult literacy (minimum value = 0 percent; maximum value = 100 percent) and of the combined primary, secondary, and tertiary enrolment ratios (minimum = 0 percent; maximum = 100 percent) with the following weights:

$E = \frac{2}{3}$ adult literacy rate (L) + $\frac{1}{3}$ combined enrolment ratio (C)

Life expectancy (L), for purposes of calculating the HDI index, has a minimum value of 25 years and a maximum value of 85 years.

Income (Y) enters the HDI as a log value of the purchasing power parity (PPP) measure of GDP per capita. As the UN Development Programme puts it (UNDP *Human Development Report 2003*: 341), "income serves as a surrogate for all the dimensions of human development not reflected in a long and healthy life and in knowledge." PPP GDP per capita income beyond $40,000 adds nothing further to the Y index.

The following shows how the HDI for 2001 was calculated for Albania. The basic data needed to calculate L, E, and Y are: Albania's life expectancy was 73.4 years in 2001; the literacy rate was 85.3 percent; the combined enrolment rate was 69 percent; and PPP GDP per capita was $3,680.

The following HDI calculation for Albania is adapted from UNDP, *Human Development Report 2003*: 341.

1 The *life expectancy index*, L, was determined as follows:
   Using the first equation above, and the minimum and maximum values for life expectancy, the life expectancy index, L, is equal to

$$L = \frac{73.4 - 25}{85 - 25} = 0.807$$

2 To determine the education index, E, a two-step procedure is necessary, again using the second equation in this appendix and the specific values for Albania for literacy and the combined enrolment ratio.

   2a First, the adult literacy index, A, component of educational attainment was computed as

$$A = \frac{85.3 - 0}{100 - 0} = 0.853$$

   2b Second, the combined enrolment index, C, the other component of education attainment, was determined as being

$$C = \frac{69 - 0}{100 - 0} = 0.690$$

Thus from 2a and 2b, the educational attainment index, E, was equal to

$E = 2/3L + 1/3C = 2/3(0.853) + 1/3(0.690) = 0.798$.

3   The income index, Y, for Albania and using Albania's PPP GDP per capita income shown above was equal to

$$Y = \frac{\log(3{,}680) - \log(100)}{\log(40{,}000) - \log(100)} = 0.602$$

The value of the HDI is then calculated as a weighted average of L, E, and Y, with each component having a value of 1/3. Since each of these is a "deprivation" measure, what is being calculated is the gap between a particular country's achievement level and what might be attained.

Thus, the HDI for Albania in 2001 is a simple weighted average of L, E, and Y, computed as

$\text{HDI} = 1/3L + 1/3E + 1/3Y$
$\quad\quad\; = 1/3(0.807) + 1/3(0.798) + 1/3(0.602) = 0.735$.

3   Development in historical perspective

After reading and studying this chapter, you should better understand:
- why and how colonialism left a lasting legacy in developing nations;
- the difference between semi-feudal/semi-capitalist social structures and capitalist social structures;
- the de-industrialization impact of colonialism and the biased nature of colonial infrastructure
- the new role credit played in the construction of neocolonial structures in the nineteenth century;
- the nature and importance of the terms of trade;
- economic dualism and its impact on colonial and post-colonial society;
- how to apply the concept of path dependency to post-colonial situations;
- the differential impact of early and mature colonialism;
- the concept of colonial drain.

Introduction

Economic development demands and entails profound cultural change, including, often, transformation of the political system, of individual behavior norms, of the culture of work and production, and most fundamentally, modifications in the manner in which society confronts, moulds, propels, and adapts itself to the requirements of technological progress that are the fount of economic growth and human development. Anyone studying the process of economic development must appreciate the wide-ranging cultural factors at work in any society. Failure to do so can result in a narrow and mechanistic interpretation of developing societies and the adoption of incomplete policy prescriptions which will, at best, diminish the effectiveness of efforts to achieve further progress.

At times, economists and others directly concerned with the process and problems of economic development have devoted too few of their efforts to understanding the historical conditions which have led to economic backwardness and underdevelopment. This failure may well arise from the fact that orthodox economists have generally been trained in the science of market behavior, with the assumption that human nature consists of, as Adam Smith maintained, a "natural propensity to truck, barter and exchange." Taking such a perspective too literally, however, can lead to the view that the peculiarities and specificities of any country's history can be disregarded. The early development economists, to be discussed in Chapters 5 and 6, did not view history as insignificant, and we would argue that many of their insights as applied to the less-developed nations were richer as a consequence.

The social conditions under which production takes place are often significantly different in the developing world from the advanced nations. Today the developing world incorporates, in shifting proportions, mixtures of neo-feudal and peasant social and productive forces, combined with some of the most advanced components of early twenty-first-century capitalist production methods (this division is sometimes referred to as economic dualism). When development economics emerged as a separate discipline in the postwar period, the primary arena of its application was Western Europe and, to a much lesser degree, Japan. In both areas, economic policy had achieved tremendous success, as the Marshall Plan and US military assistance funds were pumped into Europe. Those economies responded rapidly to this stimulus, quickly regaining and then overtaking their past levels of development. In the early 1950s, then, fresh from this experience, the task of promoting economic development in the newly independent, less-developed nations did not appear daunting to policy-makers.

The relatively easy success of Europe and Japan in spurring output and employment formed the crucible for development thinking regarding the less-developed regions. One noted text of the 1950s, Benjamin Higgins's *Economic Development*, recounts an episode from the postwar period that seemed to justify such optimism. A small Pacific island community was overrun by US military personnel, resulting in the rapid transformation of their culture. Higgins drew a conclusion from this that was widely shared in the 1950s and early 1960s:

> This experience suggests that an almost complete transformation of a society can take place within *a few years* if the external "shock" to the society is powerful enough.
> (Higgins 1959: 312)

Higgins shared with most development economists of that time a strong presumption that whatever the nature or magnitude of the social, psychological, political, or historical obstacles inhibiting economic growth and human development, these barriers could be quickly overcome. The enduring structural distortions of economic dualism, deeply embedded in society because of historical factors which had given rise to economic retardation, were not, however, adequately appreciated at the time.

The 1960s were cast as the First Development Decade by the United Nations, and already Higgins's "few years" for promoting development had been lengthened to ten, but the implication was essentially the same: economic backwardness would yield quickly to the expertise of the development specialists and to informed development advice.

Yet, after that First Development Decade had ended, the level of world poverty and despair had receded only marginally. In some nations, the standard of living had declined or remained roughly the same. In those nations where great leaps in overall economic performance had been achieved, such as Brazil, too often aggregate success had been accompanied by a lower standard of living for a significant portion of the population, as economic inequality worsened even as total output expanded. Few keen observers believed the Brazilian situation merely reflected the lead-up to the threshold income level suggested by Kuznets's inverted-U hypothesis, and time has proved them correct on this point. By the 1970s, much of the optimism about how quickly world poverty might be overcome had been muted, but development economists only rarely turned their attention to the study of historical and cultural factors to try to broaden their understanding of the stubborn persistence of world poverty. In the early twenty-first century, however, there has been a significant change in perspective, with some development economists focusing on the question of the legacy of colonial practices and institutions. Let us briefly turn to a consideration of some of these issues as they relate to the less-developed nations, most of which, it is worth remembering again, reached political independence only after the Second World War.

The origins of economic development

Sustained increases in output and income per capita over time are of relatively recent historical origin. For much of known human history, population and total output tended to grow at about the same rate, so that per capita income remained roughly constant. Lloyd Reynolds has called this the period of extensive growth (Reynolds 1986: 7–9). What this meant was that for many centuries, until the early sixteenth century, the trend line of per capita production and income rose only very slowly, as shown in Figure 3.1. Most production was rurally based, there were few large urban settlements, and most people lived on and from the land, sometimes selling small surpluses in the village marketplace for other goods. Artisan and industrial-type products, such as textiles, and services, such as transportation, were also produced in the countryside, but on a very small scale. Besides agricultural production, families also produced non-agricultural goods, from clothing to cutlery to farm implements to soap and alcoholic beverages, primarily for family own-consumption.

Production methods were relatively simple during this extensive period of growth, and technology was very primitive. Such technology, as Reynolds (1986: Chapter 1) argues, was not static, however. Technological methods were constantly adapting to the growing demands of population growth, to changing land conditions, and to new crops and strains of seeds. Such technological change tended to be sufficient to keep pace with population

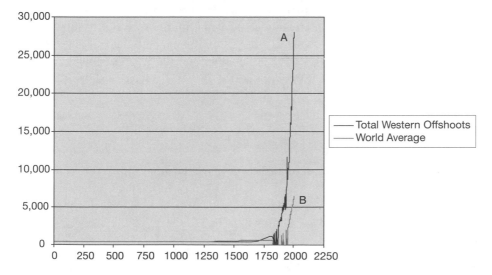

Figure 3.1 Historical growth trend of per capita income.

expansion and to maintain income per person roughly constant over long periods. Annual aggregate output during the period of extensive growth was subject to periodic ups and downs, but that was primarily due to exogenous factors, such as the weather, wars, and other crises.

The major "turning point" for world economic progress occurred with the transition from feudal production and social organization to the emergence of capitalist forms of production in Europe. Feudalism, an agricultural-based and hierarchical system of production organized around manors and based on the labor of serfs tied to the land, began to break down in the Middle Ages, especially in England, where the Industrial Revolution heralded the advent of the capitalist factory system as a new means of social and economic organization. With incipient capitalism, the purpose of production changed from survival and stasis to the pursuit of ever-increasing profit. Capitalist production was based fundamentally on the application of new knowledge and ever-greater quantities of physical capital that could produce more, at lower cost, with the same or fewer inputs to production. Industrial capitalism established the foundation for intensive production methods, which for the first time in history created the reasonable possibility of higher levels of output and income per person *without* increases in population or other resources. Output and income did not depend predominantly upon the availability of resources with intensive production and industrial capitalism, as they had in pre-capitalist forms of production, including feudalism. Now, the level of output depended upon the efficiency with which available resources were used and upon the application of technology to save on the use of such resources, so that more output and income could be produced from what was available. In Figure 3.1, the trend line of income per person (Line A) begins to rise after 1750 or so, when the capitalist system, with its factories and machines, began to triumph in some Western European countries. Due to those nations where capitalism did not become firmly planted, thus failing to displace traditional pre-capitalist methods of production, as in most of the less-developed world, the trend line of world income per person (Line B) does not show the sharp upward trend that characterized income growth in the developed capitalist world along the path of Line A.[1]

It is important to keep in mind, then, that the possibility of sustained increases in income per person, that is, in economic growth and development, is a relatively recent historical phenomenon, dating back only some 270 years. Further, high levels of economic success have been, to date at any rate, strongly associated with the spread of capitalist methods of production and the displacement of pre-capitalist methods, in both agriculture and industry. Why have such methods of production, and the ways of thinking and doing that are associated with such production, developed so strongly in some regions of the world – the developed nations – and apparently so weakly in others – the less-developed countries?

Colonialism

As noted in the last chapter, most of the less-developed nations today were colonies of one or, sometimes, more than one powerful capitalist country during their history. The period of imperial expansion after the "discovery" of the Americas by Columbus in the late fifteenth century led to a scramble by the European powers for land around the globe. Parts of Asia, Africa, and the Americas fell into the hands of incipient capitalist nations bent on winning the competitive race by controlling as much of the world's resources as possible. Not only British colonies, on which, truly, "the sun never set," but Dutch, French, Belgian, German, Spanish, Portuguese, and Italian colonial possessions multiplied, sometimes changing hands, but always attained and held in the interests of what, charmingly if inaccurately, was called the "mother country." The good of the native peoples of the colonies was of little concern to the colonizers, except in so far as they might best serve to the advantage of the colonizer.[2]

As a consequence, during the long epoch of European colonialism (until the 1930s), little thought was given to the question of economic development *per se* in the colonies. The colonizing powers repeatedly referred to their "civilizing" and often "Christianizing" missions in the colonial regions. Political leaders in the colonies occasionally commented upon their willingness to uplift natives through the introduction of Western education and modern science. It was almost taken as a truism by the colonizing powers that their presence in those "uncivilized" countries could not help but be beneficial to the natives, who so often seemed to be ungrateful for the sacrifices made by the colonizers. The colonial powers even defended European involvement in the nefarious slave trade on the grounds that slavery was widespread in Africa anyway, that Africa not Europe had invented it, and that life on a West Indian or Brazilian plantation often was preferable to death in an African tribal war or to a lifetime of slavery in Africa.

Even Karl Marx seemed to believe that the processes which European colonialism unleashed in the underdeveloped regions ultimately would be beneficial and were undoubtedly necessary if these regions were ever to make any substantial progress. For Marx, it was both inevitable and desirable, as part of his stages view of human progress (see Chapter 4), that pre-capitalist societies be swept away. The capitalism introduced by the colonial powers had a destructive and regenerative function. Antiquated, backward cultures and patterns of behavior in the colonies needed to be eliminated if development was to occur, and the introduction of the capitalist, market society would lead to a higher standard of living and an all-round better life for the natives. As difficult and brutal as the colonial process might be, the inevitability of such progress was not called into question by Marx, as his writings on British colonialism in India clearly demonstrated. Nor did there seem to be any doubt that the destruction of the old societies brought on by colonialism, traumatic as that might be, was desirable in the final calculation.

Unlike the early apologists for European colonialism, or those who emphasized the destructive and regenerative nature of a process largely regarded as inevitable, many modern development economists, particularly in the 1950s, were careful to emphasize that the development process and development policy should be critically aware of the need to preserve and constructively alter elements of the post-colonial societies which were, in the view of the particular less-developed country, worthy of retention. Many Westerners, including perhaps surprisingly Marx, might have found this perspective incomprehensible. Yet in the areas of art, literature, handicrafts, music and dance, herbal medicine, the nurturing of children, cuisine, and attitudes toward mutual support among the family, the so-called backward cultures may be imbued with valuable social institutions worthy of preserving and adapting within more modern social and productive societies.

As developing societies evolve, a fusion of old but still functional societal elements with new forces and processes should be the goal; development does not have to mean the complete destruction of what makes any people and culture special and unique. In Latin America, the contradictions of pursuing modern development are sometimes summarized as follows: "Americans know how to work, and Latin Americans know how to play." The limits of a one-dimensional society are well-drawn in this saying. There are positive lessons that less-developed societies can learn from the already developed nations, but the obverse also is true.

The lasting effects of colonialism and path dependency

To some observers, the era of colonialism might seem, on first glance, to be merely a subject of historical import, devoid of any apparent immediacy as regards the problems of development in the less-developed nations today.[3] Colonialism, however, entailed more than the plundering of a militarily and economically weaker culture by a more powerful nation. Colonialism often resulted in severe demographic crises. This was particularly the case with the Spanish in Mexico and Peru, and with the British, Dutch, French, Portuguese, and Spanish in Africa.[4] Although demographers and anthropologists dispute the magnitude of the demographic crisis in Latin America between 1540 and 1640, there is no question that the indigenous population was drastically reduced in a labor draft system which sent millions into the gold and silver mines to finance Spain's Siglo de Oro. Spain's forced labor system disrupted traditional Indian village systems of production, sent men and boys into the mines to toil without pay and then die, and left women and children to plant and harvest crops which had to support the males working in the mines.

In his fascinating account of the history of Spain in the New World, Eduardo Galeano (1973: 50) refers to research that suggests that Latin America's population declined from an estimated 70–90 million in 1540 to 3.5 million by 1690. Others question these figures, placing the original indigenous population figure at a lower level. But whatever the numbers, the sheer loss of life, whether from overwork, disease, or from struggle against better-armed adversaries, is stupefying. What consequences did this demographic crisis impose upon the Indians? To what degree was their culture decimated? What were the lasting effects upon the indigenous people who survived? How did these terrible events shape social attitudes in the region toward change in future generations? (See Focus 3.1.)

In Africa, a demographic crisis of similar proportions was spread over a period of nearly 400 years. The slave trade furnished one part of the colonial world with labor to fill the vast lands acquired by the colonial powers, at the cost of depopulating Africa. Between 1600 and 1900, approximately 12 million Africans were sold into slavery and brought to the Western hemisphere, with an additional 36 million dying as a result of constant warfare throughout Africa, or on the long march to the coast, or in the slave pens awaiting shipment across the Atlantic (Stavrianos 1981: 109). From 1650 to 1850, Africa's share of world population fell from 18 per cent to 8 per cent, as a result, at least partly, of the effects of the slave trade.

The slave trade had other effects that illustrate the lasting impact of colonialism: a new economic role for African chieftains was created, that of facilitator and regional beneficiary of the slave trade. Authoritarianism was strengthened and resistance to the status quo made more difficult by the new gains to be made from warfare on neighboring tribes. Furthermore, the constant wars encouraged by the slave traders, but perpetrated by the tribal chiefs in order to realize the potential gains of selling conquered tribes into slavery, tended to impede the emergence of inter-regional trade patterns, while at the same time it encouraged the importation of European manufactured products. Thus to the effects of depopulation through slavery, one should add the partial destruction of native manufactures and the hardening of authoritarian rule in Africa brought on by colonialism. Vertical trading patterns between Africa and Europe were often substituted for horizontal trade patterns across Africa, which could have contributed to the more robust development of linkages between the local economies. Such trade patterns might have acted as a check on tensions between tribes and regions in Africa which would have depended more on one another rather than on trade relations with Europe.

FOCUS 3.1 PATH DEPENDENCE AND COLONIAL STRUCTURES

The term "path dependence" has been used to describe the important role which historical events and historically formed institutions have in determining the future range of possibilities for a nation. Once institutions have been formed, they tend to lock-in a certain evolutionary path for the nation.

If the previously formed institutions are socially constructive, then the evolutionary path of the economy can be *virtuous*; the process of cumulative causation leads to an upward spiral of social progress. But if the institutional basis of a society has been formed through a long process whereby inhibiting institutions and social practices have become deeply entrenched, then it is more likely that the future evolutionary path will be one of *vicious circles* of cumulative causation leading to low levels of income and achievement.

Institutions may come into existence because they are desirable and superior to what has gone before. But retarding institutions may be imposed, if they serve the interests of powerful groups or nations. Even historians who are hesitant to fault colonial policies, such as David Fieldhouse, acknowledge that under colonialism only the ability to produce and export agricultural products or raw materials, such as minerals and forestry products, mattered. Colonial industry was ignored, as was any supporting matrix for industry, such as education, a financial system, or technical training.

With rare exceptions,

> colonial states constituted an arbitrary break in the historical process, sometimes splitting regions with some natural connection, elsewhere bringing together societies which had no capacity to co-operate; and in either case doing so at a speed that made it impossible for forces to operate satisfactorily. In this respect colonialism bequeathed an impossible heritage to the rulers of the new states.

History matters, then, according to path dependence theory. And, in the case of the underdeveloped nations, once free of colonialism, the weight of history continued to play a role in shaping the path of economic and social change of the future. This is not to argue that nations, once burdened by inhibiting institutions, are condemned mechanistically to repeat the processes and behavioral patterns established in the past. Rather, it is to argue that the past must be carefully understood, including the colonial past, in order to comprehend the nature of the challenges and limits which developing societies now confront. Path dependency helps us to understand why and where countries are today in their process of evolution. The concept is also helpful in beginning to grasp what is required to alter adverse path dependency by decisions that can lead to a higher level of growth and development in the future.

Sources: Fieldhouse 1981: 15, 68; Acemoglu 2003; Acemoglu, Johnson, and Robinson 2001

Forms of European colonialism

Spain: a case of absolute depredation

The earliest colonial empires, those of Spain and Portugal, while imposing devastating social and economic changes on the colonial regions, were, ironically, of no lasting benefit to the imperial powers either. As gold and, later, silver poured into Seville for roughly 200 years after 1500, Spain's quasi-feudal economy became steadily less cohesive. As these precious metals circulated as money, the rapid inflow of gold and silver resulted in severe inflation which undermined domestic Spanish industry, handicrafts, and agriculture. Conspicuous consumption among the Spanish elite, however, was enabled to reach new heights as a result of the flow of wealth emanating from the overseas colonies. Unproductive investments in government buildings and private villas and castles soared, and cheaper luxury goods and manufactures were increasingly imported from Holland and England rather than being produced in Spain. The tremendous economic surplus transferred from the mines of Mexico and Peru led to virtually no expansion of the productive capacities of Spain; technological development was restricted to addressing the most immediate necessities in mining and shipping, labor skills were not enhanced, corruption was not addressed, and authoritarian management techniques were never questioned.

A popular saying well described the economic process which vitiated both Latin American and Spanish progress: "Spain held the cow, and the Dutch milked it." The "cow" was Latin America, and its wealth of gold and silver passed quickly to Holland and England from Spain to pay for the goods the Spanish elite coveted. But, when the last of the mining booms was exhausted in the 1700s, Spain's economy imploded, as did the economies of Mexico and Peru, now saddled with the backward institutions which Spain had imposed. However, the other economies of Europe, which had been providing the manufactured goods which the Spanish devoured, flush with plundered wealth, could only get gold and silver by *producing* things Spain wished to buy, so their economies flourished and continued to do so. Ironically, then, the wealth of Spain, based on colonial plunder, was illusory; the real "wealth" was that created by production, and that wealth was being built in the emerging and expanding factory system in an increasingly capitalist Europe which traded with Spain.

Merchant capital: from old colonialism to new colonialism

Spain's economy in the sixteenth century had been dominated by semi-feudal interests, hence the emphasis on war, plunder, slavery, and short-term gain. Because there was as yet no capitalist logic of maximum profit at work, Spanish policies in the Western hemisphere epitomized the old colonial system. While Spain and its colonies sunk into a morass of backwardness, European colonial policy continued to evolve. As new powers were drawn to colonial adventures, a complex half-way transition between feudalism and capitalism emerged. This transitory period in Europe is sometimes known as the era of merchant capitalism, which gave rise to the new colonial system.[5]

The Dutch system, in particular, exhibited the characteristics of merchant capitalism, beginning roughly in the mid-seventeenth century and spreading rapidly in the early eighteenth century. The Dutch established the first sugar plantation systems in Latin America and later in the East Indies. The plantation system sought to maximize agricultural yields from a given amount of land, using slave labor, and the goal of production was clearly profit. The earliest plantation systems, prior to 1750, intentionally set such a demanding pace of work for the slaves that they survived, on average, perhaps no more than ten to fifteen years. (At that time, African slaves were cheap and readily available, since the drain on Africa's population was small relative to the late eighteenth and nineteenth centuries.) Thus the Dutch plantation system combined capitalist-type behavior, such as expanded production, as represented by the maintenance of a fixed investment in plantation lands, and the profit motive, with quasi-feudal attitudes toward labor.

The Dutch, and others who followed the Dutch plantation model, were quick to respond when slave prices soared in the mid-eighteenth century.[6] Labor conditions improved, the pace of work was made less arduous, and slaves lived longer. While the colonial powers under the sway of merchant capitalism took into account the necessity of maintaining the productive capacity of their colonial systems, the primary emphasis of merchant capitalism was on the short-term gains of trade and finance. The ethos of merchant capital was, above all, that of speculative gains. Adjustments toward economic rationality, including the introduction of technical change, were intermittent and limited to attempting to maintain the basis of social wealth for the colonizer. Extensive investments and training of workers were out of the question, as these would have absorbed current returns. The colonies were to be plundered at the lowest cost possible; they were not places in which to invest for the future.

British rule in India: the transition from merchant capital to industrial capital

Spain's and Holland's colonial legacy can be contrasted with that of the British in India. Britain, like many other powers, had gained access to coastal trading cities in India prior to the eighteenth century. In 1757 the British won a determinate military victory in India. In 1763, as a result of major military victories over France, Britain began to expand its sphere of control in India, eventually dominating much of the subcontinent in the course of the nineteenth century. When formal colonial status descended on India in the nineteenth century the British sought to "rationalize" the system of production by eliminating complex customary concepts of landed property that commonly allowed for overlapping claims (Kaiwar 1994). Instead, the British sought the one-owner rule, even over water that had been used collectively for millennia. Small peasant farmers were often those who held the new land titles, and they, in turn were the main target of Britain's land revenue tax. Over the course of Britain's rule from 1757 to 1947 per capita income likely never grew, and life expectancy declined. During the last half of the nineteenth century per capita income may have fallen by 50 percent (Hyndman 1919: 22). In addition, calculations of per capita income do not capture many forms of depredation, such as the British tax system that raised funds to support the British military and police (25 percent of India's public expenditures) that maintained Britain's rule and to finance international expeditionary forces (Hobson 1993: 480). Famously, the British restructured agriculture, forcing specialization in indigo (synthetic dyes eventually destroyed this crop), cotton – which could be used as inputs into the British textile industry – and wheat to keep workers' wages down in England. (Opium poppies were another specialization, bought by the colonial government and then profitably shipped to China.) British rule imposed heavy taxes on agriculture that led to small farmers abandoning subsistence agriculture such as rice cultivation for indigo, or to take up cotton and grain cash-crop cultivation in order to gain income for tax payments. This system, plus the functioning of market forces in grain production, resulted in sizeable grain exports from India to Europe, even during the several devastating famines that swept India in the latter half of the nineteenth century (Davis 2001: 311–40). The opening of the Suez canal in 1869 was a watershed event as it drove down the transport costs of India's exports, making them much more profitable for British merchants and financiers. Thus the wheat boom began – the value of annual average wheat exports from the Central Provinces (today roughly the large state of Madhya Pradesh) increased by 500 percent from the 1871–6 period to the peak years 1886–91, while for India as a whole the volume of grain exports went up over 300 percent from 1875 to 1900 (Davis 2001: 299).

Specialization meant the near-absence of crop rotation, which, combined with over-expansion into marginal lands, set the stage for erosion, soil depletion, and eventual collapsing yields. Meanwhile the British privatized the common lands of the villages to expand their tax base. No improvements of significance in techniques of agricultural production occurred; necessary investments were never made either by British or Indian merchant capital or the British colonial state – which spent less than 2 percent of its budget on agriculture and education (Stein 1998: 263). As is common in commodity booms, over-production occurred in India (in the northern state of Punjab cultivators had access to canals), and Argentina began to push massive amounts of wheat onto the world market in the 1890s, causing prices to collapse. But the peasants still had to pay "average" taxes based upon high yield years, and interest payments to moneylenders. This tax system had several variants, such as that of south-western India, where the British forced payments under extreme conditions:

> In the late nineteenth-century Bombay Deccan … the annual process of revenue collec-tion began with the impounding of grain in village stockyards. In order to eat from their own harvest, the [peasants] had to immediately borrow money to pay off the taxes. Typically the moneylenders bought the crop at half the current market value but lent money at a usurious 38 percent interest. If the peasant was unable to promptly repay the principle, the exorbitant rates ballooned to astronomical dimensions.
>
> When [peasants] balked at payment, Indian courts applied English civil law with the deadly efficiency of a Maxim gun.
>
> (Davis 2001: 325)

When, in the 1890s, the monsoon rains disappeared, wheat exports from the mostly un-irrigated Central Provinces continued at slightly above levels achieved at the opening of the Suez canal. But the fact that they continued was remarkable as famine spread across west and central India (an area of 420,000 square miles) and yields fell in broad areas by 66 to 88 percent. There was practically no public agency to distribute food to the starving because the British *laissez-faire* colonial state largely refused such a role (Davis 2001: 141–75). Britain had built a "Famine Fund" but much of it had been drained off to fight an expeditionary war in Afghanistan. The famines allowed Indian moneylenders and grain merchants to acquire vast tracts of peasant lands. A new parasitic stratum of Indian absentee landlords arose from the process of opening up the interior of India to the British market in commodities, and the rapidly expanding colonial rail system served as the wedge in the process. Indeed, in the process of building some 9,000 miles of state-owned railroads the British began to deplete the supply of lumber (used for ties and fuel). This resulted in the colonial state in the 1870s taking over all forest areas that heretofore had been vital "commons" areas for the peasantry, providing lumber (for carts and ploughs), fuel, medicinal plants, and many other necessi-ties. As British rule proceeded, the social structure was transformed, and everywhere the peasantry was squeezed. Although British rule in India was without doubt harsh, the extent of British transgression in India never reached the depths attained by the Spanish in Latin America.

British policy toward India changed during the course of the late eighteenth and early nineteenth centuries, as merchant capital and mercantilist ideas steadily lost ground to industrial capital and capitalist views within Britain, with the triumph of the Industrial Revolution and the steady rise of the factory system. Yet the process of pushing aside merchant capital and mercantilist policies was exceedingly complex. Even in the nine-teenth century, British policy toward India clearly failed to conform to the axioms of free trade championed by the industrial capitalists and classical economists in Britain of the period. The precepts which underlay merchant capitalism, beliefs that basically assumed that the wealth of a nation depended upon its control over trade, were radically different from those of the classical economists like Adam Smith and David Ricardo (see Chapter 4).

Merchant capital, by contrast, emphasized the *relative terms* under which exchange took place. Controlling trade and controlling wages either through slavery or by decree meant that the relative terms of exchange would be extremely advantageous to Dutch and British merchants, and thus, it was assumed, the economic wealth and power of these nations would be augmented. By way of contrast, classical economists analyzed trade relationships upon the premise that each participant in a market, both buyer and seller, had sufficient resources to *withdraw* from the market if the price was not to their liking. Slaves, uprooted natives, and colonial regions, by contrast, had no ability to withdraw from the colonial system, and merchant capitalists were not to be swayed by the logic of the classical economists (see Focus 3.2). To understand the developmental consequences of the rise to cash-crop cultivation in India in the late nineteenth century, for example, a volatile mixture of factors, rarely if ever carefully examined by the classical economists, needs to be considered:

> the forcible incorporation of smallholder production into commodity and financial circuits controlled from overseas tended to undermine traditional food security. Recent scholarship confirms that it was *subsistence adversity* (high taxes, chronic indebtedness, inadequate acreage, loss of subsidiary employment opportunities, enclosures of common resources, dissolution of patrimonial obligations, and so on) not entrepreneurial opportunity, that typically promoted the turn to cash-crop cultivation. Rural capital, in turn, tended to be parasitic rather than productivist as rich landowners redeployed fortunes that they built during the export booms into usury, [exorbitant rents] and crop brokerage. ... Whether farmers were directly engaged by foreign capital ... or were simply producing for the domestic market subject to international competition ... commercialization went hand in hand with pauperization without any silver lining of technical change or agrarian capitalism.
>
> (Davis 2001: 289–90)

Britain developed a colonial system which combined elements of merchant and industrial capitalism. For some twentieth-century observers, such as the Austrian economist Joseph Schumpeter, this blending of the precepts of merchant capital and industrial capital in the British colonies was a glaring contradiction, an anomaly which could only be explained as a throwback to an earlier pre-capitalist era (Schumpeter 1951). The American economist Thorstein Veblen, by contrast, maintained that whatever the stage of capitalist development, residual elements of earlier economic eras tended to maintain a foothold, both physically and ideologically, and "recrudescences" were likely to arise, particularly during periods of prolonged economic stagnation or cyclical downturn (Hunt 1979: Chapter 13).

Politically, the planters of the West Indies and the merchants operating in India were able to exercise a quotient of power, even when the industrial capitalists and their ideology dominated British policy-making. Merchant capital was able to maintain a certain limited autonomy regarding policy within the colonial system; policies that might have been increasingly anachronistic in Britian continued to coexist in the colonies, which lived a divided and incomplete existence, pulled in different and contradictory directions.

FOCUS 3.2   WHAT DIFFERENCE INDEPENDENCE? THE UNITED STATES VERSUS MEXICO

Sometimes the following question is posed by those skeptical of the force of colonial rule: If colonialism imposed such a burden, why did some nations seem to shrug off the legacy of colonialism, while others languished after independence? A comparison of the United States and Mexico may help to answer this question.

Just prior to independence, the estimated *net burden* of colonial rule in the thirteen colonies of North America came to 0.3 percent of their national income. In contrast, the estimated annual burden of Spanish colonialism, measured in terms of the taxes paid to Madrid and the cost of being prevented from trading freely with other nations, has been estimated to be 7.2 percent of annual income during the last twenty-four years of Spanish rule over Mexico. Thus, in this method of measuring the net drain imposed by colonialism, the relative burden of Spanish rule was twenty-five times greater than that of British rule!

In 1800, Mexico's per capita income was 44 percent of that of the United States. By 1910, the gap had widened; Mexico's per capita income was a mere 13 percent of that of the US! Why did the gap widen so rapidly? John Coatsworth's comparative research points to two factors: first, the United States had a relatively good river system which allowed bulky goods to be transported cheaply. A similar transport system in Mexico would have reduced the difference between each nation's growth rate by about one-third.

The remaining differential Coatsworth attributes to Spanish feudalism. In theory, independence in Mexico in 1821 could have begun to dissolve the rigid institutions of Spanish rule. In fact, internal and international social and political conflicts left Mexico exhausted and directionless for more than fifty years. Reform of the colonial fiscal system was only completed in the 1890s, while new legislation regarding commerce, mining, foreign trade, and banking came into existence in the 1884–1908 period. These long-awaited reforms, unfortunately, largely served to facilitate an expansion of foreign ownership and control over the Mexican economy, rather than contributing to local development.

In the US, the institutions of British rule were only rarely feudal, such as the acceptance of slavery, the slave trade, and the plantation system. A costly civil war, which also stimulated industrialization in the North, had to be fought to rid the United States of its colonial legacy, and its neocolonial links with Great Britain.

Spanish colonialism of an essentially feudal nature thus lasted longer, penetrated deeper into the behavioral dynamics of Mexican society, and was more difficult to eradicate than British rule in the North American colonies. Elsewhere in the British Empire, however, the systematic colonialism of white-settler rule championed by John Stuart Mill was replaced by a more retarding blend of British institutions, such as the plantation economy of Jamaica. There and in India and other colonies under the Union Jack, the burden of British control was much heavier than in North America.

Sources: Coatsworth 1978: 84; Thomas 1965

The functional role of colonialism

Merchant capital and industrial capital are indeed distinct forms. Yet, in the colonial system they could be complementary. In analyzing the history of the less-developed regions, it is important to understand that they played a notable, if sometimes overlooked, role in contributing to the British Industrial Revolution. For example, recent estimates place the mass of profits deriving from the British slave trade in the eighteenth century at £50 million. Profits from the British West Indian sugar plantations were between £200 and £300 million in the same period (Crow and Thorpe 1988: 16). Between 1757 and 1812, the inflow of profits from India was estimated at between £500 million and £1 billion (Digby 1969: 33). Digby's estimate, originally published in 1901, has been viewed as an exaggeration by some, but a more recent analysis estimated that the British imposed a drain on India equivalent to 5–6 percent of GNP during the period (Bagchi 1984: 81; see Focus 3.3).

While these capital flows from the colonies were exceedingly large, the fortunes acquired in the British colonies were often squandered in conspicuous consumption in England. None-theless, there can be no doubt that a portion of these funds entered the British banking system, thereby adding to liquidity, driving down interest rates, and releasing a flow of investment funds which could be tapped by the early British industrialists for their industrialization

FOCUS 3.3 THE COLONIAL DRAIN

The Dutch ruled Indonesia for more than 300 years, beginning in the early 1600s, making substantial investments over this period. But Angus Maddison's research reveals that though "there had been a consistent and substantial trade surplus for 300 years, it is clear there was never any net transfer of funds from the metropole and that foreign claims on Indonesia arose from reinvested earnings of the colonists."

How does a colonizing nation assure a net outward transfer? In the 1700s, coffee was a major export crop. The Dutch guaranteed a net drain of income from their colony by forcing delivery of coffee from native cultivators and then "paying" the cultivators for only a fraction of the total. One practice was to receive delivery of 240 lb of coffee but pay the cultivator for only 14 lb. The remainder the Dutch simply appropriated!

How much income did the Dutch drain off from Indonesia in a given year? Maddison calculated that the drain amounted to 15.6 percent of the net domestic product of Indonesia in 1930. That is, 15.6 percent of Indonesia's net output went to either Dutch corporations, Dutch nationals living in Indonesia, or to the Dutch government. In all, he estimates that the *total* income of the Dutch increased by 12.8 percent as a result of their ability to control Indonesia. What would have happened if Indonesia could have used much of the 15.6 percent of net income to increase its own productive base? Clearly, a drain of this magnitude would have been sufficient to undermine the development prospects of any nation.

For comparison, Maddison calculated the drain from India to the British in 1931. India lost approximately 5 percent of its net income, while British incomes were increased by 3.3 percent. At this time, India was the "Jewel in the Crown" of the British empire, but Britain was also in a position to drain colonial income from roughly 50 smaller colonies in 1931.

Had the Dutch in Indonesia, or the British in India, invested heavily in infrastructure, technology, and labor-training, and struggled to improve the social and economic organi-zation of their colonies, this drain might not have been of fundamental, determining importance. This is so because the drain would have constituted a less significant net flow from an ever-expanding productive base. The expansion of the productive base would have benefited the colonial region after independence and might have altered the nature of path dependency.

But the evidence in the case of Indonesia, India, and many other colonies indicates that the colonial rulers, except in the rarest of instances, never made sufficient investments in infrastructure, industrial production, technologically sophisticated agriculture, or in any of the other areas which would have served to expand the productive base sufficiently to more than offset the drain resulting from colonial control.

The colonial drain constituted lost income, caused by the institutions of colonialism. It quantified a national humiliation of major proportions, arising, in many instances, from land which had been appropriated and/or monopoly incomes attributable solely to the power of colonial domination.

Sources: Furnivall 1967: 40; Maddison 1990: 360, 364, 369

projects. Colonialism also added to aggregate demand, without driving up British wage rates. An external market for ships and for traded goods in Africa, such as woolens, guns, iron and steel products, and a market for sugar refining equipment in the West Indies further stimulated British investments, production, and employment. Such a chain of events had not occurred in Spain in the sixteenth century, because Spain had lacked an industrial base and industrialists, both destroyed by raging price inflation with the massive inflows of gold and silver from the colonies; Spain also lacked a sophisticated banking system which might have functioned as an efficient intermediary between savers and investors.

The colonial elite: the enduring significance of collaboration

At the same time that merchant capital and industrial capital were establishing a basis for complementary interaction in Britain, and to a lesser degree in Holland, merchant capitalism was consolidating its hold over the indigenous elite in the colonies which served as the medium of colonial dominion. Colonial rule was based upon a system of collaboration between the indigenous elite and the colonial power, as the case of India illustrates.

> British rule consolidated itself by creating new classes and vested interests who were tied up with that rule and whose privileges depended on its continuance. There were the landowners and the princes, and there were a large number of subordinate members of the services in various departments of the government, from the *patwari*, the village headman, upward. ... To all these methods must be added the deliberate policy, pursued throughout the period of British rule, of creating divisions among Indians, of encouraging one group at the cost of the other.
>
> (Nehru 1960: 304)

Ronald Robinson sketched the pivotal role also played by the indigenous elite in Africa and Asia in the nineteenth century:

> Although potentially the power was there in Europe, in reality only a tiny fraction of it was ever committed to Africa or Asia. Europe's policy normally was that if empire could not be had on the cheap, it was not worth having at all. The financial sinew, the military and administrative muscle of imperialism was drawn through the mediation of indigenous elite from the invaded countries themselves.
>
> Its central mechanism, therefore, may be found in the systems of this collaboration set up in the pre-industrial societies, which succeeded (or failed) in meshing the incoming process of European expansion into indigenous social politics and in achieving some kind of evolving equilibrium between the two.
>
> (Robinson 1976: 131)

It is important to note that this process of elite formation was conditioned by the behavioral parameters and norms of merchant capital rather than industrial capital. Speculative behavior, monopoly practices, favoritism, and patronage in employment, corruption within government, intermittent changes in technology, the absence of labor rights and labor norms, authoritarian governments, and profits based upon cunning trading of commodities and usurious banking practices, were all constituent elements of merchant capitalism. All were transplanted to the colonial regions where they thrived, grew, and became entrenched, even as they were being surmounted in Europe by emerging capitalist methods. The new collaborative elite in the colonies became consummate masters of the artifices of merchant capital at the same time that their colonial masters were abandoning such systems at home.

De-industrialization in the colonies

Once this new indigenous elite was consolidated and corrupted by colonial rule, there were few social forces which could emerge within the social formation of the less-developed regions to challenge the sway of merchant capital and mercantilist ideas. Two case-studies illustrate this point. In the late eighteenth century, Britain accelerated its expansion in India, which then had a thriving textile industry that had for centuries sold high-quality cotton products throughout India, in much of Africa, and in the Middle East. Large factory towns existed where skilled laborers were able to produce cloth so cheaply that the British East India Company could buy from native industrialists, ship the product to England, and still sell their cargoes at a full 100 percent mark-up over cost. Thus, Indian manufacturing early on had the capability of successfully challenging the leading sector of the British economy at the very moment when the British "take-off" into industrialization was under way.

The British reacted to this potential challenge both economically and politically. The two reactions combined illustrate the political economy of British policy at a pivotal moment in both British and Indian history. On the purely economic terrain, British textile industrialists reacted to the challenge of Indian manufactures by increasing their investments in productive equipment, by raising the amount of capital that each worker utilized and by increasing the complexity and productivity of the production process by using ever-more mechanized forms of production. These changes helped to drive down their unit costs of production, making them more competitive with Indian producers.

At the political level, British textile industrialists demanded and received protection from imported Indian textiles. By 1814, textile interests in Britain had placed a tariff of 70 to 80 percent on all imported Indian textiles, thereby pricing them out of the British market. At the same time, they forced open the Indian market to British-made textile exports. On the other hand, Britain accepted the import of raw cotton from India to be used in British production, without any tariffs being applied. The East India Company and British merchants in India then switched from textile exporting to the exporting of raw cotton to Britain. As a consequence, the Indian textile industry, which had exported to England in large part so that the British could re-export their products to the world market, lost one of its largest markets, and began to deteriorate.

At the same time, cheaper made *machino*-factured textiles from Britain were pouring into India, underselling the higher-cost *manu*-factured textiles of India. By the mid-nineteenth century, India's industrial base in textiles had been decimated, and India had been de-industrialized as a result of British policy. India no longer produced its own textiles, but now exported raw cotton to Britain only to import British-made cotton textiles, which soared from 1 million yards in 1814 to 53 million yards in 1844 (Stavrianos 1981: 247). As a result, the number of Indian textile workers (spinners and weavers) fell from an estimated 6.3 million to only 2.4 million between 1800 and 1913. While the spinners declined the handloom weavers sought to remain competitive through a precipitous drop in their wages. They "survived" by executing their own ruin, while their pauperization deprived the internal market of much-needed purchasing power, driving down further the Indian economy (Amsden 2001: 34, 37, 50).

India ceased to be a leading manufacturing country of the precapitalist era and was reduced to the position of a supplier of agricultural goods and raw materials to the industrializing economies of the West, particularly Britain.

The long process of deindustrialization of India started with the catastrophic disappearance of cotton manufactures from the list of exports of India ... For more than seventy-five years up to 1913, India remained the major importer of cotton goods from Britain, often taking more than forty percent of the British exports. ... Other rural or urban manufactures were ruined partly by the rise of alternative sources of supply and by government restrictions.

(Bagchi 1984: 82)[7]

Britain's anti-industrialization policies toward India changed after 1930, when passive support for industrialization began as part of a larger effort to forestall rising nationalist opposition to colonial domination. But upon independence in 1947 manufacturing accounted for only 7 percent of the national product and a mere 2 percent of the labor force were employed in factories (Kohli 2004: 248, 251). The First and Second World Wars allowed for some resurfacing of the textile industry, the jute export industry expanded, a steel industry began in 1907, and several other industrial areas responded to the rise in the import tariff from 5 percent in 1900 to 25 percent in 1930. The tariff was seen as a way of keeping Japanese and German manufactures out of India and as a means of raising revenues for the colonial state. While all this led to the creation of a new stratum of Indian industrialist the economy at large continued to languish, with per capita income falling from 1900 to 1947.

A somewhat similar situation occurred in Egypt between 1820 and 1840 under the leadership of Muhammed Ali. Ali sought to develop Egypt through industrialization. He borrowed extensively, developed a new strain of cotton called Egyptian long-staple, and advanced seeds to peasants to encourage cotton cultivation. Ali then constructed a series of textile factories and attempted to export high-quality textiles to the world market. The British, while championing modernization in the pre-capitalist regions, and officially wedded to a free-trade ideology, were appalled by this emerging challenge to their dominance in the global textile market.

Ali had other major enemies beside the British; his civil service worked against his dreams of a powerful and modern Egypt by appropriating whatever they could of an increasing national income through corruption and other means of skimming income. Meanwhile, Ali's plans to "hothouse" industrialization compelled the artisan class into the new factories, where hours were long and extremely onerous working conditions led to theft, sabotage, and low morale. Peasants were forced to sell cotton to the government purchasing monopoly at a very low price, while Ali's state-owned factories sought the highest price on world markets for their excellent manufactured products. Internal forces of opposition and resistance certainly hindered the potential of Ali's experiment, but Ali also was undone when the British encouraged the Turks to make war on Egypt. The Turks were defeated, so the British intervened, and Ali was forced to grant free-trade access to British products, foreigners were granted free access to land, and Egypt became a typical raw material exporter rather than an industrial country, at least partly as a consequence of British opposition.

Under the protection of the capitulatory treaties [of the war with Turkey and Britain] European speculators and adventurers were free to operate in Egypt outside the jurisdiction of the native courts and subject only to consular control. Many grew rich by smuggling opium and tobacco and invariably were protected by the foreign consuls. ... These foreigners, who were completely exempt from taxation, also served as agents in arranging for loans and contracts on extortionist terms. In 1873, for example, the [Egyptian Government] accepted a loan at face value of £32 million, but after heavy commissions and discounts received only £9 million.

(Stavrianos 1981: 221)

Colonial industrialization?

Why not manufacture textiles in India or refine minerals and petroleum products in the less-developed nations where they originate? In analyzing international trade and production patterns, it is important to recognize that the colonial powers encouraged the production of tropical products, and often contributed to increases in the efficiency of the processes of production in these goods. At the same time, they also actively discouraged the production of those goods in the colonies which might have competed with their own exports. This created patterns of distorted development, serving to internally disarticulate the less-developed economies, while contributing to the internal articulation and further development of the colonial power. Neighboring nations, if they were dominated by different colonial powers, were deprived of whatever natural complementarities existed between them, as regional trade patterns were prevented from emerging. The colonies themselves had infrastructural systems which primarily served the interests of the colonial power (see Focus 3.4). Often major cities and regions within the colonies were not well connected with one another, and what infrastructure there was had been designed to facilitate the movement of tropical commodities to the coast and onward to Europe to be consumed. In the course of the nineteenth century, an increasing number of colonies became mono-exporters, or exported, at best, a very limited range of primary products, such as agricultural goods and raw, unprocessed minerals, because that is what the colonial powers wanted, not because that was the optimal productive structure.

The process of internal disarticulation in the colonies could often be found in the disparate tendencies of peasant agriculture and export agriculture, the latter carefully stimulated by colonial policies. In India, commercial export agriculture benefited via improved organization, mechanization, enhanced infrastructure, bank credits, and ready access to the sophisticated talents of primarily British exporters. Peasant agriculture, by contrast, languished. Peasants were shunted off to poorer lands, where cultivation practices deteriorated, and where labor-intensive methods were unable to compensate for lower-quality land and the lack of financing and knowledge needed to increase worker productivity on the land. Table 3.1 records the divergent tendencies of agricultural production under colonial rule in India, reflecting the neglect of indigenous small producers and the benefits extended to exporters.

Table 3.1 Peasant versus commercial export agriculture in India, 1891–1941 (annual average growth)

	Peasant agriculture (food grains) %	Commercial export agriculture (cash crops) %
Output	−0.11	+0.67
Productivity	−0.18	+0.86

Source: Fieldhouse 1981: 89.

FOCUS 3.4   AFRICA'S COLONIAL INFRASTRUCTURE

Huge outlays, often supported with forced labor, were necessary to build an infrastructure of highways, irrigation and flood control systems, communication systems and railways in the colonies. But, as can be readily illustrated in Africa, this infrastructure lacked a developmental rationality for colonies. The purpose of colonial infrastructure was to facilitate the movement of tropical products and minerals from the colony to the ports and then on to Europe.

> [The railways] were not laid down to facilitate the internal trade in African commodities. There were no roads connecting different colonies and different parts of the same colony in a manner that made sense with regard to Africa's needs and development. All roads and railways led down to the sea. They were built to make business possible for the timber companies, trading companies, and agricultural concession firms, and for white settlers. ... In Europe and America, railway building required huge inputs of capital. Great wage bills were incurred during construction, and added bonus payments were made to workers to get the job done as quickly as possible. In most parts of Africa, the Europeans who wanted to see a railroad built offered lashes as the ordinary wage and more lashes for extra effort.

As a result of the Berlin Conference to partition Africa in 1884, Belgium's King Leopold II seized the vast territory of the Congo Free State in Central Africa. To draw out the coveted red mahogany, ivory, and rubber of the Congo, Leopold built a 241-mile railway from the mouth of the Congo river to Stanley Pool, eliminating a three-week porterage. In the first two years of the construction project an estimated 3,600 of the 60,000 workers died.

> The railway was a modest engineering success and a major human disaster. Men succumbed to accidents, dysentery, smallpox, beriberi, and malaria, all exacerbated by bad food and relentless floggings by the two-hundred-man railway militia force. Engines ran off tracks; freight cars full of dynamite exploded, blowing workers to bits. ... Sometimes there were no shelters for the people to sleep in, and recalcitrant laborers were led to work in chains. ... When bugles sounded in the morning, crowds of angry laborers laid at the feet of European supervisors the bodies of their comrades who had died during the night.

On the use of forced labor, historian Walter Rodney wrote:

> The French got Africans to start building the Brazzaville to Point-Noire railway in 1921, and it was not completed until 1933. Every year of its construction, some ten thousand people were driven to the site – sometimes from more than a thousand kilometers away. At least 25 per cent of the labor force died annually from starvation and disease, the worst period being from 1922 to 1929.

The infrastructure was necessary to convert resources into plantation land and mines. That is "resources" were transformed into privately-owned assets – production arrangements that would generate income and allow for wealth accumulation. But few Africans found much benefit in this process of conversion. By 1958 the Belgian colonists (and other foreigners) were a mere one percent of the population of the Congo, but they received 42 percent of the national income as a result of owning 95 percent of the Congo's assets.

Sources: Hochschild 1999: 170–1; Peemans 1975: 181; Rodney 1974: 209, 166

Measuring the impact of colonialism

Colonialism took an often bewildering number of forms, yielding various effects and outcomes difficult to gauge and combine. No one test, or set of quantitative tests, could measure the complex economic impact of colonialism. Nonetheless, a comprehensive study sheds some light on an issue which has received less attention than it deserves. In his study "Colonialism, Decolonisation and Growth Rates," Alam (1994) measured the average annual growth rates of eleven politically independent nations, which he classified as either "sovereign lagging countries" or "dependencies." Sovereign lagging countries were those which were able to some degree to resist subordination to the Great Powers of Europe. Dependencies were either nations which were independent through history, or former colonial nations. These nations, while independent, operated with considerable constraints because of the influence of either disadvantageous trade treaties or the presence of foreign capital with a strong influence over trade and investment activities.

The sovereign nations were compared with a group of colonies or quasi-colonies (such as China). The test included the Group I countries (sovereign nations which had income per capita of less than half that of the United States in 1900), and the Group II colonies for which data were available. Together the sample included 59 percent of the world's population for 1980.[8] For the period 1900–50, prior to the independence of all the Group II countries, the Group I countries had an average annual rate of growth of per capita income of 1.6 percent. The Group II countries had an average per capita growth rate of 0.0 percent per year (Alam 1994: 250). After colonial rule had ended for all the countries in the study, early in the 1950–73 period, the Group I countries achieved a 3.5 percent annual growth rate of per capita income, while the Group II rate of growth rose to 2.8 percent. The results, then, tend to confirm that colonialism mattered in a negative way. First, the dramatic difference between absolute stagnation of the Group II colonial nations and the growth of the independent Group I economies is a notable result of the 1900–50 period. Second, Group I nations grew at a 25 percent faster rate in the 1950–73 period, which tends to confirm the idea that after formal independence the institutions and path dependence established by colonialism continued to exert an influence which constrained growth. Alam's thesis has recently been broadened and further strengthened with the publication of his book-length treatment of these issues (Alam 2000).

The terms of trade and comparative advantage

While colonialism and neocolonialism[9] played a dominant role in imposing a particular global pattern of production and trade on the less-developed nations in the course of the 100-year period 1780–1880, so too did global market forces. The result was an international division of labor in which the less-developed countries emerged as exporters of primary products to world markets and importers of manufactured goods; the more-developed nations exported manufactured goods and imported primary products. From the late eighteenth century to the 1880s, the terms of trade, measured as the quantity of imports which will exchange for a given quantity of exports, moved steadily in favor of the colonial regions as the prices of primary exports relative to manufactured imports rose, leading to an increase in the value of the terms of trade index for colonial exports.[10] This was the consequence of technological progress and competition among the powerful nations of Europe and the United States, which pushed the prices of manufactured products downward, while the demand for tropical products and minerals rapidly expanded, but without commensurate increases in production efficiency in the less-developed regions producing these goods, leading to rising prices for these commodities in international exchange (Spraos 1983; Singer 1989). Increasing competition for raw materials and the relatively low level of technical change in agriculture meant that a given quantity of exports from the colonial regions was able to purchase more imported manufactures from the more developed nations. On the other hand, Britain, whose terms of trade were moving in the opposite direction, had to export roughly two and a half times more manufactured products, on average, in 1880 than it had in 1800 in order to obtain the same quantity of tropical products and raw materials from the less-developed regions.

As a result of this upward movement of the terms of trade for tropical commodities, it appeared to many in the less-developed regions that a primary export economy was a viable vehicle for enhancing their nation's income and wealth. Little, if any, diversification of production for export was encouraged. Investment in primary production remained low, because of technological stasis in agro-export and mineral export activities, and because high profits could be made by producing more using extensive techniques. At the same time, as wealth was acquired rapidly and easily in colonial agriculture and mining without the need for massive investments, any profits generated tended to be squandered in ostentatious displays of conspicuous consumption. The financing and distribution of imports and exports, in particular, became an active arena for quick profit-making. Argentina became a particularly notable example; the nation seemed to have mushroomed into a developed nation by the beginning of the twentieth century with virtually no additional effort. A small cadre of cattle ranchers, meat packers, grain growers, bankers, and traders dominated Argentine society. The ships transporting Argentine beef were made in Europe, however, as were the meat-packing facilities, the rails, freight cars, and engines which carried Argentine commodities to the ports for shipment to Europe, a pattern of external reliance that would not bode well for future development.

Argentina's economic miracle lasted somewhat longer than did the general commodities boom of the nineteenth century, but it too foundered when the terms of trade began to turn down sharply. From the 1880s onward, the terms of trade moved against commodity and mineral producers, with the exception of the periods of world war. The dangers and pitfalls of a global trading system and export production focused on a limited array of primary products became all too apparent, too late, to many in the less-developed nations. What had once appeared to be a successful process of natural selection, whereby the economy of a given colony tended to be centered on the basic production and export of one or two primary commodities, now was revealed to be a flawed strategy. With declining terms of trade, mono-exporters were on a treadmill which they had few means of getting off. They had to export more and more in order to buy the increasingly more expensive imported machinery and equipment if they were to maintain the production base of their agro-export or mineral-export economies and to sustain the consumption of the elites (see Focus 3.5).

In thinking about the concept of comparative advantage (analyzed more fully in the next chapter), it is important to recall that in Britain, France, Germany, and the US, the leading trade sectors were forged through conscious state involvement such as subsidies, tariffs, selective construction of infrastructure, labor training, and prohibitive trade restrictions. As we shall see in later chapters, this too has been at the base of the successful development experiences of South Korea, Taiwan, Japan, and a handful of other East Asian countries. In contrast, colonialism imposed a pattern of production and trade on the pre-capitalist, less-developed regions, a pattern that did not reflect the actual, potential, or conceivable dynamic comparative advantages of those nations. Their trade patterns reflected the needs, desires,

FOCUS 3.5 TRENDS IN THE TERMS OF TRADE

There is a large literature which attempts to measure trends in the terms of trade, some of which we shall consider again in Chapter 6. However, the following estimates give some idea of the direction of change of the terms of trade for primary product producers.

% change per year, primary export nations

1	1801–1881	0.87
2	1882–1913	−0.42
3	1876–1938	−0.95
4	1900–1986	−0.52 to −0.84[a]
5	1979–1993	−4.00

Note
a The Grilli and Yang (1988) study breaks down the trend in the terms of trade for various sub-categories of primary product exports (for example, raw material; fuels; cereals; foodstuffs). They find a long-term downward trend for the terms of trade for all primary products in international trade with the exception of tropical drinks, which had a trend of 0.63.

Line 1 shows that over the early to late nineteenth century, the terms of trade for primary product producers were moving upward at the rate of 0.87 percent per annum. In effect, each unit of primary product export was able to purchase 0.87 percent more imports each year. Over the entire period, 1801–81, the purchasing power of the average primary producer doubled in terms of ability to purchase imports with the same quantity of exports. This was the period over which it appeared that the primary product export focus of many of the now less-developed nations, and hence the productive structure created by colonial powers, was validated.

However, lines 2 to 5, based on estimates of the terms of trade of primary product exporters derived from different sources, tend to confirm that the longer-term, and certainly the modern, trend of the terms of trade for primary product producers is downward. Thus, the path dependency created by a primary product export focus turned out to be a long-term burden for economies which remained with such exports. (Note that the fall since 1979 (through 1993) was the most severe since the Great Depression, with real commodity prices 45 percent below their 1980 level by 1990!)

Sources: Grilli and Yang 1988; Maizels, Palaskas, and Crowe 1998;
Sarkar 1986; Spraos 1983

and (sometimes) whims of the colonizer. Later, as these patterns became ingrained, altering adverse path dependence was made more difficult even after political independence.

Credit and underdevelopment

In Latin America, once formal colonialism had been ended by the wars of independence in the 1820s, neocolonial mechanisms of credit allocation and debt financing replaced overt political domination, but they contributed no less to the distorted patterns of production and trade implanted several hundred years earlier by the Spanish and the Portuguese. In the nineteenth century, abundant credit became readily available to the colonial regions of Africa and Asia and to the neocolonial regions of Latin America for several interrelated reasons.[11]

1   As the scale of modern industry increased in the late nineteenth century, large US, German, British, and French manufacturers, working closely with major banks, often extended credit to finance the exportation of their products bought by elites in the less-developed

regions. Financial markets increased both in size and sophistication, thereby enabling major banks to shift from regional and national markets to global markets.

2   The second industrial revolution, in the latter part of the nineteenth century, which saw the application of chemistry to the industrial process, the adaptation of steam power to ships and agricultural machinery, electricity, the telephone and telegraph, the internal combustion engine, time-and-motion studies in the factories, and so on, created new demands for tropical products and raw materials produced by less-developed nations and colonies. This was particularly true for rubber, for example, the demand for which grew rapidly for production and consumption purposes in the developed nations. Better and faster shipping meant that tropical commodities, such as bananas and pineapples, could become part of the diet in the developed nations. Increasing quantities of minerals were needed to furnish the demands of the industrial sectors of the great powers. Railways penetrated deeper into the hinterlands of the less-developed regions as new geological discoveries were made, and cheaply produced mining products from the less-developed nations flooded the world market. In order to sustain these new activities, massive investments were typically necessary to build ports, railway systems, communication systems, and roads. Credits were readily extended to private, often foreign, firms by colonial governments and the independent governments of Latin America to create such infrastructure.

3   Government entities in the less-developed regions often borrowed large sums in order to build needed infrastructure, loans that would presumably be paid from the increased output the country could expect from a more productive infrastructure. However, the borrowing entity, imbued as it was with the ethos of merchant capital, was rarely willing or capable of making a sound economic calculation of the costs, benefits, and risks of new loans. Such loans often were squandered by a corrupt governmental elite. But borrowing had another important function; it could mask economic downturns and extend a faltering boom period for the primary-product-exporting colonial or newly independent economy.

Borrowing from abroad was a seductive choice for many less-developed nations, in the past as now (see Chapter 17); it promised an immediate benefit, while the costs could be deferred. Lord Cromer, the British Consul-General in Egypt from 1883 to 1907, aptly sketched the attractions of credit, which often formed the basis for extended control by the European powers over the less-developed areas when loans could not be repaid.

> The maximum amount of harm is probably done when an Oriental ruler is for the first time brought in contact with the European system of credit. He thus finds that he can obtain large sums of money with the utmost apparent facility. His personal wishes can thus be easily gratified. He is dazzled by the ingenious and often fallacious schemes for developing his country which European adventurers will not fail to lay before him in the most attractive light. He is too wanting in foresight to appreciate the nature of the future difficulties which he is creating for himself. The temptation to avail himself to the full of the benefits which a reckless use of credit seems to offer to him are too strong to be resisted. He will rush into the gulf which lies open before him, and inflict injury on his country from which not only his contemporaries but future generations will suffer.
>
> (Cromer 1908: 58–9)

The growing sophistication of international banking extended the power of the advanced nations over the less-developed regions, even after the end of formal colonialism, often leading to new and more subtle forms of control and influence. Tied loans became commonplace; credits were extended to the less-developed areas on the condition that the bulk of the loan be used to purchase equipment from the lending nation. This often meant not only higher prices for the borrower, but possibly inferior equipment as a consequence. Tied loans also discouraged the development of indigenous suppliers of such products and other inputs. Even semi-skilled labor was normally imported to complete major projects. The economic stimulus from the construction stage provided by external borrowing thus was exceedingly limited, and it was usually restricted to a modest and brief tightening of the casual labor market. Meanwhile, much of the downstream benefit of the loan in terms of the increased future production of tropical commodities or minerals was forgone because of the drain of future interest payments and special loan fees attached to the loans.

The new imperialism: 1870–1914

The nineteenth century was fascinating not merely because new processes of control *vis-à-vis* the less-developed nations were being forged through the medium of credit. Much more startling was the revival of wars of conquest and seizure at the very time when virtually all the political leaders of the great powers were singing the virtues of free trade. Colonies multiplied at a stupefying rate during the so-called "Century of Free Trade." In 1800, the European powers effectively controlled 55 per cent of the total global land mass, including former European colonies. By 1878, this control had increased to 67 per cent, and by 1914, colonial holdings stood at 84.4 per cent! As David Fieldhouse emphasized: "Expansion continued; by 1939 the only significant countries which had never been under European rule were Turkey, some parts of Arabia, Persia, China, Tibet, Mongolia and Siam. In addition to new colonies, there were new colonial powers: Italy, Belgium, USA, and Russia" (Fieldhouse 1967: 178). Table 3.2 records the magnitude of some of the major colonial systems holdings of the European powers and the United States at the outset of the First World War. The ranking is in terms of the population in the colonies. Of the total subjugated population under the dominance of the Europeans and the US, some 530 million in 1914, nearly 100 million had been added over the period 1870–1914, when the scramble to take control of Africa peaked. Almost half of the territory controlled by the colonial powers in 1914 had been acquired in Africa after 1879.

How does one account for the widespread acceptance of the precepts of free trade between sovereign nations at the very moment when colonialism was reinvigorated? The answer, it

Table 3.2 Selected colonial systems in 1914

Colonial power	Number of colonies	Population of colonies	Size (sq. miles)	Colonial pop./ National pop.	Colonial territory/ National territory
United Kingdom	55	391,583,000	12,044,000	8.52	99.20
France	29	62,350,000	4,111,000	1.57	19.90
Netherlands	8	37,410,000	762,863	6.13	59.80
Belgium	1	15,000,000	910,000	1.98	79.80
Germany	10	13,075,000	1,231,000	0.20	5.90
US[a]	6	10,545,000	172,091	0.14	0.05
Portugal	8	9,680,000	804,440	1.12	22.70
Italy	4	1,397,000	591,250	0.04	5.30

Sources: Hobson 1965: 23; Stavrianos 1981: 264.

Note
a Data from 1905.

seems, is that free-trade theory was only to be applied to relations between the powerful nations. As for the colonial regions, the most charitable interpretation, often utilized by supporters of colonialism, was that the less-developed nations were being readied for free trade, as enlightened colonial rule would "uplift" the colonial peoples and their economic system and prepare them for participation in the global economy.

Mature colonialism and progressive colonialism

Colonialism was an uneven institution; different colonial powers encountered different regions at different moments in history. The outcome, while perhaps never unique, was sufficiently varied, thereby making sweeping generalizations about colonialism difficult to establish and support. Throughout its long history, many came forward to sing the praises of the so-called colonizing mission. And, viewed carefully, there seems to be some support in two instances for the notion that colonialism could be somewhat benign, at least in some respects.

British and French colonialism in West Africa: 1945–65

The European powers faced a new set of relationships after the Second World War, and this led to a fundamentally new approach to the issue of colonial rule. By then most of the colonial regions had engendered an emerging nationalist element which began to exert considerable pressure on the colonial powers. The nationalists' aspirations to political independence and national autonomy resonated in the capitals of Europe, where many of the new nationalist leaders in the colonies had lived, studied, and learned to aspire to ideals of political independence championed by a pantheon of European philosophers and political thinkers. The colonizers responded to this pressure by attempting to address issues which heretofore had been ignored.

First, money was poured into infrastructure, industry, and, more generally, economic development projects. In many West African nations, the colonial governments formed marketing boards to purchase the production of native cultivators and ship their output to the world market. Additional funds came via governmental outlays derived from the colonial powers, with the bulk of these outlays being used to develop a system of paved roads. From 1945 to 1960, the paved road system of West Africa increased by a factor of ten (Hopkins 1973: 282). In the nine-year period 1947–56, the French invested twice as much in West Africa as they had over the previous fifty years. Similarly, British expenditures for 1946–60 exceeded those for 1900–45 (ibid.: 280).

During this period, sometimes known as "mature colonialism," colonial administrators practiced a new policy, known as "indigenization," which involved the hiring of Africans in the mining industry and on the staffs of the large trading companies which dominated economic activity in the colonies. Indigenization was broadly aimed at involving colonial peoples in a wider range of economic activities. The policy extended to the promotion of export agriculture for native cultivators. At the same time, the colonial governments became alert to the need to diversify and balance the economic activity of the region. They thus began to promote some industrialization, and local firms were granted relief from taxes, provided with tariff protection from imports, were guaranteed state purchases of their output, and were extended bank loans at subsidized interest rates; occasionally outright grants were provided. As a result, many of the large trading companies began to produce a range of light consumer products. As impressive as this *volte-face* may appear, the overall results were far from sufficient to reverse the structural biases and adverse path dependence created by colonialism.

In 1955, for example, only 0.09 percent of Nigerians were employed in manufacturing; in the Gold Coast (Ghana), the figure stood at 0.44 percent; in Kenya, 0.7 percent; and in the Congo, 0.87 percent of the labor force was employed in manufacturing (Fieldhouse 1981: 102). Reviewing in some detail the period of mature colonialism in French West Africa, historian David Fieldhouse concluded:

> At the end of the colonial period French West Africa had hardly begun to industrialize and the great majority of even those industries that did exist were owned and run by expatriates. Such facts provide strong arguments for those who hold that colonialism was incompatible with "balanced" economic growth in the dependencies.
>
> (Fieldhouse 1981: 102)

Progressive colonialism

Could colonialism ever confer net benefits on a nation? It would be difficult to answer this question in the affirmative, because of the complex array of factors which would have to be considered and weighted to derive an answer. In most instances, it would appear that the list of advantages of being colonized would be quite short. However, it is common to accord some progressivity to Japanese colonial rule among all the colonial powers. The overall presence of the Japanese was greater in their occupation of Taiwan and Korea than was Dutch colonial power in Indonesia, but the Japanese brought technological improvement to agriculture in their colonies, and they injected a skilled technical labor force into Korean industry. Japan also invested heavily in colonial industry, and as a consequence skills were transferred to the colonies and their educational level was advanced. The colonial state left a legacy of "a rationalized currency system, banks and other institutions that the state controlled, long-and short-term economic plans, production oriented new technology and a variety of direct and indirect subsides" (Kohli 1999: 133). There was no drain on Korea's balance of payments, as was the norm for other colonies; in fact, Japan was a net provider of capital (Maddison 1990: 365). Over the period 1929–38, the annual rate of real GDP growth in Taiwan and Korea was 1.8 percent and 3.5 percent, respectively. Industrial growth averaged nearly 10 percent per year from 1910 to 1940 in Korea (Kohli 2004: 48). By comparison, the rate of growth of GDP in India over the same period was a mere 0.5 percent, and in Indonesia it was 1.6 percent (Maddison 1985: 19). In making this comparison, it is important to recognize that in India, at least, the British were then pursuing a "dual mandate," which entailed the idea that the purpose of colonial policy was to pursue economic development, including an attempt to industrialize India. It would appear that Japan's colonial policies, on the surface, were more successful in this regard.

> [T]he Japanese were late developers who on their own had perfected a state-led model of development ... This was the model they transmitted to Korea ... A state-led economy at home also enabled the Japanese in Korea to coordinate the interests of those Japanese firms mainly interested in exporting manufactured goods to Korea as well as of those mainly interested in exporting capital and establishing manufacturing in Korea. The Japanese pattern of colonialism was thus considerably more transformative, leaving in its wake a state that was simultaneously brutal and capable of introducing socioeconomic change, on the one hand, and a growing economy with an industrial base, on the other hand.
>
> (Kohli 2004: 410)

While the contrast of the Japanese empire to other colonial powers is interesting, it is important to keep in mind that a larger portion of the growth in Taiwan and Korea in the period cited above was enjoyed by Japanese nationals, not the colonized subjects. And the loss of national identity and the imposition of alien and often arbitrary and cruel colonial practices by the Japanese raises serious questions regarding the extent to which colonialism was ever progressive in an overall sense anywhere.

Decolonization

Only in the closing years of the Second World War was it clear that the colonial regions, "readied" or not, would be released from their formal bonds of domination. Part of the impetus for this abrupt change came from the United States. Having won its independence from Britain via armed struggle, the United States had long declared its willingness to uphold the concept of national self-determination. President Woodrow Wilson had been particularly eager to impose this ideal on Europe's colonial system immediately after the First World War, but the United States had been too weak then to achieve it.

In the closing days of the Second World War, the United States faced weakened European powers, unable to maintain their colonies without US financial assistance. In some instances, the United States was willing to prolong European dominance over colonial areas, particularly where Cold War considerations tipped the scales, but the basic thrust of US policy was clear: the colonial systems would have to be dismantled relatively quickly. Altruistic motives may have driven US policy to some degree. But the United States also was anxious to see the end of British dominance in much of the Middle East, where American oil companies were keen to extend their leases and exploratory activities. Likewise in Asia and Africa, US-owned mining companies expected to have equal access to resources, something the colonial powers had resisted granting their global economic competitors. Furthermore, the United States was haunted still by the image of the Great Depression; virtually every major American economist held that the end of the Second World War would mean the onset of economic stagnation or, worse, another depression. Hence there was a widespread appreciation of the possibilities of selling US products to former colonial regions, if only they could be opened to American products by being released from European colonial dominance.

Another part of the impetus toward the break-up of colonialism came from within the colonies themselves, particularly from India.[12] The Indian anti-colonial struggle was carefully observed, giving rise to new hopes, and suggesting tactics to opposition leaders in other colonies. Indian nationalists had long struggled for independence prior to the Second World War, and during the war the British were forced to borrow heavily from the Indian treasury. Indian military forces also were extensively used to aid the British war effort, fighting valiantly and nobly. The *quid pro quo* for such compliance, reluctantly agreed to by the British, was Indian independence after the war. India's example helped other colonial areas in their determined resistance to colonialism. Still, decolonization was far from an orderly or peaceful process. The French, in particular, bitterly resisted national independence in Algeria and Vietnam, with disastrous consequences and costs for the economic development prospects of the colonies.

Point Four Aid

From the end of the Second World War until 1949, the colonial regions were not the focus of attention of the great powers. For the US, in particular, the postwar economic breakdown of

Europe, the presumed truculence of the Soviet Union, and the question of the future role of atomic weapons crowded out the issue of colonialism. Largely unnoticed, as early as 1939, with the world falling into war, the US-based Council on Foreign Relations began to raise the theme of an international long-term bank, the need for technology and learning transfers, and the creation of infrastructure as part of a "world development program." In England in 1941 Paul Rosenstein-Rodan began work on his classic study of development discussed in Chapter 6 (Arndt 1987: 26–8).

In 1949, the less-developed regions were suddenly brought into the foreground again with President Harry S. Truman's inaugural address. Truman stated that he had "four points" to make; in the fourth point:

> He called for a "bold new program" for making the benefits of American science and industrial progress available to "underdeveloped" countries ...
>
> The old imperialism – exploitation for profit – had no place in the plan, Truman said. Half the people in the world were living in conditions close to misery, and for the first time in history the knowledge and skill were available to relieve such suffering. The emphasis would be on the distribution of knowledge rather than money.
>
> (McCullough 1992: 730–1)

Truman's speech suggested that the United States could "supply the vitalizing force to stir the peoples of the world into triumphant action ... against ... hunger, misery and despair." The main thrust of US activity, however, placed "particular emphasis ... (on) the stimulation of a greatly expanded flow of private investment" (US Department of State 1949: 4). The State Department, in articulating the policy initiatives which had given rise to Truman's speech, emphasized that the chief concern of the United States would not be private investment in general, but investment in resources:

> Location, development and economical processing of mineral and fuel resources is a major aspect of the program of a technical cooperation for economic development of underdeveloped countries.
>
> (US Department of State 1949: 20)

In the more sober, calculating terms of the State Department, the ostensible global struggle against misery appeared to be as much in the self-interest of the developed nations as it was an act of magnanimity on the part of a great power: "many underdeveloped mineral resources in the areas which will participate in the cooperative effort are of considerable importance to the more highly developed nations of the world including the United States" (US Department of State 1949: 20).

Whatever the conceptual and policy limits of Point Four Aid, the shift in US policy was of fundamental importance. It marked the concrete beginning of a move away from an almost exclusive concern over European recovery after the Second World War. It brought to life a new consensus that: "By 1945, economic development of underdeveloped nations had become an accepted objective of national and international policy of the developed countries" (Arndt 1987: 25). Not only were US funds and research now to be directed toward economic development in the less-developed world, but more importantly, the International Monetary Fund (IMF) and the World Bank (see Chapter 17 for a discussion of these institutions) began to restructure themselves in the early 1950s as a result of Point Four. From the early 1950s onward, these multinational institutions would grow in power and prestige, and their policies toward the underdeveloped regions would become of the utmost importance. Furthermore, the European powers followed the lead of Point Four, particularly in the policy formulations of the Organization for European Economic Co-operation. Economists who had been concerned with recovery in Europe now found new careers open to them as development economists within government, in institutions such as the IMF and World Bank, with major foundations, and in the universities.

Economic dualism

There can be no doubt that colonialism fundamentally altered the economies of the underdeveloped areas. Having endured for centuries in many areas, the path-dependence effects of colonialism were not to be swept away in a matter of years, or a Decade of Development. One of the worst features of colonialism, as it evolved in Africa, Asia and Latin America, was the creation of what economists have termed the "dual economy." The Dutch economist J.H. Boeke was one of the earliest economists to make this distinction. Boeke, after decades of research in Asia, maintained that:

> Social Dualism is the clashing of an imported social system with an indigenous social system of another style. Most frequently the imported social system is high capitalism.
>
> (Boeke 1953: 4)

Professor Boeke regarded dualism as a form of *disintegration*, which would last interminably and would undercut all prospects for development. Others have employed the concept without adopting either Boeke's pessimism or many of his assumptions regarding the impermeable nature of the pre-capitalist social system. After subjecting Boeke's general analysis to a withering critique, Benjamin Higgins stated:

> there can be no question about the phenomenon of dualism; it is one of the distinguishing features of underdeveloped countries. Virtually all of them have two clearly differentiated sectors: one confined mainly to peasant agriculture and handicrafts or very small industry, and the trading activities associated with them; the other consisting of plantations, mines, petroleum fields and refineries, large-scale industries, and the transport and trading activities associated with these operations. Levels of technique, productivity and income are low in the first sector and high in the second.
>
> (Higgins 1959: 281)

Thus dualism posited a "two-sector model" where a pre-capitalist, transitional form of production was juxtaposed with a modern, capitalist sector. These two sectors had nothing in common other than the fact that they existed side-by-side within one social formation, and that the pre-capitalist sector provided labor to the modern capitalist enterprises. The modern sector exists as a virtual enclave within the larger pre-capitalist and semi-capitalist sector, operating within the same overall social and economic structure, but also somewhat distanced from it.[13] The modern capitalist sector does not fully supplant this semi-capitalist sector; rather the pre-capitalist sector is slowly dissolved over an intermediate, and indeterminate, time period, as both the pre-capitalist and semi-capitalist sectors exhibit a determined capacity to resist the forces of change that capitalist methods of production attempt to implant. Peasants struggle to maintain their grip on marginal plots of land, mercilessly working themselves and their families to eke out an existence that is often near, or even below, subsistence. Landless agricultural workers struggle to acquire land, while those pushed into the cities often send a part of their meager wages to their families in the countryside.

Governments in colonial dual societies often exhibited a profound urban bias (see Chapter 11 for further discussion). Taxes taken from throughout the social formation tended to be spent close to the capital city and on the highest cadre of "public servants," who often lived like potentates, and only then on the public facilities of the cities. The best infrastructure was and remains to be found in the major cities. The countryside remained starved of irrigation, roads, transportation, schools, and health clinics. Without roads, water, technical assistance, capital investment, training, and education, the countryside atrophied, further sharpening the dualist nature of colonial society.

Everett Hagen was one of the early development economists who found the dualistic framework useful to analyze economic underdevelopment. For Hagen, the social–psychological distinctions to be made between the two sectors were profound: "In a psychological sense, the elite [i.e. the 'modern' sector] and the villagers of the peasant society live literally in different worlds and have extremely few interests in common" (Hagen 1957: 28). Hagen maintained that in the pre-capitalist and semi-capitalist sectors, one found the dominance of crude concepts of the physical world, primitive production methods, and extremely low literacy rates that affected the possibilities for future progress in these rural sectors.

Even in the modern sector, Hagen found fundamental weaknesses. In particular, he noted that the social elite tended to be self-reproducing and isolated. The lack of a "middle" class was notable and troubling: "In a technologically progressive society, ... there is a more rapid circulation of the elite, more social mobility through economic success, and a substantial middle class" (ibid.: 28). These elements were missing in most less-developed nations. Hagen also noted that in both the modern and traditional sectors there was a pervasive disdain for both modern business practices and forms of labor which entailed physical effort.

Summarizing Hagen's conclusions regarding the necessary changes to be made for development to occur in less-developed nations, Higgins emphasized that "The individual's view of his relationship with the world must change radically, scientific knowledge and the scope of experience must widen, occupational values must undergo basic alteration, class relationships must alter in their social, economic and political aspects" (Higgins 1959: 306). Hagen emphasized that "drastic change in *any* one variable in the peasant society while the others remain at their peasant society level seems unlikely [to be able to foster development]" (Hagen 1957: 59). Yet he nonetheless believed that, while quite difficult, a completion of the transition to a technologically dynamic society could be achieved in one generation.

In analyzing the modern or capitalist sector of the dual society, Paul Baran emphasized that it would be a grave mistake to believe that this sector always functioned precisely in the manner one might expect. The capitalist sector in less-developed nations continues to manifest distinct structural characteristics which reveal the continued influence of merchant capital and pre-capitalist ideas. For example, Baran noted that one would expect that large-scale investments in public goods such as railways, highways, electrification projects, and so on would generate external economies by lowering the cost of production of a variety of branches of the economy. Under pure capitalism such social investments create a virtuous-circle effect: more social investment → lower costs for private producers → greater incentive to invest → increases in construction activity → increases in employment → increases in consumption → increases in GDP → increases in tax revenues → increases in social investments, and so on. This fortuitous relationship, however, is not normally to be found in the dualist less-developed regions, given the weakness of the modern sector and the size of the pre-capitalist sector:

it is not railways, roads and power stations that give rise to industrial capitalism: it is the emergence of industrial capitalism that leads to the building of railways, to the construction of roads, and to the establishment of power stations. The identical sources of external economies, if appearing in a country going through the mercantile phase of capitalism, will provide, if anything, "external economies" to merchant capital. Thus the modern banks established by the British during the second half of the nineteenth century in India, in Egypt, in Latin America, and elsewhere in the underdeveloped world became not fountains of industrial credit but large-scale clearing houses of mercantile finance vying in their interest charges with the local usurers. In the same way, the harbors and cities that sprang up in many underdeveloped countries in connection with their briskly expanding exports did not turn into centres of industrial activity but snowballed into vast market places providing the necessary "living space" to wealthy compradors and crowded by a motley population of petty traders, agents and commissionmen. Nor did the railways, trunk roads, and canals built for the purpose of foreign enterprise evolve into pulsing arteries of productive activities; they merely accelerated the disintegration of the peasant economy and provided additional means for a more intensive and more thorough mercantile exploitation of rural interiors.

(Baran 1957: 193–4)

Baran's insight into the modern capitalist sector of the dual society serves to clarify the magnitude of the embedded distortions within the modern sector deriving from colonialism. This sector is modern or capitalist in relation to the pre-capitalist and semi-capitalist sector within the less-developed country, but it remains backward when compared to the advanced economies. One of the weakest and most debilitating components of the modern sector in the less-developed world is a continuing pervasiveness of merchant capital within the circuits of banking and finance. Rather than serving as a complementary force supporting industrialization and development, banking and finance are the locus of widespread speculative activities which absorb a large portion of the potentially loanable funds which could be used to support socially useful public and private investments.

Summary and conclusions

For many former colonies, the lingering effects of colonial control are not quickly or even easily cast off. Colonization created productive structures designed not to exploit the potential comparative advantage of the dominated economy and its people. Rather, the colonizer organized production, particularly export production, around an extremely narrow array of tropical agricultural products, minerals, and other primary commodities to supply the colonizer's needs. Cost considerations were not particularly important, since production did not take place within a free-market context, but rather within a framework of domination and control. Thus, colonial regions acquired productive structures, skills, education systems, infrastructure, institutions, and organizations shaped to the interests of the colonizer. Created as mono-exporters of agricultural, mining, and other primary products, these path-dependent structures, including their embedded power structures, were carried over into independence.

One of the difficulties faced by former colonies, then, is that of altering past path dependence in ways that can lead to economic growth and human development. Countries, then, do not start as open books, as *tabulae rasae*. Rather, they begin with a complex past that has brought them to the present and will take them to the future. Making changes to the array of factors contributing to past path dependence, through proper policies, can establish a new path dependence promising a better future.

Questions for review

1 How did merchant capitalism function to retard and distort the developmental potential in the colonial regions? How is it different from industrial capitalism?

2 How did the movement in the terms of trade in the nineteenth century lead to the widely held view that a primary product export economy was both desirable and, in some sense, good economics? What has happened to the terms of trade for tropical commodities in the twentieth century? How does this affect the conclusion that a primary product export focus can contribute to economic development?

3 Does it make sense for any country to have a majority of its export income derived from one or two exports, that is, to be a mono-exporter? Why, or why not? Do developed countries have a limited array of exports? Why do most less-developed countries have such a limited array of exports?

4 Why and how were dualist structures fostered in the colonial regions, and how did they create barriers to further economic development?

5 In the era of industrial capitalism, how did institutions introduced under colonial rule act as a brake on economic development and constitute a schism with the historical pattern of evolution in the colonized areas? What role did de-industrialization play in this process? Why did the colonizers require de-industrialization in their colonies? Who benefited and who lost?

6 All countries are subject to path dependence. This simply means that past decisions, and past history, affect the present conditions and possibilities for the future. What is meant by *adverse* path dependence? What role did colonialism play in creating adverse path dependence? How can countries that were former colonies overcome adverse path dependence? What specific changes would you suggest be undertaken by now-independent countries with economic structures shaped by colonialism?

Notes

1 In the developed capitalist and industrial nations, variations in income and output were increasingly the result of business cycles, that is, they were due to factors that affected the profits of producers and their willingness to produce. Variations in income and output due to purely exogenous forces, like the weather, became much less powerful as industrial production increasingly replaced agriculture as the motor force of society (as discussed in Chapter 9). Of course, some exogenous factors, such as wars and plagues, did from time to time adversely affect income levels, but the control exercised over the environment in which humans reproduced themselves via production was remarkable after the Industrial Revolution and the spread of the factory system of production.

2 Later, at and after the turn of the twentieth century, both the United States and Japan, relative late-comers to the capitalist revolution, also joined the ranks of the colonizers.

3 The wave of decolonization that created most of today's less-developed nations, with exceptions, like China, occurred after 1945. Many of today's independent nations in Africa and the Caribbean did not win freedom from colonialism until the 1960s and in some instances not until the 1970s.

4 There were notable exceptions. First, in relatively unpopulated areas such as the United States, Canada, Australia, and New Zealand virtual extermination of the native peoples was achieved quickly, and the subsequent "white settler" societies achieved self-governance and positive economic stimulus from the international economy. Second, Japan took control of Korea and Taiwan early in the twentieth century with results that, in many respects, diverge from that found throughout Africa, Asia, Latin America, and the Middle East.

5   Maddison (1982: 4, 13) dates the period of merchant capitalism from 1700 to 1820. It is during this period, he notes, that plunder is important to the progress of the colonizing nations.

6   In contrast, adaptation was never part of the old colonial system. Thus, the Spanish did not readily utilize the new plantation system, nor were there fundamental adjustments in colonial policy in light of the depopulation of Mexico and Peru brought about by the liquidation of indigenous labor. Rather, as trade and commerce collapsed following the breakdown of the mining boom, the great *latifundio* system of the hacienda, which had been subordinate to the mining economy in the Spanish colonies, came to dominate the Latin American economy. As Francois Chevalier pointed out:

> The return to the soil helped revive in Mexico certain medieval institutions and customs recalling the patriarchal existence of Biblical times – the [hacendado's] peculiar mentality was not conducive to thinking in terms of efficient production. He acquired land, not to increase his earnings, but to eliminate rivals and hold sway over an entire region. His scorn for extra profits sometimes went to such lengths that he destroyed perfectly good equipment on land recently purchased.
>
> (Chevalier 1970: 307, 311)

John Coatsworth (1978: 86–93) has maintained that the generalizations of Chevalier, and many others, are not supported by a broad range of studies conducted in the 1970s which indicate that given the existing institutional structure of Latin America, the haciendas were economically rational. The institutional structure, however, was not.

7   Others, it must be noted, have argued that British rule regenerated India. Proponents of this perspective often stress the restoration of several canals and the renovation and expansion of major irrigation systems by the British, starting in the 1820s. Further, by 1914, India had obtained 34,000 miles of railways, and 25 million acres of land, including Burma, were under irrigation. Moreover, the agrarian plantation economy was diversified in the course of the nineteenth century, with major investments in tea and coffee, indigo and sugar plantations, a sizeable jute mill industry, as well as coal and mica mines.

Commenting on this more favorable evaluation of British colonialism in India, Tom Kemp has argued that:

> although India was perhaps unique among underdeveloped countries in having an organized sector (factories) partly under native ownership, as well as railways, ports, banks and other attributes of a modern economy these remained localized in their influence. To put it another way, they had not initiated a genuine process of industrialization or fundamentally transformed the agrarian structure.
>
> Indeed, although part of agriculture production was hinged to the market, there was no shift of population out of agriculture; if anything the proportion of the population dependent on the land tended to rise. The existence of some advanced industries did little to raise per capita income or to initiate economic growth.
>
> (Kemp 1989: 93)

8   Group I countries were Finland, Italy, Norway, Sweden, Japan, Argentina, Brazil, Chile, Colombia, Mexico, and Peru. Group II countries were Bangladesh, China, India, Indonesia, Pakistan, the Philippines, South Korea, Taiwan, and Thailand.

9   Colonialism involves both political and economic domination. The colonial power administers the political structure of the economy. Neocolonialism is economic domination of one nation by another, without the necessity of direct, political control.

10   Technically, the terms of trade is a composite index defined by the ratio of two price indices. Taking P_M as the price index of imported goods and P_X as the price index of exported goods, then the terms of trade index (TOT) can be defined as $TOT = (P_X/P_M) \times 100$.

11   For an excellent account of the role of British finance in Latin America and India, see Cain and Hopkins (1993: Chapters 9 and 10).

12   The United Nations was also an important forum for the decolonization movement, and the growth in membership in that body is due to the end of colonization.

13   It is not unusual, however, to find home workers and small artisan-style workshops with a direct

link to large national and even transnational corporations. It therefore may appear that there is little basis on which a strict separation can be made between the semi-capitalist sector and the capitalist sector.

It is important to realize that the distinction between two sectors in the dualistic models is based upon an interpretation of the motives and behavioral patterns characteristic of the distinct forms of production and not on formal interaction. A home worker or contract artisan workshop, while possibly linked to a world-straddling web of production and distribution, nonetheless may operate on a survival basis, using the labor of family members, with little mastery of technology, little or no access to credit, no power in dealing with the company it supplies, no strategy regarding cost minimization or production efficiency, and, most likely, little effective recourse to the legal system in the event that basic contract agreements are violated. While such producers may be an *appendage* of the capitalist system of production, they do not exist as capitalist producers themselves, but rather as semi-capitalist artisan workers. This is a question of symbiosis, not a case of fusion between the two sectors.

References

Acemoglu, Daron. 2003. "Root Causes," *Finance and Development* 40, 2 (June): 27–30.

Acemoglu, Daron, Simon Johnson and James Robinson. 2001. "Colonial Origins of Comparative Development: An Empirical Investigation," *American Economic Review* 91 (December): 1369–1401.

Alam, M.S. 1994. "Colonialism, Decolonisation and Growth Rates: Theory and Empirical Evidence," *Cambridge Journal of Economics* 18: 235–57.

——. 2000. *Poverty from the Wealth of Nations.* London: Macmillan.

Amsden, Alice H. 2001. *The Rise of "the Rest": Challenges to the West from Late-Industrializing Countries.* Oxford: Oxford University Press.

Arndt, H.W. 1987. "Development Economics *Before* 1945," pp. 13–29 in Jagdish Bhagwati and Richard Eckaus (eds.), *Development and Planning.* Cambridge, MA: MIT Press.

Bagchi, Amiya. 1984. *The Political Economy of Underdevelopment.* Cambridge: Cambridge University Press.

Baran, Paul. 1957. *The Political Economy of Growth.* New York: Marzani & Munsell.

Boeke, J.H. 1953. *Economics and Economic Policy of Dual Societies.* New York: Institute of Pacific Relations.

Cain, P.J. and A.G. Hopkins. 1993. *British Imperialism: Innovation and Expansion, 1688–1914.* London: Longman.

Chang, Ha-Joon. 2007. *Bad Samaritans: Rich Nations, Poor Policies, and the Threat to the Developing World.* London: Random House.

Chevalier, Francois. 1970. *Land and Society in Colonial Mexico.* Berkeley, CA: University of California Press.

Coatsworth, John. 1978. "Obstacles to Economic Growth in Nineteenth-Century Mexico," *American Historical Review* 83 (February): 80–110.

Cromer, Lord. 1908. *Modern Egypt.* London: Macmillan.

Crow, Ben and Mary Thorpe. 1988. *Survival and Change in the Third World.* New York: Oxford University Press.

Davis, Mike. *Late Victorian Holocausts.* London: Verso.

Digby, William. 1969. *"Prosperous" India: A Revelation from Official Records.* New Delhi: Sagar Publications.

Fieldhouse, David. 1967. *The Colonial Empires.* New York: Delacorte Press.

——. 1981. *Colonialism 1870–1945.* New York: St. Martin's Press.

Furnivall, J.S. 1967. *Netherlands India.* Cambridge: Cambridge University Press.

Galeano, Eduardo. 1973. *Open Veins of Latin America.* New York: Monthly Review Press.

Grilli, E. and H. Yang. 1988. "Primary Commodity Prices, Manufactured Goods Prices, and the Terms of Trade of Developing Countries: What the Long Run Shows," *The World Bank Economic Review* 2: 1–47

Hagen, Everett. 1957. "The Process of Economic Development," *Economic Development and Cultural Change* (April): 193–215.

Higgins, Benjamin. 1959. *Economic Development*. New York: W.W. Norton & Co.

Hobson, John. 1965. *Imperialism*. Ann Arbor, MI: University of Michigan Press.

——. 1993. "The Military-Extraction Gap and the Wary Titan," *Journal of European Economic History* (Winter): 466–507.

Hochschild, Adam. 1999. *King Leopold's Ghost: A Story of Greed, Terror, and Heroism in Colonial Africa*. New York: Mariner Books.

Hopkins, A.G. 1973. *An Economic History of West Africa*. New York: Columbia University Press.

Hunt, E.K. 1979. *History of Economic Thought*. Belmont, CA: Wadsworth Publishing Co.

Hyndman. H.M. 1919. *The Awakening of Asia*. London: Cassell & Co.

Kaiwar, Vasant. 1994. "The Colonial State, Capital and the Peasantry in Bombay Presidency," *Modern Asian Studies* 28 (October): 793–832.

Kemp, Tom. 1989. *Industrialization in the Non-Western World*. London: Longman.

Kohli, Atul. 1999. "Where do High-Growth Political Economies Come From? The Japanese Lineage of Korea's 'Developmental State'," pp. 93–136 in Meredith Woo-Cumings (ed.), *The Developmental State*. Ithaca: Cornell University Press.

——. 2004. *State Directed Development*. Cambridge: Cambridge University Press.

McCullough, David. 1992. *Truman*. New York: Simon & Schuster.

Maddison, Angus. 1982. *Phases of Capitalist Development*. Oxford: Oxford University Press.

——. 1985. *Two Crises: Latin America and Asia 1929–38 and 1973–83*. Paris: OECD.

——. 1990. "The Colonial Burden: A Comparative Perspective," pp. 361–76 in Maurice Scott and Deepak Lal (eds.), *Public Policy and Economic Development*. Oxford: Clarendon Press.

Maizels, Alfred, Theodsios Palaskas and Trevor Crowe. 1998. "The Prebisch-Singer Hypothesis Revisited," pp. 63–85 in David Sapsford and John-ren Chen (eds.), *Development Economics and Policy*. London: Macmillan.

Nehru, Jawaharal. 1960. *The Discovery of India*. New York: Doubleday-Anchor.

Peemans, J. P. 1975. "Capital Accumulation in the Congo under Colonialism," in P. Duigana and L.H. Gann (eds.), *Colonialism in Africa: 1870–1960.*,Cambridge: Cambridge University Press.

Reynolds, Lloyd G. 1986. *Economic Growth in the Third World*. New Haven, CT: Yale University Press.

Robinson, Ronald. 1976. "Non-European Foundations of European Imperialism," pp. 117–42 in Roger Owen and Bob Sutcliffe (eds.), *Studies in the Theory of Imperialism*. London: Longman.

Rodney, Walter. 1974. *How Europe Underdeveloped Africa*. Washington, D.C.: Howard University Press.

Sarkar, P. 1986. "The Terms of Trade Experience of Britain since the Nineteenth Century," *Journal of Development Studies* 23 (October): 20–39.

Schumpeter, Joseph. 1951. *Imperialism*. Oxford: Basil Blackwell.

Singer, Hans. 1989. "Terms of Trade," pp. 323–8 in John Eatwell *et al.* (eds.), *The New Palgrave: Economic Development*. New York: W.W. Norton.

Spraos, J. 1983. *Inequalising Trade?* Oxford: Clarendon Press.

Stavrianos, L.S. 1981. *Global Rift*. New York: William Morrow & Co.

Stein, Burton. 1998. *A History of India*. London: Blackwell Publishing.

Thomas, Robert. 1965. "A Quantitative Approach to the Study of the Effects of British Imperial Policy upon Colonial Welfare," *Journal of Economic History* 25: 615–38.

US Department of State. 1949. *Point Four, Cooperative Program for Aid in the Development of the Economically Underdeveloped Areas*. Washington, D.C.: US Department of State.

Part 2

Theories of development and underdevelopment

4   Classical and neoclassical theories

After reading and studying this chapter, you should better understand:

- Adam Smith's contribution to understanding how a capitalist market economy operates, including the importance of the invisible hand, competition, specialization, and the law of capital accumulation and how these interact to affect the rate of economic growth;
- Thomas Malthus's theory of population, how and why he believed rapid population growth was so likely and the implications of rapid population growth for the living standards of the poor;
- David Ricardo's theories of diminishing returns, of comparative advantage, his argument in favor of free trade and how these relate to the pace of economic expansion;
- Karl Marx's critique of capitalism and the theory behind his belief in the ultimate collapse of that system;
- the logic behind a Solow-type neoclassical growth model, the importance of saving and investment in determining the level of per capita income and why the neoclassical model predicts "conditional convergence" of income levels among nations over time;
- the Harrod-Domar model's importance to subsequent growth theories and strategies;
- the commonality of an emphasis on physical capital as a fundamental determinant to economic growth in all these growth models.

Introduction

As we learned in the previous chapter, the pursuit of economic growth and development as a socially desirable goal is of relatively recent origin, being more-or-less contemporaneous with the rise of capitalism as an economic system. The Industrial Revolution in England in the mid-eighteenth century provides a convenient date for the emergence of systematic and intellectual interest in understanding how and why economic development occurs. It also marks the emergence of economics – or **political economy**, as it was called at that time – as a separate sphere of scholarly inquiry. Not at all coincidentally some of the most distinguished and most enduring thinking about the process of economic development was produced in

Great Britain during and following the transition from feudalism to capitalism, where long-term economic expansion and rising income per capita first materialized on an extended scale (Maddison 1982).

Many of the great political economists whose ideas have shaped economic inquiry down to this day lived through the early changes brought on by the Industrial Revolution. These so-called classical political economists attempted not only to explain the reasons for the rapid expansion of total economic wealth that accompanied industrialization. They also tackled the enigma of the extremes of wealth and poverty that attended this process and the lack of development affecting a large segment of the population. It was during this era that *An Inquiry into the Nature and Causes of the Wealth of Nations* was composed by the Scottish philosopher and political economist, Adam Smith. *The Wealth of Nations*, published in 1776, provided a theoretical structure and explanation for the workings of the increasingly dominant market system at the center of the new capitalist industrial economy. It argued brilliantly for capitalism's superiority as a system of production compared to feudalism and its mercantilist tendencies. Smith's writings continue to provide the foundation for a good part of the optimism inherent in modern economic theory concerning the possibilities of progress in market societies.

In the late eighteenth and early nineteenth centuries, Thomas Malthus's pessimistic musings on the future of capitalism, based on his famous theory of population, darkened enthusiasm for capitalism's future – but only temporarily. David Ricardo helped to make sense of the changes in economic structure and institutions that emerged as a consequence of the spread of capitalism across Europe, and he added analytical tools to the economist's toolbox that remain central to economic analysis to this day.

And of course, there is Karl Marx. Though not a British subject, Marx spent many of his most productive years in England, much of it in the Reading Room of the old British Library in Great Russell Street, writing both a theory and a critique of capitalism which appeared in the three volumes of *Capital*. Marx's analysis of the dynamics of capitalist development contain very important insights that have become central both to Marxist thought and, though many do not realize it or refuse to acknowledge it, to non-Marxist enquiry into economic growth and development.

In the first part of this chapter, the ideas and theories of these classical economists will be briefly summarized as they relate to economic and social progress. These political economists are called **classical** because they provided the framework and bedrock ideas of economics as a separate field of enquiry. Their analysis predates **neoclassical** economics which emerged after the 1870s in reaction particularly against the radical implications of Marx's version of classical theory.

Classical economists had an interest in the wider issues of the day, not only in how society produced its output and wealth but also in how it was distributed among competing groups with a claim on that income. The classicals were concerned with explaining not only how economic growth took place but also how to reduce the numbers living in poverty. However, except for John Stuart Mill and Marx, the classicals were similar to the neoclassicals who followed in assuming that the capitalist order was a "natural order" that represented the highest achievement of human development.

Neoclassical economists shifted the emphasis of economics from the broader macroeconomics of growth and development to a much narrower concern with the allocation of a fixed quantity of scarce resources to their best use with given institutions (something like this was probably the definition of economics you learned in your first course). This turn to *efficiency* as a focus led to a more static and marginalist perspective for economics. Growth and development, which often require substantial qualitative change in society and not just small quantitative change, disappeared for quite some time from the economist's view. Supply and demand and price determination became "economics."

In the latter part of this chapter, the influential neoclassical-type growth theories of Harrod and Domar and the Solow model are assessed. These theories have an affinity in form and assumptions, if not always in their conclusions, with the classical models discussed in the first part of the chapter. They focus on the requirements for achieving an equilibrium level of economic growth, with a strong emphasis on the saving behavior of society as the determinant variable. Similar to the classical view, however, is an emphasis on the accumulation of physical capital – machines, tools, building, etc. – as the fundamental lever for economic growth. If there has been one common theme among early economists on what generates economic progress, it has been this, the accumulation of physical capital.

Neoclassical growth models of the Solow type have been extremely influential in concentrating the attention of economists and policy-makers to spotlight critical variables and tools for accelerating economic development. These often very abstract models have shaped public policies on how to best stimulate growth. No student can truly hope to understand how economists think about economic development without a rudimentary understanding of the simple foundational models reviewed in this chapter.

Adam Smith: a theory of competitive capitalism and growth

Adam Smith provided one of the earliest and most enduring metaphors for the operation of the capitalist market system: the *invisible hand*. What Smith called the "invisible hand" is simply what we now refer to as the forces of supply and demand working to attain equilibrium in a competitive economy. In such an environment, the individualistic desires of consumers for goods and services, combined with the self-interested drive to maximize profits by the producers of these goods and services, will tend toward deterministic levels of output and prices. This is the equilibrium price and quantity where the supply curve crosses the demand curve. At equilibrium, both consumers and producers gain from exchange, and there are no shortages or surpluses. All of this happens more or less automatically in an unfettered market system in which no one intends a result that nonetheless ends up benefiting everyone. Smith's words continue to be worth recalling:

> As every individual, therefore, endeavours as much as he can both to employ his capital in the support of domestic industry, and so to direct that industry that its produce may be of the greatest value; every individual necessarily labours to render the annual revenue of society as great as he can. He generally, indeed, neither intends to promote the public interest, nor knows how much he is promoting it … he intends only his own gain, and he is in this, as in many other cases, led by an *invisible hand* to promote an end which was no part of his intention.
>
> (Smith 1973: 423)

Smith believed there was a harmony of interests among consumers and producers and among workers, landlords, and capitalists and other groups in society which the competitive market capitalist system mediates to the benefit of all. The purely self-interested, even selfish and greedy behavior of consumers and producers of goods is not an evil to be despised or a lamentable flaw of the capitalist, market system. Such self-interested behavior is functional and in fact virtuous, since it leads an economy to higher levels of economic welfare. One of Smith's most famous quotations says it best:

> It is not from the benevolence of the butcher, the brewer, or the baker, that we expect our dinner, but from their regard to their own interest. We address ourselves, not to their humanity, but to their self-love, and never talk to them of our own necessities but of their advantages.
>
> (Smith 1973: 14)

Smith's concept of the invisible hand is well known by most first-year undergraduates. Often neglected, forgotten, or ignored is the equal importance Smith placed on *competition* within his philosophy of the gains expected from the market system. Competition acts as a *counterweight* to and a brake on the possible excesses that greedy and self-interested behavior might engender in its absence. An effective competitive environment is essential in restraining the actions of producers and owners/capitalists who constantly are tempted to form cartels or monopolies in an effort to increase their individual profits at the expense of both consumers and workers.

Smith's belief in the virtues of the capitalist market economy was thus not an uncritical view that emphasized only the market's harmonizing effects. In the absence of competition, Smith did not assume that "greed is good" and that individual actions automatically would benefit everyone. Nor did Smith presume that private and societal interests were always identical. Smith was suspicious of the intentions of naturally acquisitive capitalists. He believed that, given the opportunity, they would eagerly monopolize markets for their own benefit at the expense of others and might create working conditions inimical to the social and individual development of their own workers.

For Adam Smith, the benefits to consumers of the market capitalist system thus rested on two, non-separable constituent components: selfish behavior kept in check and regulated by the forces of competition. When competition is threatened by the self-interested actions of producers/capitalists, it is one of the responsibilities of government to create the legal framework and to put in place the appropriate enforcement mechanisms to defend and maintain a competitive environment so that the potential benefits of the market system might be achieved for the largest number. While Smith is often, correctly, singled out as a champion of *laissez-faire*, his was not a naïve or uncritical view of the workings of the capitalist economy. He foresaw an essential role for government within this emerging and powerful market system, a symbiotic relation between the invisible hand of the markets and the visible hand of the state.

Smith's views on economic development

What is the relation of Smith's analysis of the invisible hand and the functioning of the market system to the forces contributing to economic growth? In a broad sense, Smith believed capitalism to be a productive system with the potential to vastly increase human well-being. In particular, he stressed the importance of the **division of labor** and the **law of capital accumulation** as the primary factors contributing to economic progress or, as he termed it, to the "wealth of nations."

The division of labor, or what also can be called "specialization," began to evolve rapidly with the spread of capitalism and the factory system. Prior to the Industrial Revolution, the division of labor was relatively limited or non-existent in the production of any particular product. For example, in producing a sweater, all the distinct steps were likely to be done by one person or at most a single family. From the spinning of the yarn obtained from the clippings of the sheep, to the weaving of the cloth from the yarn, to the cutting, sewing, and finishing of the final garment, a single individual might have been involved in performing many, or even all, of the tasks of production. There was little or no specialization in such non-capitalist, non-exchange production prior to the Industrial Revolution. As might be expected, only a small quantity of output can be produced if one person must undertake all the steps required to make a product. Think how long it would take you to finish even a single T-shirt if you had to gather the cotton, weave the cloth, cut, sew, and so on. And now imagine the quality! That is a situation of no division of labor and no specialization. Both the quantity of output and quality typically suffer.

With the Industrial Revolution in Great Britain and the emergence of the factory system, the organization of production began to change, especially as peasants and farm laborers were pushed from the land and into the villages and cities by the Enclosure Movement. The factory system increasingly required that workers should come to designated locations to perform their tasks rather than producing at home.

Over time, the distinguishing characteristic of the factory system became the intensive use of machinery powered by water and steam. The pace of work was increasingly determined by the machinery with which employees toiled. With the expanded use of tools, the momentum toward specialization and the dividing of tasks (hence the term, division of labor) into ever smaller and finer components was both accelerated and made more feasible. With specialization, the process of producing clothing, for example, was changed. Some workers would be involved only in the spinning process, others in carding the wool, others in loading the yarn on to the machines, still others in moving the finished wool cloth to storage, in cutting cloth to patterns, and so on. Tasks would be divided and subdivided again and again, depending on the level of technology and the sophistication of the machinery available. Besides this extraordinary division of labor within factories, there was an ever more refined division of labor between industries, as specialization took place amongst those producers of consumer goods, producer goods, services and so on.

This division of labor and specialization of work within the factory, while often boring and repetitive for the workers involved, did unleash an extraordinary increase in the *productivity* of labor. More output could be obtained from the same number of workers than if they individually had produced a product from start to finish. Greater efficiency through specialization in factories contributed to increases in total national output and income, resulting in an increase in the living standard for larger numbers of the population. This upward movement of average income per capita following the Industrial Revolution was shown in Figure 3.1 of Chapter 3, and it was due to the "intensive" nature of factory production in a capitalist market setting.

In Smith's view, capitalism had a natural tendency toward this broadening and deepening of the division of labor, since doing so contributed to lower costs and increased output, thus enhancing the profit-making opportunities for producers. The naturally acquisitive behavior of producers in search of higher profits would tend to contribute to more specialization that could increase efficiency in production economy-wide. Smith's advocacy of free trade among nations also was based on this logic, for the larger the market of potential consumers – and what market was larger than the consumers of every country? – the greater were the possibilities for more specialization and for ever higher levels of output.[1] Owners of firms had a definite incentive to introduce the latest and best machinery and the newest ways of doing things since doing so would tend to increase efficiency and profits by further extending the division of labor and by making workers even more productive. This "law of capital accumulation" was inherent to the competitive capitalist market economy, and for Smith it was a human characteristic that capitalism unleashed.

In Smith's analysis, then, it is the accumulation of physical capital, technological progress, the specialization of labor and free trade that are the intertwined sources of expanding economic wealth. Economic growth will continue as long as capital is accumulated and new technology is introduced. Both competition and free trade contribute to making this process cumulative, and a competitive market environment provides the framework for all the benefits of an expanding market system to accrue to ever larger numbers of consumers, producers, workers, and owners. Smith's analysis of the widespread benefits of a nearly automatically expanding world capitalist order made him one of the most optimistic of all the classical economists. He truly thought that all the world's peoples would be lifted up on a wave of economic prosperity as capitalism spread.

Smith was keenly aware that the institutional structure of a society played a crucial role in determining the likelihood of continued progress. After all, his sustained criticism in *The Wealth of Nations* of England's mercantilist policies, the fettered trade relations it fostered, and the feudal remnants of production in the countryside had provided evidence for Smith's impassioned defense of capitalism, natural liberty, and a smaller state as being essential to economic expansion. *The Wealth of Nations* is essentially about how a transformed institutional environment unleashed dynamic forces of growth via a competitive capitalist economy from which the greatest number might benefit. These constituent elements – capitalism, capital accumulation, efficiency through specialization, free trade, and institutional innovation – continue to be essential elements in thinking about economic development to this day. They are not all of what is important to sustained progress, but Smith definitely provided the foundations for thinking about how economies grow.

Malthus's theory of population and economic growth

Thomas Robert Malthus, educated at the University of Cambridge, was a parson and later a professor of political economy. He is best known for his theory of population. Malthus published the first edition of his major work, *An Essay on the Principle of Population*, in 1798, when the effects of industrialization and the path of economic progress in England and Scotland looked quite different to him from how they had appeared to Adam Smith, the great optimist of classical political economy.

What observers of late eighteenth-century and early nineteenth-century England witnessed was a world not of a harmony of interests in which all gained, as Smith had postulated, but appalling conditions of degradation for a large part of the citizenry. (Read any of Charles Dickens's novels of that period to get an idea of living conditions.) Only a tiny minority of factory owners and some large rural landlords seemed to be benefiting from the spread of the industrial factory system. What had gone wrong in the last third of the eighteenth century to so alter the hopeful vision of the capitalist economy envisaged by Smith?

Malthus attempted to explain this disturbing state of affairs through his theory of population, which argued that the poor were responsible for their own misery. At a time of rising class conflict and resentment, Malthus suggested that the rich were not the enemy of the poor, but rather the poor were the architects of their own fate. Worse, he argued there was not much anyone, including government, could do about this state of affairs. The existing division between the wealthy few and the impoverished many was the natural outcome of the capitalist system. Let's take a look at his thinking.

Malthus's theory of population

Malthus assumed population would grow whenever average incomes rose above the level necessary for subsistence. Why? Because of the "animal nature" of human beings, specifically "the labouring poor', whom Malthus viewed as morally inferior to the land- and property-owning rich. What was the connection between income levels and population growth in Malthus's view?

If average income per person were to rise as a result, say, of good weather and the higher agricultural output that resulted, there would be more food and other necessities to go around. As incomes and food supplies rose above what was required for mere subsistence of the existing population, more children (and others) would be enabled to survive as the quantity of food per person rose. As a result, the effect of rising incomes coupled with the "unquenchable sexual desires of the poor" (these are Malthus's words) meant population could be expected to double about every generation, or every twenty-five years, if there was no limit on such growth.

In Malthus's famous formulation, population increases in a "geometric progression," that is, the number of people tends to grow at the rate of 2, 4, 8, 16, 32, 64, 128, 256, 512, 1,024, 2,028, and so on. For Malthus, this principle of the tendency toward the doubling of population over every generation when wages rose above subsistence was the major factor for understanding why the poorer classes remained poor. How, though, does population growth *per se* lead to poverty?

Malthus posited that the ultimate limit on population expansion was the inability of the land to produce sufficient food to continue to sustain the population surge. The production of basic foods could not keep up with geometric population growth because of the natural tendency of the fertility of the soil to be lower as additional land was brought under cultivation. Land best suited for food production already was in use. Any new land brought under production would produce less output per unit of land than more productive lands, so the growth in total food output would slow while population growth continued unabated.

Malthus believed that agricultural output could only increase in "arithmetic progression," that is, at the rate of 1, 2, 3, 4, 5, 6, 7, 8, 9, 10, and so on, certainly more slowly than the geometric growth rate he assumed governed population growth. An increasing population would sooner or later bump up against the obstacle of the slower-growing production of basic foods and other goods required for subsistence. Not only could income per person not continue to increase, it would actually begin to fall if population growth continued. Eventually incomes per person would fall *below* what was required for subsistence. Of course incomes below the minimum required for survival meant misery, starvation, death, and a declining rate of population growth, maybe even a population decline. "Equilibrium" would be attained when population grew again at a pace consistent with increases in food production. Malthus's theory is one that predicts a "vicious circle of poverty," that is, the equilibrium level of income per person (for the poor anyway) is one of subsistence only. Any deviations from that level of income lead to population growth or contraction that return incomes to the poverty level (see Basu 1997: 17–23).

Malthus noted some forces that could slow the natural rate of population growth before the ultimate barrier of incomes falling below subsistence was reached. Since the natural population growth rate depends upon the difference between the birth rate and the death rate, anything that tended to reduce the birth rate and/or to increase the death rate would tend to slow the natural rate of population growth.[2]

Malthus identified, first, what he called *preventive* (or *voluntary*) checks. These are factors that might be expected to reduce the number of births through human restraint, such as late marriage and sexual abstinence.

When these preventive checks to population growth on the birth-rate side were absent or weak, as Malthus assumed them typically to be among the poor, a second restraint on population growth, the *positive checks*, came into play. These constraints affected the other side of the population growth rate equation by increasing death rates through war, diseases, plagues, natural catastrophes, and the ultimate check, starvation. It was this apparent inevitability of poverty, squalor, disease, suffering, and death among the poorer classes that seemed imbedded in *laissez-faire* capitalism that had prompted Thomas Carlyle to voice his apprehension about economics as "the dismal science."

Malthus's vision of what seemed to be an inescapable dilemma flowing from economic growth to a population explosion to misery for the poor led him to oppose all efforts at charity directed at the poorer classes, including better health care and hygiene, since they could only delay the unavoidable drift of living standards toward subsistence. Indeed, acts of charity, be they private or public, might even be expected to lead to a *decrease* in the willingness of the poor to work by diminishing their fear of starvation, hence reducing total national production and income and thus actually accelerating the pace of decline toward subsistence.[3]

Of course, we now know that Malthus made a critical error in his analysis. He ignored the importance of technological progress to increasing productivity and output, even from relatively fixed inputs, like land, over the long run (as discussed in Focus 4.1). Malthus assumed

FOCUS 4.1   WAS MALTHUS RIGHT?

Was Malthus right about the rate of growth of food production? What factor important for increasing the level of output did Malthus overlook, even on land that may not seem suitable for farming?

If you guessed that Malthus was neglecting or not anticipating the advances in production that *technological change* in agriculture would permit, you are correct. Since the time of the Industrial Revolution, fewer and fewer persons working less and less land have been involved in producing more and more agricultural output, at least in the more developed nations. The reason is quite simple. Better technology in the form of machinery, seeds, fertilizers, irrigation, pesticides, and better-trained farmers have all contributed to a dramatic increase in agricultural output per unit of land. Fewer farmers in the rich countries feed ever-larger numbers of persons around the globe by being able to produce with ever-greater efficiency on the same or even less land.

Sachs (2005: 27–8) has two very interesting graphs. In one, he shows the rapid increase in population that begins about 1700. In a second graph, he shows the rapid increase in per capita income that begins at precisely the same time! So, if anything, world population growth and income per capita have been positively related to one another, not negatively, as Malthus predicted.

What the now developed nations experienced with the rise of capitalism was not only an industrial capitalist revolution. They also accomplished an **agricultural revolution** that increased food output and permitted higher living standards with less effort. At the time Malthus wrote, this great agricultural revolution was still somewhat in the future. But it was coming … and the Malthusian specter of starvation and unbridled population growth was a view that could not be sustained. We will revisit this perspective in Chapter 12, as there remain those who still stubbornly insist that "there is too much population growth" and that it is that which causes people around the world to be poor.

a constant productivity of any piece of land over time. To use modern terminology, Malthus envisaged a constant aggregate production function, *TP*, as shown in Figure 4.1, which never shifted. Improvements in technology, however, are precisely what permit a shifting upward of a nation's production function such that more output from the same resources is possible as shown by the higher total output curve, new *TP*, with technological change in Figure 4.1 (compare the level of output using L^* units of labor before and after a change in technology). It is through increases in technology and higher productivity of society's inputs that a growing population can be accommodated. Further, with output growing rapidly enough, there is no necessary reason for income per capita to fall, and sufficient technological progress can easily raise total output and income per person.[4]

What, then, might have accounted for the miserable living conditions among the poor that Malthus witnessed, if they were not due to a fundamental imbalance between limited food production and rapidly growing population as he believed? Most likely they were the result of transitional growing pains caused by the radical structural changes taking place in Britain as feudal society was becoming more capitalist. The benefits of the Industrial Revolution to larger numbers of people awaited institutional changes and the further spread of technology that were still in the future.

One thing Malthus demonstrated was that there was no *automatic* mechanism by which all classes in society necessarily gained from the increased productivity of the new capitalist structure. Fundamental institutional changes – particularly government initiatives – that could contribute to the sharing of the fruits of increased productivity had yet to be devised. The new capitalist order which Smith had so praised did have its natural tendencies – greater aggregate productivity, efficiency, technological change – but the productive system existed

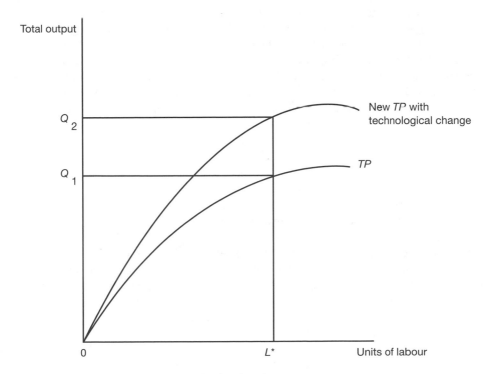

Figure 4.1 A classical aggregate production function.

within a social, human, and institutional context which needed time and evolution to adapt to the new productive structures. There was more to reaping the benefits of the capitalist market system than Smith had envisaged.

Ricardo's theories of diminishing returns and comparative advantage

David Ricardo was an English contemporary of Malthus. Indeed, they were good friends and intense intellectual rivals. While Ricardo accepted elements of Malthus's population theory, he parted ways with him over the dynamics of the capitalist system and, in particular, over the relative significance of landowners and capitalists. Ricardo believed industrialists to be at the dynamic center of the workings of the capitalist economy. With economic and population growth, landowners would receive higher, but economically unjustifiable, incomes. A shift of society's income toward landowners threatened the capacity of the capitalist system to continue to grow since this meant a reduction in profits of the industrial sector. What landowners gained in income with population growth, industrialists lost. Ricardo's views on this problem of growth in capitalist economies, or at least in England in the early nineteenth century, were based on his famous theory of diminishing returns.

The law of eventually diminishing returns

Every economics undergraduate early on encounters Ricardo's law of "eventually" diminishing marginal returns. In Ricardo's (and Malthus's) formulation, when economic growth occurs, land of progressively lower productivity is brought into use, the reasonable assumption being that farmers will make use of the best, most fertile lands first.[5] As marginal land is brought into use, the overall price of food will rise because of the rising marginal cost of producing additional food from less productive land. For those producing on land *more* productive than the marginal lands, the higher price that their output would now command will generate for them a *windfall* gain. This is because the price of the output from more productive land will be the same as that sold from less productive land, but the costs of production will be lower on the farms with more fertile land. This results in what economists call "economic profits" on all land more productive than the most marginal land. Economic profits are not necessary to bring forth the existing level of output. From a social perspective, profits above normal, i.e. economic profits, are unproductive.

In Ricardo's language, these windfall profits to landowners were called "rents." These rents increase as a share of total income as population grows. As a consequence, less and less of society's total income is available for wages and for the profits of capitalists, who will be unable to invest and expand industrial production. As Ricardo wrote, "the interest of the landlord is always opposed to the interest of every other class in the community" (in Rogin 1956: 113).

It is from the law of eventually diminishing returns to agriculture that Ricardo deduced that every economy had a maximum level of income per person that could be produced from an optimum quantity of inputs. Any attempt to further expand production by adding more inputs would set off a decline in per capita income as food prices rose. Eventually, a stationary equilibrium state would be reached where, as was the case in Malthus's analysis too, workers received only subsistence wages.

This state of affairs was not absolutely binding for Ricardo, however. Economic growth in capitalist society thrived on cheap food, since that meant industrial wages could be lower, and lower wages meant higher profits for capitalists. Higher profits for capitalists meant greater possibilities for continued capital accumulation in industry that could result in higher levels of production and higher income levels for the economy as a whole.

Ricardo believed it was the productivity of labor in agriculture, rather than in industry, which was the principal basis for sustaining economic growth. Only then would food, the indispensable and predominant component of the consumption of workers in industry, be produced at a lower cost. Ricardo believed greater productivity on existing land could be achieved over the longer run from technological change. In the short term, however, it was overseas markets, especially the colonies, which could supply food to Europe to counteract rising food prices that the law of eventually diminishing returns implied at home. It is this perspective on how the dilemma of short-run diminishing returns might be escaped that illuminates Ricardo's other contribution to economics, his emphasis on the advantages of *free trade*.

Ricardo favored the lifting of existing restrictions on imports of grains into England from the Continent and elsewhere. Opening the doors to free trade would flood the English market with imported grains, particularly wheat, a basic food item for workers at the time. This increase in supply would contribute to keeping wages lower by keeping the price of food down, though this would come at the expense of landowners at home who would see their economic rents dissipated by the lower prices they would now receive for their grain production as a result of increased competition. However, for Ricardo, this was a desirable outcome, since it meant higher profits and more capital accumulation by industrialists.

For Ricardo, free trade and an *open economy* contributed to offsetting the adverse effects of the law of eventually diminishing returns from agriculture in the short term, thus permitting industrial workers' real wages to continue to rise even with population growth. A subsistence income was not the necessary outcome provided that food prices could be kept sufficiently low. At the time Ricardo was writing that meant bringing down the barriers to imported food to England that the Corn Laws had erected.[6]

For countries today, achieving reasonable food prices and output in sufficient quantities may require the equivalent of an agricultural revolution. This would mean the adaptation of new technologies for farming, the use of new seed strains as with the Green Revolution, better pest control, irrigation, better training of farmers, and a range of other strategies that can increase agricultural productivity and keep food prices, and hence basic wage costs, from increasing so rapidly that industrial production is made less profitable. As in Ricardo's time, food prices may be kept lower through freer trade, but greater production possibilities from the use of new technologies and better training are also essential (these issues are discussed in more detail in Chapter 11).

The theory of comparative advantage

If there is one economic theory that the vast majority of economists accept as universally valid, it would be Ricardo's theory of comparative advantage. This theory argues that unrestricted exchange between countries will increase total world output *if* each country specializes in those goods it can produce at a *relatively* lower cost compared to its potential trading partners. Each country will then trade some of its lower-cost goods for others that can be produced elsewhere more cheaply than at home. With free trade among nations, all countries will find that their *consumption possibilities* have been expanded by such specialization and trade beyond what would have been possible from their domestic production possibilities alone, i.e. from a situation of **autarky**. Because of this compelling argument, economists tend to favor free trade, since it is presumed to be "welfare enhancing" in that the aggregate level of world income is increased.

Using Ricardo's own numerical example can demonstrate the logic behind the comparative advantage argument (see Table 4.1; from Hunt 1979: 105). The first and second columns of the table show the number of hours it takes to produce one unit of cloth or one unit of wine in England and Portugal. Note, first, that Portugal actually is able to produce a unit of both wine and cloth with less labor than does England. Portugal thus has an *absolute advantage* over England in the production of both goods. Economists before Ricardo, including Adam Smith, often thought that a country with lower absolute costs should produce those goods and trade them to other countries for goods others could produce at less absolute cost.

Ricardo, by making use of the concept that we now call **opportunity cost**, showed that it was not absolute costs that really mattered. Ricardo focused on the *internal* trade-off in production of one good for the other, that is, on the *internal opportunity cost of production* within each country for one unit of each good in terms of how much of the other must be sacrificed. Ricardo's approach is based on *comparative* (or *relative*) advantage.

The third and fourth columns show the opportunity costs of producing one unit of each good in terms of the number of units of the other good that can no longer be produced once a certain quantity of hours has been used up. For example, producing one unit of wine in England requires 120 hours of labor. Once that one unit of wine has been produced, those 120 hours are not available for use in the production of cloth.

How much cloth is forgone in England when one unit of wine is produced? The 120 hours expended in the production of wine would have been able to produce 1.20 units of cloth (120 hours to produce one unit of wine/100 hours to produce one unit of cloth). For each unit of wine produced in England, the opportunity cost is 1.20 units of cloth that cannot be produced from the same hours once one unit of wine is produced (this value is shown in column 4).

Likewise, the opportunity cost of producing one unit of cloth in England is 0.833 units of wine that cannot be produced once the hours are allocated to producing cloth (100 hours expended to produce one unit of cloth/120 hours needed to produce one unit of wine; this value is shown in column 3). The same method applies to determining the opportunity costs of wine and cloth in terms of forgone production of the other good in Portugal.

Ricardo recognized that what was important in determining what each country should produce for trade was the *relative cost* of producing each good within individual countries, not the absolute cost. Looking again at Table 4.1, it is clear that it is *relatively cheaper* to produce a unit of cloth in England, where the opportunity cost is 0.833 units of forgone wine, than it is to produce cloth in Portugal, where the opportunity cost is 1.125 units of wine forgone per unit of cloth produced. England sacrifices less wine to produce a unit of cloth than is the case in Portugal. England is the lower cost producer of cloth.

Table 4.1 Number of hours required to produce one unit of cloth and wine in England and Portugal

	Cloth	*Wine*	*Opportunity cost of: 1 unit of cloth produced in terms of wine forgone*	*Opportunity cost of: 1 unit of wine produced in terms of cloth forgone*
	(1)	*(2)*	*(3)*	*(4)*
England	100	120	0.833 wine	1.200 cloth
Portugal	90	80	1.125 wine	0.888 cloth

Just the opposite is true for wine production. Portugal produces wine at relatively less cost (0.888 units of cloth forgone for each unit of wine produced) than does England (1.2 units of cloth forgone for one unit of wine produced).

What Ricardo's theory of comparative advantage says is that if England specializes in the production of cloth, the good for which it has comparative advantage, and Portugal specializes in wine production, the good in which it has comparative advantage, then world output can be increased above what it was when each country did not specialize. If the two countries now trade with one another for the good they do not produce, both countries can be better off. How is that possible?

When countries specialize and then trade with one another, each country will be able to *consume outside its own production possibilities frontier*. The benefits of specialization do not require that each country completely forgo producing the good with the higher opportunity cost to gain from trade. It is only necessary to shift resources *toward* the good(s) that can be produced at relatively lower opportunity cost, that is, toward those goods with comparative advantage relative to potential trading partners. Let's see how these gains from specialization and trade can materialize.

Both countries will gain from specialization and trade in the example in Table 4.1 provided the international trade price between England and Portugal for 1 unit of cloth is between 0.833 and 1.125 units of wine or, to say the same thing, if the price of 1 unit of wine is between 0.888 and 1.20 units of cloth given up. The trade price between the countries needs to be somewhere between the **internal opportunity cost** trade-offs for the individual countries shown in the last two columns of Table 4.1. To see the benefits of specialization and trade more concretely, consider the following example.

If the trade price at which the two goods are traded is, for example, 1 cloth for 1 wine, then England would be able to produce 1 unit of cloth – the good in which it specializes – and trade it to Portugal for 1 unit of wine in exchange. How is that better for England? If England had instead produced that 1 unit of wine itself, it would have been necessary to have sacrificed the production of 1.2 units of cloth, since the production of one unit of wine in England requires 1.2 times as much labor as one unit of cloth. Clearly England benefits by being able to trade 1 unit of cloth and get 1 unit of wine from Portugal rather than having to "pay" 1.2 units of cloth to produce 1 unit of wine itself.

Portugal also benefits from the exchange at this trade price. In return for the 1 unit of wine traded to England, Portugal obtains 1 unit of cloth. If Portugal produces cloth itself, it would be necessary to give up 1.125 units of wine to release a sufficient number of workers (= 90 hours of labor) to produce that 1 unit of cloth (column 3 of Table 4.1). Portugal also benefits from the specialization and trade.

Ricardo's analysis of comparative advantage strongly suggests that specialization in production and free trade, that is, trade between countries with a minimum of tariff and non-tariff barriers, is the best policy for countries to follow.[7] Specialization and free trade increase world production and the consumption possibilities for each country by increasing the degree of internal efficiency in production in individual countries so that there is more available for all to consume, as shown in Figure 4.2.

The curve labeled PPF in Figure 4.2 is Portugal's *production possibilities frontier*.[8] When there is no trade between England and Portugal, the PPF is also equal to Portugal's consumption possibilities frontier since what is available for consumption depends exclusively upon domestic production. What Portugal produces is all that Portugal has available to consume in a world with no trade. So, for example, with no specialization and trade, i.e. in a situation of autarky, Portugal might choose to produce at point A on its PPF. At A, there are 1,666.67

units of cloth and 1,875 units of wine produced, and the same quantity of these two goods would be what was available for Portugal to consume without specialization and trade.

However, when Portugal specializes in the production of wine for which it has the comparative advantage and then trades wine with England for cloth at a mutually beneficial trade price, such as 1 cloth for 1 wine, Portugal will be able to consume more of both goods if it chooses to do so. For example, if Portugal completely specializes, it will produce 3,750 units of wine and no cloth. At a trade price of 1 cloth:1 wine, Portugal's **consumption** possibilities frontier lies *outside* its **production** possibilities frontier, as shown in Figure 4.2. (The 3,750 value on the wine axis is total production with specialization; the 3,750 value on the cloth axis would be the maximum quantity of cloth that could be consumed assuming all the 3,750 production of wine was traded at a 1c:1w price; of course any intermediate combination of both goods on the consumption possibilities frontier could be consumed.)

With specialization and then trade, Portugal actually can consume more of *both* goods compared to what was possible *without* specialization and trade. As shown in Figure 4.2, anywhere on the line segment *BC*, Portugal can actually consume both more wine *and* more cloth *with* specialization and trade. (Can you see how the values at points *B* and *C* were determined? Use the trade price of 1 wine for 1 cloth, which is nothing but the slope of the line, and the values at point *A* to calculate.) Of course, the same is true for England. Both

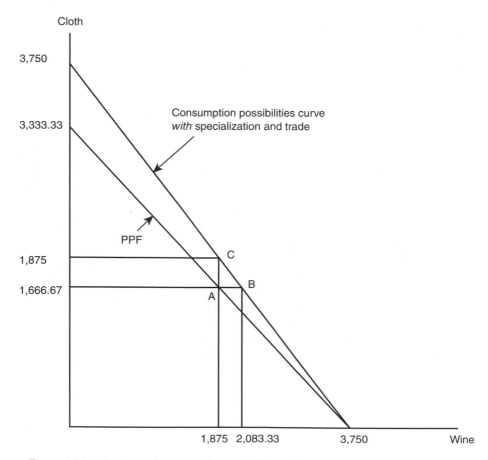

Figure 4.2 Production and consumption possibilities with and without trade.

more wine and more cloth can be consumed with specialization and trade (you will be asked to show this in a problem as the end of the chapter!).

This is a truly remarkable result, one that gives at least one of your authors goose bumps each time he teaches comparative advantage (if you got goose bumps, too, maybe you should be an economist!). There is no magic here, however. Specialization allows each country to provide to the world market those goods and services that it can produce most efficiently. It is this shift toward greater efficiency in the use of inputs that increases total world output. Then, via mutually beneficial trade, every country can be better-off than if each had simply produced and consumed goods in isolation. It is little wonder, then, that Ricardo's theory of comparative advantage has had such a profound effect on economic policy and in providing an argument for more open trade among nations.

A brief evaluation of Ricardo's theory of comparative advantage

There have been many criticisms of Ricardo's analysis of comparative advantage and the free trade conclusion to which it leads. It is important to remember some of the restrictions Ricardo applied to his theory. It was assumed that the factors of production – natural resources and land, labor and capital – were immobile and that both (all) countries had the capacity to produce both (or all) goods. Any imports are perfectly balanced by an equivalently valued export flow; thus no country incurs a trade deficit which must be financed.

Further, Ricardo assumed that perfect competition prevailed and that all resources in each country were fully employed. In fact, with less-than-fully employed resources, tariff or other protection to block imports and to increase domestic employment could well be the preferred policy to free trade, since the key allocative issue would be an internal mobilization of domestic resources to their full use rather than a reallocation of fully employed resources among alternative uses.[9]

While these are important considerations to do with the validity of assumptions, there are other concerns about a blanket endorsement of the comparative advantage argument and free trade recommendations that go beyond assumption bashing. The late British economist Joan Robinson's comment on the effect of following Ricardo's free trade advice and specialization, at least as far as Portugal was concerned, remains provocative:

> the imposition of free trade on Portugal killed off a promising textile industry and left her with a slow-growing export market for wine, while for England, exports of cotton cloth led to accumulation, mechanisation and the whole spiralling growth of the industrial revolution.
>
> (Robinson 1978: 103)

Portugal's experience highlights a potentially valuable historical lesson on the consequences of simply following *current* comparative advantage, a conclusion supported by our discussion of path dependence and the effects of colonialization in Chapter 3. It is not just specialization that is important for a country, even if one grants all of Ricardo's restrictive assumptions. Specialization and free trade may not always result in more rapid progress over time. Why?

Portugal specialized in a commodity that did not have the same growth potential as did cloth for England. Portugal's economy suffered consequently, as the productive structure and institutions were molded in the direction of wine production. In fact, after trade was rapidly expanded following the Methuen Treaty in 1703, Portugal was left with a sizeable bilateral trade deficit as its exports to Britain fell short of its imports from Britain. The boom in Portuguese–British trade fortuitously coincided with a gold rush in Brazil, Portugal's colony, enabling the Portuguese to cover their deficit for a time with a colonial gold flow, but the benefits of specialization and trade over the longer term were illusive.[10]

It may not be specialization *per se* that is so important for a country's future growth prospects as is the *choice of what to specialize in*. Some commodities are more likely to have expanding world demand over the future, as with England's cloth production. Other commodities may be more likely to benefit from the application of science and technology that reduce their production costs over time, further contributing to economic expansion. Thus the critical issue for an economy becomes what goods and services *should be* produced over the future, and this requires a vision about the possibility of *finding new comparative advantage* in goods and services that provide more promise for the future than the current mix of production. It is this more dynamic way of understanding the theory of comparative advantage and the nature of the path dependence associated with any decision to produce particular goods which would seem to account for much of the success of the East Asian economies in recent years, as will be discussed in later chapters.

Such a forward-looking comparative advantage perspective certainly presents the policy-maker with more problems – projecting demand, prices, technology, and other variables into an uncertain future – but also with more possibilities. Finding the right goods for specialization can contribute to a dynamically evolving economic system with a greater opportunity for contributing to sustained development, for overcoming the negative effects of past path dependence, including declining terms of trade, and for shifting production toward higher and more efficacious paths of development over the future.

As will be discussed in Chapters 5, 9 and 10, Ricardo's theory of *static* comparative advantage is no substitute for a more future-oriented analysis of *dynamic or created comparative advantage*. The latter is a view of comparative advantage that looks to the future possibilities associated with the production of particular goods (*dynamic* comparative advantage) rather than to a consideration of what it is best to specialize in among the goods currently produced (*static* comparative advantage). Nonetheless, among many economists, Ricardo's theory of static comparative advantage retains a particularly strong intellectual hold, one that often uncritically informs policy recommendations. We do not feel that the success of most late-developing economies is consistent, however, with the static version of comparative advantage theory, but rather with a more dynamic understanding of that theory as suggested here, based on a more robust understanding of Ricardo's theory.

A classical model of economic growth

Let us now consider a classical-type model of economic growth which builds upon Smith and Malthus but depends especially on Ricardo's formulation.[11]

The aggregate production function for an economy, which shows how inputs are turned into outputs, has land (N), labor (L), capital (K) and technology (T) as the inputs to production.

$$Y = f(N, L, K, T) \tag{4.1}$$

This production function is subject to the following restrictions: $f_N, f_L, f_K, f_T > 0$ and $f_{NN}, f_{LL}, f_{KK}, f_{TT} < 0$, which simply states that the marginal product (f_i) of each input, i, is positive, but each also is subject to the law of diminishing returns ($f_{ii} < 0$). In other words, as additional units of each input, *i*, are added to production, all others held constant, output rises but it rises at a decreasing rate.[12]

The rate of economic growth over time (= d*Y*/d*t)* depends, then, on the productivity and the rate of expansion over time of the four inputs in the production function in equation 4.2.

$$dY/dt = f_N dN/dt + f_L \, dL/dt + f_K \, dK/dt + f_T \, dT/dt \tag{4.2}$$

It seems reasonable to take d*N*/d*t* = 0, since the available quantity of land, or more generally, natural resources, can be taken as given. The growth in the labor force, d*L*/d*t*, can be presumed in the short term to be proportional to the rate of capital accumulation, d*K*/d*t*, since adding more physical capital requires more workers to operate these new machines and tools of production. Thus we can write d*L*/d*t* = *q*d*K*/d*t* (*q* > 0), where *q* is the number of workers required for each new unit of physical capital, *K*. If we also assume for simplicity that technology is given, or exogenous, in the short term, then $f_T = 0$.

Given the above conditions, equation 4.2 can be re-written as follows:

$$dY/dt = (qf_L + f_K) \, dK/dt \tag{4.3}$$

The rate of economic growth in the classical model thus depends essentially on the rate of physical capital accumulation, *K*. The more rapid the pace of capital accumulation, *K*, the faster the rate of economic growth. The rate of physical capital accumulation is determined by the rate of profit earned by capitalist investors. For Ricardo, the ultimate limit on the rate of capital accumulation, and hence on the rate of economic growth, was the binding nature of the law of diminishing returns. This can be seen from equation 4.3, since f_L, the marginal product of labor, decreases as *L* rises until eventually the point is reached when per capita income reaches a steady-state level (population growth performs the same function in Malthus's formulation of economic growth).

The important point to remember is that for the classical economists *physical capital accumulation* is the determining factor in affecting the pace of economic progress. We shall see below in considering the neoclassical economists that physical capital remains at the center of their analysis of the causes of economic growth.

Marx's analysis of capitalist development: a brief digression

Unlike Smith, Malthus, and Ricardo, and most other classical economists, Karl Marx did not assume capitalism to be immutable or to be the natural order of society. Marx believed capitalism to be but one stage of a society's historical development, which began with primitive communism and then evolved toward slavery, feudalism, and eventually to capitalism, though this historical progression did not take place in all countries simultaneously nor at the same speed.

Marx believed capitalism ultimately would break down and from it would be created a socialist economic system and, in due course, communism. Our interest here is not in Marx's historical-materialist philosophy, however, but rather in his analysis of the dynamics of capitalism, as traditional, feudal society was transformed and ultimately left behind. Chapter 3 touched upon some of Marx's ideas pertaining to the colonial regions, drawn largely from his observations of the effects of British policy in India. In this section, we shall explore in more detail Marx's analysis of the dynamics of the capitalist economy that most other classical economists, John Stuart Mill excepted, took for granted as the ultimate stage of human development.

Marx's great economic work was *Capital*, only the first volume of which was published during his lifetime. Marx died in 1883, and the other two volumes of *Capital* were edited and published in 1885 and 1894 by Marx's close friend, collaborator, and benefactor, Frederick Engels, from notebooks Marx left. A further volume, *The Grundrisse*, which some have called the fourth volume of *Capital*, was not published in English until the 1970s. Marx's analysis of the broad dynamics of capitalism differs only slightly from the other classical economists in many respects. For example, in his study of the relentless drive toward capital accumulation that motivates capitalists and the resulting division of labor there is little to distinguish Marx from Smith. It was in the *implications* of this process that Marx parted ways with the classicals.

Marx greatly admired the vast productive power of capitalism, a system that had succeeded, he noted, in creating more wealth in a hundred years than all other modes of production in previous human history (see Focus 4.2). What appalled Marx was the human cost involved in producing such wealth and the extremely one-sided distribution that resulted from its production. Marx believed, and his analysis of the creation of surplus value attempted to demonstrate this, that it was only the working class, which he called the "proletariat," that created wealth through their labor power. Capitalists appropriated a disproportionate share of society's total income solely by their "virtue" of being the owners of the means of production, particularly the physical capital in factories and businesses, required for producing society's commodities.

Marx argued that the uneven distribution of the ownership of society's means of production was the result of a historic process in which former peasants lost access to land for their own production and were forced into cities to become workers because of the Enclosure Movement in England and similar processes at work around the globe. He thus argued that the ultimate distribution of income in capitalist society was unfair and a reflection of historical power relationships, not productivity. He believed that, over time, workers, as they came to grasp the nature of their exploitation by capitalists would seize political and economic power from the minority class of owners. Marx, however, did not think this transition toward

FOCUS 4.2   MARX ON CAPITALISM

Marx and Engels wrote in the *Communist Manifesto*:

> The bourgeoisie, during its rule of scarce one hundred years, has created more massive and more colossal productive forces than have all preceding generations together. Subjection of Nature's forces to man, machinery, application of chemistry to industry and agriculture, steam-navigation, railways, electric telegraphs, clearing of whole continents for cultivation, canalisation of rivers, whole populations conjured out of the ground – what earlier century had even a presentiment that such productive forces slumbered in the lap of social labour?

The "bourgeoisie" was the capitalist class, which dominated the capitalist market system. Are you surprised Marx could heap such praise on a system he thought was immoral? Don't be. He admired the productive powers of the capitalist economy made possible by its accumulation of physical capital and the continual introduction of new technologies. What Marx objected to was the distribution of the gains of production, given that it was workers (the proletariat) who produced the wealth of society while the bourgeoisie (the capitalists) appropriated these gains not because of their productive contribution but by virtue of their ownership of the productive facilities.

socialism would be initiated until capitalism had reached a sufficiently high degree of development in its use of capital and technology. For Marx, a relatively high level of income per capita within a capitalist economic environment was a precondition for the future socialist and communist economic systems he believed would follow.

Like the other classical economists, Marx's perspective on the dynamics of capitalist economies rested on physical capital accumulation which spurred greater productivity, all in the relentless pursuit of more profit. This accumulation, however, created greater wealth and income, albeit unequally shared, which is the outcome that caused Marx such despair and concern.

Neoclassical growth models

Interest among economists in examining the sources of economic growth and in understanding the trajectory of capitalist society disappeared from view for a time with the neoclassical, marginalist revolution in economic thinking after the 1870s, perhaps in reaction to the revolutionary implication of Marx's version of classical theory which predicted an overthrow of the capitalist order by disenfranchised workers. Neoclassical economic analysis was resolutely micro-oriented with a focus on the utility-maximizing behavior of individuals and the profit-maximizing actions of perfectly competitive firms. The macroeconomic perspective inherent in a concern for economic growth and in the distribution of income among classes that had motivated the classical economists gave way to a narrower interest in the conditions required for equilibrium prices and quantities in individual markets.

A Solow-type neoclassical growth model

One of the most influential neoclassical growth models, and one that has shaped much modern thinking about the process of economic growth, has been that of Nobel Prize-winning American economist Robert Solow (1956). A Solow-type model can be depicted by a simple, aggregate production function like that shown in equation 4.4.

$$Y(t) = A(t)K(t)^{a}L(t)^{1-a}, \tag{4.4}$$

where $0 < a < 1$. Just as in the classical models, with which it shares strong similarities, the Solow-type growth model exhibits diminishing returns to both K and L in the short run, while there are constant returns to scale from changing all inputs by the same percentage over the longer term.[13]

$A(t)$ is *exogenous* technological progress which affects the production function's position but not its general shape. Exogenous technological change is assumed to be available to all economies and with the same effects, regardless of the current level of development of any specific country. Figure 4.3 shows a short-run neoclassical aggregate production function and the impact of exogenous technological change.

Just as in the classical production function shown in Figure 4.1, a change in $A(t)$ leads to an upward shift of the production function, $Y(t)$, such that more output can be produced with the same inputs. It is this *exogenous* technology which is basic to higher levels of income per capita over time. As Figure 4.3 shows, without technological change, the increased use of inputs in production, via more investment, K, has a limit in terms of total income that can be produced and hence (assuming L constant) in terms of per capita income, as shown by

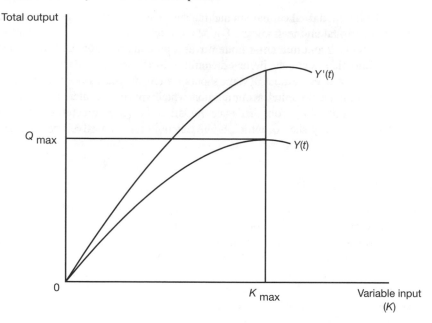

Figure 4.3 A Solow-type production function.

K_{max}, Q_{max}. This is nothing more than the familiar effect of decreasing marginal returns in the short term.

If technology and the rate of increase of L, the labor force, are constant and assuming the labor force is always fully employed, a Solow-type growth function predicts that, for any given rate of savings and investment, there is a constant, steady-state level of real per capita income that can be attained.[14] This result follows directly from the assumption of diminishing returns to K in the short term. Given a constant rate of saving (= investment, by definition), the return to capital for investors falls as the stock of capital rises[15] until, ultimately, the total amount of capital also reaches a steady-state level, and all new investment is just sufficient to replace old capital that has worn out. When that happens, the level of per capita income of a country will have reached its maximum level, given the rate of savings, its population growth rate, and assuming zero technical change, which is exogenous anyway.

An even more interesting and perhaps astounding implication of the Solow-type neoclassical model for economic development is that poorer nations would actually be expected to grow *faster* than richer nations, assuming equal rates of saving and investment and growth rates of population. In other words, the Solow model predicts the *convergence* of per capita income amongst different nations sharing similar "fundamentals." Two countries with the same rate of saving and the same population growth rate will tend to have, ultimately, the same level of real per capita income.[16] Hence if one starts at a lower non-equilibrium level of income, that economy will grow faster until it reaches the steady-state equilibrium income level associated with the rate of savings and population growth.

However, according to the Solow formulation, and somewhat controversially, as we shall see in Chapter 8, it is *not* possible for a nation to increase its **rate** of economic growth by dedicating more of its income to installing more physical capital goods. Why is that? Very simply, the law of diminishing returns means that more rapid accumulation of physical capital will simply result in the country reaching its target level of per capita income more quickly. At this point, the maximum steady-state (constant) level of income per person would have been reached and growth stops.

Higher levels of saving and investing do contribute to a higher level of real per capita income. Thus nations that save and invest 25 percent of their output will have a higher steady-state level of per capita income than those which save and invest 15 percent of their income (assuming the same rate of population growth). But a higher level of saving and investment that adds physical capital machinery *faster* to the production process does **not** lead to a higher **rate** of growth of income that can persist over time. Regardless of the rate of saving and investment, there is a ceiling on the level of per capita income for that level of S and I. As an economy approaches that level of income, the rate of growth of per capita income decreases because of diminishing returns, eventually reaching zero as the steady-state income level is attained and the optimum level of physical capital is reached.

Without belaboring the mathematics behind this conclusion, the level of per capita income of a country according to the Solow model will be:[17]

$$y = Y/L = (s/n)^{a/(1-a)} \tag{4.5}$$

where s is the percent of total income saved, n is the exogenous rate of growth of population and a and $1-a$ are the income shares of capital and labor in total income (Solow 1956: 76–7).[18]

This formulation shows how differences in income per person across countries are explained as the consequence of different rates of saving (which determine the level of physical capital accumulation) and population growth rates, assuming equal shares of income accruing to capital and labor across countries as expressed in the value for a and $1-a$. This formulation makes clear that a higher rate of saving, s, will raise the steady-state level of per capita income, all else being the same, since that will increase the level of physical capital in the economy.

Countries that are poor and not growing are thus poor, according to the Solow formulation, because they are not saving and investing a sufficiently high proportion of their income. Countries that wish to increase their average standard of living can do so by increasing the rate at which national income is saved and invested, that is, by accumulating physical capital at a higher rate.

This recommendation to accumulate physical capital so as to reach higher levels of income per person has been a fundamental policy insight common to virtually all the strategies recommended by economists for developed and less-developed nations alike.[19] It is important to keep in mind the basic insights of Solow's growth model. It continues to be a central starting point for many economists in theorizing about the underlying forces at work which influence the process of economic growth in real-world economies. It is a theory which has had profound policy implications, with, again, a focus on how to speed up physical capital accumulation being in the forefront of what is essential.

The Harrod-Domar model: a Keynesian approach

The Solow-type, neoclassical growth model was formulated not to try to explain income levels and differences in the standard of living among real-world economies, though such empirical work has been done and that has been the real importance of Solow's contribution to economic growth theory and to development economics in particular (Mankiw *et al.*

1992). Solow actually developed his theory in response to the troubling implications about economic stability suggested by the Harrod-Domar model. Sir Roy Harrod of the University of Oxford in the UK and Evsey Domar of the Massachusetts Institute of Technology in the US simultaneously developed in the late 1930s broadly similar explanations for the aggregate economic growth process.

The Harrod-Domar model makes the following assumptions about how economic growth occurs:

1   The labor force, L, grows at a constant rate $n = \Delta L/L$.
2   Net saving, S, and investment, $I = \Delta K$, are fixed proportions of total output, Q, such that $S = I = sQ$, where $0 < s < 1$. The usual Keynesian income multiplier relation is operative, where $1/s$ is the value of the income multiplier. $S = I$, *ex post*, as is typically assumed in growth models.[20]
3   The two inputs to production, K and L, are used in fixed proportions. There is no substitution of K and L in the production process.[21] To produce any level of output, Q, there is a minimum level of each of the inputs required, as given by the following: $L = bQ$ and $K = vQ$, where $0 < b$, $v < 1$, and b and v are the labor–output and the capital–output ratios, respectively.

Harrod and Domar introduced the concept of the *warranted rate of growth*, g_w, which is the rate of growth of output consistent with equilibrium in both the input and output markets. This growth rate of total output turns out to be equal to the ratio, s/v, which is the fixed savings rate, s, divided by the constant capital–output ratio, v. If output, Q, also grows over time at the same rate, s/v, the economy will be in steady-state equilibrium, such that Q, K, and K/L all grow at the same rate. What the growth rate of total output, s/v, shows is that an increase in the savings rate (which allows a higher level of investment and capital goods creation) will increase the growth rate of the economy, *ceteris paribus*. This is the now familiar result of virtually all the classical and neoclassical writings on economic growth: it is an expansion of total physical capital goods as a share of total output, i.e. higher levels of investment, that creates higher income levels. This is accomplished via a higher rate of savings, s, out of total income.

What was startling in the Harrod-Domar model, however, was that this equilibrium growth rate was found to be quite unstable. If output, Q, for some reason grows at a rate faster than s/v, then the growth rate of Q in the next period will be even larger, as investors react by investing and producing even more output. If the rate of growth of output is less than the warranted rate, s/v, the economy slows down even more in subsequent periods, as investors invest and produce even less. [22]

What the Harrod-Domar model suggested was that there was a *knife-edge* equilibrium. If an economy was not growing at *precisely* the rate required by current rate of saving, s, and given the current capital–output ratio, v, then the economy would veer further and further away from equilibrium, either growing too quickly, and eventually igniting inflationary pressures, or growing too slowly, leading to unused capacity and rising unemployment as the economy spiralled away from equilibrium.[23]

It was but a small step from this startling deduction of the Harrod-Domar model – that equilibrium would be but a fluke – to the implication that government action, especially to alter the fixed rate of saving, s, could be the means, perhaps the only recourse, for averting economic crisis. Otherwise, without the precisely right savings rate, s, the Harrod-Domar analysis predicted the alternative abysses of either self-perpetuating inflation or spiralling unemployment. This, of course, is a view squarely in the spirit of the Keynesian macroeconomics revolution of the time they were writing. Keynesian economics rejected the *laissez-faire*, full-employment assumption of classical theory and argued that central government intervention was necessary to approach full-employment equilibrium. Unlike the classical economists, Keynesians did not believe that full employment was the automatic outcome of advanced capitalist economies. Without government oversight, inflation or unemployment were as likely to result, perhaps more likely to result, than a fully employed economy.

While it would be perhaps an overstatement to insist that the Harrod-Domar instability problem suggested the importance of state planning of development in the less-developed world, it certainly is the case that the identification of key variables – the rate of saving, the level of physical capital accumulation, and the capital–output ratio – that are amenable to public policy decisions eased the way for strategies to manipulate behavior and influence decisions to affect the pace of economic development by planners and economists, theories which are considered in Chapters 5 and 6.

The neoclassical response to Harrod-Domar instability

Solow's contribution to the economic growth literature was one among many in response to the unstable disequilibrium behavior of the Harrod-Domar model (see Focus 2.3).[24] Solow showed, however, that the Harrod-Domar result was the particular consequence of assuming that production required *fixed* ratios of the inputs to production ($L = bQ$ and $K = v$) (see Solow 1956).

Solow made what is now the standard neoclassical assumption that the capital and labor inputs are infinitely substitutable in production, though such substitution was subject to the law of eventually diminishing returns. Rather than assuming that production isoquants for firms and for society formed right angles, implying no substitution of inputs as in the Harrod-Domar model, Solow assumed production isoquants to be smoothly convex to the origin as they typically are drawn in most economic theory texts. As a result, instead of running into the dilemma of requiring $g_w = s/v$ for all variables if steady-state equilibrium was to be attained, an outcome that could only be fortuitous without some sort of manipulation of the variables by government, Solow's equilibrium, as shown in equation 4.5 earlier, did away with the problem of the knife- or razor-edge problem. For any rate of saving, s, there is a steady-state equilibrium level of income per person, and the unbridled instability of the Harrod-Domar model disappeared.

Still, Solow's model leaves the door open for public policy to impact the rate of growth and the level of per capita income, if not the long-run rate of growth, via the saving rate, s, and the rate of population growth, n. Policy that can increase the rate of savings, by increasing the proportion of total output that is invested in physical capital, can increase income per person. So can policies that reduce the population growth rate. In subsequent chapters we will consider just how public policies might be shaped to impact the level of income in real-world economies.

Summary and conclusions

In this chapter, we have considered the views on economic development of some key classical and neoclassical economists whose theories and writings provide the foundations of much economic thinking. Adam Smith, Thomas Malthus, David Ricardo, Karl Marx, and Robert Solow are pioneers in economics whose work has informed all who have followed. What they wrote and thought, in some cases over a hundred years ago, still resonates and affects analysis and policy down to the present.

FOCUS 4.3   ROBERT SOLOW

Robert Solow (US, b. 1924) won the Nobel Memorial Prize in Economics in 1987 for his body of work, but especially for his contributions to economic growth theory. His influence, and sharp sense of humor, shaped a generation or more of graduate students at the Massachusetts Institute of Technology (MIT), where he began teaching in 1949, as well as researchers around the world who have been influenced and challenged by his contributions and insights. He also has served in the public sector, including on President John F. Kennedy's Council of Economic Advisors.

In his Nobel lecture in Stockholm on December 8, 1987, Solow spoke of how the implications of the Harrod-Domar model had both disturbed and stimulated his thinking:

> the possibility of steady growth would be a miraculous stroke of luck [in the Harrod-Domar model]. Most economies, most of the time, would have no equilibrium growth path. The history of capitalist economies should be an alternation of long periods of worsening unemployment and long periods of worsening labor shortage. ... An expedition from Mars arriving on Earth having read this literature would have expected to find only the wreckage of a capitalism that had shaken itself to pieces long ago. Economic history was indeed a record of fluctuations as well as of growth, but most business cycles seemed to be self-limiting. Sustained, though disturbed, growth was not a rarity.

How did Solow overcome the surprising, but not very realistic, instability of the Harrod-Domar theory? By positing a relatively smooth production function for turning inputs into outputs, i.e. smooth isoquants with varying capital–output ratios were possible, not the right-angled isoquants of production implied by the Harrod-Domar model:

> allowing for a reasonable degree of technological flexibility accomplished two things. In the first place, the mere existence of a feasible path of steady growth turned out not to be a singular event. A range of steady states is possible, and the range may even be quite wide if the range of aggregative factor-intensities is wide. There are other ways in which an economy can adapt to the Harrod-Domar condition, but it still seems to me that variation in capital-intensity is probably the most important.

Since Solow, growth models have tended to be in this spirit, allowing a substantial degree of substitutability between the inputs. As we shall see in considering some of the "new" growth theories in Chapter 8, the growth models developed by economists continue to generate controversy and to inform thinking and policy.

Source: http://nobelprize.org/nobel
prizes/economics/laureates/1987/solow-lecture.html

If we had to single out one commonality of these theories, it is the centrality of physical capital accumulation financed by saving out of an economy's total income. Machines, tools, buildings, and all the other produced inputs to production that make up what economists call "capital" are a common theme "explaining" long-term growth. We shall see in subsequent chapters that as important as physical capital is, there is more to spurring economic growth and becoming developed than this.

Questions and exercises

1   For Adam Smith, the capitalist market system can yield considerable benefits to both consumers and producers *if* two basic assumptions about the economic system are satisfied.

   a   Explain these two conditions and why both are required if a "harmony of interests" among producers and consumers is to prevail.

   b   Is it reasonable to presume that both of these conditions exist in most of the less-developed nations?

   c   If one or both of the stipulations upon which Smith's conclusion of a harmony of interests among consumers and producers in capitalist society is absent, what might be the effects on society and different groups of the unregulated operation of the market system? Who would be likely to gain? To lose?

2   Why are savings so important for economic growth? If there are no savings, what would that mean for an economy? See if you can use the macroeconomics definition for a very simple economy where $Y = C + I$ to explain the significance of total savings to economic growth (and also explain, then, the significance of the savings rate, s, which is simply equal to the ratio S/Y, that is to the percent of an economy's total GDP that is saved). *Definitions*: Y is total GDP; C is total consumption; I is gross investment; S is total savings.

3   Show the importance of savings to economic growth using a production possibilities frontier (PPF) where the two goods available are consumption goods and physical capital goods. Remember that any particular PPF represents a specific value of GDP at one point in time, with PPFs further out measuring higher levels of total GDP. Show how the choice of the mix of consumption and physical capital goods chosen by an economy at any one point in time affects the level of GDP over the future. What would happen to the PPF and total GDP in the future if all GDP produced now is consumed and none goes to physical capital goods?

4   This problem is designed to give you practice in understanding the profound implications of Ricardo's law of diminishing returns and its meaning for economic growth. Pangea can produce the levels of output shown in the table near the end of the problem by varying its labor force (the variable input) working with the following fixed inputs. The fixed inputs are the currently available 36 square miles of arable land and Pangea's existing 14 factories with the machinery and technology they have installed. The actual level of production in the country depends upon how much of the variable input labor is combined with these fixed inputs.

   a   Use the data in the table to draw a graph of Pangea's production function. If you can use Excel, input the data beginning in cell A1. Then, highlight it and choose a scatter diagram with lines (measure employment on the horizontal axis, total output on the vertical). Your graph should look like that in Figure 4.1. It clearly illustrates Ricardo's law of eventually diminishing returns. Of course, you can draw this using graphing paper.

   b   Show on a *separate* graph exactly at what level of employment *diminishing returns* to production begin by drawing a marginal output graph (put employment on the horizontal axis and marginal output on the vertical). You will have to calculate these values in the *marginal output* column. Remember: marginal output is the additional output produced by adding one more unit of the variable input. In this, example, marginal output = Δ total output/Δ labor input; you should be able to write a formula for this in Excel to calculate these values or do them by hand.

c   What are the implications of the law of eventually diminishing returns *for the maximum level of output*? What is this maximum?

d   Can total output ever be increased beyond 155? How? Show this in the graph you drew in part a.

Employment	Total output	Marginal output
0	0	
4	19	
7	42	
9	62	
13	93	
16	111	
18	120	
22	132	
29	149	
36	155	
41	155	
43	149	

5   Copy the table you inputted above for problem 4a, and paste it into a new page in Excel. Or begin anew if you are doing manual calculations.

a   You now are going to invent *new numbers* to replace those shown in the *total output* column above. Continue to use the *same total employment* levels shown! What numbers should you choose? The values you invent *must* be such that Pangea *never, ever encounters* diminishing returns to production, i.e. the value of marginal output never decreases in the last column of your new table. Be sure to calculate and show the marginal output column too, just to be sure you do not encounter diminishing marginal returns.

b   Draw the production function graph for your new example using the chart function in Excel. Again, highlight the data and choose a scatter diagram with a line.

c   What are the implications for total output if there are never diminishing returns to adding more workers to production? What is happening to total output in your example as you add more workers to the production process? Is there a maximum level of production?

d   Does it seem likely that an economy could never encounter diminishing returns to production? Why? If there are no diminishing returns, how much land would it take to produce the world's supply of food?

6   The following example gives you practice in determining which country has the comparative advantage in the production of two goods, jewelry and fish.

	Jewelry	Fish
New Zealand	500	180
India	400	220

These numbers represent the *hours* it takes to catch 1 unit of fish (in tons) and to make 1 unit of jewelry (measured in utes).

a   Which country, if any, has the comparative advantage in producing which good? (Hint: you must find the internal opportunity cost of producing each good in each country and then find which country produces which good most cheaply.)

b   What "price," or better what range of prices, would be advantageous to both countries such that they would be willing to trade? This price will be in physical units

7   Refer back to Ricardo's original example of comparative advantage in Table 4.1 to answer this question. Let's assume England has 500,000 total labor hours available per day for production to produce cloth and wine and that Portugal has 400,000 labor hours available per day to produce the two goods.

a   Assume, first, that England and Portugal *do not* trade with each other and that currently England devotes one-half its available labor to the production of each good, while Portugal uses 40 percent of its labor force to produce clothing and the remainder for wine production. How much output of each good will each country be able to produce? What is the total "world" output of both commodities without trade? Input these values into the following table. This is a situation of **autarky**, that is , with no trade where what each country consumes is determined exclusively by what it produces.

	Cloth	Wine
England		
Portugal		
Total world output		

   A. Production without specialization or trade

b   Now assume that England and Portugal both *completely specialize* in the commodity in which each has comparative advantage. How much output of each good will be produced by each country? What is the total "world" output of both commodities with specialization but *prior* to trade? Show the values of production of both goods for each country with complete specialization in the following table.

	Cloth	Wine
England		
Portugal		
Total world output		

   B. Production with specialization but prior to trade

c   Is it possible for both countries to benefit from trade, such that each has *at least* as much of one commodity and more of the other available for consumption after specialization and trade than was available prior to specialization and trade? How? Can you show this result in the following table? Remember, to show this you must choose a mutually acceptable trade price, as was done for the example used to derive Figure 4.2.

	Cloth	*Wine*
England		
Portugal		
Total world output = consumption		

C. Consumption after specialization and trade at the trade price of _____

8   The Solow equilibrium income equation 4.5 in the text says that $y = Y/L = (s/n)^{a/1-a}$, that is, that income per person, y, which is simply total GDP (Y) divided by the population (L), is determined by the ratio of the savings rate, s, (which is the percent of GDP = Y saved) divided by the population growth rate, n, raised to the power, a/1−a, where a is the share of total income, Y, received (and produced) by owners of physical capital and 1−a is the share of total income received by labor.

    a   What is equilibrium GDP per person, y, if a country has $s = 0.3$ (i.e. 30 percent), $n = 0.022$ (i.e. 2.2 percent) and $a = 0.33$ (i.e. 33 percent)? (Assume y is calculated in $1,000 of US dollars.)

    b   Now, what will equilibrium income per person, y, be, in $1,000 of US dollars, if population growth is now 0.8 percent, all the other variables the same?

    c   What is equilibrium y if the savings rate is 14.5 percent, labor's share of income is 60 percent and population growth is 1.4 percent?

9   Assume two economies have exactly the same values of population growth, n, and labor's share of income, a, but that the savings rate in one economy is 22.2 percent and in the other is 18 percent. What can you say about the relative equilibrium level of income, y, in the two economies?

10 If you have access to the internet, go to http://www.j-bradford-delong.net/macro_online/interactive/2002-11-14-Solow_growth.xls for an Excel-based interactive exercise on the Solow growth model. You can input different values for the variables in the Solow equation, and the spreadsheet will automatically show how these values affect the steady-state value of y and the time path followed in reaching equilibrium. There are also graphs showing how the equilibrium values change when you vary the fundamental parameters. (Note: the spreadsheet uses a more sophisticated form of the Solow income equation discussed in note 18.)

Notes

1 The expansion of the market tended to decrease per unit costs of production as the benefits of economies of scale in production could be exploited at higher levels of output.
2 A detailed discussion of population growth and of birth and death rates and their determinants can be found in Chapter 12.
3 Implicit in Malthus's argument that poor relief would reduce the willingness to work is the assumption that the poor, unlike their more wealthy brethren, are not maximizers of their income and consumption opportunities. Apparently the poor were presumed to have relatively low "target" income and consumption levels which would satisfy their limited desires. In modern language, the poor were presumed to be "satisficers" rather than maximizers; they functioned with a different set of beliefs and motivations than capitalists and their presumed "betters."
4 Additionally, as we shall see in Chapter 12, rising incomes lead to fewer births per woman over time, not more, as Malthus posited. This is related to the demographic transition discussed in that chapter.

5 Since Ricardo, the theory of diminishing returns has focused on the eventual decrease in the *marginal product* of a homogeneous variable input, as increasing quantities of that factor are added to production, all other inputs held constant. Ricardo's formulation had greater inputs of land of decreasing quality being added, that is, the input being added was actually heterogeneous, as successive units of land brought into use were of lower fertility.

6 Corn used to mean grains in general, but the Corn Laws were concerned primarily with wheat. The Corn Laws mandated tariffs on imported grains, tariffs that helped to keep domestic prices higher. By 1846, the last remnants of the restrictive Corn Laws had been banished from the statute books.

7 There is one exception that Ricardo made to his argument that free trade was the best policy: "It is evident, then, that trade with a colony may be so regulated that it shall at the same time be less beneficial to the colony, and more beneficial to the mother country, than a perfectly free trade" (quoted in Hunt 1979: 109). Given this caveat, it perhaps seems reasonable to wonder why, if it is possible for a country to improve upon the free trade outcome with a colony by regulating trade, it would not also, under some circumstances, be reasonable to suppose that the proper policy for a nation *vis-à-vis* nations other than colonies might also be other than free trade? We will consider the possibilities of how countries might be able to improve upon the free trade outcome in later chapters. This quotation from Ricardo reinforces, too, the discussion in Chapter 3 of the role that colonies played in contributing to the well-being of the more advanced countries and the adverse impact that colonial policies by the colonial powers had on the possibilities for economic progress in the colonies.

8 Normally, a production possibilities frontier (PPF) is assumed to be concave to the origin, indicating that inputs to production are specialized and that there are increasing marginal opportunity costs of production associated with producing more of any one good. Here we make the simplifying assumption that it is possible to produce more of one good at a constant marginal opportunity cost of production in terms of the other good sacrificed at the constant trade-off shown in Table 4.1 and by the straight line PPF in Figure 4.2. You will remember that a PPF summarizes all the efficient combinations of two goods that a country can produce given existing resources and technology.

In deriving Figure 4.2, it is assumed that Portugal has 300,000 hours of labor available per day. Using the information in Table 4.1, it is easy to calculate that if only cloth is produced and zero wine, the maximum quantity of cloth that can be produced per day is 3,333.33 units (300,000 hours ÷ 90 hours to produce each unit of cloth). Similarly, a maximum of 3,750 units of wine can be produced if no cloth is produced (300,000 hours ÷ 80 hours to produce each unit of wine). At production Point A, to produce 1,666.67 units of cloth rather than the maximum of 3,333.33, 1,666.66 units of cloth have been given up. Given the internal trade-off in production from Table 4.1 between cloth and wine for Portugal, reducing cloth production by 1,666.66 units releases enough labor to produce 1,875 units of wine (1,666.66 × 1.125, since for every one unit of cloth not produced in Portugal enough labor to produce 1.125 units of wine is released).

9 Modern analyses of the advantages of specialization and free trade, like the Heckscher-Ohlin theory, are based on Ricardo's original analysis, extending it to take into consideration differences in factor costs and other complications. The implications about specialization, however, remain essentially the same, especially as they relate to recommendations for indebted less-developed nations (Chapter 16) and as a basis for regional trade associations.

10 Between 1700 and 1770, more gold was mined in Brazil than the Spanish extracted from their colonies in the entire period from 1492 to 1800! Over 25 million pounds sterling of gold was transferred to Britain via Portugal between 1700 and 1770 (Fisher 1971: 128).

11 For a comprehensive mathematical approach to economic growth theory and economic development in general, see Basu 1997.

12 Marginal product is simply the change in total output due to a one unit change in one of the inputs, all other inputs being held constant. Mathematically, it is the first derivative of each of the inputs.

13 $dY/dK = aK^{a-1} > 0$ and $dY/dL = (1 - a)L^{-a} > 0$; $dY^2/(dK)^2 = a(a - 1)K^{a-2} < 0$ and $dY^2/(dL)^2 = -a$ $(1 - a)L^{-(1+a)} < 0$, which demonstrates the short-run existence of diminishing returns to each factor, holding the other constant. The aggregate production function 4.4 is also "linearly homogeneous," that is, multiplying both variable inputs by the same scalar value, v, changes production by vY: $A(vK)^a(vL)^{1-a} = Av^aK^av^{1-a}L^{1-a} = v(AK^aL^{1-a})$, when $0 < a < 1$, i.e., the production function exhibits constant returns to scale. In this formulation of the production function, a, which is the elasticity of

output with respect to a change in the capital input, can be interpreted as the share of total output or income received by the owners of physical capital (as profits, dividends, rents and so on) and $1 - a$ is the share of total output or income received by labor as wages. In this form, this is an example of the famous Cobb-Douglas production function.

14 It is important to remember that saving and investment are in an accounting, or *ex post*, sense always equal. In a closed economy, and assuming no government spending, national income and output, Y, are equal to consumption by households, C, and investment by business, I. We thus can write total output, or GDP, as $Y = C + I$. Rearranging, we can write $Y - C = I$. By definition, saving, S, is any income not consumed. Thus, $Y - C = S = I$, showing that saving equals investment always, *ex post*. Further, $I = \Delta K$, that is, the current level of investment is equal to new physical capital stock, I, being created, so $S = \Delta K$.

15 This is because each additional unit of capital produces less output than the previous unit due to the law of diminishing returns. Given a constant cost per unit of capital, costs of production will increase as more K is used, and thus the rate of return to all K will decline.

16 It is actually more accurate to state that the Solow-type neoclassical model predicts *conditional convergence* of per capita income. Poorer countries with the same savings rate as an already richer country will, all else the same, tend to have a faster growth rate than the richer country, so that income per capita would tend to catch up with that of the richer nation. However, the poorer nation may have a higher rate of growth of population, n, that prevents per capita income from reaching the level of the richer nation. Convergence of per capita income levels, then, is conditional on the identity of the so-called "fundamentals," particularly the rate of saving and investment and, secondarily, on the rate of population growth. Convergence of income among nations, then, depends on the rough equality in capital/labor ratios and savings behavior among economies. See Mankiw *et al.* (1992) for a recent effort that suggests that an augmented Solow model provides a reasonable explanation for cross-country income differentials based on differences in fundamentals.

17 See Jones (1998: 20–8) for a simple derivation of this result.

18 In this simple formulation, and to facilitate our understanding of the fundamental relationships, depreciation of physical capital is assumed to be zero. Also, exogenous technological change, A(t), which has the same constant value for all economies, is assumed to simply be a scalar value of 1. If depreciation of capital and the value of technological change are taken into consideration, the equilibrium Solow equation becomes:

$$y = A^{1/(1-a)}\,[s/(n+d)]^{a/(1-a)}$$

where d is the rate of depreciation of physical capital. As can be seen from this statement, countries with the same "fundamentals," i.e. with identical values of s, n, d, and a, will reach the same steady-state, equilibrium level of income per person (see Jones 1998: 34–9, for an alternative derivation).

19 In order to avoid drawing any inappropriate conclusions from the Solow model or to simplify its conclusions unduly, it is important to keep in mind the assumptions of the model, one of which is that the society has an "efficient" institutional structure which will readily transpose increased savings into increased capital formation. In Chapters 5 and 6, we will encounter some of the embedded characteristics of many of the less-developed societies which often render inapplicable the assumption of an automatic, direct and smooth link between increased savings, increased investment, and income growth.

20 However, s, the savings rate, is a constant value, and this rigidity is responsible for instability in the Harrod-Domar formulation of the economic growth process.

21 This means that all production isoquants form right angles, and there is a constant K/L ratio which is most efficient, that is, least cost, in production. This Harrod-Domar assumption also is known as a Leontief, or fixed-proportions, production function.

22 Harrod (1948: 72–100) explained this instability as illustrating the Keynesian problem of booms and busts, and the real-world reality that full-employment equilibrium without inflation was not an automatic outcome of the workings of a capitalist market system. Also see Chapters 1 and 2 of Sen (1970), which includes the original published journal contributions of Harrod (in 1939) and Domar (in 1946).

23 Consider the following simple numerical example from Sen (1970: 13). If $s = 0.2$ and $v = K/Q = 2$, then $g_w = s/v = 0.2/2 = 0.1$, or 10 percent. A rate of growth of 10 percent would mean that if $Q_{t-1} = 90$, then $Q_t = 100$ (measuring growth as a proportion of Q_t). If investors expect $Q_t = 100$, then $\Delta K_t = I_t =$

$v\Delta Q_t = 2 \times 10 = 20$. Given a savings rate of 0.2, the Keynesian income multiplier will be equal to 5, so Q_t = multiplier × Δspending = $5 \times 20 = 100$, so investor expectations are realized ($S_t = I_t = 20$) and steady-state equilibrium is attained and maintained, as long as expectations remain the same.

However, imagine that investors *expect* $Q_t = 101$, so that the expected $\Delta Q_t = 11$. Then, $\Delta K_t = I_t = v\Delta Q_t = 2 \times 11 = 22$. By the multiplier formula, then actual Q_t = multiplier × Δspending = $5 \times 22 = 110$. Investors will feel they have under-invested by anticipating too low a level of Q_t and in the next period will invest more, thus pushing the economy further away from equilibrium. The same dynamic works if investors under-anticipate the level of GDP, with continued decreases in GDP following.

If the labor market is also added to the model, such that the labor force grows yearly by the rate n (= $\Delta L/L$), then the trick of reaching and maintaining equilibrium in the Harrod-Domar model is exacerbated. Then, to avoid rising unemployment, even when $\Delta Q/Q = s/v$, this warranted rate, g_w, must equal the natural rate of growth, g_L, of the labor force, n. Thus a steady-state equilibrium requires $g_w = s/v = n = g_L$. The knife-edge equilibrium problem is even more exacting and the possibility of steady-state equilibrium even more remote when a growing labor force is introduced into the model.

24 In fact, a whole body of growth and income distribution literature – so called Cambridge growth models – predates the Solow model, but this perspective had a smaller impact on development economics than Solow's formulation would have. The Cambridge models tended to focus on savings behavior and the adjustment to equilibrium growth. See Sen 1970, esp. Chapters 2 and 3.

References

Adelman, Irma. 1961. *Theories of Economic Growth and Development*. Stanford: Stanford University Press.

Basu, Kaushik. 1997. *Analytical Development Economics: The Less Developed Economy Revisited*. Cambridge, MA: MIT Press.

Fisher, H.E.S. 1971. *The Portugal Trade*. London: Methuen.

Harrod, R.F. 1948. *Towards a Dynamic Economics*. London: Macmillan.

Hunt, E.K. 1979. *History of Economic Thought: A Critical Perspective*. Belmont, CA: Wadsworth.

Jones, Charles I. 1998. *Introduction to Economic Growth*. New York: W.W. Norton & Co.

Maddison, Angus. 1982. *Phases of Capitalist Development*. Oxford: Oxford University Press.

Mankiw, N. Gregory, David Romer and David N. Weil. 1992. "A Contribution to the Empirics of Economic Growth," *Quarterly Journal of Economics* 107 (May): 407–37.

Robinson, Joan. 1978. *Aspects of Development and Underdevelopment*. Cambridge: Cambridge University Press.

Rogin, Leo. 1956. *The Meaning and Validity of Economic Theory*. New York: Harper & Bros. Publishers.

Sachs, Jeffrey D. 2005. *The End of Poverty*. London: Penguin Books.

Sen, Amartya (ed.). 1970. *Growth Economics*. Harmondsworth: Penguin Books.

Smith, Adam. 1973. *An Inquiry into the Nature and Causes of the Wealth of Nations*. New York: The Modern Library.

Solow, Robert. 1956. "A Contribution to the Theory of Economic Growth," *Quarterly Journal of Economics* 70 (February): 65–94.

5 Developmentalist theories of economic development

> **After reading and studying this chapter, you should better understand:**
> - the concept of hidden development potential in less-developed nations;
> - the possibility of market failure and the role of positive externalities in creating virtuous circle effects;
> - the importance of social overhead capital and a nation's augmentable initial endowments to growth;
> - balanced versus unbalanced growth strategies and their shared paradigmatic perspective;
> - the theory of export pessimism;
> - backward and forward linkage effects and their key role in development;
> - the idea of hidden comparative advantage;
> - the potential role of surplus labor as a stimulant to growth in Lewis's dualist framework for transition;
> - Rostow's stages of growth theory, particularly the "take-off" stage.

Introduction

After the Second World War, and particularly after the quick success of the United States-financed Marshall Plan in helping to rebuild the European economies, several economists who had been directly involved either in the Marshall Plan or with institutions such as the United Nations and the World Banks turned their attention to the question of the economic development of less-developed regions. Among these early pioneers of development thinking were the Finnish economist Ragnar Nurkse, the Austrian economist Paul Rosenstein-Rodan, the German-born economist Albert Hirschman, the West Indian and later Nobel Laureate economist Sir Arthur Lewis, and the American economic historian Walt Whitman Rostow. Only Lewis remained outside of the policy-making institutions in the late 1940s and early 1950s, but by 1957 he too was employed by the UN.

In a broad sense, the ideas of these early development economists were mutually supportive. They formed a loose school of thought on the issue of economic development, emphasizing a less theoretical and more historical and practical approach to the question of how to develop – particularly in relation to those who stressed the applicability of neoclassical models, such as the Solow model discussed in the last chapter. Like any such school of analysis, there were differences of emphasis and interpretation between these theorists. These differences are particularly striking in the work of W.W. Rostow, who stressed a descriptive approach while emphasizing the near inevitability and predictability of economic development, based on the premise that the industrial past of Europe presents a rough picture of the approaching future of the developing nations. The others emphasized analytical constructs and were not striving to construct a megatheory of economic history. Yet they shared many fundamental propositions. Above all, they coincided in believing, in Rostow's words, that "the tricks of growth are not that difficult" (Rostow 1960: 166). They also felt that the time period necessary for achieving economic development in the less-developed world would be relatively short, a matter of a decade or perhaps a generation, rarely more.

Rostow predicted that, with US aid, by 1970 nine nations (including India) would pass the crucial threshold into a condition of self-sustaining economic growth. His bold ideas heavily influenced US President Kennedy, who then made a proposal to the UN, which was subsequently accepted, to name the 1960s the **United Nations Decade of Development** (Toye 2004: 176–9). While this initiative raised expectations in the underdeveloped nations, with its anticipation that aid-driven GDP growth could achieve a targeted rate of five percent a year, the concept was largely a feat of public relations. By 1965 the US and other major donor nations had lost their enthusiasm for the concept and aid began to decline.

Furthermore, all these economists shared, to different degrees, an affinity for the work of British economist John Maynard Keynes, whose views on macroeconomics had swept the economics profession in the late 1930s and 1940s. Thus, they emphasized *aggregate* phenomena, such as the rate of saving, measured by the share of income not consumed in gross national product (S/Y), and the rate of investment (I/Y), as fundamental variables, a perspective which fits well, too, with the Solow-type model of the previous chapter. They agreed with the Keynesian assumption that poor economic performance reflected a lack of aggregate demand, rather than a shortage of, or limits to, resources. Keynes had come to this conclusion based on his knowledge of the advanced capitalist nations, not from studying the dualistic, less-developed economies to which this insight would be applied.

These early development economists also manifested a notable preference for industrialization as the driving force of economic growth, believing industrialization would release a tide of prosperity lifting all other sectors of the economy. Finally, while these **developmentalists** had a profound respect for market forces, they were not hesitant to advocate large-scale, short-term governmental intervention into the economy, very much after the Keynesian manner, if that might be expected to force economic growth. Markets were perceived as a *means* to realizing the end of economic development; they were not an end in themselves. Markets could achieve some objectives rather well, but there were other spheres in which the market worked less well. Under certain conditions, an assertive, and even a leading, role for government was to be encouraged and was perhaps necessary. In the long run, however, the developmentalists expected that an economy would achieve its best results with a competitive market interacting with a responsive and efficient governmental apparatus, and thus the interventionist role of government in development would be reduced to its stabilizing function, as in the already-developed nations. In this sense, the developmentalists had very conventional economic ideas, but only in the very long run.

In this chapter, some of the leading theories of the developmentalists are examined. Their theories and recommendations are more pragmatic and operational than the neoclassical or classical formulations. The theories were devised with an eye to directly affecting public policy in the less-developed countries. We shall see that their influence on the thinking of many economists remains strong, though there have been, and need to be, further refinements of their analyses.

The theory of the big push

One of the early theories about how a country might create the conditions for economic progress, where growth and development had not already arisen spontaneously, was formulated by Paul Rosenstein-Rodan on the basis of research he had conducted during the Second World War. After analyzing the economic structures of a number of poor Eastern and South-East European nations, Rosenstein-Rodan drew a number of conclusions which became basic building blocks for the field of development economics emerging after the war.[1]

Rosenstein-Rodan was noted for his effort to call attention to the **hidden potential** for economic development in less-developed regions. Much of his work centered on taking advantage of the increasing returns that could be realized from large-scale planned industrialization projects that encompassed several major sectors of the economy simultaneously. A "big push" of concurrent industrial investments could launch a chain reaction of virtuous circles and complementary investments that would then ripple in many directions through the economic system. Large-scale investments in several branches of industry would lead to a favorable synergistic interaction between these branches and across sectors. If economic development was to get a start in the now less-developed nations, Rosenstein-Rodan argued, it would have to come from a concerted and substantial "push" from government to create, effectively, an entire industrial structure in one huge and interlocked undertaking (see Focus 5.1).

FOCUS 5.1   VIRTUOUS CIRCLES

Although Rosenstein-Rodan does not detail this point, one can sketch such virtuous circle effects: large-scale investments in steel-making could lead to research in metallurgy which would have "positive external" effects on companies which use metal products. Perhaps stronger alloys could be found that could then be used in the metal-fabricating industries, reducing wear and fatigue and downtime for the machines in this sector. All this could reduce costs to another branch of industry, perhaps in railway equipment manufacturing. Lower costs in the rail equipment could then be passed on to farmers, in the form of lower transport costs.

Farmers, in turn, would now be able to invest in better mechanical equipment from the metal-manufacturing industry, creating a further surge of positive ripple effects. Each branch of industry, or at least many branches of industry, would be caught in a web of interacting and mutually complementary activities. The more efficient are supply conditions, the lower costs of production will be, and the greater the demand for the product. Cross-sector positive externalities will also be transmitted, for example, from industry to agriculture.

In recent years interest in Rosenstein-Rodan's big-push theory has grown. His ideas were formalized by Kevin Murphy, Andrei Shleifer and Robert Vishney (1989) and his views are increasingly invoked by proponents of **endogenous growth theory** (see Chapter 8). This more recent work tends to highlight the role of demand **spillover effects** which, like the examples above, stress the virtuous circle effects which occur when an expanding manufacturing sector that raises productivity then stimulates income growth that, in turn, leads to Increasing demand for the products of the expanding manufacturing sector. Increasing growth in this manufacturing sector could lead to increasing demand for inputs that – because they are produced on a larger scale – lead to economies of scale in the production of these inputs. This virtuous circle will then lower the costs of production for the manufacturing sector, which could lead to increasing demand and growth – another virtuous circle!

Source: Hoff and Stiglitz 2001: 401–13

While concentrating on the hidden potential of large-scale future investments, with each successive increment to investment having an increasingly strong impact as output expanded at a rising rate,[2] Rosenstein-Rodan simultaneously maintained that these potential gains could not be realized within a purely market frame of reference. Individual entrepreneurs would be unlikely to invest enough to "push" the less-developed economy forward at its maximum potential rate, because under the profit-and-loss calculations of private entrepreneurs, their frame of reference would be too limited. Profit-maximizing steel producers are not concerned about whether their own private investments, if sufficiently large, will induce other investments and technical change in metallurgy which will then make that industry more profitable. Backward linkage effects which may be provoked by the investment actions of the steel industry are not taken into consideration by private decision-makers in the steel industry, because those firms cannot profit from these spin-off industries or even calculate the likelihood of the emergence and success of such linked firms.

Using Rosenstein-Rodan's terms, the steel industry cannot "appropriate" the future potential benefits to be gained in other sectors that are external to their business, and hence they do not take these effects into account in making their private investment decisions. Because of this information and appropriation failure, market decisions will lead to a sub-optimal level of investment from the standpoint of society as a whole.[3] Rosenstein-Rodan was convinced that there were many such hidden potentialities for expanded production in less-developed economies that went unexploited because of the inability of the market economy to coordinate the multitude of simultaneous investment decisions that needed to be made.

Insufficient economic development would occur, because the private sector mechanisms in place in less-developed societies lead to economic decision-making which is sub-optimal. More investment was needed, and in many places at one time, in order to shift the economy away from its low-level equilibrium trap and toward rapid and sustainable growth. Of particular importance to this process is the provision of social overhead capital or infrastructure: roads, bridges, docks, communications systems, hospitals, schools, utilities, irrigation and flood control projects, and so on, which also generate substantial positive external benefits to society as a whole.

> The market mechanism alone will not lead to the creation of social overhead capital, which normally accounts for 30 to 35 percent of total investment. That must be sponsored, planned, or programmed (usually by public investment). To take advantage of external economies (due to indivisibilities) requires an "optimum size" of enterprise to be brought about by a simultaneous planning of several complementary industries.
>
> (Rosenstein-Rodan 1984: 209)[4]

For example, if schools are built and operated under the profit motive, then they will be available only for the child whose parents can pay. Bright and ambitious children of poor parents will be less likely to gain needed skills, and society's labor force will be under-skilled and operating below its potential as a consequence. The hidden potential of the future labor force may never be realized if the market is left to provide social overhead capital, such as schools. This is the framework that Rosenstein-Rodan and others utilized when they argued that the market mechanism will not adequately create social overhead capital.[5]

In terms of the sequencing of investment decisions, Rosenstein-Rodan prioritized social overhead capital as an essential initial endowment, albeit one that nations have to actually create. Social overhead capital is not an initial endowment in the same sense that, say, land is.

Because of indivisibilities and because services of social overhead capital cannot be imported, a high initial investment in social overhead capital must either precede or be known to be certainly available in order to pave the way for additional more quickly yielding directly productive investments.

(Rosenstein-Rodan 1976: 635)

Rosenstein-Rodan's idea of the need for creating a "big push" of investment simultaneously in a number of branches of industry, and his emphasis on social overhead capital as fundamental to the success of the development project in less-developed nations are his best-known contributions to the literature, but they are not the whole of what he had to say about the development process. Summing up his own contributions in the area of development economics, Rosenstein-Rodan claimed that he had made four innovations.

First, he had stressed **disguised unemployment**, that is, those workers, particularly in agriculture, who receive very low or no pay and whose work effort results in relatively little increase in total output. Their labor could be tapped to create the vast public works of social overhead capital which would be necessary for development, without reducing output in the economy.[6]

Second, by emphasizing the complementarity, and the external economies, of distinct investments, Rosenstein-Rodan demonstrated that large-scale investments could have an impact on overall economic growth greater than might be expected based on the calculations of individual entrepreneurs alone. It is necessary to take into account the positive externalities of one investment on others and on the possibility of increasing returns from successive units of investment. In order to achieve these serendipitous effects, however, economic planning of a limited nature would be necessary. Key industries or branches of industry would have to be targeted for expansion, and their initial investments would need to be subsidized if they were to occur at all.

Rosenstein-Rodan's third innovation was his emphasis on social overhead capital. Such investments, he argued, should precede the expansion of consumer-goods manufacturing investment if the latter is to be successful. As we shall discover in Chapter 8, this is a view supported by recent research on endogenous growth models.

And fourth, a "big push" of investment through the economy could result in **technological external economies**. These effects he defined in terms of workforce training. Large-scale industrialization could contribute to a socially beneficial level of labor training that would have spread effects to other sectors throughout the economy, whereas incremental, market-driven development would not have the same impact, or at least dependence on the market would result in sub-optimal social quantities of such training. Private businesses would not invest in the socially optimal level of labor training, again because any individual employer will be unable to appropriate the increases in income created by the new skill, especially if a worker moves on to another employer, who would not need to make any investment to benefit from the worker's increased skill level. However, under the big-push approach, labor training could be funded as part of a more general development plan. A broader time and planning horizon could be entertained by government, which could determine the training needs of an entire industrial complex and calculate the social profitability of any investment of additional educational expenditures and labor training. As we shall see in Chapter 8 in the discussion of endogenous growth theories, Rosenstein-Rodan was ahead of his time in maintaining that appropriate labor training was of equal, or perhaps even greater, importance than capital accumulation in the process of industrialization and economic development.

A theory of balanced growth

Ragnar Nurkse, like Rosenstein-Rodan, emphasized above all the need for a coordinated increase in the amount of capital utilized in a wide range of industries if the critical threshold level of industrialization was to have a chance of being achieved. Nurkse agreed that a massive injection of new technology, new machines, and new production processes spread across a broad range of industrial sectors held the key to igniting the development process in less-developed nations.[7]

Export pessimism and the need for domestic industrialization

This perspective of how to initiate rapid economic growth needs to be contrasted with what was, in the 1940s, a received doctrine in trade theory: to foster economic progress, less-developed regions were counseled to concentrate on increasing their exports of tropical products and raw materials, products in which, it was suggested, such countries had a comparative advantage. In Nurkse's view, this rather standard prescription for accelerating economic growth in less-developed countries was likely to yield meager results for two basic reasons. First, Nurkse maintained that in future the world demand for tropical products and raw materials would be relatively limited and slow to expand. An increase in supply under such conditions would result in a decrease in the market price. The reduction in price could be of such a magnitude that the total revenue received (= unit price × quantity of the product sold on the world market) after an increase in supply could be less than the export income that was received prior to the drive to increase such exports.[8]

Nurkse did not devote himself to proving this point; rather he seems to have utilized this insight more as a working assumption based upon the weak pattern of prices for traditional primary exports from the less-developed nations he observed in the first half of the twentieth century. Because of this break with the orthodox view that the colonial and post-colonial regions had a comparative advantage in tropical products and raw material exports which could be further exploited through even more ambitious and pragmatic economic policy to expand such exports, Nurkse was branded an "export pessimist" (see Focus 3.5 for details).

The second reason for his rejection of the export-led road to development was based on Nurkse's interpretation of the propensity to import.[9] In orthodox trade theory, it was assumed that a less-developed nation with the ability to export either tropical products and/or raw materials would use the income earned to import machinery, equipment, and manufactured consumer goods for domestic consumption. Trade would balance, that is, the value of exports would equal the value of imports, at least over an intermediate period of time. To challenge orthodox assumptions, Nurkse utilized a socio-psychological theory which explains why consumption continues to rise as income rises. This theory assumes that some "wants" are not innate, but rather are socially created. In this framework, some new goods are "demonstrated" to be desirable, because they are consumed by higher-income recipients in society. These goods confer social status and are therefore sought by others with less income.[10]

Nurkse believed that the less-developed regions would be very vulnerable to the pernicious affects of this international demonstration effect. High-income consumers would spend inordinately on imported luxury products to "keep up with the Joneses" of the richer nations. Not only would there be an upward bias toward imports, especially of consumer goods, but the already limited potential supply of savings in the less-developed nation that might have been directed toward much needed domestic capital formation would be drawn down, as consumption as a share of total national income rose. Furthermore, the drive to show status through the importation of luxury commodities would conceivably cut into the ability of the economy to purchase imported machinery for industry, as the two forms of demand for foreign exchange competed for a limited stock of foreign exchange earned from primary product exports.

Less-developed regions were poor, according to Nurkse, because productivity per worker was low, and productivity, in turn, was low because savings were low, just as in the Solow model. With a low capacity for savings, the level of investment would, by necessity, be low, and consequently, with only a modest amount of capital equipment available to each worker, the end result had to be a low level of per capita income because output per worker would be low. Small, incremental increases in capital formation would not solve the problem, in Nurkse's view. The market-based approach would more than likely fail, because as an individual business or a single industry alone attempted to raise its output level by increasing its individual capital investment, it ran the risk of not finding a market for its product because of the low level of overall average income. Alternatively, Nurkse emphasized that by attempting to solve the problem of underdevelopment via an expansion on the supply side alone, that is, through the expansion of production capacity, one ran the risk that the lack of demand for new output would short-circuit the attempt to move the economy forward.

The only solution that Nurkse foresaw, as had Rosenstein-Rodan, was via balanced growth. Large-scale increases in supply sweeping across a large number of industrial sectors would, at the same time, be met by a large-scale increase in demand created by the same expansion.[11] The essential demand-side stimulus would come from industries that were expanding as a result of the overall, balanced investment program; they would need more inputs of raw materials, intermediate or semi-processed products, and labor, and their act of buying inputs would create income for their suppliers. This income would then be transposed into a further expansion of demand by other firms and by workers in those firms buying the increased array of domestic goods available. But this widespread expansion could happen only if the initial effort at development was "balanced," that is, only if supply increases were coordinated with simultaneous demand increases across the economy.

Although Nurkse's theory of balanced growth is very similar in many respects to the big-push formulation of Paul Rosenstein-Rodan, Nurkse's work was not merely a repetition. He did not advocate planning, as did Rosenstein-Rodan, nor was his approach open to the charge of being statist or of being dependent on the dominance of the public sector, a criticism that might be leveled at Rosenstein-Rodan. Rather, Nurkse felt that dynamic *fiscal policies* could have a very positive effect on the prospects for development without large-scale government involvement in production decisions or large-scale planning projects. Specifically, Nurkse advocated **forced savings** through an increase in taxes on upper-income recipients. The government, then, could repress the level of consumption out of national income, thereby increasing the level of overall savings. Then, the increased investment funds generated could be allocated to the most promising industrial sectors, possibly via government-operated development banks (see Focus 9.3 for details) designed to identify and promote industrialization in the private sector or via private sector banks.

Industries would be encouraged to increase their capital formation and to raise their productivity, both because of the availability of loans from the development banks and because of the effects of infant industry protection, in which government would raise tariffs against cheaply manufactured imports from the advanced nations that might compete with the production of the new enterprises. Thus, both supply and demand factors would be addressed. The supply of savings would be expanded, leading to an increase in the supply of available domestic output via enhanced capital formation. At the same time, a market for domestically produced goods would be created, because potentially competing imports would be deflected via tariffs to the purchase of lower-priced domestically produced goods, a strategy which, later, became known as **import substitution industrialization** (discussed in detail in Chapters 9 and 10).

Like Rosenstein-Rodan, Nurkse felt strongly that less-developed regions possessed the hidden potential for greater progress; the resources and talents of society simply needed to be coordinated and released.

Unbalanced growth

Not all developmentalist economists believed, however, that the resources needed for implementing a big push or a balanced growth strategy actually were available, though ideally this might be the optimum path in some abstract sense. One who voiced such concern was Albert O. Hirschman. Like most of the pioneers in the field of economic development, Hirschman was involved in the postwar economic reconstruction of Europe. However, this experience was followed by a four-year stint in Colombia, where his role as adviser to the National Economic Planning Board arose as a result of the recommendation of the World Bank (Hirschman 1984: 90). Hirschman's experiences in Colombia were formative; he would draw on a fund of experiences within this less-developed country to provide specificity to his emerging ideas on development. His work since that time has continued to convey a sense of immediacy and applicability that was at times lacking in the abstract and aggregative approaches employed by Rosenstein-Rodan, Nurkse, and other developmentalists.

Because Hirschman employed the term unbalanced growth in his major work (1958) on economic development, and because his seminal work came considerably later than the ideas expressed by Rosenstein-Rodan and Nurkse, it has been commonly assumed that Hirschman's work was to be interpreted as an attack on the theory of big-push or balanced growth. It is important, therefore, to note that Hirschman agreed with the vast bulk of the ideas expressed by both Rosenstein-Rodan and Nurkse. He supported an "industrialization first" strategy, and he firmly believed that the key to rapid industrialization was to be found in large-scale capital formation in several industries and sectors. Hirschman also shared the optimistic opinion that less-developed nations harbored significant hidden reserves of talent, that potentially complementary relationships were waiting to be released, and that there were major potential externalities which would be instrumental in speeding the thrust toward industrialization. Hirschman's own interpretation of the relationship of his work to that of Rosenstein-Rodan and Nurkse was that he was a dissenter *within* the framework of the big-push/balanced growth paradigm.

The less-developed economies did indeed need a big push; without it, there would be either a snail's-pace rate of economic and societal change, or perhaps no discernible progress at all. But Hirschman advocated a big push for only a limited range of industries, with the idea that by inducing development in key sectors first, overcapacity would be created in these sectors, while supply bottlenecks would simultaneously increase production difficulties elsewhere in the economic structure. These bottlenecks would create pressures for new investments to resolve the supply inadequacies. In other words, Hirschman deliberately advocated the unbalancing of the economy, creating disequilibrium situations, for two basic reasons.

First, he maintained that there were resource limits in the less-developed regions and that this would necessitate prioritizing some areas of industry over others for the use of limited investment funds. It was impossible to move forward on a "broad front" in all industries at the same time as was envisioned in the big-push and balanced growth theories. Second, in deliberately unbalancing the economy and in creating excess capacity in some areas and intensifying shortages in other areas, he believed that the pressures created would result in subsequent reactions that would speed the development process by opening up opportunities for profit for new entrepreneurs.

In industries where overcapacity was generated, the output of these sectors would be made cheaper than previously, as a result of economies of scale; as output grew, unit costs of production would decrease as the firm moved down the average total cost curve. Hirschman believed this decrease in costs, assuming these were passed on to the final consumer, would then contribute to stimulating **upstream investments**. Hirschman's theory might be illustrated with the following example: by deliberately oversupplying electrical power, and thus lowering its price to users, sectors of the economy which used large amounts of electrical power as an input into their production process could be stimulated by this lowering of their marginal and average costs. Hirschman argued that in conditions of limited resources, as applied in the less-developed world, where it would be impossible to simultaneously increase electrical power-generating facilities and still have sufficient investment funds to stimulate industries that were intensive users of electrical power, it was the task of economic development economists to prioritize one of these two possible areas of growth. Then, rely upon the positive effect of disequilibrium imbalances to push the economy forward as private entrepreneurs responded to the possibilities created by bottlenecks via the market.

The priority sector could be the upstream or the downstream industry. Excess capacity in social overhead capital could lead to the rapid expansion of private sector investments, which would then subsequently utilize the excess capacity generated in the public sector, thus justifying its initial creation. On the other hand, were private sector investments to be prioritized, the need for a rapid increase in social overhead capital would subsequently manifest itself as the demand for electricity outstripped the supply; the profitability of more social investment would be made manifest. Bottlenecks and shortages of some inputs would create opportunities for profits for private entrepreneurs to fill in the gaps. These profits would attract other investors in search of profit windfalls created by such bottlenecks. Investments would flow into under-supplied sectors, where prices and profits were rising. Perhaps this response would overshoot the needs of the market, thereby creating downstream opportunities for other businesses that could turn the new excess capacity and falling prices to their advantage.

Imbalances, or disequilibrium situations, would be conducive to further change; doing things "the wrong way around" could provide greater benefit than any other strategy in Hirschman's view. Basically, what Hirschman was explaining was how a market system responds to shortages and surpluses, but his contribution was to suggest how development planners might utilize market disequilibriums to stimulate economic progress.

Backward and forward linkages

One of Hirschman's best known and most creative ideas was that of **industrial linkages**. When one industry expands, it requires inputs from other industries to be able to produce. These are called **backward linkages**, that is, they are induced effects on the output of supplying industries. For example, coal mining and iron ore mining constitute backward linkages from a steel mill. On the other hand, when an industry sells and transports its production to other firms and sectors in the economy, these are the **forward linkages** of the original producer, that is, the induced effects of the output of the first industry in the direction of the final consumer. The metal fabrication industry and the chemical and paint manufacturing industry which use the output of the steel industry as their inputs would be forward linkages to the steel industry, and these industries might have further forward linkages to, say, the production of household stoves. Railroads or alternative forms of transport would enter the example as both backward and forward linkages to steel production and at each stage of production.

Thus, the production of one firm in one industry has a multiplicity of backward and forward linkages with firms in other industries in the domestic economy and, perhaps, abroad as well. In communicating the induced effects from one sector of the economy to another via shortages and excess capacity in Hirschman's unbalanced growth process, the size of potential backward and forward linkages were of paramount importance in evaluating where to locate the initial investment. Development strategies could be built around the maximization of the estimated stimulus of promoted industries in generating domestic backward and forward linkages.

Hirschman argued that the case could be made for large-scale capital-using projects, such as steel mills, if these investments could stimulate significant backward and forward linkages. Indeed, such investments could spark the creation of whole new industries, providing not only increased output, but also increased employment and, with rising levels of production, lower costs and lower prices to consumers as the benefits of economies of scale were reaped. Nor would such large-scale capital-intensive investments necessarily displace workers, as is sometimes alleged. In an empirical study which analyzed the relationship between industrial structures and employment in Latin America, Hirschman found that:

> once the indirect employment effects (via backward and forward linkages) are taken into account, investment in large-scale (capital-intensive) industry turns out to be just as employment-creating as investment in small-scale (labour-intensive) industry for the industrially advanced countries of Latin America.
>
> (Hirschman 1984: 97)

How might such linkages be measured? Even at the time Hirschman was writing, **input–output** analysis of national economies was being elaborated, based on the pioneering work of Wassily Leontief at Harvard. Using input–output tables, it is possible to calculate the impact of a change in the output of one industry on supplying backward-linked producers and simultaneously on the production of forward-linked industries that use the originating output as inputs. An input–output table is a matrix showing the multiplier effects of the impact on other industries per unit change of output in another industry, as well as on labor use, imports, and final demand. For any country seriously thinking about stimulating development, at least a simple input–output table and the required calculations are almost essential for effective decision-making and monitoring of effects.

Changing the social organization of the labor process

Hirschman advanced an additional reason for promoting a capital-intensive, unbalanced industrialization program in less-developed nations. Many social scientists had argued that an attitude of "achievement" needed as a precondition for industrialization was missing in both the labor force and in management in less-developed nations. It had been suggested that standards in the workplace were exceedingly lax in less-developed countries, and that neither workers nor managers were willing to take responsibility for errors in production. Slack management techniques often made it impossible to assign culpability when tasks were left uncompleted or were not completed within the time-norm set for a particular task. Hirschman did not take issue with this characterization of the work place in the less-developed nations. Rather, he noted that with the introduction of more advanced, machine-paced techniques, it would become easier both to calculate reasonable work-norms and to evaluate both success and failure in completing tasks (see Focus 5.2).

Hirschman thus advocated new forms of production on the shop floor that might "hot-house" the completion of the less productive handicraft and manufacture stages of industrialization and allow the less-developed countries to move quickly to the machino-facture stage and its higher level of productivity. Under simple, relatively labor-intensive manufacture, the human operative has a great deal of control over the pacing of and output of a machine, since the worker chooses how quickly to work and how much effort to put into the production process.

Under machino-facture, or more capital-intensive production techniques, however, norms and rates of production are pre-determined to a great extent by the pace at which the machines are engineered to operate. Workers and managers are faced with a situation that is much more "all or nothing": maintain the pace of work and the quality of output determined by the machines, or risk losing employment. This situation, argued Hirschman, forces a change in the labor process which could lead to a rapid rise in productivity and could force institutional and behavioral changes that would be conducive to further economic development. This is another example of a Hirschmanian "pressure point," or disequilibrium process, designed to disrupt the production process and society in a way that promotes a positive outcome.

New attitudes and expectations regarding the labor process, both at the level of the shop floor and in management, could be inculcated as a by-product, or positive externality, of this more capital-intensive industrialization as the pace of work is increasingly dictated by machines. Both traditional labor practices and often ritual management responses would be made untenable with the new rules of the game, and a new cadre of workers and managers would be created as a complementary effect of industrialization, with positive and cumulative

---

FOCUS 5.2   ACHIEVEMENT ORIENTATION IN THE WORKPLACE

A study of Mexican corporations conducted by the international consulting company, Vertex, may illustrate the significance of achievement attitudes. In comparing output per worker in Mexico with similar firms in advanced nations, Vertex found that productivity was 50 percent below international work-norms. In the most complex operations relating to production and maintenance, productivity was only 40 percent of what might be anticipated elsewhere.

Only 55 percent of the work day was devoted to work; 17 percent of time was spent in office gossip and coffee drinking, and 28 percent of the day was lost to (1) inefficiency of personnel, (2) communication problems, (3) repeating work because of errors, and (4) repeating instructions to employees. Among the difficulties cited by Vertex were the lack of motivation of workers as a result of the unwillingness of management to delegate authority, the lack of communication skills and proper training of workers, and the high turnover of workers with minimum loyalty to the firm. These conditions, they stated, tended to create apathy and negligence and an "it can't be done" mentality in the workforce.

Source: Crevoshay (1994: 11)

spin-off effects for other industries. Hirschman felt that innovative attitudes toward efficiency and responsibility on the job would also be transmitted to society at large. A system built upon merit and performance would eventually threaten the outmoded social structure built upon privilege and ceremony, a system which far too often remains a source of inefficiency in the less-developed world.

Antagonistic growth

Like all the developmentalist pioneers, Hirschman was extremely optimistic about the possibility for progress in the less-developed world in the 1950s. In his *Strategy of Economic Development* (1958: 5), he stated that:

> development depends not so much on finding optimal combinations for given resources and factors of production as on calling forth and enlisting for development purposes resources and abilities that are hidden, scattered, or badly utilized.

In a self-review of his own work in the 1980s, Hirschman struck a more sobering note. He defended his argument that development via excess capacity, or unbalanced growth, could be a viable strategy, while acknowledging that problems arising from resource scarcity also need to be given a more central role in conceptualizing the development process. Under conditions of resource scarcity – and all less-developed nations face scarcity, be it of investment funds or of skilled labor – an over-emphasis on a certain sector, such as industry, can mean that another sector, especially agriculture, fails to receive the inputs and support it needs to progress at a reasonable or desirable pace. Thus unbalancing development in one sector can leave another sector worse off, leading to what Hirschman termed an antagonistic growth process. In such a situation, Hirschman warned, further economic growth along the same lines will serve only to exacerbate existing levels of economic inequality. And this, of course, can lead to difficult if not explosive political struggles. So, both efficient allocation and effective reallocation of resources must be considered at the same time. It is not one or the other that is most important for development.

Growth with unlimited supplies of labor

Another of the most important pioneers of early development economics is Sir Arthur W. Lewis, who, along with Gunnar Myrdal, is one of only four development economists to have been awarded the Nobel Memorial Prize in Economic Science. Lewis's most cited work, and one of the best-known models in development economics, is his classic article on unlimited supplies of labor (1954). From 1970 to 1974, Lewis, who was born on St. Lucia in the Caribbean, was President of the Caribbean Development Bank, having previously held high-level positions at the UN in the area of development policy.

Like the other developmentalists discussed in this chapter, Lewis was quite optimistic that hidden reserves of strength could be tapped in the less-developed nations, and that by doing so, economic development could rapidly be promoted. He also shared their conviction that industrialization was the route the less-developed nations needed to pursue to escape poverty and reach a higher level of economic and social progress. Lewis's reasons for supporting industrialization, however, were quite distinct. He was not an "export pessimist." In fact, Lewis produced a major research work (Lewis 1969), the purpose of which was to demonstrate that tropical products and raw materials exports, the traditional primary exports of less-developed nations, were *not* subject to falling international prices resulting from supposed limits of the advanced nations to absorb these products. On the contrary, he drew the conclusion that rising incomes and rising levels of production in the already-developed nations would call forth a stronger demand for tropical products and raw materials. Thus, the promotion of such exports promised higher levels of export income in future.

Despite this latent potential, Lewis nonetheless insisted that the wage level of the less-developed nations was moving upward at much too slow a pace; workers' incomes in the less-developed nations were falling further behind that of their counterparts in the developed nations. Lewis believed this growing disparity was the result of differences in the productive structures existing between the two areas. The already-developed nations had large industrial and manufacturing sectors, where many workers were employed, and relatively small agricultural sectors, using a relatively small proportion of the labor force. Just the reverse structure prevailed in the less-developed nations, where most of the labor force was occupied in rural areas, with agricultural production their primary activity.

Higher wages were paid to workers in the manufacturing sector compared to agriculture in both the developed and less-developed nations, though the gap was smaller in the already-developed nations, because productivity per worker was higher in both the industrial and agricultural sectors. Especially low incomes prevailed in the agricultural sector of the less-developed countries, where most of the population lived and worked, since output per worker also was quite low, primarily because of the lack of capital and the relatively primitive technologies in use. Thus the higher average income in the already-developed nations was a structural function of having more workers in the higher-productivity, higher-wage industrial sector relative to the less-developed regions.

While the less-developed nations often were portrayed by economists and policy-makers as having a comparative advantage in the production of tropical agricultural goods and raw materials for export that should continue to be exploited, Lewis suggested that they also had a potential, hidden, dynamic comparative advantage in some types of manufacturing. At the time, this was still a somewhat unconventional view as applied to the promotion of manufacturing. It arose from his observation that wages in the manufacturing sector in less-developed nations were relatively low compared to those of the advanced nations. Since wages were an important component of costs in labor-intensive manufacturing processes, such as textile production, if the less-developed regions could restructure their economies toward this type of manufacturing, they could perhaps create comparative advantage based on their relatively lower wage costs.[12]

Lewis actually was an "export optimist," believing that the small net addition to global manufacturing exports coming from less-developed regions would be easily absorbed by a growing world market. Thus a higher level of manufactured exports from the less-developed nations need not spark a defensive reaction in the advanced nations in terms of new tariffs and other barriers, because Lewis believed that the increases in labor-intensive manufacturing exports added by the less-developed nations to total exports would be dispersed throughout the global economy. He thus did not believe that any developed country would face a serious threat from manufactured export competition coming from the less-developed regions. Consequently, the developed nations would not resort to protectionism to stop the flow of new manufacturing exports.

Lewis wanted to advocate shifting labor away from agriculture and into industry. But, as a well-trained orthodox economist, he had been taught that switching labor from agriculture to industry would mean that agricultural production must surely decline with such a reallocation, assuming the marginal product of labor in agriculture to be greater than zero.

Consequently, food prices might be expected to rise, as fewer farmers would be producing less output for a growing number of non-agricultural workers.[13] With rising food prices, industrial wages would need to rise to ensure at least a subsistence wage, and the potential comparative advantage of the less-developed country in producing labor-intensive manufacturing goods for export would disappear with the rising wages. Was there no way out?

Surplus labor

It was at this point that Lewis brought into development economics an important construct which had been widely utilized by Keynesian economists in analyzing the Great Depression (1929–39) within the industrial countries in writing about disguised unemployment. What if labor in the agricultural sector was being utilized in an extremely inefficient manner, to the degree that, by taking agricultural workers out of this sector and employing them in industry, agricultural production would not decline at all, while industrial output was increased with the influx of greater employment? What if there were actually a *surplus* of agricultural workers, such that by transferring some labor from agriculture to industry the remaining workers could work longer hours, or more efficiently, and total agricultural production could remain constant or even rise?[14] Or, alternatively, agricultural producers who had been selling to the export market could replant their fields with an eye to the potential profits created by the growing domestic market resulting from the process of industrialization. In any event, Lewis reasoned, if there was surplus labor in agriculture, then that "hidden reserve" could be tapped for industrialization, and development perhaps would not prove to be so difficult to attain after all.

If industrialists were to pay a wage somewhat, say 30 percent, above the average wage prevailing in agriculture to cover the costs and discomforts of migrating to industrial areas and to compensate for the higher cost of urban living, then industrialists could hire all the labor they might want at a constant wage, as long as surplus labor conditions prevailed in agriculture. Industrialists could look forward to a double advantage. First, the absolute level of wages would be above but close to subsistence, yet domestic wages would be far below the wage prevailing in the advanced nations. Second, as industry shifted to higher and higher levels of production over time, more and more surplus agricultural laborers would be brought into the industrial sector. But wages in that sector would not have to rise at all, because the cost of food, the basic determinant of the wage level, would remain constant until the labor surplus was exhausted.

The Lewis surplus labor model

We can formalize the Lewis model along the following lines. Lewis presumed that the typical less-developed nation was **dualistic**, not only in having two key sectors, but in the sense that these sectors had little interconnection. There was a traditional, low-productivity rural and predominantly agriculture sector, where the great bulk of the population worked and produced what it consumed. But there also existed (or there could be created) an incipient modern capitalist sector, where production was more technologically driven and, accordingly, worker productivity was higher than in the traditional sector. The modern sector bought food, and perhaps other inputs, from the traditional sector for use in the production process, and the traditional sector provided labor to industry in the cities, but otherwise the links between the two sectors were weak.

It was in the labor supply link between the two sectors that Lewis found a transformation dynamic. His model can be explained by examining Figure 5.1(a) and (b). Figure 5.1(a)

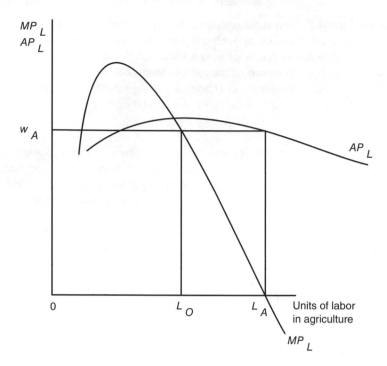

Figure 5.1(a) Lewis's surplus labor model: agriculture.

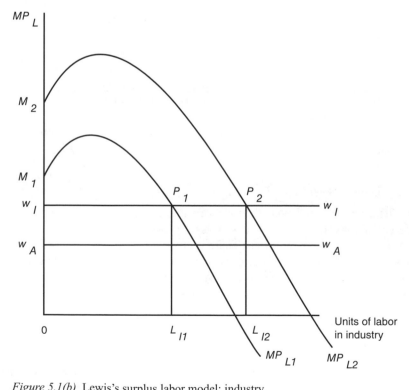

Figure 5.1(b) Lewis's surplus labor model: industry.

shows the marginal product (MP_L) and average product (AP_L) of labor curves in agriculture. Since Lewis assumes a surplus of labor in agriculture, it can be presumed that the $MP_L = 0$, so that L_A workers are employed in that sector. However, unlike the usual neoclassical assumption that workers are paid their marginal product, which, in this case, would mean agricultural workers would be paid nothing – clearly an impossibility – workers actually receive a wage, w_A, equal to their average product when L_A workers are employed. Why? In the traditional sector, it is presumed income is shared by the members of extended families. One can think of the production process being organized around the household, rather than by and for individual decision-makers. Work often is done collectively on family farms, where the marginal product calculation of the optimal use of labor inputs would be a wholly alien concept.[15] All family members may contribute to production in their own fashion; and all share in the fruits of the labor process more or less equally, regardless of the individual contribution to production.

If the industrial sector pays a wage w_I that is above w_A, then labor will be attracted from agriculture to industry (Figure 5.1(b)). Industrial capitalists, who are presumed to be profit-maximizers, will hire L_{I1} workers: additional labor will be used until the industrial wage is equal to the MP_{L1} in the industrial sector. The industrial sector's total output is equal to area $0M_1P_1L_{I1}$; the workers' share of that income is equal to area $0w_IP_1L_{I1}$, while the capitalists' share is area $w_IM_1P_1$.

When this profit or surplus is reinvested, in whole or in part, depending on other costs and considerations, the addition of new physical capital, and the technology embodied in that capital, will shift labor's marginal product curve in the industrial sector upward and outward, since the effect of more capital and more technology is to increase the productivity of labor. With increased investment, and hence the new MP_L curve, M_2P_{L2}, and given the labor surplus which keeps the industrial wage at w_I, L_{I2} workers now will be employed in the industrial sector. Thus, with continuing reinvestment from the profits of the modern sector, the transfer of labor from agriculture to industry is accomplished in the Lewis model, especially if the capital–labor ratio in industry does not rise very much – that is, as long as production remains labor-intensive. Employment in industry will rise, along with total national output.

The process of transferring labor from agriculture to industry will slow and eventually come to an end, of course. As labor leaves agriculture, the marginal product of labor, and its average product, must eventually rise as the labor surplus is exhausted. In Lewis's view, the upward pressure this puts on wages in agriculture will force producers in that sector to become more productive via the adoption of better technologies, thus forcing the "modernization" of the primary sector as well. Of course, this process happens gradually, rather than discretely, as some agricultural producers embrace modern methods of production earlier than others, but the effect of a growing scarcity of labor in agriculture will require the use of greater amounts of capital and technology to save on labor. In the process, productivity and incomes in agriculture also will rise.

To keep this "virtuous circle" of labor transfer going once started, there would have to be more and more capital formation in manufacturing capacity, which would necessitate a higher level of savings which then could be transformed into investment. In Lewis's view, only the fledgling capitalist sector would save. Large landowners, monopoly bankers, mine owners, and other wealthy strata of traditional society, including the political elite, would be more likely to squander their economic surplus in ostentatious consumption and/or capital flight out of the country. Only by increasing the share of national income which accrued to industrial capitalists, Lewis reasoned, could the less-developed regions move forward, and this would be accomplished by the transfer of labor from agriculture to industry, shown in Figure 5.1(b).

The distribution of income

As Lewis defined the problem, his surplus labor model suggested a very rapid dynamic process would unfold. A significant and rapidly rising share of national income would be shifted to the national, industrial capitalist strata. As this class increased its productive investments by plowing back its profits into new investments in pursuit of ever-greater profit, total national output would rise. But since wages would not rise as long as the labor surplus remained, a growing share of a growing total national income would accrue to the capitalist class. They, in turn, motivated only to increase production and profits further, would reinvest at an accelerated rate, thereby ensuring that national income would rise further. A perpetual-motion machine would be put into play, moving faster as time went on.

What would happen, though, when the unlimited supply of laborers was finally depleted? Lewis was unconcerned. At that point, the objective of the transformation of the economy would have been achieved. Wages for workers would rise, the standard of living would improve, and the gap between the poor and rich nations would have closed considerably. This Lewis saw as the inevitable and desirable end of the process he envisioned.

Lewis often has been accused of advocating a worsening of the distribution of income as a means to promote development. In his model, the share of income going to relatively well-off capitalists rises over time, as can be seen in Figure 5.1(b). Meanwhile, a small gap opens between the average wage in the agricultural sector and that of the industrial sector, to the disadvantage of agricultural workers, whose income remained relatively stagnant as long as there was surplus labor. Lewis was well aware of this criticism, but he felt that it missed the mark. Painful as it might be to contemplate, Lewis found no other way to foster growth. He pointed out that he was not advocating a worsening of the distribution of income. What he was advocating was economic development and a general rise in the standard of living, and he could see no other way to exploit the "hidden surplus" of disguised unemployment in agriculture without such an adverse, but temporary, increase in inequality between agriculture and industry (see Focus 5.3).[16]

Joan Robinson put the matter well in another context: "The misery of being exploited by capitalists is nothing compared to the misery of not being exploited at all" (Robinson 1966: 46). In other words, the wage of the industrial worker is likely to be higher, and the standard of living better, than for the rural peasant or rural worker. The transition from agricultural poverty to a higher standard of living in industrial production was desirable, even if it engendered temporary inequality. One suspects that Lewis would have agreed with Robinson's pithy comment.

Lewis subsequently broadened his definition of what contributed to a labor surplus, or disguised unemployment, to include:

1   individuals unemployed because of technical change in agriculture and industry;
2   the underemployed in rural areas;
3   the movement of women from the household to the labor force;
4   the surplus labor generated by rapid increases in population.

Of these factors, he considered the last the most powerful force for creating a labor surplus (Lewis 1984: 133).[17]

FOCUS 5.3 OTHER DUALIST MODELS OF STRUCTURAL TRANSFORMATION

The Lewis model of unlimited supplies of labor is but one, though perhaps the best known, of a number of dualist models examining the transfer of labor from agriculture to industry.

The Fei-Ranis model: This was an extension and elaboration of the basic Lewis model, a major distinction being an upward-sloping labor supply curve after some amount of labor has been extracted from agriculture to industry. The Lewis model also envisages such a tendency, though it is not formalized as it is in the Fei-Ranis model. This was a theoretical contribution, and it does not detract from the basic Lewis conclusion that labor will be attracted from rural areas to urban industrial centers by a wage higher than that paid in agriculture, and that it is that transfer which contributes to the desired structural transformation of production (which will be examined in Chapter 9).

The idea that total national output and income per person could be increased by such a strategy of labor transfer, where the marginal product of labor in industry exceeded the marginal product of labor in agriculture, is the key insight of both the Lewis and Fei-Ranis models.

The Harris-Todaro model: Though traditionally the Harris-Todaro model is not categorized as a dual economy model, but rather one explaining rural–urban migration and urban unemployment and underemployment, it is in the tradition and spirit of the Lewis model. The Todaro model envisages workers in agriculture rationally choosing to migrate to urban, industrial centers in the pursuit of wages that, with some probability, are expected to be higher than in rural areas. Urban wages are higher on account of many forces: higher productivity of workers, higher living costs of cities, and, perhaps, the "wedge" of unionization pushing wages above the market-clearing level.

As a consequence of a "too"-high differential between urban and rural wages, too many migrants continue to be attracted to urban areas relative to the number of urban, industrial jobs available in the formal sector. As a consequence, many migrants are forced into informal sector employment in low-productivity, low-income jobs: domestics, street vendors, beggars, jugglers, newspaper vendors, day laborers, and so on.

Further, urban slums emerge and grow, as the urban formal sector wage wedge relative to agricultural wages continues to draw migrants hoping to find formal sector employment. Thus the disguised unemployment or underemployment of some rural migrants becomes open unemployment, or the disguised underemployment of the urban informal sector.

Sources: Fei and Ranis 1964; Harris and Todaro 1970

Utilizing the economic surplus

Although Lewis is best known for his article on unlimited supplies of labor, he later took a somewhat different approach to the development problem. He felt that more attention should be paid to the inordinately high level of consumption as a share of total income in the less-developed regions. Much of the income generated in less-developed countries was squandered in conspicuous consumption, and not just by capitalists, who were too small in number to have much of an impact and who, in any case, were presumed to save and invest much of their income in pursuit of future profit. Rather, it was residual classes, like landowners and plantation barons, as well as new groups such as financial manipulators and a political elite who were skimming off part of aggregate income that could have been used for investment, who engaged in superfluous consumption (Lewis 1976: 257).

In order to reduce this waste, Lewis advocated raising the tax burden on the top 10, or perhaps the top 20 percent of income recipients to the point that government would receive 20 percent of national income. The state, in turn, would devote roughly 60 percent of those revenues, or 12 percent of national income, to basic public services, such as schools, hospitals, social security, and so on, and 40 percent of tax revenues (8 percent of national income) to public capital formation or social overhead capital. Thus, the mature version of the Lewis model should include *two* forms of investment that would be promoted: private-sector investment in manufacturing and industry deriving from the private capitalist, and public investment in social overhead capital, such as roads, communications systems, energy, and so on, deriving from government decisions as to priorities. Of the two, Lewis felt that the role to be played by the state in taxing the unproductive elite and allocating national income to socially productive purposes to be far more important in future.

By 1984, Lewis had determined that political and economic matters could not be separated. Development was as much a matter of "getting public policy right," as of providing a constructive environment for the private sector, a view with a strong Keynesian resonance. Achieving development, Lewis seemed to say, was as much a question of political will as it was of finding the technical means. Sir Arthur continued to advocate a large increase in savings and investment, but he also emphasized that the only way to achieve this was to reduce the unproductive and wasteful consumption levels at the top of the income pyramid, especially of unproductive classes who continued to control significant economic and political resources.

> Nowadays in most underdeveloped countries people know what economic growth requires; the difficulty is to make available the quarter of the national income which it costs. Personal consumption which should only be 75 per cent of the national income is nearer 85 per cent, leaving for the public services and for capital formation together only about 15 per cent instead of the 25 per cent they need.
>
> (Lewis 1984: 256)

The legacy of the Lewis model

The Lewis model has continued to have an important influence in development economics (we shall use it again in Chapter 9). Subject as it was to a great deal of critical scrutiny, it is not surprising that many objections were raised. Most telling were two. First, the model ignored institutional factors which influence the level of wage determination in the industrial sector. Governmental labor standards, including minimum wages, and unions are absent from the model. In fact, many less-developed nations have introduced relatively advanced labor legislation, and unions often have been able to negotiate a wage far above that determined by the free play of market forces.

Many of these institutional factors were introduced by, or were a reaction to, foreign multinational firms in mining and agriculture. These firms could easily afford the increase in their costs which would improve working conditions. However, via "target bargaining," such improved conditions can quickly become the bargaining norm for unions and workers in other industrial sectors not linked to the multinationals. The end result often has been to ratchet up wages for those workers in the industrial sector who have permanent jobs (i.e. who are not hired on a day-by-day or per-job basis). Thus rather than a constant industrial wage with some premium above the agricultural wage, industrial workers in some countries have been able to achieve substantial increases in wages, thereby eroding the potential comparative advantage in wage costs and undercutting Lewis projections for economic development by reducing the absorptive capacity of the industrial sector.

A second major objection concerned the socially virtuous behavior which Lewis assumed the capitalist strata would engage in, that is, the continued reinvestment of earnings in new production. Some have argued that the native capitalist strata may short-circuit the growth process through capital flight, rather than plowing profits back into production; of course that possibility certainly exists. Lewis assumed that capitalists would have a high propensity to reinvest and that their earnings would not leak out of the country via capital flight or via the conspicuous consumption of luxury imports. Whether capital flight or reinvestment take place, however, is not something that can be assumed. Governments interested in promoting economic and social development can help to create an internal economic environment attractive to domestic investors, particularly by keeping the inflation rate relatively low and stable. There are other aspects of the internal balance that are important, but there is no guarantee that capitalist profits will be reinvested, especially in an increasingly global capitalist economy.

There can be no question that capital flight played a major role in many less-developed nations in the 1980s, often contributing to an external debt crisis. However, to criticize the Lewis model in this context would appear to be inappropriate, for two reasons. First, Lewis's model was developed in the early 1950s, when international currency and financial markets were in a shambles, and most nations maintained strict currency controls. Second, given Lewis's strong advocacy of governmental intervention in order to tap the economic surplus of high income recipients, it is doubtful that Lewis would oppose the reinstitution of currency controls to block capital flight. Nations, such as Brazil, that imposed currency controls in the 1980s suffered relatively little capital flight.

Stages of growth theory

The last developmentalist theory to be examined in this chapter is Walt Whitman Rostow's stages of growth analysis (1960). Rostow's writing on the economics of what he called the "take-off" into sustained growth quickly became influential, in large part because of his remarkable ability to use metaphors, such as that of the take-off, and his deft compaction of European economic history. Like Marx before him, Rostow sought a *universal* interpretation of history, and this he provided in his stage model. He argued that all nations pass through five phases: the traditional society, the preconditions for take-off, the take-off, the drive to maturity, and the age of mass consumption. Rostow built his theoretical analysis upon the history of Britain, as had Marx. In doing so, he utilized a framework that most economists and other social scientists knew quite well. The plausibility of his argument seemed to many to be well-anchored in historical dynamics, both because it seemed to fit quite well the British experience, which had long been the basis for countless generalizations in economics, and because many economists did not have a ready grasp of the economic history of the less-developed regions. Thus, the model projected by Rostow seemed to generally conform to what many economists knew, or at least believed, to be true.

Stage 1: traditional society

In defining his first stage of historical and economic development, Rostow was rather vague. He likened traditional society to that of medieval Europe, and more broadly to any society that was pre-Newtonian. That is, traditional society was pre-scientific. Scientific progress might occur from time to time, but there was no *systematic* mechanism which led to the introduction of scientific knowledge into the production process on a continual basis. Traditional society was dominated by a perspective which Rostow defined as "long-term fatalism." According to his formulation, traditional society was predominantly agricultural, with landholders playing a dominant role in the determination of political and economic power.

Although Rostow attempted to demonstrate a general theory of historical stages, it would seem his sketch of traditional society best fits Europe prior to the sixteenth century, during its feudal period. He made virtually no effort to extend his analysis to the Third World. Were these vast regions, from 1500 to 1800, similar in any meaningful way to Europe, *circa* 1400? Certainly the information surveyed in Chapter 3 on colonialism demonstrates that this vast region was not traditional or unchanging – on the contrary, the changes imposed by colonialism were revolutionary. Rostow neglected to forge the link between traditional (European) society and the societies in the Third World – because none exists.

Stage 2: the preconditions for take-off

After his brief sketch of traditional society, Rostow moved forward to the second stage, the preconditions for take-off. Here, under one stage category, we find two processes at work: the beginnings of a sweeping destruction of traditional society, and the gathering of societal forces which will propel it forward into the subsequent take-off stage. But in his emphasis on the destruction of traditional society, usually through an outside source, probably colonialism according to Rostow, he blurred the line between a nation which becomes colonized and the colonizing nation itself. The presumption is that both colonizer and colonized are swept forward through this stage, both benefiting from events which stimulate development. But, in the case of the colonized nations, Rostow fails to entertain the likelihood that the process of destruction will be so thorough that the colonized society will be set on a path that does not lead to take-off, but to stagnation.

Thus the processes of both entering and leaving a major transformational epoch are commingled in the same stage, without a detailed analysis as to how these two processes unfold. Rather than doing so, Rostow presents a shopping list of changes which he expects to arise during this stage, without much apparent regard to either causality or sequence. He states that new types of entrepreneurs and managers will appear in the private and public sectors, banks will appear and investment will increase, particularly in infrastructure. Modern businesses will be created which will make use of new and sophisticated methods of production. As this process unfolds in the colonial or post-colonial regions, "reactive nationalism" sets the less-developed region on a new course, the drive for modernization (see Focus 5.4).

Stage 3: the take-off into sustained growth

Our brief review of Latin America in the nineteenth century in Focus 5.4 suggests that neither the role of "reactive nationalism" nor the existence of the profit motive appeared to be sufficient conditions to launch Latin America into its take-off stage. Rostow does not explain the movement from one stage to the next, and since he does not provide his reader with an interpretation of the nineteenth-century economic history of Latin America that would support his views, the Rostovian framework may be less universal than Rostow had hoped. Nonetheless, given the importance of Rostow's work in the field of development economics, it is useful

FOCUS 5.4 TESTING ROSTOW'S CONCEPT OF REACTIVE NATIONALISM: THE CASE OF LATIN AMERICA AFTER INDEPENDENCE

In attempting to test Rostow's hypotheses regarding the preconditions stage, the situation in Latin America in the early nineteenth century would appear to be an important case. Here we find, however, that the breaking of the colonial bonds did not lead to a full rupture with the past. Factions within the new nationalist elite fought among themselves for political control for another half-century, and then split into independent nations that mirrored the separated colonial vice-royalties that had kept the colonies divided from each other prior to independence. Moreover, the new nationalist elite classes were not interested in, or were not capable of, transforming their newly independent countries along the path that had been followed in Europe and the United States, that is, following a dynamic capitalist and industrial revolution. Rather, the goals of these new elite classes were relatively limited. They wished to gain the class privileges Spanish colonial policy had for so long reserved exclusively for pure-blooded European immigrants. Such a backward-looking elite was content to continue the pattern of exporting primary commodities begun under Spanish rule. This new dominant class of large landowners, merchants, and politicians was certain to enrich itself through the expansion of such exports.

As we have noted in Chapter 3, throughout nearly the entire nineteenth century, raw material prices soared and the terms of trade moved, perhaps fortuitously, in favor of such products. Trade with the advanced industrial nations permitted the nationalist leaders to import the manufactured luxury goods to which they aspired as emblems of their social status. With easy access to vast reaches of land, much of it expropriated from the Catholic Church and native Indians, the new nationalist elite was able to prosper by producing in the same technologically backward manner while utilizing more land, that is, using *extensive* forms of production.

Thus the Latin American elite bypassed one of the prime defining characteristics of the Rostovian second, preconditions, stage; they were not forced to utilize the latest technological advances in an effort to make each unit of land more productive, that is, they did not pursue *intensive* production methods. Contrary to Rostow, there was an obvious lag in the development of Latin America's essential infrastructure, such as banks, communications systems, and roads. And this, in turn, tended to reinforce the lag in the modernization of the productive apparatus, that is, a delay in the introduction and use of machinery, equipment, knowledge, and managerial strategies in tropical agriculture, mining, farming and ranching, let alone in industry. It was in the period after 1870 that Latin America's pernicious pattern of limited export diversity was consolidated. In some countries this was manifested by mono-export production.

Source: Dietz 1995: Chapter 1

to briefly analyze what he considers to be the key stage in the development process: the take-off. This stage is defined as emerging under the following simultaneous conditions:

(1) a rise in the rate of productive investment from, say, 5 percent or less to over 10 percent of national income; (2) the development of one or more substantial manufacturing sectors with a high rate of growth; [and] (3) the existence or quick emergence of a political, social and institutional framework which exploits the impulses to expansion.

(Rostow 1960: 39)

Furthermore, Rostow states that there must be a sweeping reallocation of resources devoted now to:

building up and modernizing the three non-industrial sectors required as the matrix for industrial growth: social overhead capital; agriculture and foreign-exchange earning sectors, rooted in the improved exploitation of natural resources. In addition, they must begin to find areas where the application of modern techniques is likely to permit rapid growth rates, with a high rate of plow-back of profits.

(Ibid.: 193)

The take-off is to occur in the space of roughly twenty to twenty-five years. According to Rostow's dating, India began its "take-off" in 1952. Thus India, with a per capita income in 2000 of only $460, ranked thirty-sixth in terms of the poorest countries in the world, should in fact have had by then a relatively strong economy. Yet in the period 1980–91, decades past the presumed take-off stage, India's per capita growth rate was a disappointing 0.7 percent per year (per capita growth rose to an impressive 4.2 percent per year in the 1990s). Following the take-off, growth at rates well above the population growth rate was expected to be the normal condition. The take-off into sustained growth had faltered in India, apparently – an event that the stage model cannot even consider.

Critical responses to the concept of the take-off

As intuitively appealing as Rostow's list of conditions for take-off may be, it is disconcerting to note that a number of development economists who have reviewed the historical record have found that the concept does not accord with the history of most of the nations which have purportedly moved beyond take-off into "self-sustained growth." For example, Albert Fishlow argues that, in the now advanced nations, there was no major abrupt jump in either the rate of investment or the rate of growth of output for most nations (stage 3 above). Rather, there was a gradual speed-up in the rate of investment and growth in most countries, and a sharp rise in investment and growth in only some (Fishlow 1976: 84–5). Simon Kuznets also argued (1971a) that a review of the economic history of the now-developed nations showed no sudden significant rise in the rate of savings during what might be considered their take-off stage. Kuznets further pointed out that when the now-developed nations moved into the take-off stage, they did so at per capita income levels much higher than those prevailing in the less-developed world currently (Kuznets 1971b: 224).

Gerald Meier elaborated on this point by concentrating his analysis on the agricultural sector. He drew a contrast between the robust agricultural sector of the nations which went through a take-off in the eighteenth, nineteenth, and early twentieth centuries, such as Britain, France, Germany, the United States, Canada, and Australia, with the weak agricultural sectors generally prevailing in the less-developed regions.

It is fairly conclusive that productivity is lower in the agricultural sector of underdeveloped countries than it was in the pre-industrialization phase of the presently developed countries. Although direct evidence of this is unavailable, it is indirectly confirmed by data suggesting that the supply of agricultural land per capita is much lower in most underdeveloped countries today than it was in presently developed countries during their take-off, and that there is a wider difference between per worker income in agriculture and nonagricultural sectors in the underdeveloped countries today than there was in the preindustrial phase of presently developed countries.

(Meier 1976: 95)

Meier pointed to another important difference between the conditions prevailing in the present-day less-developed regions compared to those that prevailed when the now-developed nations entered into their initial period of rapid development: population pressures were relatively moderate in the past, whereas today an annual population rate of growth of 1.5–3 percent necessitates a much higher level of investment in order to move the economy forward fast enough just to keep per capita income constant. That is, what would have been considered a remarkably fast rate of aggregate economic growth during Britain's industrial revolution, 3 percent per year, is often the minimum rate of aggregate growth that must be attained in many less-developed nations today in order simply to maintain the existing, low standard of living per capita.

Furthermore, migration played a tremendous role in the economic performance of the now advanced nations during their early industrial period. For some nations, like the United States, Canada, and Australia, the influx of trained, ambitious young immigrants was a clear economic boon. At the same time, the out-migration of young workers from Europe tended to eliminate both potential unemployment and social problems that might have arisen from structural unemployment. Lacking surpluses of labor, many of the now-developed nations had a strong incentive to adapt new machinery and equipment which would dynamize the productive process.

Criticisms of the take-off have continued to be published. Nicholas Crafts' research confirmed the analysis of Fishlow and Kuznets. On the basis of more recent work, he suggests that we "discard Rostow's linear model":

> Rostow's notion of the takeoff seems to be completely discredited. GDP growth [in Britain 1780–1830] exhibited at steady acceleration over perhaps half a century ... and there is no sign of the rapid doubling of the investment rate postulated by Rostow. The notion of a leading sector has also fared badly.
>
> (Crafts 2001: 312)

Stages 4 and 5: maturity and high mass consumption

Rostow's last two stages, maturity and high mass consumption, are defined sequentially as:

* a period wherein growth is sufficiently high so that there is significant increase in per capita income. The economy becomes diversified and technologically sophisticated, such that the society can now produce anything, but not everything, it chooses;
* a subsequent period where production is largely for the purpose of consumption, with relatively little concern for the need to further build production capabilities. Society is now devoted to the pleasures of consumer choice, the pursuit of security, and the enjoyments of the arts and leisure.

Rostow's legacy

In spite of the fact that it has been his fate to serve as a lightning-rod for criticisms from virtually all schools of thought in development economics, Rostow clearly made a powerful contribution. He forced other economists to review the experiences of the now-developed nations and to demonstrate the tremendous gulf that exists between the historical conditions which gave rise to the developmental success stories of the eighteenth, nineteenth, and twentieth centuries and the experiences with patterns of distorted development, stagnation, and economic decay that prevail in the less-developed world today. Rostow also opened the debate to another question in development economics. Did colonialism lead to the entrenchment of backward socio-economic forces and processes in less-developed nations which could not be displaced easily once political independence was achieved? A full exploration of this matter will be left for the following chapter, where we will review the work of a number of analysts who clearly argue that Rostow's main analytical error was to be found in his failure to incorporate the retarding and inhibiting forces of colonialism into his model.

While today little remains of Rostow's analysis which is of general use in the field of development economics, Rostow was clearly a pioneer in opening up new areas for study, debate, and analysis. Without his "big-picture" approach, many major issues might not have received a critical airing. Furthermore, Rostow's willingness to express his ideas within the difficult terrain of political economy forced those who would refute him to consider a broad range of factors at the analytical points of intersection of historical dynamics, political processes, and economic forces.

Questions and exercises

1   Contrast Nurkse's "export pessimism" with Lewis's views on development. In what respects do their apparently contrasting views on exports actually coincide, and where do differences remain?

2   In what sense would you argue that the economists discussed in this chapter formed a school of thought? What ideas did they tend to share?

3   How can a fair test of Rostow's stages model be formulated? Analyze the history of a specific economy to see if such a test can be made.

4   Why and how did Hirschman argue that by putting things the wrong way around, by actually creating disequilibrium, economic development could be promoted?

5   Why might unbalanced growth be easier, and less costly, for a poor economy to follow than a balanced growth strategy?

6   Briefly explain the ideas of virtuous circles. Can you give two different examples of virtuous circles that might affect a less-developed economy? Summarize the various forms of positive external effects and virtuous hidden effects which Rosenstein-Rodan utilized to argue that development could be achieved quicker than one might expect. Can you speculate on what a "vicious circle" might be?

7   What did Lewis mean when he wrote that there was a surplus of labor in agriculture? How does one measure that surplus? To what standard is labor in surplus, that is, in surplus relative to what?

Notes

1   Rosenstein-Rodan became an influential policy-maker after the war. He held a top-level post within the World Bank from 1947 until 1953, and from 1962 to 1966 he served on a key directive committee of the United States-sponsored development programme for Latin America, known as the Alliance for Progress.

2   This is the situation of increasing returns to successive inputs of investment, so that if investment increases by x per cent, output rises by more than x percent. For an aggregate production function of the form $Q = f(K, L)$, where Q is total output, K is capital and L is labor, this means that both $f_K, f_L > 0$, but also that $f_{KK}, f_{LL} > 0$, that is, diminishing returns to the inputs to production have not yet been reached. If one draws the aggregate production function, it will have both a positive and increasing

slope. Interestingly, the possibility of increasing returns, which seems to go against the grain of so much of both classical and neoclassical economic thinking and the law of eventually diminishing marginal return, is one of the pillars of the new, endogenous theories of growth considered in Chapter 8 that have become increasingly influential since the late 1980s.

3 Rosenstein-Rodan's argument illustrates an important example of a larger phenomenon in economics, called **market failure**. Whenever there is a divergence between private and social benefits, as in this instance, and/or private and social costs, an unfettered market economy may fail to produce the socially optimal level of output. What is desirable is to have the marginal social benefits of any action equal to the marginal social costs, but private calculations of benefits and costs may, and often do, differ from the social values. Basically, Rosenstein-Rodan was arguing that the inability of any single private entrepreneur to appropriate all the social benefits – in this case profits – of an action will result in an under-estimation of the total value of any private action. One entrepreneur's private investment decision, such as that of the steel firm, creates positive externalities that accrue to other potential entrepreneurs, such as the metallurgy industry, and/or society in the form of increased opportunities, higher demand, and lower costs that resulted from the decision of another. Government intervention may be required in such circumstances, particularly when many persons or firms are involved, if the social and private benefits and costs are to be equated, and if the optimal and socially desirable level of output is to be reached.

4 The term "indivisibilities" was another of Rosenstein-Rodan's favorites. Unlike neoclassical economic analysis, which assumes that capital can be combined with labor in precisely optimal amounts on the assumption that there is an infinitely divisible set of combinations of capital and labor available, the concept of indivisibility is intended to illustrate production situations where fixed, minimum amounts of capital (or labor) are necessary. A little less, and the product cannot be produced. For example, in building a steel bridge, one cannot simply and infinitely substitute labor for capital inputs and still produce the bridge; obviously labor cannot completely substitute for capital and other inputs, like steel or bolts. The bridge will be engineered in such a way that a specific amount of structural steel will be needed; an amount somewhat less and there will be no bridge at all. Likewise in oil drilling, the drilling company either buys *all* of a drilling rig, or none. It is not a divisible item. In general, social overhead capital tends to be of this nature. Often Rosenstein-Rodan referred to the "lumpiness" of capital in this context.

5 Of course, government-sponsored projects can lead to over-investment or under-investment in social overhead capital. The developmentalists did not naïvely believe that every action of government was *per se* justified. If government does not employ *transparent* methods whereby officials can be held accountable for their actions and their spending of public funds, then the government itself can become one of the primary sources of social inefficiency. Without an efficient government bureaucracy, the state itself often becomes an arena where individual fortunes are amassed through the manipulation of public funds. Unfortunately, in many less-developed nations the most promising avenue for upward social mobility lies within the governmental apparatus where accountability is nearly non-existent and corruption is rife. This barrier to progress is one we shall have occasion to comment on again later in discussing "economic rents" and the relative economic success of the East Asian nations in recent decades.

6 This theme of "surplus" labor in agriculture is one that recurs again and again in the development literature. One of the leading theories of development, that of Sir Arthur Lewis, considered below, makes this basic assumption central to the structural transformation required for economic development.

7 Nurkse is best known for his book *Problems of Capital Formation in Underdeveloped Countries* (1953). His remarkable essay "Patterns of Trade and Development" (Nurkse 1962), which constituted an attack on the idea of trade as the "engine of growth," was finished only a month prior to his untimely death in 1959.

8 This adverse effect of a lower price and greater quantity will occur, assuming demand to be constant, as supply increases if the demand for the good is price inelastic. In such cases, the larger quantity of export sales will be insufficient to compensate for the lower price, and hence total export revenues will decline.

9 The **propensity to import** is technically defined from the statement, $M = mY$, where M is the value of imports purchased, Y is national income (GNP or GDP), and, m, which has a value $0 < m < 1$, is the "marginal propensity to import," that is, it is the proportion of income that society chooses to spend on imported goods and services. This proportion depends upon the level of average income, the income distribution of society, and social and cultural factors.

10 In modern economic analysis, such consumption items are referred to as **positional goods**.

11 It is not sufficient to simply produce more to have economic growth; if the increase in output is to be sustainable, it must find a market and be sold, or capitalist enterprises will stop producing.

12 This is simply an extension of the insight that was formalized early in the 1920s in the Heckscher-Ohlin theory of trade, which suggested that countries with an abundance of one factor of production over another, would, with free trade, tend to export those goods using the abundant, that is, relatively cheaper, input because that is where their comparative advantage would exist *vis-à-vis* other nations. Thus less-developed economies, with their abundant labor and scarce capital, could be expected to export those goods, be they agricultural or industrial, that were labor-intensive in their production and, by the Stolper-Samuelson theorem of international trade, this would be expected, over time, to lead to the equalization of income for the different factors of production within and among nations, assuming free mobility of capital and labor and perfect competition.

13 In effect, as labor left agriculture, the supply of agricultural output might be expected to decrease as the quantity of labor, L, in agriculture falls, while the demand for agricultural goods would, at best, stay the same, and might even be expected to rise if workers in industry have rising incomes. Thus, from simple supply and demand analysis, if the supply of agricultural output decreases (the supply curve shifts inward), while the demand rises (an outward shift), the equilibrium price of agricultural products must increase, given the assumptions.

14 In effect, what if the marginal product of labor, MP_L, in agriculture, at the current level of labor usage, is such that $MP_L \leq 0$? In such a case, extracting L from agriculture will not reduce agricultural output, if $MP_L = 0$, and will result in an increase in agricultural output if $MP_L < 0$. As long as the MP_L in manufacturing $> MP_L$ in agriculture, a shift of labor from agriculture to manufacturing will increase aggregate output.

15 In this instance, given w_A, which can be interpreted as the subsistence wage, the optimal quantity of labor to be employed in agriculture would be L_O, which is clearly less than L_A, the actual level of employment with the household calculation of labor usage in which income is shared and average income is distributed among family members.

16 Such an outcome in the transition from a surplus labor economy might be one explanation for the Kuznets inverted-U hypothesis considered in Chapter 2, which also prognosticated a worsening of income distribution with economic growth, up to a threshold level of per capita income, after which the income distribution might be expected to improve.

17 Two very important theoretical models related to the Lewis model are the Fei-Ranis and the Todaro models. These are briefly explained in Focus 5.3.

References

Crafts, Nicholas. 2001. "Historical Perspectives on Development," pp. 301–34 in Gerald Meier and Joseph Stiglitz (eds.), *Frontiers of Development Economics*. Oxford: Oxford University Press

Crevoshay, Fay. 1994. "Complejos, Confusiones y Autoritarismo, Barreras para la Aplicación de la Calidad Total en México," *El Financiero* (21 abril): 11.

Dietz, James L. (ed.). 1995. *Latin America's Economic Development*, 2nd edn. London and Boulder, CO: Lynne Rienner Publishers.

Fei, John C.H. and Gustav Ranis. 1964. *Development of the Labour Surplus Economy*. New Haven, CT: Yale University Press.

Fishlow, Albert. 1976. "Empty Economic Stages?," pp. 82–9 in Gerald Meier (ed.), *Leading Issues in Economic Development*, 3rd edn. Oxford: Oxford University Press.

Harris, J.R. and M.P. Todaro. 1970. "Migration, Unemployment, and Development: A Two-Sector Analysis," *American Economic Review* 60 (March): 126–42.

Hirschman, Albert O. 1958. *The Strategy of Economic Development*. New Haven, CT: Yale University Press.

——. 1984. "A Dissenter's Confession," pp. 87–111 in Gerald Meier and Dudley Seers (eds.), *Pioneers in Development*. Oxford: Oxford University Press.

Hoff, Karla and Joseph Stiglitz. 2001. "Modern Economic Theory and Development," pp. 389–459 in Gerald Meier and Joseph Stiglitz (eds.), *Frontiers of Development Economics*. Oxford: Oxford University Press.

Kuznets, Simon. 1971a. *Economic Growth of Nations*. Cambridge, MA: Harvard University Press.

——. 1971b. "Notes on Stage of Economic Growth as a System Determinant," pp. 243–68 in Alexander Eckstein (ed.), *Comparison of Economic Systems*. Berkeley, CA: University of California Press.

Lewis, W.A. 1954. "Economic Development with Unlimited Supplies of Labour," *Manchester School of Economic and Social Studies* 22 (May): 139–91.

——. 1969. *Aspects of Tropical Trade*. Stockholm: Almqvist and Wiksell.

——. 1976. "The Cost of Capital Accumulation," pp. 256–7 in Gerald Meier (ed.), *Leading Issues in Economic Development*, 3rd edn. Oxford: Oxford University Press.

——. 1984. "Development Economics in the 1950s," pp. 121–37 in Gerald Meier (ed.), *Pioneers in Development*. Oxford: Oxford University Press.

Meier, Gerald. 1976. "Future Development in Historical Perspective," pp. 93–9 in Gerald Meier (ed.), *Leading Issues in Economic Development*, 3rd edn. Oxford: Oxford University Press.

Murphy, Kevin, Andrei Shleifer and Robert Vishny. 1989. "Industrialization and the Big Push," *Journal of Political Economy* 97 (October): 1003–26.

Nurkse, Ragnar. 1953. *Problems of Capital Formation in Underdeveloped Countries*. New York: Oxford University Press.

——. 1962. "Patterns of Trade and Development," pp. 282–336 in Gottfried Haberler and Robert Stern (eds.), *Equilibrium and Growth in the World Economy*. Cambridge, MA: Harvard University Press.

Robinson, Joan. 1966. *Economic Philosophy*. Harmondsworth: Penguin.

Rosenstein-Rodan, Paul. 1976. "The Theory of the 'Big Push'," pp. 632–6 in Gerald Meier (ed.), *Leading Issues in Economic Development*, 3rd edn. Oxford: Oxford University Press.

——. 1984. "Natura Facit Saltum," pp. 207–21 in Gerald Meier and Dudley Seers (eds.), *Pioneers in Development*. Oxford: Oxford University Press.

Rostow, Walt. 1960. *The Stages of Economic Growth: A Non-Communist Manifesto*. Cambridge: Cambridge University Press.

——. 1984. "Development: The Political Economy of the Marshallian Long Period," pp. 229–61 in Gerald Meier and Dudley Seers (eds.), *Pioneers in Development*. Oxford: Oxford University Press.

Toye, John. 2004. *The UN and Global Political Economy*. Bloomington, IN: Indiana University Press.

6 Heterodox theories of economic development

After reading and studying this chapter, you should better understand:
- the importance of the distinction between the center and the periphery in structuralist theory;
- the Prebisch-Singer hypothesis on declining terms of trade for primary product exporters and the debate surrounding it;
- the role of import substitution industrialization (ISI) according to the ECLA economists and their subsequent critique of this policy;
- Ayres's concept of inhibiting institutions and the importance of education and technology to the institutionalist perspective;
- Gunnar Myrdal's seminal ideas about spread effects and backwash effects as examples of cumulative causation;
- the distinction between associated dependent development and the dependency perspective of underdevelopment;
- Furtado's structuralist perspective on dependency;
- Baran's view of the equilibrium trap of underdevelopment;
- the distinction between stagnationist dependency analysis and the classical progressive Marxist view of development as presented by Bill Warren.

Introduction

This chapter discusses and analyses the ideas of economists and social scientists who have broken with economic orthodoxy and moved beyond the framework of the developmentalist economists considered in the previous chapter. These heterodox economists do not believe that relatively minor changes in economic conditions, such as an increase in foreign aid or a sudden increase in investment, will be sufficient to create the "big push" or the "take-off" into sustained growth, as did the developmentalists. In fact, many of the heterodox economists would argue that such limited changes, within the context of the existing structures and institutions prevailing in less-developed societies, might result in a strengthening of backward socio-economic frameworks, consolidating adverse path dependence. For the heterodox economists, the changes required to propel the development process forward are more fundamental, more sweeping, and more profound.

Included among the heterodox grouping are a number of thinkers who hold no more in common than the fact that they vigorously dissented from the general premises and propositions of the developmentalist economists, and of orthodox economists, as well. In this chapter, then, we will trace the ideas of the Latin American structuralists, represented by Raúl Prebisch and Hans Singer; the institutionalists, represented by Clarence Ayres and Gunnar Myrdal; the dependency school, represented by Paul Baran and Fernando Henrique Cardoso; and the classical Marxist approach in its more modern form, represented by Bill Warren.

The heterodox thinkers reached their maximum point of influence within the field of development economics in the late 1960s and early 1970s.[1] Indeed, the impact of some of their views was so profound that their ideas exerted some indirect impact on the leading development institutions, most notably the World Bank. In the 1970s, these institutions embraced the basic needs (BN) approach, which is discussed in Chapter 17. As we shall see, the heterodox thinkers had much more ambitious hopes for change than those embodied in the limited goals of the basic needs approach.[2]

The Latin American structuralists

In 1948, as the result of a Chilean initiative, the UN agreed to form the Economic Commission for Latin America, known best by its acronym, ECLA. Unlike the UN's more technically oriented Economic Commission for Asia and the Far East, created in 1947, or the Economic Commission for Africa (1958), the ECLA was destined to become a center of advocacy for a distinct Third World perspective and a hotbed of controversy. It was in and around the work of ECLA that a Latin American school of structuralist economics was forged. The structuralists argued that the less-developed countries of the periphery were structurally and institutionally different from the developed nations of the center in ways that made some aspects of both orthodox economic theory and developmentalist theory inapplicable. In particular, the Latin American structuralists were quite suspicious of the Ricardian theory of comparative advantage and the alleged benefits of free trade among nations that supposedly derive from specialization and trade.

In introducing the possibility of conflictive or adversarial relations in trade, the Latin American structuralists challenged the "harmony of interests" assumption in market transactions that had been a cornerstone of economic thinking since Adam Smith (see Chapter 4). As Gabriel Palma explains, structuralism is concerned with the *totality* of a social system and the many forms of interaction of the component elements within that system.

> The principal characteristic of structuralism is that it takes as its object of investigation a "system", that is, the reciprocal relations among parts of a whole, rather than the study of the different parts in isolation. In a more specific sense this concept is used by those theories that hold that there are a set of social and economic structures that are unobservable but which generate observable social and economic phenomena.
>
> (Palma 1989: 316)

The structuralism of Raúl Prebisch

Perhaps the best-known Latin American structuralist economist was Raúl Prebisch (1901–86). As a young man finishing his MA degree in economics at the University of Buenos Aires, he had already published six articles on economics, and his views and analysis were impeccably mainstream, orthodox, and neoclassical. During Prebisch's formative years, at least to the early 1920s, Argentina seemed to symbolize an outstanding example of the validity of the theory of comparative advantage, with producers having a cost advantage in producing beef and wheat for the world market. From the 1860s through to the second decade of the twentieth century, the Argentine economy grew at a rate that can only be described as spectacular, and the country's standard of living rivalled that of the great European powers. It certainly seemed that specializing in the export of a limited range of primary products to the world market was successfully contributing to the overall development of the country.

In the 1920s, Argentina began to experience difficulties with its primary trade partner, Britain, as the prices for its main exports began to fall. As the country incurred a growing foreign debt burden, trained observers, including Prebisch, viewed Argentina's troubles as transitory. By the 1930s, however, Argentina faced both the adverse effects of the Great Depression and the growing dominance of the world economy by the United States. In the late nineteenth century Britain's thirst for Argentina's exports had seemed unquenchable; now Argentina had to confront the troubling reality that the United States had a relatively modest propensity to import, compared to Britain. Even worse, the United States had a surfeit of domestically produced beef and wheat and did not want or need Argentinian exports to the same degree that Britain had.[3]

Like most Argentinians who had experienced the favorable conditions of the late nineteenth and early twentieth century, Prebisch was extremely reluctant to revise his views on the Ricardian doctrine of comparative advantage (see Chapter 4). Nonetheless, he eventually did so, with consequences which were particularly far-reaching. Much of Prebisch's work on questions of development policy pivoted on his willingness to draw a distinction between the timeless constructs of neoclassical economic theory and what he saw as the dynamic effects of real economic forces, particularly those existing between the already-developed center nations, such as the European powers and the United States, and the less-developed **periphery nations** of Latin America, Asia, and Africa. Prebisch began to learn and grapple with the fact that behind the laws of demand and supply there often lurked power relations and quite dissimilar forms of production between nations.

In particular, Prebisch noted that during the Great Depression, the export prices of agricultural and other primary products fell much further and faster than did the prices of manufactured, or secondary, products. At that point, in 1934, Prebisch did not as yet have a theory as to *why* this asymmetry in the behavior of the export prices of primary and secondary products might be occurring, but he did begin to develop a critical perspective on neoclassical economic theory. According to Prebisch's calculations, in 1933, Argentina had to sell 73 percent more of its primary agricultural products into the world market in order to import the same amount of imported manufactured products as it had in the mid to late 1920s, as a result of the asymmetric behavior of world export prices.

By 1937, Prebisch and his colleagues at the Argentine central bank had begun to develop a theory which would explain the relative collapse of the agricultural markets. In manufacturing, they reasoned, the supply of output was relatively price elastic; thus as demand decreased (from D_0 to D_1), so did the quantity supplied. The equilibrium price would fall, of course, but in a somewhat more limited manner, depending on the value of the supply elasticity, as shown in Figure 6.1, along supply curve S_M. In the extreme case, as with supply curve S_E, which is perfectly elastic, the decrease in demand has no effect on price, but only on the quantity traded in the market.

On the other hand, in the agricultural markets, supply conditions are dramatically different; suppliers, many of whom were small farmers with limited land, tended to plant or grow as much as possible, year-in and year-out. Supply was therefore relatively price inelastic. When demand decreased, the quantity supplied did not fall by much, but prices quickly and dramatically decreased, as along supply curve S_A in Figure 6.1. In the extreme case, which

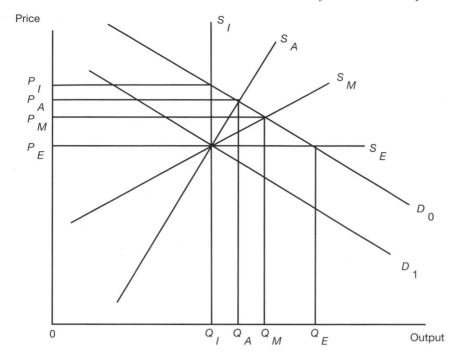

Figure 6.1 Elasticity of supply and equilibrium price adjustment.

might be somewhat more common in agriculture than in manufacturing, the momentary supply curve would be perfectly inelastic, as for supply curve S_I, and all the decrease in demand would be transmitted as a lower equilibrium price for the agricultural good.

What might account for these differences in the supply response of primary product prices and for manufacturing good prices? Prebisch's early explanation was somewhat vague. Industrial producers of manufacturing goods could control supply, at least to some degree, whereas in agriculture, producers had failed to organize their production and control their output. In 1933, Prebisch became active in the attempt to form an agreement among the major wheat-growing nations of Argentina, Australia, Canada, and the United States to try to stabilize the world market price. Unfortunately, all the participants had violated the terms of the agreement by late 1933. This experience undoubtedly helped form Prebisch's perspective on the meager possibilities of coordinated actions undertaken among nations with the goal of controlling global agricultural output. But, at this point in time, Prebisch's explanation for the differences in the supply behavior of primary agricultural products and secondary manufactured goods in the face of changes in demand was mostly incipient.

The terms of trade

In 1949 Prebisch joined ECLA, and in 1950 he was appointed its executive director. At ECLA, Prebisch made a major and lasting impact with his study *The Economic Development of Latin America and its Principal Problems* (Prebisch 1950). This study was largely made possible by a UN report entitled *Relative Prices of Exports and Imports of Underdeveloped Countries* (UN 1949), which provided an empirical basis for a thesis that soon would become associated with Prebisch: given the existing international division of labor, in which the developed center countries produced manufactured goods for export to the periphery and the less-developed peripheral countries produced primary products for export to the center, *all* the benefits of trade would accrue to the center and none to the periphery.

The periphery would have to produce more and more agricultural or raw material products simply to obtain the same quantity of imported manufactured products. Technically, this result was the outcome of a long-term deterioration of the terms of trade for the primary exporting peripheral countries.[4] Based on the years from the late nineteenth century to the late 1930s, the UN study had concluded that "On the average, a given quantity of primary exports would pay, at the end of this period, for only 60 per cent of the quantity of manufactured goods which it could buy at the beginning of the period" (UN 1949: 7), and it was this data Prebisch used in reaching his conclusion on the detrimental effect of the existing trade patterns on the periphery.

Prebisch was soon to be the target of a number of attacks by those who argued that the methodology of the UN study was flawed. Unfortunately, the study was flawed, particularly in the sense that the prices used were not really comparable. The study measured British manufactured exports in terms of "freight on board" (FOB) values, while British raw material imports were measured in terms of "cost including freight" (CIF) values. The prices of exports at FOB prices did not include shipping charges, while those of imports did. During the late nineteenth century, rail and steamship charges dropped rapidly thanks to improvements in technology. Thus, by capturing the price benefits of technological change on only one side of the equation, British imports of raw materials, and excluding such changes on the other side, British exports of manufactured goods, the method utilized by the UN biased the results.

Was the conclusion Prebisch reached therefore incorrect? Controversy has stirred over this matter for almost sixty years. Correcting for changes in both shipping costs and the changing quality of traded goods, studies conducted by J. Spraos have continued to support the basic hypothesis of Prebisch, as has research conducted by Prabijit Sarkar (Spraos 1983; Sarkar 1986). Spraos, for example, found that from 1950 to 1970, the terms of trade for primary products (in relation to manufactured products) decreased by 25 percent (Spraos 1980: 121–6). In a more recent study, D. Sapsford found a 1.2 percent decline per year in the net barter terms of trade (NBTT) from 1900 to 1982 (Sapsford 1985). Perhaps most startling is the recent confirmation of Prebisch's view by A. Maizels, T. Palaskas, and T. Crowe, who show a decline of the NBTT of roughly 4 percent per year from 1979 through 1993 (Maizels, Palaskas, and Crowe 1998: 74). Even the IMF found support for the Prebisch-Singer hypothesis (IMF 1994: 350–2, based on Borensztein *et al.* 1994); More generally, Sapsford and J. Chen demonstrate that since Prebisch's ECLA study *none of the ten major published empirical studies has refuted the Prebisch finding* – although two found no trend, perhaps on account of the time period under analysis (Sapsford and Chen 1998: 28–9). Recently, José Antonio Ocampo and María Angela Parra examined twenty-four studies published from 1985 to 2005. Only five found no significant trend, but this research *did reveal* long-term deterioration of the terms of trade: the remaining nineteen showed a significant negative trend (Ocampo and Parra 2007: 163–5). When we examine the contribution to this debate made by Hans Singer, below, we shall elaborate on the mechanisms by which such a deterioration in international purchasing power might be explained.

If Prebisch was correct in believing that the terms of trade would move against the developing nations, then a successful development program would, of necessity, force a nation to either:

- adopt a programme that emphasized *internal* changes which would restructure the peripheral economies more toward the domestic market and away from exports, or
- develop a new export strategy which would emphasize manufacturing and processing and other secondary production activities, rather than the export of raw materials, food-stuffs, and other primary products.

Abandoning raw materials exports, or de-emphasizing them, was viewed as a radical and theoretically unfounded step by the more orthodox within the economics profession, who continued to insist that it was in these goods that the less-developed nations had comparative advantage.[5]

Import substitution industrialization as a response to declining terms of trade

At ECLA, Prebisch became known as the chief advocate of the "development from within" approach, a strategy that is often associated with **import substitution industrialization**, or ISI.[6] With ISI, a country begins to manufacture the simple, consumer non-durable goods that are being imported. As we shall examine in more detail in Chapter 9, this stage of industrialization involves relatively simple production and does not require either large physical or financial capital outlays or the use of sophisticated technology. If, in fact, the terms of trade were tending to shift against the periphery because of the structure of export production, an argument could be made for industrializing the peripheral economy so that it became more like the center nations in terms of its productive and export structure.[7]

Furthermore, even if the declining terms of trade argument proved to have no validity or was weaker than Prebisch had supposed, no one contested the fact that over the course of a normal business cycle, primary product prices tended to rise much faster during an expansion and to fall to a much greater degree during a contraction. Thus, there was a second argument for industrialization: greater overall economic stability could be maintained if the degree of industrialization were increased. Third, an industrial base might facilitate the transmission of technological advances from industry to agriculture – that is, a growing manufacturing base could create technological externalities in agriculture which would increase productivity and income.

The success of ISI required that governments restrict imports of goods that might compete with the new ISI industries through the imposition of effective tariff barriers. ISI also entailed an activist governmental policy in providing and allocating public expenditures to those areas where the highest rate of return could be anticipated. In Prebisch's words:

> The structural changes inherent in industrialization require rationality and foresight in government policy and investment in infrastructure to accelerate growth, to obtain the proper relation of industry with agriculture and other activities, and to reduce the external vulnerability of the economy. These [are] strong reasons for planning. … International financial resources [are] to complement and enhance a country's capacity to save, while changes in the structure of trade [are] necessary to use these savings for capital goods imports. Planning should help obtain these resources and accomplish the latter objective. Planning [is] compatible with the market and private initiative. It [is] needed to establish certain basic conditions for the adequate functioning of the market in the context of a dynamic economy. But it [does] not necessarily require state investment, except in infrastructure and development promotion.

(Prebisch 1984: 180)

Prebisch did have some reservations regarding ISI. First, in order to promote industrialization, it would be necessary to import a considerable amount of technology embedded in machinery and equipment, or to obtain it under licensing agreements. Thus a new drain on already scarce foreign exchange earnings would be created. Furthermore, some of this technology would be more capital-intensive than previous production methods, meaning that expansion in the industrial sector would absorb a relatively modest amount of labor unless the level of investment increased substantially. There was thus a danger of structural unemployment, as young workers entered the labor force and migrants from rural areas entered the cities in search of industrial jobs at a rate faster than they could be absorbed. Finally, the domestic market was too narrow to permit the most efficient use of imported machinery and equipment. The economies of scale to be anticipated from large-scale industry would be achieved only if equipment was utilized at its peak rate, and given the relatively low incomes of much of the population, the demand for industrial output would quite likely fall short of what was required to move to the most efficient level of production. In spite of such reservations, Prebisch maintained that the anticipated benefits of leaving the treadmill of the agro-mineral peripheral export economy clearly outweighed the costs of industrialization.

Prebisch's advocacy of ISI did not initiate such policies in Latin America. ISI had been adopted in a number of Latin American nations since the 1920s, and in some as far back as the 1890s. For the most part, these ISI programmes were extremely successful in their initial or "easy" stage in spurring growth in the Latin American economies. By the 1960s, however, the easy ISI stage had ended. As Prebisch moved on to head the UN Conference on Trade and Development (UNCTAD) in 1963, ECLA itself became the source of increasingly strident attacks on ISI, as the optimism for what such a strategy might achieve, which ECLA had projected in the early 1950s, disappeared. ECLA's structuralist critique of ECLA's ISI concluded that these policies had resulted in:

1   a failure to diversify exports and a continued reliance on one or a few raw materials or agricultural products for export;
2   a shortage of foreign exchange earnings;
3   an increase in foreign debt;
4   a weak domestic agricultural sector, leading to major food imports; and
5   increasing foreign ownership of the economy by transnational corporations, leading to a drain on scarce foreign exchange as profits were repatriated.

(Kay 1989: 39–46; Sunkel 1990: 137–9)

Thus ECLA, originally the crucible for initiatives which were based upon optimistic projections, became one source of critical analysis known as dependency theory. Dependency theory, to be discussed below, nearly inverted the early optimism of ECLA; development came to be viewed either as an impossible task, or one that demanded a major reorientation of the policies originally pursued by ECLA. We will argue in Chapter 10 that what was necessary was to go beyond ISI, something ECLA had promoted, but which governments in their policies failed to do, in Latin America at any rate. It was not so much ISI which had failed, but the deficiency of policy follow-up.

The contribution of Hans Singer to the terms of trade debate

Hans Singer (1911–2006), a German-born economist, received a PhD from the University of Cambridge in 1936, precisely during the period when J.M. Keynes's influence was reaching its zenith. In 1947 Singer, an ardent Keynesian, went to the United Nations as one of the first three economists to be employed in the newly created Economics Department. He remained there until 1969, when he became associated with the influential Institute for Development Studies at the University of Sussex in England.

Singer is perhaps best known for a widely cited research paper, the research of which preceded and provided the basis for Prebisch's theory of the tendency of the terms of trade to fall for the periphery (Toye 2004: 113). Thus, in development economics, the theory that the terms of trade tend to move against raw materials, agricultural and primary producers is known as the Prebisch-Singer (P-S) hypothesis.

The Prebisch-Singer hypothesis

Prebisch had analyzed the relations between nations at unequal levels of development using the spatial imagery of the center and periphery. In this perspective, the more advanced center countries tend to reap the gains from international trade and investment at the expense of the less-developed periphery. Indeed, trade relations between the center and periphery reinforce higher levels of development in the center countries, while maintaining a relatively lower level of development and poverty in the periphery. In Prebisch's and Singer's analysis, then, free trade can actually be harmful to the peripheral, less-developed nations. This view, of course, is in diametric opposition to the very basic orthodox economic contention, from the time of David Ricardo at least, that the pursuit of comparative advantage in international trade will benefit all participating nations and that, in time, income levels between different regions of the world should tend toward equality as a consequence of the equalizing tendencies set in motion by the movement of goods and factors of production with free trade.

The reasoning behind the Prebisch-Singer hypothesis, that the relations between the center and the periphery are antagonistic and detrimental, rather than complementary and harmonious, is derived from three bases. In essence, the existing economic, productive, and labor market structures of the center and the periphery are sufficiently different to the degree that engaging in trade can be detrimental to the periphery, for the following reasons.

The application of technology to traded goods, predominantly manufactured goods for the center and primary products from the periphery, has quite different consequences. The advanced center countries are dominated by oligopolistic industries with a substantial degree of control over the prices of their final products; in other words, they are "price-makers." Further, unions and widely accepted social convention dictate that rising worker productivity from technological change be rewarded with higher incomes. In the periphery, on the other hand, most primary products, that is, agricultural goods and many minerals, face substantial domestic and, especially, international competition in trade, so the supply price is difficult to control by individual producers, who are classic, competitive "price-takers." Labor, particularly unskilled labor, is generally in some degree of surplus in the periphery, and this puts downward pressure on wages. Unions and pro-labor social attitudes, particularly in the primary sector, are not as strong in the periphery, so the institutional mechanism present in the center for raising wages with increased productivity as a result of advances in technology is lacking.

Given these structural differences, the application of new, cost-saving technology in the center would contribute to greater worker productivity and hence higher wages. However, there would be little tendency for output prices to reflect falling unit costs, because of oligopolistic pricing by firms. Corporations would thus see their profits rise, as they shared with workers the fruits of technological progress in higher incomes. In the periphery, however, where something closer to the competitive "ideal" is common in many primary product lines, the introduction of new technology results in falling output prices, as the industry supply curve shifts out and downward with technological progress. Stagnant and perhaps even declining wages for workers are the result, given the labor surplus conditions characteristic of the rural sector and the lack of social mechanisms for demanding higher incomes with greater productivity.

Thus, according to the P-S hypothesis, the center nations gain doubly from new technology and trade with the periphery, while the periphery becomes worse off as a result of a deterioration in their terms of trade that results from the price movements on center exports and periphery exports. In effect, with the constant spread of new production technologies in the world economy, the P-S hypothesis predicts that the prices of what the periphery sells on the world market will decline, while the import prices of what the periphery purchases from the center remain about the same. Just the reverse is true for the center nations, which find their terms of trade, and hence the purchasing power of their exports, rising.

As a result, the center nations are able to buy the periphery's cheaper imported primary products with their own higher-profit manufacturing exports and with higher wages for workers, while the periphery nations find that new technology only forces the prices of their exports down on the world market, thus requiring more to be exported just to be able to purchase the same quantity of manufactured imports from the center. All the benefits of new technology, which is constantly advancing, thus accrue to the already-developed nations, as their incomes rise and the prices of what is imported from the periphery fall.

The center realizes all the benefits from trade over time; the periphery gains nothing. Any benefits from comparative advantage were realized long in the past in the first period of specialization, when a shift of production in the direction of the lowest relative opportunity cost (as discussed in Chapter 4) result in a one-time gain in world efficiency. Since that one-time gain, however, the P-S hypothesis argues that the declining terms of trade for the particular goods in which the periphery has specialized have made primary product specialization by those nations a source of impoverishment, rather than a means to increase income and welfare.

Embedded in this critique of trade is an obvious policy recommendation. To avoid declining terms of trade for its exports, the periphery should become more like the center, particularly through greater industrialization. With time, imports of manufactured goods would become less necessary. Basically, the escape from the Prebisch-Singer dilemma requires the periphery to follow a path of structural change similar to that traced by the center nations before them; as we shall see in Chapter 9, that is what import substitution industrialization as an initial strategy for development was at least partly about.

According to the P-S hypothesis, then, less-developed countries that continue to follow traditional comparative advantage by persisting with primary products exports will not benefit from trade, because of the tendency for their terms of trade to deteriorate. The theory of comparative advantage may provide a one-off boost to world production such that all countries gain, but over time, primary product exporters will not profit from staying with that static comparative advantage. Singer believed that he and Prebisch had been quite successful in alerting the developing countries to their dilemma, and that these countries had, in many instances, responded correctly by either diversifying their exports or developing their own internal markets via ISI policies. "We do not know what the data would have been without such action – the deterioration in terms of trade would presumably have been even sharper than it was" (Singer 1984: 283).

Additional factors contributing to declining terms of trade

Besides the tendency for the ever-changing impact of technology to result in declining terms of trade for the primary product, given the existing domestic and international structures of production and trade, Prebisch and Singer identified two additional forces at work in the world economy that tend to move in the same direction and which reinforced the Prebisch-Singer effect.

First, differences in the income elasticities of manufactured versus primary commodities, especially agricultural goods, work over time to the detriment of the periphery.[8] In essence, as world income grows, the demand for manufactured goods, which have an income elasticity > 1, rises faster than the demand for agricultural products, with an income elasticity that is positive, but < 1 (this is the essence of **Engel's Law**), thus contributing to the secular, or long-term, deterioration of the terms of trade for the periphery. The differences in income elasticities for the exports of the center and periphery simply reinforces the need for peripheral industrialization, as suggested by the P-S hypothesis, along with the need for international commodity agreements to stabilize primary product prices, and regional integration to expand existing markets and increase competitive pressures on firms.

The second contributing factor to declining terms of trade for many peripheral countries, and certainly those in Latin America, was the lower level of the import coefficient in the United States than in Great Britain, already mentioned. As the United States replaced Great Britain as the world's major economic power, it became more difficult for some countries to expand traditional exports to be able to earn the foreign exchange required to purchase the desired manufactured imports, again supporting the argument for expanded industrialization in the periphery.

There is by now a substantial body of research into the P-S hypothesis, evidence that generally supports the P-S prediction of the long-term evolution of primary product export

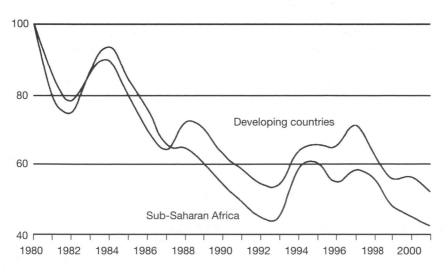

Figure 6.2 Declining real commodity prices: 1980–2001[a] (1980 = 100).

Source: World Bank Economic Policy and Prospects Group, World Bank, *Global Development Finance*, www.worldbank.org/prospects/gdf2002/.

Note
a   Excluding petroleum products.

prices and the deterioration of the terms of trade facing nations that specialize in the export of these commodities. Oil, of course, has been a partial exception to this tendency in some decades, and a limited number of other primary-based goods (e.g. tropical drinks) show a long-run tendency toward rising prices. And a few countries in the region, at least since the Second World War, have even had rising terms of trade over some periods, but the overall trend would seem to be downward for primary product exports (as shown in Figure 6.2).

Structural characteristics and the terms of trade

Singer has taken pains to clarify a point that neither he nor Prebisch had adequately emphasized in their early work; it may be more important to analyze the *structure* of a nation than it is to simply distinguish between the nature of exports. That is, economic structure may be a more important explanation of the direction of the terms of trade than whether a country is a raw materials or manufactured goods exporter.

> It will be noted that some of the ... explanations for a deteriorating trend in terms of trade of developing countries relate as much or more to the characteristics of different types of *countries* – their different level of technological capacity, different organization of labor markets, presence or absence of surplus labor, etc. – as to the characteristics of different *commodities*. This indicates a general shift in the terms of trade discussion away from primary commodities *versus* manufactures and more towards exports of developing countries – whether primary commodities or simpler manufactures – *versus* the export products of industrial countries – largely sophisticated manufactures and capital goods as well as skill-intensive services including technological know-how itself.
>
> (Singer 1989: 326)

There is a growing body of evidence that supports this insight that declining terms of trade may be associated not so much with the structure of exports, as with the institutional and economic structure of the less-developed countries *per se*. Thus, even as the periphery diversifies exports and adds manufactured exports to its tradables, the deterioration in the terms of trade may still be observed.

Not only did relative price conditions continue to move against the poorest nations in recent years, Singer also emphasized that relative changes in the volume of trade had also cast the poorest nations in a disadvantageous position:

> in overall terms, and in spite of the group of fast-growing LDC [less-developed countries] exporters of manufactures, the volume lag of LDCs is clear. Between 1948 and 1970, world trade volume (excluding the socialist countries) increased by 7.3 per cent a year, but the export volume of LDCs by only 5.3 per cent. In the decade 1970–80, the figures are 5.8 per cent and 3.1 per cent respectively. For the least developed countries, typically primary exporters, the respective growth rates were only 4.4 per cent [for the 1948–70 period] and a dismal −0.4 per cent for 1960–70. At least in this relative sense, volume changes have increased any gap created by the worsening terms of trade and in that sense trade pessimism has not been proven wrong.
>
> (Singer 1984: 295)

Like Prebisch, Singer remained a strident critic of neoclassical policy-making and of the effects which unmediated market forces tend to impose on the poor nations. Nonetheless,

José Antonio Ocampo and María Angela Parra maintain that too much attention has been given to the terms of trade debate, displacing attention from more relevant factors that Singer had noted. For them, the *main* argument for industrialization arises from the externalities and dynamic economies of scale to be realized from industrialization (Ocampo and Parra 2007).

Indeed, in his original article on the subject Singer had urged industrialization because it generated strong technological externalities and other indirect benefits such as "its general effect on education, skill, way of life, inventiveness, habits, store of technology, creation of new demand, etc." (Singer 1950: 476). In other words, the terms of trade debate can at best

FOCUS 6.1 ARE THERE ADVERSE TERMS OF TRADE FOR SOME MANUFACTURED GOODS?

Using official International Monetary Fund and United Nations data, the results on manufacturing terms of trade are conflicting. For the period 1960–80, UN data show a 0.77 percent per year increase in the terms of trade of manufactured exports from less-developed countries. Covering a slightly different period, IMF data reveal a –0.88 percent per annum *decrease* in less-developed country manufactured goods terms of trade.

If the latter figure is correct, it may suggest that, at this point in time, less-developed countries tend to produce and export manufactured products in highly competitive international markets, for example, for textiles, shoes, and toys. The same pressures on prices when there is technological change would be likely to be working on these commodities as on primary products and agricultural products, just as the Prebisch-Singer hypothesis suggested. This downward tendency of the terms of trade for manufactured exports would fit Singer's concern that it is not the products, *per se*, being exported by the less-developed economies, as it is the structural characteristics of the countries (surplus labor) and of the markets where the exports are sold (highly competitive) that is important. In a study of the terms of trade for manufactured products between developing nations and the EU, Maizels, Palaskas, and Crowe found an annual decline of –0.30 1960–94, with the decline accelerating after 1980. They note that the volume of manufactured products exported to the EU has risen faster than the fall in prices. East Asian high-technology exports fared better in terms of their terms of trade than did any other region. Ocampo and Parra found that a price index of manufactures exported by developing countries versus manufactures exported from developed nations (2000 = 100) fell from 125 in the 1980–5 period to 80 in 2004.

If Singer and other observers are correct, then countries need to look to produce commodities, be they agricultural or manufactured, for which the demand is more income elastic and for which competition is perhaps not so fierce. For example, one agricultural export that has been successful for Chile has been wine. Wine is a **non-traditional** primary product export, and it is one for which demand is quite income elastic. Further, competition is not perfect, so countries with outstanding or niche products have a chance to experience increasing terms of trade. This should be taken as a warning that passive nations that do not engage in continual upgrading of the technological content of their exports can face declining terms of trade for manufactures *vis-à-vis* more dynamic manufactured products. Nations also have to build deep supplier bases where national firms are able to share in technological innovations and applications even when they are exporting intermediate to high-tech products. Otherwise there will be no significant spread effects from industrialization if their nation has a shallow and dependent relationship with foreign-owned manufacturing export firms.

Sources: Delgado, Wise, and Cypher 2007; Ocampo 1995; Ocampo and Parra 2007;
Maizels, Palaskas, and Crowe 1998: 75–83

provide an argument for avoiding a structural quagmire. Singer felt that it is a more powerful argument that – terms of trade issues notwithstanding – a nation will still have a higher long-run rate of growth if it builds its own diversified industrial base. And in some instances nations can further their advance by adopting learning policies that lead to technological upgrading of its manufactured export products.

The role of foreign aid

Convinced as he clearly was of the unequal effects of market outcomes for the poor relative to the advanced nations, it is hardly surprising that Singer advocated non-market offsets to compensate for the effects of *laissez-faire*. Singer was, indeed, perhaps the most outspoken and relentless advocate of foreign aid among the heterodox economists. He maintained that aid could take many forms, such as buffer stock purchasing programmes for primary products to temporarily offset falling raw materials prices, and "soft loans," that is, lending made at below the market rate of interest to the poorer nations to permit them to build up their infrastructure and/or make other long-term social investments. Such projects, Singer believed, would very rarely, if ever, find private-sector backing. Singer devoted much of a decade to an attempt to create a soft-loan fund at the UN to be known as SUNFED, the Special United Nations Fund for Economic Development. Because the UN expected to control this fund and to distribute much-needed credits on a multilateral basis, and without regard to the foreign policy priorities of either the United States or the United Kingdom, these nations systematically blocked attempts led by Singer to operationalize this fund. Instead, a similar fund was created, the International Development Agency in 1960 at the World Bank, where the US and Britain could exercise overwhelming influence in soft lending patterns to the most impoverished nations (Toye 2004: 172–4).

The institutionalists

Institutionalists believe that the institutions of an economy, that is, the forms of production, ownership, work processes, and ideologies which combine to create an economy and society, are the proper subjects for economic analysis. Since, furthermore, such institutions are subject to evolutionary change, the process of studying economics should also properly be evolutionary. This is clearly not the case for those who postulate that economics is the science of choice and that the function of economics is to discover the laws of the economy, just as a physicist might attempt to understand the laws of physics. While institutionalists have not made development economics their primary focus, there have been notable contributions. We shall consider but two, the American economist Clarence Ayres and the Swedish Nobel Prize winner in economics, Gunnar Myrdal.[9]

The Ayresian view of development

Clarence Ayres (1891–1972) was one of the leading proponents of an American school of institutional economics, centered from the 1930s to the 1960s at the University of Texas, Austin. Ayres was dismissive of much of mainstream economics, and his references to development economics occur within a much broader framework. Ayres was interested in a "megatheory" of development, which would have application to the advanced and the poor nations alike. At the center of Ayres's theoretical structure on the "how" of economic development are two fundamental forces: technology and ceremonialism.

Technology

Ayres placed more emphasis on technology than on any other factor which contributed to economic development. Technology, to Ayres, arose from a combination of tools and human beings, with the latter actually defined as "tool-users." Past tools lead to future tools, because human beings are so constituted as to be endowed with "the inveterate restlessness of human hands and brains" (Ayres 1991/5):

> the technological process can be understood only by recognizing that human skills and the tools by which and on which they are exercised are logically inseparable. Skills *always* employ tools, and tools are such *always* by virtue of being employed in acts of skill by human beings. Once the dual character of the technological process is understood, the explanation of its dynamism is obvious. Technology advances by virtue of inventions and discoveries being made. ... But all inventions and discoveries result from the combining of hitherto separate tools, instruments, materials, and the like. These are capable of combination by virtue of their physical existence. ... no one ever made a combination without there being something to combine. Furthermore, the more there is to combine in any given situation the more likely inventions and discoveries become.
>
> (Ibid.: 90–1)

For Ayres, technological progress and economic development were virtually synonymous.

Ceremonialism

Unfortunately, this "restlessness" which speeds forward the technological process can be curbed or limited by **ceremonialism**, the dichotomous opposite of technological dynamism. Ceremonialism imposes a curb on human creativity; in its essence, it is any past-binding behavior that tends to thwart the forward progress that technology imparts. There are five ways in which ceremonialism intrudes on any society, according to Ayres: (1) the nature of social stratification or class structures; (2) via social mores or conventions of what is acceptable behavior; (3) ideology which justifies the existing social stratification and mores and which further attempts to emphasize the negative consequences of changing either the social strata or the mores; (4) a social system of indoctrination which emotionally conditions individuals to accept the dominant ideology, mores, and class and social stratification; and (5) social patterns of ceremonial behavior designed to reinforce the first four factors.

Which of the two elements – past-binding ceremonialism that tends to retard the pace of change, or technological dynamism which expands human potentiality – is dominant at any point in time is the determining factor in establishing a country's pace and level of development. For Ayres, all societies, developed and less-developed, have ceremonial and technological forces at work in them at the same time, often within the same organizations and institutions. Ayres insisted that economic development is the consequence of the successful triumph of technology over ceremonial behavior. Ceremonial structures assign privileges to some classes, while they condition the population to resist social and economic change. Successful development, in the Ayresian view, thus requires a revamping of those institutions, and the behavioral patterns that accompany them, which continue to be detrimental to the creation of an indigenous technological capacity (this need is discussed more fully in Chapter 13).

The central role of education

In Ayres's view, the way to diminish the negative effects of ceremonialism on technological progress was via expanded education, which he defined as the diffusion of knowledge and skills. Of course, organized educational institutions can be hostile to "educating" and be a determined element in society's efforts to inculcate and perpetuate the prevailing ceremonial structures. Indeed, this is often the case with educational institutions in poorer nations, even through the university level. Still, Ayres felt strongly that expanded educational opportunities for larger numbers, or what we will later call **human capital accumulation**, was the surest means for any society to promote economic and social progress: "[T]he most important factor in the economic life of any people is the educational level ... of the community. A technically sophisticated community can and will equip itself with the instrumentalities of an industrial economy. There is no instance of any such community having failed to do so" (ibid.: 94).

Economic development in the Ayresian perspective is thus indistinguishable from technological progress, and without continuing technological change economic development falters.

Technological change is the result of scientific discovery, experiment, and innovation. The successful introduction of technology into the domestic production process in any country, what can be called domestic innovation, requires a scientific establishment capable first of adopting and adapting foreign-produced technological knowledge to local conditions and, later, of conducting its own research, designing its own experiments, and recognizing the potential and sometimes actual dangers of its own discoveries when applied to the domestic economy. In short, a developing nation must attain an independent technology learning capacity. This is the first step toward greater technological self-sufficiency.

While Ayres's work does not address the particularities of any developing society, and while it is difficult to link his unique form of analysis to that of the other heterodox thinkers, he addressed issues of crucial importance which complement the other perspectives presented in this chapter. And while Ayres had no major influence on mainstream thinking, his views on the importance of technology, the significance of education and other human capital creation, and the need for creating an appropriate institutional structure that is supportive of sustainable economic and human progress is one that is quite compatible with the viewpoint of the endogenous growth theories to be examined in Chapter 8. Thus, by isolating issues stressed by Ayres, one can explain a very significant proportion of the successes of the East Asian economies in recent decades (We consider such matters directly in Chapters 8, 9, 10, and elsewhere in the remainder of this text.) So although Ayres's own writings perhaps exerted little influence at the time, the thrust of his approach and his insights into the sources of growth and of the barriers to progress are substantially the same as the perspective behind much of the recent scholarship on the growth process.

The institutionalism of Gunnar Myrdal

Gunnar Myrdal's contribution to the social sciences has been remarkable, particularly for its breadth. A Swedish-educated economist, Myrdal (1898–1987) won the Nobel award in economics in 1974, ironically sharing it that year with one of the most fervent supporters of the free market, Frederick von Hayek. G.L.S. Shackle, a noted Cambridge economist, maintained that had Keynes not achieved renown for his revolutionary innovations in macroeconomic theory, the early work of Myrdal indicated that he would have supplied the same theory. Myrdal and his wife, Alva, made fundamental contributions to the development of the welfare state in Sweden, and Myrdal's study of American racism (1944) has remained a classic study of race relations. His massive *Asian Drama* (1968) established his reputation as a development specialist, which began in earnest in 1957 with his *Economic Theory and Underdeveloped Regions*.

In this latter book, Myrdal drew three main conclusions which he sought to further support and demonstrate in his subsequent research.

1 "In the absence of counteracting policies inequalities would tend to increase, both inter-nationally and within a country" (Myrdal 1984: 152).
2 International trade theory was biased against the poor regions, particularly in the contention that trade in commodities would tend to equalize factor prices, especially wages.
3 Greater income equality, rather than inequality, was the correct basis on which to achieve enhanced economic growth.

We shall examine briefly the significance of each of these three propositions.

Cumulative causation and backwash effects

Each of these three propositions was, in Myrdal's view, directly linked to the others, and all could be understood through an appreciation of what Myrdal termed **cumulative causation**. This concept sought to account for dynamic economic effects which progressively moved a society away from equilibrium. Myrdal assumed that there were notable inequalities between the regions of poor nations – that is, there was "dualism," as discussed earlier. What happens when a less-developed nation receives a stimulus to growth? If, as is likely, this stimulus is experienced in the more prosperous region of the economy, then that region will surge even further ahead, leaving the more economically deprived regions of the economy lagging behind.

This cumulative causation will occur for many reasons, only a few of which can be summarized here, but all of the reasons lead to a movement in society away from equaliza-tion among regions and sectors and toward increasing inequality. First, more ambitious and better-trained workers will migrate from the poorer regions to the growing regions. This will leave behind a bifurcated population of the young and the old in the poorer areas, a population largely composed of dependants and low-productivity workers compared to those who leave. At the same time, in backward rural areas, there is likely to be a higher rate of fertility, leading to a more rapid rate of population growth that puts increasing demand on a smaller number of the least productive workers, pushing down income per person in these poorer rural regions. Thus movements in any one direction tend to be cumulative, exacer-bating poverty and sustaining low levels of development where they exist and favoring and expanding upon economic development and progress where they already exist. The cumu-lative movements which tend to economically weaken a region were termed **backwash effects**.

Secondary backwash effect also might be anticipated. If the economic stimulus took the form of the expansion of industry in the economically more advanced region of a country, the output of the new firms might well compete with the peasant and artisan production methods prevalent in the poorest region. Artisan production might then be undercut by the economies of scale realized by manufacturers in the more advanced region of the country, slowly disrupting and then displacing artisan and small manufacturing industry in poor, rural regions. Such effects could be accelerated if the more economically advanced region of the country became more involved in international markets.

The **spread effects**, or positive externalities, of such a new growth stimulus might induce other, linked domestic manufacturing needed to support an expanded export sector, à la Nurkse's "balanced growth" or Hirschman's "linkage" models considered in the previous chapter. One might think that such effects would be a plus for development. Myrdal, however, cautioned that proper analysis demanded an understanding of both the positive impact of spread effects and the negative impact of backwash effects. Benjamin Higgins neatly summarized this aspect of Myrdal's thinking:

> The spread effects could outweigh the backwash effects only if income and employment in the leading sectors grew relative to that of the laggard sectors, as they did in the now advanced countries. In underdeveloped countries, however, the historical pattern of growth has been weak. The rural sector did not produce the raw materials for the expanding industrial sector, nor did the expanding industrial sector rely heavily on the rural sector for foodstuffs. Thus the growth of the industrial sector did not much expand the market for cash crops of the rural sector.
>
> (Higgins 1959: 351)

The pattern of production in most less-developed countries reflected the legacy of colonialism and neocolonialism. The structure of the economy was one wherein a predominance of backwash effects arose because of past institutional arrangements, rather than through the workings of the laws of comparative advantage. The failure of investments in the export sector to generate multiplier effects sufficient to swamp the backwash effects arose from the lingering effects of colonial policies and adverse path dependence. In the advanced nations, investments in the raw material sector created new opportunities for manufacturing and processing, as well as for banking and shipping. But Myrdal argued that in most Asian and African countries, colonial policy was concerned only with advancing the key sectors owned or controlled by the advanced nations. Therefore, the stimulus to banking and insurance, shipping, processing, and manufacturing occurred primarily in the advanced nations, rather than in the colonial or post-colonial regions. The very weakness of the spread effects, coupled with the strong backwash effects, virtually guaranteed that the latter would dominate the former in the poor nations.

The state

For Myrdal, a crucial difference between the advanced nations and the poor nations was to be found in the strong state in the former and the weak (or soft) state in the latter (Myrdal: 1970 Chapter 7). With a strong state, the advanced nations could develop a coherent national policy which could address the question of the manner in which the benefits of economic growth might be spread through the economy. This was due to the fact that, to some degree, the state has some power to influence and direct the growth process. On the other hand, in the poor nations the state lacks effective policies to either ensure that there is a movement toward national economic integration or to address the impact of backwash effects.

Myrdal noted that one of the major weaknesses of the state in the less-developed nation is that it is an institution of, and for, the top social strata. He did not believe it likely that redistribution of wealth and income could be achieved via income and wealth taxes. The rich would only evade these, since they effectively controlled the taxing authorities through their political power. The elites thus did not fear state power. On this point, Myrdal noted that in Singapore, economic development proceeded to a certain degree, because it was "one of the few States in the underdeveloped world which actively fought against corruption" (Myrdal 1984: 158).

Myrdal's institutionalism

Myrdal utilized an institutional approach, but in a manner largely distinct from Ayres. Myrdal believed that one could not understand the sources of economic underdevelopment nor address the problems of underdevelopment as long as analysis was restricted to the intellectual constructs of orthodox economics, such as the theory of comparative advantage.

> The institutional approach meant enlarging the study to include what in a summary way I referred to as "attitudes and institutions". They were found to be largely responsible for those countries' underdevelopment and would have to be changed in order to speed up development.
>
> (Myrdal 1984: 153)

Only radical institutional reforms would allow for development. Some examples of such changes needed might be land reform, a campaign against corruption, and displacement of the elite from the commanding heights of state policy. In short, the causes of underdevelopment and the cure for poverty were to be found in the study of and changes in the "attitudes and institutions" of the less-developed nations. Economic theories about saving and investment, "big push," "balanced" or "unbalanced" strategies were hardly enough.

Dependency analysis

Dependency analysis became extremely fashionable, particularly in Latin America, and later in Africa, in the late 1960s. Dependency analysis built on the ideas of the structuralists, specifically Prebisch's distinction between the center and the periphery. The center was viewed as *cause* and the periphery as *effect*. According to dependency writers, the less-developed nations had to be understood as part of a global process. Their fate was merely to provide the inputs to the advanced nations or to receive their cast-off, low-wage manufacturing processes under trading conditions which were likely to worsen. Dependency theory found the causes for the lack of development to be *external* to the socio-economic formations of the less-developed nations (see Figure 6.3). Thus, alleged internal backward or dysfunctional institutions of the less-developed nations were not treated seriously by dependency writers as a subject of analysis, or were seen as extensions of external domination. Internal institutional structures, such as the role of state corruption, large and unproductive land holdings, the extreme concentration of wealth, unresponsive political institutions, and so on, were played down. Instead, the negative influence of transnational corporations, multilateral institutions like the World Bank and the International Monetary Fund, and the extensive influence of foreign governments in the internal affairs of less-developed nations were highlighted.

Several factors contributed to the rise of dependency analysis. Of utmost importance was the influence of "modernization" theory on social science analysis and policy, which promised quick and sweeping development, as suggested in the developmentalist theories considered

Underlying conditions:

1   The export sector dominates the economy, imports are large in relation to the GDP
2   Exports are dominated by one, or a few commodities
3   Export firms are primarily foreign-owned
4   Mineral/petroleum commodities are produced under conditions of vertical integration
5   Foreign ownership dominates the financial sector and the industrial sector

Structural results:

1   Income, employment, and growth are determined by:

    a   prices and demand conditions in international markets
    b   the willingness of transnational corporations to invest

2   Income, employment, and growth are conditioned by:

    a   economic fluctuations abroad
    b   changes in taste and fashion or technologically created substitutes
    c   changes in the price and type of imports

3   Foreign capital, foreign technology, and management are dominant economic actors
4   Profits are normally repatriated, not re-invested
5   Production for the export industries is dependent on imported inputs
6   Backward and forward linkages in export activities are rare
7   Economic growth is not self-activating

Figure 6.3 Characteristics of economic dependency.

Source: Authors, adapted from Girvan (2006: 334).

in Chapter 5. As was noted there, Rosenstein-Rodan, Nurkse, Hirschman, Rostow, and others had maintained that the attainment of development for the less-developed countries was only a matter of time. Since most nations had already reached the "pre-take-off" stage, using Rostow's stage categorization, spectacular results were to be anticipated in little more than a decade.

Yet in the 1950s and 1960s in most of the less-developed nations, growth was only modest. Population growth had slowed gains in per capita income. Furthermore, confirming Myrdal's work, a process of cumulative causation leading to greater dualism could be observed. Economic growth had created poles of prosperity in a sea of despair. Shanty-towns and slums ringed the new and fashionable city centers. Water quality was abysmal, state schools were pathetically incapable of offering an adequate education, for most people health care remained either non-existent or minimal, transportation was a daily nightmare, and the average diet remained rudimentary and inadequate. New woes arose, or were first analyzed, in these decades: environmental pollution and degradation accelerated, while workplace hazards mounted, as new chemicals and substances were introduced into the production process.

True, a new techno-bureaucracy of government functionaries, applied scientists and engineers, financial operatives, and managerial cadres now shared some of the income with the agro-export elite in some nations. A skilled middle class had formed, and they had experienced tangible social mobility. But for the working classes and small farmers who made up the bulk of the population, the changes wrought in the 1940s through to the 1960s were both traumatic and cruel.

FOCUS 6.2   CELSO FURTADO: A GIANT OF STRUCTURAL AND DEPENDENCY ANALYSIS

Celso Furtado was one of the few young Brazilians to serve in Europe during the Second World War. After the war Furtado remained in Europe to complete a doctorate in economics from the elite Sorbonne, University of Paris. His life (1920–2004) spanned a period when Brazil's economy was united under the Estado Novo in the 1930s and started to grow at a rapid pace under import substitution policies (ISI) until the debt crisis of the 1980s.

When Furtado returned to Latin America in 1949 he went to work at the Economic Commission for Latin America (ECLA), the UN's new research center in Santiago, Chile. Shortly thereafter Raúl Prebisch made him Director of the Economic Development Division. From that date through 1957 Furtado worked at ECLA with the many talented economists who had clustered there, including Aníbal Pinto and Osvaldo Sunkel, who would soon become famous as the Latin American structuralists.

Leaving ECLA Furtado spent a year at the University of Cambridge, where he became acquainted with some of the most creative Keynesian economists, including Joan Robinson and Nicolas Kaldor, both towering figures in economics in the 1950–1970 period.

Returning to Brazil in 1959 he published one of his many classic studies of development, *The Economic Growth of Brazil*, which retains its great usefulness today. Unlike Prebisch, Furtado sought to analyze economic underdevelopment through the unfolding of long-term historical periods, such as the colonial era, when Brazil was "outward oriented," and the ISI period, when Brazil was "inward oriented."

Rather than using Prebisch's term "periphery" Furtado preferred "colonial structure" to describe Latin American nations and to emphasize the conditioning legacy of the colonial period. Eventually Furtado wrote thirty books, which have been translated into fifteen languages, with over two million copies sold. Furtado gave relative weight in his analysis of development issues to the pre-capitalist, mainly agrarian, sector.

Unlike Lewis (see Chapter 5), Furtado did not argue that agrarian surplus labor would be absorbed through the process of industrialization. Dualism, far from dissolving, would be perpetuated because only modest amounts of labor are needed from the pre-capitalist sector as developing nations apply inappropriate capital-intensive technologies (technological dependence) to expand the industrial base.

The new industrial part of the economy is marked by increasing concentration of income received by foreign and domestic owners and the professionals and financial specialists who manage and operate the manufacturing firms. With wages low, with the agrarian pre-capitalist sector enduring, and with only a small number of upper-middle-class families (about 9 percent of the population) enjoying the rising incomes flowing from the industrialization process, firms cannot sell much and so they also are unable to achieve economies of scale. Operating at low levels of production to supply the restricted local market, profit levels remain low, as does the level of investment, so the economy fails to grow as fast as it could without its endemic structural problems.

Demand plays a major role in the structure of the economy – demand is defined by "cultural colonialization": the elite and the upper middle class (the top 10 percent that receive well over one-half of national income) avidly buy goods that are consumed by the affluent in the advanced industrial nations.

Brazil was very dependent upon Foreign Direct Investment (FDI) in its efforts to utilize ISI to speed-up economic growth.

> [There was an] ironic heavy dependence of new industries on foreign investors – ironic because the strategy of [ISI] was often justified in terms of building national industrial-

Continued

capacity. It would seem that the real reason for pursuing import substitution was some what different: The ruling elite, with only a shallow sense of nationalism, sought a growing economy and growing incomes via industrialization. Given the limited capital and technology readily available within Brazil ... elites invited foreigners to handle the industrialization, which otherwise would not have been possible. State and foreign investors cooperated to develop chemicals, machinery, transportation equipment, shipbuilding, electrical equipment, and engineering goods, all rapidly growing industries [from 1947–64].

Furtado maintained that there was a necessary link between FDI-led growth and rising internal inequality. He was one of the first economists to use the term "dependency" and to argue that development and underdevelopment were two aspects of one economic structure. To overcome dependence the underdeveloped nations would have to create their own economic analysis – the tradition of Smith, Ricardo, and the other European classical economists was not suitable to an analysis of the dualistic, dependent structure of nations such as Brazil.

Returning from England, Furtado took charge of Brazil's most illustrious development institution – the national development bank or BNDES (see Focus 9.3 for further comment on BNDES). At BNDES Furtado focused on the north-east, Brazil's poorest region, where the income gap between the poor subsistence farmers and that of São Paulo was greater than the gap between average income in São Paulo and Europe in the 1950s.

Furtado soon created SUDENE, designed to promote industrial development and land reform (see Chapter 11) in the north-east to counteract "internal colonialism" as manifested in the exclusion of the north-east from the benefits of Brazil's economic growth. The north-east was in a double bind according to Furtado's research: it faced falling terms of trade for its commodity exports, and falling terms of trade in relation to its income earnings on the industrial goods the region bought from Brazil's industrial core in São Paulo and Río. Development and underdevelopment were one totality, constantly reproduced within the structure of the economy.

Furtado's direction of SUDENE continued until the military coup of 1964, after which (in exile) he returned to the Sorbonne as a professor from 1965–85, becoming the first foreigner to attain such an appointment. With the return to democracy in 1985 Furtado became Brazil's ambassador to the EU, and then served as the Minister of Culture. In short, Furtado was always a "public intellectual." But he also formed part of a cadre of highly competent and reliable state operatives at BNDES, while constantly advancing his own research and economic analysis of development issues. Furtado supported the election efforts of Lula, Brazil's President since 2002, and Lula responded by re-establishing SUDENE in 2003.

Furtado stated that both Keynes and Myrdal had greatly influenced his thinking concerning the link between the economy and power, the crucial role of the state and the ways in which the international economy influenced or constrained national economies. The latter found expression through the domination of the US over Latin America, in Furtado's view. Nonetheless, before the military coup of 1964, Furtado took the position that industrialization in Brazil would not be difficult. His focus was then on the necessity of incorporating Brazil's vast population of poor workers, farmers, and marginalized people into a process of inclusive *social development*.

In his view at that time, industrialization would unleash new social forces and pressures which would drive Brazil toward a process of inclusive social development reaching far beyond the question of industrialization *per se*. But with the military coup "the essence of Brazil's political economic strategy became strictly that of industrialization thereby intensifying the process of social exclusion. This created a profound divide: development could no longer be a social project."

The coup demonstrated Brazil's dependence: US corporations funded Brazilian insti-tutes that were active in funneling money to those plotting the downfall of the elected government. The US State Department and the CIA also significantly facilitated the under-mining of the government. In dispute was the new policy of limiting the amount of profits which foreign corporations (overwhelmingly US) could take out of the country in a year and SUDENE's project for land reform in the lower Amazon region. In addition, the government decided to buy out a number of petroleum refineries, primarily owned by US transna-tionals, converting them into part of the state-owned petroleum firm Petrobas.

With the coup everything changed. The civilian government had been starved for aid funds and had faced a drop in FDI, but within weeks of the coup the military government had received $650 million in aid from the US government, which also arranged an addi-tional $450 million in loans. The military government dutifully responded with new mining laws, an end to land reform, and to the idea of putting the oil refineries under the control of the state. As Furtado moved into exile the term "dependency" now resonated as never before in Brazil.

Until the coup Furtado had been a great optimist, believing that Brazil was a nation that would surely advance, a nation that had a national social project. But the coup "Produced a form of development that was completely perverse having no other objective but to accumulate and concentrate."

After the coup Furtado put much emphasis on the fact that a successful ISI policy would pass through phases of greater and greater complexity wherein the creation of a balanced economy would necessitate the production of durable goods and later machinery and equipment (see Chapters 9 and 10 for further analysis). Yet when Brazil attempted to push its productive system into these higher phases the structural weaknesses and imbalances of the economy would be ever more critical.

In the *absence of* state intervention (see Chapter 7 for a discussion) to provide for *social development*, the economy would be limited by the small internal market combined with production processes that were ever-more capital-intensive, and an unbalanced and imitative pattern of consumption would drive the production process. Brazil could not overcome the narrowness of the domestic market via manufactured exports because of the absence of an export mentality among its industrialists, and because the trans-nationals had set up their Brazilian branch plants only to have privileged access to the Brazilian market.

Lacking any agency for endogenous development and change, Brazil would face a constant drain on its production system to make external payments in the form of debt payments, charges for the use of foreign technology, and transference of a large portion of profits to the external powers that ultimately determined the rhythms of the economy. All this, in fact, would seem at least partly to explain the unbalanced debt-led growth of the 1970s and the very low growth Brazil achieved in the 1981–2005 period.

Sources: Colby and Dennett 1995: 440–55; Kay 2005; Kohli 2004: 188;
Love 1999; Mallorquín 1998: 96–7

It is not possible to find one dependency writer who could serve as an exemplar of this school of thought. Indeed, in what may well stand as the classic attempt to summarize and detail the ideas of the Latin American dependency writers, Cristóbal Kay referred to their works as a "Tower of Babel" (Kay 1989). While the gradations and subtleties of positions defy condensation, we have, following Kay, utilized a logical division: Marxist dependency analysis and non-Marxist dependency thought. Even this distinction, unfortunately, is less crisp than might appear at first glance. The dependency writers were nothing if not eclectic, and borrowing from Marxism and employing Marx's categories and concepts was never treated as "trespassing," even by the non-Marxist theorists.

Marxist dependency analysis

Paul Baran was, at the high-water mark of McCarthyism in the 1950s, the only known Marxist economist to hold a tenured professorship at a major US university, Stanford. Unlike Marx, who believed that capitalism had a dual role of "destruction and regeneration" to play in the colonial regions, Baran emphasized the destructive side of capitalism in less-developed regions, but could find scarce evidence of "regeneration." Rather, twentieth-century **monopoly capitalism**, unlike the earlier form of competitive capitalism which Marx had scrutinized, had, according to Baran, a vested interest in maintaining backwardness and dependence in the periphery.

It might be argued that Baran initiated the analytical process which later led to the flowering of the pessimistic and stagnationist dependency school in Latin America and Africa. Baran's favorite example of the destructive effects of capitalism was that of India. He found that many Indian social scientists had discussed and developed concepts very similar to those employed by the dependency writers, but that they had done so as early as the late nineteenth century, having experienced the full force of British imperialism (see Chapter 3).

Baran's theoretical point of departure was an analysis of what he termed the **economic surplus**. This is defined as the mass of resources, actual and potential, which a society could have at its disposal in order to facilitate economic growth; it is the amount that might be reinvested in productive ways to increase the future level of social output. This "surplus" is that residual left over out of total income after a society's basic needs have been met for food, clothing, shelter, and human companionship. But this surplus may be grossly misused. It may be utilized to erect sumptuous and multiple residences for the rich, or it may be wasted through a variety of other forms of conspicuous consumption. The military or the church may make tremendous demands on the surplus, or it may be drained away by a foreign power via plunder or simple profit repatriation, as a result of foreign control over a less-developed economy's most important industries. Baran's study of the history of the less-developed regions under colonialism led him to argue that the source of their poverty was to be found in the extraction of this surplus. Had this surplus, or a large portion of it, been used for investment rather than for waste, then the poor regions would have been transformed.

Colonialism, however, blocked the potential for change. Baran summarized in one short paragraph the broad history of colonialism, condensing in the process a tremendous amount of material, striking at the very essence of the colonial legacy:

> To oppression by their feudal lords, ruthless but tempered by tradition, was added domination by foreign and domestic capitalists, callous and limited only by what the traffic would bear. The obscurantism and arbitrary violence inherited from their feudal past was combined with the rationality and sharply calculating rapacity of their capitalist present. Their exploitation was multiplied, yet its fruits were not to increase their productive wealth; these went abroad or served to support a parasitic bourgeoisie at home. They lived in abysmal misery, yet they had no prospect of a better tomorrow. They existed under capitalism, yet there was no accumulation of capital. They lost their time-honored means of livelihood, their arts and crafts, yet there was no modern industry to provide new ones in their place. They were thrust into extensive contact with the advanced science of the West, yet remained in a state of the darkest backwardness.
>
> (Baran 1957: 144)

Reviewing the history of colonialism, Baran drew an extremely powerful conclusion.

Thus the peoples who came into the orbit of Western capitalist expansion found themselves in the twilight of feudalism and capitalism, enduring the worst features of both worlds.

(Ibid.)

National capital, foreign capital, and the state

Potentially, Baran argued, there were three forces which could both increase the economic surplus and harness it for economic development. These three potential sources for socio-economic change were national capital, foreign capital, and the state.

Regarding the first, Baran acknowledged that in some of the poor nations import substitution industrialization (ISI) had changed the structure of the economy. But he also maintained that ISI had failed to go far enough, and that, in fact, the end result of ISI would be the perpetuation of a fragmented and disarticulated national economy dominated by pervasive monopoly and oligopoly firms.

> The new firms, rapidly attaining exclusive control over their markets and fencing them in by protective tariffs and/or government concessions of all kinds, blocked further industrial growth while their monopolistic price and output policies minimized the expansion of their own enterprises. Completing swiftly the entire journey from a progressive to a regressive role in the economic system, they became at an early stage barriers to economic development rather similar in their effect to the semi-feudal landownership prevailing in underdeveloped countries. Not only not promoting further division of labor and growth of productivity, they actually cause a movement in the opposite direction. Monopolistic industry on one hand extends the merchant phase of capitalism by obstructing the transition of capital and men from the sphere of circulation to the sphere of industrial production. On the other hand, providing neither a market for agricultural produce nor outlets for agricultural surplus labor and not supplying agriculture with cheap manufactured consumer goods and implements, it forces agriculture back towards self-sufficiency, perpetuates the idleness of the structurally unemployed, and fosters further mushrooming of petty traders, cottage industries, and the like.
>
> (Baran 1957: 176)[10]

As to the second potential source of change, Baran agreed with Hans Singer, whom he cited in this regard, that foreign investment, while clearly a *potential* source of development, actually failed to have an impact on more than a narrow, isolated portion of the national economy. Not only did he emphasize the enclave effect of foreign investment, Baran took the analysis one step deeper, arguing that foreign capital diminished the possibilities of economic development.

This was so, Baran argued, because in order for the foreign mining and agro-export capitalists to gain a foothold in the less-developed areas, it was necessary to form an alliance with the merchant capitalists who dominated politically and economically within these regions. These relatively backward elements, with semi-feudal and semi-capitalist ideologies and behavioral traits at one and the same time, were actually strengthened by foreign investment. And, in turn, the institutions which they sought to perpetuate, Ayresian-type ceremonial or retarding institutions, also were bolstered by the enhanced revenues which flowed into the possession of the national strata of bankers, speculators, semi-feudal landlords, and political operatives.

In Baran's view, foreign investors in mining, oil and gas, and agro-export firms learned quickly to become hostile to genuine economic development as promoted through ISI. He listed four reasons for such opposition.

1   higher wages and tolerance of unionization meant lower profit margins;
2   foreign capital would become a targeted source for increasing state revenues, meaning that higher taxes and royalty payments would be imposed;
3   foreign exchange controls limiting the amount of funds which could be taken out of the country as repatriated profits would be imposed; and
4   tariffs on imported wage goods would be utilized to protect domestic manufacturing, thereby raising the likelihood that workers would demand higher wages to maintain their living standard, thus cutting into profits.

As to the third potential source of the surplus, in theory the state could break this deadlock by opting for new programs which would make ISI ever more dynamic and successful. In fact, however, the state in the less-developed regions seemed incapable of performing the crucial role or making the decisions needed to move forward on any front that would advance development.

For Baran, following the capitalist road in the less-developed regions was to steer a course which would eventually lead not to Rostow's society based on mass consumption, but rather to an economic and social graveyard. Only by turning to socialism could the less-developed countries reasonably expect any relief from their poverty.[11]

Associated dependent development: non-Marxist dependency theory

One of the most noted non-Marxist dependency writers was Fernando Henrique Cardoso, who has had an active career as a Brazilian sociologist/economist with a worldwide reputation, and also as a powerful Brazilian politician, rising to be President of Brazil from 1994–2002. While most dependency economists argued that the nations of the periphery were capitalist, they suggested it was a particular kind of *peripheral* capitalism. One of the defining characteristics of this mutation was economic stagnation, or "the development of underdevelopment," in the catchy rhetoric of Andre Gunder Frank, another of the eminent dependency writers.

Cardoso, however, did not embrace this stagnationist perspective. Rather, he maintained that the economies and societies of the periphery had evolved and could continue to do so (Cardoso and Faletto 1979). There had been three major stages in the economic history of the less-developed countries. First was the agro-export stage of the colonial period, when economic dualism was prevalent. During this stage, the pre-capitalist sector of artisans, petty producers, and peasant producers had accounted for the bulk of all economic activity. Some sectors of the economy were integrated into the world economy, particularly the production of precious metals, minerals, and tropical products which were exported to the world markets. Production of these export products often took place in a modern semi-capitalist enclave.

Secondly, after the First World War, a major transformation in some of the less-developed economies, especially those of Latin America, had occurred with the creation of what Cardoso called the "developmentalist alliance." The strategic locus of this transformation was import substitution industrialization (ISI). A new social structure of accumulation had been formed on the basis of common or cooperating interests of industrial workers, industrialists, governmental workers, and some powerful individuals in shipping, banking, and the agro-export sector who had made the change from the agro-export model of accumulation to that of ISI.

Eventually, however, the developmentalist alliance had been replaced by an authoritarian-corporatist regime. In this third stage, the populist orientation of the state, which had been characteristic of much of the ISI stage, had given way to drastic curbs on democracy, unions, the universities, and other areas of society where dissent might be encountered and tolerated. The weak welfare state developed in the ISI stage, in which social security and minimum wage legislation, public health care, and public education had been expanded for at least some part of the population, gave way to drastic cuts in the public service aspect of the state's budget. Above all, in this stage, the transnational corporations (TNCs) were welcomed and accommodated in the less-developed nations. In fact, the TNCs became pivotal in the new process of accumulation and were central to the growth process.

Although this new capitalist model was extremely accommodating to the interests of the TNCs, Cardoso argued, the TNCs were not all-powerful. The nations of the periphery needed the TNCs because of their ability to control and reproduce technology and complex capital goods. But the TNCs also needed the nations of the periphery, as their middle- and upper-income consumers had become an important source for final TNC sales. The peripheral labor force, kept docile and cheap by the authoritarian state, was necessary to keep costs down in an era of global competition.

Under this new regime, in which the authoritarian state and TNCs cooperate, some economic growth and development does occur. GDP rises; even the standard of living for the masses may improve. The continued stagnation that some dependency writers, like Frank, argued was the fate of the less-developed nations was neither theoretically plausible, nor, even more importantly, argued Cardoso, was it empirically founded. One should not antici-pate economic stagnation, or be surprised at a certain degree of economic progress in less-developed nations. Nor should one view the peripheral nations as powerless to shape their destiny, simply buffeted about by outside forces. Rather, a new form of capitalist accumula-tion was at work, which Cardoso termed **associated dependent development**.

Cardoso did not view this new stage, or its particular characteristics, as immutable. The poor nations had a certain capacity to bargain with the TNCs and the advanced nations, and they had certain, but limited, opportunities to develop their own technological capabilities. The question was how, within this new structure, the poor nations were to respond. Innova-tion could have certain rewards. On the other hand, Cardoso found that the yearnings for a revolutionary rupture with the world system, as voiced by many dependency writers, was unfounded.

By attempting to portray a situation of submissive dependency and stagnation, many intel-lectuals had hoped to stimulate a political shift toward revolution. Cardoso disagreed with the thrust of this analysis; the economic situation of most less-developed nations no doubt was difficult, the state had ceased to attempt to combat some of the most noxious problems in their nations, but the growth created by the new alliance between domestic capital and the transnationals under dependent development opened up some new possibilities for elements of the working class, the techno-bureaucracy, and the state to progress.

At least for some less-developed nations, there was reasonable hope for modest reform and some limited autonomy, within the context of a new, more globalized, system of production. Less-developed nations may "depend" upon outside technology and finance via TNCs, but Cardoso believed that good state policy would permit less-developed nations to take advantage of the reciprocal needs of the TNCs in the less-developed countries, so that the poorer countries could obtain some of the positive effects of TNC investment and some of the benefits of economic growth would be shared within the poorer countries (see Focus 6.3).

Dependency analysis lost much of its following in the late 1970s. Yet, as Norman Girvan noted, this turned out to be one of the great ironies of development economics. In the Caribbean, but also in most other regions, a **new dependency** has flourished:

> The paradox is that the *actual* dependence of Caribbean economies became much more acute in ... the 1980s and 1990s. Heightened foreign indebtedness ... [has] increased the economic vulnerability of Caribbean countries, exposing them to pervasive external intrusions into domestic policy-making in the form of conditionalities imposed by the Washington-based international financial institutions and bilateral donors. The agreement establishing the World Trade Organization in 1994 ...significantly constrict[s] the "policy space" previously available to developing countries. National development of the kind that was the accepted objective in the era of decolonization has been replaced by the mantra of "integration into the global economy." The new dependency associated with globalization is presented as *inter*dependence in the effort to obfuscate the asymmetries. The wheel has come full circle from the 1960s, and there is a new orthodoxy that calls for a renewed critical analysis from an updated dependency perspective.
>
> (Girvan 2006: 345)

Classical Marxism

While the dependency and other heterodox perspectives discussed in this chapter were under heavy attack from more orthodox development economists, an attack was also mounted from the political left.

Bill Warren, a former lecturer in Economics at the University of London, provided a cutting and intelligent critique of both non-Marxist and Marxist dependency analyses. His ideas were extremely controversial, and his untimely death in 1978 foreclosed the possibility of a meaningful dialogue with his many critics.

Warren's position was that capitalism continued to be a progressive force for change wherever it operated. The capitalism sweeping into the less-developed regions of the world at a rapid rate may manifest signs of social pathology, but they were of a transitory nature, similar to the problems of early capitalism in England after the Industrial Revolution. Capitalism, Warren argued, had brought trauma and social dislocation in its wake wherever it had been established. But, he maintained, it had also brought an incomparably higher standard of living to the masses than any previous socio-economic system (you will recognize this, from Chapters 3 and 4, as Marx's view, too). Furthermore, as the less-developed regions industrialized at a rapid rate, their industrial working force expanded. This social class would eventually bring socialism to those countries, but only after the initial triumph of capitalism, which was a necessary stage of social and economic development.

Leaving aside Warren's prediction of a shift toward socialism somewhere in the undefined future of the less-developed regions, what is one to make of Warren's claims of the progressiveness of capitalism in the periphery? He made use of statistical data to show that in the 1950s and 1960s overall annual per capita growth in the poor regions had been relatively high: 2.4 percent in the 1950s and 2.6 percent in the 1960s. He implied that the pace was improving over time, noting that in the early 1970s, the average rate of growth of per capita income reached 3.8 percent.

FOCUS 6.3   DEPENDENCE AND THE SEMI-PERIPHERY

By the late 1970s a chorus of voices dissented from the simple center–periphery dichotomy of many dependency writers. The periphery, as destined to stagnation without a break with the world capitalist system, was increasingly seen as an incomplete, and inaccurate, description of the socio-economic conditions and the dynamic of change at work in some parts of the less-developed world, as Cardoso also argued.

It was true that some nations seemed caught in a post-colonial torpor, continuing to specialize in one or a few raw material exports. These non-industrializing nations, it was suggested, could best be described by what did not exist, but needed to be in place, if they were to develop. These nations were thus described as the **dependent economies**, stuck on the periphery of progress. They seemed incapable of autonomously altering their economic structures, stuck with adverse path dependence born of colonial structures carried over into independence.

Some less-developed nations, however, were growing and industrializing rapidly. For these economies, the term **dependent development** was applied by those who accepted this new way of looking at center–periphery relations. These were countries in the periphery, but which seemed to be changing their economic structures. Economic growth, often quite rapid growth, was taking place. These countries (Mexico and Brazil were often singled out) did not fit the stagnationist perspective of the original dependency analysis, but neither did they fit the pattern of independently developing nations.

In another path-breaking attempt to present an alternative to the stagnationist dependency perspective, Peter Evans defined "dependent development" as a situation which included

> both the accumulation of capital and some degree of industrialization on the periphery. Dependent development is a special instance of dependency, characterized by the association or alliance of international and local capital. The state also joins the alliance as an active partner, and the resulting triple alliance is a fundamental factor in the emergence of dependent development.

Although economic growth is achieved, countries engaged in a process of dependent development suffer a variety of ills:

> a regressive profile of income distribution, [an emphasis on] luxury consumer goods as opposed to basic necessities ... underutilization and exploitation of manpower resources ... [and the] frequent reliance of foreign firms on capital-intensive technologies [which] increases rather than solves the unemployment problem.

Politically, a nation at the stage of dependent development is categorized as being on the semi-periphery, neither in the periphery nor the center. Could nations undergoing dependent development ever graduate to the status of "core" nations? Dependent development theorists, such as Evans and Cardoso, did not rule out the possibility.

Cardoso did not see dependency as necessarily a "zero-sum" game, in which the periphery lost and the center nations gained, as the stagnationist dependency writers believed. Rather, the current world economy provided opportunities for "positive-sum" games in which both the developed and less-developed nations could "exploit" each other. Growth in the periphery was possible, but achieving it depended on having the appropriate internal policies to gain advantage *vis-à-vis* the TNCs.

Sources: Evans 1979: 32; Evans and Gereffi 1982: 113

Warren maintained that overcrowding, slums, and chronic unemployment arose from population growth, but that this growth itself was a fundamental indicator of an improvement in living standards. For Warren, all institutions within the less-developed nations which were ceremonial or dysfunctional from the standpoint of economic development were by-products of the colonial era and earlier modes of production. That era had ended after the Second World War, according to Warren, and a new era had dawned with political independence. And this, he argued, was sufficient to thwart whatever impediments to social and economic progress could be attributed to either the policies of transnational corporations, the multi-lateral institutions, or the governments of the advanced nations. The spread of capitalist methods of production would sweep away outmoded institutions and structures, and the now less-developed nations would be brought into the modern era, just as Britain was, by the imperative forces of capitalist progress.

In the heady days of the early 1970s, Warren's thesis had a ring of plausibility; there can be no doubt that, like the developmentalists with whom he quarreled, he shared a fundamental optimism about the possibility, even inevitability, of progress. However, the aggregate data utilized by Warren need to be carefully analyzed in terms of their representative nature. Warren's results were strongly influenced by the performance of the East Asian miracle economies. Without detracting from the great strides made in these nations, which are discussed in Chapter 8, it should be noted that there has been a significant decline in their rate of growth in recent years. Thus, the Asian miracle economies had a tendency to skew the aggregate data after the 1950s and through the early 1970s. Warren, and others who use similar forms of analysis, should have presented disaggregated data, showing the overall growth of less-developed nations both with and without the miracle Asian economies. This would have been a more reasonable basis for attempting to evaluate the thesis that "capitalism has struck deep roots [in the less-developed regions] and developed its own increasingly vigorous dynamic" (Warren 1980: 9).

Events would seem to have overtaken Warren's brash analysis. The durability of the retarding factors which disturbed the heterodox development economists became, if anything, more significant for most developing nations in the 1990s, as noted by Girvan, above. Ayres, Baran, Myrdal, Prebisch, and Singer would not, we suspect, have been surprised by the difficult conditions faced by many less-developed nations since 1980, nor by the anemic responses to these conditions from so many of these economies. It is not that progress is impossible; it is just that, contrary to Warren, it is unlikely that it is *inevitable*. Becoming developed requires the right decisions and the proper policies; it does not just happen to all countries like manna from heaven, just as a consequence of the spread of capitalism.

Questions and exercises

1   Using the definition in note 4 for the terms of trade:

   a   calculate what happens to the terms of trade index for some country between 1995 and 1997, if, in 1995, the price index for its exports was 110 and the price index for its imports was 108; and in 1997, the price index of exports was 105 and the price index of imports was 112. Has there been an increase or a decrease in this country's terms of trade? If the country wishes to buy exactly the same physical quantity of imports in 1997 which it purchased in 1995, how much more, or how much less, will it have to export, in physical terms, in 1997 compared to 1995?

   b   examine what has happened to the terms of trade for two countries of your choice over a period of at least five years, using data in either the *World Development Report* or the *Human Development Report*. Does the trend you discover tend to support or refute the Prebisch-Singer hypothesis? Explain.

2   What is meant by the "international division of labor"? What function does the periphery play *vis-à-vis* the center countries in this division of labor? Who benefits from it?

3   Why do you think Raúl Prebisch's use of the terms "center" and "periphery," and the idea that relations between them were antagonistic, was such a challenge to orthodox economists?

4   Imagine you are an adviser to your government and that your economy faces a problem of declining terms of trade for its exports. Discuss the possible policy changes for the economy and any other strategies you would recommend to avoid declining terms of trade in the future.

5   What are the problems faced by primary product exporters? Are there primary products that countries might export which would, perhaps, not be subject to the same difficulties? Can you give some examples of so-called non-traditional primary products which it might be desirable to export? In general, what makes one export a "good" export and another less desirable?

6   Distinguish between backwash effects and spread effects. Are these the same as vicious circles and virtuous circles? How do these two ideas of Myrdal's relate to the concept of cumulative causation?

7   What similarities are there between the classical Marxist view of Bill Warren and the views of the developmentalist economists reviewed in Chapter 5? What differences are there?

8   Contrast the institutionalist approach to development with the dependency approach. Are there strong similarities, as well as differences?

Notes

1 As we shall see in Chapter 8, however, the ideas of the institutionalists concerning the central role of education, technology, institutions, and path dependency have been "rediscovered" by the new development theorists, though without attribution.

2 The basic needs (BN) approach to development issues was a retreat from the optimism of the 1950s and 1960s, which had anticipated that within a decade or two the poor nations, or many of them, could achieve sustained growth and development. By the 1970s, such optimism had been shaken. Among the reasons for this was the unexpected durability of social institutions which were to have been swept away by the forces unleashed via the developmentalist path. In lieu of the high hopes projected by the developmentalist perspective, the basic needs approach substituted a more modest and immediate agenda: some significant part of development funds was to be expended on projects that had a direct and tangible effect on the well-being of the poor, for example, self-help housing projects, water treatment projects, health clinics, schools, and so on. Much of the BN approach attempted to address an uncontrolled result of economic change in the less-developed world: the phenomenal growth of urban slums and blighted mega-urban areas.

3 The propensity to import, m, is equal to the share of total national income spent on imports, thus $m = M/GNP$. For the United States, this ratio was much smaller than was true for Britain, meaning that imports were less important for the United States economy and that exporters to the United States would have less bargaining leverage on prices as a consequence.

4 Specialists in the area of international trade have used at least four separate concepts under the heading of "terms of trade." We will utilize the most basic concept, which is the ratio of the price of exports to the price of imports in a given period compared to some earlier (base year) period. The terms of trade is an index number. Thus $(P_{x,i}/P_{m,i}) \times 100$ where $P_{x,i}$ is an average price index of exports in year i and $P_{m,i}$ is the average price index of imports in year i. This measure of the terms of trade is sometimes referred to as the **net barter terms of trade**.

Another measure of the terms of trade that captures changes in productivity between nations is called the **double factorial terms of trade**. We will not attempt to consider this or any of the other terms of trade measures which might be used. Students wishing to do so should turn to any text in international trade.

Both the annual *World Development Report* and the *Human Development Report* include data on the terms of trade for all countries covered.

5 In 1996–2000 the share of primary commodities and resource-based manufactures dropped to roughly 40 percent of all exports for Latin America, the Middle East, North Africa, and South Asia, but in Sub-Saharan Africa and for the poorest of developing nations reliance on the export of commodities remained.

6 The "development from within" approach, correctly understood, encompasses more than ISI, however. It is an evolutionary strategy of development that depends upon domestic sources of finance, domestic entrepreneurship, and domestic innovation to produce for both export and the domestic market. However, in practice, "development from within" has sometimes been too focused on the domestic market only, so that it has become "inward-oriented" development. This, however, was not Prebisch's own view, though it has incorrectly been attributed to him (see Sunkel 1993 for a finely detailed look at development from within).

7 Certainly, complete industrialization in all sectors would not be urged on all of the national economies of the periphery. Prebisch's experience with industrialization programmes was primarily with relatively large economies, like Argentina, Brazil, Chile, Mexico, Peru, and Venezuela. The smaller economies, such as Costa Rica, Sri Lanka, the Caribbean countries, and some African countries, could not hope to have large and diversified industrial sectors. For smaller economies, Prebisch advocated enhanced common market-type arrangements so that sharing of markets could accomplish what was possible internally in large economies. The development problems facing small nations may sometimes be a bit more difficult, but, as the successes of Singapore and Hong Kong in recent decades suggest, the situation is far from hopeless. Size, *per se*, does not seem to be a particularly powerful explanatory variable.

8 Income elasticity measures the change in consumption resulting from a change in income. Technically, it may be written as

$$E_Y = \frac{\%DQ}{\%DY}$$

Where E_Y is the income elasticity, Q is the level of consumption of some good or service, and Y is income.

9 There are two newer branches of institutionalism besides the dominant strain discussed in this section. One is European institutionalism, organized around the efforts of the European Evolutionary Economics Association. The other, grounded in the work of another Nobel Prize winner in economics, Douglass North, is called the "new institutional economics." For recent applications of the latter view, and a number of critical evaluations, see Harriss *et al.* (1995).

10 In Marx's writings, a major distinction was made between economic activities which took place in the "sphere of circulation" and those which took place in the "sphere of industrial production." In the former, activities such as banking, insurance, stock, and bond markets, were to be found "circulating" funds from various groups within a social stratum, for example, savers and investors. In the sphere of production were to be found workers and capitalists, investment activity, production of manufactures and raw materials, and, most importantly, technological development. The sphere of circulation was viewed as unproductive, although to some degree necessary for the economy to function, while the sphere of production was viewed as productive. Hence, an expansion of the sphere of circulation indicated that the surplus was being diverted and development opportunities thwarted.

11 Recall that when Baran died, in the mid-1960s, the Cuban revolution was viewed quite positively by many, and China seemed to be making forward strides in many areas as well. We will not attempt to speculate on how Baran might have viewed the issue of capitalism versus socialism from the perspective of the 1990s. He greatly admired the Cuban revolution and seemingly agreed with his close associate Paul Sweezy that the Soviet Union had became a "state-capitalist" society dominated by a bureaucratic stratum of state-managers, and that progress would be only for a narrow elite.

References

Ayres, Clarence. 1991/95. "Economic Development: An Institutionalist Perspective," pp. 89–97 in James Dietz (ed.), *Latin America's Economic Development*, 2nd edn. London and Boulder, CO: Lynne Rienner Publishers.

Baran, Paul. 1952. "On the Political Economy of Backwardness," *The Manchester School of Economics and Social Studies* (January): 66–84.

——. 1957. *The Political Economy of Growth*. New York: Monthly Review Press.

Borensztein, Eduardo, Mohsin S. Khan, Carmen M. Reinhart, and Peter Wickham. 1994. *The Behavior of Non-Oil Commodity Prices*. Occasional Paper no. 112. Washington, D.C.: IMF.

Cardoso, Fernando Henrique and Enzo Faletto. 1979. *Dependency and Development in Latin America*. Berkeley, CA: University of California Press.

Colby, Gerard and Charlotte Dennett. 1995. *Thy Will be Done. The Conquest of the Amazon*. New York: Harper Perennial.

Delgado Wise, Raúl and James Cypher. 2007. "The Strategic Role of Mexican Labor under NAFTA," *Annals of the American Academy of Political and Social Science* 610 (March): 120–42.

Evans, Peter. 1979. *Dependent Development*. Princeton, NJ: Princeton University Press.

—— and Gary Gereffi. 1982. "Foreign Investment and Dependent Development," pp. 111–68 in Sylvia Hewlett and Richard Weinert (eds.), *Brazil and Mexico: Patterns in Late Development*. Philadelphia, PA: Institute for the Study of Human Issues.

Girvan, Norman. 2006. "Caribbean Dependency Thought Revisited," *Canadian Journal of Development Studies* 27 (3): 329–52.

Harriss, John, Janet Hunter, and Colin M. Lewis. 1995. *The New Institutional Economics and Third World Development*. London: Routledge.

Higgins, Benjamin. 1959. *Economic Development*. New York: Norton.

IMF (International Monetary Fund). 1994. "Adjustment, Not Resistance, the Key to Dealing with Low Commodity Prices," *IMF Survey* 23 (October 31): 350–2.

Kay, Cristóbal. 1989. *Latin American Theories of Development and Underdevelopment*. London: Routledge.

——. 2005. "Celso Furtado: Pioneer of Structuralist Development Theory," *Development and Change* 36 (6): 1201–7.

Kohli, Atul. 2004. *State Directed Development*. Cambridge: Cambridge University Press.

Love, Joseph. 1999. "Furtado, las ciencias sociales y la historia," pp. 136–55 in Jorge Lora and Carolos Mallorquín (eds.), *Prebisch y Furtado: El estructuralismo latinoamericano*. Puebla, Mexico: Benemérita Universidad Autónoma de Puebla.

Maizels, Alfred, Theodosios Palaskas and Trevor Crowe. 1998. "The Prebisch-Singer Hypothesis Revisited," pp. 63–85 in David Sapsford and John-ren Chen (eds.), *Development Economics and Policy*. London: Macmillan.

Mallorquín, Carlos. 1998. *Ideas e historia en torno al pensamiento económico latinoamericano*. Mexico, D.F.: Plaza y Valdes.

Myrdal, Gunnar. 1944. *An American Dilemma*, 2 vols. New York: Harper & Row.

——. 1957. *Economic Theory and Underdeveloped Regions*. London: Duckworth.

——. 1968. *Asian Drama*, 3 vols. New York: Pantheon.

——. 1970. *The Challenge of World Poverty*. New York: Vintage Books.

——. 1984. "International Inequality and Foreign Aid in Retrospect," pp. 151–65 in Gerald Meier and Dudley Seers (eds.), *Pioneers in Development*. Oxford: Oxford University Press.

Ocampo, José Antonio and María Angela Parra. 2007. "The Continuing Relevance of the Terms of Trade and Industrialization Debates," pp. 157–82 in Esteban Pérez Caldentey and Matías Vernengo (eds.), *Ideas, Policies and Economic Development in the Americas*. London: Routledge.

Palma, Gabriel. 1989. "Structuralism," pp. 316–22 in John Eatwell *et al.*, *The New Palgrave: Economic Development*. New York: W.W. Norton and Co.

Prebisch, Raúl. 1950. *The Economic Development of Latin America and Its Principal Problems*. New York: United Nations.

——. 1984. "Five Stages in My Thinking," pp. 175–91 in Gerald Meier and Dudley Seers (eds.), *Pioneers in Development*. Oxford: Oxford University Press.

Sapsford, D. 1985. "The Statistical Debate on the Net Barter Terms of Trade: A Comment," *Economic Journal* 95 (September): 781–8.

Sapsford, D. and J. Chen. 1998. "The Prebisch-Singer Terms of Trade Hypothesis," pp. 27–34 in David Sapsford and John-ren Chen (eds.), *Development Economics and Policy*. London: Macmillan.

Sarkar, Prabijit. 1986. "The Singer-Prebisch Hypothesis," *The Cambridge Journal of Economics* 10 (December): 355–72.

Singer, Hans. 1950. "The Distribution of Gains between Investing and Borrowing Countries," *American Economic Review* 40 (May): 473–85.

——. 1984. "The Terms of Trade Controversy," pp. 275–303 in Gerald Meier and Dudley Seers (eds.), *Pioneers in Development*. Oxford: Oxford University Press.

——. 1989. "Terms of Trade and Economic Development," pp. 323–8 in John Eatwell *et al., The New Palgrave: Economic Development*. New York: W.W. Norton and Co.

Spraos, J. 1980. "The Statistical Debate on the Net Barter Terms of Trade," *Economic Journal* 90 (March): 107–28.

——. 1983. *Inequalising Trade?* Oxford: Oxford University Press.

Sunkel, Osvaldo. 1990. "Reflections on Latin American Development," pp. 133–58 in James Dietz and Dilmus James (eds.), *Progress Toward Development in Latin America*. Boulder, CO: Lynne Rienner Publishers.

—— (ed.). 1993. *Development from Within*. Boulder, CO: Lynne Rienner Publishers.

Toye, John. 2004. *The UN and Global Political Economy*. Bloomington, IN: Indiana University Press.

UN (United Nations). 1949. *Relative Prices of Exports and Imports of Underdeveloped Countries*. New York: United Nations.

Warren, Bill. 1980. *Imperialism: Pioneer of Capitalism*. London: Verso.

Part 3

The structural transformation

7 The state as a potential agent of transformation

From neoliberalism to embedded autonomy

After reading and studying this chapter, you should better understand:
- the neoclassical perspective on the role and nature of the state in the economy;
- P.T. Bauer's critique of developmentalist theories and his case for spontaneous development;
- the origins and importance of market failure versus government failure;
- the nature of the so-called New Political Economy and DUP activities;
- the importance of government leadership versus government followership;
- how state activities can result in crowding-out or crowding-in of private investment;
- the crucial role of a meritocracy of state employees to successful development;
- the debate over corruption, development, and the state
- the characteristics of the non-cohesive, the fragmented-intermediate, and the developmental state;
- the meaning and significance of embedded autonomy and state capacity;
- the four roles of the developmental state.

Introduction

This chapter concentrates on one of the most disputed areas of development studies, the role of the state in the process of economic transformation. It begins by framing the discussion within the context of major socio-economic realignments of the 1980s which set the stage for a renewed debate over the role of the state. It concludes with recent research which attempts to reaffirm the potential of the state as an agent of economic growth, a view widely held by the early developmentalists as well as the heterodox thinkers discussed in the previous two chapters.

While England was passing through the agonies and ecstasies of the Industrial Revolution (1750–1840), a group of industrialists, pundits, and economists urged unrestrained *laissez-faire* as the best means to advance the wealth of the nation, and they made an impression in national political-economic debates of the period. Because many were located in the thriving industrial town of Manchester, they became known as the "Manchester Liberals." In their view, if the British government would only eliminate almost all regulations and constraints on market behavior, then England would forge ahead even faster.[1]

Economic liberalism receded into the background in the latter part of the nineteenth century, however, and it seemed to have all but disappeared by the time that Keynesian economics dominated policy-making and economic theory, from the 1940s to the mid-1970s, except among economists associated with the Austrian school and monetarist doctrines. As Keynesianism appeared unable to cope with the turmoil of inflation, instability in global commodity markets, and recurrent business cycles that swept the advanced nations in the 1970s, a counter-revolution in economics began to emerge. At first this new liberalism appeared to be restricted to the economic policies of the United Kingdom under the prime ministership of Margaret Thatcher (1979–90) and of the United States under President Ronald Reagan (1981–9), but the political changes in those countries opened the door wide to a rethinking of many economic concepts.

Very briefly, this counter-revolution in economic thinking found its way into development issues. Perhaps most telling was the Cancún Conference in Mexico in 1981, when the Mexican President José López Portillo (1976–82) hosted the assembled dignitaries of the "North" and "South" in what was to have been the first in a series of global conferences designed to establish a **New International Economic Order** (NIEO).

The NIEO concept had arisen in the course of the 1970s; at best, it constituted a hazy vision of a revised global economy wherein the needs and aspirations of the developing nations were to be given new and greater consideration by the already-developed nations. The NIEO concept reflected the fact that in the 1970s in many less-developed nations a new optimism and assertiveness had replaced the caution and uncertainty of the 1960s *vis-à-vis* the developed nations.

The Organization of Petroleum Exporting Countries, OPEC, above all, had made great strides in its bid to confront the transnational oil companies of the advanced nations by pushing up oil prices via a classical cartel arrangement. The funds earned by OPEC were to a large degree deposited in private banks in the major financial centers of London, New York, Frankfurt, and Tokyo. Dubbed "petro-dollars," these funds were subsequently recycled back to the less-developed nations, where they became an important means of financing new, often grandiose, development projects, and, just as often, conspicuous consumption contributing to the debt crisis which overwhelmed many less-developed nations in the 1980s (see Chapter 16). Privately owned corporations in many less-developed nations also had been courted assiduously by investment bankers from Europe, Japan, and the United States, who sought to offer loans without serious investigation of these firms' repayment capacities.

At the Cancún Conference, both Mrs. Thatcher and President Reagan attacked the NIEO concept, expressing their distaste for the stabilization of raw material export prices and the enhancement of foreign aid spending from the developed nations that formed two key planks of the NIEO proposal. At the same time, though, Mrs. Thatcher's and President Reagan's call for a greater reliance on the free market as the vehicle for promoting economic development seemed to fall on deaf ears. But not for long.

By late 1982, the debt crisis was in full swing, and as a result of a recession in the advanced nations which had begun in 1981, oil prices fell rapidly and the terms of trade began to move strongly against the less-developed nations. Economic crisis spread through the world economy, hitting many less-developed nations particularly hard, especially the Latin American and African nations which had accumulated huge, and unsustainable, external debts. Not all the less-developed nations had borrowed heavily, however; or if they had, some had apparently used their loans more productively. Nor did all the less-developed economies have their economic dynamic closely tied to the export of raw materials, which especially suffered from the world recession.

A small number of East Asian nations, South Korea and Taiwan in particular, seemed able to adjust to the changing economic circumstances of the 1970s and 1980s with a minimum of distortion to their economic and social growth. Most less-developed nations, however, were not so fortunate. With the global economic environment so drastically changed, the basis for the hopeful assertiveness of the less-developed nations apparent at the beginning of the 1970s, which had been based on a growing world economy, quickly evaporated. The ideas and policies advocated by Mrs. Thatcher and President Reagan soon became central to the new economics of the late 1970s and beyond. And there was to be no subsequent North–South conference to give voice to the concerns of the less-developed nations. Brief and never very productive, even the idea of a "North–South" dialogue seemed moribund.

Giving initial shape to the new economic policies advocated by Thatcher and Reagan were a group of economists known as **monetarists**. Like the Manchester Liberals before them, monetarists abhorred government regulation, advocated a minimalist role for the state to enforce property rights, to maintain order and social stability, and to provide for the public defense. They interpreted the economic turmoil of the 1970s as largely the result of too much governmental intervention in private markets. In time many monetarists became associated with a new school of thought termed "neoliberalism," since the new policies they would recommend went beyond the old monetarist formulations.

The neoliberal program was broader and more fundamental in advising novel policies in all spheres of the economy, compared to the earlier monetarist policy package which centered on limiting the rate of growth of the money supply to control inflation and spur growth. By the mid-1980s, the term neoliberal had supplanted monetarism as a label to describe the predominantly *laissez-faire*, market-driven economic policies sweeping across the globe from advanced countries to less-developed nations and to the newly formed republics emerging after the collapse of the Soviet bloc in 1989.

Origins of the neoliberal paradigm

P.T. (Lord) Bauer (1915–2002), a Hungarian-born economist whose research work in England elevated him to the peerage in 1983, was an early pioneer in development economics, with a strikingly different perspective from any discussed in previous chapters. Lord Bauer attributed his distinctive insights to reasonably long stints in the tropics, first studying colonial rubber production in Malaysia and later examining the role of traders in West Africa who provided both inputs to the production of cocoa, peanuts, cotton, and kola nuts and then, later, acted as intermediaries when they bought the cash crops for sale on the world market.

Based on his field experience and his interpretation of cause–effect relationships, Bauer boldly rejected many of the most widely used concepts that had become central to the emerging field of development economics. For example, he denied that there was any evidence of vicious circles of poverty in less-developed nations or "cumulative causation," as Gunnar Myrdal had called these mechanisms which exacerbate poverty where it already exists. At the same time, in observing key export crops such as rubber, cotton, and cocoa, he maintained that the benefits of expanded production of these crops spread down to even the very small farmers; there were no "enclaves" in the export-oriented economy that did not gain from export expansion. Thus, Bauer returned to the Smithian idea that the market "harmonizes" the interests of all participants: everyone gains. Even major investments in infrastructure by government, he claimed, were not necessary to start off, accelerate, or push the process of development forward, a view distinctly contrary to what other development economists had claimed, as we read in Chapter 5.

Bauer's criticism of traditional development economic ideas is so sweeping that it is worth citing him at length, to capture the breadth and intensity of his views.

The historical experience I have noted was not the result of conscription of people or the forced mobilization of their resources. Nor was it the result of forcible modernization of attitudes and behavior, nor of large-scale state-sponsored industrialization, nor of any other form of big push. And it was not brought about by the achievement of political independence, or by the inculcation in the minds of the local people of the notion of national identity, or by the stirring-up of mass enthusiasm for the abstract notion of economic development, or by any other form of political or cultural revolution. It was not the result of conscious efforts at nation building or the adoption by governments of economic development as a formal policy goal or commitment. What happened was in very large measure the result of the individual responses of millions of people to emerging or expanding opportunities created largely by external contacts and brought to their notice in a variety of ways, primarily through the operation of the market. These developments were made possible by firm but limited government, without large expenditures of public funds and without the receipt of large external [aid].

(Bauer 1984: 30–1)

For Bauer, then, it was not government intervention, a driving vision of the future, a desire for development, infrastructure creation, a "big push" of industrialization, or anything other than the pursuit of individual gain by individual members of society, mediated by the market, that resulted in economic growth and development. Bauer's view, then, is little more than a restatement of Adam Smith's praise of the invisible hand as a coordinating mechanism and of how the decisions of individuals to accumulate capital in the pursuit of profit lead to social progress. But it is important to draw the distinction between Lord Bauer having *concluded* this is how development was taking place in the less-developed nations and his providing any evidence as to whether, in fact, this is what was actually happening.

The free market, exports, and the nature of colonial rule: a case-study of British West Africa

How is one to assess Bauer's view that development is really a very simple process that results from allowing unimpeded market forces to work, thus permitting individuals to freely pursue their self-interest in a free market setting? This is an important question to pursue. A complete answer would take us into a complex study of British West Africa and Malaysia, subjects far from the theme of this chapter. Nonetheless, a brief discussion is in order, and our comments will be limited to the situation in West Africa.

To begin, it is necessary to restate the obvious: in Ghana (known as the Gold Coast in the colonial era) and Nigeria, it was British colonial policy in the era described as "mature colonialism" in Chapter 3, rather than unregulated and impersonal free market forces, which determined economic results. Furthermore, in the case of tropical West Africa, it is important to understand that the leading theorists of colonial rule were committed to the concept of **native paramountcy**; they sought to preserve indigenous cultural patterns and structures of production. Foremost in taking this position was F.D. Lugard, who was born in India and made a career in the British military and as an administrator of the British empire.[2] (In pointed contrast, in East Africa the British sought to introduce large plantations and turned over the bulk of the economically desirable resources to British subjects. The case of land settlement in Kenya is described in Chapter 11.) In West Africa there were few large mineral deposits which could form the basis for a mining enclave economy.

Many West African peasants had established skills in the cultivation of export products. After the elimination of the slave trade in the nineteenth century, many small farmers, through the intercession of traders, maintained centuries-old trade links with the global economy. Peasant agriculture, geared to the rapidly expanding global market, became the new motor-force of the West African economy. When the British expanded their colonial empire into West Africa in the late nineteenth century, Lugard's new principles of colonial rule were easily adapted to fit the West African situation. This created a modicum of stability, permitting the British to operate profitably within an established economy based on peasant production for the global market:

> [The] first principle was that African colonies should be supervised by strong central British governments, but that actual administration should be left to "native authorities," preferably hereditary chiefs, who must be both "unfettered" and yet "subordinate." "Unfettered" meant that they were largely autonomous, with their own treasuries, courts, laws, etc. "Subordinate" implied that they lost control over foreign relations, obeyed laws made by the colonial government and the order of the British officials, and contributed part of their revenues to the colonial treasury. Thus the system tried to balance native autonomy and imperial authority, enabling non-Europeans to take an active part in their own government without weakening British control.
>
> (Fieldhouse 1967: 299)

What quickly becomes obvious, then, is that whatever the merits of Bauer's observations, he managed to conduct his research in an area of the British empire which was extremely atypical, even in relation to the rest of Africa, where plantation-based and/or mining enclave economies were the rule, not the peasant-based, export-oriented structures found in West Africa.

The British sought to press their advantage in West Africa via their control of inputs and outputs, leaving direct cultivation of crops to native cultivators. By all accounts the peasant cultivators did respond to market (or price) incentives. Yet it is important to recognize that while small farmers were free to respond to price changes, they did not own the land they farmed. Villages and tribes owned this land and determined individuals' access to it. Custom, therefore, served as a barrier to the emergence of a landed aristocracy. Consequently, one of the basic elements of a market economy, a free market in land, did not exist.

Perhaps the greatest stimulus to increased export production arose from strategic government investments in infrastructure. For example, between 1898 and 1932 the colonial government built 2,100 miles of railways and 6,000 miles of roads in West Africa. The new transportation system permitted peasants to deliver their crops more easily from the hinterlands to the global markets. Previously, cultivators had been restricted to transporting marketable surpluses via small river canoes and human porterage over crude trails where no draught animals were used.

Furthermore, the native crops proved to be atypical, in that prices generally rose over time, with the terms of trade either working to the advantage of West African commodities, or at least not moving strongly to the disadvantage of such commodities (Kemp 1989: 180–1). Nigeria was atypical, too, in that it sold a small but diversified range of commodities, such as cotton, peanuts, palm oil, rubber, and cocoa, which generally maintained their value in the global market. Therefore, it was not dependent on merely one cash export crop. Moreover, the absence of mineral resources encouraged the development of indigenous cultivators.[3] Thus, based upon native cultivation and strong prices, an indigenous middle class began to emerge, composed of prosperous peasants, small tradesmen and shopkeepers, astute middlemen traders, and well-trained African employees of the colonial administration.

But the West African situation left the indigenous population dependent on foreign manufactured goods, since colonial rule had precluded industrialization. Meanwhile, large, usually British-owned, trading companies eventually bought the commodities produced in Africa and made profits on shipping, insurance, and finance. A division of labor imposed by colonial rule, not by the market, permitted the West African middle class to share in the economic prosperity, though this was not wholly of the market's making. And, although Bauer dwelt upon the individual initiative of the native cultivators, major changes in agricultural technique were, in fact, brought about by the government's Agricultural Department in the 1920s and 1930s, not by small-scale decision-makers in the fields (Kemp 1989: 179).

The Depression of the 1930s and the turmoil of the Second World War ushered in a fifteen-year period of debate and experimentation, leading to an attempt by the British to foster economic development in West Africa via an activist role for government. Bauer, writing in the early 1950s, deemed this experiment a failure. His critique concentrated on the role of marketing boards which, beginning in Ghana in 1939, began to buy up all the main export crops, ostensibly in order to maintain and stabilize prices. Under this scheme, individual West African middlemen buyers could still negotiate with peasant cultivators, but they were forced to sell to the government at a fixed price. Rather than actually benefiting the peasants, the marketing boards were a disguised means to help finance Britain's war effort. To understand the size of the wedge which the government had driven into the export market, immediately after the war the marketing boards were absorbing 42 percent of the value of the Nigerian cotton crop, 40 percent of the peanut crop, and 39 percent of the cocoa (Kemp 1989: 182). Compounding difficulties was the fact that prices began to fall in the 1950s, and the terms of trade started to turn against West African primary producers. Meanwhile, the marketing boards used their vast surpluses to finance colonial rule and to subsidize a range of infrastructural investments and development programs (Helleiner 1966: 32–3). As one result, British-financed public investment flowing into British West Africa was greater in the period 1946–60 than it had been in the previous forty-five years (Hopkins 1973: 280).

Examining the role played by the marketing boards, long after Bauer had chronicled their failure to either stabilize prices or help the small producers, Gerald Helleiner argued that Bauer had misrepresented the changing objectives of colonial rule. For Helleiner, the boards were to be judged not as instruments to protect the interests of the small cultivators, but as devices to facilitate the economic development of Nigeria. He concluded that, on the whole, the marketing boards had used their surpluses wisely, investing in agricultural research, road construction and local industry (Helleiner 1966: Chapter 10). In doing so, hypothesized Helleiner, they had successfully forced the prosperous peasantry to save and invest a portion of output that would otherwise have been spent on imported consumer goods. The marketing boards, then, were instrumental in helping to break the vicious circle of the open economy, whereby the lack of a balanced infrastructure and industry had forced West Africa to depend upon and perpetuate a primary commodity-based development strategy, which had reached its limits by the early 1950s, if not earlier.[4]

No one seems to question the entrepreneurialism and market responsiveness of the peasant cultivators of Ghana and Nigeria. Yet those characteristics alone have been insufficient to lift West Africa from economic backwardness, Lord Bauer's analysis notwithstanding. By all accounts, West Africa's relative success with an open economy based upon the supposed comparative advantage in commodities such as cotton, palm oil, peanuts, coffee, and cocoa had been exhausted by the early 1950s, when the terms of trade moved against West Africa, as they tend to do for most primary products.

Today, Nigeria, despite its good fortune in having discovered massive petroleum reserves since Bauer conducted his research, is one of the poorest nations in the world. In the World Bank's listing of 133 nations, Nigeria was thirteenth from the bottom ($930 in PPP), with a per capita average income of $390 per year in 2004. For the period 1990–2000, average per capita income *decreased* by 1.0 percent per year, while rising oil and commodity prices pushed per capita GDP growth to a respectable 4.7 percent rate in 2002–5.

On the human development index, Nigeria ranked eighteenth from the bottom out of 177 countries (down seven since 1999), with an HDI value of 0.45. Life expectancy at birth was only 43 years (down 17 percent since 1999!), while only 52 percent of the population had access to safe (potable) water, and 71 percent lived on less than $1 per day in 2003. Ghana (with $2,280 in PPP) had a much higher ranking – thirty-ninth from the bottom in the World Bank's 2004 listing. Ghana enjoyed modest per capita growth of 1.7 percent per year, 1990–2000, but its per capita income peaked in 1978. On the HDI Ghana was forty-one from the bottom (down two positions since 1999), with an HDI value of 0.53, life expectancy at birth was 57 years, and 25 percent of the population lacked access to safe water.

To what degree have forces totally beyond the control of these nations been instrumental in their development experience? How much of what has occurred, or has not occurred, since the 1940s in terms of development can be accounted for by factors stressed by the developmentalist and/or the heterodox economists discussed in the previous two chapters? In order for Bauer's view to be accepted, he would have to address these issues with care. This he never did, as John Toye has argued (Toye 1987: Chapter 3).

Did Bauer actually uncover through his studies evidence that the market and *laissez-faire* are key to economic development, or did he merely observe an unusual series of virtuous circles operating at a point in time that led him to be unduly optimistic about what the market might achieve on its own? Michael Lipton has maintained that Bauer observed situations that were extreme and atypical, and that it would be inaccurate to draw broad conclusions from such research.

> Export-crop production and trade in Dutch and British colonies in some areas received significant inflows of private foreign capital from 1900 to 1940. The local farmers and traders in a few such areas – having much spare land and enjoying population growth well beyond present rates in poor countries – built significant growth, quite widely shared, upon these inflows. Because rubber (and tin) and, in the early stages, cocoa and robusta coffee faced promising markets, international commodity cartels – or even agreements – were nuisances, not necessities. But were these realities too specific and temporary to allow us to transfer the lessons to other situations?
>
> (Lipton 1984: 48)

Lipton is of the opinion that Bauer failed to demonstrate the generality of his examples. As a counter-example, Lipton offered the case of Bangladesh, where the two main exports are jute and tea; both faced a price-inelastic world market demand. Bangladesh failed to attract foreign capital inflows, unlike Ghana and Malaysia, there is little spare land, and the population has a low capacity to save and invest that could allow them to shift production to other crops that might be more advantageous or to industrialize (Lipton 1984: 49–50). Lacking the fortuitous inflows of foreign capital may account, at least partly, for the extremely low level of per capita income of $380 in Bangladesh in 2000, the thirty-fourth-lowest among the 133 larger countries the World Bank lists, with an HDI value of 0.470, one hundred and thirty-fifth out of 175 in ranking.

Ethnicity and race

For Bauer, growth is due to both reliance on the free market and intangible characteristics which he believes are "natural" to certain ethnic groups. For example, Bauer made the following comparison: "Indians have many valuable economic qualities, especially when they are not hampered by a very restrictive social environment, they are nevertheless generally less ingenious, energetic, resourceful and industrious than the Chinese, as is suggested by the relative performance of Chinese and Indian emigrants" (Srinivasan 1984: 52–3). T.N. Srinivasan cites a study conducted by an Australian expert invited by the Japanese to analyze their economy in 1915 that offered similar "cultural" observations to those of Bauer:

> My impression as to your cheap labour was soon disillusioned when I saw your people at work. No doubt they are lowly paid, but the return is equally so; to see your men at work made me feel that you are a very satisfied easy-going race who reckon time no object. When I spoke to some managers they informed me that it was impossible to change the habits of national heritage.
>
> (Srinivasan 1984: 53)

No development specialist would agree with such a characterization of the Japanese today (or of the Indians and Chinese). For institutional economists, such as Ayres (see Chapter 6), the great change in the Japanese workforce arose through evolutionary change in the institutions of Japanese society and economy that brought on changes in attitudes and work behavior. The "nature" of the Japanese was not immutable for all time, assuming that the characterization in the above quotation was ever reasonable. And, one would presume, had evolutionary changes identical or similar to those in Japan taken place in other nations, or were they to take place in the future, they too would exhibit a history of emerging economic development, as the "traits" of the population changed to fit the evolving social and productive structure's needs. Racial and ethnic theories of development have been dismissed by careful empirical research, yet they seem to resurface in subtle ways in some scholarly circles again and again for those looking for easy explanations for differences in levels of development among nations.

Government in the process of development

Bauer's perspectives have been applied selectively by the advocates of neoliberal economics. For example, race and ethnicity do not play an explicit explanatory role in neoliberal thinking. Yet one of Bauer's major themes has become the pivotal point of neoliberal analysis: the essentially negative role of government. If one were to express in a sentence the essence of the neoliberal approach to development issues, it would be the following: "Nations are not poor because they are poor, that is, because of vicious circles; rather they are poor because of too much government interference." Bauer and others have constructed their criticism of the state on three pillars:

1   The public sector has become over-extended in the economy.
2   The public sector has over-emphasized capital formation and mega-investment projects.

3   The public sector has caused the proliferation of economically distorting controls in the economy that create incentives for inefficient production and ineffective economic structures.

One difficulty with the first proposition is that Bauer and others fail to demonstrate an operational definition of the proper size of the public sector; thus "over-extended" becomes little more than an ideological construct, sometimes supported by anecdotes of government inefficiency suggesting the need for a smaller state.[5] Regarding the second statement, Bauer maintained that relatively little initial capital investment is needed to foster more rapid development, and consequently foreign aid is unimportant, as is any "big push" to kick-start the economy.

On this detail, Bauer is very much the exception within the neoliberal school. Neoliberals in power typically regard foreign aid and technical assistance as extremely important instruments of influence which can be utilized to impose their policies on less-developed nations that otherwise risk forgoing such assistance. In the 1980s and 1990s, the World Bank and the International Monetary Fund became extremely influential in curbing the public sector in the less-developed world, and in the transitional economies of the former Soviet bloc, by using the threat of withholding aid and loans as their prime instrument for gaining policy agreements with less-developed nations that were consistent with neoliberal precepts.

Furthermore, Bauer's position suggesting but a modest role for capital formation in the process of economic growth has not received much theoretical or empirical support (remember the neoclassical growth model of Chapter 4; see Chapter 8 on endogenous growth theories). Clearly, however, there have been instances when mega-projects, such as a huge irrigation complex of dams and canals, have been poorly thought through and executed and where, alternatively, small sums spent on large numbers of individuals, small farmers for example, ultimately could have benefited society more than the mega-project. At the same time, one can find instances when funds spent on small businesses and micro-industries were squandered or poorly conceived from a social point of view. Such anecdotal information, however, proves nothing (see Focus 7.1).

In many instances, the size of government is determined by the degree of market failure in society, that is, by the extent to which unregulated market outcomes are inefficient or by situations when the market does not perform the desired function at all. In societies where there are pervasive monopoly and oligopoly forces, government action is clearly called for to reconstitute competitive forces. Likewise, if there is widespread hunger and malnutrition, subsidized food programmes aimed at the needy poor may be both a social and political necessity, as well as being economically sound, since healthy and adequately fed workers are likely to be more productive as well.

If employers are few and powerful, that is, if there is monopsony in the labor market, a government policy of minimum wages and protection for unions may be called for. Many essential infrastructure and social overhead capital projects, including the provision of universal public education, will not be provided via the free market, because the *private* rate of return is too low, and the payout period too long, to interest private investors, though the *social* rate of return can be quite high and the benefits to future economic and social growth large.

The list of possible situations wherein there may be a need for corrective or complementary government action in the private sector could easily be extended, but the point is that because of the failure of the market system to deliver results that are either economically

FOCUS 7.1   GOVERNMENTAL INEFFICIENCY AND GROWTH

The World Bank's *World Development Report* for 1983 argued that governmental policies led to large-scale price distortions and that such distortions negatively affected the
growth process. The study was based on thirty-one less-developed nations, and it did
show that governmental controls over the foreign trade sector, such as over- or under-
valued exchange rates, tariffs, and subsidies, which introduced large price distortions,
were, in fact, correlated with slower growth rates.

However, such large distortions could explain only 25 to 34 percent of the variance in
growth between nations. The World Bank could not account for the most important factors
which determined differences in the growth process between nations. At least part of the
remaining two-thirds to three-quarters of the determinants of growth divergences may be
due to positive effects associated with government spending on infrastructure, education,
public health, and other government-induced forms of expenditure. Analyzing the World
Bank's conclusions, John Toye noted "[The World Bank study] cannot be expanded into a
justification for ... the unrestricted play of market forces and government non-intervention
in economic life."

Following a close study of the East Asian economies (see Chapter 8 for more details),
the World Bank has suggested the extreme importance of human capital formation to
economic development. And government action in this arena is a fundamental source
of such investment, which so positively influences future growth rates and the level of
per capita income. Government intervention of this type is a kind of "policy distortion"
that is favorable. As we shall see, there is no doubt government policies *can* adversely
affect growth and development. However, there is nothing about the experiences of the
successful developers to suggest that this must be the outcome. There is good state
policy and there is bad state policy creating "good" distortions and "bad" distortions.

Sources: Toye 1987: 86; World Bank 1993

efficient or socially acceptable, there is a legitimate role for government that most economists accept as necessary to improve the operation of the entire economy, including the
private capitalist sector.

Where to draw the line between legitimate and illegitimate public sector activity cannot be
determined without a careful examination of the needs and situation of each nation. Should
a government own the railways, or a bicycle factory, subsidize health care, provide subsidies
to export businesses, tax imports, provide low-cost loans, or control the price of life-saving
pharmaceuticals? There is no a priori answer that is correct for all time and all circumstances.

For neoliberals, however, the answer to these questions is almost invariably, no. Government should do as little as possible and never should it favor one sector of the economy
over another, what neoliberals call trying to "pick the winners." Commenting on this, John
Toye draws the contrast between the neoliberal interest in proving "government failure" and
their corresponding lack of interest in studying, or sometimes even acknowledging, market
failure.

> All the well-known causes of market failure – including various types of monopoly – are
> brushed aside as insignificant, while "government failure," in the form of corruption,
> centralization of power and loss of individual liberty is brought to centre stage. But the
> ploy of using government failure to outweigh that of market failure is a shallow one.
> Apart from the fact that the methods for balancing one kind of failure against another
> cannot be specified, the underlying assumption that the two types of failure are separate

and unconnected is false. All markets are made within some legal, social and political framework of institutions. One of the most familiar causes of market failure, for example, public goods externalities, is precisely an explanation of why this must be so. ...

But just as importantly, the causal link also works in the other direction, from market failure to government failure. Technical externalities are a source of monopolistic behavior and oligopolistic behavior. Monopoly or oligopoly firms which are also large can usually exercise considerable political power and influence. This is not just a matter of contributing to political parties' funds. It extends more subtly to other forms of patronage ... [e.g. good jobs to former state employees].

(Toye 1987: 67)

This argument reveals another cornerstone of neoliberal analysis: the market is presumed to be the repository of efficiency. Government, on the other hand, is the root of inefficiency. The two sectors of the social economy are treated as autonomous, as if there were a firewall between them.

What if, however, government inefficiency arises, at times, from powerful economic interests, such as an agro-export-financial elite, who exercise determinant power over government policy in certain areas? Shrinking the size of government under these conditions actually might increase the latitude of power of these private sector groups which are unconstrained by competitive markets.

This result is assumed not to occur, however, because neoliberal economists make the critical, if typically unspoken, assumption that less-developed nations operate within a framework that is essentially a competitive market system. What happens if one drops the competitive assumption? Then, as Adam Smith understood (see Chapter 4), much of the supposed efficiency of markets disappears as more powerful interests can manipulate the market system in their favor. The need for government and public sector action as a counterweight becomes more compelling.

The neoliberalism of Deepak Lal

Deepak Lal was professor of political economy at University College, London and is currently at the University of California, Los Angeles, and has conducted a great deal of research under the auspices of the World Bank. He is perhaps best-known for his 1985 book *The Poverty of Development Economics*. He had earlier assisted in an influential compendium under the editorship of Ian Little which was critical, but not dismissive, of the role of the state in development (Little *et al.* 1970).

In his 1985 book, Lal attempted to dismiss virtually the entire body of thinking, analysis, and research conducted by the developmentalist and the heterodox thinkers discussed in the previous two chapters. Utilizing a polemical style, Lal maintained that heretofore development economics has been subject to what he termed a "dirigiste dogma," that is, a preference for state-led development strategies. He suggested that development economists had embraced instinctively the notion that the price and market system should be "supplanted (and not just supplemented) by various forms of direct government control ... to promote economic development" (Lal 1985: 5).

Lal, however, offers not a single example of such thinking. One might reasonably ask, exactly where in their writings have the major contributors to development economics advocated the elimination of market processes? Certainly there were some who strongly advocated development planning to propel forward certain projects and sectors. But this, in itself, falls far short of "supplanting" markets throughout an economy and replacing them with "direct government control."

Within the broad spectrum of development ideas there is, as noted in earlier chapters, a healthy skepticism regarding the degree of efficiency of many markets in less-developed nations. This skepticism has not arisen, however, from a "dogmatic" rejection of markets, nor from any lack of knowledge as to what markets can accomplish when they function well. Rather, it is due to an understanding that markets often do not function properly in a society that is in transition from a pre-capitalist, dualistic social formation to a fully articulated capitalist society.

The need to supplement the market process in many areas has been vigorously advocated, but supplanting the market has not been a major or even a minor theme of development economics. Virtually *no* economist would deny the importance of the information and coordination functions of properly functioning markets. Markets are an essential component of any well-functioning economy, and the more efficient such markets are, the better. The role of government will likely be less when markets work well, but every society needs some degree of state intervention to have a well-functioning social system, of which the economy is only a part, albeit an important part.[6]

Lal further attacks development economics for its emphasis on macroeconomic considerations, such as growth, industrialization, investment, and employment, rather than on micro-efficiency. This, of course, is a valid observation. But the corrective is not to be found in the direction which Lal advocates: emphasizing micro-efficiency, while assuming that the "big picture" macro-issues will somehow take care of themselves as a result of the focus on the microeconomic matters.

Refutation of Lal's microeconomic perspective has come from various respectable quarters, for example the eminent development economist Gerald Meier and, more recently, the World Bank. The Bank has shown that the successful less-developed economies, such as South Korea and Taiwan, owe their success not to "getting prices right" (i.e. micro-efficiency) but to finding the right dynamic strategies at the macro-level and the micro-level that can accelerate growth and improve productivity (World Bank 1993).

Meier shows that the arguments made in favor of import substitution industrialization, emphasizing the dynamic effects of policies while devoting relatively little attention to micro-inefficiencies which may either arise or be exacerbated by such policies, actually have their application in the so-called export-led success cases (Meier 1990: 155–69). Hla Myint, another admirer of the neoliberal school, makes a similar observation:

> Is it really true that the export-oriented countries are free from trade distortions in the neoclassical sense? … the export-oriented countries, such as Korea, appear "to have intervened virtually as much and as 'chaotically' on the side of export promotion as others have done on the side of import-substitution" and their success cannot be attributed to "the presence of a neoclassically efficient allocating mechanism *in toto* in the system".
>
> (Myint 1987: 117)

What is most interesting here is that the study cited by Myint in support of government intervention (Bhagwati and Krueger 1973) was written by two of the most prolific and influential contributors to the modern neoliberal school! In looking at some countries, the least successful less-developed nations, neoliberals argue that government intervention has slowed economic growth. In other cases, such as Japan and East Asia, they suggest that government intervention has *not* slowed growth and may even have accelerated it. So even from their own observations it would seem that it is not *whether* there is government intervention into the economy, but rather the *nature* of such intervention. Again, policy can be either good, enhancing growth and human development, or it can be bad, consistent with stagnation.

A third component of Lal's critique of development economics concerned the abandonment of the theory of comparative advantage, as a result of export pessimism (declining terms of trade). He maintains that the East Asian "miracle economies" have employed a policy of virtual free trade (Lal 1985: 47–8), by which he seems to mean that the Asian economies tampered just enough with market outcomes, and that a little fudging against the doctrine of *laissez-faire* is permissible if one ends up promoting exports. An observer might reasonably ask, "Why is it wrong to promote industrialization policies designed to expand the internal market (ISI), but correct to utilize the same degree of government policy guidance to promote the external market?" Why term one approach "dirigiste dogma" and the other "virtual free trade"? Cannot both be equally effective?

Such questions are not adequately addressed by Lal. However, in much neoliberal analysis it is argued that the state can, and perhaps should promote exports, but only as long as the domestic economy is "open" to the world market. The need for openness arises from the desire to achieve micro-efficiency. It is argued that if domestic producers are cut loose from all price supports, tariffs, and subsidies they will be *forced* by the market to either become competitive with imports, or die.[7]

This "do-or-die" imperative can have unfortunate collateral effects, however. It can flood an economy with imports, thereby creating a balance of payments crisis. It can also produce a general business slump. In other words, the search for micro-efficiency via the neoliberal shock treatment may create macroeconomic instability. Furthermore, the idea of both promoting exports and forcing a *laissez-faire* regime on domestic producers is logically flawed. Countries on the receiving end of export promotion policies may wish to retaliate, for good reason, when such policies affect their domestic production and employment. Furthermore, an extensive econometric study by Dani Rodrik points to the conclusion that "there is no economic argument for government policies that favor export activities" (Rodrik 1999: 37)

> The claims made by the boosters of economic integration … are frequently inflated or downright false. Countries that have done well in the postwar period are those that have been able to formulate a domestic investment strategy to kick-start growth and those that have had the appropriate institutions to handle external shocks, not those that have relied on reduced barriers to trade and capital flows. Policymakers therefore have to focus on the fundamentals of economic growth – investment, macroeconomic stability, human resources, and good governance – and not let international economic integration dominate their thinking on development.
>
> (Ibid.: 13)

Other difficulties with Lal's analysis arise when he seems to simultaneously decry all government interventions, and hold up government policy as the chief source of economic growth:

> It can be argued that the very large increase in infrastructure investment, coupled with higher savings rates provides the major explanation of the marked expansion in

the economic growth rates of most Third World countries during the postwar period, compared with their own previous performance and that of today's developed countries during their emergence from underdevelopment.

(Lal 1985: 72)

This would seem to be a justification of government intervention, at least as it extends to the provision of infrastructure. But, only a few pages on, government seems to again have become the root of all evil!

Most of the more serious distortions in the current working of the price mechanism in the Third World countries are due not to the inherent imperfections of the market mechanism but to irrational government interventions, of which foreign trade controls, industrial licensing and various forms of price control are the most important. In seeking to improve upon the outcomes of an imperfect market economy, the *dirigisme* to which numerous development economists have lent intellectual support has led to so-called "policy-induced" distortions which are more serious than any of the supposed distortions of the imperfect market economy it was designed to cure.

(Ibid.: 77)

Why, one might ask, if governments were so astute as to create the proper amount of infrastructure, were they so incapacitated in pursuing policy elsewhere? Lal's all-out attack on earlier development economists has provoked a strong response, particularly from John Toye, who has analyzed the propositions and analytical constructs of the neoliberal school:

The idea that development economists approve all forms of economic controls, whatever their defects, and whatever their costs, is a total misrepresentation of other people's views. ... It can easily be shown that, for example, Gunnar Myrdal, who is named by Lal as an arch *dirigiste*, published his criticisms of economic controls in India *before* the publication of the OECD volume [Little *et al.* 1970] and that the details of the criticism are very similar.

(Toye 1987: 77)

The new political economy

From 1982 to 1987, Anne Krueger was the chief economist of the World Bank, the largest economic research organization in the world. During that period, the World Bank's shift toward neoliberalism was consolidated. In 2001 Krueger was appointed First Deputy Director of the International Monetary Fund, the second-ranked position in that vastly influential organization.

Professor Krueger has authored numerous books and articles on development policy, and she is one of the most renowned advocates of the neoliberal perspective. Although Krueger draws extensively on the work of Bauer, Little, and Lal, her own research lacks the stridency of tone and/or the broad sweep of much of the work of the other major contributors to the neoliberal perspective. Professor Krueger has concentrated on the economic waste and social distrust and instability which occur when the state has the capacity to redistribute income to selected elements of society. For example, import licenses create monopolies and permit the earning of economic profits for those who receive the licenses. If the price of the license is less than the economic advantage of owning such a license, the fortunate importer is in a position to receive revenues that have not been earned. Such revenues are "windfalls" which constitute unearned sources of income, or **rents**. Krueger has argued that the large state sector in many less-developed nations creates widespread opportunities for such rents, and under such conditions one should expect a pathological result: the **rent-seeking society**.[8]

The factional state and rent-seeking behavior

In Krueger's interpretation, the state is a ready source of rents via subsidies, tax exemptions, tariffs, and a wide range of government policies. Once such rents have been captured by certain interests, those groups have a vested interest in keeping such policies in place. The implication seems to be that state activities drain the economy of its dynamism. Wrong-headed policies are maintained, because groups with an interest in the rents to be derived from such policies exert pressure on the state to maintain those policies. As a consequence, consumers end up paying unnecessarily high prices, production costs are too high, and tax revenues are squandered, as state functionaries fail to pursue the general welfare in deference to vested interests.

The above is a description of what Krueger depicts as the "factional state" (Krueger 1993: 66). The factional state can be either democratic or authoritarian. In either case, such a state can be riddled with corrupt and inefficient behavior. Under such conditions, what can be done? Krueger and neoliberal thinkers advocate the shrinking of the state to a minimum by selling off government-owned firms via privatization programs, the elimination of tariffs and import licenses, the end to special subsidies, and the elimination of any policy that might create gains for special interests.

An assessment of the neoliberal theory of the state

This school of thought has made a contribution to mainstream economic theory by arguing that the state should not be treated as *exogenous* and given in constructing economy theory and analysis. Rather, the state should be seen as *endogenous* to the economic system. This insight, hardly a path-breaking advance for heterodox theorists, who have taken such a position from the outset, could be the building block for a much more powerful understanding of the development process. How this can be achieved will be the subject of the remaining sections of this chapter.

Development economics needs a detailed theory of the state, and it also needs a body of research which reveals the extent to which rent-seeking prevails both within the structure of the state and within the private sector. Since by definition rent-seeking is socially wasteful and usually regarded as parasitic, it is often a difficult task to conduct research on such a topic. How can reliable research be conducted when those who receive rents and those who permit such rents to occur are determined to hide their activities?

The assumption that rents arise uniquely in the state sector is unwarranted. It is presumed that within the private sector there is either perfect competition or enough "workable" competition to eliminate rents. Throughout the developing world, however, there is scarce evidence to support such a proposition. One of the conditions for perfect competition is that all participants in the market have equal access to knowledge of the conditions of the market – the perfect, or symmetrical, knowledge assumption. Knowledge is a scarce commodity, however, often closely guarded. This is part of the problem. Also, there is often an absence of knowledge or information. In a society that has not reached a certain level of development, the mechanisms to produce and diffuse knowledge, such as journals and professional associations and their congresses, often do not exist, or do not exist to a sufficient degree. Public records may be either incomplete or very difficult to obtain. The difficulty in obtaining information means that there is a greater cost involved, compared to more developed nations, in terms of time required to search out relevant information, and even though the value of time may be lower in poorer nations, inaccessible information is just that – inaccessible, at least to some. Participants in the market will have different access to knowledge (asymmetric information), at least partly because of their varying ability to pay in terms of time devoted to the search for accurate information.

Of course, perfect competition entails much more than symmetric knowledge. The definition of free competitive markets is so restricted that even in the advanced nations there are few sectors that come close to this "norm" of orthodox economics. To make the assumption that the less-developed nations have efficient competitive markets, and are merely saddled by a corrupt state, as do the neoliberals, serves only to undermine the neoliberals. At the very least, the burden of proof is on those who boldly assert the existence of competitive markets. The literature which we have reviewed in this chapter does not present such a proof, nor does it explore this all-important theme.

Has neoliberalism run its course, to be replaced by yet another major focus in the early twenty-first century? There is strong reason for thinking this to be the case. First, the countries which have received the strongest inducements to shift toward neoliberalism have fared rather poorly, with the case of Chile requiring careful interpretation (Cypher 2005).

The largest social experiment with neoliberalism has been conducted in Mexico. The neoliberals strongly believe in using aid from World Bank funds, IMF funds, and bilateral institutions to induce a shift toward neoliberal policies. Mexico received more assistance from such sources than any other nation in the late 1980s and early 1990s. The shift toward neoliberalism seemingly succeeded in bringing inflation under control. But, since 1987, the primary device used to control inflation has been a tripartite agreement between the government, business, and organized labor, such that major prices have been set by decree, exactly the opposite mechanism from that advocated by neoliberals. The government's deficit was eliminated, but this was due in large part to the massive one-time sell-off of most of the government-owned firms. Where will the government find revenues once the funds from privatization have been spent?

While the neoliberals are anxious to point out their victory over inflation and their taming of the government's deficit, the Mexican economy has been plagued by modest growth, declining or stagnant living standards, massive migration into the United States, and the near-elimination of much of the small-business sector. As the Mexican economy slid into recession in 1995, neoliberals seemed to lose interest. Yet, the lessons are there to be learned. Neoliberalism did not revive the Mexican economy (Cypher 2001a; Delgado Wise and Cypher 2007). And, given the magnitude of the effort and the willingness of the Mexican policy-makers to introduce neoliberal policies, it is doubtful that a better case study of neoliberalism can be found (Cypher 2001b).

Neoliberalism faces a deeper difficulty than the failed experiment in Mexico, however; it falsely claims that the Asian miracles of Taiwan, South Korea, Singapore, and Hong Kong were models of free market economies which successfully developed. In the following chapters, we discuss the process of development in these nations, showing how this process radically diverged from the market-driven interpretation of the neoliberals. For the moment we cite only the conclusions of an important study of the industrialization policies of Taiwan and South Korea. Here Robert Wade poses the question: "Did government policies lead the industrialization process, or did government policy *follow* where the free market would have taken these nations?" If the first part of Wade's inquiry is answered in the affirmative, then Taiwan and South Korea would be seen as successful examples of state-led development. If the latter part of his question is answered in the positive, they would be seen as having received a modest boost from the government, arriving at the same destination as they would have without any government intervention. Here are his major findings:

> We began with the mainstream interpretation of East Asian success within economics, which I called the self-adjusting market theory. It gives government an important but background role as regulator and provider of public goods. Whatever else we conclude from the present evidence, we can surely say that the governments of Taiwan and South Korea have gone well beyond this theory – beyond the role described for them in neoclassical accounts, and beyond both the practice of Anglo-American governments and the neoclassical principles of good economic management.
>
>   The second conclusion is that much of this intervention has been of a leadership rather than just a followership type. It has done more than assist private producers to go where they have gone anyway.
>
> (Wade 1990: 260)

As a result of the critical scrutiny of the state that the neoliberals undertook in the 1980s, a new and more robust conception of the role of the state in the development process has begun to emerge. By forcing such a reassessment, the neoliberals have made a positive contribution to our understanding of the process of development. This reassessment is based upon the concept of the endogenous nature of the state. It is increasingly understood that *all* successful development has depended on an activist state (Adelman 2001; Chang 2002; Morris and Adelman 1988).

Working with a set of studies conducted by the World Institute for Development Economics Research (WIDER), Shapiro and Taylor demonstrate that "getting prices right," the neoliberal recommendation for the ills of less-developed nations, is not enough. They find that only if attempts at price reform are coupled with large-scale state interventions, such as aggregate demand manipulation, export subsidies, public investment, and barter trade deals, can countries improve their economic performance (Shapiro and Taylor 1990).

The neoliberal school often cites Turkey as an example of a successful development path based on free market principles. Shapiro and Taylor point, however, to a WIDER study which discovered the following set of relationships almost the reverse of the account offered by the neoliberals.

> Turkey's export "miracle" in the first part of the 1980s rested upon a preexisting industrial base created by ISI, policies leading to contraction of domestic demand for manufactures, attempts at general price reform, subsidies of up to one-third of export sales plus related incentives, and rapid growth in the demand for the products the country could produce by culturally compatible buyers in the region (the Gulf countries and both sides in the Iran-Iraq war). Had any one of these factors been missing, the boom probably would not have occurred.
>
> (Ibid.: 866)

Research conducted by WIDER also shows that public investment tends to stimulate private capital formation; this is in direct opposition to the presumed relationship postulated by the neoliberal school. For them, public investment crowds out private investment. A large body of research suggests that this is simply not true. Indeed, these studies suggest that on average every dollar of public investment *induces* one dollar or more of private investment. In other words, public spending results in the **crowding-in** of private investment.

The practitioners of the "New Political Economy" believe that the state should be a maximizer, rationally finding the right combination of minimalist policies which free the "natural" development forces in an economy. According to their view, nations such as South Korea owe their success to their willingness to follow the guidelines of neoclassical economic theory. Writing on the Asian miracles, Gottfried Haberler flatly stated: "These economies pursue, on the whole liberal market-oriented policies. ... Their success is fully explained by, and confirms, the neo-classical paradigm" (Haberler 1987: 62). Such a perspective is totally alien to specialists who have studied these economies. Tun-jen Cheng notes that factors never mentioned by neoliberals, particularly colonialism, transnational firms, and the World Bank, had much to do in shaping development strategies which were spearheaded by the state (Cheng 1990: 141).

As the logical critiques mounted and as the empirical research proliferated, those who continued to favor the neoliberal theory of the state faced deepening skepticism within the field of development economics. Major theoreticians and researchers, particularly the Nobel Prize recipient Joseph Stiglitz, have sought to advance the discussion of the role of the state. By the late 1990s Stiglitz was urging the creation of a "Post Washington Consensus" that would refocus the entire discussion of the state toward (1) concepts and policies originally advocated by the Developmentalists (see Chapter 5); and (2) a detailed emphasis on lessons to be learned from the experience with successful forms of state intervention in selected developing nations (Amsden 2001; Evans 1998; Stiglitz 2001). It is to that discussion that we now turn in the closing sections of this chapter.

Embedded autonomy

Peter Evans has made great strides in the development of a robust theory of the state in less-developed nations. Evans maintains that it is possible to identify three archetypes of the state: (1) the predatory state; (2) the intermediate state; and (3) the developmental state (Evans 1995). In his conceptualization, states can vary, depending on the historical evolution of specific societies. States are the result of complex historical forces and relationships, but they are also actors or agents potentially capable of shaping and influencing the ongoing process of historical evolution:

> States are the historical products of their societies, but that does not make them pawns in the social games of other actors. They must be dealt with as institutions and social actors in their own right, influencing the course of economic and social change even as they are shaped by it.
>
> (Ibid.: 18)

In Evans's richly detailed study one finds a thorough depiction of both intermediate and developmental states. These are states where the structures and capacities deployed by the state serve as *agents* of societal transformation and growth. In these states and societies, there exists a viable joint project, wherein civil society (the private sector) and the state managers are able to constructively and dynamically interact to engage in societal transformation.

While Evans offers a theoretical conceptualization of states, he does not present a dynamic analysis of why and how his three archetypical states come into existence, how they are perpetuated, or how they metamorphose from one archetype to another. In this dynamic sense, he does not offer a complete theory. Subsequent research following the opening created by Evans has been impressive, but the terrain is vast and many questions remain. Most of this research has been focused on East Asia and China and on the concept of the developmental state. Research on the intermediate state has been focused on India, and has brought that giant nation into closer focus (Chibber 2003; Kohli 2004; Pinglé 1999). Atul Kohli's comprehensive study *State-Directed Development* addresses the question of the origin of state types. The *type or form* of colonialism which was imposed on the nation determines to a great degree the nature of the state form that will endure long after formal independence (Kohli 2004: 27–61, 225–55, 301–23).

> Colonialism has proved to be the most significant force in the construction of basic state structures in the developing world …
>
> Much of the developing world was dragged into the modern era by colonialism. However one judges it, this is a historical legacy with which all scholars interested in the political economy of development … must come to terms. Colonialism everywhere was a system of direct political control created to enhance the political and economic interests of the ruling power … These colonial constructed political institutions, in turn, proved to be highly resilient, influencing and molding the shape of sovereign developing country states.
>
> (Ibid.: 409)

In brief, Kohli finds that to an important degree the distinct type of colonialism the Japanese imposed – what we have termed progressive colonialism in Chapter 3 – helped put Korea (and Taiwan) on a very different path that positioned it well to catch the opportunities thrown up in the 1950s. But this was not the case for India.

The British evolved a contradictory combination of institutions, many retarding, while some were highly functional in terms of operating a state system that would nurture the growth process. Thus the case of India is one where the concept of the intermediate state can be applied. Meanwhile in Nigeria (and in British West Africa) where P.T. Bauer had maintained that promising results were to be expected, the British imposed a distinct form of state structure and colonial rule, constructing a set of retarding institutions that have been entrenched through adverse path dependence. Once a nation becomes "locked in place" state forms tend to be reproduced and perpetuated (Chibber 2003). Military coups, democratic surges, and other factors that can lead to regime change may also fundamentally alter the structure of the state. So too might incremental change, but solid advance on this question awaits detailed case-studies.

The non-cohesive state

The non-cohesive state (termed "predatory" by Evans) is one where the appropriation of unearned income via rent-seeking has become endemic and structural. Everything is for sale: the courts, the legislature, the military, the taxing authority, etc. Government employees use their authority to maximize, in the shortest possible time, their accumulation of wealth. Political offices are held not for the reason of providing service to a nation, but for the purpose of individual gain in a society which may offer few alternative avenues to wealth accumulation. With corruption endemic, "rational" individuals may prepare for their own economic demise by establishing secret bank accounts in Switzerland or other havens for flight capital.

Evans did not devote much of his research to the non-cohesive state, and a critical review of this construct has stressed the fact that he here neglects the possible causal linkages between a predatory private sector and the state as the two collude (Kohli 1999: 99). He does show, nonetheless, that this formulation closely fits the Congolese state, and probably aptly describes many other states in Africa, Latin America, and the Middle East.

In the non-coherent state, we find a vitriolic mixture of traditionalism and arbitrariness characteristic of pre-capitalist societies. There is a scarcity of trained bureaucrats, and an absence of both a meritocracy and rule-governed behavior throughout the state apparatus. The state operates according to the whims of a strong president or leader who functions in the "patrimonial tradition" of an absolutist ruler. Around the president is clustered the "presidential clique" of perhaps fifty people who control the state apparatus and use it for their own ends, as a result of their personal and perhaps familial ties to the leader. Beyond the inner circle lies the "presidential brotherhood," the second circle of power, where state managers seek to both plunder society and continue to pledge their allegiance to the inner circle of power. Some of the most notorious features and results of the predatory state are (Evans 1995: 12, 248):

- "Predatory states extract at the expense of society, undercutting development even in the narrow sense of capital accumulation."
- "Predatory states lack the ability to prevent individual incumbents from pursuing their own goals."
- "Personal ties are the only source of cohesion, and individual maximization takes precedent over pursuit of collective goals."
- "The predatory state deliberately disorganizes civil society."[9]

Evans's general concepts fit well into an analysis of Nigeria: "The British ... ran Nigeria on the cheap" (Kohli 2004: 291–2). The British were unwilling to commit the expertise and financial support needed to create a viable centralized state. The British approach in Nigeria (unlike that in India) was to foster indirect rule (using existing structures of power and control), giving rise to a state riddled with personalistic leaders who were unconstrained by strong institutional structures. Public officeholders used their positions to control and privatize public resources.

Nigeria's colonial state was formed with weak and incompetent bureaucracies, as no strong civil service developed. The state was so weak and decentralized that no effective means of direct taxation was achieved. "The British slowly but surely ceded power to a variety of indigenous forces that were divided along ethnic and tribal lines" (ibid.: 292) giving rise to a geographical division between the north and the south-east and south-west. State power was never directed toward promoting a *national project* of economic development. The Second World War changed the dynamics of the economy and society in Nigeria as the British sought expanded production of commodities and imposed greater state control regarding production. But the paucity of administrators caused by the war led to more power being exercised by the three key regions, fragmenting Nigeria further. All this led to a disunited anti-colonial/nationalist perspective that lacked cohesion.

In 1960 the British ceded independence to the Nigerians, who were divided by tribal, personal, and regional interests, while the northern interests scarcely participated in the push for independence. But it was the British state that created, facilitated, and exacerbated many of the regional tensions of Nigeria with its divide and rule on the cheap strategy.

In lieu of creating a national civil service that might have been a uniting force, by 1945 the British employed only 75 Nigerians as senior civil servants. The remaining 1,375 British senior civil servants, selected without a rigorous merit-based process, ran the infrastructure and government agencies (ibid.: 318) Subsequently, "Nigerianization" led to a haphazard process whereby between 1955 and 1960 Nigerian senior civil service employees surged from 550 to 2,308 – most poorly trained and selected less on merit than political considerations (ibid.: 319).

Nigeria is not the story of failed developmental efforts, but rather of the failure to ever make the effort to make a commitment to a vision and a policy of economic development. This failure of vision includes the lack of promotion of an indigenous cadre of entrepreneurs, the neglect of a strategy to focus on possible applications of modern technology – particularly in agriculture – and the omission of a policy to engender a technologically competent, disciplined working class.

The problem with the indigenous business managers was not one of "willingness," but rather "ability," while the state had no strategy to enhance the technical and organizational capabilities of this vital stratum. That is, the state failed to set up business schools, large-scale engineering programs or forms of technical training for selected business owners. Little effort was made to find a way to initiate the transference of know-how via "learning by doing" and other forms of spin-off from the foreign firms to indigenous managers and technicians. Nor were efforts made to train the working class.

Instead, from 1966 to 1970 the military exploded from 11,000 to 270,000, while the number of federal employees soared from 65,000 in 1965 to 300,000 by 1984. Including regional governments, para-state firms, etc., over 2 million worked in the public sector in 1986 (ibid.: 344–7). The oil boom of the 1970s led to a policy of undisciplined public sector job creation without regard for the broadening/diversification of the oil-dominated production base.

Oil revenues as a share of all governmental revenues leapt from 25 percent in 1970 to between 70 and 80 percent throughout the 1970s and 1980s. As a consequence investment jumped from 12 percent of GDP in 1950 to more than 30 percent in the1970s. But little of lasting value occurred, as the state spent on grandiose construction projects such as stadiums and a new capital city, Abuja, or infrastructural projects (many abandoned in the 1980s, when oil prices declined). Costs were driven to unknown levels (200 percent above those of Kenya) as a result of expensive imports, incompetence, the paucity of technical workers, and corruption in contract management (ibid.: 356). When oil prices declined in the 1980s Nigeria lost close to 50 percent of its manufacturing production (ibid.: 351).

The fragmented intermediate state

Many states are *fragmented intermediate* states where inconsistencies reign, yet (unlike the non-cohesive states) they are able to mount and sustain a development project. Such states do, at times and within specific sectors, exhibit the loathsome features of the predatory archetype. But they also exhibit a complex range of attributes which cannot be explained within the neoliberal paradigm which accepts the non-cohesive state as an inevitability.

The fragmented intermediate state exhibits "pockets of efficiency," where state managers demonstrate both their professionalism and competence in designing, promoting, and completing imaginative and important projects, either jointly with the private sector, or on their own through state-owned enterprises (SOEs). A particularly good example of this is to be found in Alice Amsden's careful treatment of the very successful Brazilian development bank BNDES (Amsden 2001: 141–5; see also Chapter 9, Focus 9.3 in the present work). But the state apparatus is not built on a pure meritocracy. Intermediate states fall victim to "bureaucratic fragmentation," where professionalism dominates in some sectors and agencies, while personal ties and/or corruption form the basis for decision-making and authority in other parts of the state apparatus.

Such a state fails to confirm the neoliberal portrayal of utterly futile and unproductive state intervention. Yet intermediate states lack the means to consistently transform society, even as they are able to engineer successful sectoral transformations.

Such societies do not suffer from too many bureaucrats, but too few, according to Evans. For Evans, invoking the concepts of Max Weber, a fully formed and fully functioning bureaucracy entails merit-based recruitment, long-term career rewards for state managers, social status for government employees, and a coherent institutional structure which can form a constructive counterpart to private-sector institutions. Intermediate states demonstrate some of these Weberian attributes, some of the time, in some sectors of society. But pervasive imbalance is endemic.[10] We can summarize the results of much research on the fragmented intermediate state – particularly as it has been studied in India – as exhibiting the following five characteristics:

- state authority is fragmented: intra-elite and elite–mass conflicts are pervasive
- while pursuing state-led industrialization the state also aspires to redistribute income and create a social safety net
- the citizenry is frequently mobilized and weak political institutions fail to channel this energy/activism
- relations between state and capital are volatile – close at some moments, distant or confrontational at others
- the state demonstrates moderate levels of professionalism among its bureaux.

These concepts can be employed to understand both Brazil and India, as discussed in Chapter 9, Focus 9.5, "Is India a free market miracle?" (Chibber 2003; Herring 1999; Kohli 2004: 219–28; Pinglé 1999; Schneider 1999). But to really understand the use of the term "fragmented intermediate," it is necessary to view this type of state in relation to Evans's third possible state form, the developmental state. Understanding this third archetype will sharpen our conceptions of the other two state forms, and it will allow us to introduce a concept which will become an integral component of the development process as described in Chapters 8–11.

The developmental state

The key characteristic of the developmental state is **embedded autonomy**. An embedded state possesses a variety of institutionalized channels where the state apparatus and the private sector continually interact in a constructive manner via a "joint project" of fostering economic development. The developmental state is clearly *endogenous*; it is broadly embedded in civil society via a dense web of networks. Some parts of the state apparatus may be tightly linked to specific sectors. These broad and dense institutionalized channels of communication and interaction provide the links whereby the state is continually in the process of constructive negotiation and renegotiation of policies and goals intended to move a society toward a higher and higher level of economic and social development (Pempel 1999: 141–60). "Embeddedness … implies a concrete set of connections that link the state intimately and aggressively to particular social groups with whom the state shares a joint project of transformation" (Evans 1995: 59).

But embeddedness alone is not enough, for there is always the danger that the state apparatus can be "captured" by the very interests and sectors it seeks to guide, promote, and control. In order to guard against the risk of capture, the state apparatus must have integrity, loyalty, and cohesiveness. In short, the state must also exhibit the characteristics of *autonomy*. Autonomy implies that the state can stand alone, above the fray and beyond the controlling reach of vested interests which would seek to capture the power of the state and turn that power to their very specific, short-term advantage.

An autonomous state has to be able to draw on its own vision of economic transformation, and this vision has to be the result of a highly competent group of state managers who have achieved their power via proven performance and professional competence which undergird the merit-based hierarchy of state employees. State managers cannot be mere visionaries; they must develop their own capability to deliver technological entrepreneurship to selected sectors of the economy (see Focus 7.2).

Obviously, the pure concept of embeddedness logically leads to the capture of state policy-making by the sectors which the government seeks to guide and promote. The pure concept of autonomy leads to the problem often exhibited by the Indian state; a merit-based state management which is culturally cut off from the wider society and which lacks the ability to find the common ground for "joint projects" leading to economic transformation. Each concept alone is an insufficient, though necessary, characteristic of the successful state. Combining the two enables the state to overcome the risk of "capture" while avoiding the trap of pure autonomy whereby there is no effective means of constructively interacting with the private sector (Evans 1998). Figure 7.1 illustrates the nature of the developmental state, focusing on three key variables – power, purpose, and capacity.

The power variable focuses our attention on the issue of compliance – the ability of the state to actually achieve coherent consent regarding the prioritization of the development project. But this power is conditioned by a deep alliance with the business elite to ensure that the nation will not be stalemated by factional disputes over state-led initiatives.

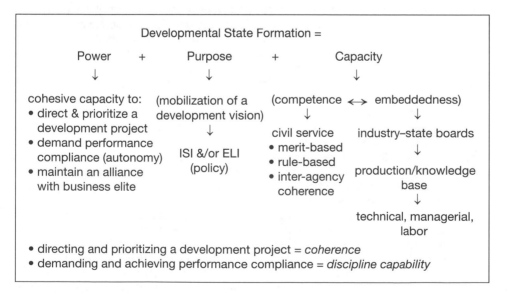

Figure 7.1 The developmental state.

FOCUS 7.2   CORRUPTION AND DEVELOPMENT: IS THERE A RELATIONSHIP?

Situated next to the US, where the contrast could not be more acute, Mexico is a nation whose citizenry frequently ruminate on the reasons for their low standard of living. The litany tends to be: Mexico has oil, gold, silver, lead, coal, and a vast range of other minerals, it has extensive farmlands and hard-working, creative people, so how can it be so poor?

Normally, the questioner has a quick, one-word answer: "corruption." Unquestionably, since the sixteenth century, at least, Mexico has had a corruption problem, partly as a residual of centuries of colonial rule when the rigid Spanish empire was commonly lubricated and drained through corrupt practices.

Corruption is difficult to measure and analyze. With that in mind, it is interesting to note that the most prosperous nation in Latin America is also widely considered to be the most corrupt – Argentina. How can Mexico's corruption be the cause of mass poverty in that nation and at the same time not generate, even when it reaches a higher level, a similar result in Argentina? Such seeming paradoxes can be repeated: Italy and Japan are both nations where corruption is considered to be widespread, yet these nations are extremely prosperous.

Given the above, development economists had not devoted much attention to corruption. But recently, as a result of the rising influence of neoliberal and neoclassical economic analysis in the field of development, the issue of corruption and "government failure" has been given much attention. Indeed, during his brief stint as president of the World Bank (2005–7) Paul Wolfowitz defined the issue of fighting corruption to be the Bank's "mission."

Following in the tradition of Peter Bauer, Deepak Lal, and Anne Krueger, the neoliberal recipe for corruption is straightforward: corruption occurs when employees of the state accept payments to provide benefits to business and other interests that they could not receive under the established rules of the society. The cure? Shrink the state to that of a simple "watchman state" through the privatization of state-owned enterprises, while eliminating as far as possible all other forms of state intervention such as tariff and trade policies and regulations designed to support infant industries, food and safety standards, and work conditions.

Implicit in this approach is the idea that if "resources" are not used by the state they will be "freed-up" for use by the private sector where a perfectly functioning free market system will automatically "allocate" these resources to their best possible societal use.

This perspective, sometimes known as "the new development economics" essentially does away, by assumption, with the entire field of development economics. The advocates of the new development economics assume that in the private sphere the operations of the market system (and the production system) are identical in rich and poor countries. Given this, what is holding poor countries back? The state, where the "unproductive," "rent-seeking" activities flourish to such a degree that the poor nation is locked into a situation of stasis, or a downward spiral.

After twenty-five years of poor results from the imposition of neoliberal and neoclassical structural adjustment policies (see Chapter 17) advocates of these policies have refused to acknowledge that such ideas are largely without substance in terms of promoting development: instead they now argue that had it not been for corruption the poor nations would have flourished with the guidance of the neoliberal and neoclassical policy prescriptions applied broadly since 1981.

Almost without exception, the role of state spending in developing nations is substantially lower than that of the advanced industrial nations. If corruption and rent-seeking behavior are destined to run rampant in the absence of a competitive market (i.e. in the state sector) – an essential tenet of the "new development economics" – why do advanced industrial nations have larger state sectors, where presumably the level of "misallocation" of society's resources would be even higher? Alternatively, why did once rapidly developing nations, such as the US in the late nineteenth century, have a small state, runaway levels of corruption, and the highest economic growth ever?

Ha-Joon Chang has noted that in Zaire (now the Democratic Republic of the Congo) under Mobutu's rule, this infamously corrupt leader removed from that terribly poor nation between 1965 and 1997 a sum equal to 4.5 times Zaire's 1961 national income. Meanwhile, in an identical thirty-two-year period (1966–98) the ruler of Indonesia, Suharto, took for his own use a sum of money equivalent to 5.2 times the 1961 national income of Indonesia. By 1997 Zaire's per capita income in purchasing power parity terms was only one-third the level achieved in 1965, while Indonesia's per capita income was 300 percent higher in 1997 than it was in 1966. (From 1966 through 2004 Indonesia maintained a strong 4 percent per year per capita growth rate of GDP.)

Chang brings into the analysis a very important issue, virtually unmentioned by the neoliberal and neoclassical advocates of the "new development economics" – capital flight. Capital flight is the rapid movement offshore (to safe banking havens such as Switzerland) of liquid funds when macroeconomic and/or political conditions are risky or when individuals receive massive payments that are likely to prove illicit. Capital flight is a serious problem for poor nations, but according to the advocates of the "new development economics" states are not to impose capital controls to limit the flow of funds across borders. Such regulations, it is argued, will interfere with the "free and rational" allocation of resources and will further serve to limit foreign direct investment by transnational corporations. What Mobutu stole of Zaire's wealth was frequently shipped offshore to Europe.

Suharto's graft was mostly redeposited in Indonesia's financial system and then circulated through this system, where it served to support whatever spending, wise or unfounded, borrowers and lenders settled upon. Eventually, then, the funds were likely turned into construction activities or business loans whereby actual production in Indonesia increased, as did jobs, etc. This tells us that corruption varies in its impact and that corruption alone does not explain the lack of development or economic growth. It also tells us that the issue is quite complex, hardly reducible to a simple prescription of "good governance."

The fact that economic development can occur, and has occurred, in nations riddled with corruption is not an argument for ignoring corruption or downplaying its negative characteristics. But the "new development economics" argues that the elimination of corruption is a *precondition* for development. Doing away with the state (constructing the minimal state and contracting out to the private sector every conceivable state-managed activity) is seen as a prerequisite to development.

One problem with this approach is that there are simply no examples of any poor countries that have first controlled corruption in a manner typical of the advanced industrial nations and then achieved high growth. High-growth developing nations such as China and India today, or Korea over the past forty-five years, were not models of "good governance" nor do they have minimal states. In fact, the causality has run the other way: state policies have been used to *create the conditions* for rapid development, in spite of the nagging problem of corruption. Indeed, the only hope for making progress against corruption seems to arise when nations have a higher standard of living, allowing them to pay public sector workers more and to institute and accelerate programs of professionalization among those employed by the state. Such steps, along with the implementation of oversight boards and procedures, have often served to damp down the level of corruption.

China's labor market has long been corrupt in every sense, often as a result of "market forces" driven by transnational corporations in collusion with captive unions and government officials. Partial resolution to this situation appeared to arrive in 2007. New policies have strengthened the lax regulatory grip of the state, now ensuring work contracts for migratory workers (guaranteeing pay), enforcing the minimum wage for these workers, and

Continued

increasing access to severance pay and many other important features extending legal protection to the majority of workers, all, presumably, arising from societal bargaining in the context of the growth already achieved by China.

Sources: Beatty 2007; Chang 2007: Chapter 8; Fine 2006; Khan 2006;
Khan and Barboza 2007; Weisman 2006

The purpose variable emphasizes the fact that the developmental state is capable of projecting a viable vision of development; often through harnessing a strong and broadly accepted conception of nationalism. This vision can find policy expression through the adoption of Import Substitution Industrialization or Export-Led Industrialization (ELI) policies (these policies are discussed in Chapters 9 and 10). Of greater importance than the discussion of preferred policies (for an Ag-led strategy see Focus 11.4) is the ability of the state to demonstrate "capacity."

Capacity breaks into two components: First, competence, which includes the capability of coordinating processes among competing agencies ("inter-agency coherence"). Second, embeddedness, which begins at the level of industry–state coordinating boards, but then reaches down into the production and knowledge bases where the society maintains and advances its production apparatus, bringing into motion and furthering its technical abilities, its managerial skills and capacities and its trained/skilled labor force. (Focuses 7.3 and 7.4 show in concrete terms the application of the concept of **state capacity** in Thailand and Korea.)

The four roles of the developmental state

Developmental states, such as those in South Korea and Taiwan, have the discretionary power to adopt several roles, depending on the needs and demands of society in general and the specific needs of sectors of the economy. Autonomy allows the developmental state to switch roles in specific sectors, as conditions dictate. Here we review the four roles described by Evans, utilizing his sometimes colorful terminology.

The custodian role

All states must have the ability to formulate and enforce rules and regulations. This role embodies the functions of the minimalist state, or the state conducting its "watchman/caretaker" activities.

The producer role

Even a minimalist state must produce adequate social overhead capital, or infrastructure, wherever and whenever there is a need for collective goods of this type. Beyond this relatively passive role, accepted as legitimate even by neoliberal critics of the state, there may be a need for the **demiurge** function. Here the state shifts to creating certain types of goods via state-owned enterprises or via joint venture schemes which link state investment funds with private-sector investors.

> When the state decides to play demiurge, it becomes involved in directly productive activities, not only in ways that complement private investments but also in ways that replace or compete with private producers. ...
>
> Playing the demiurge implies strong assumptions about the inadequacies of private capital. Local capital is presumed incapable of becoming a "transformative bourgeoisie,"

FOCUS 7.3 PERFORMANCE STANDARDS AND STATE STIMULUS IN THAILAND

Thailand would seem to have a fragmented intermediate state. This nation adopted meritocracy as its civil service employment standard in 1932. Many of the best-trained university students were attracted to government employment – particularly with the Board of Investment (BOI) – the key institution that oversees the promotion of industry in Thailand. The BOI was created in 1960 as the result of the Promotion of Industrial Investment Act.

"A very large number of investment projects grew up under the BOI's wing. ... According to the BOI's own estimates it was involved in roughly 90 percent of Thailand's major manufacturing projects covering both the private and public sectors and foreign and local firms." As the BOI's influence rose after 1960, the average annual rate of growth of manufacturing production surged by 60 percent in the 1960s to 9.1 percent and then to 10.1 percent in the 1970s. As the share of manufacturing climbed the BOI used a variety of forms of industrial stimulus, but only to the degree that *reciprocity* occurred in the form of *performance*.

Many of the forms of stimulus and the performance standards devised by the BOI are listed below simply in order to put in a more concrete form how both *intermediate* and *developmental states* might proceed to both encourage and influence the process of industrialization. For example, companies were granted targeted tax exemptions, but only on the condition that they would "perform" by meeting export targets. Failure to comply meant the end of the exemption.

Stimulus policies	Performance standards
1 Tax exemptions	Export targets
2 Tariff protection	Local-content standards
3 Subsidized credit (loans)	Debt/equity ceilings
4 Developmental banks	National ownership floors
5 Entry restrictions	Operating Scale Minima
6 Special benefits to	Hiring local managers
foreign firms	Technology transfers
7 Import duties on luxuries	Investment timetables
8 Duty exemptions on machinery	Regional location
(not made in Thailand)	requirements

The BOI has been viewed as "daring" and innovative, but also, at times, as indiscriminate in its support. Thus, while the rules of "micro"-efficiency may have been violated this has been considered insignificant in light of the growth achieved by the BOI's policy of tying programs of economic stimulus to tailor-made performance standards.

While Thailand's growth was interrupted by the Asian crisis of 1997, nonetheless annual per capita income growth in the 1990s was a respectable 3.3 percent, and in the 2002–5 period it has averaged a strong 5.1 percent.

Source: Amsden 2001: 20–4

of initiating new industries and sectors. Transnational capital is presumed uninterested in local development. If local capital is indeed unable, and transnational capital is in fact unwilling, to develop a new sector, then taking the role of demiurge may be the only way to move industrial development forward.

(Evans 1995: 79)[11]

But, Evans cautions, the demiurge role is potentially dangerous, because it may create a climate wherein the state is tempted to expand beyond a point where it can effectively

FOCUS 7.4   ADVANCED ELECTRONICS AND EMBEDDEDNESS IN KOREA

In the 1970s, the Korean government isolated the electronics industry as a key sector for promotion. For the two previous decades, Korea had developed a robust electronics assembly industry. Now it was to make the leap into the production of high-value-added products, commodities demanding advanced technologies in both production and design. To enable the electronics industry to make such a change, the Korean government took many steps to assist the growth of the industry. Among these was the creation of the government-funded and -run Electronics and Telecommunication Research Institute (ETRI).

By the mid-1980s, ETRI employed 1,200 highly skilled technicians and research personnel. ETRI was then deeply involved with industrial giants Samsung and Goldstar, and many other firms, to develop the technology for the production of large-scale computer chips. The objective was for Korea to match the pace of technological advance in the semi-conductor industry set by Japan. Cooperative research conducted by the industry and the government, and careful monitoring of technical progress by ETRI, was one major component of the process.

Selective prodding by the government, along with the allocation of generous loans, was the other major component for achieving success. All the companies eventually involved in the project acknowledged the constructive and crucial role of government cooperation with the private sector. Korea achieved its goal of shifting from low-value-added assembly electronics to technology-intensive, high-value-added electronics production over the planned period. As a result, workers' wages were able to rise, too.

Sources: Amsden 1989: 81–3; Evans 1995: 141

marshal its limited capabilities to act as an agent of economic transformation. Further, organizational problems may surface when state managers seek to expand or diversify an SOE into an area where it performs poorly and where the motivation to expand arises from the organizational structure of the SOE, rather than from the imperatives of transformational development. Finally, Evans points out that both the custodial role and the demiurge role arise from essentially negative conceptions of the private sector and of market structures.

The midwife role: a "greenhouse" policy

Here the developmental state acts as a facilitator by steering, assisting, and inducing the private firms to attempt new production challenges in areas which are of high priority. The state can lower risks, or increase the rate of return on investment, by allocating credit, limiting import competition, or even by providing subsidies. Essentially, midwifery entails the shifting of production activities into new areas which are believed to be conducive to development and which would not be areas where private capital would venture if left to market forces alone.

The role of husbandry: a policy of prodding and supporting

Husbandry tends to accompany and complement the role of midwifery. Often, in creating a new industry, there are related tasks which the state can undertake in order to help ensure the successful emergence of a new industry. Such activity will vary greatly with circumstances. Examples might be the state setting up research and development facilities or laboratories which undertake research which is complementary to a new industry. It might entail the establishment of state-owned facilities to produce the most technologically challenging inputs into an industry which the developmental state seeks to foster.

Depicting state forms

In Figures 7.2(a) and (b), we sketch the outlines of the Brazilian and South Korean states in order to exemplify the archetypes of the fragmented intermediate and developmental state. In both instances, the state essentially arises from two interrelated foundational pillars. Supporting the state on one side is its internal organization. Here one finds the characteristics which serve to define the cadre of the state employees. In Brazil (Figure 7.2(a)), one finds pockets of efficiency, but in general there is endemic organizational weakness – particularly because the 60,000 state workers who gain positions with each election are an *appointive* bureaucracy that is not embedded.

> Officials in an appointive bureaucracy rarely have the time to develop the long-term relations of trust and reciprocity with business that characterize developmental states in Asia because officials move to another job in another area of the State or the private sector whenever ... presidents change.
>
> (Schneider 1999: 304)

Imbalance reigns between the competent and cohesive portions of the state apparatus, and the wider areas where professionalism is in short supply. This gives state policy its *ad hoc* and irregular character. The state lurches toward viable projects, only to slide toward a morass of futility. But it does not stay mired. It demonstrates integrity *and* incompetence. It cannot generalize its successes, however.

The second foundational pillar undergirding the state is the state–society relation. Here, argues Evans, the Brazilian state has been unable to achieve embeddedness with industrial interests, because of the continuance of a strong agrarian sector of huge landowners who seek to utilize the power of the state to further their own interests. To a degree, because of its lack of autonomy from backward-looking agrarian interests, the Brazilian state is unable to pursue industrialization with all of its resources and capabilities. It has divided loyalties. It is partially captured by the agro-export interests, and therefore only intermittently does it exercise its transformational potential by establishing and nurturing a strategic industrial sector. Thus connecting the two foundational pillars is problematic. The state is "shaky" because at the foundational level there is some "interactive dissonance." Adding to this tension, the regional states exercise some autonomy, as they are not fully subordinated to the Federal State. At the crucial point of linkage between the two foundational pillars, we find both vicious circles of dissonance *and* virtuous circles of interaction.

A depiction of the Korean state

Our last consideration in this chapter is to turn to a description of the Korean state. Figure 7.2(b) depicts the concept of embedded autonomy. Notice that within the pillar of internal organization we find that employment is based on merit. Therefore a professional, coherent state bureaucracy is able to exercise autonomy *and* utilize its power to deliver administrative guidance to the civil society. At the same time the second pillar, state–society relations, is

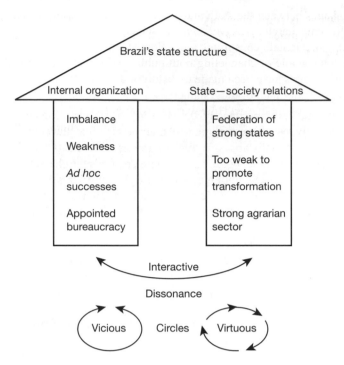

Figure 7.2(a) The Brazilian state: the intermediate state.

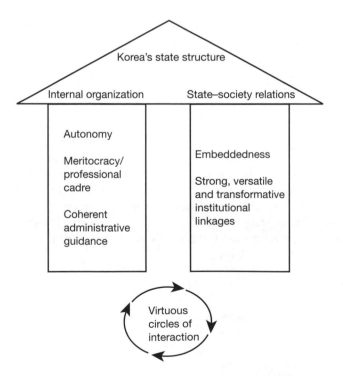

Figure 7.2(b) The South Korean state: the developmental state.

defined by institutional linkages between the state and society which are strong, versatile, and transformative. In short, state autonomy is *embedded* in society.

Consequently, the South Korean state constitutes a developmental state, with an endogenous basis of transformation capable of channeling both public and private investment to strategic sectors. Numerous attempts have been made to distort or discredit the record of the Korean state, particularly in the aftermath of the Asian crisis of 1997, because it constitutes the greatest challenge to the neoliberal theory. However, Ha-Joon Chang has demonstrated that the Asian crisis did not arise from any endemic failings of state intervention. Rather, it was the turn *away* from industrial policy after 1993 and the weakening of the state apparatus which facilitated duplicative investments in the 1993–7 period (Chang 2000). As we will see in the following chapters, the concepts of the state developed here have wide application and profound implications for the process of development.

Summary and conclusions

Our journey through the debate over the role of the state in the developmental process has led to the insights offered by Peter Evans and many others. The archetype constructions of the non-cohesive, fragmented intermediate and developmental states will be of use in understanding the role states play in given societies. Can intermediate states become developmental states? Evans argues that such a metamorphosis can be a daunting, but not an impossible, endeavor.

> existing public bureaucracies, certainly in Latin America and even to some degree in Africa, are not the irredeemable cesspools of incompetence that they are sometimes painted by neoliberal rhetoric. There are dedicated individuals working in public service in almost all countries … Most state bureaucracies, at least in Latin America, contain key agencies that at least in certain periods have displayed many of the institutional traits of "Weberian bureaucracies". Such agencies have performed with levels of efficiency comparable to those [of] their East Asian counterparts, despite being surrounded by a public sector that is much less effectual overall.
>
> (Evans 1998: 80)

He warns that: "The concept of embedded autonomy is a useful analytical guidepost, not an engineering formula that can be applied, with a few easy adjustments" (Evans 1995: 244). The goal of state policy must be to induce private investment and to channel such investment to strategic sectors. But embeddedness is easier to describe than attain. "Connecting state and society is the more difficult problem. Capacity without connection will not do the job" (ibid.: 244). Evans also warns us that the state-led successes in East Asia will not be easy to follow, because of the fact that state and society were well connected there as a result of what may be rather unique historical circumstances. Still, Evans illuminates a path to follow, while showing there is no simple road map to development. At the same time, Atul Kohli, after exhaustively examining the role of the state in Brazil, India, Korea, and Nigeria, reminds us that we ignore at our own peril the fact that:

> There are hardly any significant examples in the developing world, now or in the recent past, where industrialization has proceeded very far without state intervention. The underlying reason is simple but powerful: Private investors in late-late-developing countries need organized help, help that effective states are most able to provide to

overcome such obstacles as capital scarcity, technological backwardness, rigidities in labor markets, and to confront the overwhelming power of foreign corporations and of competitive producers elsewhere. ... state intervention in more or less successful industrializers varies, not so much by quantity as by type and quality. It is therefore patterns of state intervention in the economy that are key to explaining successful late-late development.

(Kohli 2004: 377)

Questions and exercises

1   Using the categories of non-cohesive, fragmented intermediate, and developmental states, review the discussion of the critique of state policies and practices offered by the neoliberals. How do these categories help you better understand the role of the state and the dangers of generalizing too broadly on the weakness of state intervention from specific instances?

2   Evans emphasizes that states have to play specific roles in order to promote development. Review the discussion of Deepak Lal and determine if the issues raised by Lal can be understood with greater precision with the use of Evans's categories. Why, or why not?

3   Review the case of Nigeria and Lord Bauer's analysis of West Africa, along with the discussion of non-cohesive state formation, as presented in this chapter. What are the lessons to be learned regarding the role of the state versus the role of the market in this instance?

4   Professor Krueger has maintained that the solution to rent-seeking on the part of state functionaries is the shrinkage of the state. Peter Evans's perspective is quite different. Compare their contrasting approaches to rent-seeking. Where do they agree, and when and why do they disagree?

5   Under what social and economic conditions are markets likely to fail? When is there likely to be government failure? Is macroeconomic inefficiency (for example, a high level of unemployment and underemployment) due to market failure or government failure?

6   Review Figure 7.1 and write a two-page essay on the state using all the terms and concepts from this figure to explain what is unique and important regarding the concept of the developmental state. How would you change this figure if you were to explain the idea of the fragmented intermediate state?

Notes

1   The classic study of the term "liberalism" is Girvetz (1963).
2   Lugard was an administrator of great renown and influence. He served as High Commissioner of Northern Nigeria from 1900 to 1906, and then as Governor of Nigeria from 1912 to 1919. After retirement he published a landmark work on colonial administration, *The Dual Mandate*. According to P.J. Cain and A.G. Hopkins, those who followed Lugard into colonial careers "were inclined to idealize rural Africa, to identify with 'natural' pastoralists and cultivators, and to view urbanized and supposedly 'detribalized' Africans with a mixture of disdain and alarm" (Cain and Hopkins 1993: 218).
3   Some mining occurred. Tin accounted for about 10 percent of Nigeria's exports before the Second World War.
4   Independence in 1960, unfortunately, did not carry with it a deep and profound consolidation of the hopeful trends and forces which had surfaced in the mid-1950s. From 1954 to 1960, Nigeria

experienced a very modest increase in annual per capita income of 0.32 percent. From 1960 to 1966, there was an annual decline of 0.72 percent in per capita income. In his interesting discussion of the Nigerian case, Tom Kemp argued that the Nigerian elite could not capture the momentum of the developmental strategy which was colonial rule's last effort in Nigeria. Nigeria's leaders had sprung from the prosperous peasantry, and their largely positive historical experience with market forces led them to adopt a relatively uncritical and passive posture regarding the limitations of markets. Thus, while the elite dabbled in developmental projects, their lack of determination and commitment to a strategy of "governing the market," as it is now termed, led to a downward spiral of dependence and decay:

> Already privileged economically and in the possession of educational advantages, they accepted personal advancement and enrichment as valid goals, modelling their expectations very much upon the life-style of expatriate Europeans in colonial times. The way was thus open for cooperation and collusion between politicians and civil servants on the one hand and indigenous entrepreneurs, of whom there was no lack of aspirants, and foreign businessmen on the other. Speculation and corruption became endemic in the new state, intertwined with regional and ethnic rivalries and favoritism which were to plague the country, bringing instability and a tragic war within less than a decade.
>
> (Kemp 1989: 184)

5 One particular target has been state-owned industries, or para-statals. The hypothesis of the neoliberals is that any activity which conceivably could be undertaken in a market environment will be more efficient if it is operated on a "for profit" basis. (Implicitly this approach assumes that the less-developed country has an efficient set of markets already in place.) Thus, in order to cut the state to its "proper" size, the neoliberals have strongly advocated privatization of state-owned industries.

Research into the issue of efficiency of state-owned industries is limited. However, one summary of the literature for Mexico, which has carried out the largest wave of privatizations in the less-developed world, indicates that many of the state-owned industries were no more inefficient than private-sector firms, while other state firms were operated "inefficiently" on purpose in order to subsidize private sector accumulation and/or to achieve other broad political goals. In other words, even though the employees and managers of these firms were government employees, that fact alone did not suffice to explain the efficiency level of the firm (Cypher 1990: Chapter 5).

6 The entire theme of the dynamic relationship between the state and the market has been brilliantly explored in a twentieth century classic, Karl Polanyi's *The Great Transformation* (Boston: Beacon Press, 1957).

7 We will discuss the impact of openness on the domestic economy further in subsequent chapters, especially 9 and 10. Some neoliberals have emphasized the possibility of accelerating technical change under the "do-or-die" imperative, while others have suggested that under such pressures indigenous entrepreneurial capabilities might blossom.

8 Rent-seeking is often subsumed under the more general category of "directly unproductive profit-seeking" (DUP) activities, such as lobbying, smuggling, bribery, monopoly, or any other activity which generates profits, but produces no goods or services directly.

9 Notice that the predatory state describes some of the features noted by Krueger, earlier in this chapter, under the heading of the absolutist state. Here, in contrast to Krueger, the dysfunctional state is viewed as an outgrowth of a specific historical condition. It is the "traditional," or pre-capitalist (semi-feudal/semi-capitalist) society, perhaps imbued with the ethos of merchant capital, which results in the absolutist state. Krueger assumes that by shrinking the state the society will be strengthened, because there is assumed to exist an ordered, structured, market-based economy. Evans avoids the dichotomous assumption "bad state/good civil society." Here a chaotic socio-economic system is complemented by a predatory state apparatus. Destroying such a state while leaving the socio-economic system untouched would not solve the basic underlying problems.

10 Notice the surface similarities between Evans's intermediate state and Krueger's factional state. Krueger finds rent-seeking, which distorts the intention of government policy by locking in place subsidies and other forms of vested interests. Her solution is shrinking the state. For Evans, rents

arise not from too much intervention, but from too little effective intervention, because of a lack of an adequately trained, professional civil service.

While far from the ideal, the intermediate state exhibits "pockets of efficiency" in the state sector, something Krueger rules out by assumption. Such "pockets" are hardly trivial; they form the basis for the creation of whole new industries. They redefine the production base, creating new forms of comparative advantage. Krueger's approach cannot accommodate such activities, which Evans presents in some detail. And, therefore, the new political economy approach has difficulty explaining the economic development of such nations as Brazil, India, or Mexico, all important instances of the intermediate state.

11 The concept of demiurge is not the same as what Lal called "dirigiste dogma." Lal refers to a situation wherein the government seeks to supplant the market, rather than supplement it. The demiurge function is limited to the creation of state-owned enterprises, or what are sometimes known as para-state firms.

References

Adelman, Irma. 2001. "Fallacies in Development Theory," pp. 103–34 in Gerald Meier and Joseph Stiglitz (eds.), *Frontiers of Development Economics*. Oxford: Oxford University Press.

Amsden, Alice. 1989. *Asia's Next Giant*. Oxford: Oxford University Press.

——. 2001. *The Rise of "the Rest."* Oxford: Oxford University Press.

Bauer, P.T. 1984. "Remembrance of Studies Past," pp. 27–43 in Gerald Meier and Dudley Seers (eds.), *Pioneers in Development*. Oxford: Oxford University Press.

Beatty, Jack. 2007. *Age of Betrayal: The Triumph of Money in America, 1865–1900*. New York: Knopf.

Bhagwati, Jagdish and Anne Krueger. 1973. "Exchange Control Liberalization and Development," *American Economic Review* 63 (June): 419–27.

Cain, P.J. and A.G. Hopkins. 1993. *British Imperialism: Crisis and Deconstruction 1914–1990*. London: Longman.

Chang, Ha-Joon. 2000. "The Hazard of Moral Hazard: Untangling the Asian Crisis," *World Development* 28: 775–88.

——. 2002. *Kicking away the Ladder: Development Strategy in Historical Perspective*. London: Anthem Press.

——. 2007. *Bad Samaritans: Rich Nations, Poor Policies, and the Threat to the Developing World*. London: Random House.

Cheng, Tun-jen. 1990. "Political Regimes and Development Strategies," pp. 139–78 in Gary Gereffi and Donald Wyman (eds.), *Manufacturing Miracles*. Princeton: Princeton University Press.

Chibber, Vivek. 2003. *Locked in Place: State Building and Late Industrialization in India*. Princeton: Princeton University Press

Cypher, James. 1990. *State and Capital in Mexico*. London and Boulder, CO: Westview Press.

——. 2001a. "Developing Disarticulation within the Mexican Economy," *Latin American Perspectives* 28 (May): 11–37.

——. 2001b. "NAFTA's Lessons: From Economic Mythology to Current Realities," *Labour Studies Journal* 26 (Spring): 5–21.

——. 2005. "The Political Economy of the Chilean State in the Neoliberal Era: 1973–2005," *Canadian Journal of Development Studies* 24 (4): 763–80.

Delgado Wise, Raúl and James Cypher. 2007. "The Strategic Role of Mexican Labor under NAFTA: Critical Perspectives on Current Economic Integration," *Annals of the American Academy of Political and Social Science* 610 (March): 120–42.

Evans, Peter. 1995. *Embedded Autonomy: States and Industrial Transformation*. Princeton, NJ: Princeton University Press.

——. 1998. "Transferable Lesson?: Re-examining the Institutional Prerequisites of East Asian Economic Policies," *Journal of Development Studies* 34 (August): 66–86.

Fieldhouse, David K. 1967. *The Colonial Empires*. New York: Delacorte Press.

Fine, Ben. 2006. "The New Development Economics," pp. 1–20 in Jomo K.S. and Ben Fine (eds.), *The New Development Economics: After the Washington Consensus*. London: Zed Books.

Girvetz, Harry K. 1963. *The Evolution of Liberalism*. New York: Collier Books.

Haberler, Gottfried. 1987. "Liberal and Illiberal Development Policy," in Gerald Meier (ed.), *Pioneers in Development*, 2nd series. Oxford: Oxford University Press.

Helleiner, Gerald. 1966. *Peasant Agriculture, Government, and Economic Growth in Nigeria*. Homewood, IL: Irwin.

Herring, Ronald. 1999. "Embedded Particularism: India's Failed Developmental State," pp 306–34 in Meredith Woo-Cumings (ed.), *The Developmental State*. Ithaca: Cornell University Press.

Hopkins, A.G. 1973. *An Economic History of West Africa*. London: Longman.

Kahn, Joseph and David Barbaoza. 2007. "As Unrest Rises China Broadens Workers' Rights," *New York Times* (June 30): A1, A5.

Kahn, Mushtaq Husain. 2006. "Corruption and Governance," pp. 200–21 in Jomo K.S. and Ben Fine (eds.), *The New Development Economics: After the Washington Consensus*. London: Zed Books.

Kemp, Tom. 1989. *Industrialization in the Non-Western World*. London: Longman.

Kohli, Atul. 1999. "Where do High-Growth Political Economies Come From? The Japanese Lineage of Korea's 'Developmental State'," pp. 93–136 in Meredith Woo-Cumings (ed.), *The Developmental State*. Ithaca: Cornell University Press.

——. 2004. *State-Directed Development*. Cambridge: Cambridge University Press.

Krueger, Anne. 1993. *Political Economy of Policy Reform in Developing Countries*. Cambridge, MA: MIT Press.

Lal, Deepak. 1985. *The Poverty of Development Economics*. Cambridge, MA: Harvard University Press.

Lipton, Michael. 1984. "Comment [on Bauer]," pp. 40–50 in Gerald Meier and Dudley Seers (eds.), *Pioneers in Development*. Oxford: Oxford University Press.

Little, Ian, Tibor Scitovsky and Maurice Scott. 1970. *Industry and Trade in Some Developing Countries*. Oxford: Oxford University Press.

Meier, Gerald. 1990. "Trade Policy and Development," pp. 155–69 in Maurice Scott and Ian Little (eds.), *Public Policy and Economic Development*. Oxford: Oxford University Press.

Myint, Hla. 1987. "Neoclassical Development Analysis: Its Strengths and Limitations," pp. 107–36 in Gerald Meier (ed.), *Pioneers in Development*, 2nd series. Oxford: Oxford University Press.

Morris, Cynthia and Irma Adelman. 1988. *Comparative Patterns of Economic Development: 1850–1910*. Baltimore: Johns Hopkins Press.

Pempel, T.J. 1999. "The Developmental Regime in a Changing World Economy," pp. 137–81 in Meredith Woo-Cumings (ed.), *The Developmental State*. Ithaca: Cornell University Press.

Pinglé, Vihba. (1999). *Rethinking the Developmental State*. New York: St. Martin's Press.

Rodrik, Dani. 1999. *The New Global Economy and Developing Countries: Making Openness Work*. Baltimore: Johns Hopkins Press.

Schneider, Ben Ross. 1999. "The *Desarrollista* State in Brazil and Mexico," pp. 276–305 in Meredith Woo-Cumings (ed.), *The Developmental State*. Ithaca: Cornell University Press.

Shapiro, Helen and Lance Taylor. 1990. "The State and Industrial Strategy," *World Development* 18 (June): 861–78.

Srinivasan, T.N. 1984. "Comment [on Bauer]," pp. 51–8 in Gerald Meier and Dudley Seers (eds.), *Pioneers in Development*. Oxford: Oxford University Press.

Stiglitz, Joseph. 2001. "More Instruments and Broader Goals: Moving toward the Post-Washington Consensus," pp. 17–56 in Ha-Joon Chang (ed.), *The Rebel Within: Joseph Stiglitz and the World Bank*. London: Anthem Press.

Toye, John. 1987. *Dilemmas of Development*. Oxford: Basil Blackwell.

UN Development Programme. 2003. *Human Development Report 2003*. New York: Oxford University Press.

——. 2006. *Human Development Report 2006*. New York: Oxford University Press.

Wade, Robert. 1990. "Industrial Policy in East Asia: Does It Lead or Follow the Market?," in Gary Gereffi and Donald Wyman (eds.), *Manufacturing Miracles*. Princeton: Princeton University Press.

Weisman, Steven. 2006. "Drive on Corruption Angers Some at World Bank," *New York Times* (September 14): C1, C4.

World Bank. 1993. *The East Asian Miracle*. Oxford: Oxford University Press.

——. 2002. *World Development Report 2002*. Oxford: Oxford University Press.

——. 2006. *World Development Report 2006*. Oxford: Oxford University Press.

8   Endogenous growth theories and new strategies for development

After reading and studying this chapter, you should better understand:
- the income convergence controversy;
- the basic structure of endogenous growth models and how they differ from the classical and neoclassical growth theories;
- the importance of human capital, learning-by-doing, specialization, research and development, and other positive externalities that can permit rapid growth rates over the long term;
- the significance of constant and increasing returns in the endogenous growth models and how these contribute to long-run growth and increased income levels;
- the possible effects of inequality of income and land distribution on the rate of economic growth;
- the importance of social infrastructure and other alterable initial endowments to the rate of economic growth;
- the significance of "technical efficiency change" to economic growth.

Introduction

Near the end of Chapter 4, the Solow neoclassical growth theory was introduced. It has been interpreted as predicting that the per capita incomes of economies will tend to converge to the same level over time. This happens as lower income nations grow faster than higher income nations, assuming they all have access to the same technology and share similar savings, investment, and population growth rates.[1] Solow's theoretical structure validated the policy recommendations of the early development economists and their policy-oriented theories, such as the "big push," "balanced growth," and "unbalanced growth" strategies considered in Chapter 5. You will remember that these focused on the expansion of the industrial capital stock and an increase in the rate of savings as the means to promote more rapid economic growth and higher income per capita.

The primacy of physical capital accumulation, the K variable in the Solow-type aggregate production function, has been a focus for development economists since the time of Adam Smith. In this view, countries need to save and invest sufficiently so as to augment their total physical capital stock if they are to reach higher income levels. A higher level of investment boosts the attainable level of income by increasing the productivity of each worker, who has more physical capital with which to work. Of course, it was recognized that many poor nations would have trouble accumulating physical capital, as their low level of income meant limited savings to finance new investments. Because of low domestic incomes and savings, the level of capital accumulation might remain insufficient to achieve higher levels of per capita income.[2]

However, as discussed in Chapter 5, flush with the success of post-Second World War reconstruction in Europe and Japan, most early development economists believed that domestic saving and investment could be complemented by external financing. Total saving and investment, and hence total income, need not be constrained by a shortage of domestic resources in less-developed nations. Rather, saving is equal to $S = S_D + S_F$, where S is total saving, S_D is domestic saving by households, business, and government and S_F is foreign saving in the form of loans, aid, and foreign direct investment. The level of investment of a country was not believed to be rigidly determined by that economy's own limited ability to save, thus breaking the link between low income and low savings that seemed to constrain the possibilities of the poorest of the less-developed nations to a "vicious circle of poverty" where being poor becomes the equilibrium outcome. External resources could add to and complement domestic financing for investment and thus spur economic growth and development.

The income convergence controversy

The 1950s and 1960s were periods of relative optimism among development economists and policy-makers in evaluating the prospects for the newly independent former colonies that emerged as new nations after the Second World War. The economic models of the day suggested that growth was essentially a technical problem to be solved through larger injections of physical capital and secondarily through measures to slow population expansion. Economists had no shortage of recommendations as to the strategic means for adding to that stock of capital, as we learned in Chapters 4 and 5.[3]

Further, the convergence of world income levels predicted by Solow-type neoclassical growth models reassured economists and policy-makers alike that world poverty might reasonably be expected to be eradicated within the not-too-distant future if countries could just undertake the right policies. The relatively rapid rates of growth of some countries in the less-developed world compared to the already-developed nations in the period after the Second World War seemed to corroborate these hopeful theoretical prognostications, at least for a time.

As Table 8.1 shows, data to support income convergence to that of the high-income economies, particularly for some regions, can be found. The rate of growth of income person (as measured by GDP per capita) in East Asia and the Pacific has been consistently a multiple of income growth in the high-income economies over the entire 1970–2005 period and in every sub-period. South Asia's rate of growth of income since 1980 also exceeded that of the high-income economies. These regions' growth experience seemed to support the income convergence hypothesis of neoclassical economics as their more rapid growth rates brought their incomes relatively closer to those of the high-income countries.[4]

However, there is at the same time evidence of income divergence between poor and rich regions. The income growth of the fifty-four *low-income economies* was close to, but still less than, the growth rate of the fifty-six *high-income economies* as shown in the last two lines of the table. As a result, average real income levels of high- and low-income economies were further apart in 2005 than they had been in 1970. Sub-Saharan Africa's growth in GDP per person was virtually nil over more than three decades, meaning a widening of the income gap

Table 8.1 Comparative growth rates

	2005 GNI per capita[a]	Average annual growth rate of GDP per capita in constant 2000 dollars (percentage)							
		1970–5	1975–80	1980–5	1985–90	1990–5	1995–2000	2000–5	1970–2005
East Asia and Pacific	1,627	3.8	5.2	5.9	5.8	8.9	5.3	7.3	6.0
Latin America and Caribbean	4,008	3.4	2.9	−1.6	−0.16	1.7	1.6	0.9	1.3
Middle East and North Africa	2,241	n.a.	0.7	1.5	−1.2	1.4	2.4	2.2	1.1[b]
South Asia	684	−0.03	1.3	3.1	3.6	3.0	3.5	4.6	2.7
Sub-Saharan Africa	745	2.0	0.07	−1.7	−0.35	−1.4	0.8	2.0	0.1
Low-income economies	580	0.4	0.9	2.3	2.7	1.7	2.9	4.1	2.0
High-income economies	35,131	2.4	2.8	1.9	2.9	1.7	2.0	1.5	2.2

Source: World Bank, *World Development Indicators Online.*

Notes
a   In current US dollars; GNI is gross national income, what used to be called gross national product.
b   1975–2005.

between that region and every other. Nor did Latin America and the Caribbean or the Middle East enjoy income convergence to the high-income economies. Further, these regions lost ground compared to East Asia and the Pacific in terms of relative income levels among the less-developed economies themselves.

The economic growth data thus provides contradictory evidence for income convergence and for the neoclassical hypothesis that one should expect faster growth *rates* for countries with lower incomes. In some cases, for example, East Asia and the Pacific, the neoclassical theory would seem to fit. For other regions, like Sub-Saharan Africa, just the opposite appears true. As one of the world's poorest regions, Sub-Saharan Africa has had the worst overall growth performance in the less-developed world. The neoclassical model would have predicted that it would have been precisely such a low-income region that would have had the greatest opportunities for profits from increased capital accumulation. Its growth rate would have been expected to be the highest, not the lowest, as it actually was.

The way we have interpreted the data in Table 8.1, however, needs to be approached with caution. It represents what is called the *crude unconditional* income convergence prediction. It is an interpretation based on the belief that in a relatively open international economy, where both physical and financial capital are relatively mobile, if capital is scarce in some countries, like those in Sub-Saharan Africa, then the lower quantity of capital will correspond to a higher expected rate of return to investors.[5] It is thought that international capital should flow toward such capital-scarce nations, thus *increasing the rate of investment* relative to total output in those economies. This would then increase the potential *level* of GDP in those countries and contribute to the convergence of incomes among nations as the stock of capital in the less-developed nations increased relative to the higher-income economies. Higher growth rates would put these economies on the path to a higher level of income, too.

As discussed in Chapter 4 and in note 1 in this chapter, the Solow-type neoclassical theory actually anticipates income convergence *only* when countries have similar savings rates and similar population growth rates – that is, income convergence is *conditional* on countries sharing the same *fundamentals* (you'll remember that it is already assumed they all share the same technology, which is exogenous to each economy). Income convergence is not dependent upon international capital flows in this view, the magnitude of which could never be sufficient to achieve convergence. Convergence of incomes is dependent on the similarity of savings and investment rates and population growth. Only then would incomes converge to the same levels. So, it is not a comparison of growth rates between regions or countries that reveals whether convergence of income is likely. Rather it is the share of saving and investment out of income that determines the future equilibrium income and hence is the determinant as to whether incomes will converge in the neoclassical perspective.

Sub-Saharan Africa has had low rates of investment and savings as a share of GDP compared to other regions (though close to those in Latin America), as can be seen from Table 8.2. Thus, even if population growth rates *were* similar between this region and the higher-income economies (which they are not; they are higher: see Chapter 12), we should *not* expect to see a convergence of income per capita between Sub-Saharan Africa and the high-income economies as a result of the large differential in the rates of investment and saving. In other words, the necessary conditions for Solow-type income convergence to occur are absent. The low growth rates of GDP in Sub-Saharan Africa relative to other regions, and the low absolute level of GDP per person, are not a surprise within the neoclassical framework. It is what would be expected from the fundamental Solow income equation from Chapter 4 (equation 4.5) because of differences in the accumulation of physical capital and the low-level equilibrium of income toward which those economies are transitioning. Low growth rates in the Solow model indicate that an economy is approaching its equilibrium income level, and in Sub-Saharan Africa that is a low-level equilibrium income.

On the other hand, East Asia and the Pacific have experienced a dramatic increase in investment and saving rates, such that investment has equaled 30 percent or more of income in many years. One would expect convergence of income levels with more developed regions on this basis, as savings and investment rates actually exceed those in the high-income economies. Growth rates of per capita income in East Asia did increase more rapidly, as shown

Table 8.2 Saving and investment by region (as a percentage of GDP)

	1970		1980		1990		2000		2005	
	S	I	S	I	S	I	S	I	S	I
East Asia and Pacific	27.2	27.7	33.0	33.0	35.0	33.5	35.8	31.6	42.9	37.7
Latin America	21.3	21.8	23.0	24.5	21.6	19.4	19.0	19.9	22.3	19.5
Middle East and N. Africa	n.a.	n.a.	26.4	29.0	18.7	26.0	25.9	23.8	26.1	27.4
South Asia	13.5	15.4	13.3	18.7	20	22.8	22.3	23.9	26.7	30.7
Sub-Saharan Africa	19.9	22.4	25.9	24.8	18.8	17.7	19.5	17.8	18.1	19.2
Low- and middle-income economies	21.6	22.2	24.9	26.6	25.4	25.2	25.2	24.0	28.7	26.6
Low-income only	13.6	15.5	13.4	18.4	17.7	21.1	21.2	22.6	25.1	28.8
High-income economies	25.6	25.2	23.6	24.6	22.6	22.9	21.5	21.9	19.9	20.5

Source: World Bank, *World Development Indicators Online.*

in Table 8.1, so the gap between East Asian incomes and incomes in more-developed nations was closing.

In fact, as the Solow model would predict (again, refer back to equation 4.5 in Chapter 4), if East Asian saving and investment rates were to remain as high as they are for a sufficiently long period of time, per capita income in the region would eventually be *even higher* than those of all other regions, when the steady-state equilibrium level of income was reached, since the region's level of investment and saving is the highest in the world (assuming similar population growth rates)! And growth rates of income would have to be high for some period of time so that the higher level of income could be attained, though as the equilibrium level of income was approached, growth rates of income would be expected to slow.

However, there remains something slightly disconcerting about the statistics contained in Tables 8.1 and 8.2. The differences in investment and savings rates, and in the aggregate size of the physical capital stock they imply, are not really that great and are unable to explain the persistence of the large *absolute* income differentials between regions. Why is the *absolute* level of income so low in Sub-Saharan Africa relative to the high-income areas given that the differences in savings and investment rates shown in Table 8.2 are not that dramatic and that new investment there should be more effective in raising incomes compared to higher-income economies, according to the neoclassical growth perspective?[6]

What other forces might be at work besides the rates of saving and investment (and population growth rates) that might be affecting not only the growth rates of GDP per person but also the absolute level of income in different economies that lead to the wide gap in observed levels of development?

Income convergence/divergence, path dependence, and poverty traps

Economist Lloyd Reynolds found what seemed to be path-dependent patterns of growth rates in his study of "turning points" in economic development. Some countries with certain shared characteristics performed better over time in terms of their income per capita growth rates than other economies with different characteristics (Reynolds 1986: 79–81). If there is *path dependence* resulting from specific growth-inhibiting characteristics that are cumulative in their effects, then catch-up by the poorest countries, which have had the lowest average growth rates and much lower incomes, obviously would be impossible. For example, the negative impact of Myrdal-type "backwash effects," or "vicious circles" discussed in Chapter 6, might account for the consistent lack of progress in Sub-Saharan Africa and slow progress in other regions, despite investment and savings rates that would have led one to believe that incomes should be higher and rising more rapidly than they have. There seems to be "something" about the Sub-Saharan economies that resists progress. In Chapter 6, we considered what some of those factors restraining progress might be.

What seems to happen is that countries that already have attained a higher level of income are more likely to grow faster, for reasons which are considered below. Countries with low absolute incomes are more likely to find themselves on a lower growth path, so that the income gap between poor and rich nations widens rather than shrinks. Consider the following data.

Of 114 economies with data on GDP per person in both 1970 and 2000, those with incomes below $1,000 per capita in 2000 (in constant 2000 US dollars) were clustered around an annual 1970–2000 growth rate of 0 percent. For economies with incomes exceeding $1,000 per person in 2000, 1970–2000 growth rates were clustered around 2 percent (calculations by the authors from World Bank, *World Development Indicators Online* data). Economies with low incomes had low growth rates, while those with higher incomes had higher growth rates, on average.

Such differences can also generate a widening gap between countries within the less-developed world as well, with the poorest remaining at the bottom of the heap, while some formerly poor nations "somehow" succeed in raising their living standards. All this is contrary to the predictions of the neoclassical models and the hopes of development economists. How well countries are performing today seems to be the best predictor of how they will perform in the future, which does not seem to be a very hopeful prognosis for the poorest of the poor. Nor does this tell us why this occurs. Only that it seems to be the pattern.

There is thus some evidence that convergence of incomes might be a reasonable hypothesis for some of the already better-off less-developed countries, but not for the poorer economies. Many of these economies appear to be in a low-level equilibrium income trap such that their incomes are diverging from world averages (Jones 1998:56–88). The Solow model thus may apply quite well to developed countries or for some upper-tier less-developed economies, but for understanding economic development for the bulk of the world's economies, especially the poorest, it would appear that more is needed.

It is important to remember that the past does not have an absolute stranglehold on the future, though. Some economies *have* found the means to escape the ravages of past adverse path dependence and what must have looked like a low-level equilibrium income trap at some point in their past. Yet they have succeeded in jumping to a higher standard of living and more rapid economic growth. The faster growth rates and rapidly rising incomes observed in some countries or regions that had been relatively low-income in the not-too-distant past, countries like South Korea and Taiwan in East Asia, for example, and now perhaps China, too, and their ability to sustain these high rates of growth over time are reminiscent of the "virtuous circles" and "cumulative causation" effects that many development and heterodox economists observed at work in their earlier historical studies (discussed in Chapters 5 and 6). It is important to remember that progress has been made in countries that previously looked as hopeless as, say, economies in Sub-Saharan Africa today. Low income does not have to be a permanent feature of economic life if the key to moving from a low income path to a higher income path can be found. That key apparently is not just the savings and investment rate of the Solow-type models, however. There has to be more to the explanation.

China's and even India's recent growth paths may hold promise for other less-developed economies mired in poverty (see Focus 8.1). It *is* possible for now-poor economies to escape from adverse path dependence and what seems to be a low-income trap. Sustained increases in income per person seem to have been maintained over a number of decades in a growing number of formerly poor economies. The challenge for development economics is finding as many of the critical variables as possible that explain this, variables that can be manipulated by economic policy so as to foment positive cumulative change over the long term for more of the world's population.

The pressing question, though, is whether high or rising growth rates of income – such as those China has attained or those of the East Asian economies shown in Table 8.1 – can be maintained over the long run. Why is this in question? It is an issue, because Solow-type neoclassical growth models imply that high *rates* of economic growth cannot be persistent. Because of the law of eventually diminishing returns, it is argued, as an economy gets closer to its equilibrium level of income determined by the savings rate and population growth, the *percentage growth rate* will decrease until it eventually reaches zero when the equilibrium income is attained. After that, income per person will only grow if there is a change in exogenous technology or if the savings rate changes or the population growth rate changes.

FOCUS 8.1   CHINA AND INDIA ON THE RISE: INCOME CONVERGENCE?

In Chapter 2, China's recent growth experience was considered. Here we examine both China's and India's growth history specifically as they apply to the income convergence controversy.

	2005 GNI per capita	Average annual growth rate of GDP per capita in constant 2000 dollars (percentage)							
	US$	1970–5	1975–80	1980–5	1985–90	1990–5	1995–2000	2000–5	1970–2005
China	1,740	3.7	5.0	9.3	6.2	10.9	7.6	8.8	7.3
India	720	0.6	0.8	3.1	4.0	3.3	4.0	5.2	3.0
United Kingdom	37,600	1.9	1.8	1.9	3.0	1.4	2.7	2.1	2.1
United States	43,740	1.8	2.6	2.3	2.3	1.2	2.9	1.7	2.1

China's overall growth rate of GDP per person since 1970 has been more than three times that of both the UK and the US, so income per capita has been converging toward US and UK levels. China's 1970 per capita GDP was $122, while that of the US was $18,150 (the values are all in constant US dollars, i.e. adjusted for inflation). US 1970 GDP per person was nearly 149 times as large as in China; by 2005, US average GDP was "only" 26 times larger than China's, as GDP per person increased to $1,445 in China compared to $37,574 in the US. The relative income gap, as measured by GDP per capita, was closing. Relative income convergence was taking place. (Think about this, though: What was happening to the *absolute* GDP per person gap between the US and China between 1970 and 2005? Calculate the difference for the two years.)

The average GNI for each country is also shown for 2005, as GNI is the amount of income that is actually available to be spent in an economy, as opposed to the income created (i.e. GDP), as you will remember from Chapter 2. India, too, was closing the relative GDP gap with both the US and the UK, though the pace of convergence in India has been significantly slower. In 2005, US output per person was still more than 64 times larger than average GDP in India, down from almost 87 times greater in 1970, as a result of the slightly larger growth rate of GDP in India compared to that in the US over the time period.

There thus has been some measurable income convergence between the two most populated economies in the world (China and India) and the third most populous (the United States). That is undoubtedly good news, as this economic growth led also to a higher average level of development in both India and China. Chapter 2 looked at the positive direction of changes in key indicators, including the Human Development Index (HDI), for both of these economies, and these showed essential progress being made in improving living standards as incomes grew.

There remains, however, a large gap in absolute incomes between China and India and the US and the UK that has become wider, not narrower, over time. It is the absolute level of income that is available for consumption and investment, not relative income. If the 1970–2005 growth rates in GDP per person shown above were to be maintained over the future, it would not be until the year 2052 for China and 2146 for India that the US 2005 level of GDP per capita would be attained.

Of course, if US GDP continued to increase, as it would be likely to do, there still would not be full income convergence by those dates as US income would have increased. If China, India and the US continued with the same rates of economic growth into the future as prevailed over the period 1970–2005, actual convergence of GDP per capita with the US would occur in 2071 for China and in the year 2479 for India!

Continued

It is important to remember that in the Solow model, incomes will be expected to converge to the same level only if the so-called "fundamentals" are the same. Specifically, the rate of savings and the population growth rates must be the same for incomes to converge to the same equilibrium level (see equation 4.5 in Chapter 4). The following table shows s/n – the savings rate divided by the population growth rate – for China, India, the UK, and the US for various years.

	1970	*1980*	*1990*	*2000*
China	10.5	27.9	26.0	49.5
India	6.5	6.9	11.2	13.8
United Kingdom	68.0	124.1	50.3	9.0
United States	15.7	20.6	14.4	14.7

Using the 2000 values of s/n, we would actually predict from the Solow model that China's per capita income sometime in the future would be the highest, followed by the US, India, and the UK, everything else the same. Of course, the s/n value shows substantial variation (using 1970, 1980, or 1990 values, the UK would be predicted to eventually have the highest equilibrium value rather than the lowest if we look only at the 2000 values), so this shows that not only growth rates might vary as the steady-state level of income per person is approached, but also the *level* of that equilibrium income is subject to variation within the Solow model as the values of s and n are not constant over time.

Source: World Bank, *World Development Indicators Online*

If, however growth *rates* are sustained over time, an economy would be moving toward ever higher *levels* of income. Sustained growth rates imply that there is no equilibrium target level of income towards which an economy is transitioning. Growth *rates* would be influencing the future *level* of income, an outcome that is not possible within a Solow-type neoclassical growth framework (Lucas 1988: 12–13). Since the real-world evidence does show growth rates remaining high for many economies for relatively long periods of time, how can this be explained in an economic model?

Endogenous growth models[7]

It was not only the question as to whether and how economies could maintain rapid growth rates over the longer-term that vexed many development economists. There was also the relatively slow progress of most Sub-Saharan African economies, as well as lagging growth rates in other regions like Latin America, that led a number of economists to question the validity of any growth model which predicts eventual income convergence based on simple fundamentals like the rate of saving or investment. This resulted in a critical re-examination of the policy recommendation to accumulate ever more physical capital, that is, to save or borrow more, that flowed from the neoclassical economic formulations. As one economist put it:

The idea that capital investment is essential to the long-run state of growth of a nation is a common, if somewhat vague, axiom of most policy discussions of economic growth and development. Yet for the better part of a generation the preeminent theory of economic growth developed by the Nobel Prize winning economist Robert Solow and the data summarized by the important contributions of Edward Denison, John Kendrick, Solow, and others have provided us with virtually no basis for making such claims. Perhaps even more striking was the fact that theory seemed unable to explain the extreme and persistent differences in living standards or growth rates across countries.

(Plosser 1993: 57)

The empirical research on growth using the neoclassical framework typically found that a significant portion of the growth rate of a country, often well over 50 percent, could *not* be accounted for by changes in the use of physical capital and labor, leaving what came to be called the "Solow residual" as the major contributor to economic growth. In other words, the K, capital, and L, labor, inputs in the Solow growth equation back in Chapter 4 were not good predictors of either levels of income per person or growth rates of income when sophisticated statistical analyses were undertaken.

Accumulating more physical capital through more savings did not explain much of what caused economies to develop in the real world. Increases in income per person were assumed to thus be the result of exogenous technology, but the Solow model had no theory of how or why technology changed, and almost everyone agreed that it was technology in some broad sense that had been responsible for a very significant proportion of the progress in most economies. Instead, something outside the Solow model was found responsible for the bulk of economic growth; savings rates and population growth and the accumulation of physical capital had an effect, but they were not the major players when the statistical analyses were done. Something was missing from the story that the neoclassical model was trying to tell.

All the diverse factors and influences that might reasonably be attributed to generating the Solow residual – such as the effects of education, technology, business organization, research and development efforts, culture, growing international trade, local politics, and so on – invited much speculation, but empirical models that might have helped to untangle, classify, and identify these possible influences on economic growth rates were slow to appear. What economists were left with for quite some time was a theory that seemed to say that "something in the air" was responsible for most economic growth and higher incomes, but we are just not sure of what that might be.

Then, in the late 1980s, so-called endogenous growth models began to emerge in the economics literature. Endogenous growth theories do not assume, nor do they find, physical capital accumulation to be the dominant factor in spurring economic growth or in explaining differences in income levels among nations. Perhaps most controversially, these models jettisoned the assumption of diminishing returns for at least some of the inputs to production. This effectively turns a nation's short-run production function into a dynamic, constantly-evolving relationship, rather than a "fixed-in-time" function where given quantities of physical inputs impose limits on how much can be produced and on income levels. And, lastly, the rate of growth of per capita income is not constrained by exogenous technological change but is internally, that is, *endogenously,* determined by forces specific to each economy.[8]

In endogenous growth models, a higher level of investment, properly defined, not only increases per capita income, but it can *sustain* high and even rising rates of income growth over the future. This is something simply not possible within the traditional neoclassical growth model, which finds that a steady-state income level, determined by the rate of saving and the population growth rate, is the equilibrium outcome of the growth process. On the path to this income level, growth rates would be expected to slow down the closer current income per person is to its steady-state value. Once that equilibrium level of income is reached, there would be no further economic growth in a Solow-type model, unless there were to be a change in savings and investment rates or a new burst of exogenous technology.

In endogenous growth models, it is possible for countries to continue to grow quickly for long periods, even when they have already achieved relatively high incomes. There is not some target equilibrium income level that is fixed by the current level of inputs to production. There is, in fact, no steady-state income level per se. There is no pre-determined maximum level of income that can be reached based on the rate of savings and investment and the limits of diminishing returns. Income per person is more of a moving target. As Young (1928: 535) long ago put it, "the more appropriate conception is that of a *moving* equilibrium."

In an endogenous growth framework, rapid growth *rates* can be sustained *without* an increase in the rate of saving or investment, an astonishing and impossible result in Solow-type models. Growth is not just a stage of development, as it is in Solow models, a stage that ends once equilibrium income is attained. Instead, growth can become a permanent feature of an economy's history.

As Warsh (2006: 207) writes in describing Paul Romer's struggle to develop one of the earliest endogenous growth models:

> the strictly empirical problem Romer was addressing was the reality that growth seems to have been speeding up for more than a century instead of slowing down, as had been expected [from a Solow-type model]. He reasoned that it must have to do with the internal dynamic of science: the more you learn, the faster you learn things. If knowledge was the source of increasing returns, then accumulating more of it should mean faster growth – which was, in fact, the record of the preceding two hundred years.

This insight about knowledge and how it is both cumulative and dynamic is a key to grasping the essence of what endogenous growth theories have to say about how economies make progress.

Endogenous growth models also can quite easily explain a widening gap in income between poorer and richer nations, because they break the link between the rate of economic growth and the law of diminishing returns. This effectively removes the ceiling on income per person for any particular rate of savings and investment that is imbedded in neoclassical theory, as represented by the production function shown in Figure 4.3 in Chapter 4. Countries that already are developed can continue to grow and grow rapidly over the future.

Endogenous growth models are reminiscent of "cumulative causation" and "virtuous cycles" discussed in Chapter 6, and they are consistent with a shift to a new, more beneficial path dependence which contributes to rising income levels. In fact, some of what seemed new in endogenous growth models was already there in Smith's view of economic growth, especially his concepts of specialization and the division of labor on an ever-widening scale. Endogenous growth models actually incorporate theories and concepts from a rich earlier economic literature on decreasing costs and increasing returns that, while not quite ignored, was not fully appreciated for its importance in contributing to economic growth.[9]

In most endogenous growth models, one of the important factors of production contributing to growth has been found to be both the rate of accumulation of, as well as the initial stock of, human capital.[10] Another key input is "research" capital, that is, research and development and the creation of *knowledge*, as the quotation from Warsh above suggests.

While these models share some superficial similarities with the capital- and saving-centered neoclassical growth models in their form, they do not predict convergence of income levels, even among countries which share similar rates of saving, investment, and population growth rates. They also treat research and development and the creation of new knowledge as a purposeful economic activity, pursued in the real world by profit-driven firms and individuals operating within a specific institutional context. The development of new technology and new products is an internally driven process that is endogenous to every economy, and it is this purposeful pursuit of profit within a particular institutional context that helps to explain how economic growth occurs over the long run and why there are differences in income levels and growth rates among real-world economies.

This insight fits better with how knowledge and technology have progressed historically. The Industrial Revolution marks a turning point in economic and human history, as we saw in Chapter 3. Why did economic growth accelerate for some countries, for those who became capitalist, with the Industrial Revolution? It was not due to exogenous technological change but rather to the decisions and actions of thousands, perhaps millions, of decision-makers, who, in the pursuit of income and profits via the market system, experimented and searched for the means to cut costs and gain an advantage over other producers. This is another sense in which economic growth is an endogenous process; in capitalist societies, there is an incentive to invent and for some to expend energy and resources to attempt to create more efficient ways to produce as a means to increase their individual income. Adam Smith saw this process as it emerged, and in his own way described it as the forces of accumulation and the ever-present drive for a further division of labor, especially through the use of machines.[11]

Endogenous growth models also place a quite different emphasis on what is required to boost a country's economic growth and development possibilities compared to the recommendations derived from the capital- and saving-centered neoclassical-type models by focusing more on institutions, knowledge-creation, and education. These theories have profoundly affected the way many economists think about policy and how they identify the most severe barriers to development.[12]

A key document signaling a shift in emphasis in thinking among economists was the World Bank study, *The East Asian Miracle* (World Bank 1993a).[13] This critical examination of the "high-performance Asian economies" – the HPAEs – of Japan, Hong Kong, South Korea, Singapore, Taiwan, Indonesia, Malaysia, and Thailand was built around insights flowing from the endogenous growth theory's methodology for identifying the crucial policy variables in the growth process. Such endogenous growth models help to explain the power of path dependence on growth rates and why growth can be cumulative, as well as suggesting what is needed if countries are to jump from lower paths of growth and development to higher paths. In other words, endogenous growth models can explain why some countries grow quickly, reaching higher equilibrium income levels, while others get stuck in what look like low-level equilibrium poverty traps.

A simple endogenous growth model with externalities

The major conceptual difference between the Solow-type neoclassical growth models and the endogenous growth models is the presumption in the endogenous models that there are not necessarily diminishing returns to all the reproducible factors of production, K, the stock of physical capital, to H, the stock of human capital, nor to technology (or more broadly, the intangible concept of knowledge), R. Rather it is assumed that constant, or perhaps even increasing, marginal returns to at least some of these inputs are possible.[14] How is this explained?

Endogenous growth models typically assume that there are positive externalities to human capital accumulation, research capital, and, perhaps, to some physical capital accumulation to the extent that new capital embodies the latest knowledge, as it is quite likely to do. Diminishing returns to H, R and maybe even K are avoided through society-wide spillover effects.[15] When the social benefits from, for example, human capital accumulation exceed the private benefits, there are positive secondary and tertiary effects from any increase in a country's average education level or enrolment ratios that reverberate through the economy. More educated and presumably more productive workers not only produce more at their own tasks, but they also interact synergistically with their workmates so that the productivity of other workers also rises, even though their level of education, that is, the quantity of enhanced labor, remains unchanged.[16]

Higher average levels of education in an economy also contribute to "learning-by-doing" effects, that is, to the capacity for workers to build upon their previous learning and training so that the same level of human capital input is actually able to improve its productivity over time in the process of producing goods and services on the shop floor, or wherever production takes place. Learning-by-doing contributes to increases in the potential level of total output of a given level of labor input without the need for an increase in any additional inputs and without any additional increase in investment. The presumption is that the higher the average level of human capital accumulation in an economy, the stronger will be such effects, again breaking the link between increases in employment and human capital accumulation and diminishing returns.[17]

In the endogenous growth theory view, the ability to use technology, to develop new knowledge and new products, and the skills of the labor force that complement knowledge creation and its application are formed and shaped by each particular economy. In other words, growth is an endogenous process, coming from within each particular economy, with each having a different production function reflecting different quantities and qualities of its inputs and their ability to adapt, develop and use knowledge about how to produce within that economy.

A very general endogenous growth production function for a representative economy would look like (Romer 1994: 16):

$$Y = F(R, K, H) \tag{8.1}$$

where Y is total output, R is research and development (R&D) done by all firms in the economy, K is the accumulated physical capital stock and H is the accumulated stock of human capital. For analytical purposes, this formulation has at times been operationalized as a particular linear aggregate production function, often called an "AK" production function, for obvious reasons, shown in equation 8.2.

$$Y_t = aK_t \tag{8.2}$$

where K is redefined as a measure of the combined stock of human, physical, and research capital and a is a constant multiplier.[18] In this very simple formulation, there are constant returns to scale to K in production (since $XY_t = aXK_t$, where X is any finite number), as well as constant marginal returns in the short-term, since $dY/dK = a > 0$ and $d^2Y/dK^2 = 0$, so that the marginal product curve, MP_K, is a horizontal line with a constant value a. Since increased increments of K are not less effective than prior additions to K, both a rising per capita income and a non-decreasing rate of growth of per capita income are possible.

In a slightly more complex formulation that captures a bit more of the "endogeneity" of the growth process, we can write the aggregate production function as

$$Y_t = A(K)_t K_t \tag{8.3}$$

where $A(K)_t$ is the "induced or endogenous technological change" imparted to the economy by the stock of physical, human and research capital particular to that country. In the production function shown in definition 8.3, different economies will have distinct $A(K)$ values, depending on the feedback mechanisms affecting knowledge adaptation and technological change specific to that economy. These are reflections of differences in human capital accumulation, the spread of specialization and the introduction of new products, micro- and macro-policies of business and government organization, social and physical infrastructure capacity, and so on. In the original Solow-neoclassical formulation, by comparison, technology, A, was "exogenous" to all economies, affecting them identically like "manna from heaven." Technology was assumed to grow at the same rate for all countries, regardless of their own resources, policies, or actions. Such technology was not subject to policies or decisions internal to any economy and did not grow at different rates for each economy.

In the endogenous growth models, technological progress as represented by $A(K)$ is dependent on the accumulation and spread of knowledge within each economy. It is dependent on the rate of capital formation, broadly defined. This includes physical, human, and research capital, and *it also includes the organizational and institutional structures of that economy*. Such structures affect an economy's capacity to effectively utilize the world supply of knowledge in production, to adapt it, and eventually to add to that knowledge.

Thus, in the endogenous growth formulation, the level of technology and the rate of its application are not determined externally to the operation of that economy. Given this formulation, countries that accumulate more H and undertake more R&D, R, will be more likely to be able to continue to grow, and even to accelerate their economic growth rates, over time, compared to nations which accumulate these inputs at slower rates.[19] Indeed, the pace of any individual country's technological progress is conditional on:

1 the level and type of education of the labor force and on the level and types of investment the society makes in R&D;
2 certain government policies, for example, tax credits for R&D, worker training and education, patent and copyright laws, and so on;
3 the economy's and society's organizational and institutional capabilities formed over time in both the private and *public* sectors.

Technology is not the A of the Solow-model, available equally and identically to all countries as if it were a costless public good. It is, at least in part, a private good that is costly to produce for each country.[20] The profits of such technology can be appropriated, to a degree, by the creators of such new knowledge, which is typically assumed to be a private firm operating in an environment of imperfect competition. Newly created knowledge will affect the production process and will spill over into the rest of the economy over time, resulting in even more new processes, to new products, to broader and deeper specialization both internal to firms and economy-wide, and in enhanced efficiency that contributes to the ability of an economy to continue to grow without necessarily facing diminishing returns.[21]

What the endogenous growth models attempt to explain is really nothing more than how a capitalist economy functions. Robert Lucas, an important contributor to the literature, wrote (quoted in Warsh 2006: 237):

A few centuries ago, some of us moved into a phase of sustained growth while others did not, and out of this ill-understood process emerged the unequal world we know today.

The "a few centuries ago" comment marks the beginning of the Industrial Revolution for Western European nations and their offshoots, like the US, Canada and Australia. As capitalism took root and advanced in those economies, the drive to earn profits created a strong incentive for the creation of new knowledge that could reduce costs and provide a competitive advantage for one producer over another. This is nothing more than the process that Adam Smith so presciently described in *The Wealth of Nations* and with so much hope for the spread of progress (see Young 1928: 528–31, who discusses how Smith's insights lead directly to a consideration of external increasing returns and specialization of industries on an expanding scale and how this is a characteristic of capitalist economies). It is this process that endogenous growth models seek to explain, including the failure of progress in the still-poor nations.

Figure 8.1 shows an endogenous-growth production function implied by statement 8.3. Also shown for comparison is a typical, Solow-type neoclassical production function which exhibits diminishing returns to K. The neoclassical production function will shift upward for all economies when there are changes in exogenous technology, but along any given production function there are diminishing returns to the variable input shown on the horizontal axis (be it capital, K, or labor, L) as can be seen by the smaller slope of the production function at higher levels of K.

However, for the endogenous growth function, $A(K)_t K_t$, there are no diminishing returns to the variable and reproducible factors of production (be they K, or human capital, H, or research and development, R). It would be even better to show the endogenous growth production function as being "flexible," i.e. as not fixed in position but capable of "stretching" as

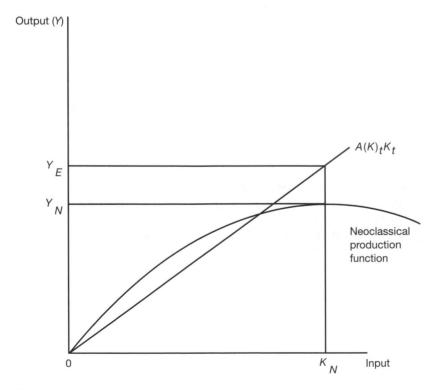

Figure 8.1 An endogenous growth production function.

spillovers from new knowledge begin to affect the nature of the productive structure of an economy.

While further investment cannot increase total output and income per person, Y_N/L, above Y_N, in the neoclassical world with its assumption of diminishing returns, in the endogenous growth formulation additional investment in K, H, and R *can* increase output beyond Y_E along the $A(K)$ production function without reaching a pre-determined maximum. Figure 8.1 shows what an exogenous growth production function would look like if there are constant returns to the reproducible inputs to production along $A(K)_t K_t$, though increasing returns could also be shown. (What would the graph look like for increasing returns?)

Given the possibility of non-diminishing returns, convergence of income levels will not occur automatically. Higher initial stocks of both capital, K, and research and development, R, contribute to even higher rates of growth in future. Different economies will evolve in a path-dependent fashion with distinct growth rates depending on past accumulation and assimilation of knowledge. In economies that have accumulated a critical mass of these inputs, spillovers will lead to more learning-by-doing, new and more specialized products, and decreasing costs of producing. This occurs not because the world pool of "best practice" technological knowledge has expanded exogenously. Rather this outcome is as a consequence of the interaction of the reproducible inputs in these economies in ways that contribute to greater efficiency, higher incomes, and to a changing economic structure in response to the effects of knowledge transmission by firms operating in an imperfectly competitive world. [22]

For economies that have failed to accumulate a sufficient stock of human, research, and physical capital, the spillover benefits will be smaller or nearly non-existent. This will be manifested in a lower level of income per person and lower growth rates of income and the possibility of a low-level equilibrium income trap. As Lucas (1988: 25) concluded after analyzing the dynamics of his endogenous growth model: "an economy beginning with low levels of human physical capital will remain *permanently* below an initially better endowed economy."

In endogenous growth theory, the key inputs to production are not perfect substitutes for one another. Physical capital, human capital and knowledge are, rather, complementary inputs. This "means the higher the capital stock, the more technology can increase productivity over the future. Instead of a one-time boost to productivity, higher rates of saving and capital investment increase the rate at which productivity rises. *There is no steady state of growth* ... the key inputs of growth – skilled labour, sophisticated capital, new forms of technology – are not independent of each other but are positively interdependent" (Landau *et al.* 1996: 6; also see Lau 1996).

Endogenous growth models suggest that government policies can affect the rate of long-term economic growth by impacting the accumulation of both physical and human capital and the effort dedicated to research and development and the creation of new knowledge. Such policies are extremely important in boosting the long-run rate of growth and the level of income by shaping future path dependence. Markets for saving and borrowing are often absent, or less-than-perfect, in many less-developed economies. Consequently, a purely market-based development strategy will *fail* to adequately tap a society's potential to the extent that investment is financed by private savings and investment decisions. Further, since firms that invest in labor training and in research and development often create positive externalities in production that spread to other producers, not all the profits from their investment activities will accrue to the firms making such investments.

Therefore, left to their own devices, private firms are likely to under-invest in socially desirable labor training, in research and development, and other such non-fully appropriable investments, since the private and social benefits of such expenditures diverge. Consequently, government action will be necessary to subsidize or otherwise augment such investment activities by private firms if the socially desired level of augmented capital accumulation is to be attained. (The theory of positive externalities and the case for government action in the face of this type of market failure are explored in detail in Chapter 12.)

At the very least, the endogenous growth models and their insistence on the existence of pervasive positive externalities and of the spread of knowledge suggest a wider arena for public policy action than is immediately evident from the simple Solow model.

Measuring the impact of key inputs in endogenous growth models: growth accounting

The work on endogenous growth often has been highly theoretical. But there also has been an applied econometric and empirical literature, too. Robert J. Barro's early research was especially influential in this regard, but there are many other contributions, including some useful review essays (Barro 1991, 1993; Romer 1994; World Bank 1993a: Chapter 1).

The endogenous growth research in its *growth accounting* form measures the contribution of various inputs to production. Table 8.3 presents the results of some of this research drawing on the World Bank's study (1993a) of the HPAEs (based on Barro's methodology) and a follow-up study by Rodrik (1994) incorporating additional factors affecting economic growth. This research is suggestive of what those working early-on in this area considered important factors to the growth process. These empirical models were based on ideas from the endogenous growth literature, including the role of human capital and institutions in the broadest sense. What the empirical studies attempt to do is to measure how much each included variable "accounts for" or contributes to economic growth.

The regression coefficients in Table 8.3 show the contribution of the various inputs to per capita income growth. They can be interpreted as follows. For the first variable, "Relative GDP," the World Bank's negative coefficient suggests, as the Solow-type neoclassical models predict, that countries with lower incomes will grow faster, holding all other factors constant, and thus incomes would be expected to converge. For example, a country with a 1960 GDP equal to 40 percent of 1960 US GDP would be predicted to grow 1.28 percent

Table 8.3 Estimates of input contributions to per capita economic growth

Variable	World Bank coefficient	Rodrik coefficient
1 Relative GDP, 1960	-0.0320^b	-0.38^b
2 Primary school enrolment, 1960	0.0272^b	2.66^a
3 Secondary school enrolment, 1960	0.0069	
4 Population growth, 1960–85	0.0998	
5 Average investment/GDP, 1960–85	0.0285	
6 HPAEs	0.0171^b	
7 Latin America	-0.0131^b	
8 Sub-Saharan Africa	-0.0099^a	
9 Gini coefficient for land, around 1960		-5.22^b
10 Gini coefficient for income, around 1960		-3.47
Adjusted R^2	0.4821	0.53

Sources: World Bank 1993a: 51, Table 1.8; Rodrik 1994: 20, Table 3.

Notes
a Statistically significant at the 0.05 level.
b Statistically significant at the 0.01 level.

(−40% × −0.0320) faster per year than the United States over the period 1960–85, *ceteris paribus*.

This "other factors remaining the same" assumption is quite important; it is an "as if" assumption, used in interpreting each variable independently. It assumes when we look at the first coefficient that the only difference between a poor nation and a rich nation is the level of relative income. All other possible differences between nations on all other variables are assumed away. Over time, then, the income per capita of poorer nations would be expected to converge to that of richer nations, provided the only difference between countries *is* this initial difference in incomes as a result of differences in the initial stock of physical capital, as discussed previously. Thus **conditional convergence** is confirmed in the World Bank model, since the first coefficient shows that being poor relative to the United States does tend to raise growth rates of output, all else constant.

However, actual convergence of income is not presumed to occur simply because of initial income differentials. There are other inputs to production in the World Bank model, especially the level and type of human capital, that can and do result in quite different rates of economic expansion. In fact, as we shall see from examining the remainder of the coefficients in the first column of Table 8.3, income convergence is predicted to occur in the World Bank study only if a poorer country has a higher than average stock of human capital which will allow it to make ever better use of the world pool of technological knowledge and to take advantage of the positive externalities which result from higher human capital investments within their own economic setting.

The second statistically significant variable in the World Bank model in Table 8.3 is the initial stock of accumulated human capital, as measured by primary school enrolment rates in 1960.[23] An increase of 10 percent in the primary school enrolment rate would, everything else the same, increase the annual predicted rate of growth of the average country by 0.27 percent (10% × 0.0272). Thus Peru, with a primary school enrolment rate in 1960 of 83 percent, would have been expected to have grown 0.95 percent faster each year than Mozambique, which had a 1960 primary school enrolment rate of 48 percent, again assuming all other variables the same (World Bank 1993a: 196–7, Table 25).

Variables 3, 4, and 5 in Table 8.3 were not found to be statistically significant in the World Bank model, that is, their coefficient values were not able to be confirmed as being different from zero, though the average investment variable (variable 5) is statistically significant when variables 6, 7, and 8 are not included in the estimates.[24] Thus, the endogenous growth model suggests the unimportance, *by itself*, of the level of physical capital investment.

What variable 6 tells us is that if a country was one of the HPAEs,[25] that status added 1.7 percent *per year* to the growth of real per capita GDP. Unfortunately, exactly *why* HPAE status had this impact is unexplained by the variable itself: it is actually a *residual*, or dummy, variable that captures all the intangible factors that affect economic growth but which themselves are not directly estimated in the World Bank model. These might include: good public administration; better organization of production at the firm level; increased product and process specialization; appropriate macroeconomic policies; more efficient use of the world pool of technological knowledge; more and better R&D expenditures; education appropriate to modern economic growth; effective institutional and financial organizations; and so on. In a broad sense, the reasons for the better performance of the HPAEs was likely due to a more appropriate and facilitating institutional environment that was conducive to rapid economic growth and development at both the micro and macro levels. The East Asian economies have had weak *ceremonial* structures since the 1950s that do not impede, and in some cases positively promoted, the growth process.

When one compares the values for variables 7 and 8 (also dummy variables) in the World Bank model, these estimates tell quite a different story from that told by the HPAE dummy coefficient. Simply being a Latin American country actually reduced a country's predicted growth rate by 1.31 percent per year over the entire 1960–85 period, all else constant.[26] For countries in Sub-Saharan Africa, their growth rates were predicted to be lower by 0.99 percent per year, all else constant. Thus if a country in Latin America were to be compared with one of the HPAE countries, even if each were identical with respect to all other measured inputs to production in Table 8.3, the Latin American economy would be predicted to have an annual growth rate per capita of 3.02 percent *lower* per year than the comparable HPAE economy (= variable 6, the HPAE dummy, minus variable 7, the Latin American dummy, or = 1.71 percent − (−1.31 percent)). For the average Sub-Saharan African economy, its annual growth rate would be predicted to be 2.70 percent below that of the average HPAE economy, all else the same.

Let's return to the interpretation of variable 5, average investment as a share of GDP. The fact that this coefficient is statistically insignificant should be interpreted with care: this does *not* prove that new capital formation is unimportant. Rather, the investment co-efficient suggests that capital formation *per se* is a necessary, but not sufficient, condition for economic growth. In the case of the high-growth Asian economies, the necessary and sufficient conditions have been met. There, a given mass of physical capital equipment is more productively utilized than in Latin America or Africa. This is likely due to organizational and institutional factors not isolated by the World Bank study but captured in the dummy variables 6–8 rather than in the contribution of investment.

Note, too, from the value of the adjusted R^2 that the variables shown in Table 8.3 can explain only about 48 percent of the growth rate of per capita income of the average economy. That still leaves quite a lot out of the picture. In fact, more than half of what determines growth remains unexplained, much as the Solow-residual left half or more of the growth rate unexplained by the inputs to production.

This unexplained difference in growth rates between regions or nations unaccounted for by differences in relative income levels, human capital, or investment is, of course, of extreme importance. This variation in performance tells us that some countries perform better with the same endowments of labor, physical capital, and human capital than do other economies. They are more efficient in producing output than other economies that are seemingly identical in the so-called fundamental economic variables, that is, initial physical and human capital stocks. Thus simply accumulating capital, be it physical or human, is not the whole story of what promotes a higher level of economic development in the World Bank's version of the endogenous growth model. It is but part of what is necessary to stimulate economic growth and to qualitatively change the nature of path dependence. There is still a lot missing from this story.

Accumulating human capital may be necessary for achieving higher rates of economic growth, but it surely is not sufficient, or more of the variation in income would be explained by the World Bank's analysis. There are other factors, such as the entire macroeconomic environment of the economy, the *types* of human capital accumulated and their effectiveness in using knowledge and physical capital, and other positive externalities associated with the production process and the creation of knowledge that interact to contribute to aggregate growth through all kinds of spillovers and learning. And, surely, there are both micro and macro organizational and institutional forces at work. But none of these additional factors is identified explicitly in the World Bank estimation. They are implicit only, which is not helpful to policy-makers.

Other empirical studies have included more explanatory variables. For example, Barro (1991) uses the number of revolutions per year as a proxy measure of political stability; it has the expected negative effect on growth. So, too, do fertility rates, though weakly. Other analyses add R&D expenditures as an explanatory variable, and this raises the explanatory power of the model. There is a danger of adding too many different variables to any growth accounting model. One wants a theory with some generality, not a grab-bag of everything that might affect growth, since virtually anything can conceivably do so. What is important is to identify those factors that are *most* significant in influencing growth and for affecting the nature of path dependence. For endogenous growth theory in the World Bank-type endogenous growth format, these have been found to be human capital accumulation, capital accumulation (if only weakly supported), R&D expenditures, political stability, fertility, and openness to international trade.

Other endogenous factors: income and wealth distribution again

Dani Rodrik, of Harvard University and the National Bureau of Economic Research (NBER), redid the World Bank study, altering slightly the explanatory variables, but otherwise following the structure of the original model (Rodrik 1994). By excluding the investment rate, secondary education, and the population growth rate (which were not statistically significant in the World Bank model shown in Table 8.3), and by including Gini coefficient measures for the degree of inequality in land ownership and in income distribution, Rodrik was able to explain more of the growth rate in per capita income – between 53 and 67 percent, as opposed to 48 percent for the World Bank estimate.[27] Since data on land and income distribution were available for only forty countries, fewer than the sample used by the World Bank, Rodrik's study is somewhat less comprehensive. Nonetheless, these findings do contribute to our understanding about other factors that may be affecting growth rates beyond the traditional variables used by the World Bank and other researchers.

Taking the Asian nations as a group, there is a significantly lower degree of inequality in land and income distribution than in other less-developed nations (see Focus 8.1). Rodrik's findings suggest that less inequality in land distribution is associated with higher economic growth. For example, a reduction in the Gini coefficient for land distribution from 0.5 to 0.4, implying less inequality, would be predicted, from coefficient 9, to increase the rate of growth of per capita income by 0.52 percent per year, a not insignificant amount for countries with low growth rates and low incomes.

From Chapter 2, Focus 2.4, we have already seen that a high degree of income inequality can be a substantial burden on economic growth rates, so it is valuable to have Rodrik's independent confirmation of precisely how adverse the effects of inequality are. Even though the Gini coefficient for income inequality was significant only at the 10 percent confidence level (variable 10), its negative value, like the statistically significant negative value for land distribution, does imply an inverse relation between inequality and per capita income.

Since both of these Gini coefficient measures were for 1960 (or close to that year), lesser inequality may be a significant initial condition for attaining a higher growth rate and a higher level of income, just as the stock of human capital was found to be (variable 2 in Table 8.3). Countries may need to reach a threshold instrumental value in inequality if future success in economic and human development is to be speeded up (which turns the traditional Kuznets curve we considered in Chapter 2 on its head). This may be due partly to the fact that if the income distribution is highly skewed, individuals may be unable to reap the private benefits

FOCUS 8.2   INEQUALITY AND GROWTH

The East Asian HPAEs individually and as a group have had substantially less inequality in both their income and land distribution patterns than is the case for most other less-developed nations, as the following table, from Rodrik (1994: 18), shows. All Gini coefficient values are for the year closest to 1960.

	Gini coefficient for	
	land	income
Hong Kong	–	0.49
Japan	0.47	0.40
South Korea	0.39	0.34
Malaysia	0.47	0.42
Taiwan	0.46	0.31
Thailand	0.46	0.41
Average, all eight HPAEs	0.45	0.39
Argentina	0.87	0.44
Brazil	0.85	0.53
India	0.52	0.42
Kenya	0.69	0.64
Mexico	0.69	0.53
Philippines	0.53	0.45
Average, selected others	0.68	0.50

It will be remembered from Chapter 2 that Gini coefficients closer to 1 (or 100) imply greater inequality, while values closer to 0 suggest greater equality of the respective distribution. It is quite impressive to note the substantially greater degree of equality in both land and income distribution in the HPAE economies compared to other less-developed nations. It is certainly relevant to examine, as Rodrik does in his study of the sources of growth shown in Table 8.3, the significance of these differences on the rate of economic growth. Rodrik found that higher degrees of inequality were harmful to the level and to the pace of economic growth, as shown by the negative values on variables 9 and 10 in Table 8.3. Inequality may be necessary to provide incentives, but there is a danger if inequality is too great.

of increasing their human capital, thus reducing the potential level of GDP and reducing the growth rate. An income distribution with "too much" inequality can act as an institutional barrier to progress and contribute to a low-level equilibrium income by limiting opportunities and aggregate demand.

Part of the reason for the lower growth rates of income for economies in Latin America and in Sub-Saharan Africa was therefore likely due to the greater degree of initial inequality in those economies. While Rodrik's work leaves unexplained other reasons for differences in income levels among economies, as evidenced by the adjusted R^2 value, the inclusion of the degree of inequality adds explanatory power as a further insight of importance for nations that remain relatively poor beyond those of the World Bank model.[28] Further, as Rodrik (1994: 22) argues,

> once initial levels of schooling and equality are taken into account, there appears to be nothing miraculous about the HPAE's growth experience ... Around 90 percent or more of the growth of Korea, Taiwan, Malaysia, and Thailand can be accounted for by these economies' exceptionally high levels of primary school enrolment and equality around 1960.

In other words, Rodrik does not believe that the East Asian economies have resorted to any "miracle" strategies, as the title of the World Bank study might suggest, in shifting from a less-developed path to one taking them toward a more developed status. What the East Asian economies achieved and what contributed to their economic growth is tangible and reproducible and was "by design". Public policies were devised to create the key "fundamentals" – in this case, human capital and greater equality – that provided the essential initial conditions conducive to future progress. In the case of primary and secondary education and increased equality, these are examples of *social infrastructure* or social capital. They are just as important to economic growth, and to human development, as are physical infrastructure, such as ports, roads, water and power grids, and communications systems. Too often, perhaps, social infrastructure has not been accorded sufficient attention by policy-makers in less-developed economies. The evidence now seems clear, and more will be adduced later, in support of more productive public policies for economic growth.

Other research supports this conclusion that there was no "miracle" that explains the rapid pace of economic progress in the East Asian economies since the 1950s. Young (1995) and Grier (2003) both argue that rapid economic growth was due to accumulating the right kind of inputs in sufficient quantities. More human capital accumulation paid off with its efficiency-enhancing, spillover effects. Greater capital accumulation that embodied new knowledge and technological innovation contributed to economic growth to the extent that the complementary human capital inputs had been formed to work with it. There were no miracles that led to productivity increases that cannot be explained primarily by more of the right inputs, that is, not just more labor and physical capital, but better trained and educated workers who could work with new physical capital embodying new knowledge in ways that expanded output even faster.

That there was no "miracle" of growth in East Asia is actually very good news for those economies that remain mired in poverty. It means that what some successful, formerly less-developed economies have done to shift to a higher growth path can be followed by others. The lessons are clear thanks to the on-going efforts of economists to clarify the specific inputs to production: provide funding and incentives for the accumulation of more human capital; create financial and legal institutional structures conducive to innovation in products and processes; and provide incentives for investments in new physical capital that embodies new knowledge. From these broad strategies comes more rapid economic progress.

Technical efficiency change

Part of the story told by the endogenous growth theories has to do with the effectiveness with which a country's endowments – human capital, physical capital, other resources, knowledge, etc. – are utilized in the production process. And in today's world, with such rapidly expanding knowledge and technology creation, countries must be "doing the right things" if growth rates are to be maintained and higher levels of income are to be reached.

One way effectiveness can be measured is by what is called **technical efficiency change**. The idea behind this concept is illustrated in Figure 8.2, which shows a standard production possibilities frontier (PPF). Technological change can be represented by an outward shift of the frontier from FF_1 to FF_2.[29]

First, let's consider an economy that had originally been producing at *A* on FF_1 and then, after the technological advance, moves to *B* on the new, higher production possibilities frontier, FF_2. This economy would be keeping pace exactly with the rate of technological advance and international "best practice" as represented by the maximum outputs that can

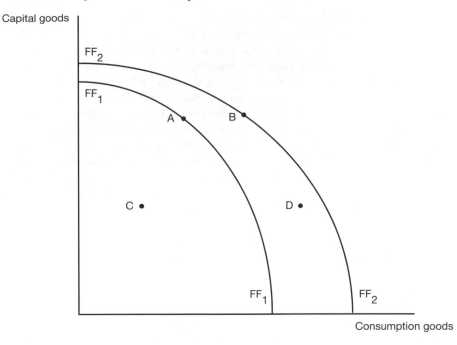

Figure 8.2 Technological change versus technical efficiency change.

be produced from the inputs on the production possibilities frontier. The potential rate of economic growth is determined by the rate of technological change and new knowledge creation, whatever its source may be. The actual rate of technological and knowledge change attained by an economy, however, is endogenous, depending on past and present investment, educational, R&D, legal, and a whole range of other decisions that determine how efficient the economy is relative to what is possible as represented by the PPF (World Bank 1993a: 49–50, 68–9).

An economy that moves from production point *A* to production level *B* is keeping pace with what is possible. It is growing at the pace of technological change (represented by the shift in the PPF) and is operating efficiently (on the PPF). For such an economy, there is zero technical efficiency change, as the economy operates at maximum efficiency both before and after a change in technology.

Now consider an economy beginning at a position like *C*, inside of FF_1, which moves to *D*, inside FF_2 after the change in technology. By approaching closer to the new production possibilities frontier compared to its position relative to the former PPF, we can say this economy has experienced *positive* technical efficiency change. The level of international best practice is being approached as the nation's productive resources are better able to capture the advantages of increases in knowledge than in the past. For such countries, their rate of economic growth will *exceed* the average rate of world technological change measured by the shift outward of the PPF.

Such economies are better able to make use of their current resource endowments in ways that enhance the overall rate of economic expansion. This permits growth rates that exceed the pace of overall, world best-practice technological change. In other words, such countries are able to combine their existing resources in more efficient combinations by being better able to capture the benefits of increases in knowledge and technology. This may be due to improvements in the stock of human capital accumulated, learning-by-doing, continued improvements in the macroeconomic or microeconomic management of the economy, or to any of a number of possible causes, internal and external, as discussed earlier in the chapter.

Table 8.4 summarizes the World Bank's estimates of how various countries and regions did relative to international "best practice" technology, that is, in terms of technological efficiency change and progress toward reaching the ever-moving optimal production possibilities frontier resulting from constant knowledge creation at the international level.

Of the HPAEs, Hong Kong, Japan, Taiwan, and Thailand were making progress toward using, and using more effectively, the best available technology.[30] This happened, the World Bank suggests (and Chapter 12 will consider this reasoning in detail) because these countries had accumulated an appropriate stock of human capital that permitted them to learn from, adapt, and use new technologies, new ideas, and new production processes discovered elsewhere, perhaps even adding to best practice methods adapted to their own economies as a consequence of trial-and-error.

Singapore, Malaysia, Indonesia, and even apparently South Korea, however, were slipping behind world best practice. Graphically this would mean that their relative position compared to the outward-shifting production possibilities frontier in Figure 8.2 was to be further inside the outward-shifting frontier, that is, further away from the expanding pool of technological knowledge and its application to the production process compared to production prior to technological advances that shifted the PPF.[31] Negative technical efficiency change does not imply that an economy is not growing. It means that it is not growing as quickly as it might have given the advances in knowledge that occurred. Such economies are not keeping pace with the expansion of best-practice technological change, but they may still be growing.

For Latin America and Sub-Saharan Africa, there also was a growing shortfall from the most efficient production methods. This situation was most severe in the case of Sub-Saharan Africa, which effectively was falling further and further behind in the ability to use its resources in ways that could positively augment production and human development. This reflects a weakness in the creation of human capital and in R&D expenditures, and perhaps is also a consequence of the inequalities in land and income distribution that rendered the Sub-Saharan economies unable to use, adopt, or adapt very effectively what the world pool of technology had to offer.

Additionally, the productivity gap between Sub-Saharan Africa and Latin America and the HPAEs was widening because of these differences in technological capacity, making even relative, unconditional convergence of incomes impossible without a substantial turn-

Table 8.4 Estimates of technical efficiency change, 1960–1989

	Technical efficiency change
Latin America	−1.4217
Sub-Saharan Africa	−3.4539
Hong Kong	1.9714
Japan	0.9876
Taiwan	0.8431
Thailand	0.1067
Indonesia	−1.2352
Malaysia	−1.7767
South Korea	−0.2044
Singapore	−3.4510

Source: World Bank 1993a: 69.

around in the level of technical efficiency change. That will require changes in the factors that the new growth theories see as fundamental to stimulating growth. More saving or investment alone is not sufficient. There must be appropriate human capital accumulation and sufficient research and development so that a critical threshold of domestic techno-logical competency is reached. It is also likely that better macroeconomic policies need to be introduced, that changes in industrial organization and business practices that reward innovation be fomented, and, following Rodrik, amelioration of severe inequality also may be a prerequisite for future progress. These are themes we will touch on in the remaining chapters, building on the endogenous growth theories and the identification of some of the fundamental policy variables.

Conclusions

Endogenous growth theories have contributed to our understanding of how some countries can maintain high economic growth rates over long periods of time. They also help to clarify why levels of income remain low in far too many economies and why others have been able to escape adverse past path dependence and attain higher levels of both economic growth and incomes. In often complex mathematical formulations, economists have attempted to model the workings of market economies with all of their real-world imperfections.

In a very general way, endogenous growth models focus on how capitalist economies expand over time. They show how new knowledge, new products, and a finer division of labor within and between firms can contribute to both economic growth and higher income levels. For such models, the institutional milieu of each economy is extremely important, though it cannot always be modeled explicitly. Where the institutional environment – government, finance, the legal system, openness of the economy to trade, incentives to entrepreneurship, the educational system, and so on – is conducive to expansion, an economy is more likely to prosper and can do so for long periods of time. And we know if the institutional environment is propitious by observing what is occurring at the macro-level of the economy. While this may sound like circular reasoning, it is not, since part of what is done empirically with these models is to examine these institutional structures.

In other economies where economic growth rates and levels of income are both low, the confluence of obstructive institutions and the failure to accumulate the appropriate human and physical capital resources can be seen to be the restraining forces to progress. It is in this way that theory can be an aid to policy by identifying what is most crucial for economic growth and human welfare. On these counts, endogenous growth theory has made important contributions to our understanding of these mechanisms.[32]

Questions and exercises

1   Distinguish between "conditional convergence" and "unconditional convergence" of per capita income. On what does "conditional" convergence of income depend in the neoclassical model, i.e., what are the conditions that must hold for incomes to converge? Does either the Solow-type growth model or the endogenous growth model predict *unconditional* convergence of incomes amongst nations? What would unconditional convergence of incomes imply for incomes of countries in the future?

2   Table 8.1 considers income convergence by looking at aggregate income by region. Using the World Bank website (http://www.worldbank.org), find income growth figures for four different less-developed economies and for the United States, the UK, and Japan

for as many years as feasible. Put the data into a table format so it is easy to compare the countries over a number of years. Has there been income convergence or divergence of the four less-developed countries you selected with the high-income economies? Discuss the evidence.

3   More than one development economist has opined that "poor countries are poor because they are poor." What might at first sound like a vacuous and not very helpful observation actually captures the essence of the neoclassical theory of economic growth. Looking at note 2 below and the material in the text related to it, explain in words why saying "poor countries are poor because they are poor" might in fact be a very rich statement reflecting some basic facts of real world economies that may impact on their ability to grow.

4   How can increased human capital accumulation which results in a higher average number of years of education contribute to sustaining a high rate (i.e., percentage change) of economic growth? What *specific* positive externalities might be expected from workers with more education interacting with other workers with education or even with workers with little education? Can you see how two (or more) workers might be more productive together than they would be if they did not interact? Can you give some concrete examples of how and when such interaction have resulted in such positive externalities? (One example: Have you ever studied with someone else? Can both learn more by such sharing than by studying alone? Is this a positive externality, i.e., a spillover effect?)

5   How can a country try to improve its rate of "technical efficiency change"? What public policies might be required? What "initial conditions" might be important if an economy is to have a positive rate of technical efficiency change? Is "knowledge or technology" something that all economies can use with the same effectiveness? Why, or why not?

6   What does it mean to say technological change is *endogenous* to an economy? How is this different from viewing technological change as *exogenous*? Does the idea that technology is country-specific fit better into the exogenous or endogenous technological perspective? Can technological change be both exogenous and endogenous at the same time?

7   Looking back at Table 8.1, how many years will it take the low- and middle-income countries to double their per capita income, assuming they continue to grow at the average annual rate which prevailed during 1970–2005? How many years will it take for the high-income economies to double their per capita income, using their average annual growth rate for 1970–2005? How long would it take Sub-Saharan Africa to double its income per person if it grew at the average annual rate which prevailed from 1970–2005? (Hint: using the *Rule of 70*, the doubling time in years = 70/annual % change; in finance, the Rule of 72 is often used in the same way. In fact, the Rule of 70 gives a very good estimate of doubling for percentage rates of 5 percent or less. The Rule of 72 gives better estimates for percentage changes between 5 and 10 percent. If growth rates are negative, what is being determined is the time to halve a value, and for negative values the Rule of 70 is more accurate.)

8   Consider Table 8.4 on "technical efficiency change." What might be some reasons explaining the negative value for South Korea? Does negative technical efficiency change necessarily mean an economy is inefficient or becoming more so? What does negative technical efficiency mean, then? (Hint: remember, technical efficiency change has to do with to what degree a country is approaching its production possibilities frontier, a frontier that is a moving target as a result of on-going knowledge creation and technological innovation.)

9   Draw a "fuzzy" or "flexible" production function showing how accumulating more

human capital (the variable on the horizontal axis) can result in different levels of per capita output (the variable on the vertical axis) depending on the spillover effects and positive externalities to the economy that human capital accumulation provides. Think, for example, of a string in the shape of a production function that is not fixed in place, but is capable of sliding upward as spillovers occur at any given level of human capital accumulation. Are there increasing returns to your input?

Notes

1 In Solow-type neoclassical models, technology is treated as if it were a pure public good available to all countries and firms freely and with the same effect on productivity when applied to the production process, regardless of any differences in organizational or institutional structures or in the levels of education or skill levels of the work force.

Income convergence among nations will not occur in the Solow model, however, if a poor country does not save and invest at the same rate as higher income countries, that is, *unconditional* convergence is not predicted by the neoclassical model. Being a model where growth is based primarily on capital accumulation, that is, on additional investment, which is equal to saving in the neoclassical formulation, the Solow model only predicts convergence of poor nations to rich nations if the poor nations save and invest a proportion of their GDP which is similar to that of the richer nations, assuming comparable rates of population growth. Income convergence is thus *conditional* on the similarity of the fundamental variables affecting the level of income per capita shown in equation 4.5 in Chapter 4.

2 The level of savings in period t, S_t, is related to the level of aggregate income. In simple models, this relation is often stated as $S_t = a + sY_t$, where Y_t is income in period t, $a > 0$ is some constant amount saved out of income each period t, and $0 < s < 1$, is the marginal propensity to save (MPS), that is, the fraction of each additional unit of income which is saved rather than spent. It is easy to see that if the constant, a, and the marginal propensity to save, s, and income, Y_t, are all small values, then so too will be S_t. To the extent that saving is required for investment, then a low level of aggregate savings contributes to a low level of aggregate investment and a lower rate of economic growth in future and a lower income per person. Other, more complex, and perhaps more realistic, theories of savings, such as the "permanent income hypothesis" and the "relative income hypothesis" can be read about in any intermediate macroeconomics text, but the "low income–low saving" relation remains in force within these more complex formulations. This is another example of a "vicious circle of poverty."

Also of interest are the Kaleckian or Kaldorian-type savings functions which disaggregate savings behavior by classes, usually the working and the capitalist class, each of which is presumed to have a different propensity to save. In such models, the higher income, capitalist class is assumed to save more than workers, and thus income inequality is presumed to functionally contribute to a higher level of investment and greater economic growth. In many developing nations, however, this may be an unwarranted assumption. To the degree that conspicuous consumption plays an important role among the remnants of the agro-export and financial elites, the rate of domestic saving may be driven down, as will the rate of capital formation, by a high degree of income inequality. This possibility is considered later in this chapter.

3 The literature is vast and often quite challenging. For a useful collection of original readings, see Stiglitz and Uzawa (1969).

4 Even though there is evidence of relative convergence of incomes in South Asia and East Asia and the Pacific, both regions have low levels of income per person in an absolute sense compared to the high-income economies. For example, in 1970, GDP per person in East Asia and the Pacific was $175 versus $13,372 in the high-income economies. East Asia's GDP per person was but 1.3 percent of that of the high-income economies. In 2005, relative incomes were $1,352 and $28,304, respectively (all data is in 2000 US dollars, i.e., adjusted for inflation), and the ratio of East Asia's GDP per person to that of the high-income economies had increased to 4.8 percent because of the more rapid rate of GDP growth in East Asia (6.0 percent per year) compared to the high-income economies (2.2 percent).

Though relative incomes converged somewhat between these two regions, the gap in absolute incomes actually widened. Whereas in 1970, GDP per person in the richer economies exceeded that in East Asia by $13,197 the absolute gap in average GDP in 2005 had grown to $26,952. If East Asia were to continue to grow at an average yearly rate of 6.0 percent, it would take until the year 2058 for East Asia's income to reach the level that the high-income economies had reached in 2005. It would take until 2089 for GDP per person to converge for both regions at a value of $173,460 per person, assuming that the annual growth rates of 6.0 and 2.2 percent are maintained.

More sobering is to realize that with a GDP per person of $562 in 2005, and a slower rate of growth per year than East Asia (2.7 percent), South Asia's income would not converge to that of the high-income economies until 2808!

5 This is due to the assumption of diminishing returns to capital. As the amount of capital, K, in use increases, its marginal product, $MP_K = df(K)/dK$, decreases. If we use the short-hand of assuming profit, r, to be the return to capital paid in units of production, then the return to capital when there are K_0 units of capital, r_0, is greater than where there are K_1 units of capital in use, if $K_0 < K_1$. Graphically, the slope of the production function gets flatter, and r decreases, as K increases.

6 Plosser (1993: 63–4), for example, notes that recent estimates of the Solow model show that if physical capital differences were to account for the fact that per capita income in the United States is about twenty times that of Kenya, the United States capital stock per person would have to be on the order of 8,000 times greater than in Kenya, when in fact it is "only" about twenty-six times larger. This leads to the suggestion that there must be factors other than the stock of physical capital and of rates of investment which account for the wide income differentials between developed and less-developed nations.

7 See Warsh 2006, especially Chapters 15–24, for a very insightful, informed, and eminently readable intellectual history of the rise of endogenous growth theory and its impact on thinking in economics.

8 The Solow-type model might be called an *exogenous* growth model, in the sense that once a nation reaches its "steady state" level of income per capita as determined in equation 4.5 of Chapter 4, income per capita will *only* grow in the future at a pace determined by the rate of exogenous, that is, externally determined, technological change taking place at the world level. On the other hand, in the *endogenous* growth models, the rate of change of both short- and long-run income per capita are internal, that is endogenous, to the workings of each economy. In these models, the pace of economic growth and of technological change depend on that economy's specific organizational structure, labor types and skills, institutions, government, and an entire range of factors we shall be discussing in this chapter.

9 In particular, there were the suggestive and profound works of Young (1928) and Arrow (1962). Rereading Young today one sees how old ideas are rediscovered.

10 Human capital accumulation is any improvement in the quality of labor, be it the result of increased education, on-the-job learning, better health care, interaction with other workers with accumulated human capital, or other influences which improve labor's productivity without adding more physical capital to production.

11 Endogenous growth models eventually accepted some form of imperfect competition as a real-world reality that needed to be built into the theories. There was no other way to understand why firms would undertake expensive research and development and invest in the search for new knowledge unless there was some way to capture a sufficient part of the expected returns from such purposeful action so as to warrant the initial investment. Assuming perfect competition also assumed away such purposeful behavior with sufficient individual returns through the assumption of perfect information imbedded in the concept. Thus endogenous growth theories became even more complicated theoretically, though more real, by presuming that imperfect competition was in play.

12 Controversy over the superiority of endogenous growth models versus neoclassical models continues. Endogenous growth theories ask economists to let go of the concept of diminishing returns in the short run for some variable inputs, especially human and research capital, a large theoretical leap given the power of neoclassical theory. For a taste of the strength of the passions, and perhaps egos, involved on both sides of this debate, see the mostly non-technical symposium on endogenous growth in the *Journal of Economic Perspectives*, Winter 1994. Leading proponents of the endogenous model, such as Paul Romer, square off against skeptics, like Robert Solow, who defends a revised neoclassical model. Warsh's (2006) book also reveals how much was and is at stake in this debate for the reputations of many economists.

13 It is perhaps worth noting that the World Bank study was initiated at the insistence of, and financed by, the government of Japan as a result of "a determination on Japan's part to get the World Bank to pay greater attention to the distinctive features of the East Asian development experience, which stood in marked contrast to development approaches the Bank was then advocating" (Fishlow and Gwin 1994: 3). As many commentators have noted, there is much in the Bank's report that would seem to reflect a criticism of past World Bank policy and an acceptance of at least some aspects of a more activist approach for certain kinds of state involvement in the support of more rapid economic growth and human development.

14 Solow (1994: 49–51) has argued that the elimination of diminishing returns to the variable inputs is one of the weakest links in the endogenous growth models. He shows that if marginal returns are increasing, then an endogenous growth model would predict an infinite level of per capita income in the finite future, a clear impossibility. Typical of Solow, known for his humorous side, he comments on this "knife-edge" instability of the increasing returns assumption: "It is one thing to say that [income] will eventually exceed any bound. It is quite another to say that it will exceed any stated bound before Christmas." So, if there are increasing returns to any factor, the theoretical model explodes to infinity. If there are diminishing returns, on the other hand, the endogenous model is reduced to the Solow model, and there will be a finite, steady-state income level. Only when there are constant returns to the variable factors does the possibility of sustained increases in long-run per capita income make theoretical sense in the endogenous growth model. Solow, however, does not think that the real world is likely to be so precise as to be of the constant-return variety.

Lau (1996: 90), however, finds increasing returns to scale on the order of 1.6 for developing economies and approximately constant returns for more mature economies, suggesting sustained growth is possible. Perhaps the real world is more precise than Solow would give it credit for, and it may be possible to have "constant" increasing returns. Perhaps increasing returns at the rate found by Lau do not "explode" the model, nor lead to infinite income by Christmas, but rather permit long-term growth of income per person for fairly long periods of time, certainly longer than would be possible in a world of diminishing returns. Park and Ryu (2006: 251, Table 3) estimate something very close to constant returns over a thirty-year time frame, but with mildly increasing returns in earlier periods for some of the East Asian economies.

Graphically, an endogenous growth production function is a bit like a piece of clay or Plasticine. It is not fixed in place but is capable of shifting upward and stretching without any new investment or labor being added to production. It does not have just one income level for each level of K or L; since the economy's production function is capable of stretching, over time, the attainable level of income increases.

15 Increasing returns are thus accruing to the economy as a whole, not to any particular individual firm through at least partial spillover of new proprietary knowledge to other producers. This is an important point, since if the increasing returns were internal that would lead to one firm monopolizing the industry. Increasing returns are external to any firm and accrue to the economy as a whole. However, these theories do not presume that there is perfect competition, but rather that there is some form of imperfect competition that leads firms to look for new products, more specialization, and new ways to produce in the hopes of maximizing their profits.

16 As Lucas (1988) observed, individuals who have accumulated human capital tend to gravitate toward locations where human capital is abundant not toward where it is scarce. Thus individuals in rural areas with more education migrate to cities, and highly educated persons in less-developed nations often migrate from the cities of their own country to the cities of more-developed nations – the so-called brain drain – to associate with others with abundant human capital. The rate of return (i.e., the private benefits in increased income) to migrants is higher in their new setting than it was in the human-capital-poor regions from which they migrated. This is an extremely important observation.

This is strong, if casual, evidence for the positive externality effect of human capital; the productivity of one individual's human capital is increased, not decreased, when it is combined with more human capital inputs similar or higher in quality. That is, this is evidence for an absence of diminishing returns to human capital accumulation and, via positive externalities, for increasing returns to such inputs when combined with complementary human capital. Myrdal, of course, made much the same point in discussing "virtuous circles" (see Chapter 6), though his theory was purely literary, not mathematical and rigorous like the endogenous growth theory literature.

One estimate of the social rate of return to an additional year of secondary schooling is 13 percent, while another finds that each additional year of schooling above three to four years added to the average years per person contributes about 5 percent to total output (Rowen 1996: 103).

17 Learning-by-doing effects are not limited to industrial and manufacturing pursuits or even to the productivity of those who ostensibly are doing the learning-by-doing. In a study of the introduction of high-yield seed varieties in agriculture, Foster and Rosenzweig (1995: 1205) found that "farmers with experienced neighbors are significantly more profitable than those with inexperienced neighbors, as they experienced positive learning-by-doing spillover benefits from those with more experience. Such spillover learning effects to other farmers suggest that subsidies to early users of new technologies may help to not only increase total output and efficiency of those particular producers, but also to contribute to the attainment of the social optimum that is even higher due to the 'teaching' they impart to neighboring farms."

The original formulation of the theory of learning-by-doing is due to another Nobel Prize-winning economist, Kenneth Arrow. Arrow's work fits very neatly with the endogenous growth theories, as one of the characteristics of his model is that it is non-linear and that opens the possibility of non-diminishing returns as productivity of a given input is able to expand over time in the process of producing.

18 The constant, a, can be interpreted as the output–capital ratio, that is, Y/K, which indicates on average how much additional output can be produced from each additional unit of capital. The value, a, may also be interpreted as the incremental output–capital ratio, that is, even though a is a constant at any point in time, it is not necessarily fixed through time. As an economy evolves and grows, the value of a can change, rising with increasing returns, falling with decreasing returns, though at any point in time, it can be taken as a constant value. A changing value of a would result in a "flexible" production function if graphed.

19 If well-trained individuals in a poor country migrate to higher-income economies where their skills are worth more because they can be combined with those of other workers with high levels of skills, a "lock-in" of a low-level income poverty trap may be more likely. Already richer countries actually benefit from the spillover of learning these individuals, the training of which took place in a poorer economy, as their human capital can contribute to more rapid growth rates.

20 Given that there are high initial costs associated with creating new knowledge or new products or processes of production, i.e., of more specialization, these fixed costs alone are sufficient to generate increasing returns, since higher levels of output are associated with decreasing costs of production. See Jones (1998: Chapter 4) for a simple and clear exposition.

21 In other words, new knowledge is not a pure public good available for adoption by any firm or economy. Some spillover is likely to occur, but for most new knowledge it is possible for its creator to exclude others from using it, at least for a time. Such knowledge thus shares one characteristic of a public good: no one's use of such knowledge prevents anyone else from using it (i.e., knowledge is a *non-rival good*). But knowledge also at least in part shares, for a time and to some degree, an important characteristic of a private good, that is, it is possible to exclude others from using it. Whether knowledge is therefore called an *impure public good* or a *quasi-public good* or a *club good* is immaterial. What is important in the endogenous growth models is that new knowledge or new technology or new goods or a new production process is created by someone or some firm with an expectation of a return on that uncertain investment.

Knowledge is different from human capital. Human capital is all the knowledge imbedded in human beings that must have been learned in some way. Such knowledge is non-transferable. Knowledge is the un-imbedded raw material that can be utilized by purposeful human action. It is this world pool of knowledge, to the extent that an economy can tap into it, that creates the possibility of increasing returns over the future.

22 For technological models of endogenous growth that are quite consistent with the Ayresian approach or Myrdal's "cumulative causation" considered in Chapter 6, see the very suggestive work of Grossman and Helpman (1991, 1994). This theoretical work puts the technological process at the forefront of the development process, a view we argue is essential in Chapter 13.

23 The primary school enrolment rate is defined as the number of all students enrolled in primary school as a percentage of primary-school-aged children. The ratio can exceed 100 percent due to the presence of students older or younger than the normal primary-school age.

24 There is a good reason to exclude the share of national output going to investment as a variable explaining the rate of economic growth, however. There is a feedback from economic growth to investment and back to income and output that makes these two variables interdependent rather

than independent. This is Rodrik's rationale for not including the investment rate, variable 5, as an independent variable in his own re-estimation of the World Bank model (Rodrik 1994: 19–20). Also see Grier (2003: 394) who models investment as endogenous.

25 Again, the HPAEs are the eight high-performance Asian economies of Japan, Hong Kong, South Korea, Singapore, Taiwan, Indonesia, Malaysia, and Thailand.

26 Recall, from our discussion in Chapter 6 Ayres's emphasis on ceremonialism as a retarding factor that can obstruct the creation, the spread, and the adaptation of new technology and the spread of new knowledge. In Latin America, such backward ceremonial institutional structures might include the extreme concentration of land ownership and income, monopoly power in certain industries, military dictatorships during certain periods and pseudo-democratic authoritarian structures.

27 The adjusted $R^2 = 0.67$ was obtained when the investment/GDP ratio coefficient was included as an explanatory variable, but since Rodrik felt it inappropriate to include investment as a separate explanatory factor for economic growth given the feedback between the two, we have reported his regression 3 results only (Rodrik 1994: 20).

28 Why should land and income inequality play a retarding role in growth performance? Two responses have been forthcoming; one concentrates on aggregate demand. Studies of Japan and Taiwan have indicated that robust demand by farmers for domestic manufactured goods contributed strongly to economic growth during the formative stages of the industrialization process. Thus a "better" distribution of land and income would contribute to a larger domestic market. The second reason for a link between higher inequality and lower economic growth has to do with social stability; societies with a greater degree of equality are likely to be more politically stable. When political instability is a recurring event, investment of all types, and hence economic growth, is likely to be reduced. Rodrik's study pointed out that the World Bank *did* recognize income distribution and land distribution as important factors in the HPAEs success, but argued that the Bank's study "[lacked] a serious discussion of equity as a precondition of growth" (Rodrik 1994: 26).

29 In this example, technological change is not neutral. Assuming equal units on both axes, production possibilities frontier FF_2 shows that technology has had a greater impact on the production of consumption goods, C, relative to the impact on capital goods, K.

30 It is not enough to simply have access to the best technologies or the most modern capital equipment if greater efficiency is to be attained. Technology transfer or technology purchases do not guarantee that a country has the capacity to make effective use of such technology. As Nelson and Winter's analogy suggests, buying the best and most advanced tennis racket available is not the same thing as having mastered the skills necessary to play the game. That is where human capital accumulation, R&D expenditures, industrial organization, and a whole range of "inputs" to production enter into determining success or failure of the development effort.

31 It may be that the very rapid economic transformation of South Korea, particularly the "compressed" nature of the industrialization process compared to the already developed countries, has meant that the ability to keep up with international best practice has been difficult. On the other hand, it may be that the measures of technical efficiency change for countries with rapid growth do not accurately measure such advances toward best practice. With very rapid physical capital accumulation, new machines typically will embody the latest technology, so some of what might be counted as technical efficiency in slower growing economies is imputed to increases in physical capital in rapidly growing economies.

32 Research continues on these issues. An interesting recent contribution, though somewhat outside the endogenous growth framework, is Jones (2007), who offers a new theoretical explanation for the widening income gaps between rich and poor countries. His model is based upon the concept of industrial linkages considered in Chapter 5 and the complementary nature of inputs in production. The latter concept allows for the introduction of a range of institutional realities that can help or hinder production in modern economies. One of the attractions of this new theory is that it does not require that there be constant or increasing returns to explain wide income differences between economies.

References

Arrow, Kenneth J. 1962. "The Economic Implications of Learning by Doing," *Review of Economic Studies* 29 (June): 155–73.

Barro, Robert J. 1991. "Economic Growth in a Cross Section of Countries," *Quarterly Journal of Economics* 106 (May): 407–43.

———. 1993. "Human Capital and Economic Growth," pp. 199–216 in Federal Reserve Bank of Kansas City, *Policies for Long-Run Economic Growth*. Kansas City: Federal Reserve Bank.

Fishlow, Albert and Catherine Gwin. 1994. "Lessons from the East Asian Experience," pp. 1–12 in Albert Fishlow *et al.*, *Miracle or Design?: Lessons from the East Asian Experience*. Washington, D.C: Overseas Development Council.

Foster, Andrew D. and Mark R. Rosenzweig. 1995. "Learning by Doing and Learning from Others: Human Capital and Technical Change in Agriculture," *Journal of Political Economy* 103 (December): 1176–209.

Grier, Robin. 2003. "Toothless Tigers? East Asian Economic Growth from 1960 to 1990," *Review of Development Economics* 7 (August): 392–405.

Grossman, Gene M. and Elhanan Helpman. 1991. *Innovation and Growth in the Global Economy*. Cambridge, MA: MIT Press.

———. 1994. "Endogenous Innovation in the Theory of Growth," *Journal of Economic Perspectives* 8 (Winter): 23–44.

Jones, Charles I. 1998. *Introduction to Economic Growth*. New York: W.W. Norton & Co.

———. 2007. "The Weak Link Theory of Economic Development," draft copy, University of California, Berkeley and NBER.

Landau, Ralph, Timothy Taylor and Gavin Wright. 1996. "Introduction," pp. 1–18 in Ralph Landau, Timothy Taylor, and Gavin Wright (eds.), *The Mosaic of Economic Growth*. Stanford: Stanford University Press.

Lau, Lawrence J. 1996. "The Sources of Long-Term Economic Growth: Observations from the Experience of Developed and Developing Countries," pp. 63–91 in Ralph Landau, Timothy Taylor, and Gavin Wright (eds.), *The Mosaic of Economic Growth*. Stanford: Stanford University Press.

Lucas, Robert E. 1988. "On the Mechanics of Economic Development," *Journal of Monetary Economics* 22 (July): 3–42.

Park, Jungsoo and Hang K. Ryu. 2006. "Accumulation, Technical Progress, and Increasing Returns in the Economic Growth of East Asia," *Journal of Productivity Analysis* 25 (June): 243–55.

Plosser, Charles I. 1993. "The Search for Growth," pp. 57–86 in Federal Reserve Bank of Kansas City, *Policies for Long-Run Economic Growth*. Kansas City: Federal Reserve Bank.

Reynolds, Lloyd G. 1986. *Economic Growth in the Third World: An Introduction*. New Haven, CT: Yale University Press.

Rodrik, Dani. 1994. "King Kong Meets Godzilla: The World Bank and 'The East Asian Miracle'," pp. 13–53 in Albert Fishlow *et al.*, *Miracle or Design?: Lessons from the East Asian Experience*. Washington, D.C: Overseas Development Council.

Romer, Paul M. 1994. "The Origins of Endogenous Growth," *Journal of Economic Perspectives* 8 (Winter): 3–22.

Rowen, Henry S. 1996. "World Wealth Expanding: Why a Rich, Democratic, and (Perhaps) Peaceful Era Is Ahead," pp. 92–125 in Ralph Landau, Timothy Taylor, and Gavin Wright (eds.), *The Mosaic of Economic Growth*. Stanford: Stanford University Press.

Solow, Robert M. 1994. "Perspectives on Growth Theory," *Journal of Economic Perspectives* 8 (Winter): 45–54.

Stiglitz, Joseph E. and Hirofumi Uzawa (eds.). 1969. *Readings in the Modern Theory of Economic Growth*. Cambridge, MA: MIT Press.

UNDP (United Nations Development Programme). 1994. *Human Development Report 1994*. Oxford: Oxford University Press.

Warsh, David. 2006. *Knowledge and the Wealth of Nations: A Story of Economic Discovery*. New York: W.W. Norton & Co.

World Bank. 1983. *World Development Report 1983*. Oxford: Oxford University Press.

———. 1991. *World Development Report 1991*. Oxford: Oxford University Press.

———. 1993a. *The East Asian Miracle*. Oxford: Oxford University Press.

——. 1993b. *World Development Report 1993*. Oxford: Oxford University Press.

——. 1995. *World Development Report 1995*. Oxford: Oxford University Press.

——. 2003. *World Development Report 2003*. Oxford: Oxford University Press.

Young, Allyn A. 1928. "Increasing Returns and Economic Progress," *The Economic Journal* 38 (December): 527–42.

Young, Alwyn. 1995. "The Tyranny of Numbers: Confronting the Statistical Realities of the East Asian Growth Experience," *The Quarterly Journal of Economics* 110 (August): 641–80.

9 The initial structural transformation

Initiating the industrialization process

After reading and studying this chapter, you should better understand:
- the need for industrialization to accelerate the pace of economic growth and development;
- the structural changes which easy import substitution industrialization (ISI) can initiate as the *first* stage of industrialization;
- the role of government in speeding-up industrialization;
- the nature of transitional inefficiencies and competition from imported goods;
- the static and dynamic welfare effects of infant industry tariffs;
- the role that development banks, financing, and other initiatives can play in supporting industrialization;
- the potential benefits and dangers of pursuing an ISI strategy;
- why easy ISI is almost assuredly necessary but definitely not sufficient for escaping past adverse path dependence.

Introduction: an industrialization imperative?

Achieving a higher level of development appears to be inextricably intertwined with the industrialization of an economy. One chronicler of the nature of structural change in the development process has written that the issue is not whether industrialization is necessary for development but only "when and in what manner it will take place" (Syrquin 1988: 218).

The structural transformation that accompanies industrialization alters not only the physical landscape of nations via urbanization, internal labor migration and the establishment of a complex of, typically, urban business enterprises. It also alters many of the cultural, social, and other institutional arrangements that have stamped a particular society and made it what it is to that point in time.

With industrialization, nations become more homogeneous in terms of what is consumed, what is read, what is seen on the television and at the cinema, and what is learned in schools and in universities. Of course, many cultural differences remain even after industrialization, since they arise from distinct historical experiences woven into the fabric of individual societies in their language, literature, law, folklore, religion, music, cuisine, and embedded in shared attitudes, perspectives, and practices.

Industrialization and development provide unmistakable benefits to society, but sacrifices also are required, as is true whenever choices must be made. One inevitable cost is an often wrenching change in social values and the everyday rhythms of life in less-developed nations. Industrialization induces adjustments that often are disruptive of ancient patterns and ways of doing things. Frequently, opposition to industrialization arises from powerful groups who benefit from the status quo and who thus oppose the possibility of a new order. In other circumstances, opposition to industrialization and the changes it sets in motion comes from religious or cultural institutions which see a spiritual or traditional way of life being threatened by the material concerns of a business society and the private acquisitiveness and individualism on which it thrives.

Opposition to industrialization is natural and expected, and the debate over how to develop, how fast, and who is to benefit are important issues for any nation to consider and evaluate. There is no a priori reason why all nations must follow the same industrialization path or must make the same sacrifices on the road to a higher living standard and an improvement in their level of human development. Since many decisions about development can have irreversible effects on the local environment or on social structures, it is wise for societies to engage in an ongoing dialogue over the present and the future. Too often, in evaluating the expected effects of development, economic and business concerns – perhaps because they are more amenable to measurement – are treated as if they are more important than are spiritual, cultural, environmental, or religious interests which are intrinsically more subjective and hence more difficult to quantify. That should not make them less important to consider, however.

Reconciling conflicting interests may slow progress, but each society must evaluate as objectively as possible to what extent trade-offs made to sustain traditional dimensions of social, political, and cultural life are worth the sacrifice. In some cases, caution in balancing growth and development versus other interests is justified. In other circumstances, an unnecessary slow-down in progress for the majority is simply the consequence of catering to narrow special interests.

Nonetheless, all nations and economies are linked and interdependent to varying degrees, making the general forces and pressures of the global capitalist economy difficult, perhaps increasingly impossible, for nations to circumvent. Given these economic bonds and the real need for less-developed nations to make progress along both economic and human development dimensions (think back to the Millennium Development Goals introduced in Chapter 1), higher levels of industrialization – even with its attendant costs – would seem to be absolutely necessary.

The data at the top of Table 9.1 suggest the close relation between the growth rate of industry and the rate of growth of total national output.[1] There would seem to be a positive correlation between the rate of growth of total output and the pace of industrial growth, though the *direction* of causation is certainly not proven by this data.

If one disaggregates further to look at the link between industrial growth and the growth of total GDP for specific countries, the relationship is also positive, as shown for China, India, and South Korea in the last lines of the table. More rapid industrial growth tends to be associated with more robust GDP growth, though again the direction of causation is not defined, and it most likely is two-way.

Looking at China, for example, as the rate of industrial growth rose from 9.5 percent annually in the 1980s to 13.5 percent in the 1990s, GDP growth increased from 9.3 percent to 10.4 percent per year. When industrial growth slowed down after 2000, so too did the GDP growth rate. Korea's pattern also shows a positive relationship between industrial and GDP growth rates; when industrial growth fell from 1980 to 2005, GDP growth also declined. India's growth of industry fell and then rose, and so too did the GDP growth rate. Again, this does not prove causation from industrial growth to GDP growth; the direction of causation

Table 9.1 Industrialization and economic growth (annual percentage growth of constant dollar GDP and industry)

	Industry			GDP		
	1980–90	*1990–2000*	*2000–5*	*1980–90*	*1990–2000*	*2000–5*
East Asia and Pacific	8.0	10.9	9.2	7.5	8.4	8.2
Latin America and Caribbean	0.6	3.2	1.0	1.1	3.4	1.9
Middle East/North Africa	4.1	3.0	2.9	3.1	4.0	4.1
South Asia	7.0	5.6	6.8	5.6	5.2	6.4
Sub-Saharan Africa	1.1	1.6	4.4	1.9	2.2	4.3
China	9.5	13.5	10.6	9.3	10.4	9.5
India	7.1	5.6	7.0	5.8	5.5	6.8
Korea	10.9	6.5	4.9[*]	8.7	6.1	4.7[*]

Source: World Bank, *World Development Indicators Online.*

* 2000–4

could be in the other direction. It is likely, though, that the causation is reciprocal, or at least that is what economic theory would suggest. But the important point is that the two growth rates *are* positively related.

In fact, not only are the growth rates of industry and GDP directly related, but so are their relative magnitudes. When the growth rate of industry is low, so is the growth rate of GDP (and vice versa). Just consider Latin America and the Caribbean or Sub-Saharan Africa in the 1980s. On the other hand, when the industrial growth rate is high, so is the GDP growth rate. Look at East Asia and the Pacific or China. There is thus not only a positive relationship between the growth rates of industry and GDP that can be observed in Table 9.1; these growth rates are closely related to one another. When one is low, the other is low; when one is high, the other is high as well.

Besides the positive relationship between industrial expansion and economic growth, there is yet a further reason for pursuing industrialization. As considered in Chapter 3 and then again in Chapter 6 in the discussion of the Prebisch-Singer hypothesis, countries which predominantly produce and export primary products and import the bulk of their manufactured goods are apt to experience instability in their terms of trade, that is, in the purchasing power of their exports. In fact, there has been a long-term deterioration in the purchasing power of these exports relative to the manufactured goods imported. Industrialization is therefore a means to create not only a more productive domestic economic structure which raises domestic incomes; it also can help to create the *possibility* for an import and export pattern more similar to that of the already-developed nations, one that tends to be more stable in terms of the purchasing power of a country's exports (see Focus 9.1).

There is thus a twofold industrial imperative: first, higher levels of industrialization can contribute to higher levels of income, and secondly, industrialization sets the stage for a desired structural transformation of import and export patterns.

Structural change and economic growth

It is not simply the expansion of the industrial and manufacturing sectors that is critical to the pace of development. The process of growth and development is the unfolding consequence of a quantitative and a qualitative reorientation of the entire economic and social structure of a nation. It involves basic changes in the education level of the population, in what they know and can do, in business organization and in the population's way of thinking about their relation to the world around them. It is as much ideological as it is economic. We know, too, from Chapter 8 on endogenous growth that higher levels of development require the accumulation and use of more of the ever-expanding world stock of knowledge.

The size of the agricultural (*primary*) sector tends to shrink with economic growth as rural workers move into the industrial (*secondary*) and services (*tertiary*) sectors. This transformation entails the migration of labor from the rural countryside to urban areas where former rural workers become urban workers available to run the machinery of industry and to work in all the supporting firms, shops, and institutions, including government, which an expanding economy requires.

During successful industrial transformations, agricultural production becomes more efficient and intensive in its use of capital, both physical and human, and in the use of knowledge and technology which increase the productivity of workers remaining in that sector. An industrial revolution without an agricultural transformation will be but a partial success (see Chapter 11). As we saw in Focus 8.2, a change in agricultural land distribution patterns in the direction of greater equality seems to be associated with more rapid progress as well. As an economy proceeds to ever-higher paths of development, there is continuing structural transformation as workers shift from the secondary sector toward the service sector to work in commerce, transportation, trade, government, finance, educational institutions, and so on.

Over time, then, more developed economies tend to have the majority of their labor force employed in industry and services. As well, the greatest part of total income is generated in these two sectors, while the relative importance of agriculture shrinks. All three sectors of production show a tendency toward converging levels of worker productivity over time if development efforts are successful, as the labor force is used to its fullest effectiveness. The spread of technology and human capital accumulation generates a trend toward homogeneity among the primary, secondary and tertiary sectors in terms of the level of output per worker (Chenery 1979: 18–21; also see Kuznets 1971, on structural change patterns that induce and accompany economic growth and development; Exercise 2 at the end of the chapter gives you some practice in examining these issues).

Table 9.2 shows the structural shift of labor usage from primary production toward secondary and tertiary activities that occurs at higher levels of development. High-income economies have less than 5 percent of employed workers in agriculture; in the low-income economies, this proportion is nearly 60 percent in the most recent period. A strong inverse relation between the share of the labor force in agriculture and the level of per capita income is

Table 9.2 Labor force distribution, by sector[a]

	GDP/person[b]		Agriculture		Industry		Services	
	1980	2001	1980	2001	1980	2001	1980	2001
High income	17,282	26,460	8.6	4.0	33.5	26.3	57.8	69.5
Middle income	1,245	1,809	62.0	36.2	18.8	19.5	17.3	40.7
Low income[c]	310	338	66.0	59.2	14.0	14.2	18.1	26.5

Source: World Bank, *World Development Indicators Online.*

Notes
a As percentage of total labor force.
b GDP per person in constant 2000 US dollars.
c For the low-income economies, because of data limitations, the data is for 1990 and 1995 only.

quite evident. The larger the share of the total labor force engaged in agriculture, the lower the level of income. At higher levels of development, the share of the labor force engaged in agriculture is relatively small.

Likewise, there is an equally strong positive relation between the share of the labor force in industry and in services and the level of development. The smaller the share of the employed labor force in industry and services, the lower the level of income of the country or region. The larger that share, the higher the level of aggregate income and development. Part of the explanation for this has to do with the increase in total output that accompanies the shift of labor from low-productivity agriculture to, typically, higher-productivity industry and service activities. As one of the fundamental structural transformations first introduced at the end of Chapter 1, this labor transfer results in a one-time boost to GDP as an economy's labor force is distributed in a more optimal manner (again, Exercise 2 at the end of the chapter illustrates the gains in output that can come from a redistribution of the labor force from low- to high-productivity activities).

The slow pace of both agrarian transformation and of industrialization of the low-income nations provides strong evidence of the compelling *correlation* for the agricultural and industrial transformations that contribute to greater development as measured by income or by the human development index (HDI).

Development thus involves both an industrial revolution *and* a reorganization of the agrarian sector.[2] Success in such a transformation requires the proper additions to human and physical capital and the attention to endogenous technological change considered in previous chapters and to which we will return in later chapters.

An industrial transformation aimed at raising a nation's level of development that fails to foment an effective agrarian transformation eventually will falter and fail, just as it will be less effective without the attention to technology and to the quality of inputs that have been identified in endogenous growth theories as central to sustained growth in income per capita.[3] All sectors of an economy must become progressively more technological and more productive as the shift in labor use from primary to secondary to tertiary uses moves forward. This typically involves a slow, then accelerating, reduction in the significance of primary production within the overall productive structure of the economy. One development economist, Benjamin Higgins, has referred to this structural transformation from agricultural dominance to industrial and service production primacy as the strategy of "getting rid of farmers" (Higgins and Higgins 1979).[4]

The Lewis dual-economy model of structural transformation: surplus labor

How does this structural evolution that shifts labor from agriculture to industry come about in practice? What sets this labor migration process in motion? A classic description, already presented in Chapter 5, was provided by Nobel Prize-winning economist Sir W. Arthur Lewis. Here we only briefly review the main points of his argument.

If there is *surplus labor* in agriculture, and by surplus labor we simply mean a lower level of *productivity* of labor in agriculture than in industry (or services), then it is possible for the more productive and higher-wage industrial (or service) sector to attract labor from the countryside to urban areas by paying wages slightly above rural wages. Shifting workers from lower-productivity activities in agriculture to higher-productivity industrial (or service) jobs will result in an increase in total national output and, of course, income per person.[5]

Lewis observed that the typical less-developed nation was dualistic, not only in the sense of having two key sectors, agriculture and industry, but also in the more fundamental sense that these sectors had little interconnection. There was a traditional low-productivity, low-technology agriculture sector where the great bulk of the population lived, worked, and produced most of what they consumed. There also existed, or there could be created, an incipient industrial sector where production was profit-oriented, more capital-using and technology-driven, and where worker productivity was higher than in the traditional sector. Those working in the modern sector bought food and perhaps some other primary inputs from the traditional sector. But the most important link between the traditional and modern, industrial capitalist sector was via the provision of labor from the primary sector to industry via labor migration.

It was in this labor supply link between the two sectors that Lewis found the transformation dynamic that could contribute to greater growth and development via expanded industrialization. Lewis maintained that with continuing reinvestment from the profits of the modern sector, the transfer of surplus labor from agriculture to industry could be accomplished relatively smoothly, especially if the capital–labor ratio did not rise significantly in industry and if the growth of the industrial sector was financed at a low cost from the profits of private industrialists (for further details review the discussion around Figures 5.1(a) and 5.1(b)). It was believed there would be sufficient new employment for rural migrants, as formal sector industries would be able to grow at a rate sufficient to absorb the labor flow from agriculture.

The Lewis model has been a powerful theory for understanding how the structural transformation of an agriculture society into a more industrial society might be accomplished. If all works more or less as Lewis envisaged, it would seem that the labor migration process is cumulative once it has begun, as the higher wages of industry attract rural workers until an equilibrium of productivity and wages is reached between sectors.

Now we shall consider how countries might foment such a migration of labor from agriculture to industry if it has not begun spontaneously on its own or if the pace of industrialization is deemed too low.

Initiating the structural transformation process: industrialization

Is there a particular development strategy that less-developed nations can follow that can help to initiate or accelerate the transition of labor from agriculture to industry and contribute to the positive transformation of the productive structure of the economy from an agricultural to an industrial base?

Historically, *import substitution industrialization* (ISI) has been the means by which governments have supported this process. In this chapter, we consider in some detail how ISI can propel an agriculture-based economy into a more modern, industrially-based economy. We will also note the pitfalls to be avoided if the potential transformative benefits of this instrumental strategy are to be reaped.

The first stage of industrialization: easy import substitution industrialization (ISI)

With the exception of Great Britain, the first modern industrializing nation, all subsequent successful efforts by nations to modernize have involved elements of import substitution industrialization (ISI) as a means to promote the expansion of a domestic industrial sector. ISI involves the establishment of firms within the domestic economy that produce for local consumption at least some of the manufactured goods currently being imported. With ISI, domestic production replaces – *substitutes for* – some imported goods, hence the name of the strategy: industrialization that substitutes for imports, ISI.

Which commodities are the most likely candidates for new or expanded domestic production when beginning ISI?

Typically, ISI begins with the production of relatively simple *non-durable consumer goods*, such as socks, beverages (soft drinks, beer, canned and bottled juices), furniture, shoes, cloth diapers, toys, building materials, and so on. These are goods with pre-existing market demands within the local economy that are currently being met by imports. The technology and know-how for producing such goods tends to be relatively rudimentary, of low cost, and frequently available "off-the-shelf" on the world market with few or no restrictions on use, as, for example, for sewing machines or bottling equipment. The demands on the skills and knowledge of the labor force is moderate, which is important since many industrial workers will be recent arrivals from rural areas with but modest levels of education and other training, certainly within a factory setting.

A focus on producing non-durable consumer goods is also consistent with the Lewis model. The surplus labor coming from agriculture will be absorbed more easily if industrial production is concentrated in labor-intensive processes, which is the case for many non-durable consumer goods. A focus on labor-intensive production can help to avoid problems of urban unemployment and underemployment by providing sufficient new employment to the flow of rural migrants. Consumer non-durable production that is labor-using conserves scarce physical and financial capital and makes use of the less-developed economy's most abundant factor of production, its labor.

Concentrating on producing goods similar to those being imported removes some of the risk for local entrepreneurs undertaking these projects since there is a pre-existing demand for low-cost goods, such as T-shirts or socks. Given a known import demand, local producers will be better able to make reasonable calculations as to the probability of the profits that can be expected from initiating or expanding production given local wage and cost conditions, the level of technology and human capital accumulation, and the expertise level of local workers, managers, and entrepreneurs.

This first stage of ISI with the focus on producing simple consumer non-durable goods for the domestic market to replace imported goods has been called *easy, primary, or horizontal* ISI.[6] We will most often refer to this stage of industrialization as simply easy ISI.

It is not necessarily desirable nor recommended that easy ISI be initiated for all non-durable consumer goods products being imported. Nor does easy ISI need to take place simultaneously for many goods via a "big push" in all sectors (Chapter 5). Some non-durable consumer goods may be better candidates for easy ISI than others. Some imports may present better opportunities for substitution later rather than sooner. Factors that need to be considered in determining the pace and reach of easy ISI include:

1 the size of the domestic market, including population size, average income, and income distribution;
2 the size and skills of the existing pool of potential entrepreneurs who would operate new enterprises;
3 the educational attainment and available skills of the labor force and the speed of migration of labor from agriculture to industry;
4 the availability of finance for the purchase of technology, needed physical capital and other inputs, and for the needed training of managers and workers;

5   the potential for growth of demand over the future for each import substitution good and the learning-by-doing potential from production; and

6   possible linkage and spin-off and spillover effects (*positive externalities in production*) that might stimulate production or knowledge expansion in other industries, including the establishment of new industries, as the consequence of initiating production in any particular easy ISI industry.

Whether a "balanced" or "unbalanced" ISI strategy in the sense discussed in Chapter 5 is followed will depend on the evaluation in each country of the feasibility of and the expected gains and costs accruing to either "blanket" or more "selective" ISI promotion of non-durable consumer goods production. If selective ISI is chosen, as will be the case in most instances, then the timing of the promotion and expansion of particular industries and firms can be decided by taking into consideration the factors listed above and by making strategic decisions based on those constraints.

Japan, India, and the larger countries in Latin America (Brazil, Mexico, Argentina, Chile, and Colombia) followed an easy ISI strategy of industrial transformation beginning as far back as the mid-1800s in the case of Mexico and by the last third of the century for the others (Amsden 2001: 43). In Japan, the conscious decision to industrialize via ISI was part and parcel of the Meiji restoration after 1868, and "all modern industries were started as import substitutes" (ibid.: 174).

ISI on an expanded scale in Latin America was to some degree forced upon the countries by the breakdown in normal trade patterns as a result of the successive crises of the First World War, the Great Depression, and then the Second World War. As a result of these disruptions, it was difficult to purchase imported consumer goods because of supply interruptions. It was equally difficult to sell agricultural and other primary exports to traditional markets to earn the foreign exchange required to purchase imports during these crisis periods (see Focus 9.1). As a result of these interruptions to world trade, local manufacturing firms were able to emerge and expand by producing for the domestic market behind the artificial barrier of these external international crises that shielded them from import competition (see the discussion on the structuralists in Chapter 6 for more details).

FOCUS 9.1   THE EXPORT STRUCTURE

A fundamental shared characteristic of many less-developed countries is the predominance of primary product exports as a percent of total merchandise exports. This, of course, means that manufactured goods are a small fraction of total exports.

Successful structural transformation, as outlined at the end of Chapter 1 and discussed in this chapter as well, not only alters what is produced domestically by shifting an economy from an agricultural focus toward industrial and service enterprises. Long-term development also requires a makeover in the export and import profiles of an economy. To avoid declining terms of trade, the export composition must be modified so that traditional primary product exports are replaced by manufactured good exports or higher value-added non-traditional primary product exports (like cut-flowers, strawberries, or shrimp) not as systematically subject to decreases in their purchasing power.

The following table reminds us of the often heavy concentration of primary product exports in total exports that still persists for many less-developed economies, particularly in Latin America and Africa. Primary exports include: agricultural raw materials, food, fuels and ores and metals.

	Primary product exports as % of merchandise exports					GNI per capita
	1965	1980	1990	2000	2004	2004
Bolivia	95.7	97.1	95.2	71.0	86.3	960
Brazil	91.6	61.4	46.9	39.5	45.9	3,000
Chile	85.9	90.3	87.4	81.4	85.9	4,930
China	–	–	26.5	11.6	8.4	1,500
Colombia	93.0	79.6	74.2	67.5	61.6	2,010
Costa Rica	84.2	65.7	65.6	34.4	37.2	4,470
Côte d'Ivoire	94.7	–	–	84.9	–	760
Ghana	97.4	98.0	–	85.2	–	380
India	51.0	41.0	27.6	21.3	26.1	630
Indonesia	–	97.6	64.5	42.9	43.9	1,130
Korea	40.6	10.1	6.4	9.2	7.8	14,040
Malaysia	93.9	81.0	45.8	18.8	23.1	4,520
Mexico	83.6	88.1	56.5	16.5	20.0	6,930
Nicaragua	94.5	86.2	91.6	92.1	88.5	830
Nigeria	97.7	–	–	99.8	–	430
Pakistan	63.9	50.9	20.9	15.0	14.6	600
Taiwan	58.5	–	7.4	4.8	7.3	15,350
Thailand	95.2	71.0	35.6	22.0	–	2,490
Venezuela	98.2	98.3	89.6	90.9	88.4	4,030
UK	17.2	26.3	18.8	16.8	17.9	33,630
US	34.8	32.1	21.2	12.8	14.4	41,440

Examining the above figures carefully, it is possible to detect some correlation between the percentage of primary exports and the level of per capita income in 2004. A larger percent of primary exports to total exports tends to be associated with a lower per capita income.[7] Consider Bolivia, Côte d'Ivoire, Ghana, Nicaragua, and Nigeria; primary exports comprise a relatively large share of their total manufactured exports. Income per capita is relatively low in all these economies.

The correlation is not perfect, however. There are countries like Venezuela with a large share of primary exports and yet income per capita is not as low as one might expect from that fact alone. Why? Does it help to know that Venezuela's major export is oil? Some primary product exports, like petroleum, may not be as associated with low average incomes as is the case for other primary product exports.

Pakistan also stands out as an exception, too, but for the opposite reason. Pakistan has both relatively low per capita income and a *small* share of primary product exports. The bulk of Pakistan's exports were concentrated in manufactured goods, but the majority of these were textile fibers, textiles, and socks, which tend to be generally low-value-added, low-income generating exports.

Clearly, then, having manufactured exports alone is not the whole of the story for becoming more developed. The concentration of exports and their diversity and type also are important. Apparently there are "good" manufacturing exports and not-so-good, just as there are "good" primary exports (like petroleum or cut-flowers, for example), while others that are not so valuable (think bananas or peanuts).

China is an interesting intermediate case. In 1990, China's GNI per person was $320 (not shown in the table); as primary exports declined over time and manufactured goods exports grew, average GNI rose to $1,500 in 2004. India's progress toward raising its income per capita has been slower, and that may be connected to the larger share of primary exports compared to China.

Source: World Bank, *World Development Indicators Online*

What easy ISI can do and what it cannot do: a foreshadowing of what's to come

For the easy ISI strategy to work so that LDCs are less likely to be subject to long-term declining terms of trade, it is necessary that the pattern of domestic production *and* exports be altered. A reorganization of the *internal structure of production* toward a higher degree of industrialization is insufficient for long-term progress *without* a fundamental reorientation of what less-developed nations export to the world market.

It is important to keep this qualification in mind as we continue through this chapter. Easy ISI can help set the stage for successful structural transformation in an economy; by itself, it is insufficient, as we hope to make very clear. But easy ISI is necessary to get industrialization under way. Without that, there is no possibility of an evolution in the export structure.

It is incorrect for countries to accept the existing export structure as immutable and definitive, as if it reflected an optimal outcome of international specialization in production, as described by Ricardo's theory of comparative advantage discussed in Chapter 4. Rather, existing patterns of trade relations might better be viewed as a single frame of a motion picture, a static snapshot. It is not the whole of the movie. Initiating easy ISI is one means to begin to create *new comparative advantage* in more dynamic product lines that promise greater gains in productivity and income growth over the future in both domestic and, if successful, in international markets.

To advance the metaphor, easy ISI is not a rapid "jump-cut" to a more efficient productive structure compared to foreign producers, but rather it is akin to a scene within the whole of a movie that ultimately advances toward the desired conclusion: an evolving industrial structure, alterations in the use of labor by sector, and evolving patterns of imports and exports that can instrumentally contribute to a progressively higher average standard of living. All of the parts are essential to the final outcome, just as all the scenes of a film are integral to the whole.

The array of productive inputs a society possesses at any particular moment is its current *resource endowment*. However, every nation is capable of modifying and making more productive and more extensive its *reproducible* resources, particularly human capital, knowledge, technology, and physical capital. Expansion in the stock and quality of these assets helps to increase the pace of economic expansion and leads to higher levels of income, as Chapter 8 argued.

Every economy has a *constantly changing* resource endowment on which it can build for the future. A country's resource endowment is not a given. Productive resource endowments are fluid, altering as population grows, as education takes place, as research and development occurs leading to technology and knowledge advances, as governments improve their operations, and so on. Of course, the pace and direction of change in endowments can be quite different across economies.

Public policy has an impact, for good or bad, on an economy's potential resource endowment. For development to continue, a society must alter and make more productive its resource base so as to keep pace with the maturation of the world economy and its changing demand patterns and new knowledge about how to produce and what to produce. Countries that fail to keep pace will find their average incomes lagging and their growth rates lower than they could be.

The products and services in which a nation has a comparative advantage are, from this perspective, subject to a substantial degree of control and design through the particular decisions made regarding investments in human capital and knowledge, technology, better organizational methods, and other policies under the full or partial control of government policy-makers and individuals.

Government and easy ISI

In an industry where no, or only a few, local firms produce goods similar to imported commodities, stimulating domestic production will typically require some sort of government intervention that can provide insulation to local firms from direct foreign competition. This is necessary because in most less-developed nations few if any local firms are likely to be able, at least initially, to produce efficiently enough to compete with imports. As relative late-comers to industrialization, new firms in less-developed economies are likely to be at a substantial disadvantage *vis-à-vis* existing foreign firms which already produce for the international market. A lack of financing for new projects, few trained entrepreneurs, low skill levels of workers and fierce competition from imports all work against the spontaneous expansion of the manufacturing sector in most LDCs.

Without an industrialization strategy supported by government, a thriving domestic industrial sector may continue to be an impossibility, particularly in this era of very open international markets with low barriers to trade among nations. New firms face start-up problems that tend to make their costs higher than for comparable firms in other countries that already supply the international market. One specific obstacle prospective manufacturers encounter is in attempting to borrow funds for projects in economies with very imperfect markets in banking and finance (see Focus 9.2). Thus without a government-sponsored industrial initiative, the high probability of market failure through institutional inadequacy will result in a sub-optimal level of industrialization and a sacrifice of potential overall economic welfare in most LDCs.

Transitional inefficiencies

New firms anywhere, but especially those in less-developed economies, are likely to incur higher per unit production costs for some time compared to foreign firms already successfully producing for the international market in the same product line. These higher unit costs are the consequence of what can be called *transitional inefficiencies*. Such inefficiencies can result from:

- inexperienced management and labor;
- low levels of technological development, technological effectiveness, and knowledge acquisition;
- a lack of experience with accounting, financial, marketing, supply networks, and other critical inputs to the production process;
- low output levels that prevent the attainment of scale economies;
- a low average level of human capital accumulation and educational attainment;
- inefficient financial markets; and
- government red-tape and other bureaucratic inefficiencies.

The list of factors that might contribute to transitional inefficiencies compared to foreign firms supplying the import demand for comparable goods could be extended almost *ad infinitum* and may differ among economies.

What is not in doubt is the *effect* of transitional inefficiencies: they raise the unit costs of production for new firms in a less-developed economy relative to established producers in other countries which export to markets around the world.

Transitional inefficiencies are reduced and overcome through "learning-by-doing," a real-time process that can be fostered only by initiating production so that workers, managers,

FOCUS 9.2   CREDIT AND MARKET FAILURE

Some economists argue that if there are sufficient expected profits to justify the creation of an ISI firm, private firms and entrepreneurs will recognize such opportunities and borrow against future earnings to establish such enterprises. If that were truly the case, there would be no need for government intervention to initiate industrialization.

However, even if such a future profit calculation is made by private entrepreneurs, any *market failure* problem in financial markets because of a weak or poorly functioning banking and financial intermediation system, or the lack of an equity capital or bond market, may make the realization of such projects unlikely by rendering borrowing difficult or even impossible.

This is an example of *institutional inadequacy* quite common in less-developed economies as a result of incomplete and poorly functioning markets. The result of such market failure will be an inefficient allocation of society's resources, both currently and into the future, and a sub-optimal level of economic and human development. When there is such market failure in financial markets, there is a strong case to be made for government remediation if industrialization is to have half a chance at success.

A further complication enters the picture when it is asked whether it is even reasonable to expect prospective entrepreneurs in LDCs to be able to make the expected profitability calculations for establishing new enterprises. This is an issue concerning the availability of information. Joseph Stiglitz and Kenneth Arrow, both Nobel Prize-winning economists, have written extensively on the economics of information.

Information is not free; it is a "good" much like any other. There is a cost to both producing information and to obtaining it. In less-developed nations with only a rudimentary industrial structure, is it reasonable to expect potential entrepreneurs to be able, at a sensible private cost, to identify the expected future profit stream of an investment that no one has yet made?

If an economy lacks the required social and physical infrastructure, appropriate human capital resources, supply networks, sources of financing, and so on, is it a reasonable possibility to think prospective entrepreneurs will be able to estimate what profits they might make if they did set up a firm?

If the answer to these questions is no, then there is a valid *economic rationale* for government action that corrects for market failure and for information costs that distort the private calculation of future benefits. Such government intervention has been shown to be able to improve upon what the market outcome would have been, that is, to increase economic efficiency. An easy ISI strategy can be one part of an effort to help the market work better over the long term, thus rendering such government intervention to correct for market failure less necessary over time.

Source: Stiglitz 1992

and entrepreneurs have the opportunity to improve their efficiency level in the actual process of producing. Transitional inefficiencies also can be addressed via more formal and typically economy-wide processes such as technology acquisition and licensing, improvements in managerial and worker education to increase the quantity and quality of the stock of human capital, and through organizational innovations like equity and bond markets and an expansion in financial intermediation via banks and other such institutions that reduce the costs of borrowing. Further, the operations of government *vis-à-vis* the business sector can be streamlined and made more efficient and transparent, and infrastructure, such as roads and communications networks, with substantial positive externalities, can be modernized. Some, perhaps all, of these initiatives are essential for surmounting transitional inefficiencies in new firms.

Figure 9.1 shows the effect of transitional inefficiencies in production: average and marginal costs will be higher for new domestic producers compared to established foreign producers providing a comparable import product. Particularly for production at less than the socially optimal level – where unit costs of production are minimized at the bottom of the average total cost (*ATC*) curve – when economies of scale have been fully realized, average and marginal costs of producing are higher than they otherwise might be because of the effects of transitional inefficiencies.

At relatively low levels of production like $Q_{current}$ for an easy ISI firm just beginning production, unit costs of production (along ATC_{new}) are higher than they would be at the same level of output for existing producers providing imports to the local market ($ATC_{established}$). Compared to the per unit costs of production ATC_O at the optimal level of production, Q_O, for an already established foreign firm, the combination of transitional inefficiencies and low production levels (i.e. unexploited economies of scale) when beginning ISI result in higher costs of production per unit of output for new producers of ISI goods. These higher per unit costs translate into higher prices for new domestic producers compared to experienced foreign firms providing a country's imports.

For many small nations and even for some larger ones, the limited size of the domestic market as a result of a small population, low average incomes, and a high degree of income inequality can constitute a significant barrier to attaining the cost reductions consistent with optimal production levels, even if the sources of the transitional inefficiencies are removed (that is, domestic output still may be less than Q_O in Figure 9.1 because of limited

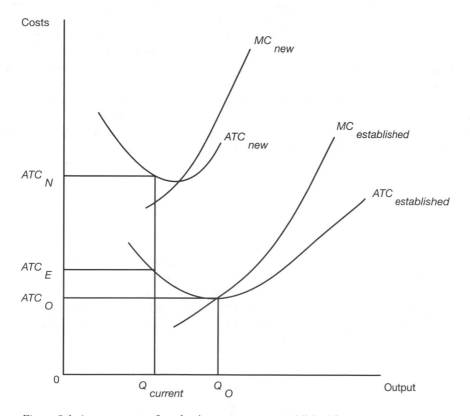

Figure 9.1 Average costs of production, new versus established firms.

domestic demand).[8] However, the domestic market is not the only potential outlet for the output of easy ISI firms. There is no inherent reason why easy ISI goods that are first produced for local consumption cannot be exported to foreign markets at some point in the future. This would contribute to an expansion in demand that could help producers achieve lower costs per unit through scale economies *once and if* transitional inefficiencies are overcome. We shall see that this is precisely what successful developing economies do.

The critical issue for us to explore is how a new firm can confront the barrier of transitional inefficiencies and be able to survive in the face of competition from imported goods. If the firm does survive, it may be able to eventually compete head-to-head with existing foreign firms. In other words, we need to consider how transitional inefficiencies might be overcome so that a new domestic firm in an LDC can become as efficient as existing producers elsewhere. At the end of the day, efficiency *must* be one of the primary goals of any successful structural transformation process if government intervention in the market is ultimately to be justified.

Infant industry tariffs: overcoming transitional inefficiencies

The higher per unit costs of production for new domestic producers compared to established foreign producers shown in Figure 9.1 translate into higher prices to consumers for the goods produced by domestic firms compared to the prices of imports of the same commodity, all else the same. Given the choice between a higher priced (and probably, initially, lower quality) domestically produced good and a foreign imported good at a lower price, there is little question which product most consumers will choose, particularly low-income consumers. In the face of external competition and given the inevitability of transitional inefficiencies, new domestic producers can hardly be expected to compete at the beginning of easy ISI. They may choose to not even initiate production under such circumstances, since the chances of success against established foreign firms supplying the import market is so stiff.

It is the difference in average and marginal costs of production between potential domestic producers and foreign firms –and the price differential the cost disparity implies –that underlies the argument for imposing *infant industry tariffs* on imported goods if domestic industrialization is to be stimulated. Raising the final price of imported non-durable consumer goods by adding an appropriate import tax on top of the price charged by the firm will make the prices of domestically produced import substitutes more attractive to consumers in the home market.[9]

The need for such protection from external competition at the beginning of the industrialization process is rooted in the difficulty for new producers to acquire the knowledge associated with the entire process of production (also see Amsden 2001: 5–6).

> The fundamental rationale for protection is found in the tacitness of technology, which implies that internationally competitive levels of productivity cannot be reached without experience-based learning which entails comparatively high costs that must in some way be financed.
>
> (Evenson and Westphal 1995: 2284)[10]

A protective tariff is one way to finance this learning process. As a tax on a specific import, it raises the price of the imported good thus making the higher-cost domestic output better able to compete, assuming no substantial consumer bias in favor of foreign goods. The final price of the imported good to the consumer will be pushed above that of the domestic import-substitute. This will augment the demand for the domestic import-substitute as substitution by consumers takes place away from imports and toward domestic goods, thus permitting the domestic producer to slide down the average cost curve (ATC_{new} in Figure 9.1) as higher rates of domestic production fill the gap in demand left by the decrease in imported goods.

From this perspective, infant industry tariffs may best be looked at as one form of investment in the economic progress of an economy. Prices are increased, yes, but that is necessary to give new domestic firms a chance to expand production and learn to produce more efficiently. For future growth possibilities, past and present "manufacturing experience matters" in learning to produce efficiently and without starting up and expanding industrialization, such learning cannot take place. As Bruton (1989: 1607) writes: "Another way of looking at this cost [of infant economy protection] is possible: the reduced availability of goods and services can be considered an investment."

There is no alternative to actually initiating production and participating in the learning-by-doing required if the beneficial path dependence of an industrial-based economy is to have any chance of being forged (Amsden 2001: Chapter 5). Easy ISI may be an essential investment in the future human and economic development of late-developing economies, as fundamental as investing in education, infrastructure, and new physical capital.

An alternative to a tariff on imports to protect new easy ISI enterprises from lower-cost foreign imports is a subsidy provided to domestic firms. A subsidy would lower the private average costs of production of new enterprises and could provide the same degree of protection from imported goods as a tariff, and it would do so without necessarily increasing the price of the good to the final consumer as a tariff will do. However, a subsidy creates a drain on public resources which are already likely to be in short supply in most less-developed nations. For this reason, infant industry tariff protection is a near universal feature of ISI programs (other forms of non-tariff barriers also are used, such as regulations, quotas, and the like).

Gerschenkron (1962: 44) noted that the more "backward" a nation is the more likely it is that industrialization will need "to proceed under some organized direction; depending on the degree of backwardness, the seat of such direction could be found in private investment banks, in investment banks acting under the aegis of the state, or in bureaucratic controls." This expresses Gerschenkron's important insight on the "substitutability" of instruments to stimulate industrialization already mentioned in note 2 to this chapter. It will usually be government providing "organized direction" to the industrialization process, but there are other possibilities.

Tariff protection is but one instrument often used to promote easy ISI. Undervalued exchange rates, low interest rates extended to particular borrowers, directed credit allocation via state-owned investment banks (see Focus 9.3), technology and R&D assistance, education and training programs, planned government purchases of private domestic firm output, and the creation of para-state firms are but a few of the alternatives available to public policy-makers to initiate, sustain, and stimulate the industrialization process. The goal is to create the desired structural transformation from an agriculturally-based economy to a more productive industrial and service economy. Successful developing countries actually use a combination of these instruments to promote industrialization, as we shall see here and in the next chapter.

FOCUS 9.3   DEVELOPMENT BANKS AND ISI

Development banks, which are state-owned and state-directed non-commercial banks, have been an important tool for directing a nation's savings and borrowed funds toward higher-risk projects which can help foment development in some economies.

One of the most successful development banks has been Mexico's Nafinsa. In 1940, Nafinsa was directed by the Mexican government to pursue the following objectives: (1) promote industrialization; (2) promote the production of intermediate and capital goods; (3) invest in infrastructure; (4) help stimulate and develop indigenous entrepreneurial talent; (5) build confidence within the Mexican private sector; and (6) reduce the role of direct foreign investment in industry.

Nafinsa went through two major stages: aggressive promotion of industrialization from 1940 to 1947 and then promotion of infrastructure and heavy industry from 1947 to the early 1960s. In making its investments, Nafinsa emphasized potential linkage effects. An emphasis on linkages is well known today, but in the early 1940s, Nafinsa engaged in innovative policy-making. In a classic study of Nafinsa, Calvin Blair emphasized the "systematic" nature of Nafinsa's investments:

> Nafinsa established in 1941 a department of promotion and began to make systematic studies of industrial development projects. With a predilection for manufacturing, it promoted enterprises in practically every sector of the Mexican economy over the course of the next several years. The roster of firms aided by loan, guarantee, or purchase of stocks and bonds reads like a "who's who" of Mexican business.

In addition to promoting para-state firms, Nafinsa engaged extensively in lending long-term capital to the private sector and in forming partnership investments with both the private sector and international firms. By 1961, Nafinsa's investments were supporting 533 industrial firms, and its long-term investments were twice as large as the sum of such loans deriving from the private banking system. Between 1940 and 1980, the Mexican economy grew at an average annual rate of 6 percent, after adjusting for inflation. Nafinsa's role was a major ingredient in what was then known as the "Mexican Miracle."

Nafinsa continued to be a prominent development agency through the 1980s, but its "golden age" was in the 1940s and 1950s, when the private sector's reluctance to commit funds to industry was particularly acute.

By the early 1990s, all but thirteen of the hundreds of state-owned firms which Nafinsa had helped to create had been privatized, merged, or liquidated. Nafinsa still continues to play a role, now channeling funds into the export sector to promote the expansion of manufactured products.

In Brazil, a development bank known as BNDES was created to channel credit to strategic sectors. At the height of the so-called "Brazilian Miracle" from 1975–9, BNDES was responsible for 48–56 percent of all industrial investment. Known for its "unusually effective bureaucracy," which was also well-paid, BNDES was the prime catalyst for Brazil's strong process of successful industrialization for decades. Brazil's economy grew at the annual rate of 6 percent from 1947 to 1962, with industrial growth leading the way at an annual rate of 9–10 percent. After a pause, extremely high rates of growth began again in 1968 and lasted through the 1970s. It was precisely in the areas prioritized by BNDES and other key state entities such as automobiles, steel, and public utilities where the fastest growth occurred.

> [BNDES and other key executive groups] brought together managers of domestic and foreign private industry and senior bureaucrats from various ministries …These groups planned the output and investment strategy of prioritized sectors and concomitantly

created appropriate public policies to support private sector needs for credit, imports, and domestic inputs. ... the state elite worked closely with business to direct and facilitate private production. These groups worked well ... because planners and implementers were the same people.

Sources: Blair 1964: 213; Kohli 2004; Krieckhaus 2002

The contribution of an infant industry tariff to the industrialization process

The effect of the infant industry tariff on the domestic market price, consumption, domestic output and on the welfare of a less-developed nation imposing an infant industry tariff can be shown using Figure 9.2. It is assumed here for simplicity that the import good currently enters the domestic market with a zero tariff.

The current (or potential) domestic supply curve of socks is S_D. S_W is the world supply curve of socks, which is drawn as perfectly elastic, reflecting the assumption that with free trade the less-developed country can purchase any quantity of socks it wishes at a fixed free-trade price, P_F. In other words, the less-developed economy is assumed to be a price-taker for socks on the international market.

D_D is the domestic demand curve for socks which reflects the per capita income, income distribution, population size and preferences of consumers. Given the premise of free trade prior to initiating the ISI program, the price of socks to domestic consumers is equal to the

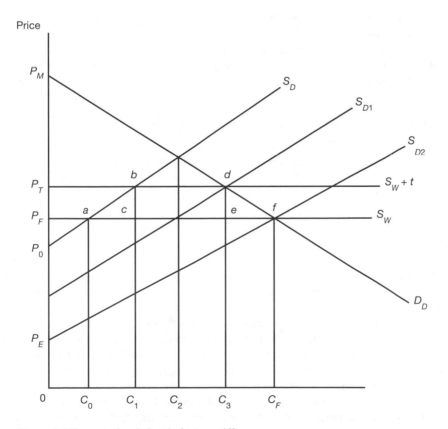

Figure 9.2 Impact of an infant industry tariff.

world market price, P_F. The total quantity of socks demanded in and supplied to the domestic market will be C_F, determined by the intersection of the S_W supply curve and the domestic demand curve, D_D.

At the world market price P_F, local firms will produce quantity C_0 of socks, determined by where P_F crosses the domestic supply curve, S_D.[11] The quantity of imported socks in Figure 9.2 is equal to $C_F - C_0$ (total quantity demanded minus domestic production), which also represents the potential market for import substitution.

If the less-developed economy imposes an infant industry tariff of a fixed amount, t, this will shift the world supply curve of socks to $S_W + t$.[12] With the tariff, the price of the imported good to consumers will be shifted upward to the new equilibrium price P_T, where the new supply curve, $S_W + t$, is equal to the domestic demand curve, D_D.

Domestic producers are now willing to supply a larger portion of the domestic market at the higher price P_T, potentially up to quantity C_1. The price of the socks produced by domestic firms, assuming they are of equal quality and in that sense a perfect substitute for the foreign good, could be as high as P_T. However, it is possible that some socks, equal to any quantity less than C_1 in Figure 9.2, might be sold by domestic producers at a price below P_T but above P_0. This price-cutting behavior by domestic producers would reduce their profit, but it may be necessary in those cases where the domestically produced good is not a perfect substitute for the foreign import as a result of quality differences or a strong bias in favor of imported goods by consumers. As shown in Figure 9.2, there continue to be imports of foreign socks even with the tariff. Imports are equal to the quantity $C_3 - C_1$, that is total quantity demanded minus the quantity supplied by domestic enterprises.

What the imposition of the tariff does is to provide space for domestic firms to expand production for the local market by shielding them from the competition and lower prices of foreign imports. It also gives them breathing room so that production can be initiated and expanded so that the possibility of learning to be more efficient has a chance of success.

Static and dynamic welfare effects of an infant industry tariff: to do or not to do?

In analyzing the impact of a tariff, t, economists typically show the *welfare loss* to society by examining the impact of the tariff on total consumer surplus. But there is more to the issue than any possible immediate welfare loss, as we argue below. Let us first examine the effect of the infant industry tariff on social welfare.

Prior to imposing the infant industry tariff on socks, total consumer surplus was equal to the large triangle $P_M P_F f$ in Figure 9.2. Consumer surplus measures the *additional* amount consumers would have been willing to pay to buy quantity C_F of the good but did not have to pay because of the fact that all units of the good could be bought for price P_F. The consumer surplus is thus the triangle-shaped area above the prevailing price of the good, P_F, and below the demand curve, D_D.

What is the effect of imposing the infant industry tariff? With the tariff, total consumer surplus now is equal to the smaller triangle $P_M P_T d$. It is easy to see that there has been a loss in consumer surplus equal to the area $P_F f d P_T$, i.e. the area of the trapezoid. That area is simply the area left after subtracting the smaller triangle of consumer surplus after the tariff from the larger triangle of consumer surplus that existed with free trade. Domestic consumers clearly have been made worse off by the tariff. They are paying a higher price for the good, are consuming less, and receive less consumer surplus than was the case at the free market price.

Who gains, if anyone, from imposing the infant industry tariff? How can such a tariff be justified if consumers, many of whom are poor in an LDC, are made worse off by paying higher prices and having less to consume?

First, not all of what consumers lose is a pure loss to society. Part of the lost consumer surplus as a result of the tariff is collected by government as tariff revenues. These revenues are equal to the area represented by the rectangle *bcde*, which is equal to the tariff, *t*, times the quantity of imports remaining after the imposition of the tariff, $C_3 - C_1$.

Second, domestic firms producing the import substitute also gain from the tariff. After all, the purpose of imposing an infant industry tariff in the first instance is to make it possible for domestic firms to begin to produce so as to learn to compete with foreign producers. With the tariff and the higher price of imports, domestic producers are able to increase their level of production from C_0 to C_1. As a consequence, they receive additional *producer surplus* equal to the area $P_F ab P_T$.[13]

So, some of what consumers lose in consumer surplus from the tariff goes to government as new tariff revenues and some of the lost surplus is received by domestic producers as additional producer surplus at the higher level of domestic production, C_1. Still, looking at the area of lost consumer surplus in Figure 9.2, it is clear that after accounting for the new tariff revenues and the increased producer surplus, some of the lost consumer surplus is not received by anyone in society. A portion of the lost consumer surplus is a pure loss.

This loss is called the *deadweight loss*. It is equal to the sum of the areas of the two small triangles, *abc* + *def*.[14] This is the remaining area of the lost (pre-tariff) consumer surplus that is not transferred either to domestic firms as producer surplus or to government as increased tariff revenues. Economists argue that there is thus a net loss in total social welfare from the imposition of the infant industry tariff compared to the free trade situation as measured by the value of the deadweight loss.

What, then, can be the justification for infant industry tariffs except as a means to increase tariff revenues or to augment the producer surplus of local firms? Consumers are worse off, paying higher prices for fewer socks. How can such a tariff (or other market-distorting policies – see Focus 9.4) ever be defensible?

FOCUS 9.4   TAIWAN'S EXPERIENCE WITH ISI IN TEXTILES

In the early 1950s, the Taiwanese government paid particular attention to the textile industry as part of the core of a loosely formulated plan for industrial development. The first textile producers were mostly relocated mainlanders, so the industry did not arise *de novo*. Nevertheless, a whole battery of market-distorting and even market-replacing methods was used to establish the industry quickly. The market-distorting methods included tariffs and quantitative restrictions on imports of yarn and finished products, restrictions on the entry of new producers to prevent "excessive" competition, and controlled access to raw materials. From 1951 to 1953, a government agency, with help from the US, replaced market allocation altogether. It supplied raw cotton directly to the spinning mills, advanced all working capital requirements, and bought up all production – and did basically the same at the weaving stage.

The supply response was dramatic. Between 1951 and 1954, production of cotton yarn went up by over 200 percent and woolen yarn rose by over 400 percent. By mid-1953 Taiwan was more than self-sufficient in yarn and cloth. There was no need for imports of these goods, and domestic producers, workers, and consumers were the winners from such promoted development.

Source: Wade 1990: 79

Remember, the purpose of an infant industry tariff is to assist an ISI industry in getting started and to give it time to overcome its transitional inefficiencies. If these new domestic firms succeed in becoming more efficient, then the domestic supply curve, S_D, will shift outward and downward toward S_{D1} (and curve S_D will no longer exist). If the domestic sock industry becomes internationally competitive, the domestic supply curve will shift all the way to S_{D2} in Figure 9.2 (and neither S_D nor S_{D1} will exist).

What would cause the domestic supply curve to shift in this fashion? First, an increase in the number of domestic producers who are able to emerge and produce behind the protective wall provided by the tariff could shift the supply curve outward. Second, and of greater importance, the domestic supply curve would be shifted outward as a consequence of:

1   increased efficiency of domestic enterprises through the use of "cutting-edge" or "best-practice" technology;
2   the more effective application of whatever technology already is available, that is, via positive "technical efficiency change";
3   better training of managers and workers in schools or special institutes;
4   "learning-by-doing" on the job, whereby both workers and managers become more efficient with practice, adaptation and even trial-and-error in the process of producing goods;
5   the application of more effective management and financial techniques and quality control;
6   improvements in banking and financial institutions to facilitate financing of production;
7   the improvement of infrastructure, such as roads, communications, ports, power, and so on.

All of these factors, and others could be added, would contribute to reducing marginal and average costs of production with the outcome being a shift in the domestic sock industry's total supply curve toward S_{D2}.

It is easy to see from the graph that with the full elimination of transitional inefficiencies so that S_{D2} intersects D_D at C_F, consumer surplus will be equal what it was prior to the imposition of the tariff (area $P_F P_M f$) *if* price is again at P_F. If that happens, however, the *domestic producer surplus* is larger than in the pre-ISI free-trade regime as the supply curve has shifted outward allowing domestic firms to capture revenues previously received by foreign firms.[15] With domestic production at C_F there would be both more industrial employment and a higher level of GDP produced by the country than was the case when the free-trade regime prevailed, assuming a shift of labor from agriculture to industry to produce the new output.

What the imposition of an infant tariff, t, can facilitate, then, is the attainment of *dynamic welfare gains* that, accruing over time, can quite easily swamp the *static* welfare losses that the tariff initially imposed on the economy. As a means to promote the transformation of an economy from agriculture to industry and to shift workers from lower to higher productivity employment, infant industry ISI tariffs can foster significant dynamic welfare gains which can easily outweigh any short-run deadweight loss of uncompensated consumer surplus. With industrialization, a country can realize both higher total income and higher income per person. Seeing the deadweight loss as one of the costs of development, as an investment in the future, assuming the ISI industries become more efficient, helps to put everything into perspective.

The use of an infant industry tariff is one example of how "getting prices wrong" (in this case, raising prices of socks above the international market level with a tariff) can yield positive development outcomes. Rather than abdicating control over the economy to past adverse path dependence and to current unfettered market forces, the conscious forging of an easy ISI sector, as in Korea, Taiwan, Brazil, Mexico, and many other large less-developed nations, can be a means to bend domestic resource allocation, production and labor usage in more productive directions via state intervention which eventually is less necessary as the market system develops.

Such "governing" of the market, as Wade (1990) calls it, does lead to market-distorting and perhaps even market-replacing policies, at least for a time. That should not be the issue; what should be asked is: What are the effects of such policies? When these policies are carried out with care and monitored for results and where vested interests have difficulty in influencing state actions, the practice of "getting prices wrong" by governing the market rather than surrendering to the neoclassical and orthodox policy of "getting prices right" and accepting existing market forces as optimal can result in substantial gains in output, income, and human development by accelerating the pace of industrialization. There are an increasing number of modern examples that support this view, from Korea to Taiwan to Chile to China and beyond.

The elimination of infant industry protection: when is enough enough?

How long should infant industry protection from lower-cost imports be extended to domestic firms? In other words, how long should it take until ISI firms are able to compete head-to-head with foreign imports *without* the artificial benefit of tariff protection?

From Figure 9.2, once transitional inefficiencies are overcome and the domestic supply curve has increased to S_{D2}, tariff protection becomes redundant and unnecessary. In that case, domestic industries can compete directly with foreign imports and at world prices, since domestic firms will have attained the same level of efficiency at output C_F as producers elsewhere.

In fact, as firms begin to achieve greater efficiency through learning-by-doing the need for a tariff at the original level, t, is diminished. It is perilous, perhaps, to put a number to this, but in the non-durable consumer goods industries in which ISI begins, seven to ten years would seem to be a reasonable target date for ending protection and for expecting domestic producers to have overcome the basic transitional inefficiencies encountered at the beginning of easy ISI.[16] For more complicated products with longer learning curves or where technology is more complex, somewhat longer transition periods may be warranted. For some goods the transitional period may be less than seven years. In instances where a society's overall level of human capital accumulation and its technological and R&D capacity needs to be improved through relatively large social investments in education and health care, the period of tariff protection may need to be lengthened. This will allow time for the necessary "initial endowments" to be formed so as to provide domestic firms a reasonable opportunity to become competitive with international enterprises.

Whatever the specific plan for the termination of infant industry protection, what is critical is that a timetable for the phasing-out of tariff protection be part of government policy and be announced to potential firms when infant industry tariffs are introduced. In this way, domestic producers do not become complacent, thinking and acting as if protection is to be a permanent fixture of the economic landscape that permits higher-cost, less efficient domestic producers to prosper, immune from outside competition.

Domestic producers must anticipate, *with certainty*, that protective tariffs will end at a determinate date, and they must either be competitive with foreign imports at that time by having overcome any transitional inefficiencies (as on supply curve S_{D2} in Figure 9.2), or suffer the consequences when foreign imports are permitted to re-enter the domestic market on an equal footing with domestic production.

The phasing-out of tariffs can be uniform over the protected period or accelerating. For example, if the domestic beverage industry is initially provided a 25 percent protective tariff, to be phased out over five years, then 5 percent of tariff protection could be removed at the end of year 1, a further 5 percent at the end of year 2, and so on until all compensatory protection has been lifted (there still might be a minimal tariff on beverages after the protective tariff is removed to cover the administrative costs of the customs service). Alternative schemes might leave the full 25 per cent protection for two years; remove 5 percent at the end of year 3; remove 10 percent at the end of year 4; and at the end of year 5 remove the final 10 percent of protection. Whatever the phasing-out pattern, it should be clear to enterprises that it is non-negotiable after start-up and that the end period for eliminating tariff protection is final.[17]

These tariffs are called *infant industry* tariffs for a reason; they are applied to new firms and industries with short-term inefficiencies. The language is evocative of a presumed reality and that is that infants do (and should!) mature and that transitional inefficiencies are indeed transitory. When the firms mature and have overcome those start-up inefficiencies, there is no reason to maintain the tariffs any longer.

If tariffs on ISI industries are not phased out, then they can become a substantial internal barrier to progress. Maintaining infant industry tariffs too long not only threatens further industrialization, but also the possibility of reaching higher levels of growth, development, and social and human welfare that are the motivating forces for initiating easy ISI in the first place. If tariff protection is not withdrawn from domestic producers, there is a strong likelihood that the static deadweight losses shown in Figure 9.2 will persist as permanent deadweight losses, thus sacrificing the potential dynamic welfare gains that should be the motivating force behind implementing infant industry tariffs. No one can be in favor of such an outcome, and as we shall see below and in the next chapter, in those countries that did not draw down infant industry tariff protection, economic progress was compromised and stalled.

Infant industry tariff protection can only be a phase, and a temporary one at that, on the path to fuller industrialization and a higher standard of living.

The importance of embedded state autonomy to successful ISI

One of the legitimate concerns many economists have had about countries that pursue an easy ISI strategy is that there is a danger of this stage becoming virtually permanent, so that tariff protection is not fully removed.[18] And that has happened. In India and many Latin American countries, high levels of protection continued for far longer than can be justified by the infant industry argument and by appeals to the transitional inefficiencies of new local firms. Producing behind a highly protective tariff wall, domestic producers gained a quasi-captive market which resulted in above-normal profits, often with minimal attention being paid to efficiency, to improvements in technology or training, to product quality, or to consumer preferences. Industrialists in an ISI sector where tariffs are not progressively removed may be able to reap long-term economic rents, that is, to earn profits higher than are necessary for calling forth the current level of production, since the tariff prevents the full force of foreign competition from being felt by domestic producers. Consumers end up paying prices that are wholly unwarranted, as local industrialists earn unjustified profits in a less than competitive environment.

When tariff protection is prolonged rather than phased out, this typically is the consequence of close links forged by entrepreneurial elites in the ISI sector with administrators in government having responsibility for the industrialization program. Such connections can diminish the independence of state decision-makers to act from broader social and economic interests. These links may be quite informal. Industrialists and government officials may belong to the same clubs. They quite likely operate in the same social circles, meeting at restaurants, the theatre, social gathering, weddings, and so on. They often are related by blood or marriage.

The contact between protected industrialists and government bureaucrats can involve substantial degrees of corruption and bribery. When governments lack relative autonomy from strong vested interests, they often respond to the specific, private concerns of those groups with the power, money, influence, and access to government to make their voice heard. In the process, more general interests of society for more efficient, more technological, more productive, more equitable, and higher-paying and expanding domestic industry are sacrificed, as the ability of the majority segment of the economy to voice its interests is circumscribed by relatively closed and exclusive political processes that respond to powerful interests first and public concerns later, if at all.

This problem of a captured state is not, however, one inherent to countries which initiate an easy ISI strategy. It is rather due to the nature of the political process and the privileged access that some groups have to state decision-making which create a barrier to the desired reduction of tariff protection on ISI industries. These elites are able to turn state economic policy in their direction for their own profit at a cost to the domestic economy and to long-run consumer interests. Whenever the state is to some degree "captured" by special interests who can create and maintain tariffs, laws, and regulations that allow them to earn a larger producer surplus and economic rents without becoming more efficient, economic policy will be distorted in the direction of those elites' interests at the expense of overall economic efficiency and social welfare.[19]

Distortions and interference in state policy by predatory elites for their own special interests, however, can arise regardless of the particular economic strategy an economy pursues. It is not a necessary consequence of the easy ISI stage, as the experience of the East Asian economies, reviewed in the next chapter, vividly demonstrates. Further, the experiences of South Korea, Taiwan, and other LDCs do not support the conclusion that permanent tariff protection and inefficient production are necessary outcomes of the ISI stage of industrialization (Amsden 2001).

The problem of continued protectionism, then, is one of domestic *politics* and is not due to the particular economic strategy in force.[20] It is purely coincidental that such "captured" states are most evident during the easy ISI stage of industrialization, but that is only because ISI is most often the natural and logical first stage of industrialization and of the structural transformation process required for higher levels of development (see Focus 9.5 on India's development trajectory).

In nations where an economic elite dominates or can corrupt the political process, tariff protection is more likely to be maintained long beyond its justifiable usefulness for infant industry protection. But it is not the easy ISI strategy that is to blame. It is not a problem of the state providing new firms with protection from import competition so that transitional inefficiencies can be addressed. Rather, it is the nature of the political process and its captured status that lead to the detrimental over-extension of tariff protection, and this is more likely

FOCUS 9.5   IS INDIA A FREE MARKET MIRACLE?

Much has been written in recent years about India's economic renaissance. Long known for its low "Hindu rate of growth," India's economy has gained sufficient momentum in recent decades, to be viewed, along with China, as an economic success story of grand proportions. How realistic is this view, and what has happened in India?

From 1995 to 2005, average per capita income grew by 4 percent per year, a monumental achievement for a nation of 1.1 billion people. From the period 1965–79 to the twenty-year period 1980–2000, annual GDP growth doubled to an impressive 5.8 percent rate – unheard of in any previous period in India. The 1980s ushered in a decade of debt-led growth (driven by both a domestic debt build-up and international borrowing) that, finally, could not be sustained.

While private sector investment was modest in the 1980s, the government boosted public sector investments in infrastructure and industry, where emphasis was placed on cheapening inputs to raise the growth rate. These expanded investments were curtailed in the late 1990s, and state investment fell from 10.3 percent of GDP in the 1980s to roughly 8 percent in the 1990s.

Popular accounts of India's recent boom rely upon a simplistic story that has some grains of truth. In 1991, the government, long active in guiding and promoting the economy, reduced a number of regulations, opening the way for greater market participation, more foreign trade, and enhanced foreign direct investment. India was nudged in this direction by a major International Monetary Fund "stabilization" program (these programs are discussed in Chapter 17) in order to obtain some relief from its unmanageable level of external debt. In any event, as public sector investment declined in the 1990s, private sector investment surged as new opportunities opened up. Private sector investment rose from 4.4 percent of GDP in the 1980s to 6 percent in the 1990–5 period and then to 8.3 percent in the 1995–8 period.

India has become famous for its service-sector-led growth in the 1990s and into the twenty-first century. What is often conveniently forgotten is that state policy changes from the 1970s through 1984 led to the prioritization of the information technology (IT) sector.

Particularly favorable promotional policies included the decline in import tariffs, the reduction in regulations – including the elimination of industrial licensing, permitting the entrance of foreign and domestic firms, the marketing of exports in international markets, the setting up of an array of industrial parks, the building of a specialized communications infrastructure, and the provision of crucial computer installations. As a result of this new cooperation between the private and public sector in the IT industry, output growth reached spectacular levels of 50 percent per year in the 1990s.

These changes also highlight not only the importance of state policy, but that there needs to be "good" state policy, that is, policies that reward and promote efficiency and competition. While India cannot be said to have come as far as Taiwan or Korea or other recent successful developers in balancing the role of the state and the private sector, there has been some positive movement.

After 1984, the Indian government reduced some of its more ambitious schemes of income redistribution and populism and adopted a more pro-growth perspective. The more pro-business stance, however, should not be taken as a retreat of the state in the economic sphere. India never had a high state capacity, such as has been the case in Korea. India's new posture reflects many elements, including the fact that from independence until the 1980s an industrial or business element had matured, and this new element was increasingly able to influence the future of the policy structure of India because of its increased effectiveness in the marketplace.

Nonetheless, it must be noted that in the early twenty-first century India's policy posture remains statist in nature. Public-owned firms loom large in the economy, import tariffs still remain significant (on average over 100 percent in 1990, falling to 40 percent by 1999), foreign investment is held to low levels, and the state inhibits the movement of financial capital into and out of the economy. It would be an inaccurate statement to assert that India's improved economic performance is a demonstration of a major shift toward economic liberalization.

To some degree India's improved economic performance is the result of the historical legacy of positive state intervention. Large public investments in technological education and capital-intensive industries from the 1940s through 1964 were to be expected to have a long gestation and a distant payoff. In the 1950s, the government created five elite universities that have trained two generations of Indian engineers in the justly world-famous Indian Institutes of Technology. Because of these institutes and a thriving university system, India has the third-largest national scientific and technical capacity in the world. This cadre of knowledge workers is a very important resource that provides India with the possibility of great change (Chapter 13 discusses in detail the importance of these knowledge workers).

India's ISI policies also generated positive externalities in terms of a growing, well-trained labor force and more efficient supplier networks.

Still, many commentators now argue that the chief bottleneck facing India is an infrastructure deficit of daunting proportions. This demonstrates that the slowdown in state investment in the 1990s, championed by some as a sign that the Indian state was shrinking, was not necessarily a good developmental decision. Today India lacks adequate roads, sea ports, airports, water, and electricity. Current plans are for massive state investment and creative public–private partnerships designed to improve essential infrastructure. The prime minister has advocated an ambitious effort to invest $300–500 billion spread over the 2007–12 period. This may be unattainable, as India is currently attracting only modest levels of foreign investment, which will be needed to generate spending of this magnitude. But at least the government is looking forward and seems to be moving in the right direction.

Sources: Hamm 2007; Kohli 2004

to occur in nations without a history of democratic experience, which is the situation many less-developed economies face. The barrier of a weak, captured, and predatory state needs to be overcome by appropriate institutional reform, culminating in the creation of a forward-looking developmental state, as described in Chapter 7.

Potential gains from the easy ISI stage of industrialization

What are some of the expected gains to countries from initiating the easy ISI stage of industrialization?

First, given the nature of the methods used to produce the typical easy ISI good, this stage of industrialization tends to be relatively *labor-intensive*. As output in this sector grows, easy ISI industries can provide increasing employment opportunities for an expanding proportion of the labor force. This will be especially important if the increasing number of migrants exiting the agricultural sector, attracted to factory jobs by the pull of higher wages in the ISI sector, is to be absorbed in productive employment.

Second, during the easy ISI phase, the industrial labor force develops both *specific* and *general human capital skills* as a result of "learning-by-doing" as they work with the modern machines and technology they encounter in the factories. General human capital skills, by definition, will be at least partially transferable to other enterprises, thus shortening the lag-time required for those firms to become more productive. This happens as some workers or managers leave one firm to work in another or to start their own spin-off venture in the same or a different industry. There is thus an acceleration of the societal learning process that can accompany the expansion of the easy ISI sector as new production linkages, both backward and forward, are created. Of course, as already discussed in the previous section, such positive externalities are more likely to appear as infant industry tariffs are lifted with some time-certainty so that the original easy ISI firms succeed in becoming competitive and shed their transitional inefficiencies. Then what is learned in these firms will be at least partially applicable in other parts of the economy.

As the endogenous growth theories of Chapter 8 suggest, such positive technological and human capital externalities can accelerate the pace of economic expansion, even with the same level of other productive resources in use. Through their interaction with the existing pool of knowledge or technology and the learning which accompanies the actual process of being involved in production, the ability of an economy's labor force to better utilize existing knowledge and technology can be improved and the growth and development prospects of the economy can be enhanced. Further, management, financial, marketing, accounting, and essential entrepreneurial skills can be acquired and improved during the easy ISI stage as a consequence of experience in producing and striving for efficiency and market share as tariffs are reduced. These are skills that are integral to successful and sustained industrialization over the long term, especially in the absolutely essential post-easy ISI stages of industrialization considered in the next chapter.

Third, easy ISI acts as a training ground for entry-level local capitalists who have an opportunity to develop their own skills in operating profit-oriented and efficiency-focused enterprises. Over time, with successful easy ISI, the initial disparity between the management skills and information levels of domestic managers and capitalists and those of foreign industrialists can be narrowed. This stage of industrialization for late industrializers, which all the less-developed nations are, facilitates the establishment, extension, and solidification of a domestic class of private entrepreneurs who will be essential to the continuation of the process of development into the future.

Every society has latent entrepreneurs. Prior to industrialization, many will be involved in trade, finance, and, perhaps, illegal activities where profit-making opportunities are the greatest. The expansion of the easy ISI sector provides these entrepreneurs with another opportunity to maximize their earnings. The difference is that the activities of entrepreneurs in the ISI sector are likely be more socially and economically productive than when the opportunities for profitable pursuits were more circumscribed in a pre-industrial setting. Providing creative space for entrepreneurs to be part of a more productive sector of the economy, and to learn and thrive there, can be one of the more fundamental transformations for the future growth and efficiency of an economy to be derived from a successful easy ISI experience.

In the easy ISI stage, the rise of the modern capitalist "business ethic" is encouraged and reinforced. The attention to detail and quality, to financial and accounting costs, to time schedules, and to contracts that are characteristic of production in more developed nations have a chance to begin to seep into the thinking and behavior of businesspeople. Where corruption and cheating of the customer might have been the norm of behavior by sellers in the past, the progressive elimination of tariff protection under an easy ISI regime can contribute to an alteration in entrepreneurial behavior that drives them to achieve levels of efficiency, stability, and responsibility to the consumer that modern industrialization demands (Gerschenkron 1962: 47–8).

Given these potential advantages, easy ISI would seem to be an imperative stage of economic and social transformation, though it is not by itself sufficient to the continued prosperity of the development process. Easy ISI is the first step, then, on a journey toward a more complex process of industrialization and development. It is not, and cannot be, the final stopping point.

Para-state firms and social capital[21]

In many instances, private sector development in less-developed economies will require assistance from state-owned firms, perhaps especially during the initial ISI transformation. Infrastructure investments such as heating oil and natural gas, electricity, ports, and tele-communications are all industrial activities that require enormous start-up costs in terms of physical and financial capital outlays. They are also industries which demand a mastery of intermediate levels of technology that may be beyond the capacity of local private entrepreneurs to provide in the early stages of industrialization.[22] The state, however, may be able to supply the necessary capital resources, the organization of production, and contribute to the shaping of a cadre of engineers and state-managers capable of providing the infrastructural base and other key inputs into the industrialization process that are required for the eventual efficient operation of the private sector of the economy.

There are those who argue strongly against the expansion of state-owned firms, even in the early ISI stage. It is most commonly alleged that state enterprises are prone to be less efficient than if they were to be privately operated. It is asserted that the prices charged by state-owned firms all too often are set too low, that is, below what the unfettered market price would be. State-owned enterprises thus often fail to recover all of their costs of production or to make a reasonable rate of return on the initial public investment in them. Any losses incurred by state enterprises are funded out of the national budget, thus creating a drain on scarce government revenues that cannot then be used for other purposes.

While it is true that state enterprises often do operate at a loss, this is not always the case, even in those instances in which a state enterprise does not recover its full costs, it is not accurate to claim that the mere existence of an *accounting* loss incurred by a state enterprise implies a *social* loss from the operation of the para-statal. To the extent that a state enterprise's operations promote the production of positive externalities accruing to private producers in the economy in the form of increased private returns, it is entirely possible that a subsidized state enterprise selling its output at a price below what unsubsidized private producers would charge will contribute to reaching the socially optimal level of production better than if the enterprise were to be in private hands.

The theory of positive externalities is quite unambiguous in asserting that, in the presence of high transactions costs such as are involved in any large-scale infrastructure investment, producers of positive externalities must be subsidized if they are to reach the optimal level of production where marginal social benefits are equated to marginal social costs. Unsubsidized producers of positive externalities most certainly will under-produce.[23] Mustering evidence of state enterprises with accounting losses falls short of providing evidence of their relative inefficiency compared to private firms. Such state enterprises may, in fact, be contributing quite effectively to social efficiency by producing the socially optimal level of electricity, water, transportation, communications, or gas by contributing the attendant positive externalities helping to make the private sector more productive, to increasing incomes, and to raising employment in the private industrial sector. Is there any evidence to support the argument supporting state provision of infrastructure to stimulate private sector industrialization?

In Taiwan in the 1950s, during that nation's phase of easy ISI, state enterprises of all types produced well over half of all of Taiwanese industrial output. Para-state activity overshadowed private firms in "fuels, chemicals, mining and metal working, fertilizer and food processing, textiles, and utilities" (Wade 1990: 78). In the glass, plastics, steel, and cement industries, state enterprises initiated production, removing the high fixed-cost investment barrier, and then, after the new firms were up and running and had reached a level of production sufficient to reduce per unit costs, these firms were turned over to entrepreneurs in the private sector to be run for profit.

The para-state solution is, however, only one among many possibilities for providing essential inputs, especially infrastructure, to an emerging industrial sector. Depending on the circumstances, joint ventures of ownership and control shared by national entrepreneurs, foreign owners, and, perhaps, the state in various combinations can substitute for a para-state firm. In other situations, for example where technology is very expensive and well-trained domestic management and maintenance personnel scarce, the most reasonable solution for obtaining the production and positive externalities from needed infrastructure investment may well best be via the intervention of a wholly-owned multinational firm. In any case, all successful ISI programmes have incorporated para-statals to one degree or another, and these enterprises were often catalytic forces in industrial transformation. Para-statals need not be, by definition, purveyors of inefficiency.

Measuring the success of easy ISI

A successful easy ISI stage of industrialization shifts a country's production possibilities frontier (PPF) outward both along the agricultural axis, if agricultural productivity is raised simultaneously, and along the manufactured goods axis, as shown in Figure 9.3.

The curve PPF_1 is the production possibilities frontier of a country prior to the initiation of easy ISI. Most of the economy's output comes from the agricultural sector. The country initially operates at a mix of production like that at A, which lies inside PPF_1 as a result of the misallocation of resources, particularly of labor, that characterizes less-developed, agriculture-based economies. Often the labor force occupied in that dominant sector has low or even zero marginal product for at least part of the year.

With the start of easy ISI and the transfer of labor from agriculture to industry and the introduction of new technology into both agriculture and industry, a new production possibilities curve, PPF_2, emerges that lies outside the former PPF_1. The new mix of production at, say, B, involves a movement toward both the industry axis and toward the new PPF_2 frontier as a result of positive technical efficiency change, as resources are better utilized, especially labor, which is shifted from low marginal productivity uses in agriculture to higher productivity occupations in manufacturing. Both the share of total production and of total employment in manufacturing rise over the transition.[24] It is precisely these sorts of transformations that lead to higher levels of income and development.

Summary and conclusions

Easy ISI is only a first step on the path toward a higher level of industrialization and development. Let us repeat this so there can be no misunderstanding:

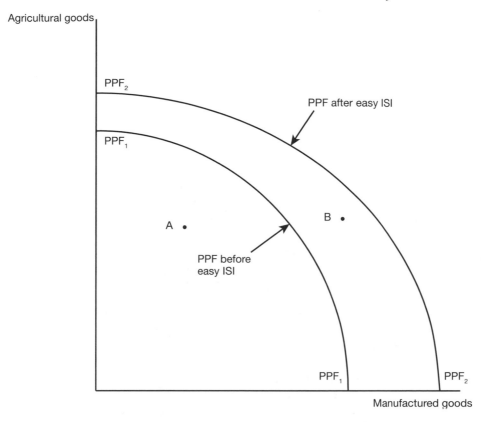

Figure 9.3 Impact of easy ISI on the productive possibilities frontier (PPF).

Easy ISI is only a first step on the path toward a higher level of industrialization and development.

But it is an **essential** first step if countries are to move to a higher growth and income path. It is true that some nations have become stuck at this stage of industrialization because of internal barriers to transforming the productive and social structures of the nation, particularly where there are powerful vested interests. It is also the case that for those nations that have successfully transitioned through easy ISI, this stage of industrialization has been fundamental in creating the conditions for future progress.

In the next chapter we shall consider the subsequent stages of structural transformation and industrialization that different economies have followed after the easy ISI stage. We shall see that there appears to be a bifurcation in possible transitions: one path – the optimal path – seems to lead toward greater opportunities to realize even more of the dynamic effects of industrialization and structural transformation, as seen in the discussion of endogenous growth theories; the other path – the sub-optimal path – reduces dramatically the possibilities for continued progress for the economy as a whole, though some sectors do benefit.

What is not seriously in question, though, is the need for initiating industrialization if poverty is to have a chance to be overcome, and easy ISI is the natural start of this journey.

Questions and exercises

1 Table 9.1 suggests a strong positive correlation between the rate of growth of the industrial sector and the rate of growth of total gross domestic product (GDP), but this is shown only for regions and three countries. In this exercise, you will further consider the relationship between these growth rates.

Select four less-developed countries other than China, India, or Korea, and record for each the rate of growth of industry and the rate of growth of GDP for at least two periods. You can typically find the data in Table 4.1 in the World Development Indicators available online at http://worldbank.org. If this source is not available, check elsewhere on the World Bank website or another source for the data. Using this data, draw a graph with the "industry growth rate" on the horizontal axis and the "growth rate of GDP" on the vertical axis. For each country, show its specific industry growth rate and its growth rate of GDP as one point on your graph for each of the time periods for which you have data.

Do you see any relationship between the two variables? Draw a straight line through the points you have graphed. Does it have a positive or a negative slope? What does that positive or negative slope tell you? Are the industry growth rate and the GDP growth rate systematically related to one another in your data? (If you have access to Excel or some simple regression program, you can input the data in two columns, one for the growth rate of industry and the other for the growth rate of GDP; use a scatter diagram to show the data. You can have Excel draw a trend line for you.)

2 This exercise will demonstrate the gains to total national output from a better distribution of an economy's labor force to higher productivity activities.

Choose a less-developed country that interests you or one you are assigned. If you wish, you can use one of the countries for which you collected data in the previous problem. Find the following:

a the share (i.e. percentage) of total output (GDP) produced in agriculture, industry, and services for a recent year. You can typically find the data in Table 4.1 in the World Development Indicators available online at http://worldbank.org. Go to the "Country at a Glance" section in the middle of the page; select your country to find the data in the "Structure of the Economy" section.

b Then find the share (i.e. percentage) of the labor force working in agriculture, industry, and services from Table 2.3 in the same World Development Indicators online. Choose data for the period closest to the year you selected for your data in part a of this question. You will have to average the male and female rates if both are given. If your country does not have data for *both* GDP and labor shares, you will need to pick another country.

c Now, calculate the productivity of *each 1 percent* of the labor force in these three sectors, i.e., what percent of total GDP is produced by 1 percent of the workers in agriculture, industry, and services (hint: divide the output share in each sector by its labor share);

d Is the labor force in this country distributed optimally, that is, could total GDP be increased by shifting labor from one sector to another? Explain.

e Is there "surplus" labor in agriculture in your country? Or some other sector? Explain what is meant by "surplus" labor (hint: there is a discussion of surplus labor in the section of this chapter on the Lewis model).

3   How does shifting labor from a low-productivity sector to a higher-productivity sector affect an economy's GDP? This exercise will show you how and why that happens.

Utilizing the data you calculated from part c of question 2 above, determine the *net impact* on total GDP for your country from transferring out 10 percent of the labor force in your country's surplus labor sector and adding that to the workforce in the sector with the highest per worker productivity (e.g., if your surplus labor sector is agriculture, reduce the agricultural labor force by 10 percent, say from 45 percent to 35 percent; then add that 10 percent of workers to the high productivity sector, increasing the labor force by 10 percent in that sector; for example, in industry, increase the labor force from 17 percent to 27 percent).

You should be able to determine the net gain to GDP from such a movement of workers as: the loss in output from a decrease in 10 percent of the workforce in the surplus sector *plus* the increase in output resulting from an increase in the labor force by 10 percent in the high productivity sector. The result you get should be a specific, concrete numerical percentage change in GDP resulting from a negative change in output in the low-productivity sector and a positive change in output in the high-productivity sector as a result of the shifting of labor.

4   Table 9.2 in the text provides evidence for a close relation between a decrease in the share of the labor force engaged in agriculture (the primary sector) and an increase in the share of the labor force employed in industry (the secondary sector) and services (the tertiary sector) and a higher level of development for a country.

You are going to draw two graphs. In the first, put the "level of development" on the vertical axis and the "share of the labor force employed in agriculture" on the horizontal. Using the same four LDCs for which you collected data in problem 1 above, find the HDI value (this is the "level of development" measure) and the share of the labor force employed in agriculture for the most recent year possible, and plot the data for these two variables (if you have access to Excel or some other spreadsheet program, input the data there and use it to draw a scatter diagram). You can find the data at the UN Development Programme website, http://www.undp.org.

On a second graph, again put the "level of development" on the vertical axis but now put the "share of the labor force employed in industry" on the horizontal. Find and plot this data for your selected countries using the same source as above (of course you already have the HDI data from the first graph).

In both graphs, draw a straight line through the points which best fits the data (if you are using Excel, have the program draw a trend line for you).

What relationship do you find in each graph as determined by the slope (positive or negative) of the "regression" line you have drawn? In your own words, explain what "story" the data tell you about the relationship between the share of labor at work in agriculture and industry and the level of development of the four countries as measured by their HDI values.

5   Carefully explain the economic rationale for imposing an infant industry tariff to protect new producers from import competition. If you can use a graph to illustrate your argument, please do so. Why are these called "infant industry" tariffs and not just tariffs?

6   Carefully explain what is meant by transitional inefficiencies? A few possible sources of transitional inefficiencies were noted in the text. Can you list two or three other sources of such inefficiencies in less-developed economies? Why are these called "transitional" inefficiencies and not just "inefficiencies"?

7   Discuss alternative ways other than tariffs that governments in a less-developed country might encourage and support easy ISI firms to produce in competition with imports. Are there things government *must do* to help the private sector be more competitive if industrialization is to be successful? Explain.

8   As noted in the text, many economists worry about the wisdom of an infant industry tariff strategy as a means to promote industrialization in LDCs. The following exercise gives you a chance to consider the effect of such tariffs.

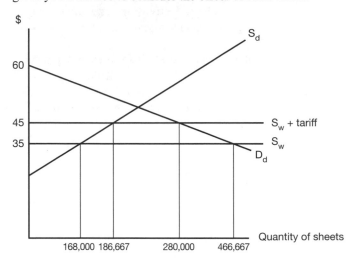

a   Calculate the consumer surplus prior to imposing an infant industry tariff. What, exactly, does this consumer surplus value measure?

b   How much was actually spent by consumers on sheets before the tariff? After the tariff?

c   Calculate the consumer surplus after the infant industry tariff is imposed. (How much *is* the tariff?)

d   What is the total loss in consumer surplus due to the imposition of the infant industry tariff?

e   What are the government's tariff revenues after imposing the tariff?

f   What is the producer surplus after the imposition of the tariff?

g   How much deadweight loss is there as a result of the imposition of the infant industry tariff?

h   Add the totals you obtained from d, e and f. How does this total compare to what you calculated for part c? Explain what you have found and what it means.

i   If domestic producers succeed in becoming as efficient as foreign producers by overcoming their transitional inefficiencies, what would be the value of consumers' surplus, assuming the infant industry tariff is removed? Show on the graph where this consumer surplus is.

j   How can this infant industry tariff be justified?

9   Explain how the accounting profits (or losses) of an unsubsidized public enterprise, the output of which creates positive externalities for other firms, are likely to overstate (understate) the true level of profits (losses) of that firm. Is it possible for a para-state firm which creates positive externalities to private sector enterprises to have an accounting loss but still be "socially profitable"? Explain.

10 Focus 9.1 shows the share of primary exports as a percentage of total exports for a limited range of countries. Choose three low-income less-developed nations not listed in the table. Does the primary product export pattern dominate in each of these as well? What potential problems do countries face when primary products are a large part of their total exports? Why is it "better" to have manufactured goods exports as a larger share of total exports?

Notes

1 The industrial sector includes the manufacturing sector. Within the industrial sector, but not classified as manufacturing industries, are electrical power generation, communications, gas and water generation, mining, transportation, and other non-manufacturing enterprises.

2 It is perhaps worth remembering the insight of an early development economist, Alexander Gerschenkron, that there exists the possibility of "substitution" in the way any particular country becomes developed. Becoming developed is not a process of simply copying what other successful countries have done before. There are patterns, of course or there would be no purpose in teaching about development, but each country must forge its own particular path within the patterns of structural change that have been identified as being crucial.

   Nobel Prize-winning economist Simon Kuznets wrote in this regard: "there is a connection between the high rate of growth associated with modern economic development and a variety of structural changes, not only economic but also social; not only in institutions but also in ideology. This does not mean that all the historically associated shifts in economic and social structure and ideology are requirements, and that none of them could be avoided or substituted for. It does mean that some structural changes, not only in economic but also in social institutions and beliefs, are required, without which modern economic growth would be impossible" (Kuznets 1971: 348).

   Further, as the endogenous growth analysis examined in Chapter 8 suggests, it is not just structural change that is the key to successful growth. Efforts at structural change alone – for example, the transfer of labor from agriculture to industry – that lack the required changes in the quality of inputs to production via human capital accumulation, funding for R&D and technology and new knowledge acquisition, and application and additions of more productive physical capital are likely to be substantially less effective. Further, as we shall consider in subsequent chapters, there are fundamental macroeconomic concerns and constraints that must also be a part of a successful development strategy.

3 Industrialization involves the transfer of what is often called surplus labor from agriculture to the emerging industrial, factory system, as is reviewed in the section on the Lewis model below. If that movement of labor is not to result in a decrease in basic food production, in higher food prices, and for the need for expanding food imports, domestic agricultural production must become more efficient at the same time, as already noted.

   One important additional and non-economic reason to transform agriculture is to remove a potential political obstacle, that is, an Ayresian ceremonial barrier, to further industrialization and development, particularly during the export-substitution stage of industrialization discussed in Chapter 10. If large and politically powerful landowners derive a portion of their wealth from their primary product exports, they are more likely to oppose the evolution of the industrialization process into diversified exporting, particularly when the aim of such a transformation is to change the export profile of the nation by replacing agricultural and other primary exports with the manufactured outputs of an emerging domestic industrial sector.

4 It is typically the case that the benefits of primary product specialization, that is, of an economic structure dominated by agricultural and natural resource extraction, tend to accrue to only a relatively small elite in the country. Industrialization opens the door, then, to a wider distribution of the gains of production and an increase in total social welfare not as easily attained if a nation remains in the primary product producer category (Chenery 1979: 35). Thus, industrialization increases the opportunities for greater income dispersion, as well as higher incomes per capita, that can contribute to improvements along the HDI dimension as well, particularly as universal primary and secondary education become the norm. To the extent that income distribution is improved as a consequence of such an evolution in the productive structure and in the accumulation of human

capital, and to the extent that an improved income distribution contributes to a higher level of development, this transformation is "growth-enhancing."

5   This can be demonstrated relatively easily by determining the productivity of 1 percent of the labor force in producing GDP in agriculture, industry, and services. In many less-developed economies, the productivity of the agricultural sector is less than 1 and substantially less than the productivity of labor in industry or services. Shifting workers from lower-productivity agriculture to higher-productivity industry will thus increase total GDP. Exercise 2 at the end of the chapter asks you to show this.

6   It is "easy" ISI in two senses. First, since the demand for a particular manufactured good already is known from the quantity of imports, the potential size of the market for that good also is known; all local producers need do is produce to service that demand. And second, this stage is "easy" because the technology used in production is relatively simple; often standardized, off-the-shelf machinery can be purchased on the world market. The term "primary ISI" recognizes this stage as a first phase of ISI, not its endpoint. The term "horizontal" ISI recognizes that the first stage of ISI is taking place within particular industries; during this stage, industrialization does not extend backward into the other, supplier industries, which is called vertical ISI, and which involves a deepening of the industrialization process.

7   As one of the poorest regions among the LDCs, Sub-Saharan Africa's exports – more than 80 percent – remain dominated by unprocessed primary products; Wood and Mayer 2001: 376.

8   This may be a further reason why too much income and wealth inequality can limit the pace of economic growth, as Rodrik's study suggested in Chapter 8. Excessive inequality limits the size of the domestic market, thus impeding the pace of domestic industrialization and growth and development by restricting total demand. Efficient levels of production cannot be reached if the market is "too small."

9   Bruton (1989) prefers the term "infant economy" protection, which perhaps better conveys that, for the less-developed economies, the transformations in production, organization, education, public policy, and so on that are required to overcome the transitional inefficiencies go far beyond any particular industry.

10 Evenson and Westphal (1995: 2284–5) argue that protection is only a second-best policy, however. The first-best policy would be to have efficiently functioning capital and financial markets, as discussed in Focus 9.2, such that protection would be unnecessary. However, in poor nations, the option of forgoing tariffs may not be open. It is not just because waiting for the maturation of financial markets may be costly in terms of long-run growth which is sacrificed. It is also because, for poor countries lacking government revenues, tariff revenues obtained from infant industry protection contribute a share of total government revenues. And given, as Evenson and Westphal note, that no program of protection of infant industry which has lacked needed investments in technological capacity has been successful, those tariff revenues provide a potential source of funding for precisely the technological development required, from research and development to the training of human capital, if they are put to good use. These issues are considered in detail in Chapters 12 and 13.

11 This quantity could be zero if the domestic supply curve begins at a reservation price, or minimum supply price, which is greater than P_F.

12 Adding a fixed tariff amount to each unit of a good imported, say £3 per unit, is to impose a *specific tariff*. Alternatively, if a tariff is imposed as a percentage of the value of the imported good, say, a 30 percent tax, then this is an *ad valorem tariff*. In this example, with a fixed international price, either an *ad valorem* or specific tax will have the same effect of causing a parallel shift upward of the world supply curve, S_W.

      However, if the world supply curve were to be drawn as upward sloping, then an ad valorem tax would result in a non-parallel upward shift of the world supply curve for the country imposing the tariff. As the price of the imported good rose, the gap between the original world supply curve and the world supply curve plus the *ad valorem* tariff would widen, since the price to which the percentage tariff was being applied would be greater.

13 Producer surplus is the extra revenue domestic firms receive above and beyond what is necessary for them to be willing to supply a particular level of output. It is equal to the area above the domestic supply curve and below the prevailing market price. In this example, *total* producer surplus at price P_T is equal to the triangle $P_T P_0 b$. However, there was producer surplus even when there was free trade at price P_F equal to the triangle $P_0 a P_F$. Therefore the additional producer surplus from the

infant industry tariff is the difference between the two areas, i.e. $P_T P_0 b - P_0 a P_F$ which is the area $P_F a b P_T$.

14 The deadweight loss equals the loss of consumer surplus minus the increase in producer surplus minus the increase in government tariff revenues. Graphically it is: $P_E f d P_T - P_F a b P_T - bced = abc + def$.

15 Prior to the imposition of the infant industry tariff, domestic firms produced output C_0 at price P_F. Domestic producer surplus was equal to area $P_0 a P_F$ with domestic supply curve S_D, the position of which reflected the transitional inefficiencies of production for domestic enterprises. With the elimination of the transitional inefficiencies, shown by the shifting of the domestic supply curve to S_{D2}, the new producer surplus, assuming a price of P_F, would be triangle $P_E f P_E$.

16 Most countries levy some minimum tariff on a large array of imports for reasons other than infant industry protection. Such tariffs, particularly when they are uniform (say, 4 percent or 6 percent) and do not discriminate against any particular good, are often assessed as a means to raise revenues to help cover the costs of customs and other border operations, such as immigration. Thus, with the end of ISI protection, tariffs do not necessarily, and most likely will not, decline to zero.

17 There may be some exceptions where tariff protection is not fully removed, for example, in the case of certain industries deemed to be critical for national security. However, even in such industries (motor vehicle production may be one such industry), there are likely to be better means to guarantee the survival of firms when full tariff protection is withdrawn, e.g., low-cost loans and government procurement programmes, that help to push enterprises to be more competitive and efficient.

18 For a critique of ISI policies in general, see Balassa 1982.

19 This effort to capture economic rents is referred to as DUP or "directly unproductive profit-seeking" activity in the economics literature. In the process of attempting to retain tariff protection, ISI firms expend resources for lobbying and perhaps graft for dishonest politicians and other public officials to convince them to maintain high tariffs or other favorable treatment. Such expenditures are an unproductive uses of society's resources, as they do not contribute to greater output or efficiency, thus increasing the net loss of a tariff to society (see Colander 1984). For a recent analysis of state structures, see Evans (1995: Chapter 7), who describes what we call a "captured" state as a "predatory" state. Perhaps Evans's language is even more evocative of what occurs when the state is dominated by special interests.

20 One need only think back to David Ricardo's analysis of the advantages of free trade and of the struggles over the Corn Laws in England discussed in Chapter 4 to realize that the search for economic rents by those with privileged access to political power is neither new nor confined to countries making use of ISI development strategies. Large English landowners struggled hard to keep European grains from entering British shores through the implementation of restrictive trade measures which kept their "rents," or incomes, artificially and unnecessarily high, at the expense of others, particularly low-income British consumers.

21 Para-state firms, or para-statals, are government-owned and -operated enterprises.

22 The standard market failure argument for government provision of such goods and services applies here. Infrastructure tends to generate substantial positive externalities that cannot be captured by the provider of the service or good and often have substantial public goods characteristics.

State production tends to lower the cost of essential inputs, like electricity, to third-party private industrialists, thus increasing their profits without any private investment. Further, the mere existence of sufficient electrical generation capacity, as one example, creates opportunities for new production to emerge.

In other words, the *social profitability* of infrastructural investment by government will be larger than its accounting profitability, and this is why state firms often seem to be unprofitable. That is true only when looking at the revenues and costs of the firm using a standard accounting approach. However, if an *economic accounting approach* is taken then the additional revenues of private firms using the state-provided input that can be imputed to the existence of the infrastructure must be added to the actual revenues received by the state firm for its services. Taxes on private profits are one means to capture at least part of the third-party benefits that result from state-generated inputs, such as electricity, water, roads, ports, telephone and other communications services, and so on. Taxing to pay for the provision of such public goods and to cover accounting losses of the state easily can be justified by the theories of positive externalities and public goods.

23 Unsubsidized private producers of positive externalities have no way of appropriating any of the additional profits that their production process creates for other firms. Concerned only about their

own private benefits of production, which, when there are positive externalities, are less than the social benefits of production, the private level of (unsubsidized) production will be less than the social optimum since the marginal private benefit curve intersects the marginal social cost curve at a lower level of output than the marginal social benefit curve intersects the marginal social cost curve. Thus, the private prices of firms affected by the positive externality will be higher than the socially optimum price and their output levels will be lower than would be desirable because of under-provision of the positive externality by private firms.

24 For those who argue that ISI breeds inefficiencies, the issue still remains whether the level of production with ISI, even if taking place inside PPF_2, results in a higher growth path than the mix of production associated with the original PPF_1 with the output mix at A. It is not transitional, static inefficiency of ISI versus an ideal growth path that is crucial but rather the impact on growth and developed associated with pursuing the ISI strategy versus staying on the status quo path. Of course continued ISI inefficiency is not desirable but that is contained in the concept of "transitional" inefficiencies, which can be reduced as tariff protection (or subsidization) is removed, as was argued above.

References

Amsden, Alice. 2001. *The Rise of "the Rest": Challenges to the West from Late-Industrializing Economies*. Oxford: Oxford University Press.

Balassa, Bela. 1982. *Development Strategies in Semi-Industrializing Economies*. Baltimore, MD: The Johns Hopkins University Press.

Blair, Calvin. 1964. "Nacional Financiera," pp. 193–238 in Raymond Vernon (ed.), *Public Policy and Private Enterprise in Mexico*. Cambridge, MA: Harvard University Press.

Bruton, Harry. 1989. "Import Substitution," Chapter 30 in Hollis Chenery and T.N. Srinivasan (eds.), *Handbook of Development Economics*, vol. ii. Amsterdam: North Holland Publishers.

Chenery, Hollis. 1979. *Structural Change and Development Policy*. New York: Oxford University Press.

Colander, David C. (ed.). 1984. *Neoclassical Political Economy: The Analysis of Rent-Seeking and DUP Activities*. Cambridge, MA: Ballinger.

Evans, Peter. 1995. *Embedded Autonomy*. Princeton: Princeton University Press.

Evenson, Robert E. and Larry E. Westphal. 1995. "Technological Change and Technology Strategy," Chapter 37 in Jere Behrman and T.N. Srinivasan (eds.), *Handbook of Development Economics*, vol. iiia. Amsterdam: Elsevier Science.

Gerschenkron, Alexander. 1962. *Economic Backwardness in Historical Perspective*. Cambridge, MA: Harvard University Press.

Hamm, Steve. 2007. "The Trouble with India," *Business Week* (March 19).

Higgins, Benjamin and Jean Downing Higgins. 1979. *Economic Development of a Small Planet*. New York: W.W. Norton & Co.

Kohli, Atul. 2004. *State-Directed Development*. Cambridge: Cambridge University Press.

Krieckhaus, Jonathan. 2002. "Reconceptualizing the Developmental State: Public Savings and Economic Growth," *World Development* 30 (October): 1697–712.

Kuznets, Simon. 1971. *The Economic Growth of Nations*. Cambridge, MA: Harvard University Press.

Lewis, W. Arthur. 1954. "Economic Development with Unlimited Supplies of Labour," *Manchester School of Economic and Social Studies* 22 (May 1954): 139–91.

Stiglitz, Joseph. 1992. "Alternative Tactics and Strategies for Economic Development," in A.K. Dutt and Kenneth P. Jameson (eds.), *New Directions in Development Economics*. Notre Dame, IN: University of Notre Dame Press.

Syrquin, Moshe. 1988. "Patterns of Structural Change," Chapter 7 in Hollis B. Chenery and T.N. Srinivasan (eds.), *Handbook of Development Economics*, vol. i. Amsterdam: North Holland Publishers.

UNDP (United Nations Development Programme). 1995. *Human Development Report 1995*. Oxford: Oxford University Press.

——. 2001. *Human Development Report 2001*. Oxford: Oxford University Press.

Wade, Robert. 1990. *Governing the Market: Economic Theory and the Role of Government in East Asian Industrialization*. Princeton: Princeton University Press.

Wood, Adrian and Jörg Mayer. 2001. "Africa's Export Structure in Comparative Perspective," *Cambridge Journal of Economics* 25 (May): 369–94.

World Bank. 1993. *World Development Report 1993*. Oxford: Oxford University Press.

——. 1995. *World Development Report 1995*. Oxford: Oxford University Press.

——. 2000. *World Development Report 2000/2001*. Oxford: Oxford University Press.

——. 2001. *World Development Indicators*. Washington, D.C.: World Bank.

——. 2007. *World Development Indicators*. Washington, D.C.: World Bank.

10 Strategy switching and industrial transformation

After reading and studying this chapter, you should better understand:
- the limits to easy import substitution as the motor of industrialization and growth and development;
- the importance of the proper sequencing of phases of industrialization and timely strategy switches to successful development programs;
- the importance of *export substitution* as a fundamental stage in industrialization;
- the costs associated with premature difficult import substitution;
- the importance of trade as a promoter of increased productivity and of more efficient technology use;
- the importance of public policy to augmenting resource endowments appropriate for future progress;
- the need to search for and promote dynamic comparative advantage and the role of "contests" in achieving this objective;
- the role of appropriate institutions in supporting warranted strategy switches.

Continuing structural change

In the previous chapter, we saw that the initial impulse toward a higher level of development comes with the movement of labor from agriculture toward industrial production. This is typically achieved with easy import substitution industrialization (ISI), as relatively simple, non-durable manufactured goods are produced for the domestic market by replacing at least some of the imports of these goods. This shift in the productive structure and of labor usage via import substitution is common to virtually all successful, and to many unsuccessful, development experiences.

Easy ISI is only the *first* step along a complex path of structural change. Easy ISI makes further progress possible but without guaranteeing success. No single development strategy is likely to be sufficient over time if economic growth and progress are to be sustained. Decision-makers, especially those in government, need to be prepared to make changes in the prevailing strategy when it no longer provides the base for continued growth. The marks of good policy-making and of relatively long and stable periods of sustained expansion are the ability to recognize the need for and to quickly and effectively make what we call **strategy switches**.

Industrial sequencing: beyond easy ISI

The stage of easy import substitution industrialization (ISI) examined in Chapter 9 has a natural limit as a contributor to sustained growth and development. When easy ISI begins, there is typically a fairly substantial increase in economic growth and the level of GDP per person. This occurs as a result of the shift of low-productivity labor from agriculture to higher-productivity activities in industry and services. However, once all the potentially viable non-durable consumer good imports have been replaced by domestic production, then further industrial growth in the domestic market will be limited to population growth plus any aggregate income expansion and changes in tastes and preferences.[1]

The pace of economic growth will slow as the ability of the manufacturing sector to lead the growth of the rest of the economy is reduced as the opportunities for shifting labor from agriculture to industry are exhausted. In fact, *diminishing returns* to the easy ISI strategy will be apparent long before all import substitution possibilities for non-durable consumption goods have been realized.

Countries thus face a dilemma. What can be done to ensure continuing economic growth and the attainment of higher levels of development? What measures might facilitate *strategy switches* in the design of a country's economic strategy to further the desired structural transformations?

The changing composition of imports

Complicating matters, during the easy ISI stage there is a change in the composition of imports. Non-durable consumer imports as a percentage of total imports obviously decline as these are replaced by domestic production via the easy ISI strategy. In their place, the new ISI industries begin to import more expensive and more complex manufactured goods. As a consequence there will be a rising share of total imports that are *intermediate inputs*, such as, needles, bobbins, dyes, and thread for, say, clothing production, and physical *capital goods*, such as sewing machines, destined for these new firms in the easy ISI sector.

To the extent that easy ISI is fairly generalized and not limited to a restricted range of goods, the percentage of total imports accounted for by non-durable consumer goods will continue to shrink as easy ISI proceeds.[2] Intermediate imports for the easy ISI industries and durable consumer goods (like motor cars, refrigerators, and computers) will loom larger as a share of total imports. Of course, these imports often are more expensive than the former non-durable consumer imports.

It was at one time thought that an easy ISI strategy could lessen the dependence of less-developed countries on the world market. By reducing the demand for non-durable consumer imports by replacing them with domestic production, it was thought that countries would produce more of the goods they consumed, which was partly true, and hence would be more self-reliant, which turned out to not always be true. Easy ISI replaced the demand for imported consumer non-durables with the need to now import many of the inputs for the expanding ISI firms.

The urgency to secure sufficient export earnings thus remained as compelling after starting domestic industrialization as before, perhaps even more so, if the inputs for the ISI industries were to be imported. Dependence on the external market simply changed its form. Certain intermediate imports became indispensable to the domestic industrial production process, to economic growth, and to continued employment within the expanding easy ISI sector.

In an important sense, then, dependence on the world market is intensified after initiating easy ISI, even though the overall *import coefficient* declined for most countries at first.[3] However, the composition of imports changed during easy ISI. Imported machinery and transport equipment and other capital goods increased during the easy ISI phase of expansion, as shown in Table 10.1. The shift toward intermediate and capital goods imports was most pronounced in the regions where industrialization has been most rapid and longest-lived, particularly East Asia and Latin America. It was this "import imperative" that ultimately forced economies to make changes to their development strategies as the easy ISI state of industrialization begins to reach its natural limits of expansion.

We have not shown the composition of imports for more recent years, since for many of the economies of East Asia and Latin America the easy ISI stage of industrialization had been completed by the 1980s. Further, the change in imports ultimately is less important over the long run than the change in the mix of exports for the development process. For countries in Africa, however, when they do begin more rapid industrialization, the problems of the import mix will show itself in the foreign exchange shortages discussed in the next section that will, at some point, require a strategy switch to resolve. And that is the importance of looking at the changing composition of imports, for the pressure it puts on the existing development strategy.

Foreign exchange shortages

Most countries that initiate easy ISI find that recurrent balance of payments problems threaten economic stability at some point.[4] Very simply what this means is that earning the foreign exchange needed to pay for the imports of manufactured inputs to keep the easy ISI industries operating and the economy growing becomes a constant struggle. This is because the bulk of foreign exchange earnings continue to be derived from the same limited array of primary product exports the country has long been selling to the international market, often since colonial days, even though the economy is becoming more industrialized internally. Easy ISI does not relieve this constraint on the balance of payments. Easy ISI changes what is produced internally and makes an economy more industrial appearing, that is true. However, what is exported does not change much during this stage in most economies. They continue to export to world markets the same primary products that were being exported before industrialization began.

Table 10.1 Composition of imports (as a percentage of total imports)

	Primary goods[a]		Machinery and transport equipment		Other manufactured goods	
	1970	*1992*	*1970*	*1992*	*1970*	*1992*
East Asia and Pacific	23	15	33	39	37	36
Latin America and Caribbean	18	16	35	40	36	35
Middle East and North Africa	26	21	32	35	39	39
South Asia	33	21	24	22	31	39
Sub-Saharan Africa	15	16	38	39	42	37
High-income economies	32	16	25	35	33	41

Source: World Bank 1994: 189.

Note
a Includes food but excludes fuels, so components do not sum to 100 percent.

Whether because of instability in commodity prices or declining terms of trade or as a consequence of inefficiencies in primary product production or a combination of these effects, the income derived from primary exports tends to fall short of what is needed to pay for the imported inputs required by the easy ISI industries and to meet the demand for imported durable consumer goods. The lack of dynamism in traditional primary product export markets limits the growth of foreign exchange earnings at the same time the need for such income to finance the purchase of industrial inputs becomes ever more pressing.

We can express this foreign exchange shortage, when export income (X) is insufficient to pay for the desired imports (M), by the inequality, $M > X$. Simplifying greatly, the gap between import expenditures and export earnings creates the need to borrow foreign exchange or take other steps to finance the expenditure excess. In fact, import spending cannot exceed export income without the borrowing of foreign exchange to pay for the excess spending.[5] We thus say there is a *foreign exchange shortage* that must be resolved *if* an economy is to have import expenditures, M, greater than export earnings, X.

A severe imbalance between export income and import expenditures thus requires external borrowing of foreign currency from foreign banks or economies. If the magnitudes of needed financing are large and persistent, they cannot be sustained by countries forever, just as individuals or families cannot spend more than their income forever by adding without limit to their debt. Countries are no different. There is a limit to how much debt is reasonable.[6]

When external debt becomes unsustainable or economies find that it has become difficult to borrow foreign exchange, then what was a foreign exchange shortage becomes a *foreign exchange crisis*. A foreign exchange crisis forces economies to achieve a balance between export earnings and import spending when it is no longer possible to borrow. More than likely it will be necessary to actually have $X > M$, that is, to earn more foreign exchange than is spent, so as to be able to make payments on the debt of foreign exchange already accumulated.

Resolving a foreign exchange crisis via a strategy switch

How does an economy go from having $X < M$ to a situation where $X > M$? How can a foreign exchange crisis be overcome over the longer term?

There are two strategies that have been followed in an attempt to ease the foreign exchange constraint that results from the easy import substitution stage of industrialization: *easy export substitution* or *difficult ISI*. Each takes an economy in a different direction in terms of its industrial structure, export and import patterns, and the impact on the balance of payments. Further, each strategy has distinctive effects on long-term economic growth and human development possibilities.

From examining the historical experience, there would seem to be a "superior" and a "sub-optimal" strategy switch for ordering industrial growth and for furthering the structural transition.[7]

Ultimately, though, the issue is not one of choosing between import substitution or exporting as overall strategies, as neoliberal economists often frame the issue. The policy choice is rather between the *sequencing of import and export substitution stages* and the nature of what is exported and at what stage in the cycle of industrialization. Proper industrial "strategy sequencing" involves the appropriate combination of exporting *and* ISI; it is not a choice between one or the other. No less-developed country has successfully made the transition to a higher stage of economic growth and development without passing through *both* import substitution industrialization *and* the stage of exporting manufactures to the world market. Industrialization and higher levels of development begin with easy ISI, but they must not end there.

Easy export substitution industrialization: the optimal strategy switch after easy ISI

Assuming infant industry tariffs have been progressively eliminated during the easy ISI phase, as is indispensable to future economic progress (remember our discussion at the end of Chapter 9), then imports will be able to re-enter the domestic market. Domestic producers will need to be competitive with these goods, or consumers will substitute toward imports and away from less desirable domestic goods as tariffs fall. Those easy ISI firms that have learned to compete with imported goods somewhere on the price-quality continuum will not only be able to survive the competition; they will then have a further option beyond the domestic market for expanding their production, sales, and profits. They now can begin to export the same non-durable ISI consumer goods to the international market.

The price-quality spectrum permits substantial substitution possibilities from "lower quality-lower price" to "higher quality-higher price" combinations compared to the average world price and average quality of any particular good. For example, some of the non-durable consumer goods China exports may be of slightly lower quality than comparable products from other countries. If those lower-quality Chinese commodities are to be competitive on the international market, they will also need to be priced lower. Goods of equal quality can be priced at the average international price and still be competitive. There is thus not one single price for a good, such as plastic outdoor chairs. There can be a variety of price and quality combinations that can be competitive on the international market.

This is why it is so important that infant industry tariffs be but a temporary means to allow domestic producers to overcome transitional inefficiencies common to new enterprises. At some point, and sooner rather than later is best, these tariffs have to be eliminated. It is this fundamental policy step that provides the "stick" of competition from imported goods that pushes domestic easy ISI firms to learn to be efficient or face the possibility of being eliminated from the market. Governments can help firms become more competitive and able to export beyond reducing tariffs. Besides the "stick" of competition, they can provide "carrots" that help to reduce costs via: international marketing assistance; an exchange rate that is not artificially over-valued and is, perhaps, mildly under-valued; low but positive, real interest rates for productive investment ("financial repression"); education subsidies; and so on.[8] The point is that for those easy ISI firms able to meet foreign competition, their potential market extends far beyond domestic consumers to regional and world markets. For smaller nations with relatively limited domestic markets and few firms in each industry, the ability to compete with foreign firms may require the *early* intervention of government to assist in pushing production into export markets so that economies of scale and technological maturity can be realized more rapidly than would be possible from depending on domestic market size alone.[9]

The advantages for countries entering export markets are many, and not solely and most obviously for the individual firms which expect to earn higher profits. From the national or social viewpoint, an expansion of total exports by selling easy ISI manufactured goods in international markets provides for the possibility of financing a higher quantity of imported goods, a faster pace of economic growth and development, higher levels of income, and more employment for rural migrants entering into the relatively labor-intensive easy ISI industrial sector. The exports of non-durable manufactured goods contribute to the foreign earnings needed to import the necessary intermediate and capital inputs required by the ISI industry itself, thus helping to self-finance the export expansion.

Further, and of great importance, to the extent that the exports of ISI firms begin to *replace and substitute for traditional primary exports*, the economy's export structure will include a greater share of manufactured good exports. This can reduce the pressures arising from the Prebisch-Singer declining terms of trade dilemma (considered in Chapter 6) that can contribute to export earning problems and to recurring foreign exchange problems.[10] To the extent that manufactured and other non-traditional exports increase in significance compared to primary product exports, then we can say that export substitution is taking place. The significance of primary exports declines in both relative and absolute terms within the export profile with easy export substitution.

In other words, for an economy pursuing easy export substitution industrialization, manu-factured exports are more than just an addition on top of the primary product export base. Over time, easy ISI manufactured exports *take the place of* primary product exports, hence the name, easy export substitution. Old exports (primary goods) are replaced by new exports (secondary goods).

Gustav Ranis (1981) has suggested that *export substitution* is the logical next stage of evolution of the industrialization strategy after easy ISI. It is this stage which was followed by the East Asian nations of Korea, Taiwan, Hong Kong, Japan, and other HPAEs ("high performance Asian economies"). And it is one that economic policy-makers in nations still in the easy ISI phase of transformation, or taking steps to deepen ISI, should be planning to implement in the not-too-distant future. Sachs (2005: 18–20) refers to this as the "develop-ment ladder," a natural progression in production which China is now climbing, too.

Exporting simple consumer non-durables allows less-developed countries to penetrate the international market at a low level in the so-called "life cycle" of manufactured good exports. It is a natural, evolutionary niche in that production tends to be labor-intensive and hence relatively low-cost because of low wages and the continuing labor surplus in agriculture in the domestic economy. Further, by continuing the expansion of the original easy ISI firms into world markets, the technology is still relatively low-level and international levels of efficiency can be more easily maintained.

The gains from easy export substitution industrialization

During the easy export substitution stage, labor-intensive production methods continue to be used, since it is simple non-durable consumer goods that are being produced for both domestic and, now, for foreign consumption. Easy export substitution deepens the industrialization process and allows for the continued growth of employment in the domestic manufacturing sector. Rising exports can help to maintain a higher rate of economic growth for a longer period of time.[11]

By increasing total production to meet domestic and export demand, scale economies in production may be more easily attained so that per unit costs of production continue to fall with higher levels of output. Of particular importance too will be the management, finan-cial, marketing, technological, and other essential capacities that can be learned from oper-ating successfully in the international marketplace. Such skills often are transferable to other domestic industries as spillover effects multiply and as the nation's pool of domestic talent is enlarged and extended to new arenas. As will be remembered from Chapter 8, these external effects can help an economy not only reach a higher level of income, but also to maintain high growth rates over the longer term.

It is the *ability to export* manufactured goods, however, not the exporting *per se* that provides the benefits to the economy, because the ability to export secondary goods requires a level of world-class efficiency having been reached somewhere on the price-quality continuum. The ability to export these goods is a signal that domestic firms have become efficient producers, and it is efficiency in production and the ability to use knowledge effectively that marks successful development over the long haul.

This prospect of *backward* and *forward linkages* in new areas of production emerging through a process of entrepreneurial-deepening is another of the potential benefits of moving into the easy export substitution phase of industrialization. This stage provides continuity in the industrialization process and helps to augment the training of the domestic entrepreneurial and professional class, as well as upgrading the skills of the labor force as they work and learn on the job. Local entrepreneurs are allowed to flourish in the international marketplace and possibly to spin off new domestic industries related to the original easy ISI firms.

Easy export substitution industrialization thus permits the local entrepreneurial class to come to greater maturity by being forced to remain competitive on price and quality and via the continuous upgrading of technological skills and training that maintain productive efficiency. It is precisely these sorts of positive externalities that endogenous growth theories envisage as fundamental to sustained growth over time, and it seems that *the capacity to export manufactured goods* helps to endogenize such behavior within the domestic economy by imbedding the search for efficiency within the productive culture of the economy.

In a study of thirty developing economies over the period 1970–82, Sebastian Edwards (1992) confirmed that trade and openness to the international economy are important not solely because exports are a contributor to growth, but because, combined with the appropriate human capital base and with supporting government policies, openness is a significant *transmission mechanism for technological learning* by domestic firms operating in the global economy.

Foreign capital and foreign technology may have a role to play in this stage of the industrial transformation process, but at least in the East Asian economies, foreign interests and foreign capital were subordinated to local interests, local capital, and local entrepreneurs (see Focus 10.1). We shall see that this was not the case in Latin America and other regions.

It has become an article of faith in recent years among many economists that an export orientation, as opposed to an inward-oriented ISI policy, is essential for economic success in less-developed nations. Exports are perceived as an *engine of growth* for the economy as a whole. Sometimes the successes of the HPAEs and Japan before them have been put forward as exemplars of the efficacy of this strategy. A greater volume of exporting *per se*, however, is no panacea for less-developed nations or the former colonies would have become developed long ago! Exporting is not a new phenomenon; the LDCs have always been exporters.

Recent research, such as that of Edwards noted above, suggests that it is not exporting, but export substitution and before that ISI, that were essential to the gains from exporting of a certain type. And even easy export substitution is *not sufficient* for successful economic development, even if it would appear to be a *necessary* stage of industrial transformation. As we know from the endogenous growth models of Chapter 8, higher and sustained rates of economic growth also require improvements in the stock of human capital and in the adaptation and use of new technologies and knowledge in production if economic growth is to be sustained.

Countries which fail to accumulate human capital at a sufficiently high rate and of the right type and to maintain knowledge acquisition ultimately will face lower growth rates than comparable countries with more human capital accumulation, even if both have identical

FOCUS 10.1   FOREIGN CAPITAL AND TECHNOLOGY IN KOREA

Korea utilized foreign investment as a strategic means to gain access to technology and skills at a lower cost than might otherwise have been possible through domestic channels alone. The Korean state's approach to investment from abroad has been anything but *laissez-faire*, taking what has been called the "eye of the needle" approach, to make certain that any foreign investment met South Korea's needs.

One study found that only 29.7 percent of foreign direct investment (FDI) in South Korea took the form of wholly-owned subsidiaries of multinational companies. This compares with 33.1 percent for Japan at the same time (1976), and an average 69.1 percent ratio for the sixty-six countries in the study. In fact, Korea's ratio of wholly-owned FDI was the lowest in the sample.

> Foreign investors were expected by their partners and by the Korean government to make a continuing contribution to Korean development, one which was complementary to, rather than at the expense of domestic manufacturing interests.

In terms of technology transfers, the government usually approved these through the Economic Planning Board or the Ministry of Finance, with input from the Ministry of Science and Technology. Technical assistance contracts were typically limited to no more than three years, except in complex processes, with the intention of forcing domestic firms to learn how to do technology themselves rather than depending on foreign consultants.

Foreign technology in Korea was viewed as a teaching tool to encourage local adaptation; it was not a fundamental cog in the development project meant to stand alone and apart from the domestic economy. FDI was one means used to facilitate such learning, but the focus was on how to upgrade the skills and efficiency levels of local factors of production, including entrepreneurs, engineers, skilled workers, and so on.

Source: Luedde-Neurath 1988: 84–5, 90–3

levels of manufactured exports. Further, they will forgo some of the potential technological gains available from the world pool of "best practice" production knowledge and sacrifice economic efficiency, even if they are exporting manufactured goods on a relatively large, or increasing, scale. Accumulating the proper human resources is a complementary cog to industrial phasing and to exporting. [12]

Are some exports better than others?

It is important that countries identify exports that have a reasonable prospect for expanding demand over time and which also promise substantial *value-added* to the domestic economy.

Value-added in production is the income created at each stage of production of a good, so the greater the value-added in production of a product the more income that is created for the domestic economy. Goods with high value-added are those which require more labor time and more machinery, technology, and knowledge to produce. Countries want to increase the production of goods with higher value-added accruing to domestically owned resources, since it is the production of these commodities for the domestic market and for export which will add most to a country's GDP.

How do countries determine which higher value-added goods to export? To create comparative advantage in goods that are dynamic and adaptive dictates an export mix dominated by commodities with *income elasticities* that are not just positive, but preferably greater than one and which promise significant opportunities for growth in export earnings over time. [13]

Many manufactured goods, such as most electronics products, computer software, recreational and sports equipment, plumbing supplies, and so on, fall into this category. Some of these can begin to be produced during the easy ISI stage.

The success of not only Taiwan and Korea in recent decades, but of Japan before them, would seem to strongly suggest that the *sequencing of industrialization* from easy ISI and then transitioning to easy export substitution of higher valued-added commodities is a design that not only builds upon the *created comparative advantage* forged during the easy ISI stage but also furthers the goal of augmenting and revealing new dynamic comparative advantage in the future.[14]

Comparative advantage changes, sometimes quite rapidly, as the result of increases in education and in the skill levels of workers and managers, with the pace of technological change and its domestic adaptation, and as a consequence of rising incomes and the changing structure of domestic demand that accompanies an expanding urban, industrial society. The economy's domestic productive base, as well as its export structure, must be evolving in concert with, or perhaps even leading, these changes.

Table 10.2 provides some information on the evolution of export structures over time for the major regions and for various countries.

East Asia, dominated by the HPAEs, such as Korea and Taiwan, and South Asia, led by India's economy, show the greatest movement toward manufactured exports among the different regions. Latin America and the Caribbean, despite a relatively high level of industrialization by some measures (for example, the share of the labor force working in industry),

Table 10.2 Export structure

	Manufactured good exports (percentage of merchandise exports)			
	1970	*1990*	*2000*	*2004*
Region				
East Asia and Pacific	32	60	80	80
Latin America and the Caribbean	16	36	58	56
Middle East and North Africa	5	2	4	4
South Asia	48	71[a]	80[b]	76
Sub-Saharan Africa	19	–	24	31
High-income economies	72	79	80	81
Countries				
Argentina	14	29	32	29
Bangladesh	65	81[a]	91[c]	90
Brazil	13	52	59	54
Cameroon	14	9	4	5
China	–	72	88	91
Côte d'Ivoire	6	11	14	20
India	52	70	77	73
Kenya	12	29	21	21
Korea	77	94	91	92
Malaysia	7	54	80	76
Mexico	32	43	83	80

Sources: World Bank 2002, 2006.

Notes
a   Predominately textiles and clothing.
b   1999.
c   1998.

has not shown as strong a movement toward manufactured exports. In 1990, little more than one-third of merchandise exports were manufactured goods.[15] By 2004, there had been a noticeable shift toward manufactured exports in Latin America, though the region still lags behind the progress made in East Asia and the Pacific.

Looking at individual countries, Korea's large share of manufactured exports in merchandise exports reflects the effects of the government's conscious efforts to promote export substitution as ISI's gains began to diminish. Among Latin American countries, Mexico has shifted its export profile more in the direction of manufactured goods than have Argentina and Brazil. India and, especially, Bangladesh have an export profile more similar to East Asia and the Pacific, but these exports tend to be concentrated in low value-added commodities. This is also the case with China, for the moment at least. For countries in Sub-Saharan Africa like Cameroon, Côte d'Ivoire, and Kenya, manufactured exports remain very low. This is due to the low level of industrialization in these economies; most are doing limited easy ISI and have not switched to easy export substitution.

The growth in manufactured goods exports of the East Asian countries was obvious in the evolution of the region's share of total manufactured goods exports. Considering only Hong Kong, Taiwan, Korea and Singapore, their combined share of manufactured goods exports as a proportion of the manufactured goods exports of *all* less-developed countries grew steadily, from 13.2 percent in 1965 to an astounding 61.5 percent of the total in 1990 (World Bank 1993: 38).

By 2004, the share of these economies had fallen to just over 50 percent, as other economies have been transitioning toward greater manufactured exports via export substitution or other policies. There is learning taking place as the benefits to being able to export manufactured goods as the East Asian economies have done is being replicated in other countries.

Latin America's share of less-developed country manufactured goods exports has declined over the same period. This shift is not surprising when it is realized that East Asia's exports, led by manufactured export expansion, grew at an annual rate of 10.5 percent over the 1980s, 11.0 percent in the 1990s and 15.3 percent from 2000–4. Latin America's total exports grew by a much smaller 2.9 percent per annum in the 1980s, increasing to 8.5 percent in the 1990s before falling back to a 4.4 percent growth rate for total exports from 2000–4. As a result of these different trends in export expansion, by 2004 East Asia and the Pacific's total exports were more than double Latin America's exports, having been slightly less in 1990.

What accounts for the relatively poor performance of Latin America's manufactured goods exports relative to the HPAEs and for the marked difference in the pace of development? How have the HPAEs been able to "leap over" the level of development of the larger Latin American countries, like Brazil and Mexico, and begin to approach the threshold of developed country status at a more rapid pace than the Latin American countries, which had a head start? And, by extension, what can other late-developing nations in Africa and South Asia perhaps learn from the two experiences?

Difficult ISI: a sub-optimal strategy switch immediately after easy ISI

One explanation for the growing gap between the HPAEs and some other economies in the less-developed world is found *partially* in the fact that an alternative sequencing of the path of industrialization was followed after exhausting the possibilities of easy ISI other than easy export substitution.[16]

The larger Latin American nations transitioned from easy ISI directly to *difficult ISI* thus *forgoing and skipping* the easy export-substitution phase followed by the East Asian economies.[17] It will be recalled from the discussion of foreign exchange crises earlier in this chapter that the structure of imports is transformed during easy ISI toward a growing proportion of intermediate and capital goods, as non-durable consumer good imports are progressively replaced by domestic production of those commodities. Difficult ISI *deepens* the domestic industrialization process by *extending* import substitution *backward* into the domestic production of durable consumption goods (like motor cars), intermediate goods (such as tires and batteries), and capital goods (like car body stamping machines).

The shift toward difficult ISI is motivated by the same two parallel concerns that led the East Asian economies to switch to easy export substitution. First, the exhaustion of easy ISI growth possibilities meant that continued economic expansion fueled by manufacturing growth is impossible without production for new markets. One possibility is to create these markets through *domestic vertical integration* by pushing the domestic production structure backward into intermediate and capital goods and consumer durables instead of continuing to import them. This creates the possibility for continued economic growth based on local demand via the usual macroeconomic *income and employment multiplier* effects of new investments and spending and the *crowding-in* of tertiary production that emerges to service the new difficult ISI industries that emerge.[18]

Second, the foreign exchange shortages fomented by persistent trade deficits due to having import spending, M, greater than export earnings, X, can motivate a decision to "strategy switch" toward difficult ISI. Thus, the decision to reduce the *import bill* even further via additional ISI beyond easy ISI does seem a logical alternative to increasing foreign exchange export earnings via export substitution, which is the alternative means for attempting to resolve the foreign exchange disequilibrium that accompanies early industrialization.

The thinking behind such a decision is based on the assumption that an additional unit of foreign exchange *saved* by a deepening of ISI is equivalent to an additional unit of foreign exchange *earned* via export substitution. After all, if a country has a foreign exchange shortage because $M > X$, and there is a need to turn this around so that $X > M$, then one way to do that is obviously to reduce import expenditures, M, further so that they are less than export earnings, X.

However, this static and purely mathematical view obscures longer-term effects that suggest that a one-unit saving in foreign exchange from reducing M is actually worth less over time than a one-unit increase in foreign exchange earnings that results from switching to an export substituting strategy that increases exports, X. The easy export substitution industrialization stage followed by the East Asian economies also had the goal of relieving the foreign exchange shortages of the easy ISI stage. However, the export substitution strategy resolves the $M > X$ inequality by increasing export earnings, X, rather than reducing imports, M. It can be seen that an industrialization strategy that increases *export* earnings not only can result in $X > M$, but it also opens the possibility of a higher level of imports too. Further, imports can only be reduced so much; they cannot go to zero. Exports, however, have no such limit. So, in a real sense, increasing export earnings, X, is a superior strategy for overcoming a foreign exchange crisis, because it can be virtually limitless.

The Latin American economies (and India) *prematurely* entered the difficult ISI phase of industrialization, however, for reasons to be explored, and they thereby short-circuited the potential for more dynamic growth and structural transformation. As a result, the period of ISI-led industrialization in Latin America was distorted and over-extended, lasting in some larger countries from the 1890s, and in others from the 1930s, to the 1950s in the easy ISI phase, followed by the stage of difficult ISI from the 1950s to the late 1970s or so. The reason why we call Latin America's – and India's – shift to difficult ISI immediately following easy ISI premature is that they were not ready to produce the more sophisticated commodities characteristic of that stage of industrialization, as will be explained more fully below.

By contrast, easy ISI as a *central* component of the structural transformation in the East Asian economies lasted only about a decade, from roughly 1953 to 1963 (though there was some isolated ISI before), and then the strategy switch was to export substitution and a more dynamic export pattern, dominated by manufactured goods as primary product exports declined in importance. We will see that when the East Asian economies eventually shifted to difficult ISI, they did so *after* the easy export substitution stage had transformed their economic structures. The economies were ready to produce the difficult ISI goods themselves, unlike in Latin America and India.

Premature difficult ISI in Latin America and India and its costs

What were the costs of skipping easy export substitution and instead strategy switching from easy ISI to difficult ISI, as happened in the larger Latin American economies and India? Why is it that transitioning to the production of more sophisticated manufactured goods, such as automobiles, steel, and other heavy industries was a sub-optimal choice after easy ISI?

1 The sacrifice of viable entrepreneurial skills

The production of intermediate and capital goods and consumer non-durables characteristic of difficult ISI tends to be more capital- and knowledge-intensive than is true of easy ISI production. The technology for producing the difficult ISI goods is not only more difficult to master, it often is based upon proprietary knowledge lodged in multinational corporations (MNCs). Countries, and this was true in Latin America and India that entered the difficult phase of ISI directly following the easy ISI stage, have done so primarily by promoting multinational investment within their borders. It is often only MNCs which control the technology and expertise, from management to engineering to quality control, required to produce the more complex products involved in producing difficult ISI goods.

The dependence on MNCs resulted in a shift in the locus of power *away from* the still-emerging class of domestic entrepreneurs who had been nurtured by the easy ISI strategy. Easy ISI had helped to create, protect, and promote the growth of an indigenous capitalist class with the potential to be world-class competitors. A premature strategy switch in the direction of difficult ISI stunted and even reversed the growth of the local capitalist class, particularly as it occurred when these domestic entrepreneurs were not fully prepared to produce the more complex array of products characteristic of the difficult ISI phase. They typically had had but limited contact with the international economy and lacked the higher levels of technological proficiency to produce even the easy ISI commodities since they had not been forced to become efficient and competitive *vis-à-vis* foreign competition in export markets as a result of the failure to reduce infant industry tariffs that would have provided the stick of competition.[19] This clearly demonstrates the importance of ending the regime of infant industry tariffs if the efficiency gains that are desired from initiating industrialization are to be realized.

This cutting-short of the maturation of the local entrepreneurial class was a crucial cost of shifting prematurely toward difficult ISI strategy rather than transitioning to easy export substitution strategy after the easy ISI stage of industrialization. Easy export substitution allows the local entrepreneurial class to continue to evolve by becoming more efficient producers, better able to weather international competition by being actively involved in international export markets. In Latin America and India, the need to depend upon multinational investment as the principal agents in producing during the difficult ISI stage made the technological learning process more difficult for local producers, who found themselves increasingly closed out of the productive process.

The dependence on MNCs to produce the difficult ISI goods was necessitated by the continued inefficiency of most local capitalists in the local and international markets. Government policy had neither pushed nor helped local firms to become internationally competitive, because infant industry tariffs had not been progressively eliminated as they should have been. What should have been a transitional policy to temporarily shield new domestic producers from foreign imports became permanent. Of course, many local capitalists thrived and became wealthy without having to learn to compete, but at a cost to society as a whole, where inefficiency was rampant.

When these economies faced the need to resolve their foreign exchange constraint so that $X > M$ rather than $M > X$, the shift to an export substitution industrialization simply was not possible, even if it might have been contemplated. Unlike in East Asia, local firms in Latin America and India had not yet become internationally competitive and thus could not export the easy ISI goods they were producing for the domestic market. Given the impossibility of shifting to a manufactured goods export strategy, Latin America and India could only do more import substitution to try to balance out export earnings (still from primary products) and import spending. Since local entrepreneurs were not even efficiently producing non-durable consumer goods, they were unable to move up and produce more sophisticated consumer durables, intermediate inputs, and capital goods characteristic of the difficult ISI stage. Thus, it was the MNCs that became the way to produce these goods, bypassing the domestic entrepreneurial class. It is in this sense that we say these economies entered difficult ISI *prematurely*; local entrepreneurs, workers and the range of infrastructure were not ready to produce difficult IS goods, having failed to become more efficient at producing even lower-level, lower-technology goods during the easy ISI stage of industrialization.

2 Insufficient labor absorption

Since production in difficult ISI enterprises is more capital-intensive than in easy ISI or easy export substitution, this strategy tends to slow the rate of labor absorption in the industrial sector, unless the level of overall investment is extraordinarily high, which it has not been. As workers continue to migrate from the rural areas to the cities, attracted by the lure of higher wages, the labor force is increasingly to be found in urban rather than rural areas.

With the premature implementation of difficult ISI, however, many migrants fail to find work in these more capital-intensive factories. Instead they often are forced to enter the *informal urban sector*, where productivity and incomes are extremely low. There they toil as artisans, petty traders, taxi drivers, day laborers, domestics, and so on, with the hope of *formal sector* employment in manufacturing at best a distant possibility.

The relatively few workers employed in the difficult ISI firms often earn higher incomes than those employed in domestically-owned easy ISI firms.[20] The growth of employment in the difficult ISI sector tends to be relatively limited, however, and thus a bifurcation of income classes tends to emerge in the urban areas, with an adverse impact on the economy's overall income distribution (look back at Focus 5.3 on the Harris-Todaro model's predictions of precisely this sort of evolution if the wage wedge between industry and agriculture was not closed over time). Urban slums ringing large cities became common throughout Latin

America and India as informal sector workers struggled to survive by building precarious housing with limited access to sanitation, water, schools, and health facilities.

Just the opposite happened in Korea and Taiwan and other HPAEs. By further expanding the labor-intensive production of consumer non-durables by pushing production outward into the international market via export substitution policies, the domestic capitalist class continued to be able to thrive and hone their skills, knowledge, and their management and production expertise in an ever more open environment in which not only domestic entrepreneurs but also the domestic labor force learned to be more efficient.

The flow of workers from the countryside was more easily absorbed by the labor-intensive nature of non-durable consumer goods production in East Asia. And with firms exporting to world markets providing increased demand for these goods beyond the local economy, employment in the industrial sector expanded rapidly. Urban unemployment rates remained low, and the informal sector employment characteristic of economies skipping export substitution was minimal. Workers and entrepreneurs upgraded their productivity and efficiency levels, though for some time this did not appear as any substantial income growth for workers, as gains from productivity growth were plowed back into further investment. The stage was being set in the East Asian economies, however, for a wider sharing of the gains of income and productivity growth among the population.

In Latin America, India, and a few other areas, premature difficult ISI resulted in continued and expanded infant industry policies to block foreign imports from entering the domestic market, as protection was now expanded to encompass intermediate and capital goods and consumer durables, in addition to the easy ISI firms already being protected. Operating behind relatively high tariff walls, domestic producers in easy ISI firms remained shielded from the external pressures that had faced East Asian entrepreneurs and forced them to become more technologically knowledgeable. Worker education and training on the job was neglected too, as these investments in higher productivity were not necessary given the high tariff levels that reduced competition from the world market.[21] The result was negative technical efficiency change, such that many economies have been moving away from "best practice" technology and away from their potential production possibilities frontier (refer back to Table 8.4).

3 High social costs

By jumping directly and prematurely to difficult ISI without fully gaining the benefits of the easy ISI stage of industrialization, the Latin American and Indian economies imposed high social costs on their populations. Governments often have been less efficient and more prone to corruption and rent-seeking behavior. The benefits of infant industry tariff policies in helping firms have time to learn to be efficient have not materialized because of the over-extension of tariffs long beyond what can be justified. Thus the deadweight losses in consumer surplus that infant industry tariffs imposed (examined in the previous chapter) were not counterbalanced by gains in efficiency and lower costs and prices that could justify their imposition in the first place.

Income distribution worsened when economies prematurely switched strategies to difficult ISI after easy ISI, as the informal sector with its low average productivity and low incomes grew in size. And human capital accumulation lagged in these economies, as raising the skills of workers was not necessary in the protected domestic environment. This lowered average worker skills and resulted in lower incomes and has made knowledge acquisition from the world that much more difficult for these economies.

Endowments and policies: explaining strategy switches

It is not enough to know that the East Asian economies followed a more optimal sequencing of their industrial path that contributed to further economic expansion, while the Latin American and a few other economies, such as India, failed to initiate an export substitution strategy following easy ISI and "chose" a sub-optimal path of industrialization. It is necessary to try to determine the underlying reasons for the strategy switches that led some countries to pursue export substitution and others to shift prematurely to difficult ISI after easy ISI if other countries are to learn from these experiences. What might explain these different choices as to the stage of industrialization after easy ISI?

Differing endowments: the resource curse explanation

One might think that having relatively abundant natural resources would be a blessing. However, Ranis (1981: 180–3) argues that for the Latin American countries, and by extension for other large countries with ample natural resources, the apparent resource base "cushion" of this *initial endowment* actually allowed those economies to continue along the same path of exporting primary commodities. It was relatively easy to earn foreign exchange with a large and elastic natural resource base and to continue their highly protected industrial policies at the same time.

Exports could be increased by simply producing more sugar or coffee or beef by using more of the abundant land via *extensive* production methods, rather than having to resort to becoming more efficient, as would have been required if land had been less abundant, i.e., by employing more intensive production methods, to use the language of Chapter 3. Even with declining terms of trade per unit of these exports, total export income could be bolstered by sufficiently increasing the physical quantity of exports if owners of resources found their export income shrinking too much.

Further, there was the continuing influence on economic and political decisions of an agricultural elite who profited from the existing primary export structure, and given that the benefits of the protected ISI sector provided both profits and relatively high wages for a small urban elite, the "many decades of import substitution growth have led to encrusted habits and strong vested interest groups able to resist reforms or even marginal policy changes" (Ranis 1981: 180). Thus a large natural resource base, given the particular institutional barriers to change that prevailed in Latin America and India, actually *hindered* the transition to the more optimal path of export substitution. An apparent resource blessing turned into its opposite, the so-called "resource curse."

> The availability of ample natural resources and/or foreign capital can thus be viewed as permitting the system to continue on its old tracks, thus avoiding the political and, at least short-term, economic pain of having to move to a different policy package. Growth rates can in this way be maintained – just by adding more fuel to the engine – and difficult decisions postponed ... While additional resources, in theory, should be able to ease the actual and psychological adjustment pains, they can be used, and in the real world are often used, to put off – or entirely avoid – difficult decisions.
>
> (Ranis 1981: 180)

In the East Asian economies, by comparison, land was at a premium. It was not possible to simply increase the quantity of primary product exports to compensate for declining terms of trade and to continue to do easy import substitution. ISI industries required a steady inflow of imported inputs and capital equipment that could be paid for only by expanding the quantity of exports. Sufficient foreign exchange earnings simply could not continue to be generated by the primary product export sector if recurring foreign exchange crises were to be avoided.

Lacking a natural resource base, the East Asian economies were forced to confront the urgency of maintaining and increasing foreign exchange earnings if the growth of domestic industry was to be sustained, and it seemed that the only means for doing so was to find new exports, specifically manufactured exports, given the limited natural resource base.

There is another factor, however, that helps to explain the different responses in East Asia and Latin America and India to the given natural resource endowment. While land distribution and ownership patterns have changed very little in this century in most Latin American countries and in much of South Asia, in East Asia, particularly in Korea and Taiwan, fundamental *agrarian reforms* were imposed after the Second World War (see Chapter 11). Thus, East Asian policy-makers did not have to concern themselves with the "encrusted habits and strong vested interest groups" that Ranis suggested might oppose the replacement and substitution of primary product commodity exports with manufactured good exports from the easy ISI industries.

The former landed class in Taiwan and Korea, as in Japan before them, had been forcibly stripped of their position, power, and prestige, and thus resistance to industrialization and industrial exports at the expense of primary product exports did not materialize. No elite group with political power was threatened by the transition to a changed export mix dominated by manufactured goods that the easy export substitution strategy implied. Fundamental agrarian reform in those countries made it feasible for those remaining in agriculture, now typically small farmers created after the agricultural revolutions, to increase the productivity of the land they worked.

Without any substantial agrarian reform in Latin America and India, any effort to shift the export structure away from agriculture encountered fierce resistance from the landed elites. This is another *institutional difference* of importance that made initial endowments and their distribution act as barriers to effective industrial transformation in Latin America and other countries with similar structures. In East Asia, these potential internal barriers to change had been dismantled as a result of war and social turmoil.

Policy choices and institutional appropriateness

But there is another dimension to the differences in the strategies of development followed in East Asia compared to Latin American economies and others that followed a similar development trajectory. East Asian policy-makers, on the whole, made *better* decisions, implemented their chosen policies *better*, monitored their policies *better,* and were willing and able to alter relatively quickly any decisions and policies if they did not bring forth the desired results.

While all governments affect the operation of their economies and the nature of future path dependence, in East Asia

> the government intervened – systematically and through multiple channels – to foster development, and in some cases the development of specific industries. Policy interventions took many forms: targeting and subsidizing credit to selected industries, keeping deposit rates low and maintaining ceilings on borrowing rates to increase profits and retained earnings, protecting domestic import substitutes, subsidizing declining

industries, establishing and financially supporting government banks, making public investments in applied research, establishing firm- and industry-specific export targets, developing export marketing institutions, and sharing information widely between public and private sectors. Some industries were promoted while others were not.

(World Bank 1993: 5–6)

This quotation from the World Bank's study of the HPAEs makes clear that policy intervention to shape the East Asian economies was pervasive. In South Korea and Taiwan, the banking system was, until quite recently, entirely publicly owned, and the Korean government has not hesitated to nationalize banks again in crisis situations that threaten the economy (such as the 1997–98 financial debacle). "Financial repression," in which interest rates were reduced and loans provided to firms that could meet the desired social, economic, and development goals, helped to speed investment, technological change, and growth.

The East Asian path of industrialization and development does not exemplify what a "market-based" approach can attain, but rather just the opposite. It shows what a "governed" market potentially can do. The East Asian experience clearly presents the possibilities of vigorous and competent policy-making with well-defined goals (look back at Focus 7.3 and Focus 7.4 in Chapter 7 on Thailand's and Korea's state policies).

In East Asia the goal was to raise the level of efficiency and technological capabilities of those economies to new levels that would permit a higher standard of living and the prospect of greater human development for a larger proportion of the population. They did this through a policy of *shared growth*, in which all classes gained from progress, albeit slowly during some periods, and by *development from within*, that is, by *depending predominantly on local capital and local capitalists* to operate industry, based on expanded human capital accumulation and an augmented technological capacity. To a great degree, East Asians did the industrialization and fomented structural change themselves and for themselves.

Critics sometimes have charged that the South Korean economy was able to grow rapidly because of severe labor repression and a long period of non-democratic rule, which ended in 1988. And there is some truth to that charge. But with time and economic expansion, and given the relatively high levels of education within the population, there have been substantial spread effects accompanying the structural transformation of the economy and society, so that average incomes have risen rapidly with a relatively low degree of inequality and with substantial progress on the key human development indicators.

In Korea in 1988, the share of total income received by the richest 20 percent of income earners as a ratio of the share of income received by the poorest 20 percent was 5.7 (= 42.4 percent/7.4 percent). By 1998, as average incomes continued to grow, income became even more equal, as the ratio of the income of the richest to the poorest fell to 4.8 (= 37.5 percent/7.9 percent). The share of income received by the poorest rose slightly, while that of the richest quintile fell, much like on the downward sloping portion of a traditional Kuznets curve.

In Mexico, by comparison, in 1984, the ratio of the income of the richest 20 percent to the poorest was 13.6, falling to a multiple of 12.8 in 2002 (= 55.1/4.3). In Brazil, the ratio of income of the richest to the poorest income earners was 32.1 (67.5 percent/2.1 percent) for 1989 and 23.9 (= 62.1/2.6) as incomes became slightly more equal, reflecting economic strategies that helped to spread incomes somewhat more equitably (World Bank 1994: 220–1, Table 30, World Development Indicators 2006).

Incomes are certainly not equal in South Korea, but the degree of inequality between the rich and the poor is much lower than in any of the Latin American countries. Given the higher rates of growth and higher income in South Korea, it would seem that economic expansion over time has tended to promote, or at a minimum sustain, equity. This trend toward greater equity also has been strengthened by the spread effects of greater human capital accumulation reaching a broader spectrum of the population, especially through education, as we shall see in Chapter 12. **Shared growth** has been a fundamental component of the Korean state's strategy for sustaining economic growth and for legitimizing its policies. It is a goal and means to other goals from which other economies could and should take heed.

The South Korean and other East Asian states can certainly be faulted for certain excesses, but there also have been undeniable accomplishments that could, if emulated, help other countries poorer than the HPAEs make substantial progress out of extreme poverty and put them closer to achieving the Millennium Development Goals.[22] One does not have to go too far back in time to when Korean and Taiwanese per capita income levels were well below those of Mexico or Brazil; today the relation is reversed (see Focus 10.2). And even though we know quite well that per capita income is not all of what development is about, it *is* an important part of what development is about.

Subsequent strategy switches

Since the 1970s, both the East Asian economies and the larger Latin American economies have further altered their development strategies, again going in slightly different directions that have once again changed the nature of their path dependence, but with important and distinct consequences.

FOCUS 10.2 COMPARATIVE INCOMES: EAST ASIA AND LATIN AMERICA

Income levels of the HPAEs, though they started off in the 1950s substantially lower, now rival those in Latin America, where industrialization has had a longer history. For all the economies of East Asia and the Pacific, real per capita income was but 7 percent of Latin America and the Caribbean's in 1960. By 2004, the ratio of East Asia's real income to Latin America's had risen to nearly one-third, as per capita real incomes in East Asia rose by 790 percent and in Latin America by only 92 percent.

	GDP per person (constant 2000 $US)					
	1960	*1970*	*1980*	*1990*	*2000*	*2004*
East Asia and Pacific	141	175	273	481	952	1,254
Latin America and the Caribbean	2,035	2,616	3,568	3,261	3,853	3,917
Korea	1,110	1,912	3,221	6,615	10,884	12,762
Mexico	2,554	3,576	5,114	4,966	5,935	6,056

If we consider one major economy from each region, the table shows that whereas Korea's per capita income in 1960 was less than half of Mexico's, by 2004 the relationship had completely reversed, as South Korea's real income per person was more than double Mexico's. This is a powerful demonstration of how the different industrialization paths of East Asia and Latin America, one more optimal than the other, have affected the rates of growth and the levels of income of countries in each region.

Source: World Bank, World Development Indicators Online

Difficult ISI with difficult export substitution: East Asia's next strategy switch after easy export substitution

Even before the export substitution boom in consumer non-durables began to slow, Korea and Taiwan (and Japan before) entered a stage of state-promoted *difficult ISI accompanied by difficult export substitution* (Ranis 1981; World Bank 1993: 123–55). In selected industries like chemicals and machinery, electronics and automobiles, and other durable consumer goods from microwave ovens to refrigerators, the state assisted in the formation of industries with *backward linkages* to existing industrial sectors. These new difficult ISI industries operated behind substantial infant industry tariff and non-tariff barriers that shielded them from international competition as they initiated production, just as the easy ISI firms before them. But the state also required that these industries be prepared to export at an increasing rate over time *as a condition* of obtaining loans or subsidies to finance domestic production or any other special considerations. And these infant industry tariffs were not to be permanent either.

Over time, these more sophisticated goods with their higher value-added and higher wages began to be exported. Slowly they began to replace – substitute for – some of the non-durable exports of the previous phase of easy export substitution industrialization. Once again, the East Asian economies consciously worked to alter their export profile, replacing relatively simple non-durable consumer good exports with the ever more complex manufactured exports characteristic of difficult ISI. These exports also tended to have higher income elasticity values. With growth in incomes in the international economy, the demand for these goods could be expected to rise rapidly, contributing to the expansion of export income and national incomes (see Focus 10.3).

The East Asian state provided constant guidance and assistance to the private sector throughout these transformations, though with an important *quid pro quo* attached. Firms receiving state subsidies or privileged access to credit or special training or whatever cost-

---

FOCUS 10.3　CREATING DYNAMIC COMPARATIVE ADVANTAGE

Korean manufacturing giant Samsung Industries began making microwave ovens in the early 1970s in a cramped old laboratory, turning out a few hundred overpriced ovens annually for the heavily protected domestic market. This was the stage of difficult ISI in the economy. By the 1990s, Samsung was making 80,000 microwave ovens a week and ranked as the world's biggest producer. How did a Korean company with almost no experience manufacturing complex ovens beat better-financed and more experienced US and Japanese companies?

The government's Economic Development Board was a key player in Samsung's success. Government officials were keenly aware that the Republic of Korea could not rely forever on low-wage manufacturing. Just as the United States had lost countless textile industry jobs to Korea, they reasoned, so Korea would one day find it could no longer compete for labor-intensive manufacturing jobs with lower-wage neighbors such as China and Indonesia. To prepare for that day, government officials, working in consultation with the private sector, developed incentives for new knowledge- and capital-intensive industries. Incentives varied widely and included government-sponsored building of industrial parks, subsidized utilities, tax rebates for exports, and the provision of cheap loans for investment in new products. By 1980, urged forward by subsidies and incentives, Korean industry had moved into steel, ships, and even automobiles and was about to leap into world-class electronics.

Source: World Bank 1993: 130, Focus 3.3

saving advantage government benefits provided were expected to meet specific *performance standards*, particularly exporting targets, if they hoped to be recipients of state assistance in the future. Unproductive rent-seeking by the private sector thus was kept to a minimum, aided by the fact that most government bureaucrats were above being bribed, unlike in other countries. Firms could and did earn above normal economic profits, but they were permitted and assisted to do so with government help on the condition that the firms continue to meet the performance standards set by the state. When firms failed that test, they lost access to subsidized credit, marketing outlets, bank loans, and so on, usually wiping out their economic profit or worse. Thus the pressures to conform to government policy by the private sector were strong, and at the same time, this persuasion by government ensured that private decision-makers' goals tended to be consistent with those of the overall development strategy. Government programs helped firms in the private sector to prosper, but only if they played by the rules of the game, with exporting manufactured goods being the yardstick for measuring success. The result of this state intervention was a private sector that was forced and helped to become increasingly more efficient and productive, and the entire economy tended to benefit from the state–private partnership through shared growth and wide spread education initiatives.

Contests: rules, rewards, and referees

MIT economist Alice Amsden (1989, 1994) identified the importance of East Asia's use of a "performance-based allocation" system as central to their success. What Japan, Korea and Taiwan did was to create a structure, what she calls "contests," wherein there were *rules*, *rewards*, and *referees* for private firms wishing to gain access to, say, credit or a license to open a branch bank. To "win" a contest, a firm had to meet the performance standards set by government (the "rules") if there was any hope for the reward of above-normal profits (World Bank 1993: 93–102). Typically, one of the rules of the contests was sustained export performance, so that firms were forced, as a condition of obtaining special access to credit or tax benefits or exclusive licenses to produce something, to become and remain internationally competitive as revealed by their ability to export manufactured goods.

This has required firms to pay constant attention to learning about and utilizing best-practice knowledge and technology, to the upgrading of labor and management skills, and generally to increasing efficiency and decreasing costs per unit of output via the utilization of superior production methods, the best physical capital, and highly trained human capital. Contest-based competition among firms meant that the possibility of earning above-normal returns and monopoly profits via bribery and other unproductive activities were substantially reduced. Instead, above-normal economic returns became the reward for efficient performance, not corruption and rent-seeking, thus forcing productive activities to dominate. East Asian policy-makers chose to take the *high path* of improving the quality of production methods and of its factor inputs as the means to reduce costs as the means to compete internationally, rather than relying on the *low path* of holding costs down by keeping wages low as other less-developed countries have so often tried to do (Amsden 1994: 635).

The capacity to export and to expand exporting over time provided the yardstick for determining which firms had become efficient. Firms that attained international levels of efficiency could compete on world markets on the price-quality spectrum, and those that did so and met their export targets were rewarded with continued access to state assistance and special treatment. Thus the East Asian governments cooperated with and assisted private sector firms in ways that increased their private profits, but only if such firms were meeting the desired social goals of greater efficiency, productivity, employment, and other targets that contributed to overall social welfare. This sounds very much like Adam Smith's idea of harmony of interests at work in capitalism.

Key to the success of the contests was the integrity of the referees. These might be banks that provided credit or government bureaucrats in charge of economic development in the issuance of licenses, subsidies, tax breaks, or other special privileges. The creation of an honest, professional, and dedicated civil service seems absolutely essential to good policy-making. A corrupt and incompetent cadre of bureaucrats will result in poor quality policy, to no one's surprise. If this is not to occur, it is important that civil servants be relatively well-paid compared to what could be earned in comparable jobs in the private sector. The lower the relative income paid to members of the civil service, the lower will be the average level of competence and the higher the probability that "informal" income, that is, bribery and corruption, will permeate the system as a substitute for income earned on the job.

Any prestige and employment security that comes with a government job cannot fully compensate for incomes that are too low. In Taiwan, public sector salaries averaged about 60–5 percent of comparable private sector income; in South Korea, public sector income averaged 82–99 percent of private sector salaries; and in Singapore, where the civil service is highly regarded, public sector salaries often exceeded comparable private sector opportunity cost earnings. The relatively high incomes of the East Asian civil service compared to the private sector at least partly accounts for the higher average quality of these government administrators.

On the other hand, Argentina's public sector workers, at every level, received between 25 and 30 percent of what could be earned in the private sector, and in Somalia, the pay was less than 15 percent of private sector incomes (World Bank 1993: 177). Can countries that pay their civil servants at these levels expect to recruit and retain the best public sector workers possible? Should bad policy decisions, and perhaps endemic corruption, emanating from such civil servants be unexpected or surprising? Low pay for government lawyers or accountants or financial analysts, for example, will attract those unable to compete in the private sector, and their average level of ability will very likely be quite low. Such civil servants may be more tempted to accept bribes to supplement their incomes to levels closer to their better paid, but also more productive, colleagues in the private sectors. Low pay for civil service workers does not save government money, however. If anything, the cost to government and society from paying public sector workers less than comparable employment in terms of low quality, bad policy decisions, and corruption as civil servants boost their incomes via bribes and pay-offs is a multiple of what it would cost to attract higher-quality public employees whose decisions will be closer to the social optimum.

Of course, if less-developed countries have bloated public sectors and if public employment is being used to provide posts for urban workers with few other alternatives for employment, it is difficult to pay higher salaries. But the reason for over-staffing in public employment often reflects a failure of the existing development program to generate sufficient employment in the private sector for those migrating from the rural areas to the cities. What is required, then, for economies that have started import substitution industrialization is a strategy switch along the lines followed in East Asia. The need for a shift toward a labor-using easy export substitution strategy and the efficiency it promotes cannot be overstated. Then there can be a phase-out of excess government employment, as the industrial strategy begins to pay dividends in increased industrial employment as the export market creates additional demand, allowing domestic industries to continue to expand production.

With the ability to shrink public sector employment rationally rather than through wholesale lay-offs that neoliberal economic policy often demands, there can be a turn toward the recruitment to the public sector of competent and dependable civil servants who can rise within a *merit-based employment system*. It is this core of government bureaucrats who can, with some integrity and relatively insulated from pressures from the private sector, oversee the policies and programs that the state in late-developing economies must implement to assist the private sector in reaching maturity, with higher efficiency, increasing private sector employment, and shared growth as the goals.

If one thinks of a competent and honest civil service as part of the essential social infrastructure required to achieve a higher level of development, then this is another area for public investment which promises a very high pay-off in terms of the positive externalities which can be expected to accrue to society at large. The relatively high pay commanded by workers in key public administration sectors, such as budgeting, economic planning, oversight, and so on, will be well worth the expenditure if economic growth, productivity and efficiency are positively affected, for it will at least partly be the result of their efforts, ideas, and monitoring of the progress of the economy.

Export promotion: the Latin American economies avoid export substitution

When the larger Latin American economies shifted from easy ISI to difficult ISI, part of the rationale had been to try to reduce imports so as to improve the trade balance and to relieve the constant problem of insufficient foreign exchange. However, during difficult ISI, the demand for imported goods continued to expand, not only for imported industrial inputs required by the ISI industries. The demand for imports also expanded because of economic growth and rising incomes for manufactured goods and services the economy did not produce at all, or did not produce in the right quantities or with the desired qualities, such as televisions, computers, sporting goods, movies, insurance, wines and liquors, designer clothing, and foreign travel. Unfortunately, the ability to purchase the increased volume of imports desired by Latin American consumers was threatened because export income continued to be based on primary products which grew only very slowly and typically only by increasing the quantity of exports. The premature difficult ISI strategy in Latin America did not solve the balance of trade and foreign exchange problem by reducing total import expenditures. The basic problem of foreign exchange inadequacy increasingly revealed itself to be a *failure to export* and to *earn foreign exchange*. Saving foreign exchange was not a sufficient solution to the balance of trade dilemma for the Latin American economies.

The countries which prematurely initiated difficult ISI faced the realization that the possibility of further reducing imports via a deepening of the import substitution process could never generate sufficient foreign exchange savings relative to the foreign exchange that might be earned by *expanding* manufactured good exports. It was at this point that the larger Latin American economies, such as Brazil, Mexico, Chile, and Argentina, perceived that saving a unit of foreign exchange via import substitution was not always equivalent to the earning of a unit of foreign exchange via exporting. Saving foreign exchange generated a *one-time benefit* that could not overcome the problem of declining terms of trade that continued to afflict their traditional primary product exports. On the other hand, creating additional export capacity and shifting from primary to manufactured good exports could, year after year, provide *cumulative returns* in terms of foreign exchange earnings, particularly if the new exports were income elastic.

What the Latin American economies turned to in the 1960s and 1970s, however, was not easy export substitution as had been the case in the East Asian economies. Instead, they began to practice what Ranis (1981) called *export promotion*. The Latin American countries began adding on to the existing primary product export structure some specially-promoted manufactured good exports, but without the intention of reducing the importance of the primary product export base within the overall export structure. In other words, export promotion was not export substitution. There was not a fundamental *underlying* change in the structure of production that put less emphasis on traditional agriculture and more on labor-using manufacturing that might absorb the surplus labor in urban centers. Instead, manufactured exports were added on top of the primary product export base.

Nor was the export of manufactured goods the natural consequence of the maturing of a *domestic* entrepreneurial elite that had learned to be more efficient and internationally competitive over a period of time, as it was with the East Asian export-substitution experience. Export promotion was rather the consequence of special subsidies extended to multinational corporations to export some of their output to the world market.[23] The residual strength of the landed agriculture and mineral elite class contributed to the difficulty of fundamentally modifying the structure of both production and exports and moving toward a more dynamic and productive economy on a higher sustained path of growth and development (see Focus 10.4).

As we shall see, the larger Latin American economies and India were eventually forced by international forces to strategy switch to export substitution to varying degrees. Not all the Latin American economies have fully made this transformation; Mexico has perhaps been the most successful in getting the most out of the efficiency-enforcing effects of producing manufactured goods for the international market (Weiss and Jalilian 2004). The inefficiencies from maintaining protected ISI industries and failing to fundamentally shift from being primary product exporters to manufactured good exporters had become impossible to sustain. From the 1980s, as a result of the international debt crisis (Chapter 17), it became impossible.

FOCUS 10.4   REGIONAL TRADE ASSOCIATIONS

One way to expand the demand for manufactured and other goods, and thus perhaps reduce per unit costs of production by sliding down the average cost curve (remember Figure 9.1 in Chapter 9?), is through regional trade associations. Such arrangements give preferential treatment to goods traded among members of the association, usually reducing tariffs on traded goods to zero. This, of course, should increase exports and imports among members of the trade association and help economic growth.

Such trade groupings have proliferated and have different structures. Take a look at the on-line encyclopedia Wikipedia, and search for "trade bloc." Then look at the table for a "comparison of trade blocs." You will see that some of the regional associations are *free trade areas* (FTAs), others are *customs unions*, and yet others involve substantially more integration among members in a *common market* arrangement (like the European Union, EU). You should be able to identify the key differences between these different types of trade associations as to internal tariffs, tariffs with non-member nations, monetary and fiscal policy, immigration, and so on.

Sometimes these regional trade associations can be a force for positive change by enforcing more competition among members. In other cases, they may be a way in which regional elites can sustain economic growth in their countries by extending the market and increasing total output via exporting but without undertaking the fundamental reforms and policy switches that have been discussed in this and the previous chapter.

Continuing strategy switches

Figure 10.1 shows a fifth phase of transformation for the East Asian economies. They have begun to move toward even higher value-added production both for the domestic market and for export in knowledge- and technology-intensive industries, such as electronics, computer technology, software, biotechnology, communications equipment, precision instruments, and so on. These are "cutting-edge" industries and services with rapidly rising demand and excellent possibilities for future growth. These are industries that build upon the existing human capital base, and at the same time contribute to additional human capital accumulation via continued learning-by-doing.

There may even be a Stage 6 or 7 that will need to be added in the future to Figure 10.1. What the East Asian economies have done, as have successful developers in the past, is to climb the product cycle from simple goods to more complicated manufactured goods and services. This has been achieved via timely "strategy switches" promoted by innovative and flexible state policy which encouraged and allowed the private sector to continue to innovate and prosper with economy-wide spillover benefits. As proficiency is gained at each level of production, ascending to the next level has been made easier by past policies that have contributed to the creation of even more advantageous path dependence.

At the base of the East Asian success have been a series of beneficial past policy decisions: expanding educational opportunities; creating a competent civil service; creating mechanisms ("contests") to promote technological adaptation and efficiency in the private sector; and supportive government spending, advice, and policies to increase profitability of firms that contribute to overall social welfare.[24]

The Latin American and Indian economies still lag behind the most successful East Asian economies on account of past policy errors, though these were often the result of ingrained political pressures rooted in deep economic inequalities that continue to slow progress. Good policies require a political environment conducive to and accepting of change, which can

	Optimal (East Asia-type)	Sub-optimal (Latin American/India-type)
Stage 1	Primary production, pre-industrial *(agriculture-based)*	Primary production, pre-industrial *(agriculture-based)*
Stage 2	Easy ISI *(first industrial stage) (opening of economy begins)*	Easy ISI *(first industrial stage) (infant industry protection continued)*
Stage 3	Easy export substitution *(primary products replaced by manufactured exports)*	Premature difficult ISI *(infant industry protection continued; primary product exports still most important)*
Stage 4	Difficult ISI with secondary export substitution *(higher value-added manufactured goods replace non-durable consumer goods exports)*	Export promotion *(pushing out of manufactured exports; primary product exports not replaced or reduced in absolute significance)*
Stage 5	Knowledge-intensive production; ISI and export substituting continue in new, dynamic industries	Export substitution begins in non-durable and durable goods and in services as economies attempt to recover from skipped stages of industrialization

Figure 10.1 Stages of structural and industrial transformation and strategy switches.

Sources: Based on Ranis 1981; World Bank 1993: Chapter 3.

be difficult to achieve when political and economic elites are resistant to change. Along with many of the countries in Africa and the Middle East, the economies of India and Latin America need shifts in political power that can open the possibilities for even more positive and sustainable economic transformation.

What can other less-developed nations learn?

Many nations of Africa and South Asia have yet to proceed as far in their structural transformations as have the East Asian or the larger Latin American economies or India, which provide our recent historical insight. Without being over-simplistic ("If becoming developed is so easy would not every country be doing it?"), following a path similar to the general outlines of the optimal East Asian strategy in Figure 10.1 promises the best outcome in a relatively open, growing world economy.

Small economies face special problems associated with market size, but even these can use the East Asian prototype as a guide to structural transformation by focusing on a limited range of ISI products and then expanding into exporting as efficiency levels are improved. For small economies, regional trade arrangements may be essential so that economies of scale become feasible and the benefits of learning-by-doing can contribute to the overcoming of transitional inefficiencies prior to beginning to export to the world market. Larger economies with a higher level of domestic demand have more opportunities for both import substitution and exporting, but they also face more potential pitfalls, especially if they are land or natural resource rich and those resources are owned by a relatively small elite, as our discussion of the resource curse suggested.

As Gerschenkron (1962) stressed in his famous *Economic Backwardness in Historical Perspective*, no nation can or should attempt to duplicate the success story of any other. Nations have been able to *build* on the accomplishments of other nations, often skipping over, and learning from, the arduous steps taken by path-breaking nations. Thus, Table 10.1 is not a blueprint for "how to develop," so much as a source of guidance for thinking about the sequence of structural change that has been most beneficial in a growing, relatively open international economy.

Institutions matter

What a close study of the differences between the more successful East Asian economies and the less prosperous larger Latin American economies reveals is how important sound policy-making by government and the private sector is to creating cycles of virtuous change. The institutions of society, the soft infrastructure, profoundly matter, from the civil service, to banks, to educational institutions, to professional bodies, like accountancy organizations, to the importance placed on honesty in business and personal relations, and so on. As Amsden (1994: 632) put it:

> Since East Asia has had some of the highest growth rates of output and productivity in the world, and since East Asia provides no evidence that any other set of policies is as good or better than its own set, why not advise developing countries the world over to adopt a variant of the East Asian model? ... why not use the [World] Bank's awesome powers of conditionality to help other countries to build the institutions and skills necessary to adopt, modify and effectively implement East Asia's approach to suit their own needs?

In other words, what other late-developers would be advised to do is to create the building blocks of the proper institutional structures that can allow them, using their human capital, physical capital, and financial resources, to replicate a variant of the East Asian experience. These institutions are pre-conditions or co-requisites of more rapid development, and what Amsden is suggesting is that the international community, especially the World Bank and other international institutions, assist countries to construct these building blocks. This can be done with the "stick" of withholding aid when such institutions are not created as planned or promised and the "carrot" of lower interest rates, easier repayment schedules, debt reduction, marketing assistance, technological sharing mechanisms, and other perquisites extended to the private sector which can lead, as the East Asian economies have shown, to rapid "performance-based" results.

Where we are headed, where we have been

Figure 10.2 schematically shows how institutions, policies, and an economy's endowments interact to contribute to the structural transformations that are aimed at achieving a society's goals of development.

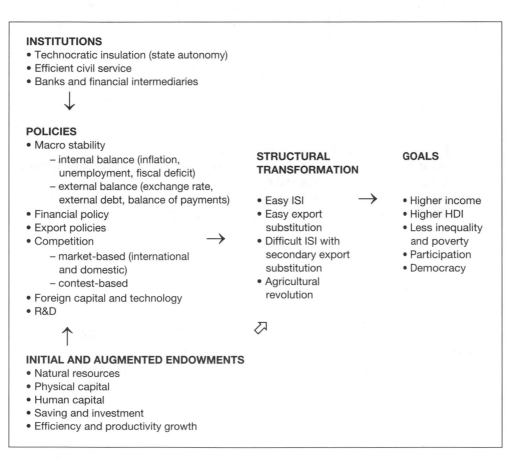

Figure 10.2 The transition to development.

Source: Adapted from World Bank 1993: 88, Figure 2.1.

To read Figure 10.2, begin from the right-hand side, Goals. These were enumerated in Chapter 2; they are the ends toward which society is directed. Moving to the left in the figure, we see that achieving these goals requires fundamental structural transformation in the productive and export structure of an economy. This structural transformation is affected both by the policies of state and by the initial and augmented resource endowments of the economy and society (with augmented endowments contributing to changing comparative advantage via state policy and as a consequence of individual decisions, e.g., education and entrepreneurs producing new goods and services). Society's institutions, only three of which are listed here, affect the efficiency of policy-making and hence the nature of the structural transformation.

In Chapters 9 and 10, we considered the industrial side of the structural transformation. In Chapter 11, the agricultural aspect will be examined. Chapter 8 considered the importance of augmenting resource endowments such as human capital accumulation, technology, and research and development (R&D) to the overall development process, themes which are examined in more detail in Chapters 12 and 13. The issues surrounding macroeconomic policy, the role of multinational corporations, financial policies, and aid are examined in Chapters 14–17.

Figure 10.2 serves to remind us that the goals of development are attained only through a complex web of institutions, policies, and endowments interacting, and at times conflicting, which impact on the structural transformation leading to the desired ends. There is much to do and much that can go wrong, but the essentials of what is required to move from being less developed to higher levels of income and human development are relatively well-defined.

Questions and exercises

1
     a   Explain what is meant by a foreign exchange shortage.
     b   What is it that typically causes such a shortage of foreign currency for LDCs during their easy ISI phase of industrialization?
     c   When does a foreign exchange *shortage* become a foreign exchange *crisis*?
     d   What, in general, do countries need to do to overcome a foreign exchange crisis situation in the future?

2   What is meant by a strategy switch? Why are strategy switches an important component of good policy-making?

3   Define easy export substitution. What exactly is being substituted for what?

4   Define difficult ISI. In what sense do we say that the Latin American countries entered this stage "prematurely" while the East Asian economies entered this stage "maturely?" What potential problems are there for countries which follow easy ISI with difficult ISI, thus skipping the export substitution stage of transformation?

5   Go to http://hdr.undp.org/hdr2006/statistics/data/ and choose "Data by Country" (you may need to change 2006 to 2007, etc. in the URL). Choose an LDC that interests you, or which you are assigned, from the drop-down menu and click on "Data."

     a   Then go to category 16 and make a table showing primary exports (as percentage of merchandise exports) for the two years in the table; manufacturing exports (as percentage of merchandise exports) for the two years in the table; and high technology exports (as percentage of manufactured exports) for the two years in the table.

b   List the terms of trade for the year in the table; what is the base year?

c   What story does this data tell you about the *particular stage of industrialization* your country might be in using Table 10.1 as a guide to the stages? Explain what it is about the data you collected in parts a and b that makes you think your country is in the stage of industrialization you have identified.

6

a   Explain why a country that is currently a primary commodity exporter and that has a relatively large land area and abundant natural resources might be more likely to remain a primary product exporter compared to another country, which is also now a primary product exporter, but which lacks abundant land and other natural resources.

b   Do abundant resources *necessarily* act as a brake on the evolution of the economic structure (this is the *resource curse* issue)?

c   Under what conditions might natural resources and abundant land be a blessing for future growth possibilities? Might there be a difference in terms of the "resource curse" effect between countries which have abundant *but equitably* owned natural resources and those with abundant but *unequally* owned resources where control is concentrated in a small elite?

7   Explain the importance of the easy export substitution stage of industrial transformation as a means to absorb labor from less productive sectors, particularly agriculture. Why is it that this stage is able to absorb more labor than the difficult ISI stage? (Hint: think about how goods are produced.) What other benefits are there to easy export substitution compared to premature difficult ISI as a stage of industrialization to follow after easy ISI?

8   How were the East Asian economies able to avoid unproductive rent-seeking by industrialists interested in earning above-normal profits who might have wanted to extend infant industry protection via the payment of bribes to government officials, while the Latin American economies seemed unable to avoid such costs? What role do "contests" play in reducing unproductive rents? Explain.

9   A competent, merit-based civil service system seems indispensable for making good policy. What steps can governments take to implement such a civil service system if one is not in place? What obstacles might be expected to be encountered in overhauling the existing civil service system in countries where corruption seems endemic?

10   One of the buzz-word issues amongst policy experts in recent years has been "transparency." This has to do with the openness and fairness with which government, in particular, carries out its activities. Are the same rules/laws/policies applied to everyone? Are the rules/laws/policies clear and worth more than the paper on which they are written? How much corruption is there? In other words, does government operate in a "transparent" way so that the "rules of the game" are fairly applied? Go to http://www.transparency.org and open the Corruption Perceptions Index (CPI) file. Record the CPI value for China, India, Korea, the UK, Nigeria, Mexico, Saudi Arabia, and one other country that interests you. What does the CPI value tell you? What are the critical cut-off values of the CPI?

11   Some observers believe that the East Asian countries have succeeded because they have followed a policy sometimes called "shared growth." Explain what shared growth is, how countries might achieve it, and why shared growth might be expected to contribute to a more rapid pace of economic development.

12
    a   What role can foreign direct investment (FDI) and multinational corporations (MNCs) play in the industrialization process as economies pass through the different stages summarized in Figure 10.1? Are they a positive force or a negative force?

    b   How was the experience with FDI and MNCs different in the East Asian development experience and in Latin America and India? Were FDI and MNCs helpful or harmful? Discuss.

13 Might some cultures or religions be more accepting of fundamental structural change than others? What evidence is there to support your viewpoint?

Notes

1   For any particular commodity, the impact of aggregate income growth on demand for that good will depend on the income elasticity of that individual good, as well as any changes in the distribution of income affecting consumption patterns.

2   Consumer goods imports, even of non-durables, are unlikely to ever be fully replaced by domestic production. There will always be some goods, say, for example, Scotch whisky, that are not produced domestically. Further, more expensive consumer non-durables, including brand names not licensed for production in the local economy, will continue to be imported for the consumption of those with higher incomes willing and able to pay both higher prices and any tariffs imposed on such items. Durable consumer goods – like home appliances, motor cars, computers – will also be part of total imports.

3   The *import coefficient* is equal to M/GDP, where *M* is the value of total imports. It is the share of total income spent on imports.

4   You will remember from the previous chapter and the discussion in Chapter 6 around the Prebisch-Singer hypothesis that balance of payments problems as a result of the difficulties in importing and exporting during war and economic crisis had pushed the larger Latin American economies on the road to easy ISI by the 1930s. In fact, it has been balance of payment crises that most often force countries to rethink and alter their strategies of economic development. This is another example of how imbalances and disequilibriums can be functional in identifying problem areas in an economy that need attention. At times, for example, with an imbalance between the quantity demanded and the quantity supplied of laundry soap, the market can most easily, efficiently, and rapidly resolve the disequilibrium. In other instances, as when the complex of economic policies guiding an economy are creating imbalances, the state will have to take some sort of action to change the direction of path dependence. This functional change undertaken by means of government policy we refer to as a *strategy switch*.

5   There is one other option: the use of an economy's foreign exchange savings or official foreign exchange reserves. The balance of payments is examined in more detail in Chapter 15. We are simplifying greatly here by assuming there are no other flows of foreign exchange in the current account besides exports and imports.

6   Chapter 16 examines the issue of external debt in detail.

7   Alternatively, we could say that each strategy creates new forms of path dependence, with one a progressive and transformative path and the other much less so. We say this realizing that the optimal path depends upon the existence of a growing world economy and relatively open trade among countries. The first condition is met over the longer term, if not always in the short-run. Relatively open and free trade among nations has been institutionalized only since the end of the Second World War, especially via the various "rounds" of talks of the General Agreement on Tariffs and Trade (GATT), which have reduced border restrictions on trade by slashing tariffs and, to a lesser degree, non-tariff barriers. If, in future, the open trade system closes, a new optimum strategy of development may need to be discovered and implemented.

    The GATT was replaced in 1995 by the World Trade Organization (WTO), a more formal and ostensibly more powerful institutional structure for maintaining an open international trade system. The WTO (and the GATT before it) is the trade "leg" of the tripartite international institutional structure for overseeing international economic relations among nations forged at Bretton Woods in 1944. The other two "legs" are the International Monetary Fund (IMF), concerned with exchange rates and balance of payments issues, and the International Bank for Reconstruction and Development (the World Bank), responsible for issues related to economic development. There is more about this division of labor among international agencies in Chapter 17.

8 Such selective interventions by government are considered "market friendly" by the World Bank (1991, 1993) in that they assist the market in doing what it would do if there were not substantial market imperfections. The World Bank has cautiously recommended such stimuli but recognizes that to be effective the preconditions for their success must be in place, including an effective and relatively incorruptible government bureaucracy and constant monitoring of the results of such selective intervention in meeting the goals of structural transformation and development.

In the opinion of some area specialists, like Wade (1990) and Amsden (1989), such interventions by government in East Asia have been more than simply market friendly. Wade terms the East Asian development strategy as one of "*governing the market*" through a variety of practices, some of which are discussed in the latter parts of this and other chapters. Such practices, it is suggested, have allowed the East Asian economies to improve upon what even a perfectly functioning competitive economy would have achieved by *bending* the allocation of productive resources in more dynamic directions than would have been achieved by the market alone. By governing the market, it may be possible to outperform what a perfectly functioning market would achieve. These policies are the "carrot" rewarding firms for becoming more efficient, and they work alongside the "stick" of reduced infant industry tariffs.

9 Nations with large domestic markets have more room for maneuver. A large domestic market means, assuming there are a number of firms in each ISI industry, that the forces of domestic competition for market share can complement the external threat of eventual foreign competition as infant industry protection is withdrawn. In such economies, like Brazil or China, domestic competition also can be a spur to greater productivity (Pazos 1985–6). Even in these economies, however, a reduction of tariff and other protection would still seem to be warranted to ensure that international efficiency levels are approached.

10 There are three developed countries with a high level of primary product exports rather than manufactured goods exports: Australia, New Zealand, and Norway. However, production in these economies is quite diversified, and there has been an evolution over time in the nature of the particular primary products exported. In other words, these countries did not remain with static comparative advantage in one or a few primary product exports but rather the primary product pattern adapted to changing external circumstances and evolving domestic comparative advantage (Lewis 1989: 1596). It may be the case that some less-developed countries can follow such a path of non-traditional primary product exporting. One such example may be Chile, which has had rising income per capita with a continued high level of primary, but diversified and changing, exports (see Focus 9.1 in the previous chapter).

11 Exports, X, are a component of the total output and income of an economy, since $Y = C + I + G + (X - M)$. Thus, increasing X, all else constant, will increase an economy's total GDP and aggregate income level. You will remember from Chapter 2, Focus 2.5, that China's rapid economic expansion since the 1980s has been driven by exports, something that worries some analysts, since the domestic market is playing a smaller and smaller role.

12 We emphasize the role of exports and the foreign trade sector, because nations must have some strategy to overcome the foreign exchange shortage that comes with easy ISI. The imbalance between import spending and export earnings need to be resolved or foreign exchange shortages will lead to increased external indebtedness and, eventually, a cessation of economic growth, as discussed at the beginning of the chapter.

Nonetheless, for any nation with a sizeable population, production for the *domestic market* will remain an important factor for long-term economic growth. In South Korea, for example, which is often put forward as an exemplar of economic growth, roughly 70 percent of all economic activity takes place within the national economy.

Although conventional wisdom often has argued that South Korea's rapid economic growth has been the consequence of its success in exporting, it is important to keep in mind that a relatively large and growing domestic economy can generate economies of scale in industry and that a viable export capability *typically follows from and builds upon* successful performance in the domestic economy as a result of the easy ISI stage of industrialization.

Actually, causality runs both ways: exports can stimulate the growth of the local economy, and the growth of the domestic economy can strengthen a nation's capacity to export via higher levels of investment, technology and research, training, education and so on, which improve productivity and increase competitiveness on the international market. Domestic and international markets are complementary to one another.

13 Income elasticity measures the relative change in consumption of a good resulting from a change in income. Technically, the income elasticity, E_Y, of good Z, is

$$E_Y = (\% \, \Delta Q_Z) \div (\% \, \Delta Y),$$

where ΔQ_Z is the change in the consumption of good Z and ΔY is the change in income, Y. If $E_Y > 0$, Z is a "normal good," meaning that as income increases, consumption of good Z also increases. If $E_Y < 0$, Z is an "inferior good," meaning that as income increases, the consumption of good Z decreases.

For normal goods, if $0 < E_Y < 1$, as income increases the consumption of the good rises, but by less in percentage terms than income rises. If $E_Y > 1$, the consumption of good Z increases faster, in per cent terms, than income increases. It is this category of "superior or luxury normal goods" that, over time, a country would like to expand within its overall export mix.

Technically, a country would like to have the sum of the weighted average of the income elasticities of all its export goods exceed one. Then, as world income increases, spending on that country's exports in the aggregate also will rise.

14 Based on an econometric study, William Cline has issued a cautionary warning about the generality of this process. He argues that the East Asian export strategy cannot be universalized for all less-developed nations. His results suggest that increasing manufactured exports in a manner similar to that achieved in the East Asian nations would require the industrial nations to import about 60 percent of their manufactured products from the developing nations. Cline argued that the less-developed nations had, by the early 1980s, reached a threshold level with their manufactures and that further incursions into the world market for manufactures would call forth a protectionist response from the more-developed economies (Cline 1988). This possibility has not yet materialized, as the international market appears to date to be able to absorb an increasing flow of traded goods.

From 1950–73, the volume of the world's exports rose by 8.6 percent per year; in the period 1973–9, this growth rate slowed to 4.8 percent, leading to the pessimism expressed by Cline. However, over the 1990–2004 period, world exports have increased at a robust 7.1 percent annual rate (Maddison 1982: 60, Table 3.7; IMF 1995: 3; World Development Indicators 2006). Given that the latter growth rate is calculated on a growing volume of trade, it does not appear that the market for exports is in danger of drying up. And there is no reason it should, as long as world incomes continue to rise over time.

15 Total exports are the sum of merchandise and service exports.

16 We say "partially explain," since the HPAEs have different endowments from other regions. We know, for example, from the studies of endogenous growth in Chapter 8, that the East Asian economies have a higher average level of human capital accumulation than other regions (this is considered again in Chapter 12). They also have had lower average inflation rates; have not had seriously over-valued exchange rates (Chapter 15); have a lesser degree of income inequality (Chapter 8); and policy-makers have generally been more adept at designing appropriate policies for growth and development, in implementing and monitoring them, and in changing policies when required to maintain the pace of both growth and development. So, there are other significant factors that contribute to overall development success besides transitioning from one stage of industrialization to another.

17 Recalling our discussion of external *barriers* to growth in Chapter 1, it is important to recognize that *timing* can be a major determinant in the choice of a development strategy. In the early 1950s, when the Latin American economies faced balance of payments crises and foreign exchange shortages due to the easy ISI strategy that required a change in economic strategy, the global economy was relatively closed, with Europe and Japan still recovering from the Second World War. Consequently, the *absorption capacity* for additional manufactured products from the less-developed economies in the international economy was highly constrained.

By the early 1960s, however, as a result of the success of reducing tariff barriers between nations and other efforts to achieve greater openness, the East Asian economies were able to ride the crest of a new wave of trade expansion when they faced the need to alter their economic strategy to handle their easy ISI balance-of-payments crises. At this *turning point*, however, the Latin American nations failed to take advantage of an historical opportunity in which they too might have advanced their economic strategy by shifting to an export substitution phase of industrialization in certain sectors.

18 From basic macroeconomics, the *income multiplier* determines the maximum change in total output and income in an economy from a one unit change in total investment (or any autonomous spending). In the simplest formulation, the income multiplier = $1/(1 - MPC) = 1/MPS$, where MPC is the marginal propensity to consume and MPS is the marginal propensity to save. Thus, if the MPC = 0.95 (95 percent of an additional £1 of income is spent on consumption), then the maximum income multiplier = $1/(1 - 0.95) = 1/(0.05) = 20$. An increase of £5 million of investment would have a maximum effect of increasing total output and income by £100 million. In more realistic, but similar, calculations, the income multiplier's maximum value will be reduced by any "leakages" from the domestic spending stream, for example, for imports or for taxes.

The *employment multiplier* measures the change in employment resulting from a change in income or total output. The size of the employment multiplier depends upon the capital–labor ratio of the economy, the *incremental capital output ratio* (ICOR) and the pace of change in total output. Thus,

$$\Delta L = \Delta L / \Delta K \times \Delta K / \Delta Y \times \Delta Y$$

which says that the change in employment, ΔL, is equal to the change in the inverse of the incremental capital–labor ratio *times* the change in the incremental capital–output ratio *times* the change in output.

Crowding-in refers to the stimulus to additional investment following from some initial investment. For example, investment in the production of motor cars may stimulate investments in battery production or glass to supply the motor car industry. This description of how an industrial structure evolves should sound familiar; it is the linkage, or strategic disequilibrium, perspective associated with Albert Hirschman's unbalanced growth theory considered in Chapter 5.

19 This shift in control over production was especially evident where MNCs tended to enter the local market through the purchase of existing production facilities, thus "denationalizing" the production process and replacing domestic capitalists with foreign capitalists (see Chapter 14).

20 These often are the economy's most skilled workers, with a higher than average level of training and education. They work in more capital-intensive activities, and their level of productivity and income tend to be higher. On the other hand, being capital-intensive, such industries cannot absorb the continued growth of the labor force arriving in the cities at a pace greater than the absorption capacity of these industries. If the easy ISI firms are no longer expanding as a result of demand limited to the domestic market, then the only place for rural migrants to go is into informal sector activities.

21 And even in the larger economies, such as Brazil and India, with large internal markets, the forces of internal competition amongst enterprises in the same industry was not always sufficient to assure a high level of technological competency.

22 South Korea repressed labor by banning labor unions and strike activity that helped to keep wages lower and contributed to the extended period of labor-intensive production in the easy ISI and easy export substitution stages of industrialization. And there is abundant evidence of high-level corruption of government officials that no one can condone. Still, neither direct labor repression (as opposed to wage restraint) nor corruption seem central to the success of South Korea's economy over the past five decades and even less so over the past decade or so.

23 For a discussion of Mexico's troubled export promotion program and its reliance on MNCs, see Cypher (1994).

24 It would take an entire book, or various books, to detail all the different microeconomic policies a country might implement in pursuit of its development goals. A careful reading of the World Bank's study (1993) of the HPAEs can provide a wealth of specifics on policies that have worked and on others which have been less successful. Policy-makers truly interested in taking positive strides toward better decisions could do worse than to *carefully* study that volume.

References

Amsden, Alice. 1989. *Asia's Next Giant: South Korea and Late Industrialization*. New York: Oxford University Press.

——. 1994. "Why Isn't the Whole World Experimenting with the East Asian Model to Develop?: Review of *The East Asian Miracle*," *World Development* 22 (April): 627–35.

Banamex. 1994. "Income Distribution," *Review of the Economic Situation in Mexico* (April): 170–90.

Cline, William R. 1988. "Can the East Asian Model of Development be Generalized?," pp. 282–97 in Charles Wilber and Keith Jameson (eds.), *The Political Economy of Development and Underdevelopment*, 4th edn. New York: Random House.

Cypher, James. 1994. "Mexico's Export Promotion Policies," pp. 191–216 in Paul Ganster (ed.), *Changes in US-Mexican Economic Relations*. Mexico City: UAM-Profmex-Anuies.

Edwards, Sebastian. 1992. "Trade Orientation, Distortions and Growth in Developing Countries," *Journal of Development Economics* 39: 31–57.

Gerschenkron, Alexander. 1962. *Economic Backwardness in Historical Perspective*. Cambridge, MA: Harvard University Press.

IMF (International Monetary Fund). 1995. *World Economic Outlook* (May). Washington, D.C.: IMF.

Lewis, Jr., Stephen R. 1989. "Primary Exporting Countries," Chapter 29 in Hollis B. Chenery and T.N. Srinivasan (eds.), *Handbook of Development Economics*, vol. ii. Amsterdam: North Holland Publishers.

Luedde-Neurath, Richard. 1988. "State Intervention and Export-oriented Development in South Korea," Chapter 3 in Gordon White (ed.), *Developmental States in East Asia*. New York: St. Martin's Press.

Maddison, Angus. 1982. *Phases of Capitalist Development*. Oxford: Oxford University Press.

Pazos, Felipe. 1985–6. "Have Import Substitution Policies Either Precipitated or Aggravated the Debt Crisis?," *Journal of Interamerican Studies and World Affairs* 27 (Winter): 57–73.

Ranis, Gustav. 1981. "Challenges and Opportunities Posed by Asia's Superexporters: Implications for Manufactured Exports from Latin America," *The Quarterly Review of Economics and Business* 21 (Summer): 204–26.

Sachs, Jeffrey D. 2005. *The End of Poverty*. London: Penguin Books.

Wade, Robert. 1990. *Governing the Market: Economic Theory and the Role of Government in East Asian Industrialization*. Princeton: Princeton University Press.

Weiss, John and Hossein Jalilian. 2004. "Industrialization in an Age of Globalization: Some Comparisons Between East and South Asia and Latin America," *Oxford Development Studies* 32 (June): 283–307.

World Bank. 1991. *World Development Report 1991*. Oxford: Oxford University Press.

——. 1993. *The East Asian Miracle*. Oxford: Oxford University Press.

——. 1994. *World Development Report 1994*. Oxford: Oxford University Press.

——. 2002. *World Development Indicators 2002*. Online.

——. 2006. *World Development Indicators 2006*. Online.

11 Agriculture and development

After reading and studying this chapter, you should better understand:

- the significance of the triple biases confronting agriculture: urban bias, gender bias, and landlord bias;
- why agricultural development is crucially dependent on governmental infrastructure investments;
- the extent and nature of the difficulties faced by mono-exporters of primary products;
- the special conditions and behavioral responses to economic variables of peasant cultivators and the concept of "de-agrarianization";
- the nature of environmental problems in the agricultural sector, including issues of erosion and deforestation, the "circle of poison" effect, and the dispute over property rights and resource depletion;
- the structural barriers created by historically defined land tenure systems;
- the Green Revolution's achievements and limitations and the prospects for a Transgenic/Biotech Revolution;
- the compelling logic of a pro-poor, "Ag first" development strategy;
- the nature of large-scale agricultural enterprises;
- the developmental limitations of plantation economies and the promise and limits of transnational agribusiness;
- the elements of successful land reform and its role in undergirding development strategies.

Introduction

Most people in the developing regions are either cultivators, farm laborers, or relatively small-scale producers of services or manufactured goods in the countryside. In 1970, 75 percent of the population of low- and middle-income countries lived in rural areas; by 2004, this share had fallen to 58 per cent. As we saw in Chapter 9, there is a strong inverse relationship between a nation's level of per capita income and the size of the population living and at work in agriculture. In 2004/5, 70 percent of the population in "low-income" nations with average per capita income of US$ 585 per year were located in the rural sector – 2.4 billion people – whereas in the "middle-income countries" with average per capita income of $2,600 per year, the rural population accounted for only 47 percent of the total population (World Bank 1994: 222–3, Table 31; UNDP 2001: 157; UNDP 2006: 300; World Bank 2007). In absolute terms in 1993 there were over 2.2 billion people involved in agriculture as producers, while another 800 million lived in rural areas; by 2004 the total rural population was essentially the same, 2.94 billion. Despite the large proportion of the population living and working in rural areas, mostly in farming activities, agriculture contributes a relatively small share of total gross domestic product.

This is why incomes are low for countries with large rural populations; agriculture tends to be a sector which generates low value-added in production. For example, among the "low-income countries," only 21.5 percent of total GDP was produced by agriculture in 2005, despite the fact that (as mentioned) 70 percent of the population lived in rural areas – most involved in agricultural production (UNDP 2006: 300; World Bank 2007). This relationship clearly highlights one of the major issues in development: the pervasiveness of low agricultural productivity. Despite this obvious problem, agricultural development is rarely the central focus of most development strategies. Why?

In studies of the development patterns of what are today the more developed nations, as was discussed in Chapter 9, it has been demonstrated that agriculture has shrunk dramatically both in terms of the percentage of the labor force occupied in this sector and of the contribution of the sector to total output. In this context agriculture has been viewed primarily as a provider of labor to industry, to the government sector, and to the service sector of the economy during the structural transformation process. Such a perspective was dramatically reinforced by the Lewis model, where agricultural labor was treated as redundant, having a very low, or even zero, marginal product. The general tendency in development economics to overlook the significance of agriculture has been of major concern to many agricultural specialists. John Mellor has noted that "it is surprising that the principal broad conceptualizations in development economics have not articulated a central place for agriculture" (Mellor 1998a: 136).

Today agriculture in the developing nations is caught in a three-way struggle. There is overwhelming pressure to transform the sector via market-driven forces toward the production of higher value-added "non-traditional" crops destined for export and the urban areas. At the same time pressures are building to address concerns for social justice, including advancing strategies to confront food insecurity (chronic malnutrition) and alter inequitable land tenure systems via land reform – both are matters that cannot be resolved through market-driven strategies. And, third, there is pressure to introduce more environmentally sustainable forms of farm management (including organic production) as issues of soil depletion, pesticide use, climate change, deforestation and desertification, soil compaction, and increasing water scarcity are treated with greater consideration.

During the 1990s the rate of growth of agricultural production dropped dramatically in relation to the 1980s, yet the consequences of this decline were partially mitigated by strong reductions in population growth rates. For the 2.4 billion people living in "low-income countries" (per capita GNP averaging only $410 in 1999) annual agricultural growth fell from 3 percent per year in the 1980s to 2.5 percent In the 1990s – a drop in the growth rate of 17 percent. The population growth rate fell by slightly less (13 percent), leaving the food situation, on the whole, somewhat more critical (World Bank 2000/1: 275, 279, 295). This discouraging trend should be considered in context – some 840 million people suffered from chronic malnutrition in 1996, and most lived in rural areas, with the figure dropping by only 20 million in 2006 (Staatz and Eichner 1998: 8; FAO 2006). More disturbing was the trend of the 1990s for "middle-income countries" (nations with an average per capita income of $2,000 in 1999). In these nations – then comprising 2.7 billion people – while population growth rates fell by an impressive 29 percent in the 1990s compared to the 1980s, the growth of agricultural output slowed more dramatically – from 3.5 percent per year in the 1980s to 2.0 percent in the 1990s (a staggering 43 percent drop in the growth rate). Nonetheless, these nations retained a strong edge over their population growth rates, as food output continued to grow at a rate that was forty percent faster than population growth (Table 11.1). Recent years have brought some changes to these trends. Population growth rates continue to drop, but much more strongly in middle-income nations, as Table 11.1 shows. But in the crucial area of output growth, for the low-income countries production has come close to stagnating (1.3 percent growth from 2000–5) falling substantially behind population growth rates. Much of this crisis situation relates to Sub-Saharan Africa, where many farmers cannot now afford fertilizers which they once almost universally applied, along with problems of soil degradation. In an otherwise generally positive environment for developing nations in recent years, this advancing crisis in food production is unquestionably a critical issue, particularly for Africa.[1] Middle-income nations, however, have substantially improved their level of food production, with rates of growth outstripping population growth rates by a ratio of 3:1.

As the world's population continues to shift out of agriculture in the coming years the need to increase food output at a rate faster than the rate of population growth will continue. It Is currently anticipated that the food needs of developing nations will increase substantially from 2005–15, primarily because it is thought that the two-thirds of all population growth in this period will be that of the urban population in developing nations – global population is anticipated to rise by 750 million in these years to reach a level of 7.2 billion (OECD-FAO 2006: 25). With cultivatable areas now considered to be largely fixed, higher productivity will be required to meet the food challenge to come, particularly since in relative terms there will be in the near future fewer and fewer cultivators. For reasons explored below, growing yields may be sufficient, yet the issue of **food security** – having the means to buy or receive an adequate diet – will remain a critical problem for hundreds of millions of primarily agrarian cultivators and laborers and their dependants. Malnutrition contributes directly to one-half of the annual deaths of the world's children, perhaps the most brutal expression of the lack of food security, an issue strongly associated with the rural population (Stringer 2001: 80–1).

Table 11.1 Declining growth rate in agricultural output in low-income countries

	Low-income nations	*Middle-income nations*
GNP per capita (2005)	$585[a]	$2,600
Population (2005)	2.4 billion	3.1 billion
Annual population growth		
1980–90	2.3 percent	1.7 percent
1990–99	2.0 percent	1.2 percent
2000–5	1.9 percent	0.9 percent
Agricultural output growth		
1980–90	3.0 percent	3.5 percent
1990–99	2.5 percent	2.0 percent
2000–5	1.3 percent	2.8 percent

Source: World Bank 2000/1: 275, 279, 295; 2007.

Note
a US dollars.

Urban bias and landlord bias

The relative neglect of agriculture may be partly explained by the theory of "**urban bias**." This perspective, pioneered by Michael Lipton (1977), argues that agriculture receives relatively little attention in the implementation of most development strategies, as a result of a complex of social forces and processes operating both in the developing and in the developed nations. As a rule, the leading economic strategists and policy-makers in less-developed nations live in the capital city or some other major urban area. They have relatively little contact with and little knowledge of day-to-day activities in the rural sector. Not only are they physically divorced from the rural areas, they are also intellectually trained in a Western academic paradigm which has little concern with or understanding of backward agricultural regions. Development is equated with industrialization, and industrialization has been predominantly an urban phenomenon. Hence, this urban bias leads to a neglect of the rural agricultural sector. Urban bias can be and has been quantified: Maurice Schiff and Alberto Valdés found that for a sample of eighteen developing nations, had the governments of these nations *not* imposed policies that were adverse to the interests of the countryside (but supportive of urban interests) the domestic terms of trade (the price of agricultural products over time measured against the price of urban produced goods and services) would have been 43 percent higher in the 1960–85 period (Schiff and Valdés 1998: 228). In spite of the fact that the research of Schiff and Valdés shows clearly that nations which have a low bias against agriculture demonstrate (1) lower rates of migration from agriculture – into the belts of urban misery; (2) increased investment by cultivators; (3) greater technological adaptation; and (4) *higher economic growth*, the bias against adequate support for agriculture remains.

As a complement to urban bias, economists and others studying the countryside have developed the concept of "landlord bias." In often remote areas of the countryside a small elite of landlords may exercise a high degree of power, particularly when rural areas interact with the central state and its agencies. Landlord bias can stall land reform initiatives (discussed below), they can exercise power over the local labor market to drive down farm laborer wages, they can insure that schemes of irrigation and flood control inordinately help their farmlands, and they can often derive the lion's share of benefits to improve the agrarian infrastructure. Whether the issue be one of tariff policies, credit available to the agricultural sector, R&D, agricultural extension, or any other, frequently the small quotient of attention and support received by the rural areas is perhaps the most unequal form of any allocation of resources in a developing nation.

Culture and caste

The relative neglect of agriculture is often traceable to the quite strong sense of a cultural divide prevalent in many poor nations. Small cultivators are often depicted pejoratively as "peasants," "tribal peoples," indigenous people, or lower-level caste groups; they often are the "others" who speak a different language or dialect, wear traditional clothing, and live in a milieu that is to a very great degree seen as primitive and beneath those who occupy positions of political, social, and economic power both in the advanced industrial nations and in the poor developing nations themselves. Wide disparities in income between ethnic groups and those of the dominant group often reflect the pervasiveness and depth of urban bias, as well as cultural and class differences (see Focus 11.1). For example, male Bolivian Indians have an average earning level that is only 40 percent of that of non-indigenous employees. This disparity reflects differences in schooling and training that are often a reflection of the lack of schools in the countryside, and

FOCUS 11.1   GENDER BIAS: WOMEN IN AGRICULTURE

In poor nations, women typically play a major role in agricultural activities. In Africa, women work both as farm laborers and as farmers on family plots. Women account for 60 percent of all cultivators and produce an estimated 75 percent of the food. In India, 48 percent of self-employed cultivators are women. In all of Asia women are the producers of more than two-thirds of the food, while in Latin America the figure stands at 45 percent.

Total work time for women in the rural areas is about 20 percent more than for men. Relative to adult males, women shoulder the heaviest burden: 53 percent of all labor time. Women in agricultural regions divide their time between unpaid household duties and paid activities, which can include direct farming and marketing, handicraft production, garment making, and brewing. In Nepal, women spend an average of nearly three hours per day in direct farm work, and nearly four hours per day gathering fuel wood and scavenging. Another three hours per day is committed to food preparation and related household activities. Rural women throughout the developing world can be seen spending long hours on the mundane task of acquiring water. In Senegal, for example, women devote an average of two and a half hours per day on water collection alone; in Mozambique, it is over two hours per day.

Women often cannot acquire legal title to land ownership, or, as in the case of Africa, maintain their customary rights to communal lands. Women cultivators have generally been ignored in land reform programmes. Lacking title to land, women face high barriers when they need credit. In Africa, women receive only 10 percent of the bank loans to small farmers, a mere 1 percent of all agricultural credits, despite the disproportionate numbers of women involved in agricultural activities. Even the multilateral lending banks (discussed in Chapter 17) ignore women farmers' credit needs, extending 95 percent of their loans to men.

Women farmers also receive unequal support from agricultural extension services. In India, most women farmers are excluded from the benefits of extension services completely. In Africa, women receive 33 percent fewer visits from farm advisers than do men cultivators. Women are the poorest portion of the rural population, and they and their dependants constitute 70 percent of all those living in absolute poverty. Indeed, if women farmers had the same level of education and inputs as men, their farm yields would increase by as much as 20 percent according to studies conducted in Kenya and Burkina-Faso. If anything, the issue of gender bias is more significant than ever as a result of the explosion in migration of millions of (largely) male small cultivators into the industrial countries in recent years. (See Focus 12.1 on women and health, which complements this material very well.)

Sources: Stringer 2001: 94–5; Tomich *et al.* 1995: 29;
UNDP 1995: 38, 93; World Bank 2001: 119

outright discrimination. In India, one in every seven of the population is lower-caste, for whom agricultural employment is one of the few occupational opportunities available.

India's caste system, while fraying at the edges, still condemns millions of talented cultivators and potential innovators to menial work with little possibility of social mobility. Bhimrao Ambedkar, the first untouchable to be educated abroad and the principal author of the 1950 constitution described the caste hierarchy as "an ascending scale of hatred and a descending scale of contempt." In the rural villages where two-thirds of the population lives, caste intermarriage is rare (Luce 2007: 14). In a poll of middle-class Indians nearly three-quarters said they would prohibit their children from marrying out of their caste (ibid.: 13–14, 298).

In Malaysia, until late in the twentieth century, ethnic Malays were confined to traditional small-scale agriculture, with the higher income-generating activities in industry and finance controlled by the ethnic Chinese. Only recently have governmental policies specifically aimed to improve the educational and training opportunities of the ethnic Malays.

In Thailand, the earnings of the northern hill people in the 1990s were more than 75 percent below the national average, and schools were attended by fewer than 30 percent of the population, so that some 85 percent of the population could not read or write (World Bank 1995: 44–6). In South Africa in 1994 the average amount of land held per person on black-owned farms was only 1.3 hectares, while whites held 1,570 hectares (Deininger 1999: 664)!

Inadequate infrastructural investment

Whatever the cause or causes, agriculture is either neglected or relegated to a subordinate position in development strategies, too often an afterthought to industrialization. This relative lack of interest takes many forms, but of paramount importance to rural cultivators, both large and small, is the inadequate provision of infrastructure and social overhead capital: schools and health clinics, roads, dams and irrigation canals, crop storage facilities, farm extension services, agricultural research, and farm credit programmes are inadequate, if they exist at all. Roads and water resources are fundamental to agriculture. Small cultivators in particular confront tremendous difficulties in bringing their output to urban areas for marketing because of substandard road systems. At their best, rural roads often are unpaved, and trucks are forced to crawl along, lest a breakdown occur. This means long hours on the road, in quite small trucks, which raises the costs of transportation inordinately and makes it more difficult for small producers to compete with larger ones. This also means more spoilage, with a smaller share of output reaching its final destination in usable form. Bad weather results in the wash-out of poorly constructed bridges, or, as is more likely, streams that cannot be forded as they rise to cover and muddy roads. The lack of irrigation means that levels of production are less predictable as a result of the need to depend on the irregularities of rain, and growing seasons are shorter than they might be if there were more control over nature that irrigation provides. In many tropical regions, irrigation would permit near year-round cultivation.

To a great degree, many of the infrastructural projects mentioned above are of an all-or-none nature. This means that for the agricultural sector, and most particularly small-scale agriculture, it is the **state** which must finance these large-scale investment programmes if productivity in agriculture is to be raised. Given urban bias, given the general lack of investment funds available to most poor nations, and given that the pay-off from investments in agriculture and in rural areas often require decades of concentrated efforts to show success, it is perhaps not too surprising that examples of successful agricultural programmes in less-developed nations are few and far between. Because such programmes would have to take place over a relatively long period of time, and because governments in most poor nations are extremely insecure and often lack adequate financial resources, the state can rarely afford to take the long-term view. Thus public funds tend to be allocated to areas where more short-term, and more limited, objectives, including political support, can be achieved, and this has typically meant stimulating industry and urban development.

In addition to physical infrastructural outlays which could directly raise agricultural productivity, other basic public expenditures are usually desperately needed in the countryside. Here we refer in particular to the urgent need for educational programs and health care, both of which contribute to enriching the human capabilities of the rural population and contribute to growth. The educational demands of rural areas may well pose special difficulties for decision-makers compared to those in urban schools. In many nations, much of the rural population may have only the most rudimentary knowledge of the dominant or official language. Adult literacy and second-language programs may be of the utmost necessity, yet the lack of trained personnel to provide such services may make it difficult to move forward in these areas. Still, these are investments which are desperately required and for which the returns, both individual and social, are likely to be quite high (see Chapter 12).

Health care, primarily through rural public health clinics, could immediately help to reduce high rural infant mortality rates and contribute to raising productivity by damping-down the widespread exposure to intestinal parasites which sap the energy of small cultivators. Public health programmes to create and then maintain sanitary water supplies and to treat waste water are essential for these goals, but they too demand sizeable public outlays, and the competition with urban areas for funds has most often been lost.

Agrarian dualism

Nearly every poor nation was once a colony of one developed nation or another at one time, as discussed in Chapter 3. Even some independent nations fell under the indirect sway of the colonizing powers. Although the first wave of colonization and control in the sixteenth century was concerned with extracting precious metals and controlling trade routes and trading stations, the focus of colonization quickly turned to agricultural commodities which could be marketed in the international markets as the flow of precious metals ultimately slowed in the mid-1600s. The production of "King Sugar" or "white gold," became of paramount importance as early as the eighteenth century. A host of other primary commodities played key roles in the determination of the agrarian structure of the less-developed nations between 1500 and 1960, when colonial rule finally ended in most nations. Tobacco, indigo, rice, tea, jute, henequen, bananas, coffee, chocolate, sugar, cotton, and spices were some of the major commodities produced through the centuries of colonial rule to meet the demands, usually of the elites, of the more-developed nations. Even items which were not driven by the logic of tropical production, such as beef and wheat, were often leading commodities exported from the colonial and post-colonial nations to the more-advanced industrial nations.

The vast trade in tropical commodities, including some such as rubber used as inputs into industrial production, carried with it a massive structural change in rural landholdings in colonial and post-colonial society. With rare exceptions, the colonial powers sought to turn over vast tracts of land to a new planter aristocracy. Often this new elite survived only because of the sophisticated slave trade which brought captive laborers to the new plantation regions. Thus, whatever the nature of landholding prior to colonialism, the indigenous population was generally forcefully relegated to the most marginally productive and, often, the most distant lands. The truly optimal tracts of fertile land were claimed by well-positioned members of the colonial powers or by colonial-born creoles, and by a select few members of the colonized society who had become instrumental in maintaining colonial rule. Thus a fundamental characteristic of colonial agriculture, one which persists to the present, emerged, creating a dichotomous production structure wherein a relatively few planters controlled vast expanses of the most productive land, while a large mass of cultivators clung tenaciously to small plots of marginally productive land at considerable distances from urban areas with the worst communication network of roads linking them.

This pattern, while established in the somewhat distant past, continued into the twentieth century. In Mexico, for example, between 1877 and 1910, under the infamous rule of Porfirio Díaz, 72 million hectares of land were appropriated from indigenous peoples and turned over to large landowners, domestic and foreign (Smith 1972: 3). In Kenya, during the course of 1903, British colonial administrators sold immense areas of the land to British growers at less than one US cent per hectare. Some of the estates acquired that year included Lord Delamere's acquisition of 311,615 acres; Lord Francis Scott's purchase of 89,032 acres; and sales to two companies known as East Africa Estates and East Africa Syndicates of 311,615 and 89,032 acres respectively (Dixon 1990: 43). The British even divided Kenya into two areas: the "scheduled areas," where the colonial settlers were allowed to hold land, and the "native reserves," to which the indigenous population was relegated. Prior to the end of the colonial era, colonial settlers in scheduled areas had acquired 36,260 square kilometers of land, where 3,500 colonial farms and estates were established on the best soil. The 4 million "native" farms were crowded on to 134,670 square kilometers. Foreign colonial settlers thus owned farms averaging 10.4 square kilometers of land each, that is, more than 2,500 acres (or 1,000 hectares), while indigenous smallholders held an average of only 0.034 square kilometers, or less than 9 acres (3⅓ hectares). There was little change in land concentration after independence. In the 1980s, 2.4 percent of the cultivators controlled 32 percent of the cultivated land, and most of the cash crop came from this land of the highest quality (Dixon 1990: 46).

Throughout most less-developed countries, this concentrated pattern of land ownership characteristic of Kenya and Mexico is repeated, and neither Kenya's nor Mexico's inequality is the most extreme. While Kenya had a Gini coefficient for landholding inequality of 0.77 in 1981, the figure for Colombia in 1990 was 0.84, for Saudi Arabia 0.83 in 1983, while Brazil's was 0.86 (UNDP 1993; Deininger 1999: 655). Translating the Gini coefficient in the case of Colombia, the top 1.7 percent of landowners controlled 42 percent of the farmland, while the *minifundistas* with less than 5 hectares (57 percent of all farmers) held a minuscule 4.2 percent of the farmland.

In virtually all less-developed countries, with the exception of those relatively few where meaningful land reform has been consolidated, this dualism and inequality is evident. Large numbers of peasant cultivators control extremely small parcels of land, while a few large landholders, who constitute the landed oligarchy, own and vie with agribusiness transnationals to control vast quantities of land. One study, published in the 1970s, analyzed six Latin American nations and found that an average of 52 percent of all the farmland was controlled by the largest landholders, though they constituted less than 1 percent of all the agrarian households in these nations. Small farms, employing no more than four family members, held approximately 25 percent of the land, while accounting for the vast bulk of the agrarian households. Counting landless peasants, they and small cultivators accounted for 94 percent of all rural households (Barraclough 1973: 326–7, 331–2).

With smallholders crowded on to the poorest and less productive land, a serious problem of overgrazing and overuse occurs, both on the land itself and in forests and wooded areas where firewood and fence materials are collected (see Focus 11.2). The inadequacy of fallowing, that is, of leaving land idle for a period of time so that it can regain its nutrients, is a result of small farm size, where families are forced into practices which abuse the natural resource base. This, combined with relatively high population growth rates in rural areas, sets up a vicious circle of excessive land use leading to greater degradation of soils via erosion, soil exhaustion, leaching of minerals, and loss of water sources, which results in declining productivity of the land and falling output levels, which, in turn, leads to even greater use of increasingly marginal land at a too-intensive rate. This is an example of the "pollution of poverty" introduced before (see Focus 2.3).

This destructive and non-sustainable cycle already could be noted in Mexico and in the Andean highlands nearly 500 years ago, as villagers were pushed up on to ever higher mountain slopes, operating on more difficult lands, receiving lower yields, reducing the nutritional content and reliability of their diet. Among the less-developed nations, only in those where successful land reform has been implemented has there been a noticeable shift from the dichotomous nature of agriculture and the overuse or misuse of land resources as a result of the need for survival brought on by small farm size. High-yield varieties of wheat, rice, corn, and some other staples, discussed later in this chapter, have brought some relief from

FOCUS 11.2   AGRICULTURE AND THE ENVIRONMENT: DEFORESTATION AND SOIL EROSION

Improvements in infrastructure in agriculture must be accompanied by a strategy to sustain the resource base. Without adequate training, adequate investment, and adequate regulation in the maintenance of forests, however, deforestation has become a major problem in much of the developing world. In Latin America in the course of the 1980s alone, over 8 million hectares were deforested annually, as trees were felled for new farms, for grazing land, for firewood, or for the wood itself. In Asia, roughly 3.5 million hectares suffered deforestation, while in Sub-Saharan Africa, approximately 2 million hectares of forest were lost each year. For the decade as a whole, then, some 165 million hectares of forest were destroyed in the poor regions of the world. From 1900 to 1990, one-fifth of all tropical forests were destroyed, and the rate of deforestation has accelerated in recent years.

Soil erosion and soil degradation are also, unfortunately, widespread. The World Bank estimates that in many poor nations soil depletion as a result of run-off and improper use of land resources reduces annual growth rates by between 0.5 and 1.5 percent. Clearly, the cumulative, long-term effect can be very large. In addition to the measured impact of erosion on agricultural output, soil erosion also undermines and damages the fragile infrastructure of roads, bridges, canals, and dams, while reducing water quality and adversely affecting freshwater fish and animal habitats.

Some studies indicate that relatively simple and inexpensive measures can effectively combat soil erosion. Mulching, for example, could reduce erosion by 70 percent or more. Contour cultivation could reduce erosion by 50 to 80 percent, while grass contour hedges can also be extremely effective. Unfortunately, such measures are too rarely employed, both because they are an additional expense and because the dissemination of knowledge regarding ecologically sensitive and sustainable agriculture is poor. It is not that farmers wish to destroy the land and the natural resource base. They simply lack the tools, including the knowledge, to be able to do different. Further, given their low incomes, the choice is often between starvation and overuse or misuse of the land.

Erosion and deforestation can have dramatic effects: in Mexico, for example, soil erosion reduces the amount of cultivable land by 317,000 acres a year. In addition, deforestation robs the country of 1.5 million acres per year. One result of these processes is desertification, which expands the deserts of Mexico at an annual rate of 556,000 acres. Deforestation is caused both by ecologically insensitive forestry practices and by the drive to introduce cattle ranching. As alarming as these figures may seem, the extent of deforestation which exists in Mexico is exceeded in other nations. In fact, annual deforestation throughout the developing nations averaged 113,000 sq. kilometres in 1990–5. (Impacting an area equal to the size of the nation of Honduras.)

> Between 1950 and 2000 roughly 2 billion of the total of 8.7 billion hectares of farmland, permanent pastures, and forest/woodlands have been degraded. Through overgrazing, deforestation, and inappropriate agricultural practices 5 to 10 million hectares per year become unusable and impossible to restore.
>
> Sources: Barry 1992: 264–8; Doolette and Smyle 1990, Pinstrup-Anderson 2003: 6, World Bank 2001: 291

this vicious circle for smallholders for a thirty-year period that ended in the late 1980s or early 1990s. In the low-income economies, land yields have remained low, and since the late 1990s rate of growth of population has consistently exceeded overall agricultural growth, pushing down the per capita level of food production, so that in 2005 food production per person was only 97 percent of what it was in 2000 (Table 11.2, see column 2).[2]

Table 11.2 Changes in per capita food production, cereal output, and irrigated land

	Food production index (1989–1991 = 100) (1999–2001 = 100)		Cereal yield (kg per hectare)	Irrigated land (percentage)
	1997	2005	2005	2001–3
Income groups:				
Low-income economies	109.4	97.1	2,055	24.4
Middle-income countries	134.3	110.4	3,382	18.5
Geographic regions:				
East Asia and Pacific	142.6	112.7	4,495	n.d.*
Latin America and Caribbean	111.4	106.8	3,310	11.4
Middle East and North Africa	121.5	105.1	2,393	32.7
South Asia	108.0	96.7	2,479	38.9
Sub-Saharan Africa	104.6	93.4	1,078	3.6
Nations:				
India	107.0	96.7	2,367	32.7
China	131.0	114.2	5,105	47.5

Sources: World Bank 2000/1: 278–9, Table 3, 288–9, Table 8; 2007: 40–2, Table 2.1, 130–2, Table 3.2, and "Data and Statistics, Agriculture."

Note
* No data.

For the middle-income countries where significant applications of Green Revolution technologies were employed (particularly in East Asia), food production raced ahead of falling population growth in the 1980s and into the 1990s, with steady gains continuing into the twenty-first century. Sub-Saharan Africa fared worse in the 1990s, and then suffered systematic reversals far deeper than any other region in the twenty-first century, thus far. Of note is the discouraging recent performance of India, which carries implications for more than1 billion people (see Focus 11.3). Also note what is partially revealed by Table 11.1 – the spectacular twenty-six-year achievement (1979–2005) of China, with a population of 1.3 billion in 2005, managing to raise food output per capita by a total of 96 percent! Directly behind China in cereal yields, East Asia has a very low degree of inequality in land owner-ship and successfully applied Green Revolution technologies.

Primary product mono-exporters

One further structural aspect of agriculture in less-developed nations is important to note. In most nations, primary product food and fiber exports account for a very high percentage of total exports. This, again, reflects the legacy of colonial rule when, in many instances, the single strongest motivator for acquiring colonial territories had been to gain access to the production of tropical commodities so desired in the more temperate center economies. In many economies, then, unprocessed agricultural exports constitute the pivot on which not only export income depends, but on which the entire economy turns. A shortfall in production and/or a decline in the world price for one or two commodities can force a less-developed nation into an economic tailspin as the terms of trade deteriorate. When a nation is largely dependent on the export of one or a very limited number of exports, the term mono-exporter

FOCUS 11.3   INDIA'S AGRICULTURAL SECTOR

In recent years, the blossoming of India's information technology firms and its back-office/call-center operations have captured much attention. India is sometimes portrayed as an economic miracle in the making, and (simplistically and inaccurately) as a successful example of the application of "free-market" policies over the past fifteen years or so.

But there are two Indias: with 1.1 *billion* people, only 1–1.6 *million* work in the info-tech sector and related industries. The bulk of India's economy is to be found in rural areas where two-thirds of the population is located, primarily engaged in subsistence cultivation. Some 750 million Indians are scattered about in 680,000 small villages. Not all of these are cultivators, but their existence in the village is based upon the foundational activity in the countryside – farming on minuscule plots. Ninety percent of India's farmers own but a hectare or two, not large enough for much mechanization or to afford a tractor or drip irrigation. In fact, average farm size is only a quarter of a hectare. One hundred million are landless villagers. As such, in 2001 more than one-third of rural households depended upon non-farm income for their existence. Many have migrated temporarily to the cities. Because of the minuscule formal sector (only 35 million jobs) these workers have been forced into the massive, precarious informal sector of vendors and casual day laborers.

In the countryside only two percent of farm output is subsequently refined or processed to add value. Meanwhile more than one-third of all vegetables and fruit rot before getting to market. In India's villages only approximately one-half of the population has electrical connections, while nearly one-half of the villages cannot be reached by paved roads. Obviously, India's rural infrastructure is in an abysmal condition, as are rural health clinics, and the primary and secondary schools. While the government claims that the burst of economic growth since 1980 has benefited the poor – overwhelmingly in the countryside – dropping the poverty rate by 29 percent from 1991 through 2001, critics dispute these claims. The government, in fact, changed its methodology for counting the poor in 1991. Using other, more accepted methods Indian specialists have claimed that poverty has either fallen only slightly, or not at all.

Agriculture was largely ignored in the first Five-Year Plan which guided public spending after Independence – the focus was on industrialization. Agriculture received only one-third of the budget in 1952. By 1957, when the second Five-Year Plan was launched, less than 20 percent of outlays were directed toward the agricultural sector where 80 percent of the populace then resided. But the Green Revolution (as discussed in this chapter) doubled agricultural yields in the 1970s and 1980s. India surpassed production levels needed for food self-sufficiency in 1991 thanks in part to Green Revolution technologies. Nevertheless, most farmers cannot afford the necessary electrical connections and pumps to obtain essentially free ground water needed to cultivate the high-yield Green Revolution crops. Larger farmers have overused water, sinking the water table and leaving smaller farmers to rely increasingly on rainwater. With the uneven pattern of ownership, technology distribution, and production in the countryside, average yields per hectare in agriculture are less than one-half those now realized in China (see Table 11.3).

The new growth in information processing and computers has created a cascading process of wealth accumulation for India's privileged classes and castes while leaving the impoverished rural population to its own state of atrophy and decay. These complacent elite classes and castes lack a sense of urgency regarding India's developmental needs, an astonishing absence of concern most apparent in the vast neglected countryside. Thus, while India's development success has been widely acclaimed in recent years, evidence suggests that from 1989/90 to 2001/2 the poorest 80 percent of the rural population – the majority of India's citizenry – did not share in the aggregate economic growth. As such, the urban–rural income gap has widened significantly.

Sources: Ghosh 2004; Luce 2007

is generally applied.[3] Table 11.3 provides some representative data for several mono-export nations. Most oil exporting nations, particularly throughout the Middle East, are reliant on oil and gas exports – Venezuela is representative, with 80 percent of exports coming from petroleum in 2002 (Table 11.3 focuses only on agricultural products). No developed economy depends upon only one or a few exports. There is an obvious value to producing a diversified array of exports; this reduces the risk to total export income, and hence to the ability to import, of any downturn in the price of any one exported good.

Dutch disease and boom-and-bust cycles

Because the prices of agricultural exports, particularly tropical exports, are prone to very wide swings in price from year to year as a result of supply variations caused by weather, disease, and other factors, a special feature of mono-export economies (economies that depend on one or two or three commodity exports for the majority of their foreign exchange earnings) is their tendency toward macroeconomic instability. This can result in boom–bust cycles, which bring about speculation on the upswing of the business cycle that, if not moderated, can result in over-borrowing and a large inflow of foreign exchange earnings as higher export prices result in growing export earnings. The widespread, but fortuitous, availability of foreign exchange earnings as a result of higher prices following a bad crop elsewhere in the world can lead to distortions in the internal structure of an economy, as imported commodities temporarily are rendered cheaper than many which are locally produced. This occurs when the exchange rate of the local currency increases in value, as will happen if exchange rates are not fixed but are determined at least in part by the market, and there is an increase in total export income because of the higher export price (see Chapter 16 for a full discussion of exchange rates).

Ironically, then, the increase in the value of the exchange rate brought on by the increased purchases of a higher-priced export makes that export, and any other exports from that country, more expensive on the international market, leading to a reduction in purchases and employment in those sectors. At the same time, the increased imports of foreign goods, made possible by the same increase in the value of the currency, can cause a downturn in production for import substitution industries whose prices are undercut by cheaper imports as a result of the exchange rate over-valuation. In addition, the greater income created as a consequence of increased export revenues can set off inflation in the domestic economy. This further exacerbates the tendencies for exports to become more expensive and imports cheaper. Particularly affected will be the prices of those goods, like transportation and local food products, that are not traded on the world market, so that both the "tradable" and "non-tradable" goods sectors of the local economy are affected. Thus, perhaps paradoxically, the higher international price of the commodity export sets in motion a series of events that tend ultimately to slow economic activity in the less-developed nation. This phenomenon

Table 11.3 Degree of export dependency, Low Income Food Deficit nations (1999–2001)

Nation	% top agricultural commodity	Nation	% top agricultural commodity
Nicaragua	23	Rwanda	42
Ghana	25	Ethiopia	45
Kenya	28	Malawi	56
Cuba	30	Guinea	88
Benin	37	Burundi	92

Source: Pingali and Stringer 2003: Figure 3.

has been dubbed Dutch disease, because its effect was first noticed following discoveries of natural gas reserves by the Netherlands in the 1960s and 1970s.[4]

When the price of the commodity export turns down in future, then export revenues will decrease, and as a result of both lower domestic income and the decrease in the exchange rate of the currency, imports will become more expensive. Thus domestic producers of import substitutes will once again find a market, as the decrease in income and in the value of the currency leads domestic consumers to be able and willing to import less. However, some firms are likely to have been priced out of the market on the upside of the "boom-and-bust" cycle, and they may not be able to swing back into production, perhaps because their businesses have been bankrupted and sold off. Machinery and equipment may now be dispersed into other parts of the economy, or have fallen into disrepair. Worse, the labor force formerly used to produce for the local market in the import substitution industries may no longer be available, even if a firm wished to expand or re-start production. Thus the domestic economy is weakened and its productive base reduced as a result of the twists and turns of the boom–bust cycle and the phenomenon of Dutch disease, and these effects are strongest for countries that are mono-exporters. But, with the strategy of export diversification, the risk of Dutch disease can normally be reduced or eliminated.[5]

FOCUS 11.4 AN AGRICULTURAL-LED DEVELOPMENT STRATEGY?

Can agriculture be a leading sector rather than a follower? Until the era of the **Green Revolution of the 1950s and 1960s** (discussed below) there seemed to be no reason to entertain such a notion. And – as we have seen in earlier chapters – no development theorist ever suggested an "Ag-led" development strategy. Yet Robert Fogel's research on British economic growth demonstrates that from 1790 to 1980 a truly impressive thirty percent of all economic growth arose from better nutrition and increased human capability arising from the improved ability of the labor force given greater energy from their food consumption (Fogel 1994). Rising productivity in agriculture, then, appears to induce rising productivity in the remainder of the labor force as food prices fall – this is an important **externality** – engendering a virtuous circle. In addition, a booming agricultural sector can be an important source of domestic industrial demand both for consumer goods which farmers will buy and farm inputs which can create economies of scale in the production of manufacturing products.

An "Ag-led" strategy can also be appealing because of the daunting needs for infrastructure in agriculture. Dams, irrigation canals, water storage facilities, roads, bridges, etc. can all be produced under very labor-intensive methods – more so than easy import substitution activities such as the textile industry. At the same time, with agricultural output growing rapidly, the demand for landless workers in the countryside will grow – thus, an "Ag-led" strategy will target some of the poorest people. Developing nations, particularly when they seek to industrialize, find that they need foreign exchange to fund needed imports. But agriculture is less import-intensive.

Research shows that if the "Ag-led" strategy is concentrated on small landowners there is a high degree of stimulus to the remainder of the economy – the "multiplier effect" of increasing agricultural output by $100 is to create an additional $80 of total output as a result of the need for both more consumer goods and farming inputs. But agriculture cannot move ahead without a serious commitment to rural education, and, many argue, a sustained effort to "reform" the agricultural sector with policies that enable smallholders and especially the landless to gain access to land by breaking up large estates – which are known to be less productive per unit of land.

Continued

However, signs of a possible reversal are to be noted, particularly with the publication of the World Bank's *Reaching the World Poor – A Renewed Strategy for Rural Development* (World Bank 2003), which advocated for a stronger focus on agriculture and the fact that the 2007 *World Development Report* is devoted to agriculture. World Bank loans to the agricultural sector increased by more than to any other sector 2001–6, rising to 7.4 percent of all loans by 2006.

Peter Trimmer credits Indonesia's development success in the 1970s and 1980s to an "Ag-led" strategy which used the rural economy as the motor force for growth. Noting that the poverty rate fell from 50 percent of the population in the 1960s to only 20 percent in 1990, he found that 40 percent of the new jobs acquired by the growing labor force between 1969 and 1994 occurred through agricultural development.

Indonesia's success combined adoption of the **Green Revolution** in the 1960s and support for the agricultural sector that centered on the needs of small landholders. An Ag-led, pro-poor development strategy focused on raising public sector investments in the agricultural sector promises to engender a virtuous circle of forces, and could be envisioned in the following manner (see diagram below). First, initiate investment in the agricultural sector, primarily through a state-led process of large-scale investments in irrigation, roads, bridges, storage facilities, canals, and research and development in seeds, cultivation techniques, animal breeding and conservation/sustainability methods. The central thrust of the Ag-first strategy would be to initiate a broad-based agrarian reform (discussed later in this chapter). Initially this will increase the demand for rural workers as cultivators and laborers, thereby quickly lowering malnutrition and food security concerns. At the same time this will raise food transfer capacity out of the agrarian sector into the urban areas. In the short-to-intermediate time-frame, supply expansion in agriculture will lower food prices which will improve the living standard of the urban working class and critically benefit the "informal sector" workers.

In order to expand farm production, urban inputs of tools, cement, and simple machinery will be needed, raising the demand for urban (and rural) workers. As fewer workers exit the rural areas the surplus of labor in the informal sector will dwindle, facilitating a rise in wages. All this will serve to enhance "human capital" by increasing longevity and health, reducing/eliminating micronutrient deficiencies among children, reducing the need to keep children working in the rural areas and thereby improving school attendance. All these factors combined in the course of a year will start to raise the GDP, which will thereby increase the amount of funds and perhaps even the percentage of GDP devoted to agricultural investment in subsequent years. This simple model will generate even higher and faster social and private rates of returns if supplemented by strategically placed foreign aid (an issue discussed in Chapter 17).

Using a "food first" strategy, Indonesia was able to shift from being the world's biggest importer of rice to food self-sufficiency in only sixteen years! While there seems to be a growing interest among agricultural specialists in the possibilities of an "Ag-led" policy (at least for some nations) the major aid institutions, such as the World Bank, shifted away from supporting agriculture until very recently. Through 1980 the World Bank had devoted 23 percent of its loans and grants to agriculture, but by 1999 this sector received less than 10 percent of total funding, which practically disappeared by 2001, when only 4 percent of all lending went to agricultural.

The decline in attention to agriculture in foreign aid has the greatest impact on countries that are lagging developmentally, currently the bulk of Africa and a few Asian countries. The front runners in development have already benefited from the period when agriculture was uppermost in technical assistance. In Asia, for example, agriculture is moving, and now rapid industrial growth is providing a demand pull to agriculture. The laggard countries are still largely agricultural, with weak institutional structures for agricultural growth and limited human resources.

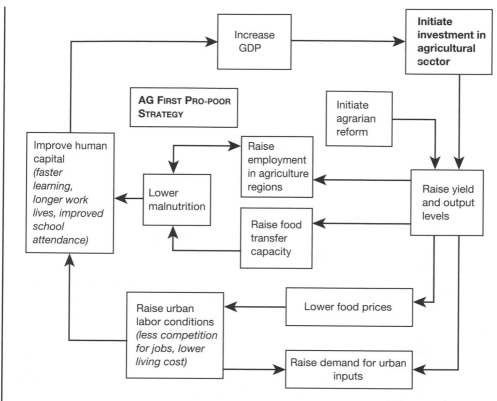

Sources: Mellor 1998b: 62; Trimmer 1998; United Nations, Department of Economic and Social Affairs 2000: 131–55; World Bank 2003

Peasant agriculture and small-scale cultivators

It is commonplace to find reference to "peasants" as a principal category of cultivators in the less-developed world who operate in a milieu of traditional agriculture. Exactly what these two terms – peasant agriculture and traditional agriculture – are intended to convey is too often left unstated. Unlike the peasants of medieval and feudal times in Europe, small cultivators in the less-developed nations are not tied to any particular landowner as serfs were bound to feudal manors. It is rare to find compulsory labor imposed on particular days or in particular seasons on small cultivators by large landholders. Nor do large landholders have "reciprocal obligations" to peasants as was the case in feudal Europe (for example, to provide protection).

Rather, what the terms are meant to convey is an emphasis on the self-sufficiency of the peasant farming operation: production for family consumption is thought to dominate decision-making. "Traditional" appears to be utilized to suggest a certain timelessness in the production process. In one telling phrase, Walt W. Rostow maintained that traditional agriculture was "pre-Newtonian" (Rostow 1960). He meant, apparently, that small cultivators farmed without regard to trial-and-error methods of cultivation, harvesting, irrigation, and seed selection. He also used the term to imply that there was a ceiling on the peasant production function, meaning, apparently, that farmers quickly encountered diminishing returns, and even absolutely diminishing returns, when they sought to raise output by working their land harder or longer. In any case, the image of traditional agriculture conveyed was one wherein productivity was abysmally low and did not rise over time, except in the most intermittent and unpredictable manner, where pure chance might bring an improvement in cultivation techniques. The application of science and technology to improving productivity or of investments in human capital were presumed to be absent from peasant or traditional farming.

Is this a realistic portrayal of the poorest and most numerous cultivators in the less-developed nations? Probably not, certainly as a generalization. First, peasants and other small-scale cultivators do not produce solely for family consumption, selling only any surplus that might remain. Peasant farms typically combine both non-market and market production. Small cultivators also often maintain modest numbers of animals and a vege-table garden for their own use to supplement what can be earned by marketing their cash crops. Since small cultivators are almost without exception very poor, and since they are very poor in large part because they are small cultivators without access to large areas of productive land, they do not need to spend all of their time cultivating the crops cultivated on their land. Maintaining animals and gardening usually occurs in an environment in which there are few other claims on the time of the cultivator. To the degree that peas-ants can find work elsewhere as day laborers on public works projects or larger farms at harvest or planting time, alternative employment is often sought, while other members of the cultivator's family, particularly women, maintain the family's non-cash production. While non-market activities are an important source of real income to the small cultivator, it is very rare to find small cultivators consuming all of what they produce, or having all their consumption limited only to what they themselves produce.

Thus, the concept of "self-sufficiency" has a relatively limited meaning in describing agri-culture in most less-developed nations today. As a defining characteristic, it would be more accurate to emphasize the relatively low degree of specialization of small cultivators. They often combine the roles of small market producer with that of family production, artisan producer, day laborer, and migratory worker, and in this categorization should be included the labor activities of most, if not all, the family members.

Traditional agriculture has virtually no applicability today if it is intended to suggest the image of a rigidly set pattern of cultivation determined by custom and impervious to change, even when a change in the method of cultivation has clearly been demonstrated to be more efficient. Anyone traveling in the less-developed world today certainly can encounter culti-vators utilizing some methods of cultivation which have been employed for centuries, if not a millennium. Wooden ploughs drawn by oxen, for example, abound. Cultivators often use a "digging-stick" to plant, pushing soil over the indentation in the earth with their feet after planting a seed. Machetes are ubiquitous. Yet these same cultivators, seen with digging-sticks and machetes, may return to their crops a few weeks after planting to douse them with synthetic fertilizers produced by one of a handful of giant transnational oil companies. They may, and often do, use herbicides and insecticides on their crops, often indiscriminately and with little apparent regard to their own health or that of the ultimate consumer (see Focus 11.3). Today the seeds in use by peasants quite often come from giant agro-industrial corporations which have spent millions of dollars to create new strains of crops to increase agricultural productivity.

If traditional agriculture means anything, then, perhaps we can take it to mean farming activities that combine the marketing of a modest-sized cash crop and some self-consumption of production, all organized around family labor. These are operations which are small and quite labor- and land-intensive in their production methods; they lack much capital, and the land in use is often marginal at best. Traditional agriculture tends to be low-productivity, low value-added, certainly as measured by output per worker, but it would be incorrect to suggest that there is no innovation or no capital in use, or that peasant farmers cannot learn-by-doing or by observing, or that they will not undertake change which can be demonstrated to be worth the risk involved.

Attitudes toward risk and change

With regard to production methods used by peasant farms, then, what is to be noted is the unevenness of production techniques. Combinations of some quite advanced methods with techniques which are ancient are not unusual or unexpected. Yet cultivators rarely cling to ancient methods simply out of some desire to maintain customs and traditions. The degree of resistance to change may often be noticeably higher in less-developed nations, but this observation is different from an assertion that cultivators are mired in unchanging techniques of production which are hopelessly out of date. Change is often slow to come in peasant agriculture for three very important reasons.

First, there is cultural resistance, as there is in any society, to change; these are the Ayresian "ceremonial" structures and institutions that are backward-looking but which exist in any society (see Chapter 6). The pace of change is likely to be slower than in the more developed, industrial nations, but peasant society is far from static.

Second, given the fact that small cultivators are very poor, they are often extremely risk averse. Unproven changes in production methods or the introduction of new seed strains or new crops may mean the taking of risks that, if the gamble is successful, can increase a family's income and perhaps take them out of poverty. On the other hand, risky changes can result in decreases in income, when the risk does not pay off, which takes the family from near-subsistence to below subsistence income.

The possibility of the down-side of the risk, with its devastating consequences, may for the rationally calculating peasant simply outweigh the potential gains of the projected change.[6] Consequently, prudence often leads small cultivators to hesitate in innovating, not because they cannot envision the conceivable benefits of change, or because they are irrational, but rather because they can only too well balance the costs and benefits of change and must do so carefully; that is, near-subsistence peasant producers may not change, thus sticking to "traditional" methods, precisely because they are rational and because they have evaluated the risks involved in changing production. However, even within the classification of "small cultivators," one finds peasants with somewhat more land and other means of economic survival, who, given their relatively greater access to resources, are more likely to accept new innovations, because failure is less likely to result in destitution.

Third, many small cultivators remain mired in production techniques which are clearly obsolete, not out of any choice they make, but because they have little or no access to cash or credit which would enable them to finance more advanced technologies, even though it is clear these could increase productivity. Or, even if financing were to be available, farm technologies appropriate to small-scale farming operations may not be available because of a paucity of demand for such technology. With only a limited number of small cultivators able to make such purchases, forms of "appropriate technologies," such as small tractors, may be unavailable because it is not profitable to provide them via the market. On the other hand, large- and medium-scale capitalist cultivators find a wide spectrum of farming technologies, and financing, more readily available on the market.

Are peasants efficient producers?

Development economists have expressed great interest in the question of the efficiency of small cultivators. The issue has been approached from three distinct perspectives. First, several of the early developmentalist economists took the position that a lack of efficiency in agriculture actually reflected another area in which less-developed nations had "hidden potential" which could be quickly and easily tapped to propel the nation on to the path of greater development. Their potential productivity simply needs to be released through proper policies. Second, one encounters the argument that peasants are, in fact, true maximizers in the neoclassical sense, who behave no differently from any other market participants. And, third, one encounters the position that peasants endure even though they are inefficient by the standards of neoclassical economics, because there is a special logic to peasant cultivation. Below we consider each of these three positions.

The hidden potential of peasant producers

The argument that there is hidden potential within the agricultural sector because of the inefficiency of peasant cultivation is rather straightforward, though the inefficiency of the peasantry is often assumed, rather than demonstrated. This was not always the case. Gunnar Myrdal, particularly in *Asian Drama*, took great pains to discuss a multiplicity of factors which he felt led to inefficient production in small-scale agriculture. If agriculture is inefficient, then there are structural changes which could lead to a rapid increase in output without any increase in inputs. Once these blockages or bottlenecks in agricultural production are identified and corrected, output should rise steadily, at least until maximum efficiency is attained.

The Lewis model is one such theory with this underlying perspective. Recall that Lewis asserted that the marginal product of labor in agriculture was zero and was certainly less than the marginal product of labor in industry (Chapter 5). Consequently, shifting labor from agriculture to the industrial sector would not reduce farm output, while industrial output would rise. Thus agriculture was viewed as a hidden reserve for development. The structural inadequacy, or bottleneck, was the surplus of labor in agriculture, and thus transferring labor from agriculture to industry was the means to overcome the barrier to progress. Quite a large number of cultivators could be withdrawn from the agricultural sector, and the remaining farmers could work a bit harder and a bit better to generate a food surplus to feed the growing number of workers in the industrial sector. Clearly, this process could not go on and on; there were limits to Lewis's virtuous circle. But such limits were not Lewis's main concern or focus. He understood quite well that agriculture would reach its limits somewhere in the not too distant future, but in the meantime he envisioned a successful transition to a semi-industrialized economy which would have much greater possibilities to improve the long-run productivity of agriculture, releasing its hidden potential.

The Chicago School approach: efficiency attained

In 1964, Theodore Schultz published *Transforming Traditional Agriculture* to challenge the idea that small-scale farmers were inefficient at all, particularly in their use of labor (Schultz 1964). Schultz took the position that small farmers were efficient; given their knowledge and access to information, and given their income levels and stocks of tools, implements and draft animals, and given their command over labor power (primarily the family unit), one could not recombine the inputs which peasants controlled so as to increase output. Nor could one reduce inputs and maintain output at the same level, as Lewis had argued. Furthermore, according to Schultz, if prices for agricultural products were increased, peasants would respond by increasing their inputs to production for those goods, just as neoclassical market analysis would predict. Consequently, Schultz concluded, small-scale agriculture was efficient.

This interpretation essentially argues that there is nothing which is unique about small-scale agricultural production in the less-developed nations. Small farmers are assumed to be quite poor, but through no fault of their own. Nor is their poverty the result of any particular cultural impediments which might be linked to a pre-capitalist or pre-modern ideology or to land ownership patterns. Rather, small farmers are poor because of government policies which either inhibit the workings of a free market in agriculture, such as price-setting for crops, or they are poor because of government policies which insufficiently assist in the workings of the market. Although this approach generally tends to emphasize the negative impact of government, Schultz also highlighted the neglect of government-provided agricultural extension and agricultural research, and the need for rural schools which would improve the managerial abilities of small-scale producers. How, then, in this view, is the low level of productivity in agriculture to be improved? New and better inputs, such as high-yield varieties, will raise output per hectare. The elimination of price ceilings and other government-imposed policies which reduce the rate of return to farmers will serve to eradicate rural poverty by removing the sources of low productivity behavior in response to the "wrong" price signals.

Schultz's interpretation has been challenged on several grounds. Most directly, the economic anthropologist Polly Hill, who spent long periods painstakingly observing peasant cultivators in Africa and Asia, rejects Schultz's analysis as being based on second-hand studies which fail to prove his argument. Hill (1986) notes that Schultz relied on only two empirical studies: one conducted on Guatemalan peasants and the other on an Indian village. She rejects the finding of the Guatemalan study because the village observed was a trading village, not a village of commodity producers. Traders, she maintained, would surely have acutely attuned responses to market incentives or they could not survive, but this proves nothing regarding the behavior of producers such as peasants who do not survive solely on the basis of trade. Further, she states that the absence of disguised unemployment or underemployment in this particular village was unrepresentative of Guatemala and of less-developed economies in general.

Second, she rejects the study of Indian farmers, because it failed to differentiate between the behavior of rich and poor small farmers. Based on her research in India, and the work of others, Hill maintains that the poorest farmers are inefficient in relation to relatively richer farmers. Rich farmers and poor farmers are not equally motivated, equally skilled, or equally informed. Hill points out that, in India, the poorest farmers are inefficient from the standpoint of the village's standards, since they cannot afford to buy manure, thus reducing their yield per acre and engendering soil exhaustion. And, even in the case of the rich small farmers, who come closest to fitting Schultz's ideas, Hill rejects the notion of the ubiquity of profit-maximizing responses. She mentions, for example, the stability of rural wages for farm laborers in spite of the seasonality of agricultural labor. Using a hypothesis based upon the universality of market-driven behavior, such as that espoused by Schultz, one might predict that wages would rise and fall with the changing demand for that labor (Hill 1986: 22). She also noted the general lack of a properly functioning market in credit and land. Hill quotes the work of two economists who had sought to demonstrate the validity of Schultz's generalizations in Palanpur, India.

> We are unable to confirm that neoclassical economics is alive and well and residing in Palanpur ... Farmers were not doing the best that they could do given their resources.
>
> (Bliss and Stern 1982: 291, 293)

Peasant agriculture as a special category

According to modernization theory, particularly as presented by Rostow, the agricultural sector should move rapidly forward with the dissolution and consolidation of traditional or backward agriculture, as inefficient, small-scale farming is phased out with structural transformation. Small farmers should be found migrating, en masse, to the industrial and service sectors. This had not been the case, until recently, in most of the Third World, despite the rapid growth of urban centers. Rather, large numbers of peasant cultivators have clung tenaciously to their landholdings. Once landless, many have continued to reside in the countryside. Small cultivators may migrate to urban areas, or they may migrate internationally, for one or more seasons per year. Yet their base often remains in the agricultural regions of the countries where they originated. Without doubt, the number of small cultivators is declining, and the realm of purely capitalist farmers is expanding, as is the extent of urbanization. But the pace of this change had been relatively slow, at least until the 1980s. To try to explain the tenacious hold land has on small cultivators, a large body of literature has emerged, some of which is summarized here.

In one study of the phenomenon, Alexander Schejtman defines "peasant economy" in the following manner.

> The concept of the peasant economy encompasses that sector of domestic agriculture activity in which family-type units engage in the process of production with the aim of ensuring, from one cycle to another, the reproduction of the living and working conditions, or, to put it another way, the reproduction of the producers and the unit of production itself. Achieving this objective generally means generating, firstly, the means of subsistence (biological and cultural) of all members of the family, active or not, and secondly – a fund designed to pay for the replacement of the means of production used in the production cycle and to deal with the various eventualities which may affect the existence of the group.
>
> (Schejtman 1992: 278)

Peasants, then, seek to attain survival or to sustain themselves. In commercial agriculture, on the other hand, the objective is to maximize profits, or to leave the agricultural sector if the market rate of return is higher in other pursuits. Peasants do not utilize the pure logic of profit maximization. Nor do they concern themselves with the "opportunity cost" of farming, exiting the agricultural sector if the wage to be obtained in the industrial or service sector is higher, as in the Lewis, Fei-Ranis, and Harris-Todaro models, or if the rate of return in the non-agricultural sectors of the economy is higher.

Exactly how widespread this behavior may be is not specified. Yet the imputation is clear; family-size farms are most likely to be part of the peasant economy. Table 11.4 provides some idea of the division of land ownership on the basis of farm size in the 1970s. For Latin America, smallholdings were defined as less than 10 hectares, while large holdings were above 100 hectares. For the Near East, the division between these two categories was taken to be less than 5 hectares and greater than 20 hectares. For Africa and the Far East, the division was less than two hectares and more than 10 hectares. In all regions, small-sized peasant farms dominate the total number of farms.

Some researchers who have studied the peasantry have defined these cultivators as either subsistence or semi-subsistence producers. In the latter category, it is assumed that only agricultural surpluses are sold in the market. Thus, there is an attempt to define the peasantry not merely in terms of its behavioral patterns, which fail to fit the model of standard market participants, but also as producers who generally operate outside a market context. There are such economic entities, but Hill believes "such communities are statistically so rare in the world that they (can) be ignored" (Hill 1986: 19). In general, a very high quotient of total production will be marketed, not merely some residual which is not consumed, and this marketing usually takes place at the peak harvest time when prices descend to their lowest point. The need to make payment on borrowed money and/or the inability to store crops for sale at a more opportune time, if the crops so permit, typically forces the smallest cultivators to sell at the worst moment.

While peasants do draw on unpaid family labor which can allow them to devote a large mass of labor power to their small plots, it is not always true that small cultivators are the most efficient in terms of yield per acre or hectare, as is sometimes supposed. For the poorest of the small cultivators, it appears that management of family labor is weak; poverty and duress force many family members to seek outside employment to support a fragile existence. This employment can come at the very moment when the family's land needs the most attention. Furthermore, since peasant farmers generally sell at peak harvest time, their return has to be balanced against the fact that the price earned on the quantity produced typically will be less than that of the richer small farmers. This is because more well-to-do small farmers are able to manage their family labor with an eye toward pushing their yield upward, while being able to afford manure and other inputs which will tend to enhance yield. Moreover, they may well be in a position to store some of their cash crop in order to await a rise in the market prices as seasonal surpluses dwindle.

As tenacious as the peasantry has proven to be, it is certainly the case that migration from the agrarian South to the industrial North has exploded in the early twenty-first century. Mexico alone sent more than 400,000 per year into the US in the 2001–6 period. The term **de-agrarianization** has been used by Cristóbal Kay and Jonathan Rigg to capture the essence of the processes currently under way in the rural sector (Kay 2006; Rigg 2006). They maintain that a profound transformation is unfolding in the countryside, with significant portions of the populace now completely de-linked from farming and land ownership, drawing their livelihood from non-farm activities including bouts of migration. Occupational "multiplicity," rather than the drive to maintain peasantry status is now widespread.

Table 11.4 Land tenure relations[a]

	Smallholdings			Large holdings		
	Average number %	Area %	Size ha	Average number %	Area %	Size ha
Latin America	66.0	3.7	2.7	7.9	80.3	514
Africa	66.0	22.4	1.0	3.6	34.0	28
Near East	50.0	11.2	1.6	10.3	54.7	50
Far East	71.1	21.7	0.7	4.0	31.1	17

Source: Dixon 1990: 71.

Note
a Medium-sized holdings not included in the table.

Numerous studies of the countryside in Asia, Africa, and Latin America show that non-farm forms of income have risen dramatically from the 1970s or 1980s to 2000. Frequently the share of non-farm income has been found to average 40 percent, and in some regions most rural families receive the major part of their income from non-farm activities. Increasing land shortages, declining yields/profitability, environmental degradation and new opportunities for employment in rural assembly/manufacturing or in internal/international short-term migration are all factors driving this process, bringing into question current understanding of the role and permanence of the peasantry. Rigg concludes that "land has lost its strategic value in the countryside" for some families in Laos – a view that, if more broadly confirmed, will hold deep implications for the rural poor, particularly the peasantry (Rigg 2006: 194). More generally, Rigg concludes that:

> No longer are agriculture and farming the desired, default position of rural households. No longer do parents desire a settled, farming life for their children. And no longer should we assume that agricultural development is the best way to promote rural development, and rural development the best means of raising rural incomes and improving livelihoods … The best means of promoting pro-poor growth in the countryside may have less to do with supporting small-holder farming, whether through land redistribution or policies of agricultural development, and more to do with endowing poor people with the skills so that they can escape from farming and, perhaps, escape from the countryside.
>
> (Rigg 2006: 195–6)

Kay, however, finds that poor peasant households are using non-farm income as a key means to retain possession of their small plots in Latin America, suggesting that the peasantry is not dissolving at a rapid pace (Kay 2006: 471).

High-yield varieties, biotechnology, genetically modified food crops, and rural productivity

Concern for the precarious economic position of small cultivators, combined with the fear that they might become a politically active group if their living standard was not improved as they gradually lost land ownership, led to attempts to improve seed varieties which could be employed in the less-developed economies on small plots to increase productivity. Such seeds, of course, were not limited to usage by or for smallholders. Nevertheless, there was widespread hope that such seeds, termed high-yield varieties, would contribute to reducing rural poverty. Research on new wheat seeds conducted in the 1940s and 1950s in Mexico provided the basis for a breakthrough in scientific plant breeding. Later, the revolution spread to rice and has more recently been extended to corn, millet, and sorghum production. Widespread application of these new plant varieties did not occur until the 1960s, however. In 1968, the term **Green Revolution** was first applied to these efforts. This term constituted not only the recognition of a major technological change undergoing rapid diffusion, but most importantly a strategy wherein it was hoped that seed technologies could be substituted for missing land reform and for more radical "red revolutions" of the socialist variety threatening to sweep across the globe at the time. In the view of those who advocated the Green Revolution (GR), the absence of high-yield varieties, coupled with growing population pressures in rural areas, would eventually result in a situation where the pressures and burdens of the small cultivators would be released in a political explosion. Poor peasants with few alternatives and little hope, it was feared, would seize plantation and estate lands, as well as those lands held by agribusiness conglomerates and transnationals.

Critics of the GR strategy predicted that the diffusion of high-yield varieties would, however, further exacerbate rural poverty and accelerate the tendency toward the concentration of landholdings. They foresaw peasants driven out of rural areas by falling prices for their crops as supplies rose as a result of better technology and higher levels of production. In this view, only rich peasants, mid-size capitalist farmers and larger landholders would be able to take advantage of the Green Revolution's promise. Critics took this position because the cultivation of these new varieties usually required irrigation and the intensive use of fertilizers. Thus the necessary complements to high-yield cultivation were thought to be beyond the reach of the mass of poorer peasants. Furthermore, such new varieties were prone to pests and plant disease, which might destroy most or all of a crop. From the theory that poorer peasants are most likely to resist change, since they can least afford the risk involved if there is a crop failure, it was argued by some that even if peasants might be able to afford to adapt to the new varieties, they could not afford to accept the risk such varieties entailed and thus the rural income divide would widen.

In some respects, the results of the GR were correctly anticipated by critics of the policy. As Keith Griffin summarizes:

> The main beneficiaries in the rural areas have been producers who control optimal production environments, i.e. farms on good soils in well-irrigated regions, and in some countries optimal production environments are frequently controlled by the larger and better-off farmers.
>
> (Griffin 1989: 147)

Michael Lipton and Richard Longhurst, in their analysis of the effects of the GR, have isolated four phases of response to the issue of high-yield varieties:

> First came the "green revolution" euphoria of 1967–70. In the second phase, there were growing fears that the MVs (modern varieties) enriched large farmers at the expense of small farmers and landowners at the expense of labourers. The later 1970s saw a third phase; several reassessments suggested that in MV-affected areas the poor gained absolutely, but lost relatively. Small farmers adopted after large ones – but did adopt and raised yields. Farmworkers found that the effects of MVs in boosting the demand for their labour seldom brought much higher wage rates – but employment rose. Above all, poor consumers gained, as extra cereals supplied by MVs restrained food prices. The big exception to this rather happier verdict on the MVs was that producers in the non-MV areas, including many poor farmers, gained nothing from the new technology.
>
> (Lipton and Longhurst 1989: 19)

Kathleen Baker and Sarah Jewitt conducted an evaluation of the impact of the GR in a state in India (Uttar Pradesh) covering a thirty-five-year period when the Green Revolution was broadly applied (Baker and Jewitt 2007). Their findings are generally positive, but the broad positive impact of the GR in this important state needs to be carefully interpreted: Uttar Pradesh has had adequate access to water and canals, and – most importantly – in 1996 the state imposed a cap on land ownership of only 7.35 hectares for irrigated land. In effect, this constituted an application of agrarian reform (discussed below) along with GR

FOCUS 11.5   AGRICULTURE AND THE ENVIRONMENT: PESTICIDES AND THE CIRCLE OF POISON

Pesticides are used moderately in Sub-Saharan Africa, but elsewhere in the less-developed world their use is widespread, commonplace, and subject to rapid growth. For example, in the period 1980–5, the rate of growth of pesticide application exceeded 10 percent per year in Indonesia, Pakistan, the Philippines, and Sri Lanka. Often pesticide use has been stimulated by government subsidies which, along with technical assistance in applying these chemicals, have been extended to large- and medium-sized farm operations. Pesticide use often is problematic, because it can poison groundwater supplies, disrupt ecosystems and cause serious harm to humans and animal life. Alternatives to widespread pesticide use do, however, exist: Integrated pest management calls for carefully timed spraying of pesticides, combined with the introduction of natural predators, pest-resistant crop varieties, and crop rotation, measures which are more environmentally friendly and which can contribute to sustainability of fragile ecosystems.

One study of farming in Guatemala indicated that peasants used three times the amount of pesticides per hectare as did large- and medium-sized cultivators. And they applied pesticides as a precaution, without regard to specific pest infestation. Furthermore, they generally failed to leave an adequate interval between spraying pesticides and harvesting. As a result, their crops often were unacceptable for export because of high concentrations of toxic agents; such commodities were sold, however, in the local market. Other agricultural products from the less-developed countries with lower levels of contamination, however, continue to be exported.

This so-called circle of poison occurs when industrial nations prohibit the domestic use of certain pesticides, but continue to allow their chemical corporations to produce and export these banned poisons to other countries. The United States, for example, controls 25 percent of international trade in pesticides, but approximately one-quarter of this output cannot be sold in the United States. Many of these pesticides re-enter the United States, however, via food exports from the developing nations which utilize the banned pesticides. The US imports as much as half of certain fresh fruits and vegetables from Mexico between December and March each year. Less than 1 percent of these items are tested for pesticide contamination. Mexico, however, continues to use DDT and BHC, more than twenty years after their patents were revoked as a result of the health dangers associated with their use. Other dangerous herbicides and pesticides such as paraquat, parathion, and ethylmercuric substances are regularly utilized to dust crops.

Indiscriminate and widespread use of insecticides and herbicides is creating new, complex, and expensive public health problems, which poor nations are ill-equipped to remedy. For example, in some of the cotton-growing regions of Central America, DDT residuals in breast milk are the highest ever recorded in humans. These are passed on to young children, with potentially devastating consequences.

Sources: Barry 1992: 269; Pingali 1998; Russell 1994: 252; World Bank 1992: 140

technologies. The imposition of land size limits did not occur through the guidance of the central state or through the agricultural ministry, but rather as a result of political pressure from organized political groups that were really social movements advocating for the peasantry. Small farmers benefited directly through self-consumption, planting HYVs of wheat and rice in alternative seasons (while working as farm laborers, construction workers, or urban informal workers when time away from farming made this possible). Average yields in Uttar Pradesh have exceeded the national average yields by roughly 50 percent since the GR began, and even the smallest farmers have experienced sustained yield increases over 100 percent. By virtue of the land cap imposed on GR cultivation large farmers have frequently sold parcels of land, and overall land distribution among the villagers has improved, while in one village the number of landless declined by 25 percent (Baker and Jewitt 2007: 324–6).

Meanwhile the amount of irrigated land increased by 66 percent from 1972–2003, although the distribution has been skewed toward larger farmers, with small farmers unable to afford wells being forced to pay very high prices for water (ibid.: 328–9). As one would expect, small farmers have not had the income (from their labor jobs) to buy adequate amounts of fertilizers – they use about 50 percent less than large farmers and as a consequence their yields are 50–60 percent less than the largest farmers. Fertilizers have been heavily subsidized, but with India's turn toward neoliberalism in the1990s it is anticipated that this subsidy will be phased out. In any case yields are declining in the most heavily fertilized areas as a result of salt deposits.

Even though land distribution among the villagers is more equal than before the GR, *and hunger has disappeared,* income distribution has widened for two reasons: (1) the small farmers have much larger families than the medium and large farmers, and this results in the further division of land into smaller plots, cutting effective per-family income from self-cultivation; (2) yields are substantially higher on larger plots of land. As a result, in 2001 medium and large farmers owned 75 percent of the wealth of the villages studied, while in 1972 they owned 45–50 per cent of the wealth. In general, the share of the wealth of small farmers went down from 40 to 20 percent, while that of the landless went up from 0 to 10–15 percent because the rising prosperity in the region created jobs in agriculture, the villages, and in the surrounding urban areas which improved the conditions of the landless (ibid.: 331–4).

While numerous other factors played an important role in the rural conditions of Uttar Pradesh, the aggregate impact of the GR technologies has been mixed – large farmers have benefited the most, but the land cap constrained this tendency to a great degree, while "multiplier effects" from higher levels of income have spilled over, creating new opportunities for the landless, and the standard of living for small farmers has improved in an absolute, though not in a relative sense. Nonetheless, doubts remain regarding the impact of salt deposits and the poisoning of well water through fertilizers, pesticides, and insecticides.

Africa was largely left out of the GR, but from 1999 to 2007 the Rockefeller Foundation focused on the development and propagation of a new GR rice, NERICA, that has brought GR yield increases to much of Africa (Strom 2006: A16; WARDA 2007). NERICA combines the yield capacities of GR rice plants developed in Asia with resistance characteristics common to Africa rice. NERICA has been identified as the major cause for six years (2000–6) of substantial and consecutive increases in rice production in Africa. Nigeria, the largest rice importer in the world, was able to reduce its 2005 rice imports by 800,000 tonnes as a result of the adoption of NERICA. Use of NERICA is spreading rapidly, with at least thirteen African nations actively cultivating this breakthrough plant in 2007.

Returning now to Lipton's analysis, above, it is possible to locate a fourth phase of plant technologies which began in the 1980s and has gathered momentum ever since. This time the emphasis is on the promise of nitrogen fixation, coupled with breakthroughs in biotechnology (including the explosion in genetically modified food crops). All this has been combined with the renewed faith that in breaking up the public sector and imposing the rule of the market (see Chapter 7), the dilemmas of the rural sector will be overcome at last. Skepticism, based on the limited impact of the GR, appears warranted. Nonetheless, the positive accomplishments of the technological burst coming from the GR also are beyond dispute: food yields did rise in many areas of the developing world. Still, the GR has not achieved the success that once appeared inevitable; in many poor regions, physical and social infrastructure is insufficient to support major yield increases. In these regions, farm advisers are lacking, roads can be non-existent, and the subsidies often needed to stimulate a shift in production technologies are unavailable (Goldman and Smith 1995).

In the early twenty-first century **transgenic crops** were being introduced into the developing nations at a faster rate than any agricultural technology had been applied before. Some 38 percent of all transgenic crops grown (or genetically modified food crops) were under cultivation in developing nations in 2005. In 2003 there were 67.7 million hectares of transgenic crops planted in developing nations – an area slightly smaller than Japan. By 2005 the rate of growth in planting of transgenic crops was higher in the developing nations than in the advanced industrial nations of Europe, Japan, the US, Canada, and Australia. However, this technology has overwhelmingly been utilized to solve production problems in high-tech agribusiness in the industrial nations. Hence the focus has been on cotton, maize, soy, and canola, with relatively few applications to food and fodder grown in the developing nations, such as cowpeas, millet, sorghum, and cassava. As was the case in the 1960s, the arrival of transgenics has created waves of research and storms of controversy in development economics (Lipton 2007; Bouis 2007; Graff, Roland-Holst and Zilberman 2006; Raney 2006).

While there has been much speculation regarding the introduction of transgenic crops (TCs), little high quality comparative research has yet been published. Terri Raney summarized several existing studies that show substantial improvements in yields (11–65 percent), and reductions in pesticide costs (−47 to −77 percent) in the planting of insect resistant cotton versus conventional cotton. However, seed costs went up substantially (17 to 530 percent), with the extreme variance in seeds related to whether a nation had the ability to either negotiate with the agribusiness transnational corporations who own patent rights to the genetically modified seeds or the ability to largely circumvent these corporations. The level of profit increased in the areas studied (Argentina, China, India, Mexico, South Africa), but the benefits to small farmers were mixed: only when a nation has institutions designed to insure that those benefiting will include small farmers (such as national R&D capacity that can independently produce forms of TCs as in China) will the new technologies have a "pro-poor" impact (Raney 2006: 2–4). Michael Lipton, however, maintains that the reduction in pesticide usage carries anti-poor implications because the TCs reduce the demand for agricultural laborers, impacting the landless most of all (Lipton 2007: 45). Yet he also notes that in the case of transgenic rice, developing nations have succeeded in negotiating with a transnational corporation to make the seeds almost part of the "public domain" (Lipton 2007: 48). This leads him to the position that for the small cultivators to benefit from TCs it will likely be necessary to recast the relationship with the agribusiness biotech firms to one where a single fee would be paid for the unlimited use of TCs, as opposed to the current situation where these firms seek royalties in perpetuity for the use of their seeds. If suitable measures can be instituted regarding the low cost application of TCs, Lipton foresees wide applications in developing nations in agro-ecologies that have been inhospitable to the standard seed-fertilizer-irrigation formula, such as applications of TCs where water is scarce or where soil salt content is high. Others, such as Howarth Bouis and Gregory Graff *et al.* emphasize the possibilities of improving the micronutrient content of TCs, thereby addressing the issue of malnutrition affecting over 50 percent of the population in the developing nations (Bouis, 2007: 80–2; Graff, Roland-Holst and Zilberman 2006: 1434).

In analyzing the above studies regarding the application of TCs it is necessary to keep in mind the fact that similar positive impressions were quickly gathered at the onset of the Green Revolution – it was only much later that evidence accumulated as to the difficulties arising from the GR. By the late 1990s there was growing evidence of a slowdown in productivity in the GR areas of Asia, and this has spurred interest in TCs. Many farmers shifted to rice intensification strategies – planting two or three crops per year instead of the customary one – and this practice has degraded the ecological system of the rice paddies. Frequently, agricultural specialists have warned that Asia's great success with the GR is coming to an end. Investment in irrigation slowed in the 1990s as more investment went into land rehabilitation.

Monocropping has led to a build-up in pests and a growing expenditure on pesticides. As fertilizer use and pesticide expenditures climb to maintain yield the gains of the Green Revolution are declining. In some instances farmers have increased their use of fertilizer at a 10 percent per year rate. India's public sector expenditures for fertilizer absorbed 80 percent of the subsidies devoted to agriculture in the early 1990s (Morris and Byerlee 1998: 470). Prabhu Pingali's research points to a number of growing weaknesses in the GR strategy. Among the problems he highlights are soil compaction, changes in soil composition, soil toxicity, increases in soil salinity because of flooding techniques employed in rice cultivation. Phosphorous and potassium depletion in the soils has been a negative externality of intensive use of nitrogen fertilizers. Loss of these soil nutrients has given rise to an unbalanced soil composition. Perennial flooding, meanwhile, has leached out micronutrients such as zinc. Pests are showing increasing resistance to pesticides, and herbicides are under scrutiny due to indications of weed resistance. Across Asia Pingali found many instances of yield declines in the 1980s, compared to the 1970s. Where yields were maintained or increased the growing use of inputs (declining productivity) was often noted (Pingali 1998). In the case of TCs, critics believe that it is merely a matter of time before pest resistance is degraded and/or adverse health implications are documented as a result of animal or human consumption.

The developmental problems of cash crop farmers

Caught between the two extremes of the agrarian dualistic structure are the cash crop cultivators, typically with mid-sized farming operations. These cultivators produce almost entirely for the market with the aid of four to twelve agricultural workers hired on a permanent basis. Such farmers are important to any successful development strategy, both because they control a significant portion of the land (23 percent in Latin America, for example) and because they provide an even higher percentage of the food domestically produced and marketed. In short, such farmers normally constitute a vital source of food for the urbanized workforce. Since food purchases constitute a very high portion of the expenditures of the industrial workforce, quite often 50 percent or higher, the search for policies which attempt to harmonize the developmental needs of the cash crop farmers with those of the industrial work force is of utmost importance. Some of the factors that make cash crop farming distinct from peasant agriculture are highlighted in Table 11.5.

Cash crop farmers face several alternatives in their decision to plant and market their output. In production, they can cultivate either staples of the population's basic diet, such as rice, beans, corn, wheat, lentils, oats, and manioc, or they can produce specialty crops, such as fruits and vegetables or export crops, including tropical products, such as coffee and tea or bananas, or non-traditional exports, such as fresh-cut flowers or wine destined for consumption at home by the more wealthy and in developed countries.

Table 11.5 Peasant production conditions versus cash crop farming

Concept	Peasant production	Cash crop farming
Production objective	Survival of the family	Profit maximization
Labor force	Family members	Hired wage labor
Productivity of labor	Maximize output, without regard to labor quantity	Productivity > wage rate
Marketing	Home use plus cash crop (low level of specialization)	Production for market
Risk	Extreme risk-aversion	Risk accepted, based on estimated profitability
Technology	Extremely labor-intensive, uneven adoption of new methods	Capital intensive, dynamically adaptive

Staple production

Staple crops are often referred to as wage goods, because they form the bulk of the diet for working people in the industrial, government, and service sectors of the economy. In many developing nations, the government forms a purchasing board to set the price of such wage good crops. Often, the purchasing board's decisions reflect urban bias in that the "buy price" is set at an extremely low level. The one-sided logic of this strategy is to favor the industrial workforce with cheap wage goods. Such a strategy allows employers to keep wages low, and profits higher, without affecting the urban standard of living, but this comes at the expense of both the cash crop farmers and their employees.

For the cash crop farmers, the low buy price paid by government, acting in its role as a monopsonist, creates a potent disincentive which can lead cash crop farmers to switch production toward speciality and export crops. Then, to compensate for a shortfall in the domestic production of staples, the government may adopt a policy of importation of cereals and legumes to make up for the shortage of domestic production brought on by its own policies. Large-scale agribusiness corporations in the advanced industrial nations often can produce these crops at a lower average price than domestic cultivators, due to the use of more advanced levels of mechanization, chemically assisted production, and a variety of subsidies. When food imports form an important part of the consumption of basic foodstuffs in a developing nation, domestic cash crop farmers will tend to be driven from the market. A vicious circle may then ensue. Urban bias leads to a shift away from basic foodstuff cultivation, which leads to cheap food imports, which leads to a further reduction in the production and marketing of basic foodstuffs (Byerlee 1992). This can lead, in the future, to a crisis in the balance of payments if total imports exceed exports for too long.

Speciality crop production

When cash crop farmers shift production toward fruits and vegetables and meat and dairy products, they both avoid the urban bias implicit in government control of the staple food markets and are, at the same time, responding to the highly unequal distribution of income in most developing nations. Luxury meat and cheese products and wines, for example, may be readily available and relatively cheap by international standards, but at the same time, there may be shortages in the domestic production of food staples that must be met by imports. Rectification of this situation may entail difficult choices and policies, such as luxury taxes on certain food products, or income taxes which could be used to support targeted entitlement programs to transfer income to the poor, instead of utilizing a too-low "buy price" program to attempt to subsidize low-income consumers. Income transfers would increase the demand for food staples via an injection of purchasing power into the hands of the poor, and the quantity supplied of such staple products would be expected to increase as the market price received by producers would rise in the absence of a government-imposed "buy price."

Export crops

In addition to the problems created when cash crop producers shift from food staple production to fruits, vegetables, and food luxury items for high-income domestic consumers, cash crop producers can also switch to export crops. Once again, such a situation can be critical when policies which have been imposed to favor the urbanized population lead to a strong counter-reaction in the countryside. Emphasis on export crops can lead to a diminution of land planted to food staples, thereby necessitating expanded food imports. In such a situation, a nation may be forced to deal with a series of exchanges and structures (in the nations from which they now draw imported food staples) which it cannot control, and may not be able to influence, in order to provide basic foodstuffs. First, there is the difficulty of obtaining foreign exchange. Second, imported food products can be affected by export tariffs and quotas (from the supplying – exporting – nations) which are beyond the control of the importing nation. Third, the vagaries of planting and domestic consumption in the exporting nations can have a devastating impact on the food-importing nations. However, the difficulties inherent in food exports are hardly new; virtually all less-developed nations, because of their colonial history, are highly involved in the export of tropical food products, as we saw in Table 11.3. The issue, then, is normally not one of pure food self-sufficiency, but whether such nations should travel further down the path wherein much of their land, and a much higher portion of their best land, is devoted to exports.

Production problems in cash crops

Medium-sized cash crop producers face a variety of barriers to production that tend to increase their costs of production, three of which are briefly considered here.

Appropriate technology

Cash crop farmers combine the use of wage laborers with a certain degree of mechanization. However, most mechanized farm implements have been engineered for use in the advanced industrial nations, where relatively high wages prevail. Thus many available forms of agricultural capital tend to be labor-saving in their design, to economize on wages. In the less-developed countries, however, labor tends to be relatively abundant compared to capital, so labor is relatively cheaper. This means that the optimal combination of labor and capital in production in most less-developed countries would utilize more labor relative to capital when compared to developed-country production techniques. Appropriate technologies in agriculture, that is, appropriate to the labor and capital mix of less-developed nations, can be of fundamental importance in finding new combinations of capital and labor which would both provide relatively more employment and capture the advantages of the relatively cheap labor so abundant in such economies. Furthermore, such technologies need to be "appropriate" in the sense that the mechanical devices in use should be relatively simple to operate, easy to repair, and durable.

Sometimes, finding the appropriate technology is a simple matter of selecting off-the-shelf products. For example, in facing the issue of irrigation, there are several ways in which cultivators can proceed. To take a simple and perhaps overdrawn case, imagine that the options are between choosing a high technology or an intermediate technology. In the high-tech scenario, laser-guided irrigation machines, integrated to computers, could be employed. Or, with intermediate technology, pipes and tubes, which can be locally produced and easily repaired without a reliance on foreign technicians and imported parts, can be employed with a much better "fit" in the developing society. Here we can view already existing alternative technologies in use, and one would suspect that few examples of the high-tech method would be utilized in the less-developed world.

In viewing the choice to plough a field, however, we do not actually see the appropriate technology. Instead, the choice is often between a modern tractor and a team of oxen pulling a wooden plough. What less-developed countries require might be a particular type of tractor which is more versatile in the often uneven terrains of small, marginal farm land, and one less prone to needing repair than the machine which best fits the production needs in a more advanced nation. But it is the latter tractor which is likely to be available, not the former. Thus engineering of the alternative tractor is waiting to be done; it typically is not available on the market as a choice for the small to medium-sized farmer. Creating such an alternative technology, however, entails a commitment to agricultural research, to mechanical research, and most particularly to basic education in the less-developed economies.

Yet as a result of urban bias and many of the factors discussed earlier, the commitment to agricultural research and development (R&D) is extremely small: in 1975 for every $100 of agricultural GDP production developing nations spent only 48 cents on agricultural R&D. Industrial nations spent $1.55 for every $100 of output in 1975, and $2.68 in 1995. Meanwhile, in 1995 developing nations spent only 62 cents per $100 of agricultural output (UNDP 2001: 110). Furthermore, it demands a commitment to the long run. Alternative technologies are too rarely developed precisely because of their distant pay-off, because of their smaller potential market, and because most less-developed nations have not yet created the required cadre of scientists and engineers who can undertake to adapt technologies to the needs of their countries.

Those few scientists and engineers who are available in less-developed nations often have received their education abroad, and this education rarely prepares them for the task of confronting the particular production problems of poor nations. Compounding the problem is the brain drain; many promising students, once they have received their education abroad, decide to remain in the advanced industrial nation, where they perceive they have greater opportunity (Adler 1987). Still, research on the impact of 85 public research institutes in 81 developing countries found that the average rate of return on a dollar invested in agricultural research, over time, was 80 cents – nearly twice the rate of return achieved in agriculture in the industrial nations (UN, Department of Economic and Social Affairs 2000: 183).

Labor supply

Cash crop farmers are further constrained by the available labor supply in the rural areas. Landless peasants and smallholders will form the basis of their labor force. But the effects of urban bias, which severely limits educational spending in the countryside, mean that the rural labor force will be likely to have limited educational skills, thus reducing their potential productivity. Irregularities in labor supply will also present a structural barrier to cash crop farmers, who must compete for the labor-time of peasants who need to tend to their own small plots, particularly at peak times such as harvests. Landless peasants will often hire out to construction projects or in a variety of other activities such as unloading cargo, hawking products in nearby villages, selling artisan wares, and so on, thereby further restricting the cash crop farmer's access to hired labor. Furthermore, low wage levels and the irregularity of employment of occasional workers, combined with the general lack of adequate public health care, again particularly acute in the rural areas, often translate into a workforce which is burdened with malnutrition and chronic gastrointestinal disorders. As a consequence, the output per worker per day can be quite low, thereby creating major impediments to the efficiency of cash crop production.

Credit markets

The financial sector tends to reflect urban bias, in that bankers infrequently establish banks in the small and medium-sized villages and towns near where cash crop farmers operate. Bankers are rarely trained in agricultural production or its special problems, and they are not necessarily receptive to the petitions of farmers for credit, particularly small and medium-sized landholders. The formal credit market tends to be urban-based and sophisticated in terms of extending business loans, financing real-estate transactions, facilitating foreign investments, and investing in the local stock and bond markets. But rural lending tends to be outside the expertise, or interest, of urban center banks with loanable funds.

Credit, then, is too often of limited availability in rural areas. As a stop-gap measure, informal credit markets tend to develop; moneylenders surface in the rural areas, who know their clients and their production capabilities and risks quite well. Two new barriers may arise, however, in dealing with this curb-side banking, as it is sometimes called.

First, as local monopolists, the moneylenders, who are often merchants or owners of larger farming operations, may be able to impose exorbitant interest charges which drain off a significant portion of the net proceeds of the farm income of small borrowers. Second, informal moneylenders normally have a very limited supply of liquid funds to lend. Consequently, the level of borrowing from such sources will likely be highly constrained. Recognizing this, many governments have specifically channeled credit through agrarian development banks, the purpose of which is to target the borrowing needs of smaller cash crop farmers who lack access to formal channels of credit. Such a policy can be highly successful in meeting the special credit needs of farmers, but, as is true of so many other programs, it needs to be targeted carefully to meet the special needs of small and medium-sized farm operators.

Large landholdings and agrarian backwardness

Throughout the less-developed world, large tracts of land owned by domestic landowners are rarely utilized to produce agricultural output in a purely capitalistic manner. What typically is found are two widespread forms of land usage, renting and sharecropping. Large owners may divide their lands into a multiplicity of small plots and either rent them out to small peasants for a fee or have sharecroppers who divide their output with the landowner. If the rental/sharecropping arrangement results in a lack of adequate mechanization, and/or increased erosion, and/or underutilization of fertilizers because the renter, or tenant, is forced to take a very short-term view, then both the renter or tenant and the landlord are likely to be utilizing the land in a sub-optimal manner, both privately and socially.

The early classical economists, particularly Adam Smith and David Ricardo (see Chapter 4), criticized the "unproductive" landlord class and strongly believed that sharecropping and land rental farming were inefficient. Later, Alfred Marshall took much the same position, arguing that sharecroppers would have little incentive to make improvements to the land. Current research, however, is much more cautious in approaching the question of efficiency. Several studies and models have indicated that it is possible to have a relatively efficient land tenure arrangement involving tenants and landlords, or at least to have a production arrangement which does not fulfill the dire anticipations of Smith, Ricardo, and Marshall (Stiglitz 1992).

Keith Griffin (1974), on the other hand, has emphasized the issue of land and income distribution, rather than that of optimal production, in his research on agriculture. He has drawn the conclusion that it is not land tenure arrangements *per se* which lead to agricultural retardation, but rather that the crucial issue is how the benefits of greater output are shared between renters or tenants and landlords.

> In our view, the problem in India and in other agrarian economies is not that some types of tenure systems are inflexible and inhibit innovation but that as long as the ownership of land is unequally distributed, and access to investment opportunities restricted, the benefits of whatever innovation does occur will be captured largely by the more prosperous landlords.
>
> (Griffin 1974: 91)

In Griffin's view, what precedes sharecropping – unequal power relations in the countryside – rather than the question of sharecropping *per se* is what is fundamental. He describes a situation in which, if production increases due to improvements made by sharecroppers, most or all the net increase in output ends up being captured by the landlord.

Why? Because while the total yield may go up, the share received by the sharecroppers can be adjusted downward, to the benefit of the landowner. This can result when the supply of potential sharecroppers steadily increases every year, as more and more peasants are forced off their land, or have to engage in sharecropping as part of their survival strategy. Thus, the bargaining power of each individual tenant farmer declines as their total supply rises, allowing landlords to renegotiate distributive shares in their favor. Alternatively, the net amount of the harvest received by the tenant may remain relatively constant in spite of increased output, if the growth in production is achieved via mechanization and/or fertilizers and herbicides, with the landlord acting as the "middleman" in providing these inputs. Landowners also can gain a larger income share by requiring their tenants to rent tractors and to buy other agricultural inputs exclusively from them. It is via such processes that Griffin maintains that the benefits of technical change will be captured, in large degree, by the landlords and not the tenants, so that it is the distributive question which must logically precede the optimal production issue.

The issues surrounding the question of land ownership, however, continue to attract attention, and some researchers have found reason to continue to align themselves with the tradition of Smith, Ricardo, and Marshall, although not necessarily for the same reasons which those authors cited. For example, an econometric study of four districts in India, conducted by Radwan Ali Shaban (1987), compared sharecropping production results with the level of output achieved on land owned by small farmers. The results quite clearly show that where property and distribution rights are clearly defined, that is, on privately owned land, both the intensity of production and the level of output exceed the corresponding levels from less-secure production and distribution schemes, such as sharecropping:

- Both inputs and outputs were greater on the land owned by cultivators than on share-cropped land.
- After controlling for variables such as irrigation, plot value, and soil quality, it was found that output was 16 percent higher on the owned land.
- Family male labor use was 21 percent higher and female labor use was 47 percent higher on owned land.
- Draft animal usage was 17 percent higher on owned land.

Summarizing the results of this study, Stephen Smith concluded: "The theory and evidence considered in this study suggest that sharecropping is less technically efficient than owner-farming or fix-rent farming in many, but not all, instances" (Smith 1994: 35). The dispute over the efficiency of different land tenure forms has not been resolved fully, but the dominant view may be once again shifting toward the classical economists' perception that the precise nature of the land tenure system and the property and distribution rights accompanying these are of fundamental importance in considering the efficient use of land.

The structuralist view

In Latin America, particularly through the 1960s, structuralist economists (see Chapter 6 for other details) argued that backward land tenure systems were at the heart of the lack of development in agriculture. Alain de Janvry nicely captures the essence of the structuralist argument.

> Structuralists claim that agricultural prices have not been particularly unfavorable in the last 40 years and that stagnation results from producer behavior under archaic land tenure systems. Survival of precapitalist relations of production imply rigidities in supply response; … absentee management and autocratic, hierarchical labor relations impede the spread of innovations. The high degree of monopoly of productive resources and of institutional services (credit, information, etc.) permits the landlords to derive enormous economic rents and social advantages even while using the land highly extensively. As a result, behavior of the landed elite is oriented more toward maintenance of the economic and social status quo than toward profit maximization and capital accumulation.
>
> (de Janvry 1981: 146)

de Janvry strongly disputes this structuralist depiction of agrarian structures in Latin America, not as an institutional–historical description, but as an adequate analysis of recent trends. His research suggests that the social structures which were conducive in the past to the landed elite's misuse of land are quickly breaking down. The semi-feudal use of land is being replaced by capitalist land usage, as the last vestiges of a bygone era are swept away by the intrusions of the logic of the purely market-based economy. The old *hacendado* mentality, wherein land was a symbol of social stature, is being replaced by a new ethos wherein land is simply another capital asset, and the rate of return on land must be maximized through optimal production techniques.

If this is a correct depiction of current land usage, the dilemmas of development may, to some degree, be compounded rather than relieved. An unfettered capitalist strategy in agriculture will likely lead to the substitution of capital for labor, to further concentration in land ownership, and to the expulsion of large numbers of peasants from their small plots and from their status as intermittent farm laborers. A new dynamic then ensues: labor expelled from rural areas gravitates toward the urban areas, circling less-developed world cities in ever-expanding belts of misery and human degradation. Restructuring in the rural areas, then, may lead to increased yields in agriculture and an increase in the marketable surplus of crops either on the domestic or international market, as a result of the increasing displacement of small cultivators from the agrarian regions. Thus far, the employment absorptive capacity in most urban areas has been deficient in relation to the need to incorporate the population flow migrating from the rural areas. International migration has surged, too, as this process of creating landless workers has accelerated. And this new migration of labor from less-developed countries, some of it illegal, has created new forms of social stress and dissent, particularly in Western Europe and the United States.

Transnational agribusiness

Since the Second World War, and particularly since the mid-1960s, a new link has been formed with some corporations in the advanced industrial nations and the agrarian sectors in the less-developed world. Modern agriculture is increasingly dependent upon research and development of herbicides, fungicides, insecticides, and synthetic fertilizers, most of which are produced by the huge petroleum transnationals through their enormous petro-chemicals divisions. The bulk of the original research on these new chemical combinations was conducted during, or shortly after, the Second World War. At first, diffusion of the new products occurred principally within the advanced industrial nations. By the mid-1960s, however, market saturation led to the desire by the agro-transnationals to extend their sales into the less-developed world. This coincided with increasing concerns with a "population time-bomb" in the less-developed world and the need for agricultural output to increase faster than the rate of growth of population. Widespread usage of, and often dependence upon, new fertilizers, pesticides, and hybrid seeds provided by the new transnational agribusiness interests has sometimes been encouraged and financed by governments in the poor nations. Another source of such technological diffusion has been the spread of contract farming, whereby large and intermediate-sized farmers agree to plant, cultivate, and harvest according to the terms set by a contractor, often a large food-processing corporation based in the advanced industrial nations.

Agribusiness corporations have also made new incursions into the less-developed world in order to control cattle ranchers who are suppliers for the hamburger chains, such as McDonald's, and other fast-food restaurants in the more developed nations. Thus vertical integration in the increasingly concentrated restaurant business has had a profound impact on certain less-developed nations, sometimes taking good agricultural land out of the available domestic supply in order to export beef, which requires a land-intensive form of production. In the process, such farming operations can contribute to deforestation, land degradation, and environmental pollution, ranging from soil erosion to global warming.

Finally, largely as a result of the increasingly sophisticated network of transportation, including automated docks, ship containerization, roll-on-roll-off truck trailers and cargo jets, exotic crops are increasingly being grown for the high-income recipients of the advanced industrial nations. Thus an array of both tropical products and traditional luxury fruits and vegetables are now generally available year-round to those who can pay. Ernest Feder described this new phenomenon as "strawberry imperialism," partly because a northern seasonal "exotic" such as strawberries could be brought to Stockholm in the dead of winter from a distance of perhaps 4,000 miles via airfreight.

Unlike the older plantation economy arrangements, the new agribusiness conglomerates tend to make minimal commitments to high fixed cost assets such as land, docks, and railroads in the countries in which the production is derived. Rather, they emphasize contract farming, relying on existing infrastructure, rather than financing their own projects. Thus labor problems and the risks of weather, as well as long-term problems such as soil erosion or contamination of groundwater and streams, along with soil exhaustion, become the problems of the medium and large farmers who contract with the agribusiness TNCs, who can then simply contract out their purchases elsewhere. In the case of the new emphasis on cattle ranching for hamburger chains, many environmentalists have voiced concern over the tendency to push back rainforests in order to open up grazing land. The fear is that delicate environmental structures, where rainfall patterns are interrupted and where the holding capacity of the ground cover is now insufficient because of the elimination of much of the natural plant life, will be further adversely affected. Soil erosion can be an extremely serious negative externality in the cattle-ranching areas, as forests are cleared and grasslands lose their capacity to hold water. This can set up a vicious circle, whereby governments dispose of large tracts of rainforest for a modest payment, ranchers convert the land to cattle-grazing, erosion makes the land unsuitable within a few years, and the ranchers then pressure the government for access to new tracts of forest and savannah lands.

In the case of so-called exotic crops, though hard currency is earned via exports, a less-developed nation will have to share such new forms of revenue with the agribusiness transnational. Net foreign exchange earnings may well be quite modest, particularly when balanced against the opportunity costs of land shifted out of domestic food consumption and the possible adoption of cultivation practices which may not be sustainable, and/or which incur large external costs in the form of erosion which fouls stream beds, water supplies, and fish-spawning areas or environmentally important wetlands.

One example of a possible outcome under the new arrangements being formed by agribusiness TNCs in the less-developed world is Senegal's alliance with the giant Castle & Cooke operation.

> In 1972 Bud Antel Inc., a large California-based food conglomerate (taken over in 1978 by Castle & Cooke), formed a joint enterprise with the Senegalese government. The subsidiary, Bud Senegal is an affiliate with the House of Bud in Brussels. Bud Senegal grew vegetables, using a virtually labor-free drip irrigation system, with plastic tubes continuously supplying water to each plant individually, to tap the vast reserves of water just below the Senegal's dry soil. Three times a week from early December until May, a DC-10 cargo jet takes off from Senegal loaded with green beans, melons, tomatoes, aubergines, strawberries and paprika. The destinations are Amsterdam, Paris, and Stockholm. The vegetables are not marketed locally, but in any event few Senegalese have enough money to buy them. Local people gained few jobs from the project, and in laying out the 450 hectare plantation Bud uprooted the indigenous baobab trees which were an important village resource, having previously provided local families with rope, planting materials, fuel, and wind erosion protection.
>
> (Dixon 1990:42)

TNCs have tended to focus on expanding their market concentration in recent years. For example, by 2005 only three firms controlled 90 percent of the global coffee trade. Increasing concentration allows the agribusiness giants more leverage over millions of small suppliers. In 1992 global coffee sales were $30 billion, with producers receiving

40 percent of this total. By 2002 sales had increased to $50 billion and the producers' share had been cut to only 16 percent, and their income actually declined by one-third (FAO 2005). In general the introduction of neoliberal policies in developing nations has proven advantageous to agroindustrial transnationals as they have been freer to transport and sell food products, as many nations have abandoned goals of food self-sufficiency and have ceased to nurture their own agricultural sector through subsidies, tariffs, directed credit, and other means. This has led to higher levels of concentration of the giant agribusiness firms devoted to processing, transporting, and distributing agricultural commodities, as they have been able to introduce new technologies and capture the benefits of scale economies in processing and distribution. For example, "controlled atmosphere" technologies are now commonly used to prolong freshness of fruit and vegetables over vast distances, giving rise to the concept of "permanent global summertime" permitting fruits and vegetables to become the fastest-growth area in agricultural commodities in recent years and enabling China and India to rise to first and second place in terms of production. All this has led to the take-over through mergers and acquisitions or joint-ventures of higher portions of the agricultural sector, particularly at the wholesale/retail level by agribusiness TNCs (Reardon and Barrett 2000).

In developing countries growth in the agricultural system is strongest at the retail level, with supermarket sales growing at the rate of 20 percent per year in some nations. This has led retail giants such as Wal-Mart, Carrefour, Metro, Royal Ahold, and a few others to rapidly advance their marketing position. Much of this growth has been due to major agroindustrial firms restructuring their production and marketing on a global basis. For example, foreign ownership of Brazil's booming agribusiness sector is soaring: from 1994 to1998 soy production went from 30 percent TNC production to 48 percent, pork leaped from 11 to 40 percent, and poultry from 8 to 34 percent (Jank and Franco 1999: 365). As production methods, diets, and transporting and distribution methods change, agribusiness has repositioned its activities to find new opportunities, always focusing on four high value-added areas: (1) inputs such as pesticides (ten firms, none from developing nations, controlled 80 percent of sales in 2004) or seeds (nearly half the world market was controlled by ten firms, none from developing nations); (2) growth areas such as fruits and vegetables and meat products; (3) food processing (dominated by US firms, including seven of the top ten in 2004); and (4) food retailing, the fastest-growing of all segments in developing nations. Setting aside China and India, where growth in expenditures has been very strong, agricultural research and development (R&D) expenditures have grown modestly in developing nations in the 1980–2000 period. Transnational corporations are commonly understood to derive much of their advantage from their ability to develop and control technology – a situation that extends to the agribusiness TNCs. Developed nations spend eight times more on R&D per $100 of agricultural GDP than do developing nations, and this is a primary reason for the continued expansion of the role of TNCs in the agricultural sector of developing nations (Alston and Pardy 2006: 22).

Government in agricultural development

Although some economists have recently turned to free markets in the hope of accelerating the development process (see Chapter 7), major agricultural specialists have long maintained that a successful development strategy in agriculture must at a minimum have some state intervention to foment needed changes. In the forefront of this discussion is the research work of Bruce Johnston and John Mellor, who, according to Peter Trimmer, advocate a "market policy" approach which would combine the advantages to be found through active government policies toward agricultural development with the benefits to be derived from properly channeled market forces.

> [The strategy] calls for government policy interventions into market outcomes but uses markets and the private marketing sector as the vehicle for those policy interventions. This "market policy" approach recognizes widespread "market failures" in agriculture as well as extensive "government failures" in implementation of economic tasks. The strategic dilemma is how to cope with segmented rural capital and labor markets, poorly functioning land markets, the welfare consequences of sharp instability of prices in commodity markets the pervasive lack of information about current and future events in most rural economies, and sheer absence of many important markets.
>
> (Trimmer 1989: 358)

One of John Mellor's major concerns has been the general lack of output response when increasing demands have been placed on less-developed world agricultural producers (this is the problem of low elasticity of supply). Mellor argues that in most instances higher prices and profits will not call forth much of an increase in the quantity supplied, as the neoliberals believe, because cultivators have tended to reach the limits of existing technologies and traditional inputs. Thus to increase agricultural output, a major shift toward new and appropriate technologies is needed, as well as massive investments in infrastructural elements that will relieve some of the bottlenecks on the supply-side of the agricultural sector. Mellor believes that a strategy which brings agricultural needs into the foreground will also have a impact on the demand for labor by increasing wages. This will, in turn, create more disposable income, which will, for the most part, be spent on food.

While Mellor does not believe that a strategy of development which pushes agriculture into the foreground will solve the unemployment or underemployment dilemmas in agriculture, it will contribute to a significant reduction in the ranks of the unemployed. Mellor would, in fact, provide more governmental support to agriculture than to industry, and he emphasizes that the success stories in food production are to be found precisely in those nations where the state was actively involved in the diffusion of food-growing technologies, particularly through a technically competent extension service.

> Agriculture, with its small-scale orientation, is more in need of public-sector support than industry. The sharp turn-around in Asian agriculture – resulting in a 30 percent increase in growth rates in basic food-staple production from the 1960s to the 1970s – impressively demonstrates the results of turning the public sector's attention to the requisites of technological change in agriculture.
>
> (Mellor 1998a: 144)

While Mellor's emphasis on the need for technological diffusion and massive infrastructural investments in agriculture is certainly well-reasoned and supported by the successes of the East Asian economies and other examples, the problems of agriculture are not purely technological. The countryside needs to be understood as an arena where gross injustices have often been perpetrated, and the powerful have behaved with impunity, often for centuries. In this environment, it is important for those engaged in economic development to understand the grievances of small cultivators. This will not be easy for "outsiders" to comprehend, because small cultivators have usually nurtured a profound distrust of anyone who, in an

FOCUS 11.6   AGRICULTURE AND THE ENVIRONMENT: PROPERTY RIGHTS AND RESOURCE DEPLETION

Many environmental problems are traceable to issues of property rights and a lack of property rights enforcement. Throughout the developing world, vast tracts of land are held as common property resources and as state property. If policy regarding land use is ill-defined, either at the community level and/or at the level of the national government, environmental problems caused by the overuse of resources are likely to arise, creating vicious circles of desertification, famine, and increasing poverty. This is the problem known as the tragedy of the commons.

In Africa, pastoral arrangements often allow for overgrazing, unbalanced forestry practices, and forest depletion through the scavenging for fuel. In India, the rural poor derive as much as 20 percent of their income from foraging and from grazing their animals on commons areas. In Latin America, vast tracts of tropical forests are national property, but the use of this land is subject to little systematic management, and the predicted over- and misuse with which the tragedy of the commons literature abounds is the consequence. In Nepal, for example, population growth led to the expansion of peasant agriculture into forest regions, resulting in the loss of 20 to 50 percent of all forests within a decade.

Neoliberal economists have often argued that overgrazing, desertification, and deforestation on common and national lands can be resolved through the establishment of private property rights. Without well-defined private property rights, it is believed, individuals will have little incentive to conserve resources. Sometimes a compelling case can be made for the market-based solution which they advocate. In other instances, however, redefining communal practices, strengthening pastoral associations, or creating governmental oversight agencies can be a solution which strengthens long-standing institutional arrangements.

There are alternatives to simply privatizing all land, forests, and the seas to prevent overuse and the tragedy of the commons outcome. Nepal, for example, has reversed its policy of open access to woodlands by strengthening village and community control over these resources.

Current research suggests that a resolution of these issues arises only when property rights are well defined and enforced. Adequate management of such resources can proceed using either a private property-based distribution or a combination of communal and national ownership, but with a critical eye on the socially optimal use of such resources. What this implies if such resources are not privately held is either limits on use of commons resources and/or fees for use.

Source: Tomich *et al.* 1995: 33

official capacity, arrives in the countryside with the intention of "doing good" or "fostering development." Based on a study of agrarian issues in ten poor nations, David Lea and D.P. Chaudhri concluded that:

> To us it seems that the role of modern inputs, infrastructure and other enabling institutions is important but grossly exaggerated. More important than these inputs is local participation, local organization and skillful use of historical experience by the policy-makers. The role of the human element, individual and collective, can hardly be overstated in this respect.
>
> Rural development successes ... on a national scale are likely to be glaring exceptions and would be the result of a balanced growth strategy pursued by an enlightened and sensitive national leadership who can inspire confidence and a sense of participatory economic justice among the rural peasantry and landless poor. Such conditions cannot

be created in a hurry. The strength of the past and continuity seems rather formidable. Change can be induced successfully if, and only if, the policy-makers and planners understand the working of the rural socioeconomic system and are prepared to hasten slowly.

(Lea and Chaudhri 1983: 337–8)

Land reform

Land reform has been used to describe a very wide variety of changes in land ownership. For example, **colonization** programs, where land is given to small farmers who are willing to conquer wastelands, jungles, and other unsettled areas of marginal productive value, often fall under this heading. Likewise, programs that are designed to partition extremely large neo-feudal landholdings into smaller parcels, while leaving virtually untouched all other large landholders, have been considered as land reforms. And land reform has sometimes meant the break-up of village agrarian systems, where land is farmed in common without individual land title; such policies often also entail the sale of previously unclaimed forests and grazing lands which had been utilized on an as-needed basis by subsistence cultivators, much as commons lands had been used in Europe centuries before.

Nonetheless, the most common usage of the term land reform refers to the conversion of most, or all, large estates and privately held tracts of land to smallholder shares. Such a shift can, but need not, entail the direct entitlement of land ownership to smallholders. Rather, land title may reside in the hands of a village system; periodic redistribution can be made as the number of families grows or declines, and to suit other demographic changes at the village level. Normally, land reform sets strict limits on the maximum size of smallholdings. While some specialists argue that land reform is a dead issue, others believe that **negotiated land reform** may give new life to this issue. Under negotiated land reform there is an attempt to create a responsive market for large landholdings and to give both grants and loans to smallholders/peasants to buy land at fair market value. This approach, which demands the participation of either federal or state governments, avoids the politically explosive issue of condemnation and confiscation of large estates. Some countries are seriously engaged in negotiated sales, such as Brazil, Colombia, and South Africa (Deininger 1999).

These programs fall more broadly under the heading of **market-led agrarian reform (MLAR)**, and they include a strong focus on the setting up of viable markets in land. Some of the methods used include "titling" programs to clear land-ownership documents, an issue of extreme importance where women may be able for the first time to gain full legal title to plots of land they farm. Other approaches seek to rationalize sharecropping arrangements. Yet another approach, backed by the World Bank in countries where large estates are farmed inefficiently, is to advocate progressive land taxes, possibly applicable only to farms above a certain minimum. The MLAR approach is thought to be more efficient, from the World Bank's perspective, than earlier state-led agrarian reform schemes because no costly ministry of agrarian reform is required, and no entrenched bureaucracy will result. Nor will the state be burdened with the funding for the acquisition of land because peasants and small cultivators will obtain loans from the private banking sector or from aid agencies to finance purchases of land. The most important factor and guiding principle of MLAR is cooperation with landlords. Another aspect of MLAR is the privatization of farm extension services – another approach to shrinking the role of the state. Saturnino Borras has conducted a broad assessment of land reform in the Philippines, where 10 million hectares of land – one-third of all land – became the target for land reform in 1988 (Borras 2005). Furthermore, 2 million hectares of sharecropping land would be converted to a leaseholder arrangement. The project was scheduled to affect 4 million peasants, 80 percent of the agricultural population. According to the official agency charged with the land reform, by 2001 5 million hectares had been redistributed to 2 million poor families – although critics put the numbers much lower (Borras 2006: 101). All the above occurred via either a mandated land transfer arrangement or via a voluntary land transfer scheme that reflected the new approach of MLAR.

Although not stressed by the government, increasingly the main focus turned to voluntary land reform. But, at this point "landlord bias" came into the process, with a very large share of the "new owners" under the voluntary scheme actually being fictional or unqualified as large landholders proceeded to transfer "reformed" land back to their possession via their children and other relatives (Borras 2005: 103–10). One top administrator estimated that up to 70 percent of the land transfers were fraudulent (ibid.: 116). Nor did the "titling" program work as the World Bank anticipated: in one flagrant case the agribusiness giant Dole effectively took control of 20,000 hectares of prime land when Dole advanced the loan funds for a land transfer to 20,000 peasant households, but only on the condition that the peasants "owners" lease the land to Dole and that they would work for Dole as long as twenty years as laborers on "their" land at the minimum wage ($3.20 per day). Officially this might appear a successful "titling" program within the concept of MLAR. In reality Dole locked in a captive labor force at subsistence wages, effectively continuing to control the land and its use (ibid.: 111–12). More generally, Borras found that in Brazil, Colombia, and South Africa under MLAR projects landowners managed to overprice land by 30–50 percent while frequently selling only marginal or excess land (ibid.: 123). In Brazil, where the state for some time since the 1990s has been engaged in the process of purchasing land for land settlement, large landowners have refused to sell to the state. Most state purchases (82 percent) have come from small and intermediate-level farmers who have sold underutilized or abandoned land (Borras 2003: 377). Most of the land acquired was in remote, roadless areas without irrigation or electricity, condemning most "beneficiaries" to income levels lower than their pre-ownership levels (ibid.: 378, 380). Hence, where large landholders farm or utilize only 17 percent of their vast holdings of 360 million hectares, the goal of reducing the power of the landed agroexport elite is not being realized.

Given the research by Borras and others into the applications of the MLAR approach, and given the renewed thrust of governments and social movements for distributing land to peasants without burdening them with loan payments and privatized farm extension services, some specialists are now advocating a return to state-led agrarian reforms that do not involve full compensation to landlords. Most adamant has been Keith Griffin, who has vigorously marshaled an array of theoretical arguments and empirical evidence urging a return to state-led land reform schemes that offer limited or no compensation to large landholders (Griffin, Khan, and Ickowitz 2002, 2004). The premise behind such an approach is that large landholders have reaped the advantages of controlled labor markets which have unjustly lowered farm-workers' incomes, often for generations. Large landowners have frequently managed to avoid justified land taxes, they have received subsidies in the form of irrigation projects, electrification and roads, and they have often acquired lands through manipulation and "arranged" land deals orchestrated by friendly governments.

As do the advocates of MLAR, Griffin *et al.* maintain that when properly measured, there are no linear economies of scale in agriculture (Figure 11.1), and that peasant farms of an indeterminate but small size are the best way in which a poor nation can achieve higher levels of food production. Figure 11.1 is presented for illustrative purposes; it is not based directly on empirical evidence. The least controversial and best established portion of the

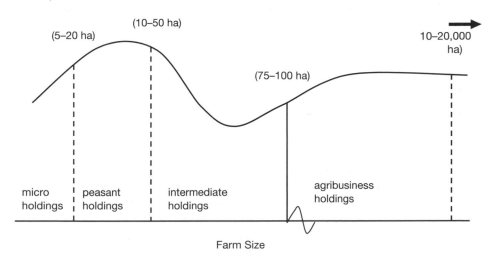

Yield per hectare

(10–50 ha)

(5–20 ha)

10–20,000 ha)

(75–100 ha)

micro holdings

peasant holdings

intermediate holdings

agribusiness holdings

Farm Size

Figure 11.1 Farm size and yields.

curving function portrayed is that which differentiates "micro holdings" from peasant holdings. As we have noted above in analyzing the Green Revolution in India, very small holdings, in some countries those below 5 hectares – but in India even lower – are less efficient than larger holdings. Further, Griffin *et al.* maintain that while peasants can deploy a great deal of labor to raise yields at little opportunity cost, intermediate farmers are at a double disadvantage – they are too large to obtain most of the labor needed from large families and must pay wages for labor inputs, yet they are too small to use machinery and equipment at full advantage and will probably pay a premium for loans either from banks or large landholders who also function as moneylenders. Then, as farms become larger – perhaps in the region of 100 hectares – economies of scale are to be found. Most important to Griffin *et al.* is the fact that while these economies exist, the average yield is never as high as that achieved by the peasantry.

Thus there is a social rate of return to agrarian reform as the farm land in a nation is distributed in a manner that will ensure maximum yield. This analysis is supported by empirical studies of Brazil, showing that peasant families have a yield more than 50 percent higher than commerical/agribusiness operations, where the average size of the peasant plots is 26 hectares and the commercial operations utilize on average 433 hectares (Griffin, Khan, and Ickowitz 2004: 369). Griffin *et al.* are careful to argue that the "inverse relationship" shown in Figure 11.1 is a tendency – not something one should anticipate universally.

These authors further maintain that while state-led land reform is currently needed in many nations such schemes will not be permanent, because as nations successfully engage in the process of economic development rural workers will eventually be drawn into industry, as the Lewis model presented in Chapter 5 anticipated (Griffin, Khan, and Ickowitz 2002: 318). The approach of these authors seemed to resonate in 2006, when the government of Bolivia announced that it would confront the unequal distribution of land, wherein 10 percent of the landowners hold 90 percent of the land. Bolivia's planned agrarian reform would impact 77,000 square miles of land if carried out (Romero 2006). But Griffin *et al.* have created a strident controversy, with their most adamant critics claiming that their advocacy of land reform is quixotic. Terrence Byres, for example, seems to echo Bill Warren (see Chapter 6) in arguing that there are in fact economies of scale in agriculture. If so, it is merely a matter of time before the peasantry are swept away and capitalist agriculture, either of the agribusiness-type or family-based cash crop farming, or both, replaces peasant agriculture and the vast reservoir of the underemployed in the countryside shifts to industrial and service sector employment (Byres 2006: 239–45).

In evaluating land reform schemes, it is important to keep in mind the fact that such programs typically seek to achieve a combination of political, social, and economic goals simultaneously. At the political level, land reform is often seen as a means to forestall or eliminate potential threats of a thorough-going social revolution by the landless. At the societal level, peasants may feel that the goal is social justice; they disregard the "big picture" issues such as "Is this socialism?" At the economic level, care needs to be exercised in assessing the outcome of a land reform program. Smallholders will, with the rarest exceptions, appropriate a larger share of agricultural output for themselves as they gain land and improve their own diets. This can mean, and often does mean, that the surplus of agricultural production above that which is consumed in the countryside can actually decline initially following land reform. For the mass of people living in the urban areas, and for the central government, land reform can create great difficulties if food scarcity becomes an issue. Such a situation can lead to a reliance on food imports and create a broad range of new political and social problems. Particularly if "urban bias" is present, critics will be quick to argue that land reform is a failure, though staying the course usually results in the marketable surplus rising.

Another issue of fundamental importance needs emphasis. The switching of ownership titles in the countryside, without an accompanying agricultural development strategy, will lead to failure and is not real land reform. Smallholders need not only title to their land; they also need the services, information, and training from agricultural extension services that can help to make them more productive. They need to be involved in research and development projects, and they need help in locating appropriate forms of mechanization, in learning about irrigation and water control projects, in gaining access to effective infrastructure, such as roads and schools, they need fertilizers and help in obtaining reasonable access to credit for future development.

In closing this chapter on agriculture, we will briefly examine two large land reform programmes: Mexico's *ejido* system, which is generally thought to have failed, and South Korea's model of agricultural development, known as the *Saemaul Undong*. But bear in mind that land reform has been achieved in a great number of other nations, such as Taiwan, China, Ethiopia, Bolivia, eastern India, Chile, and Iran. Currently land reform efforts are under way in Zimbabwe, Malawi, South Africa, Guatemala, El Salvador, Brazil, Bolivia, Venezuela, and Colombia.

Land reform in Mexico

As a result of the Mexican revolution (1910–17), which included widespread peasant revolts, particularly in land areas where plantation-style estates abounded, land reform was a *fait accompli* of the armed struggle. After the revolution, successive governments sought to complete the land reform, essentially breaking up tillable holdings in excess of 200 hectares. By 1976, 43 percent of land had been turned over to *ejidos*, which are village councils responsible for distributing land to their members. *Ejidos* were prohibited from renting, selling, or mortgaging the land. Unfortunately, the 28,000 *ejidos*, which provided land to 43 percent of all the farming families in Mexico, held only 16 percent of the irrigated land. The large landholders, a mere 2.5 percent of all landholders, were able to produce 40 percent of the food on 20 percent of the land. They were able to do so because, despite land redistribution, they had managed to hold on to and control the best land. They were able to finance irrigation projects themselves or, in the more likely instance, to benefit from government-created irrigation projects specifically aimed at large farms. And the large landholders had a near monopoly on credit. For example, between 1956 and 1969, the private commercial farmers received 85 percent of all agricultural credits granted by financial intermediaries (de Janvry 1981: 215).

At first it appeared that the *ejido* system was a social, political, and economic success. From 1938 to 1951, agricultural output leaped ahead at an annual rate of 4.3 percent. From 1951 to 1970, agricultural output growth exceeded 6 percent per annum. Then, however, Mexican agricultural growth virtually stopped. From 1970 to 1976, agricultural output per capita fell by more than 15 percent (de Janvry 1981: 217; Cypher 1990: 90). Grain imports soared; between 1970 and 1979, they totaled 689,000 tons, and in the 1980–9 period, they rose to 26 million tons (Russell 1994: 194). By 1996, 6 million tons of corn, more than 30 percent of national consumption, was imported from the US.

The great failure of small-scale Mexican agriculture following land reform was the result of several factors. In the 1970s, when greater emphasis should have been placed on agriculture because of the tightening of the "scissors" between land yields and population demands, the Mexican state became increasingly involved in industrial development, neglecting agriculture. Second, with the onset of the oil boom (1976–82), the Mexican government took the position that it would be more efficient to export oil, which commanded a high price at the time, and import food.

When the oil boom collapsed, however, and the debt crisis ensued, Mexico adopted neoliberal policies which reduced the size of governmental investments, particularly in the agrarian sector, and drastically reduced the subsidized credits which had been allocated to the smallholders, or *ejidatarios*. Subsidies which had been granted on fertilizers were virtually eliminated, and electricity prices were increased by 60 percent under the "get prices right" or "real prices" doctrine of neoliberalism. In order to trim its budget, the government lowered the buying price of corn and other staples, further squeezing the *ejidatarios*. Not surprisingly, agricultural growth fell well below the rate of growth in population.

In 1992, Mexico instituted sweeping changes in agriculture, essentially allowing *ejidatarios* to sell and rent their land and to use it as collateral for credit, while allowing corporations, both domestic and foreign, to buy such properties. In essence, by the 1990s, the Mexican effort at land reform had ended. Critics charge that these new trends will lead to a renewal of land concentration, expelling as many as 10 million rural residents (largely drawn from the 2.8 million former *ejido* cultivators and their families) from the countryside into Mexico's huge urban areas, or into international migration and ending the *ejido* system.

Korea's *Saemaul Undong*

Prior to Japanese colonial rule in the early twentieth century, the rural landholding nobility in Korea, the *yangban*, had held both the land and the peasants in a vice-like grip for over 500 years. By the late nineteenth century, much of the Korean countryside had been swept with unsuccessful peasant revolts and risings. Japanese rule brought some limitations on the *yangban*, as some Japanese adopted Korean landholdings. For the peasants, however, conditions and land concentration, as described in the following quotation, generally became worse under colonialism.

In 1914, only 1.8 per cent of the households owned 51 per cent of the cultivated land. Rents ranged from 50 to 60 per cent of the crop with tenants, who bore the costs of production, left with 20 per cent or less of the final production. As in many Asian countries in the colonial period, the change from sharecropping to fixed rents in rural Korea meant in bad years there was no relief from starvation. Contracts were verbal and could easily be manipulated or terminated by landlords and protestors faced possible imprisonment by the colonial state.

(Douglas 1983: 192–3)

In 1953, in the aftermath of the Korean war, which had left 10 million Koreans homeless in the devastated cities, a thorough-going land reform was instituted. Compensation paid to the *yangban* was minimal, 150 percent of the value of the annual harvest, with full payment spread over several years, an amount that was insufficient to compensate for the capitalized value of the land. Land was then distributed to the peasants, with an upper limit of 3 hectares. Once instituted, the land ownership pattern in South Korea has remained stable.

In the early years, Korean land reform had the appearance of a "title switching" program; peasants were forced to sell their surplus staples to the government, which redistributed them to the cities, with the price paid being so low that costs of production could not be covered. At first, Korean farmers were forced to compete with food-aid imports which came into Korea virtually free from the United States. Such difficult conditions in the countryside led to a massive out-migration of farmers. Such a demographic shift, however, was largely accomplished without an expanding underclass, as the South Korean industrialization program, and its emphasis on maintaining labor-intensive production via export substitution (see Chapter 10), helped to absorb the inflow of former agricultural workers. Still, the relative neglect of agriculture, and the migration it fostered, was telling; in 1969, 29 percent of the dwellings in Seoul were classified as slum/squatter dwellings, where many former peasants resided.

The neglect of agriculture created a poverty syndrome which had several dimensions. Low rural incomes meant ineffective demand for agricultural inputs ... Evidence for this period shows widening disparities between rural and urban incomes there is evidence to suggest that rural welfare, although not at the level of desperation of the 1950s, was not advancing. Real rural incomes stayed nearly the same for the decade (1960–70), while urban incomes doubled.

(Douglas 1983: 190–1)

Fortunately, government planners recognized the critical conditions in the agricultural sector in the course of the 1960s, and reforms were introduced. For example, interest rates above 20 percent per year on crop loans were declared illegal, and there was a general expansion of irrigation facilities. In 1972, with the third five-year plan, the government turned to an integrated strategy of agricultural development, the *Saemaul Undong*, which has successfully moved land reform from title switching to a genuine program of rural development. The strategies employed in South Korea contrast sharply with the growing neglect of small-scale producers in Mexico. The third five-year plan dealt with the slow growth in agricultural output – only a 2.3 percent increase per year in 1967–71 – via four integrated strategies:

- the general diffusion of high yield varieties of seeds, the domestic production of fertilizers, and greater application of pesticides;

- the mechanization of agriculture;
- state management of grain storage facilities; and
- a program of housing construction, rural electrification and feeder road construction.

During this period, the government allocated an extraordinary 28 percent of its budget to agricultural development! As a consequence, the differential between rural and urban living standards was greatly diminished. By the late 1970s, South Korea's program of agrarian development had been consolidated. In real terms, agricultural output increased by over 500 percent between 1970 and 1991. In 2004 Korea had a relatively large population of 48 million and a relatively modest population growth rate of 0.8 percent. With but limited land for cultivation – Mexico, for example, has nearly ten times the amount of land per capita – Korea has continued to import grains. But with its tremendous strength in manufacturing exports, Korea can afford to sustain heavy grain imports as it creates true dynamic comparative advantage in production with greater value-added, while paying high wages.

While Korea's experience with land reform and agricultural development has, of necessity, taken place within certain physical limitations, and while it has not eliminated the need to import cereals, it does demonstrate that a productive relationship between the state and the rural population can be achieved, within the context of a strong program of land reform. In Korea's case, the successes achieved in agriculture have always depended upon state intervention and a successful program of state-directed industrialization. Neoliberalism has played virtually no role in South Korea's success, nor has the program succeeded as a result of an "agriculture first" or an agriculture-led policy. Instead there has evolved a balanced policy of both agrarian and industrial development.

To the extent that export-led industrial growth has made rural development possible, the use of such terms as "self reliant" to describe Korea's rural development is extremely misleading. The emphasis on private ownership has, in general, meant that increases in production have been generated by state intervention into the market rather than through an increase in a local corporate capacity to develop. It also suggests that the future of Korea's agricultural-cum-rural development will depend upon the ability to keep the export engine of growth in high gear.

(Douglas 1983: 208)

Questions and exercises

1   In discussing appropriate technology for less-developed nations, we noted that given the relative labor abundance and relatively lower wages in the less-developed nations compared to the more developed economies, and the relatively higher price of capital, in many situations the optimal combination of labor and capital that should be used in the less-developed nations would be more labor-using and less capital-using compared to a higher-wage developed country.

a   In a graph with the quantity of capital, K, measured along one axis and the quantity of labor, L, measured along the other, draw one convex-to-the-origin production isoquant, representing, say, 1,000 units of output for every combination of L and K on the curve. Also draw in an isocost line for a developed country which is tangent to the isoquant at some point. (You will remember that the slope of the isocost line is determined by the relative prices of K and L.) Note the quantity of K and L used on the axes.

Now, assuming that the price of a unit of *K* in the less-developed country is the same as in the more developed, but the wage rate is lower, show that the optimal combination of *K* and *L* to produce 1,000 units of output in the less-developed nation would use more labor and less capital than in the more developed economy. Prove, too, that the less-developed country would be the lower cost producer of the 1,000 units.

b   What difference does it make to the way you draw the isoquant if, now, we assume that not all combinations of labor and capital are technologically feasible to produce 1,000 units of output? What will the isoquant look like if there are only two different combinations of *K* and *L* available, for example? What choice of technique (i.e. which combination of *K* and *L*) will the developed country and the less-developed country producer select?

2   Advocates of the Green Revolution have argued that the technologies employed are "scale neutral." That is, seeds and fertilizers are easily divisible, and no appreciable change in unit costs is involved in altering the quantities used. Therefore, they hypothesized, the Green Revolution should benefit both poor and wealthy farmers alike, without an appreciable relative advantage to one or the other in use. Contrast this technical view of the impact of the Green Revolution with a more "institutional" view.

a   Assuming that the unit cost of inputs are nearly "scale neutral," why did the many institutionalists predict that the Green Revolution would increase intraregional and interregional income disparities rather than diminish them?

b   What other considerations are there besides costs of the new inputs in deciding whether to use a new seed, a new fertilizer, or any new technology in agriculture?

c   Can the response of poorer and richer farmers differ? Why?

3   Available research suggests that when peasant farmers are impacted by deforestation and desertification, women are particularly affected. Why is this so? How are women affected adversely?

4   Some peasants are quite "risk-averse," for reasons discussed in this chapter. Imagine a group of poor pastoralists struggling with the effects of a famine and drought.

a   Why might it be "rational" for them to actively, if unintentionally, contribute to the acceleration of environmental degradation, and to their own famine, via overuse of grazing land, if they are concerned with guarding against the exhaustion of their animal herds? Is this situation an example of a market failure?

b   What could be done to prevent overgrazing of land?

c   Are these people poor because they overgraze the land with the animals, or are they overgrazing the land because they are poor?

5

a   Explain, using supply and demand curves, how a low "buy price" (i.e. a price below market equilibrium) by government for a staple product, such as rice in India, may lead profit-oriented staple crop producers to switch to other crops.

b   On the same graph, show the effect of targeted income subsidies to low income consumers on the quantity and price of rice traded in the market, assuming the "buy price" program is abandoned.

c   Discuss the pros and cons of subsidized prices for staple commodities versus targeting income subsidies as strategies to help the poor to purchase staple food products.

6

    a   How is true land reform different from a redistribution of landholdings? What political purposes might each have?

    b   What are the economic reasons for pursuing land reform? For a redistribution of landholdings that falls short of full land reform?

7   How important are improvements in the productivity of the agricultural sector relative to efforts to increase productivity in industry? Can a country become developed without an industrial and agricultural "revolution" in the economic sense of the term?

8

    a   Are food imports necessarily an indication of weakness in the agricultural sector of an economy? Under what conditions might food imports, rather than domestic production, be desirable and economically rational?

    b   Under what conditions would rising food imports indicate a weakness in the overall economic strategy? Do countries have to produce everything they consume?

    c   Looking back at Table 11.1, for which countries would you guess that falling food production per person is an indication of problems and for which might such a result not be a problem?

Notes

1 A vicious circle has overtaken Sub-Saharan Africa, where a combination of public health issues (malaria and AIDS, in particular), water scarcity and lack of water infrastructure, inability to irrigate, soil compaction (sometimes from overgrazing), a decline in public sector resources devoted to agricultural extension and R&D, desertification, political instability, and sometimes warfare and rising input prices, especially for fertilizers, has stalled and nearly stopped forward momentum in agricultural production. With a prevalence of subsistence farmers and very poor agricultural laborers, the rural population cannot avail themselves of the plentiful food stocks available around the world. The availability of foreign aid, analyzed in Chapter 17, is crucial. For further discussion see Sachs (2005), especially chapters 3, 10, and 13.

2 Note, however, that declining per capita food *production* is not the same as declining per capita food *consumption*. For some newly industrialized nations, agricultural and food production should, with successful structural transformation, fall in relative terms compared to industrial and service production. The poorer a country, however, and the lower its level of human development, the less likely it is that the structural transformation has taken place.

3 Note that this term is intended to signify extreme dependence on a very limited range of primary product exports, be they agriculture or raw material exports. It is not strictly intended to mean that an economy is literally dependent on only one export for its foreign exchange earnings.

4 It perhaps goes without saying that, though this phenomenon was only "discovered" at that time, this does not mean that the effects of commodity price swings had not been in operation for some time. This instability of prices, and the macroeconomic consequences, had been a focus of much of the critical concern of heterodox economists, as discussed in Chapter 6, and of policy-makers in the less-developed world who had to periodically confront such crises.

5 How can a country prevent a temporary and exogenous export price increase from having such adverse effects? One way is to sterilize the increased inflow of export revenues, to prevent an increase in the currency's exchange rate value *vis-à-vis* other currencies. This can be done if the central bank of the country sells more of its own currency, thus buying up foreign exchange. This will increase the supply of its own currency, to balance the increased demand for that currency by non-residents resulting from the higher prices of the export. Effective sterilization also requires that government, with the increased revenues it earns and increased foreign exchange reserves, exercise restraint in spending these "savings."

6 Technically, the expected losses from the gamble failing exceed the expected gains from the gamble succeeding, where in this case, the gamble being considered is a change in peasant production (such as a new technology, or a new seed, or a new fallowing technique) where the probabilities of success and failure are still subject to some degree of uncertainty.

References

Adler, Emanuel. 1987. *The Power of Ideology: The Quest for Technological Autonomy in Argentina and Brazil*. Berkeley: University of California Press.

Alston, Julian and Phillip Pardy. 2006. "Developing Country Perspectives on Agricultural R&D," pp. 11–29 in Philip Pardy, Julian Alston and Rogley Piggott (eds.), *Agricultural R&D in the Developing World*. Washington, D.C.: IFPRI.

Baker, Kathleen and Sarah Jewitt, 2007. "Evaluating 35 Years of Green Revolution Technology in Indian Villages of Bulandshahr District, Western UP, North India," *Journal of Development Studies* 43 (February): 312–29.

Barraclough, Solon (ed.). 1973. *Agrarian Structure in Latin America*. Lexington, MA: Lexington Books.

Barry, Tom (ed.). 1992. *Mexico: A Country Guide*. Albuquerque, NM: Inter-Hemispheric Resource Center.

Bliss, C.J. and N.H. Stern. 1982. *Palanpur: The Economy of an Indian Village*. Oxford: Clarendon Press.

Borras, Saturnino. 2003. "Questioning Market-Led Agrarian Reform: Experiences from Brazil, Colombia and South Africa," *Journal of Agrarian Change* 3 (July): 367–94.

——. 2005. "Can Redistributive Reform Be Achieved via Market-Based Voluntary Land Transfer Schemes?," *Journal of Development Studies* 41: (January) 2005: 90–134.

Bouis, Howarth. 2007. "The Potential of Genetically Modified Food Crops to Improve Human Nutrition in Developing Countries," *Journal of Development Studies* 43 (January): 79–96.

Byerlee, Derek. 1992. "The Political Economy of Third World Food Imports: The Case of Wheat," pp. 305–26 in Charles Wilber and Kenneth Jameson (eds.), *The Political Economy of Development and Underdevelopment*, 5th edn. New York: Random House.

Byres, Terrance. 2006. "Agricultural Development: Towards a Critique of the 'New Neoclassical Development Economics' and of 'Neoclassical Neo-Populism'," pp. 222–48 in Jomo K.S. and Ben Fine (eds.), *The New Development Economics*. London: Zed Books.

Cypher, James M. 1990. *State and Capital in Mexico*. London and Boulder, CO: Westview.

de Janvry, Alain. 1981. *The Agrarian Question in Latin America*. Baltimore, MD: Johns Hopkins Press.

Deininger, Klaus. 1999. "Making Negotiated Land Reform Work: Initial Experience from Colombia, Brazil and South Africa," *World Development* 27: 651–72.

Dixon, Chris. 1990. *Rural Development in the Third World*. London: Routledge.

Doolette, John and James Smyle. 1990. "Soil and Moisture Conservation Technologies," in John Doolette and James Smyle (eds.), *Watershed Development in Asia*. Washington, D.C.: World Bank Technical Paper 127.

Douglas, Mike. 1983. "The Korean Saemaul Undong," pp. 186–214 in David Lea and D.P. Chaudhri (eds.), *Rural Development and the State*. London: Methuen.

Eicher, Carl and John Staatz. 1998. "Agricultural Ideas in Historical Perspective," pp. 8–38 in Carl Eicher and John Staatz (eds.) *International Agricultural Development*, 3rd edn. Baltimore MD: Johns Hopkins Press.

FAO (United Nations Food and Agricultural Organization). 2006. FAONewsroom. http://www.fao.org/newsroom/en/news/2006/100043/index.html.

——. 2005. "The Role of Transnational Corporations," http://www.fao.org/docrep/005/4671e/.

Fogel, Robert. 1994. "Economic Growth, Population Growth and Physiology," *American Economic Review* 84: 369–95.

Ghosh, Jayati. 2004. "Income Inequality in India," *IDEA*. Online at http://www.networkideas.org/news/feb2004/news09_Income_inequality.htm.

Goldman, Abe and Joyotee Smith. 1995. "Agricultural Transformations in India and Northern Nigeria: Exploring the Nature of Green Revolutions," *World Development* 23 (March): 243–63.

Graff, Gregory, David Roland-Holst and David Zilberman 2006. "Agricultural Biotechnology and Poverty Reduction in Low-Income Countries," *World Development* 34 (August): 1430–45.

Griffin, Keith. 1974. *The Political Economy of Agrarian Change*. Cambridge, MA: Harvard University Press.

——. 1989. *Alternative Strategies for Economic Development*. New York: St Martin's Press.

Griffin, Keith, Azizur Khan and Amy Ickowitz. 2002. "Poverty and the Distribution of Land," *Journal of Agrarian Change* 2 (July): 279–330.

——. 2004. "In Defense of NeoClassical Populism," *Journal of Agrarian Change* 4 (July): 361–86.

Hill, Polly. 1986. *Development Economics on Trial*. Cambridge: Cambridge University Press.

Jank, Marcos Sawaya, Maristela Franco, Andre Meloni and Paulo Faveret. 1999. "Concentration and Internationalization of Brazilian Agribusiness Exporters," *International Food and Agribusiness Management Review* 2 (3/4): 359–74.

Kay, Cristóbal. 2006. "Rural Poverty and Development Strategies in Latin America," *Journal of Agrarian Change* 6 (October): 455–508.

Lea, David and D.P. Chaudhri (eds.). 1983. *Rural Development and the State*. London: Methuen.

Lipton, Michael. 1977. *Why Poor People Stay Poor*. Cambridge: Cambridge University Press.

——. 2007. "Plant Breeding and Poverty: Can Transgenic Seeds Replicate the 'Green Revolution' as a Source of Gains for the Poor?," *Journal of Development Studies* 43 (January): 31–62.

—— and Richard Longhurst. 1989. *New Seeds and Poor People*. Baltimore, MD: Johns Hopkins Press.

Luce, Edward. 2007. *In Spite of the Gods: The Strange Rise of Modern India*. New York: Doubleday.

Mellor, John. 1998a. "Agriculture on the Road to Industrialization," pp. 136–54 in Carl Eicher and John Staatz (eds.) *International Agricultural Development*, 3rd edn. Baltimore MD: Johns Hopkins Press.

——. 1998b. "Foreign Aid and Agriculture-Led Development," pp. 55–66 in Carl Eicher and John Staatz (eds.) *International Agricultural Development*, 3rd edn. Baltimore MD: Johns Hopkins Press.

McCalla, Alex. 1998. "Agriculture and Food Needs to 2025," pp. 39–54 in Carl Eicher and John Staatz (eds.) *International Agricultural Development*, 3rd edn. Baltimore MD: Johns Hopkins Press.

Morris, Michael and Derek Byerlee. 1998. "Maintaining Productivity in Post-Green Revolution Asian Agriculture," pp. 458–73 in Carl Eicher and John Staatz (eds.) *International Agricultural Development*, 3rd edn. Baltimore MD: Johns Hopkins Press.

OECD-FAO (Organization for Economic Co-operation and Development – Food and Agricultural Organization). 2006. *Agricultural Outlook 2006–2015*. Paris: OECD.

Pingali, Prabhu. 1998. "Confronting the Ecological Consequences of the Rice Green Revolution in Tropical Asia," pp. 474–93 in Carl Eicher and John Staatz (eds.) *International Agricultural Development*, 3rd edn. Baltimore MD: Johns Hopkins Press.

—— and Randy Stringer. 2003. "Food Security and Agriculture in Low Income Food Deficit Countries," paper presented to the International Conference on "Agricultural Policy Reform and the WTO," Capri, Italy, June 23–26. Online at http://www.ecostat.unical.it/2003agtradeconf/Invited%20papers/Pingali%20and%20Stringer.

Pinstrup-Anderson, Per. 2003. "Food Security and Trade, the Challenges Ahead," paper presented to the International Conference on "Agricultural Policy Reform and the WTO," Capri, Italy, June 23–26.

Raney, Terri. 2006. "Economic Impact of Transgenic Crops in Developing Countries," *Current Opinion in Biotechnology* 17: 1–5.

Reardon, Thomas and Christopher Barrett. 2000. "Agroindustrialization, Globalization and International Development," *Agricultural Economics* 23 (September): 195–205.

Rigg, Jonathan. 2006. "Land, Farming, Livelihoods and Poverty," *World Development* 34 (January): 180–202.

Romero, Simon. 2006. "Manitoba Journal: Bolivian Reforms Raise Anxiety on Menonite Frontier," *New York Times* (December 21). Online at http://select.nytimes.com/search.

Rostow, Walt W. 1960. *The Stages of Economic Growth*. Cambridge: Cambridge University Press.

Russell, Phillip. 1994. *Mexico under Salinas*. Austin, TX: Mexico Resource Center.

Sachs, Jeffrey. 2005. *The End of Poverty*. New York: Penguin Books.

Schejtman, Alexander. 1992. "The Peasant Economy: Internal Logic, Articulation and Persistence," pp. 276–304 in Charles Wilber and Kenneth Jameson (eds.), *The Political Economy of Development and Underdevelopment*, 5th edn. New York: Random House.

Schultz, Theodore. 1964. *Transforming Traditional Agriculture*. New Haven CT: Yale University Press.

Schiff, Maurice and Alberto Valdés. 1998. "The Plundering of Agricultural Policy in Developing Countries," pp. 226–33 in Carl Eicher and John Staatz (eds.) *International Agricultural Development*, 3rd edn. Baltimore MD: Johns Hopkins Press.

Shaban, Radwan Ali. 1987. "Testing Between Alternative Models of Sharecropping," *Journal of Political Economy* 95: 893–920.

Smith, R.E. 1972. *The United States and Revolutionary Nationalism*. Chicago: University of Chicago Press.

Smith, Stephen. 1994. *Case Studies in Economic Development*. New York: Longman.

Stiglitz, Joseph. 1992. "The New Development Economics," pp. 261–75 in Charles Wilber and Kenneth Jameson (eds.), *The Political Economy of Development and Underdevelopment*, 5th edn. New York: Random House.

Stringer, Randy. 2001. "Food Security in Developing Countries," pp. 70–104 in B.N. Ghosh (ed.), *Contemporary Issues in Development Economics*. London: Routledge.

Strom, Stephanie. 2006. "Two Foundations Join in Africa Agriculture Push," *New York Times* (September 13): A16.

Tomich, Thomas, Peter Kilby and Bruce Johnston. 1995. *Transforming Agrarian Economies*. Ithaca, NY: Cornell University Press.

Trimmer, Peter. 1989. "The Agricultural Transformation," pp. 358–61 in Gerald Meier (ed.), *Leading Issues in Development Economics*. Oxford: Oxford University Press.

——. 1998. "The Role of Agriculture in Indonesia's Development," pp. 539–49 in Carl Eicher and John Staatz (eds.) *International Agricultural Development*, 3rd edn. Baltimore MD: Johns Hopkins Press.

UNCTAD. 1987. *Handbook of International Trade and Development Statistics*. Geneva: UNCTAD.

UN, Department of Economic and Social Affairs. 2000. *World Economic and Social Survey 2000*. New York: United Nations.

UNDP (United Nations Development Programme). 1993. *Human Development Report 1993*. Oxford: Oxford University Press.

——. 1994. *Human Development Report 1994*. Oxford: Oxford University Press.

——. 1995. *Human Development Report 1995*. Oxford: Oxford University Press.

——. 2001. *Human Development Report 2001*. Oxford: Oxford University Press.

——. 2006. *Human Development Report 2006*. Oxford: Oxford University Press.

WARDA. 2007. "NERICA Contributes to Record Rice Harvest in Africa," May 3. Online at http://www.warda.org/warda/newsrel-riceharvest-may07.asp.

World Bank. 1992. *World Development Report 1992*. Oxford: Oxford University Press.

——. 1994. *World Development Report 1994*. Oxford: Oxford University Press.

——. 2000/1. *World Development Report 2001*. Oxford: Oxford University Press.

——. 2002. *World Development Report 2002*. Oxford: Oxford University Press.

——. 2003. *Reaching the World Poor – A Renewed Strategy for Rural Development*. Washington, D.C.: World Bank.

——. 2007. World Development Indicators Database (April 2007). Online at http://devdata.worldbank.org/external/CPProfile.asp?PTYPE=CP&CCODE=LIC

12 Population, education, and human capital

After reading and studying this chapter, you should better understand:

- the connection between population growth rates and the level and growth rate of income per capita;
- the importance and causes of the demographic transition and its effect on birth and death rates;
- the direction of causation is from poverty to population growth and not the reverse;
- the key determinants of the fertility rate and population growth, particularly income per person and the level of education of women;
- the idea of the "opportunity cost" of having children and the impact on fertility and population growth;
- the importance of education and human capital accumulation to economic growth and human development;
- the particular significance of scientists, engineers, and other technically-trained workers who apply R&D to the development process;
- the role for government action to overcome market failure in the creation of human capital.

Introduction

The most malleable factor of production available to any economy is its population. It is not stretching the truth to say that an economy's labor force is its most significant resource endowment, and it is one that can be made more productive over time. Our consideration of endogenous growth theories in Chapter 8 and of the recent successes of the "high performance East Asian economies" (HPAEs) in Chapters 9–10 have highlighted the importance of an educated labor force to economic growth. A better educated and trained labor force increases what economists call "human capital." Education is the means by which a nation is able to appropriate from and share in the gains arising from technological and knowledge advances at the world level by augmenting the economy's stock of human capital.

A properly educated labor force is absolutely necessary for sustained growth and for achieving full human development. An economy that succeeds in avoiding all the other pitfalls of developing societies considered in the next part of the book but which neglects education will not succeed in developing as quickly or to such a high level as would be possible with more and better human capital.

The accumulation of a productive stock of human capital is thus one of the fundamental keys to development.[1] There is often a lingering question, however, about how population growth affects the level and pace of economic growth and development. So, prior to considering in more detail the importance of the human capital input to development, it is necessary to briefly examine the nature of what, since the time of Thomas Malthus, has been called the "population problem."

A population problem?

The so-called population problem is based on an assumption that rapid population growth can cause the total population to exceed a nation's productive capacity so that real income per person falls or rises unnecessarily slowly. Deep down, concerns about a population problem is simply a reassertion of the Malthusian specter of population outstripping output growth considered in Chapter 4. We can, perhaps, see why some might think that population growth is the cause of poverty if we remember from Chapter 2 that

$$\% \, \Delta\text{income per person} = \% \, \Delta\text{total income} - \% \, \Delta\text{population.} \qquad (12.1)$$

This is a definition, that is, it is a mathematically true statement. This says that the change in real income per person over time depends both on the growth rate of aggregate real income (measured by GNI or GDP) minus the rate of population growth. Obviously the faster that total income grows, with population growth held constant, the more rapid will income per capita rise. The faster that population grows, the slower will be the expansion in income per person, for any given rate of aggregate income growth. This, however, does not mean that faster population growth *causes* slower growth in income per capita or that slower population growth *leads* to a faster increase in income per person.

So statement 12.1 says nothing about whether population growth affects income per person or vice versa. It simply states that both population growth and total income growth are important for what happens to income per person. It does not imply anything about causation. If population is growing 2 percent per year, total income must grow by at least 2 percent just to keep income per person constant. If total income only grows 1 percent, then per capita income will decrease by 1 percent with 2 percent population growth. But this does not mean that population growth causes income per person to decrease. Both the growth of total income and the growth of population are important, and we need to try to uncover which of the two affects the other.

We shall in fact argue that causation actually runs in the direction of income to population growth and not vice versa.[2] Very simply, an increase in average income in an economy leads to a lower population growth rate, all else the same.

Let's consider some initial evidence. In Table 12.1, look first at the broad groupings of countries ranked as "low-income," "middle-income," and "high-income." From these averages, it is clear that population growth rates are lowest for the high-income economies and highest for the low-income economies for the different time periods shown. Of course, this alone still does not tell us whether population growth affects income or vice versa. But it is suggestive evidence.

Looking at individual nations, the population growth rate tends to be highest for low-income economies and lowest for countries in the "high-income" grouping. The "middle-

Table 12.1 Actual population growth rates, by region and selected countries

	Population growth rate, annual percent			Share of world population[a]	
	1960–70	*1970–80*	*1990–2004*	*1980*	*2000*
Low-income economies	2.3	2.1	2.0	36.3	40.6
China[b]	2.3	1.8	0.9		
India	2.3	2.2	1.7		
Pakistan	2.8	2.6	2.4		
Somalia	2.8	2.9	1.3		
Zimbabwe	2.6	3.0	1.4		
Middle-income economies	2.5	1.9	1.1	45.8	44.9
Argentina	1.4	1.6	1.2		
Côte d'Ivoire[c]	3.8	4.0	2.5		
Jamaica	1.4	1.3	0.7		
Senegal[d]	2.3	2.9	2.5		
South Korea[e]	2.6	1.8	0.8		
High-income economies	1.1	0.8	0.8	17.8	14.9
Ireland	0.4	1.4	1.1		
Japan	1.0	1.1	0.2		
United Kingdom	0.6	0.1	0.3		
United States	1.3	1.1	1.2		
Less-developed regions					
East Asia and Pacific	1.9	1.5	1.1	31.5	30.6
Latin America and Caribbean	2.4	2.0	1.6	8.1	8.5
Middle East and North Africa	2.9	3.0	2.0	3.9	4.9
South Asia	2.3	2.1	1.9	20.4	22.4
Sub-Saharan Africa	2.7	2.9	2.5	8.6	10.9

Sources: World Bank 1983: 184–5, Table 19; 1994: 210–11, Table 25; 2002: 48–51, Table 2.1; *World Development Indicators 2006*: 46–8, Table 2.1.

Notes
a   Total world population in 1980 was estimated as 4,429.3 million and 6,057.3 million in 2000.
b   China was reclassified as "middle-income" in 1999.
c   Côte d'Ivoire was reclassified as "low-income" in 1994.
d   Senegal was reclassified as "low-income" in 1995.
e   South Korea was reclassified as "high-income" in 2003.

income" countries might seem to show more variability, but two of these countries have been reclassified as "low-income" (Côte d'Ivoire and Senegal) and one, Korea, has been advanced to the "high-income" category. The pattern of population growth rates being lower for economies with higher incomes tends to be confirmed among individual countries.

Another important tendency can be seen by looking at what has happened to population growth rates over time. Reading across the columns, population growth rates have been falling over time, slowly for the "low-income" and "high-income" economies and more rapidly for the "middle-income" countries. The same pattern is observed for individual economies and in all the regions at the bottom of the table. As we will argue, falling population growth rates are closely associated with rising income levels, though with a lag.

To return to the question that headed this section, we argue that there is not a population problem. If anything, there is an income problem. Rather than an increase in income per person resulting in ever more rapid increases in population, as Malthus had argued, the relation is actually the other way around. Income per person and population growth rates are inversely related, not directly related, for reasons we shall consider more fully below. The best way to reduce population growth rates, then, is for a country to increase economic growth and achieve higher income per person. Population growth is a fundamental consequence of the level of income and not the reverse. It is income that needs to be increased, and then population growth naturally and inevitably declines.

The natural and the actual rate of population growth

What accounts for differences in population growth rates among countries and regions? To explain this, we need to define both the *natural rate of population growth* and the *actual rate of population growth*.

In a purely accounting sense, the *natural* rate of population growth can be defined as

$$p_n = (\text{CBR} - \text{CDR})/10 \qquad (12.2)$$

where p_n is the annual natural rate of population growth; CBR is the crude birth rate, which is the number of live births per 1,000 population; and CDR is the crude death rate, which is the number of deaths per 1,000 population.[3]

Using statement 12.2 for Côte d'Ivoire, for example, in 2004, with a CBR of 37 and a CDR of 17, the natural rate of population growth was $p_n = (37 - 17)/10 = 2.0$ percent. Crude birth and crude death rates are shown in Table 12.2 for the same countries and regions as in the previous table. The listings of the countries within each grouping is now shown not alphabetically, however, but from the country with the lowest income to the country with the highest income per person within each grouping. This is done to help us see if there are any patterns we can detect connecting crude birth rates (CBRs) and crude death rates (CDRs) to average income levels.

The natural rate of population growth, p_n, calculated in Table 12.2, often is quite different from the *actual* population growth rates shown in Table 12.1 (note that these are averages for longer periods than the per year calculations in Table 12.2 for the natural rate). For example, in 1970, the p_n for Côte d'Ivoire was 3.1 percent, while the actual annual population growth rate over both the 1960s and the 1970s was well above this figure. The natural rate of population growth thus understated the actual rate of population growth for Côte d'Ivoire. Considering Somalia in 2000, just the opposite is true; the natural rate of population growth overstates the actual trend of population. For Japan, the natural rate of population growth predicts the actual population growth rate quite closely.

What accounts for the difference between the natural rate of population growth and the actual? The *actual rate of population growth* shown in Table 12.1 depends not only on the natural rate, p_n, as a result of births and deaths. The actual population growth rate also takes into consideration migration flows between nations. We can define the actual rate of population growth, p_a, as

$$p_a = p_n + m \qquad (12.3)$$

where m is net migration: $m = (\text{immigrants}/100 \text{ population}) - (\text{emigrants}/100 \text{ population})$ and p_a, the actual rate of population growth is a percentage. Thus, the actual rate of population growth is equal to the natural rate of population growth plus or minus net migration.

Table 12.2 Crude birth rates, crude death rates, and the natural rate of population growth[a]

	Crude birth rate[b]			Crude death rate[b]			p_n, %		
	1970	*1993*	*2004*	*1970*	*1993*	*2004*	*1970*	*1993*	*2004*
Low-income economies	39	28	29	14	10	11	2.5	1.8	1.8
India	41	29	24	18	10	8	2.3	1.9	1.6
Pakistan	48	40	27	19	9	7	2.9	3.1	2.0
China	33	19	12	8	8	6	2.5	1.1	0.6
Zimbabwe	53	38	30	16	12	23	3.7	2.6	0.7
Somalia	50	48[c]	45	24	17[c]	17	2.6	3.1[c]	2.8
Middle-income economies	35	23	16	11	8	7	2.4	1.5	0.9
Côte d'Ivoire	51	49	37	20	15	17	3.1	3.4	2.0
Senegal	47	43	36	22	16	11	2.5	2.7	2.5
Jamaica	34	21	18	8	6	6	2.6	1.5	1.2
Argentina	23	20	18	9	8	8	1.4	1.2	1.0
Korea	30	16	9	9	6	5	2.1	1.0	0.4
High-income economies	18	13	12	10	9	8	0.8	0.4	0.4
Ireland	22	15	16	11	9	7	1.1	0.6	0.9
United Kingdom	16	13	12	12	11	10	0.4	0.2	0.2
United States	18	16	14	10	9	8	0.8	0.7	0.6
Japan	19	10	9	7	8	9	1.2	0.2	0.0
Less-developed regions									
East Asia and Pacific	35	21	15	9	8	7	2.6	1.3	0.8
Latin Americaand Caribbean	36	26	21	10	7	6	2.6	1.9	1.5
Middle East and North Africa	45	33	25	16	7	6	2.9	2.6	1.9
South Asia	42	31	25	18	10	8	2.4	2.1	1.7
Sub-Saharan Africa	47	44	40	20	15	18	2.7	2.9	2.2

Sources: World Bank 1994: 212–13, Table 26; 1995: 212–13, Table 26; 2002: 48–51, Table 2.1; *World Development Indicators* 2006: 46–8, Table 2.1

Notes
a Countries are ranked in terms of their 1993 GNI per capita, from lower to higher incomes within income groupings.
b Per 1,000 population.
c 1992.

For countries with little immigration or emigration, or in which these flows are relatively balanced, the actual rate of population growth will be very similar to the natural rate. For countries with a high level of emigration relative to immigration, that is, with more people leaving the country than entering, the natural rate of population growth, p_n, will overstate the actual rate of population growth, p_a, as in Somalia. In countries, like Côte d'Ivoire, where net migration is positive, the actual population growth exceeds the natural rate, as population inflows exceed population outflows.

But we still have not answered a critical question for understanding population growth and the relation between income levels and population. We need to understand what it is that explains differences in CBRs and CDRs among countries, and hence population growth rates, and their trends over time. Why do CBRs and CDRs differ among nations?

To understand this, it is helpful to consider the issue within a somewhat longer time frame. A look at the so-called *demographic transition* will illustrate the factors affecting population growth rates via the impact over time of various forces at work on the levels of the CBRs and the CDRs.

The demographic transition

If we were to go back a century or so and examine natural population growth rates, we would find a quite different picture from that shown in Table 12.2. Crude birth and crude death rates were both higher, so that most countries had natural rates of population growth in the neighborhood of about 1 percent per year.[4] High death rates tended to nearly cancel out relatively high birth rates, so population growth rates were quite low by the standard of many LDCs today. Births and deaths were in a sort of perverse balance, so that there was no population explosion. Natural population growth rates at 2, 3 and 4 percent are primarily twentieth- and twenty-first-century phenomena.[5]

What changed to make such historically high rates of population growth a reality in some LDCs, while population growth remained low in richer economies?

The demographic transition and the now-developed economies

What changed was the spread and speeding-up in some countries of the structural transformation toward industrialization and capitalist expansion (examined in Chapters 9–10) and higher levels of income and development, which contributed both to falling birth rates in the nations experiencing accelerated development and to a worldwide trend toward lower death rates in nearly every nation, rich and poor. For nations on the road to industrialization, especially Western Europe, the United States, Canada, and Japan, both crude birth rates and crude death rates fell relatively rapidly, so that their natural population growth rates remained close to 1 percent. In these countries, there was no increase in natural population growth rates.

In these now-developed nations, rapid economic growth resulted in improvements in living standards, incomes, and education which led people to choose to have fewer children, thus significantly reducing birth rates. At the same time, these economies experienced falling death rates, as improved economic conditions contributed to better health and longevity.[6] When modern medicine set out to tackle major public health hazards, like malaria, measles, smallpox, cholera, typhoid, diphtheria, poor sanitation, and so on, death rates fell even more rapidly, especially after 1900 or so. The systematic understanding, production, and use of antibiotics beginning in the early twentieth century also contributed to lower CDRs.

With these decreases in both the CBR and the CDR, the now-developed nations were in the process of completing what is called the *demographic transition*. This occurs when *both* the crude birth rate and the crude death rate have fallen to a level equal to less than 20 per 1,000 of population. As a result of this transition, population growth rates typically are at, or even below, 1 percent per annum.

The demographic transition and the LDCs

In the less-developed nations, however, where the structural transformation toward more productive industrialization and capitalist development was either absent, very primitive, or dualistic (especially prior to decolonization in the late 1940s but also after), crude birth continued to be significantly higher than in the now-developed nations. However, crude death rates decreased in the LDC economies after 1900 or so, often to levels equal to or even below those attained in the developed nations.[7]

The fall in death rates in the LDCs was not wholly the result of economic, social, and health improvements taking place within these nations themselves. Instead, the sharp drop in worldwide crude death rates, especially after 1945, was the consequence of the public good characteristics of and positive externalities associated with the great strides in public health and sanitation measures (water and sewage), immunization for childhood diseases, pest control, and similar measures that had originated in the developed world. However, because of the positive spillover benefits of many of these measures, the gains were transferred to and available in much of the less-developed world as well.

However, with CBRs remaining high, the effect of a period of rapidly decreasing CDRs was to open a growing breach in the less-developed nations between their birth rates, which fell only slowly as incomes increased slowly, and their rapidly declining death rates. This asymmetry led to an inevitable ratcheting upward in the rate of population growth in the less-developed nations as the gap between slowly falling but still relatively high CBRs and rapidly falling but quite low CDRs widened.

You will remember from statement 12.2 above that the natural population growth rate is the difference between the CBR and the CDR (divided by 10 to state the result as a percentage rate). Thus, if the CDR decreases quickly, as happened in most LDCs around the 1940s, the result is an increase in the population growth rate, no matter what the CBR was. And that is what happened. As a result, LDCs all of a sudden found themselves facing a higher population growth rate due to the positive spread effects of public health measures pursued by the developed countries that reduced worldwide crude death rates but which did nothing to reduce CBRs in the LDCs.

Most of the less-developed countries have thus passed through but one-half of the demographic transition. Death rates have fallen significantly and are more in line with levels associated with higher incomes per person in more developed economies, but they did so not because of what happened internally in those economies but as a result of public health measures at the world level that reduced CDRs everywhere. As a result, in nearly every country of the world, CDRs have passed through the 20 per 1,000 population threshold. Birth rates, however, have remained relatively high in the less-developed economies, reflecting their relatively low income levels, though CBRs have been falling as incomes have increased over time. It is a cruel twist of fate that visits on the less-developed nations some of the best of the developed world – low CDRs – and the worst of the less-developed world – relatively high CBRs – simultaneously.

Graphing the demographic transition

Figure 12.1 is a stylistic representation of the phases of the demographic transition and the changes over time in crude birth rates and crude death rates and their effect on population growth.

In Phase I, prior to the Industrial Revolution and the spread of capitalist methods of production within the now-developed world, both birth and death rates were high for all countries, so population growth was relatively slow everywhere. The gap between the CBR line and the CDR line graphically measures the rate of population growth.

In Phase II, death rates began to decline in the more-developed nations due to both the effects of higher incomes that improved health care, but also as a consequence of worldwide health measures which brought mortality rates down for all countries, regardless of income level, as discussed already. In Phase II, the developed nations experienced declining birth rates due to rising income levels at the same time that their death rates were decreasing, so population growth did not accelerate. The gap between the CBR line and the CDR line remained relatively stable as both CBRs and CDRs decreased at somewhat the same pace.

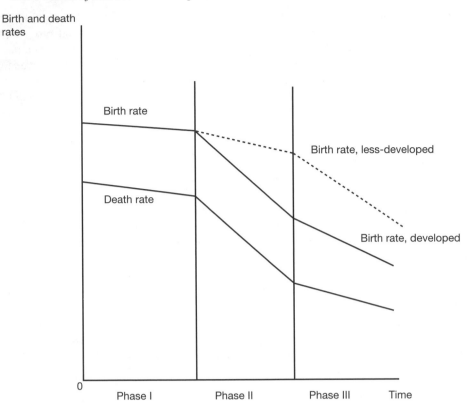

Figure 12.1 The demographic transition.

In the less-developed nations, on the other hand, in Phase II, crude birth rates remain high. They do decrease, but only very moderately as incomes slowly rise. As a result, population growth rates actually increased, as can be very clearly seen from the widening gap between the birth and death rates lines. Again, this was due to the worldwide benefits of health measures that reduced CDRs in poor and rich nations alike, not from anything endogenously occurring within the LDCs themselves.

It is only in Phase III, which has not yet been attained for most less-developed nations, when their birth rates also decline below 20 per 1000 population that they also will complete the demographic transition. For those less-developed nations which fail to make the necessary structural transformations considered in previous chapters and which have lagging per capita income levels, population growth rates remain high as these economies are mired in Phase II of the demographic transition with high CBRs (> 20) and low CDRs (< 20). The result of this imbalance is a relatively high population growth rate. This is the situation facing countries like Pakistan, Côte d'Ivoire and Senegal shown in Table 12.2.

Some countries in Sub-Saharan Africa are facing an even graver situation because of the HIV/AIDS crisis. Zimbabwe suffered a nearly two-fold *increase* in its CDR between 1993 and 2004 (Table 12.2) as a result of the effects of HIV/AIDS. Having passed through half the demographic transition (with CDRs < 20), by 2004 CDRs were again above 20 per 1000 population, as Zimbabwe's transition moved back in time. As a result of this perverse trend, the population growth rate declined from 2.6 percent to 0.7 percent. However, unlike lower population growth rates attained in the "high-income" economies as a result of lower birth and death rates, what we might call a "good" low population growth rate, Zimbabwe's lower population growth rate represents a retrogression to the high CBR, high CDR demographic pattern characteristic of a pre-industrial world economy and, within the current context, is a "bad" low population growth rate. Focus 12.1 looks at this demographic, economic and human tragedy of HIV/AIDS in more detail.

FOCUS 12.1 A RETURN TO THE PAST: THE HIV/AIDS CHALLENGE IN SUB-SAHARAN AFRICA

After 1980, life expectancy began to fall in Sub-Saharan Africa. Why? Lots of reasons: malnutrition, malaria, prolonged droughts, isolation from the world economy, geography, and failed economic policies. And then there is HIV/AIDS. Consider the following data.

	1980		1990		2000		2005		HIV
	LE	*CDR*	*LE*	*CDR*	*LE*	*CDR*	*LE*	*CDR*	*2005*
Africa	48.1	12.9	49.3	16.6	46.7	17.3	47.2	17.3	5.8
Zimbabwe	59.3	10.3	58.6	9.7	39.8	20.6	37.3	22.9	20.1
Kenya	57.8	11.4	57.9	10.2	48.4	14.7	49.0	14.5	6.1
World	62.6	10.4	65.9	9.2	66.7	8.9	67.6	8.6	0.9

While life expectancy (LE) in the world has been moving upward and crude death rates (CDR) down, in Africa as a whole and in Zimbabwe and Kenya as two concrete examples, the trends have been in the opposite direction. The downturn in life expectancy in Zimbabwe has been especially sharp, falling from nearly 60 years in 1980 to less than 40 years in 2005. As noted earlier in the chapter, Zimbabwe has suffered a more than two-fold increase in its CDR, an unprecedented reversal of the demographic transition. The major explanation for this human tragedy is the high incidence of HIV/AIDS, which was in the 20 percent range for adults in 2005. (These figures may be revised downward, but the relative magnitude of the HIV/AIDS crisis is all too real, even if the incidence rate is actually somewhat lower.)

The reasons for the higher incidence of HIV/AIDS in Africa than in other parts of the world are complicated, too complicated to discuss here (for a short but very useful overview, see Sachs 2005: Chapter 10). But the need to stop the disease in its tracks is undeniable, on both human and economic grounds. The costs to countries and families of HIV/AIDS treatment is immense. And it's not just the direct costs of the antiretroviral drugs that save lives and give people hope. It is also the opportunity costs of providing health care (that is, what if other expenditures are sacrificed to care for HIV/AIDS patients that might have been dedicated to economic development?) and the impact on worker productivity for the current generation, but also for future generations.

How are future generations harmed? Because many children are being orphaned and their education and futures short-circuited. The impact on economic growth and development in those countries will reverberate for some time. More needs to be done, not just by the countries affected, but by the international community. Remember, Goal 6 of the Millennium Development Goals is to "have halted by 2015 and begun to reverse the spread of HIV/AIDS." One of the exercises at the end of the chapter asks you to see how the world is doing on this goal.

Sources: Sachs 2005: Chapter 10; World Bank,
World Development Indicators Online

Determinants of the crude birth rate: understanding the dynamics of population growth

Let's return to Table 12.2. First, look at the crude birth rate for, say, 1993. Read down that column. What do you observe? As we scan down, the CBR tends to decrease, it is true, which is the inverse relation between the CBR and income that we noted earlier. That is one worthy observation. But we also note the relatively large variance in the CBR from a high of 49 in Côte d'Ivoire to a low of 10 in Japan in 1993.

Now read down the crude death rate column for 1993. There does not seem to be any systematic relation between the level of income of a country and the CDR, certainly nothing as clear-cut as for the CBR. Further, the crude death rate tends to be dispersed within a relatively narrow band (a high of 17 in Senegal and a low of 6 in Jamaica) as a result of the spread of world public health measures like vaccinations and mosquito control that have lowered death rates worldwide.

The difference in the patterns of the crude birth rate and the crude death rate is because each country's CBR is determined by family-specific national determinants particular to each individual economy, while the CDR is affected to a substantial degree by world health measures and their positive external effects, though national health policies do have an impact. For crude birth rates, the most important country-specific determinants have been found to be (a) family income and (b) the education level of women.[8]

There are, of course, country-specific cultural and religious factors which impinge on birth rates in particular nations and regions, but even when these are factored in, the evolution of family income and women's education in each country are the most important determinants of birth rates over time. Reading down the CBR column in Table 12.2 for 2004 confirms the general tendency for the CBR to decline with higher income, as discussed earlier. Reading across the columns from 1970 to 2004 for each individual country and for all regions, it can also be observed that the CBR declined, too. Since average incomes rose in most countries over this period of time (more about this in the next section), this is additional evidence for the inverse relation between income and CBRs.

The CBR in China has decreased rapidly, such that the population growth rate is more like what one might find in a high-income economy. Why is that? Easy. China's "one-child policy" instituted in 1979 enforces large fines on additional children in urban area, thus increasing their cost and deterring many families from having more children.

The CBR and fertility rates

To review, population growth rates depend on the evolution of CBRs and CDRs in any particular country. A key determinant of CBRs is the average level of income in each economy. Another significant factor affecting CBRs has been found to be the level of education of women, and not simply because women become more aware of birth control. The issue is rather more complicated and is economic at root, as is discussed more fully below. But keep in mind that both higher average income levels and higher education levels for women are the key variables that affect CBRs in every economy, and they do so via fertility rates. We thus need to briefly consider this connection between the CBR and the fertility rate.

The total number of children that the average woman is expected to have is called the *fertility rate*. The fertility rate tends to be lower in regions with higher incomes and higher in regions with lower incomes, as can be seen quite clearly in the top part of Table 12.3. Since the CBR depends upon what happens to fertility rates over time, the inverse relation between

Table 12.3 Fertility rates, income, and women's education

	GNI	Total fertility rate[a]			Ratio of girls to boys[b]		
	per capita ($)[c]	*1970*	*1990*	*2004*	*1970*	*1990*	*2005*
All regions							
Low-income economies	580 (4.2%)	5.9	4.4	3.7	59	n.a.	87.8
Middle-income economies	2,241 (6.2%)	5.1	2.6	2.1	n.a.	84	–
High-income economies	35,131 (7.3%)	2.4	1.8	1.7	94	96	99.9
Less-developed regions							
East Asia and Pacific	1,627 (7.5%)	5.7	2.4	2.0	n.a.	89	99.0
Latin America and Caribbean	4,008 (5.5%)	5.3	3.4	2.5	95	100	101.4
Middle East and North Africa	2,640 (2.4%)	6.8	4.8	3.0	53	82	93.5
South Asia	684 (4.9%)	6.0	4.1	3.1	51	71	88.4
Sub-Saharan Africa	745 (3.2%)	6.6	6.1	5.3	58	80	86.5

Sources: World Bank, *World Development Indicators 2002; World Development Indicators 2006; World Development Indicators Online.*

Notes
a Total fertility is the number of children that would be expected to be born alive to the "average" woman if she were to live to the end of her child-bearing years and have children according to age-specific fertility rates.
b The number of females per 100 males in primary and secondary school.
c 2005. Number in parentheses after GNI per capita is the average growth rate of GNI per capita, 1970–2004 (1979–2004 for the Middle East and North Africa).

fertility rates and income also manifests itself in the relation between average income in an economy and the crude birth rate as changing fertility rates affect the number of children women choose to have.

Within all regions over the period 1970 to 2004, the fertility rate decreased. Those regions that have shown the fastest growth in income per capita and that have reached higher levels of income per capita, as in Latin America and the Caribbean and in East Asia, have demonstrated the most rapid decline in fertility and birth rates within the less-developed world (see Birdsall 1988). All regions have experienced declining fertility rates as income per capita has increased; Table 12.3 shows average income in 2005 and the annual percentage change in GNI per capita in every region since 1970.

Table 12.3 also shows the number of females per 100 males attending primary and secondary school. Higher ratios in 1970, indicating a reduction of the education gender gap, are associated with lower fertility rates in 1990 and 2004, underscoring the importance of women's education as a means of reducing fertility and population growth rates.[9] Women's education increases opportunities for earning income and is a key factor in leading women to choose to have fewer children. Note that in Latin America and the Caribbean there are more girls than boys attending primary and secondary school.

It will be noted that the Middle East and North Africa still have a relatively high fertility rate and population growth rate compared to other less-developed regions, despite a narrowing of the education gender gap and a relatively high income level per capita compared to both South Asia and East Asia, which have lower fertility rates.[10] This is likely to be the result of distinct cultural factors, perhaps partly reflecting the role of women in Islamic societies, which have prevented as rapid a reduction in fertility and population growth that the impact of more female education and rising income would incline us to predict. The same is true for the higher fertility rates in Latin America compared to some lower income regions.

Nonetheless, abstracting from these regional and country-specific factors that can make fertility rates higher or lower for cultural or religious reasons, the fact remains that over time, as average incomes and women's education rise *within* any economy or region, fertility rates *do* fall. Higher incomes and more education for girls result in a smaller number of children born per woman, and hence a lower birth rate, irrespective of the cultural, religious, or other specific factors. That this has occurred in the Middle East and Latin America can be confirmed by looking at what happened to fertility rates in both regions from 1970 to 2004.[11] Over time, fertility decreased with rising income and education levels.

Family planning, the availability of and knowledge about contraception methods, social, moral, and legal views on and access to abortion services, and a whole range of other factors can result in fertility and population growth rates that are higher or lower than might be expected given income per capita or the level of female education in any particular country. Such interventions can help to speed the process of reducing CBRs so that countries pass through the demographic transition threshold more quickly. However, these measures are unlikely to be substitutes for economic growth and the expansion of educational opportunities for women as the most effective means to reduce fertility rates and crude birth rates.

As family income and women's education rises, then, there is an unmistakable tendency for birth rates to fall, as was confirmed in Table 12.2, because fertility rates decrease.[12] This means that average *family* incomes will tend to rise over time as per capita income rises, assuming no strongly adverse changes in the income distribution, since family size will fall over time.[13] This is almost certain to raise family well-being.

The role of children in less-developed and developed economies

Though Table 12.3 suggests that fertility and hence birth rates tend to be inversely related to the level of per capita income and the education of women, the *explanation* for such a link needs to be clarified. At root, the reason is primarily economic.

We can formalize the relation between fertility rates and their determinants as

$$F = f(y, e, S) \tag{12.4}$$

where F is the total fertility rate, y is per capita income, e is the number of females per 100 males in primary school, and S measures the social, cultural and political factors specific to each country that also may affect fertility. It is expected that the first derivatives, $f_y, f_e < 0$, that is, fertility is negatively related to income and education levels, while the relationship between S and fertility (f_S) is indeterminate. The reason for expecting an inverse relation between fertility and income is predicated on the different roles children perform in low- versus high-income economies. Let's examine this assumption.

In economies at lower levels of per capita income, children play multiple roles for their parents. Even at young ages, children can provide an additional source of labor on family farms thus contributing to total family income and welfare. Within the household, older girls can care for younger siblings and help with the cooking, cleaning, fetching of wood and water, and other simple but essential tasks that contribute to the family's overall well-being.

Just as importantly, children often are a form of insurance for poor parents in their old age, ensuring that they will be provided for. This effect is strongest in countries lacking broadly-based social security and old-age pension systems. It is for this reason that the so-called *extended family*, in which grandparents, parents, children, and perhaps aunts and uncles and cousins live in the same house or in very close proximity to one another, is so much more common in the less-developed world than in more developed economies. Without an old-age social security system in place, poor elderly parents often may be forced to live with their children and grandchildren as a means of survival, and the natural-ness of such arrangements is deeply inculcated in all members of the family as a reciprocal relationship. It should be remembered, nonetheless, that such arrangements are born out of necessity and are at root a result of economic necessity as much as they may seem to be desired social arrangements.

Another link between higher fertility rates and low incomes is found in infant and child mortality rates shown in Table 12.4. Families in poor economies are aware that the proba-bility of losing a child either at birth or at a young age is high, but they do not know precisely how many, if any, of their children will fail to reach maturity. According to the table, in Sub-Saharan Africa, the probability of mortality of a child before age five was nearly 1 in 5 in 2004, and this probability is higher the poorer the family. Thus, to the extent that children are at least partly a form of old-age insurance and given that the risk of losing a child is highest in Sub-Saharan Africa among all the less-developed regions, we would expect fertility rates to be higher there than other regions because of the greater risk of loss. And that is precisely what Table 12.3 confirms.

These multiple roles of children, and the perceived risks of mortality, thus lead parents in poorer nations to "choose" to have more children for income and social security reasons. Children are an economic resource for poor families. This does not reflect on how much parents love their children, but simply represents an economic perspective on how families "choose' the number of children to have. Children are a valuable resource to their families in poor families and poor economies.

There is another aspect of this "choosing" which comes into play in both low- and high-income economies. This has to do with the opportunity costs of bearing children. Let's consider this by considering why parents choose to have children in high-income economies.

What is the "role" of children in richer economies? How does it differ? At higher levels of per capita income, fertility declines, because the *cost* of having children rises in terms both of the care required and educational and other direct expenses. But there also is another

Table 12.4 Infant and child mortality rates

	Infant mortality rate[a]			*Under-five mortality rate*[b]		
	1970	*1990*	*2004*	*1970*	*1990*	*2004*
All regions						
Low-income economies	134	94	79	209	147	122
Middle-income economies	79	43	30	125	57	37
High-income economies	21	9	6	26	11	7
Less-developed regions						
East Asia and Pacific	79	43	329	126	59	37
Latin America and Caribbean	84	43	27	124	54	31
Middle East and North Africa	134	60	44	200	81	55
South Asia	138	86	66	209	129	92
Sub-Saharan Africa	138	111	100	222	185	168

Sources: World Bank, *World Development Indicators 2002 and 2006*: Table 2.19.

Notes
a The number of children who die before age one, per 1,000 live births.
b The probability of a newborn baby dying before reaching age five, per 1,000 live births.

important cost to having children, and this is their *opportunity cost* to their parents, but especially for the mother. At higher levels of income, the time spent caring for, feeding, washing, taking children to and from school, dancing, and sports practices, and so on has a higher value than at lower levels of per capita income in terms of forgone income. This is true particularly for working mothers who have to take time off from paid employment to nurse sick children, pick them up from school, get them to the dentist's office, or whatever it is that takes them away from the workplace. Simple economic analysis would suggest that the number of children "demanded" would decrease as income rises since the (opportunity) cost, or implicit price, of an additional child is greater at higher income levels.

Women remain the primary care-givers of children in every country regardless of shifting responsibilities of men *vis-à-vis* women, and women thus bear the burden of this opportunity cost (see Focus 12.2 for another view of the role of women within the household). As their education level rises, women's income-earning power increases and their relative contribution to family income grows. As a consequence, women begin to choose to have fewer children because of the rising opportunity cost, as additional children mean a larger amount of forgone income (see Sachs 2005: 64–5 on Iran's experience).

At higher income levels, the lost income from children is greater than at lower income levels, so the number of children a family chooses to have is inversely related to family income. As women's and family income rises, there are fewer children naturally "chosen" for good economic reasons. At lower income levels, families "choose" to have more children since the cost (which is the implicit price) of each is less in terms of forgone income. This also explains why women who do not work outside the home, even in richer economies, may choose to have more children, since the "price" of an additional child in terms of forgone income is lower. It is a simple price and quantity-demanded decision based on the logic of the downward-sloping demand curve you learned in basic economics.

In richer countries, parents do not have children as either investments in their futures, as a substitute for social security, or as potential workers. As one of our more perceptive students once put it, in richer economies (and in richer families in poor economies) children might be better seen as a source of "entertainment" for their parents. They are doted on, dressed in designer clothes, groomed from infancy for pre-schools and beyond, and generally treated as objects of consumption rather than as investments, as is the case in poorer economies.

As objects of consumption who require that spending be undertaken, children are expensive and are more expensive the higher the income of the family having them. The prevalence of the "nuclear" family – mother and father and one or two children – is thus the norm in economies with higher average income as the economic rationale for the extended family tends to dissipate. Children are less likely to be the source of income for their elderly parents, as developed economies have created old-age security systems and many workers have pension plans. As people age, fewer are dependent on family members for their living arrangements and well-being.

There is another reason why families in both poor and richer nations may choose to have children: to carry on the family name. Since family names typically are passed to the next generation via male children, this results in a bias in favor of male over female babies. Nobel Prize-winning economist Amartya Sen has written passionately about how this predilection has led to abortions and undernourishment of female children through what he calls "natality inequality." In a famous study of Asia, he writes of the "one hundred million" missing women (Sen 1990). In part, the abnormally low number of women to men in India and Pakistan and in other countries in Asia and Africa – roughly 93 to 100 rather than the more typical average of 98 – is the result of the "role" of male children in transmitting the family name to the next

FOCUS 12.2 WOMEN'S EDUCATION, INCOME, AND HEALTH

It is not only fertility rates that decline with higher levels of education for women. Health indicators, and hence family welfare, also improve.

In Africa, studies have shown that a 10 percent increase in female literacy rates reduced child death rates by 10 percent; by comparison, changes in men's literacy rates had no effect on child mortality rates. In Thailand, it was found that women with some primary education were 30 percent more likely to know how to treat diarrhea in their children – using homemade salt and sugar solutions or other oral rehydration methods we considered in Chapter 1 – than were mothers with no education, thus reducing infant deaths.

In studies in Indonesia, Kenya, Morocco, and Peru, the strong positive correlation of years of women's education and a reduction in child mortality rates was confirmed again and again. In all instances, women's education was more important than men's education in reducing the death rate of children.

Further, income earned by women is spent differently within the household. In Jamaica, a household study found that women spend more of their income on goods for their children than do men – and less on alcohol. "In Guatemala, it takes fifteen times more spending to achieve a given improvement in child nutrition when income is earned by the father than when it is earned by the mother."

What do these results say about the role of men's and women's incomes and education levels within the household? What explains these differential effects? Why is the marginal contribution of men's income and education to household welfare less than women's? These are worthy subjects of discussion and research.

Source: World Bank 1993a: 41–3

generation. This results in girls not receiving the same level of medical care or nutrition as boys, deficiencies that often are carried through life and contribute to higher mortality rates than would be expected for females relative to males.

Human capital accumulation: augmenting initial endowments

Beginning in the 1960s, economists began to seriously study labor not just as a homogeneous factor of production, L, but as a differentiated and moldable input to production, that is, as human capital. This suggested that nations could invest in people via education, work training, on-the-job training, nutrition, health care, sanitation, and so on to increase the quality of the employed labor force, just as investment could take place in increasing the quantity and quality of physical capital via technological innovation. The dissatisfaction with the inability of neoclassical growth theories to fully explain the sources of economic growth by the accumulation of more physical capital and by the growth in the labor force led economists to consider more fully education, training, and technology, which might account for more rapid growth in some economies than in others.

Our consideration of endogenous growth theories in Chapter 8 and the successes of the high-performance Asian economies (HPAEs) confirmed the importance of a well-trained population and labor force within the development process. It is certainly not the only factor in successful development, but it is important. Human capital accumulation is not sufficient to guarantee success (think of the former Soviet Union), but it certainly would seem to be necessary for success (for a critical view see Easterly 2001). In this section, we examine in greater detail the contribution that human capital accumulation, especially schooling, can have on the prospects for economic growth and human development.

The contribution of education to development

In the World Bank's study (1993: 52–3, Table 1.9) of the HPAEs, they found that enrolments in primary education in 1960 predicted the following proportion of economic growth over the period 1960–85.

	% of total predicted growth
Hong Kong	86
Indonesia	79
Japan	58
South Korea	67
Malaysia	73
Taiwan	69
Singapore	75
Thailand	87

These are astounding and instructive results. The level of primary education was far and away the most important contributor to the predicted growth rates of the HPAEs and Japan. Further, the accumulated and improving human capital stock of the HPAEs contributed to their ability to be able to adopt, adapt and endogenize the ever-expanding pool of "best practice" technological knowledge being created at the world level. As a consequence, in most of these economies, because of the qualities and relatively high level of training of the population and labor force, levels of productivity and of "technical efficiency change" were able to grow quickly (look back at Table 8.4 for confirmation of this). In other words, most of the HPAEs were able to move closer over time to the ever-shifting-outward production possibilities frontier of "international best technological practice" by becoming more technologically efficient as their growth rates of what economists call total factor productivity (TFP) have exceeded the rate of exogenous, best practice technological change. We will be examining TFP in much more detail in the next chapter.

Table 12.5 provides some data on the level and pace of human capital accumulation for various countries. Years of schooling is used as a proxy measure for the human capital stock. This is a typical assumption made by economists that presumes that better educated workers are more productive workers. A higher average level of education is taken to be an indicator of a higher level of human capital accumulation.

The data in the table are quite suggestive. Countries were more likely to be middle- or high-income in 1993 if their 1970 level of primary education coverage was close to universal, that is, 100 percent. Among the less-developed regions, East Asia and the Pacific had the second-highest stock of human capital in 1970 as measured by primary school enrolments. Further, the mean value of schooling, shown in the last column of the Table 12.5, was higher at higher levels of income and at higher levels of human development, as measured by the HDI (see UNDP 1994: 138–9, Table 5). For example, while Indonesia is ranked among the low-income economies, it is ranked as having "medium human development" according to the HDI. South Korea, an upper-middle-income nation by the World Bank's income rankings at the time, was ranked thirty-second among all nations on the HDI index and was among the countries with "high human development." The level of schooling in both these economies is one important reason for these results.

Note that the "average years of school" measure is the mean value for adults aged twenty-five or more. To the extent that more years of school on average is a measure of greater human capital accumulation and potential for growth, this trend augurs well, by itself, for the

Table 12.5 Education and human capital accumulation

	Primary[a]		Secondary[b]		Tertiary[c]		Primary student– teacher ratio			[d]
	1970	*2004*	*1970*	*2004*	*1970*	*2004*	*1970*	*1998*	*2004*	
Low-income economies	66	100	18	46	3	9	43	42	43	
Bangladesh	54	106	n.a.	51	2	7	46	59	54	2.6
India	78	107	24	52	5	11	41	72	41	5.1
Indonesia	80	116	16	62	3	16	29	22	20	5.0
Kenya	62	111	9	48	1	1	34	28	40	4.2
Middle-income economies	94	111	28	75	3	24	30	22	22	
Senegal	39	76	9	19	1	5	45	49	43	2.6
Mexico	106	109	23	79	5	22	46	27	27	7.2
Jamaica	119	93	46	84	5	19	47	31	30	5.3
Korea	103	105	42	91	7	89	57	31	30	10.8
High-income economies	100	100	77	105	27	67	26	17	16	
Canada	101	101	65	105	53	57	23	18	17	12.2
Japan	100	100	87	102	18	52	26	21	20	10.8
United Kingdom	104	101	73	170	14	63	23	19	17	11.7
United States	88	100	84	95	47	83	27	15	15	12.4
Less-developed regions										
East Asia and Pacific	90	113	24	69	1	17	30	23	22	n.a.
Latin America and Caribbean	107	121	28	87	6	26	33	28	25	n.a.
Middle East and North Africa	70	104	24	67	4	23	34	24	24	n.a.
South Asia	71	103	23	49	4	10	42	66	42	n.a.
Sub-Saharan Africa	51	93	6	30	1	5	43	40	49	n.a.

Sources: World Bank, *World Development Indicators 2002* and *2006*: Tables 2.10 and 2.11.

Notes

a Total ("gross") enrolment in primary school as a percent of primary school-age children (often 6–11 years). If this is greater than 100, it indicates that some children younger and/or older than the standard age are enrolled in primary school.

b Calculated the same as in the previous note, but as a percent of secondary school-age children (often 12–17 years).

c Determined by dividing the number of students enrolled in all post-secondary education (college, university, technical, etc.) by the population aged 20–24.

d Most recent year, for population aged 15 and above.

less-developed nations approaching universal primary school coverage. Of course, quantity is not enough; the quality of the education received is fundamental too, though this is inherently more difficult to measure.

The "primary student–teacher ratio" in Table 12.5, which measures the number of students per teacher in primary schools, can be interpreted as one indicator of the *quality* of education. The ratio is positively related both to the mean years of schooling and to the level of income of the country. It suggests that those countries most focused on enriching and enlarging their stock of human capital will be those which strive to increase both the average number of years of schooling, what we can call *human capital broadening*, and those which improve the quality of schooling, what we can call *human capital deepening*, which is measured here by smaller class size. The assumption is that in smaller classes teachers can give more individual attention to students and that "more learning" is likely to take place.

Look at Bangladesh's record. From 1970, human capital broadening definitely took place at the primary school level so that by 2004 universal education had become the norm. However, the primary student–teacher ratio suggests that it is likely that the quality of schooling suffered as there was an average of fifty-nine children per teacher in 1998 compared to forty-six in 1970. Yes, Bangladesh was educating more students, but was it done at the sacrifice of quality as students were shoved into ever more over-crowded classrooms without the attention from teachers to make the learning experience of real value? It certainly looks like that might be the case.

The situation was even worse in India over the same period as the average number of students in each primary school classroom dramatically increased to seventy-two in 1998. And if one thinks of the other complementary inputs to education – books, pencils, paper, desks – is it likely that either Pakistan's or India's over-burdened teachers had sufficient numbers of these for the larger number of students they were trying to teach?

By 2004, however, human capital deepening had begun to take place in both Bangladesh and India, as average class size per teacher fell. In India the decrease from 1998 to 2004 was quite dramatic. Nonetheless, average class size in these and in the low-income economies remained, on average, about twice or more that of the middle-income and high-income economies.

Korea, on the other hand, has continuously reduced the number of students per teacher over the entire period, suggesting that there was constant improvement, or at least no deterioration, in the quality of education in each classroom on average, at least as measured by the student-to-teacher ratio.

So while universal primary and secondary education and human capital broadening should be important goals for countries wishing to increase the level of development, it is also important that sufficient financial and other resources be allocated so that the quality of such education, that is what we call **human capital deepening**, is not compromised in the interests simply of increasing the coverage ratio of the percentage of students in school. Though this is not noted in Table 12.5, it is also of importance to maintain balance in the pursuit of universal primary school coverage, keeping in mind the need to address and reduce the gender education gap and the rural–urban education gap in designing human capital broadening and deepening programmes.

Goal 3 of the Millennium Development Goals from Chapter 1 was to "promote gender equality and empower women" and specifically to "eliminate gender disparity in primary and secondary education preferably by 2005 and in all levels of education no later than 2015." Our tables do not look at these disparities in detail, but a good out-of-class exercise would be to go to the World Bank website and look at the data on the so-called gender gap in primary, secondary, and tertiary education. Is the gap closing, as the MDGs prescribe?

Human capital accumulation and market failure: what is the role of government?

The evidence on the importance of education as a specific form of human capital to accelerating economic growth rates seems incontrovertible (but again, see the views of Easterly 2001).[14] Nations with a larger stock of human capital tend to grow faster than those with less human capital, and they are able to reach higher levels of income per person. The endogenous growth models reviewed in Chapter 8 are unambiguous on this, and much of the vast economics literature on human capital is dedicated to exploring the "value" of education to individuals and to society (see the classic articles by Mincer (1958) and Schultz (1960)). One of the important reasons why growth rates do not necessarily fall with increased human capital accumulation, that is, one possible reason for the absence of diminishing social returns to human capital investment, is that human capital accumulation creates substantial positive externalities as the exogenous growth models argue.

An important issue, however, is what role does government have in the provision of education? If a better educated labor force is so important to economic growth and human welfare, should government intervene to augment that stock of human capital? Or should these decisions be left to individuals? Let's consider this matter in the following way.

When an individual undertakes schooling, that person is, of course, likely to earn more income over his or her lifetime as a consequence of the higher level of skills and knowledge attained that increase their individual productivity. There is an abundance of sophisticated economics research in labor economics that demonstrates the individual or private benefits to receiving additional years of education. In fact, it is the positive return to more schooling that is typically the personal motivation for undertaking more years of education in the first place (either that or parents that insist on university study no matter what!).

However, besides the private benefits of increased income received by individuals who have themselves received more schooling, there also are social benefits that accrue to the economy as a whole as the result of those many individual decisions to accumulate more human capital. Such social benefits can include: new knowledge created by more educated individuals that adds to the well-being of others through new products, new medicines, safer production processes, and so on; more efficient workers who thus reduce the costs of production and prices of products and services paid by all consumers; a more educated workforce which may be more inclined toward democratic processes and tolerance of differences; and more educated workers interact with other people, so that the level of productivity of all workers rises through the synergistic effects that endogenous growth theories hypothesize, thus increasing the incomes of all involved, not just those who individually sacrificed to undertake additional schooling.

What this means is that the *social benefits* of education exceed the *private benefits* of education as a result of the existence of *positive external effects* that accrue to society at large and to individuals who did not undertake additional schooling themselves. We can write this as:

$$\text{social benefits} = \text{private benefits} + \text{positive external effects of} \\ \text{additional schooling} \qquad (12.5)$$

There is a large literature in economics dealing with this and similar situations where there are benefits accruing to third parties, that is, when there are positive externalities to some action, in this case, to undertake additional years of schooling. From the research, we know that the choices of individuals as to the level of education to pursue will result in less education *on average* being undertaken than is socially desirable. This is a classic example of market failure in the presence of positive externalities that requires some sort of government intervention to bring private and social benefits in line with one another for the overall social good. In effect, government intervention is necessary to reach the most efficient level of average education in society that maximizes the net social benefits from education.

Figure 12.2 illustrates this divergence between the privately chosen level of education and that which would be socially optimal. The curve labeled *MPC* = *MSC* = *S* assumes that the marginal private costs of education (*MPC*) to individuals are equal to the marginal social

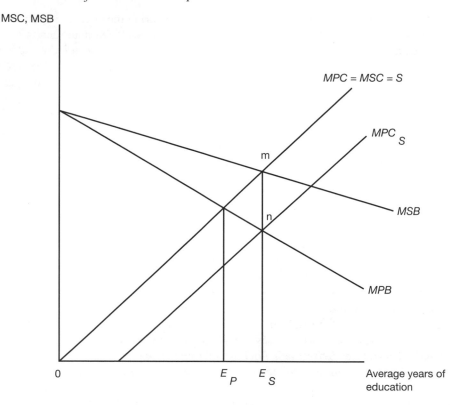

Figure 12.2 The private optimum and the social optimum level of education.

costs (*MSC*) of providing education, and that these can be viewed as the supply curve (*S*) of education, measured in terms of years of schooling on the horizontal axis. In other words, the *S* curve shows the costs of providing education at each level of schooling, irrespective of who receives the education or how that level of education is paid for.

The cost of schooling and the benefits are measured on the vertical axis. The private market demand curve for education by individuals is shown by the curve *MPB*, which measures the marginal private benefits of additional years of schooling accruing as increased income and other benefits to those individuals who actually undertake the schooling. If individuals choose how much education to attain based on their own private decisions alone, the average quantity of education which is optimal for them to choose is E_p, where the supply curve, *S*, crosses the individual market demand curve, *MPB*. This is nothing more than the textbook demand and supply equilibrium learned in first-year economics now applied to the specific case of the (private) demand and supply curves for years of schooling.

As noted already, however, some of the benefits of schooling are received indirectly by others who are not themselves actually "consuming" additional years of education. These spin-off or third-party benefits can be in the form of higher incomes, improved product quality, lower prices, new goods and services, increased social cohesiveness, a higher level of technological development, and so on accruing to others beyond those who actually have undertaken additional schooling. Thus the marginal social benefits (*MSB*) of education curve, which can be thought of as society's total demand curve for education, lies outside and to the right of the *MPB* curve, the private demand curve for education.

The gap between the MPB and the MSB curve measures the value of the positive externality to society of any particular level of schooling, that is, from statement 12.5 above, it is equal to

positive externality = social benefits − private benefits (12.6)

at any particular level of education. This gap widens as more years of education are accumulated, reflecting the presumption that learning-by-doing, association effects, and other indirect gains from increased education levels generate even more beneficial effects to society at higher versus lower average levels of education, as the research considered in Chapter 8 confirmed.

The socially optimum level of education, then, is E_S years, where the supply curve of education crosses the marginal social benefits curve, that is, where society's supply curve intersects society's demand curve for education, *MSB*. This is the equilibrium of supply and demand once again, but now it is the equilibrium from society's perspective.

For the socially optimum average level of education, E_S, to be reached, however, some sort of state intervention will be required to induce private decision-makers to undertake more years of education, since they will not, based on their own private maximizing calculations, accumulate years of schooling beyond the level E_P where their *individual* benefits are maximized.

A subsidy to private individuals equal to the amount *mn* would, however, lead private decisionmakers to choose to undertake E_S years of education. That is because the subsidy will reduce the *individual* costs of any level of schooling by the amount, *mn*, so that now there will be a *new* marginal private costs curve shown by MPC_S in Figure 12.2. This new private cost curve of education, representing the direct costs to be paid by individuals actually undertaking additional years of schooling, lies below and to the right of the old marginal private cost curve, MPC, by the amount *mn* at every level of education individuals might choose.

Individuals will now rationally choose the socially optimum level of education, E_S, as is desired, since the subsidized marginal private cost curve of education MPC_S, which can be interpreted as the new private supply curve, intersects the *MPB* curve, the private demand curve for education, at the socially desired average years of education.[15] Once again, private individuals are maximizing their own net benefits of schooling where (private) demand equals (the new private) costs, but so too is society, since at E_S society's demand curve for education, *MSB*, is also equal to society's supply curve of education, *MSC*. This is the most efficient level of education from society's viewpoint. It is the level of schooling that generates the maximum level of net benefits from education to both individuals and to society. The subsidy to education brings private and social interests into alignment.

Figure 12.2 illustrates the theoretical rationale for not expecting individuals to absorb the full cost of their education. Some of the benefits of that education accrue to others and not to the person undertaking it. There thus is an *efficiency reason* for subsidizing the cost of education and, by simple extension, subsidizing a larger proportion of the costs the lower the income of the individuals being schooled. Even those who do not have children or who do not undertake additional education themselves gain from the positive externalities of those who do receive more education. There thus is a rationale for taxing and then subsidizing education and other forms of human capital accumulation so that the socially desired outcome might be reached.

The assumptions of perfect markets and perfect information, often made in analyzing more developed economies, is even more inappropriate in the less-developed countries. Poor households lack access to financial resources or the ability to borrow to capitalize future expected earnings from education, so the market failure problem extends beyond that caused by the divergence between private and social benefits. Social returns to education have been estimated to be nearly 20 percent from primary education. Given the imperfect markets and imperfect information facing the population in the less-developed economies, there is a strong *prima facie* case on efficiency and equity grounds for providing free, universal primary schooling, and, over time, extending this coverage to secondary education as well.

In the World Bank study on the HPAEs it was noted that:

> the allocation of public expenditure between basic and higher education is the major public policy factor that accounts for East Asia's extraordinary performance with regard to the quantity of basic education provided. The share of public expenditure on education allocated to basic (i.e., primary and secondary) education has been consistently higher in East Asia than elsewhere.
>
> (World Bank 1993b: 197–203)

Thus it makes good economic sense, as well as contributing to improvements in equity via shared growth and broader based human development, to allocate schooling expenditures first to primary education with a goal of universal coverage of males *and* females, with secondary education close behind in terms of spending priority (see Focus 12.3).

FOCUS 12.3   PRIMARY EDUCATION IN BOLIVIA AND INDONESIA

In the early 1980s, Bolivia and Indonesia were, superficially, at about the same level of development in terms of income per capita – in the low to middle $600 range. Illiteracy ran at about 20 percent of the population, and girls were especially disadvantaged. Both nations were predominantly agricultural. And both countries were spending an identical percentage of their total GDP on education: 2.3 percent.

What each did with this share differentiates the two countries markedly.

Indonesia spent 90 percent of its education budget on primary education. By 1987, 91 percent of rural children were enrolled in primary school, compared to the national average of 92 percent. And the gender gap between boys and girls in primary education had virtually disappeared. Free education was extended through the ninth grade.

By contrast, Bolivia spent only about 41 percent of its education budget on primary education, so only 60 percent of primary school-age children attended school on average. In the rural areas, only 45 percent of schools even offered education to the fifth grade, with the remainder providing only three years of primary education. With such low attention to primary education, the gender gap was larger than in Indonesia. Drop-out rates and grade repetition by girls were significantly higher than for boys. Worse, the textbook ratio was only one per ten students, indicating weakness in the quality of education and problems in achieving significant human capital deepening.

Indonesia's income per capita grew at a 4.2 percent annual rate, 1980–93, while Bolivia's growth rate of per capita income was –0.7 percent per year. While not all of the variance in growth rates can be attributed to differences in the attention paid to creating essential human capital resources via funding universal primary schooling, what we know about the importance of primary education to future economic growth suggests that Indonesia's policies were paying off.

Source: World Bank 1993a: 201, Box 5.1

Post-secondary schooling, which is important for creating the indigenous capacity to adopt and adapt world-level best practice technological knowledge and for improving total factor productivity that we will discuss in the next chapter, should not consume too large a level of government resources at early stages of development. In fact, for low-income economies, there are alternative avenues for financing tertiary education besides large subsidies from the state. These can range from requiring university students, who are likely to be from higher-income families anyway, to pay the major portion of the full costs of their education via tuition and fees,[16] "targeting" state subsidies (via, say, scholarships) only toward those with both ability and financial need. Further, it may be more efficient and most likely much cheaper for some period of time to subsidize higher education for domestic students by sending "the best and the brightest" to study abroad at institutions of high quality rather than attempting to invest in the expensive infrastructure and training that university-level teaching and research demands.

Population growth and human capital accumulation

In the first part of this chapter, we argued that the rate of population growth in many less-developed nations has tended to rise because of the incomplete nature of the demographic transition. Death rates have declined rapidly, but birth rates have fallen much more sluggishly as a result of slower changes in fertility rates. Though family-planning programs have had some success in some nations, the primary determinants of declining fertility and lower birth rates have been increasing family incomes and an expansion of women's education.

Population growth is thus a dependent variable rather than an independent, exogenous factor subject to easy manipulation. It is not rapid population growth which causes low incomes; it is low incomes and low education levels that engender high population growth rates through higher fertility rates, as discussed in full above.

This perspective, however, does not deny that rapid population growth can create problems for less-developed economies, and typically these are greater in economies which can ill afford them. One of the consequences of a rapid natural rate of population growth over an extended period of time will be a reduction in the average age-profile of the population.[17]

The dependency ratio is a convenient, if imperfect, demographic measure that provides some idea of the impact of population growth and demographic changes on society (Table 12.6). It indicates for each potentially employed worker, the number of non-employed workers that must be supported by one worker's production.

In Somalia, for example, with a high and rising population growth rate, the dependency ratio rose. This means there was a rising proportion of young people in the population so that those who were working had to produce enough not only for themselves but for a growing proportion of the population that was young and non-productive. On the other hand, in Korea and with a slowing rate of population growth between 1970 and 2000, the dependency ratio fell dramatically, so that rising output per employed person could go to increasing per capita income and not solely to be spread over a larger number of non-workers.

The table also shows the commitment of governments to education as measured by the educational expenditures as a percent of gross national income (or gross total income). The World Bank study on the HPAEs (World Bank 1993b: 194–6) found that in Korea, Thailand, and Singapore the absolute number of school-age children actually fell, while in Sub-Saharan Africa the numbers of those of school age rose as a consequence of a more rapid pace of population growth. Thus, the increase in spending on education as a share of GNI for Korea shown in the table was applied to a smaller number of students, and this permitted a focus on improvements in the quality of education and in the quality of the human capital

Table 12.6 Dependency ratios, population age profile, and public expenditure on education

	% of population of working age (15–64 years)		*Dependency ratio[a]*		*Public expenditure on education (% of GNI)*	
	1970	*2000*	*1970*	*2000*	*1970*	*2000*
Low-income economies	54.8	58.7	0.84	0.71	2.36	2.83
China	56.0	68.3	0.79	0.48	1.20	2.03
India	55.9	61.5	0.79	0.63	2.47	3.35
Pakistan	54.6	54.5	0.98	0.82	1.01	2.39
Somalia	51.5	49.6	0.94	1.01	1.05	n.a.
Zimbabwe	48.6	51.6	1.08	0.76	3.26	7.47
Middle-income economies	56.3	66.0	0.79	0.52	2.48	3.76
Argentina	63.7	62.6	0.57	0.60	1.35	3.20
Côte d'Ivoire	51.9	54.8	0.93	0.85	4.70	4.54
Jamaica	47.5	61.3	1.11	0.61	2.58	6.84
Korea	54.6	72.1	0.83	0.39	2.62	3.38
Senegal	52.6	53.2	0.90	0.91	3.76	3.44
High-income economies	63.5	66.9	0.58	0.49	4.17	4.81
Ireland	57.7	67.1	0.74	0.49	4.01	5.49
Japan	68.9	68.1	0.45	0.47	2.87	4.63
United Kingdom	62.8	65.3	0.59	0.53	n.a.	4.69
United States	61.8	66.0	0.62	0.51	4.49	4.70
Less-developed regions						
East Asia and Pacific	55.3	66.8	0.81	0.50	1.63	2.47
Latin America and Caribbean	53.4	63.1	0.88	0.59	2.67	4.21
Middle East and North Africa	51.3	58.6	0.96	0.69	3.97	4.75
South Asia	55.3	60.3	0.82	0.66	2.27	3.09
Sub-Saharan Africa	52.3	52.6	0.91	0.89	3.43	4.73

Source: World Bank, *World Development Indicators 2002*.

Note
a   Calculated as [(population < age 15) + (population > 64 years of age)] ÷ population aged 15–64.

being created. The large decrease in the average student–teacher ratio in Korea (Table 12.5) is another quality indicator of the gains that can be attained from lower population growth rates on the capacity of a nation to accumulate human capital and hence to be able to both grow faster and to reach a higher level of income per person.

Other countries, such as Zimbabwe, also spent more of their government budgets on education (the last column of Table 12.6), but these were expenditures needed, at least partly, to keep pace with the growth of the school-age population so as to maintain the extent of coverage of primary and secondary schooling, making any increase in enrolment ratios (Zimbabwe now has universal primary coverage, but less than 50 percent secondary coverage) more expensive than would have been the case with slower population growth. Faster population growth and having a large young population skews the need for spending in the direction of education and other social services aimed at younger persons, for example neonatal and natal health care, just to keep pace with population growth, leaving less for other development purposes. These trends, however, are being mitigated as population growth slows with declines in fertility rates, as discussed above.

Summary and conclusions

This chapter builds upon the theory of the structural transformation which has been our focus since Chapter 7. Economic and human development are inextricably linked to the structural transformation of poorer nations from agriculture-based productive patterns to industrial and service-based economies. However, this transformation is not just one of changing what is produced but of fundamentally altering *how* production takes place. The endogenous growth theories in Chapter 8 alerted us to the importance of augmenting the stock of human capital, especially through education, since higher levels of human capital are strongly associated with higher income per capita, higher rates of economic growth, with progress on the human development indicators, and with greater equity via shared growth.

In this chapter, we have examined some of the details of human capital accumulation, drawing attention to universal primary and secondary coverage and reducing both the gender and urban–rural education gaps if less-developed nations are to build the base for future growth and development. At low levels of income and development, university education expenditures should not consume too much of the state's education budget; 25 percent might be the maximum warranted amount, leaving the remainder for primary and secondary funding.

This chapter also reinforces the positive role the state can perform, this time in the education arena, by helping to overcome the market failure problem that arises from the positive externalities associated with increasing the average level of education. In this vein, university education should not just be left either to the whims of academics or to the current demands of students. Rather, part of the guiding function of the state is to direct government funding for tertiary education and to shape incentives so that a critical mass of scientists, engineers, and technicians are properly trained. In this way, the human capital stock can be augmented so as to be ready to take advantage of the rapidly changing technological and knowledge innovations occurring at the world level. (This essential type of investment will be discussed more fully in the next chapter.) With the proper incentive structure via scholarships, employment, and so on, government can contribute to the formation of a dynamic labor force capable of contributing on an on-going basis to an economy's level of development over the long run.

Questions and exercises

1 Using data you can find at the World Bank website (www.worldbank.org; look under "Data and Research" then "Data by Topic") on the CBR and the CDR:

    a   calculate the *natural* rate of population growth for two LDCs not shown in Table 12.2.

    b   Then compare these values with their *actual* rates of population growth and *calculate* the amount of net migration for each country.

    c   Have either of these two LDCs passed through the demographic transition or any part of the demographic transition? Explain.

2 Using data from the previous problem, calculate the doubling time of population for both the natural and actual population growth rates for both of the LDCs.

3 Crude death rates in Table 12.2 tend to fall within a smaller range than crude birth rates. However, Sub-Saharan Africa countries like Zimbabwe, Senegal, and Côte d'Ivoire have somewhat higher crude death rates than other nations within their grouping (and

in some cases, the CDR actually has been rising). What factors might account for these higher death rates?

4   In Table 12.5 the number of students per teacher is used as an indicator of human capital deepening, that is, as a quality measure. What other possible measures might be utilized to get some idea of the quality of education? Can you find data on these measures that tells a different story for some country in the table, for example, Pakistan?

5   Focus 12.3 looked at the different experiences of Bolivia and Indonesia in their approaches to providing primary education. Let's bring the perspective in that focus up to date. Find data on each country's public expenditures for: all types of education as a percentage of GDP for some recent year; the percentage of total public expenditure on education spent on primary and secondary education; enrolment rates for primary and secondary education for males and females for the same (or a recent) year; and the growth rate of per capita income for a recent period of time. Does the "story" of Focus 12.3 that the importance of concentrating spending on primary (and now secondary) education still apply for Bolivia and Indonesia? How have things changed in both economies, at least according to the data you have collected compared to the late 1980s? (Try looking for the data at www.undp.org, Human Development Data, then click on "Data and factsheets by country.")

6   Note 8 to this chapter, which refers to the section on "Determinants of the crude birth rate," and the accompanying discussion in that section, argue that the inverse relation between per capita income and crude death rates is much weaker than the inverse relation between per capita income and crude birth rates shown in Table 12.2. A simple econometric exercise can test these two hypotheses.

Using Excel, and beginning in cell A1, create a spreadsheet like the following, using data from the World Bank website (www.worldbank.org; look under "Data and Research" then "Data by Topic') or some other source. Input data for eight countries on their CBR, CDR and income (either GNI or GDP) per capita for a recent year in the corresponding columns. Try to choose countries from different parts of the world. (If you do not have access to Excel or some other spreadsheet program, draw two scatter diagrams for the data and fit, by hand, the best straight line to the data.)

Country	CBR	CDR	Income per capita

a   You are first going to draw two scatter diagrams (choose the one with no line!). The first will have the crude birth rate as the dependent variable shown on the vertical axis and income per capita as the independent variable on the horizontal axis. The second scatter diagram (with no line) should have the CDR on the vertical axis and income again on the horizontal.

b   Right click on one of the data points in each graph and then have Excel "add trend-line" (choose linear) and under "Options," display the equation and R-squared.

c   What were the expected signs on the per capita income variable in each equation? Do the coefficients on income have the expected signs in your regression results?

d   How "good" is income in explaining what happens to crude birth and crude death rates, at least according to the R^2 values you obtained for your limited sample?

7   China's CBR and CDR values in Table 12.2 are more typical of a high-income country than for low-income economies as a group.

a   Find data on what has happened to China's fertility rate since, say, 1970. (A good place to look is at www.undp.org where you can find data from the UN *Human Development Report*. Look under Human Development Data, and then "Data and factsheets by country.") How does China's fertility rate compare to the average among low-income economies shown in Table 12.3?

b   What might explain any differences between China's CBR and fertility rate relative to the average for low-income economies shown in Table 12.3? If you don't know about China's "one-child policy," try reading something about it and summarize the policy here. There are lots of good sites on the internet. Check Wikipedia, too.

c   How does China's one-child policy fit into the "opportunity cost" explanation as to why families in poor (or rich) economies choose how many children to have? Does the one-child policy affect the opportunity costs of bearing children in China? Explain.

8   If you have studied consumer indifference curves, try the following analysis of a family's decision about choosing the "optimum" number of children which can help you to understand better why income and fertility are inversely related from a neoclassical economic perspective.

   Draw axes where you measure the "number of children" on the horizontal axis and "family income" on the vertical axis. Draw in a few normally shaped, convex-to-the-origin indifference curves. The shapes of the curves indicate that income (a proxy for "all other goods") and children are substitutes for a family in providing satisfaction or utility.

   Draw and label a "current income" budget line and find the "optimum" number of children, given that income level. You will remember that the optimum will be at the tangency point of that linear budget line and the highest attainable indifference curve. Show on the horizontal axis the number of children "chosen"; label that quantity C_0.

   Now, let income increase, but at the same time let the "price" of children also increase (in terms of the opportunity cost of lost income for time spent in caring for children by, for example, women with greater opportunities for employment). Thus the new budget line will both shift out and be *steeper* than the original line, indicating an increase in the relative "price" of children compared to all other goods as income rises.

   You should be able to show that it is quite possible that the new optimum number of children, C_N, that a family now chooses is fewer because of the higher relative price of children (as a result of their higher opportunity cost) at the higher income level.

9   This is a question that challenges you to see if you have understood one of the major points of this chapter. Discuss the following quotation using the concepts of and the interaction between: the CBR, the CDR, the fertility rate, and the demographic transition.

   "There is no population problem in less-developed countries. There is only a development problem."

10 Differentiate between human capital *broadening* and human capital *deepening*. Is one more important than the other? Discuss.

11 For a country that interests you or that you are assigned:

a   Find the ratio of pupils to teachers in primary and secondary school for two years, if that is available.

b   Has there been "human capital deepening" over that period? Explain what that means. (Go to http://portal.unesco.org/uis/ev.php?URL_ID=5187&URL_DO=DO_ TOPIC&URL_SECTION=201 and then click on pupil–teacher ratio near the middle of the page.)

12 One of the side-benefits of expanding education can be an increase in equity or, at least, no strong increase in inequality. Extending primary and secondary education to all residents of a country contributes to individual productivity and individual incomes and may be important in creating a regime for shared growth. Compare enrolment rates and income inequality for five less-developed nations (use the ratio of income of the top 20 percent of income earners to the bottom 20 percent of income earners, or the Gini coefficient, as the measure of inequality). Do countries with lower enrolment coverage for primary and secondary education have more or less inequality than economies with higher enrolment ratios? Are there any systematic differences amongst the countries you have selected? Why, or why not? What other factors might be at work which contribute to or detract from the possibility for shared growth?

13 Millennium Development Goal 4 is to "reduce by two-thirds, between 1990 and 2015, the under-five mortality rate"; Goal 5 is to "reduce by three-quarters, between 1990 and 2015, the maternal mortality ratio"; and Goal 6 is to "have halted by 2015 and begun to reverse the spread of HIV/AIDS" and to "have halted by 2015 and begun to reverse the incidence of malaria and other major diseases."

Examine the data by regions at the World Bank website under Statistics and MDGs. You can click on each goal and then examine the data in map, table, or chart form. Which regions are on target? Which are not? Does it look like, globally, these MDGs will be met by the 2015 target date?

Notes

1 Easterly (2001: Chapter 4 especially, but throughout) takes a decidedly contrarian perspective on the role of education. A close reading of his essays suggests, however, that education is important, but in the right context, which is what we have argued. There is no single approach that, by itself, guarantees successful development. There are a number of complementary policies that must be carried out more or less simultaneously.

2 We say the "normal" relation is from income to population growth, but there actually are instances of more rapid population growth leading to an increase in output and income, as in the United States in the early to mid-nineteenth century, or in Australia later in that century. In both cases, high population growth rates resulting from large inflows of migrants contributed to, rather than subtracted from, the expansion of production. New migrants helped to fill a void in labor supply and contributed to an increase in total output beyond population growth and did not act as a drain that reduced income per person.

3 We divide by 10 in equation 12.2, because both the crude birth rate, CRB, and the crude death rate, CDR, are stated per 1,000 population. When we divide by 10, these are converted to rates per 100 of population, thus permitting us to interpret the difference as a percentage. Crude birth and death rates depend upon the age distribution of the population, death rates for different age groups (including infant mortality rates), the fertility rate of women, and other demographic characteristics of the population. The adjective "crude" is used in the sense of an "average."

4 Rapid population growth is a very recent historical phenomenon. It has been estimated that in AD 1 world population was about 300 million. It took 1,500 years for population to double from that level, an annual rate of population growth of less than 0.05 percent. From 1750 to the early twentieth century, world population grew at a rate of about 0.5 percent, increasing the doubling time of world population to less than 150 years. From 1950–87, world population doubled again from 2.5 billion to 5 billion as the doubling time further decreased, and world population grew at a rate approaching 2 percent per annum (Birdsall 1988: 479).

5 The average rate of population growth in the less-developed nations was 0.6 percent from 1850–1900, rising to 1.3 percent by the 1920s, 2.0 percent in the early 1950s, and to 2.6 percent in the early 1970s (Reynolds 1986: 50). It is quite easy to determine, in an approximate fashion, how fast population doubles at these rates of growth by using the Rule of 70, which is

doubling time (in years) = 70 ÷ annual percent rate of change of population.

Thus, if population is growing at 2 percent per annum, population will double in approximately thirty-five years; at 3 percent per annum, the doubling time is reduced to twenty-three and one-third years.

6 Maddison (1982: 189, Table B6) reports the following crude birth rates for a few of the now-developed countries, illustrating their trend rate.

	1820	*1900*
France	31.7	21.3
Germany	39.9	35.6
Japan	–	32.4
United Kingdom	30.3	28.7
United States	55.2	32.3

7 This can happen when, as is the case of a country whose population has been growing rapidly, a large proportion of the population is relatively young compared to that which is elderly. A nation's crude death rate is a weighted average of the death rates of different age groups, so with a younger population the average death rate can be quite low, even for a poor economy, given the large number of young people relative to older persons.

8 In 2005, the crude birth rate (CBR) varied between 53 per 1000 of population in Niger and 8 in Japan, while the crude death rate (CDR) varied only between 27 per 1000 of population in Botswana and 2 in Kuwait. Of course the crude death rate has some association to per capita income levels, with countries with lower per capita incomes tending to have higher per capita crude death rates. However, the link between income and death rates is significantly weaker than the link between income and birth rates. Infant mortality rates are strongly inversely correlated with women's education, just as birth rates are (World Bank 1991: 49).

9 Birdsall (1988: 514) notes that the inverse relation between women's education and fertility rates is noted only for more than four years of schooling. For 0–4 years of education, women's education and fertility tend to be positively related.

10 China's fertility rate fell from 5.8 children per woman in 1970 to 2.1 in 1990 and 1.8 in 2005.

11 When crude death rates are high, high rates of fertility and high crude birth rates are quite functional for maintaining the survival of entire populations. In such circumstances, cultural, religious, social, ideological, and family values have tended to advocate high birth rates and women's role as caretaker for the family. The already-developed nations had a longer time period, in some cases a century and more, during which the demographic transition was taking place at a more measured pace, so their religious and cultural value systems, particularly concerning the reproductive role of women, were able to evolve more in line with the falling rate of mortality. The less-developed nations, particularly those newly independent since 1945, have had much less time for their social value systems to catch up with changing economic and structural conditions.

12 The same trend for fertility rates to decline is observed when, instead of using average income as an indicator, the level of human development is used. Countries with a low HDI value in 1992 had an average fertility rate of 5.1; those with medium HDI values had an average fertility rate of 3.0; and in those nations with a high HDI value, average fertility was 2.8 (UNDP 1994: 174–5, Table 23).

13 All family incomes could theoretically rise even with a worsening income distribution if those with higher incomes have a faster rate of growth in their incomes than those with lower incomes. We simply want to focus here on the direct link between family income and lower birth rates, abstracting from income distribution changes, although such changes would be important to know and to analyze as to their impact on fertility and birth rates.

14 In Chapter 13 we shall consider the importance of specific types of education to economic growth, specifically the role of scientists and engineers in taking the process of development to higher levels of income and human realization, and especially their role in fomenting technological change. It is thus not just universal primary and secondary education that are important over the long term for sustained success, though these provide the base upon which further progress can be made.

   Once again, things are more complicated, and yet are not. Universal primary and secondary education are important in their own right for providing a broader-based and more skilled labour force that can contribute to greater efficiency and productivity. Building on this base of secondary students, the needed core of workers with higher level skills that come from having undertaken tertiary education can be attained more easily. One goal follows another, with each having its own complementary importance.

15 The subsidy amount of mn is found by determining the vertical difference between the MSB and the MPB curves at the socially optimum level of education, E_S.

16 Students from high-income families are more likely to attend university than are students from low-income families, both because the out-of-pocket costs for low-income families are a higher proportion of their income, and because the opportunity cost of attending university or other post-secondary education compared to total income is larger. Thus when post-secondary, particularly university, education is funded via low tuition fees to all students regardless of need, it is higher-income students, who could afford to pay a larger proportion of the actual costs, who disproportionately benefit from such subsidies. That is why targeted subsidies, rather than blanket subsidies extended to all regardless of need, tend to be both more efficient for the goals designed and tend to contribute to greater equity in society.

17 Rapid population growth caused by immigration often is the consequence of positive economic forces that pull migrants from low-wage, low-opportunity countries toward higher-wage, higher-opportunity economies. In these cases, as in the large migratory flows from Europe to North America, Argentina, and Australia in the 1800s, migrants are older, and they often bring valuable skills and education formed elsewhere. Such migrants add to the labor force and human capital pool of the receiving nation and contribute immediately to increasing aggregate output. This is different from the situation discussed here where the growth of population is the result of natural forces and not of migration flows.

References

Birdsall, Nancy. 1988. "Economic Approaches to Population Growth," in Hollis B. Chenery and T.N. Srinivasan (eds.), *Handbook of Development Economics*. Amsterdam: North Holland Publishers.

Easterly, William. 2001. *The Elusive Quest for Growth: Economists' Adventures and Misadventures in the Tropics*. Cambridge, MA: MIT Press.

Maddison, Angus. 1982. *Phases of Capitalist Development*. Oxford: Oxford University Press.

Mincer, Jacob. 1958. "Investment in Human Capital and Personal Income Distribution," *Journal of Political Economy* 66: 281–302.

Reynolds, Lloyd G. 1986. *Economic Growth in the Third World: An Introduction*. New Haven, CT: Yale University Press.

Sachs, Jeffrey D. 2005. *The End of Poverty*. London: Penguin Books.

Schultz, T.W. 1960. "Capital Formation by Education," *Journal of Political Economy* 68: 511–83.

Sen, Amartya. 1990. "More Than 100 Million Women are Missing," *New York Review of Books* 37 (December 20): 61–6.

UNDP (United Nations Development Programme). 1994. *Human Development Report 1994*. New York: Oxford University Press.

World Bank. 1983. *World Development Report 1983*. New York: Oxford University Press.

——. 1991. *World Development Report 1991*. New York: Oxford University Press.

——. 1993a. *World Development Report 1993.* New York: Oxford University Press.
——. 1993b. *The East Asian Miracle.* New York: Oxford University Press.
——. 1994. *World Development Report 1994.* New York: Oxford University Press.
——. 1995. *World Development Report 1995.* New York: Oxford University Press.
——. 2002a. *World Development Report 2002.* New York: Oxford University Press.
——. 2002b. *World Development Indicators 2002.* New York: Oxford University Press.

13 Technology and development

After reading and studying this chapter, you should better understand:

- what is meant by "technology";
- the distinction between an "independent technology *learning* capacity (ITLC) and an "independent technology *creating* capacity" (ITCC);
- the connection between specific forms of human capital accumulation, technological progress and the level of development;
- the role of facilitating and obstructing institutions in the spread of technology;
- the imbedded nature of technology in a particular society's institutions and organizational structure;
- the fact that technology is country-specific;
- the importance of appropriate state action in helping to provide the complementary inputs for capturing the benefits of "best practice" technological change;
- the need for a strategy of "technological autonomy" based upon domestic sources of financial capital, entrepreneurship and science to create a dynamic "national technology".

Introduction

The significance of technological change to economic growth and development has been verified again and again in empirical studies. The endogenous growth theories considered in Chapter 8 and in the World Bank study (1993) of the East Asian economies are part of this ever-growing literature. The research based on neoclassical growth models has found that the basic factors of production, capital and labor, cannot explain all, or even much, of economic growth. It is often the "residual," that is, the unidentified variables, which contribute the most to increased productivity. The non-included variables, which can encompass such diverse items as technology, business and governmental organization, institutional structures, the legal system, property rights, and so on, carry the weight of "explaining" economic growth over time and the differences in growth rates amongst countries.

In this chapter, we consider in more detail what is meant by technology, one of the most important contributors to economic progress. We will focus on the required *preconditions* for an economy to be able to make effective use of technological knowledge as the structural transformation process discussed in previous chapters moves forward. We also consider what countries need to do to take better advantage of the ever-expanding world supply of technological opportunities available to almost any economy.

What is technology?

Technology is knowledge applied to the production process. It permits an outward shift of a nation's production possibilities frontier (PPF) and creates the *potential* for greater output and income from the same resources. Technological progress reduces costs, increases productive efficiency, conserves society's resources, and establishes the capacity for a higher standard of living for greater numbers of persons.

It is primarily due to technological advances that humankind has been able to progress so rapidly since the Industrial Revolution. Without technological change, the specter of hunger and deprivation that Malthus expected might have come to pass, as the law of diminishing returns would have worked its inexorable logic on fixed resources with unchanging productivity. However, by shifting the production possibilities frontier outward and the aggregate production function upward, the static effect of diminishing returns was overcome by technological change that improved the productivity of all the factors of production, thus releasing resources for an ever higher level of output. The upward trend line of income per capita following the Industrial Revolution shown in Figure 3.1 in Chapter 3 was the consequence of this ever more intensive application of new knowledge to production.

Nonetheless, technology is often a difficult concept to understand. This is because it is not any particular object, but rather is a *way of doing things and a way of thinking*. Technology involves not only the entire accumulated complex of scientific and machine-tool knowledge and the tools and machines which encapsulate this knowledge. It also encompasses the *country-specific* human understanding, skills, education, and training essential for making use of this knowledge, the machines, and the tools. Evenson and Westphal (1995: 2213) describe technology as:

> tacit, not feasibly embodied and neither codifiable nor readily transferable. Thus, though two producers in the same circumstances may use identical material inputs in conjunction with equal information, they may nonetheless employ what are really two distinct techniques owing to differences in understanding of the tacit elements [of that technology].

Technology is thus specific to each economy. The same physical manifestations of technology, such as a computer or a lathe, can have quite different effects on productivity since these tools are combined with labor forces in each economy, even each firm, with specific accumulated skills operating within a larger institutional and organizational framework. Technological knowledge is thus economy-specific, depending not just on the tools, machines, and other manifestations of technology in place, but also dependent on the skills and effectiveness of the operators and users of those tools and that knowledge.

The more rapidly technological knowledge is able to be adapted and put to work in an economy, the more rapid will be the pace of economic growth. This requires that workers and entrepreneurs have hands-on experience using such ideas in the act of producing. That is the tacit part of technology noted in the quote above. Slower technological progress means, *ceteris paribus*, slower economic growth and reduced possibilities for augmenting or creating the social mechanisms that promote greater equity and the higher level of human development that technological progress makes feasible.

What has not been well understood in thinking about technology is how some of society's social and economic institutions – including the existing class structure, land tenure relations, institutions for finance and banking, ideology, religion and superstition, the commitment of society to education and free inquiry, the openness of the state to change and to shared development, the legal structure and property rights, and the nature of the ties between industry and the scientific and educational infrastructure – can be powerful forces in determining to what extent technology is able to perform its dynamic and transformative functions.[1] Many of the above are *Ayresian-type ceremonial institutions* examined in Chapter 6. They tend to engender tradition-bound modes of behavior that operate on other than scientific principles. It is inconceivable, however, to have any socio-economic system where there are not some such ceremonial institutions, structures which are by their nature past-binding and status quo-oriented.

Nonetheless, in economies where this ceremonial structure is relatively weak, facilitating, and complementary to change, or can be made so by appropriate state policies, technological knowledge has a better chance of being combined in the production process to contribute to greater productivity and to higher levels of output. On the other hand, in societies where the ceremonial institutional structure is retrograde, especially powerful, and non-facilitating of change, and where the state does not act to debilitate these adverse structures and ways of thinking, new knowledge is less apt to be applied to production.

The importance of technology has been widely identified as a major contributor to economic growth beginning with the empirical work of Edward Denison (1967: 299, 315). His research found technology to be responsible for over 40 percent of growth in the US and the UK over the period studied. Simon Kuznets's work also identified the significance of technological change, broadly interpreted, to productivity and economic growth. Solow (1988: 314) noted that perhaps over 90 percent of the increases in output can be accounted for by the combined forces of technology and education, which in our view are interlocked variables.

The magnitude of this technology effect should not be too surprising. In Chapter 8, we looked at how endogenous growth models have identified the importance of both technology and of human capital as fundamental *complementary inputs* affecting the rate of economic growth and the level of per capita income. The endogenous growth theories also showed how the ability to apply technological knowledge varies dramatically amongst economies, so that a convergence of income has not taken place in the simple fashion suggested by the neoclassical growth model. This is because technological knowledge in use is economy-specific as a result of differences in the capacity of end-users to apply knowledge in the production process.

This way of looking at technology focuses attention on the need for social investment in specific human capital and organizational inputs if such knowledge is to be utilized to its full effect. This way of understanding technology also recognizes that there can be *technology gaps* among economies and that each economy must develop its own relatively unique technological base. Technology is *specific knowledge*, not general knowledge. It cannot be applied everywhere in the same way. Each country must make a substantial investment in its social and human resource capital base if it is to gain the capacity "to do" technology in a way that maximizes the gains that are implicit in any particular component of knowledge applied to production.

In the past, many economic growth models envisaged technology as an exogenous public good available to every economy, as in the Solow-type, neoclassical formulation, rather than understanding *technology as a process of knowledge-in-practice*.[2] Technology is not something that just happens to economies, like some *deus ex machina*. It is a process that countries need to consciously and actively promote and nurture if the potential benefits of technological knowledge are to be effectively achieved.

To an important extent, the current level of technology-in-use in any economy is *path dependent*, that is, it hinges crucially on past decisions that affect current outcomes, though this lock-in on path dependency is never absolutely binding. Countries can do something about *adverse* path dependency in their use of technology by investing in the complementary inputs, particularly education and research and development (R&D), which contribute over time to each country's specific capability to effectively make use of the world's supply of technological knowledge. It is precisely these areas of social investment that can spell the difference between successful and less-successful development over time; they are the *necessary preconditions* for future progress.

A technological strategy of development

In a meaningful sense, economic development is indistinguishable from the ongoing application of technological knowledge to production.[3] Without continuing technological change, economic growth slows and eventually development falters. In their comprehensive overview of technology, Evenson and Westphal (1995: 2216) quite unequivocally state that "[n]o LDC has to date achieved rapid economic growth without continued technological investment."

Technological change is the result of scientific discovery, experiment, and innovation which must be financed either by the private sector or the state. The successful introduction of technology into the domestic production process in any country, what can be called *domestic innovation*, requires a domestic scientific establishment capable, first, of understanding, adopting, and adapting new, often foreign-created, technological knowledge to the specific needs of the domestic economy. Machines and tools often have to be customized to fit local conditions. This is the *adaptation stage* of technological progress where existing knowledge is "borrowed" from the world supply and made to fit the local economy.

Later, some countries might move into the *creation state* of technological progress, which involves the conducting of new research, the designing of experiments, and the dissemination of new knowledge that adds to the world supply of technological competency and to the possibility of ever higher standards of living.

Ronald Dore (1984: 65–8) refers to these two distinct stages as, respectively, an *ITLC* and an *ITCC*: an "independent technology *learning* capacity" and an "independent technology *creating* capacity." An ITLC might also be called, interchangeably, *technological autonomy*.

Creating an ITLC and achieving technological autonomy is the first step toward greater self-sufficiency, a higher level of domestic efficiency and the creation of an internal dynamic for any economy. It is an ITLC that undergirded the Japanese, Korean, and Taiwanese development successes. The easy import substitution and easy export substitution phases of industrialization in those countries provided the creative space for domestic entrepreneurs and workers to be able to attain higher levels of skill that permitted them to become increasingly technologically competent. It is this learning capacity which permitted the East Asian economies to grow faster, on average, than other less-developed countries which apparently shared roughly the same initial endowments, such as the level of investment. Looking back at Table 8.4 in Chapter 8, with the exception of Singapore (which is a service-intensive economy), the East Asian economies did better at keeping pace or catching up with international "best practice" technology than did nations in Africa or Latin America.

The ability to *create* technology and to add to the world pool of knowledge and practice, that is, for a country to have an ITCC, comes later with the further maturation and deepening of the ITLC process which preceded it. An ITCC is most likely to appear as more resources are devoted to R&D and as economies complete difficult ISI and difficult export substitution and move into the knowledge-intensive phase of structural transformation (see Figure 10.1 in Chapter 10).

An ITLC is essential to sustaining high rates of economic growth and to make progress on the path to fuller development. An ITCC may be necessary to sustain this progress over the longer term after the gains from the ITLC strategy become more difficult to sustain and after a country has learned to be as efficient as world-level best practice techniques.[4] It was an ITCC that Great Britain and then the US created and which contributed to their phenomenal progress over long periods, while each was the leading force for the creation of new technological standards and knowledge for the world.

Recent empirical studies have found that a nation's research and development (R&D) expenditures are significant in explaining sustained growth rates over time. Other research has suggested that within the overall goal of increasing the stock of human capital, scientists and technicians involved in R&D are an important sub-category of human capital which should be emphasized to better appropriate the benefits of technology. There is now little doubt that both R&D and the training of R&D researchers contribute to the creation of specific national technologies and to the learning required to be able to utilize technological knowledge effectively. Table 13.1 provides data on the number of R&D researchers and the share of total gross domestic product (GDP) devoted to R&D for a variety of economies.

The story the table tells seems quite unambiguous. Countries at higher levels of development, here measured by the human development index (HDI), tend to have larger numbers of R&D scientists and technicians directly involved in research and development activities with close links to the production process than do countries with lower HDI values. But even among these economies, there are evident differences.

Korea's and Singapore's attention to R&D researchers is especially noteworthy among even the high human development countries, though all the less-developed countries have a stock of technology-oriented researchers that still falls well short of what has been achieved, on average, in the already-developed countries.[5] Singapore's and Korea's R&D spending is also quite high, particularly when compared to other LDCs among the high human development category, such as Argentina, Chile, Mexico, and Malaysia. Looking at gross national income (GNI) per person in 2005, both Singapore and Korea distinguish themselves from the other high human development economies shown. There clearly seems to be a very positive relationship between R&D researchers and expenditures and not only the level of development, as measured by the HDI, but also in terms of income.

Among the economies that have achieved medium human development, China's number of R&D researchers and its level of R&D expenditures is worthy of note. Given China's large population, this represents a substantial core of R&D workers who can fuel the ITLC process and continue to help the economy achieve the high levels of economic growth that have been attained over the past two decades. China's income per capita is low relative, say, to Brazil, but the chances are quite good that soon China will surpass Brazil given the rapid pace of change and given the technological focus.

For the low human development economies, the low and at times negligible levels of R&D expenditures and R&D researchers manifests itself in, and is partly the consequence of, low levels of income per person. There is clearly a path-dependent effect at work in all economies in that there is a feedback mechanism from the level of ITLC to income and the level of human development and vice versa. The data is difficult to controvert: more attention to R&D has a long-run effect on the level of development and income. Look at Japan among

Table 13.1 R&D scientists and technicians

	R&D scientists and technicians (per 1,000,000 pop.)	R&D expenditures (% of GDP)	GNI per capita (US dollars)
	1990–2003	2000–2003	2005
High Human Development (HDI > 0.800)	2,968	2.5	
Argentina	720	0.4	4,470
Chile	444	0.6	5,870
Korea	3,187	2.6	15,840
Malaysia	299	0.7	4,970
Mexico	268	0.4	7,310
Singapore	4,745	2.2	27,850
Medium Human Development (0.500 < HDI < 0.800)	523	0.9	
Brazil	344	1.0	3,550
China	663	1.3	1,740
India	119	0.8	730
Pakistan	86	0.2	690
Thailand	286	0.2	2,720
Low Human Development (HDI < 0.500)	–	–	
Guinea	251	–	420
Nigeria	–	–	560
Zambia	51	–	500
All Developing Countries	416	1.1	
Developed Countries	3,748	2.5	
Japan	5,287	3.1	38,950
US	4,484	2.6	43,560

Sources: UNDP 2006: 327–30, Table 13; World Bank 2007: Table 1.1.

the developed economies. The attention paid to learning to do technology as revealed by the large share of R&D researchers and the investment in R&D out of total income is part of the story of why Japan became a powerful economy in the half-century after 1945.

While the rate of economic growth and technological change *are* path dependent in the sense of being the consequence of *past decisions* on the economic strategy, on expenditures for human capital purposes, on the exchange rate and inflation rate, and so on, modifications of the path are always possible when a country decides to make a change. What can be inferred from the Korean and Japanese experiences is that, though the current rate of economic and human development may be path dependent, the future path has multiple branches at any moment in time.

The decisions the state sector makes on expenditures for education, health, the military, on tariffs, on tax laws, on patents and other intellectual property rights, on the treatment of multinational corporations, and on a whole range of other factors today will determine along which path the economy and society will traverse in future. Private firms, individuals, and the state make decisions within the confines of the parameters for economic decision-making determined by the state and within the cultural and historical confines of each specific society.

They choose the paths now via spending and other decisions which affect future growth and development prospects and determine the future path dependency of the economy.

While Table 13.1 does not prove causality, the endogenous growth models and research work by other scholars (see Grossman and Helpman 1994) do find that there is a *serendipitous effect*, what we would call a positive externality, associated with a larger number of scientists engaged in R&D activities who are then able to interact with others also possessing a high level of skill and knowledge. R&D scientists and technicians are one specific category of human capital which seems to be unambiguously associated with a positive pay-off for growth, all else the same.

This does not change the conclusion of Chapters 8 and 12 on the importance for countries to pursue a more *generalized* human capital accumulation process in which universal primary and secondary education are extremely important. It does suggest, however, that resources do need to be directed to tertiary education as well, including funding specifically targeted at the training of essential R&D scientists and technicians as the level of per capita income and the level of human development rises. Further, this argument underscores the importance, in the modern global economic environment, of primary and secondary education with a substantial *technical focus*, with both mathematics and science training given particular emphasis if today's students are to have the skills and adaptability which tomorrow's economy will demand.

Table 13.2 provides more direct evidence on the relation between the level of technological capability and other key indicators. The seventy-five less-developed countries with Level 1 technological capacity had, at most, some industrial research capacity in the public sector, but not in the private sector, where production takes place. In agriculture, the capacity for doing technology ranged from nil to relatively advanced.[6]

Table 13.2 Technological capability and development capacity

	Level 1 LDCs	*Level 2 LDCs*	*OECD*
Real GDP growth (1965–90)			
Per capita	0.5–1.5	2.4–7.1	2.5
Total	2.5–2.8	4.7–8.1	3.5
R&D/GDP (1990)			
Public	0.2–0.3	0.4–0.6	0.7
Private	0.0–0.02	0.05–1.0	2.3
Science/GDP (1990)			
Public	0.02–0.03	0.04–0.10	0.40
Private	0.0	0.0	0.05
S&E/GDP	0.2–0.4	0.6–1.3	1.0
IPR (index)	0–1	2–4	5.0

Source: adapted from Evenson and Westphal 1995: 2242–3, Table 37.1.

Note
Level 1 less-developed countries have "traditional technology" to some "islands of modernization"; *Level 2* developing countries have technology ranging from "mastery of conventional technology" to newly-industrialized countries. OECD are the high-income economies. *R&D/GDP* is the percent of gross domestic product spent on research and development. *Science/GDP* is the percent of gross domestic product spent on science. *S&E/GDP* is the availability of scientists and engineers relative to gross domestic product. *IPR* is an index measuring the strength of intellectual property rights; it ranges from 0 (no IPRs) to 5 (complete IPRs).

There were only twenty less-developed countries with Level 2 technological capacity (all the East Asian economies were at this level), which means they had at least a basic ITLC capacity in key sectors of their economies.

It is clear from the first and second lines of Table 13.2, and even clearer from data that is even more finely disaggregated but not shown here (see Evenson and Westphal 1995), that the level of technological capability was positively correlated with the pace of economic expansion over the period 1965–90. For Level 2 less-developed countries that had achieved a higher level of ITLC, the rate of growth of aggregate GDP was higher than for the Organisation for Economic Co-operation and Development (OECD) industrialized economies and was at least double the pace of growth for Level 1 countries with less capacity for an ITLC.

The last line of Table 13.2 gives some notion of the institutional, including legal, support provided to R&D endeavors in terms of protection for intellectual property rights (IPRs), such as patents and copyrights. Most Level 1 countries have no patent protection for domestic IPRs and provide virtually no protection for foreign IPRs. In Level 2 countries, there are laws providing intermediate protection for foreign IPRs, but IPRs in the domestic economy remain weakly defined, except for the four East Asian economies. Protection of domestic intellectual property rights is particularly important as economies become more adept at adapting foreign knowledge to the domestic sphere.

Lacking such protection, private firms and private inventors may be hesitant to invest in the development or introduction of new ideas for fear of theft of their innovations. But more importantly, a well-developed legal apparatus which affords IPRs proper and needed protection is a signal that an economy recognizes the significance of technology and the importance of the application of new knowledge in the process of production. Laws concerning IPRs are complementary to efforts to build an ITLC, and they reflect the attention to organization and institution-building characteristic of economies forging new paths toward a higher level of development. Thus the legal structure of economies must keep pace with efforts to augment other endowments for development, such as human capital resources. The positive relationship between the IPR protection and the pace of economic growth is quite clear from the table.

Total factor productivity and national technology

Economists often assess the impact of various inputs to production on economic growth using a *growth accounting* methodology. Basically, this is an attempt to measure how much of any increase in an economy's output can be accounted for by additional units of the inputs added to production, for example physical capital (K) and additional labor (L). Any economic growth left unaccounted for by increases in the quantity of the physical inputs is called *total factor productivity*, or TFP.[7]

Countries able to combine both new capital, which typically embodies new technological knowledge (read about the Salter Effect in Focus 13.1), and a growing and improving human capital stock which is better able to make use of and unlock the technological knowledge incorporated in new capital, will be better equipped to move toward and keep pace with the world production possibilities "best practice" frontier and will tend to have the highest rates of TFP. The World Bank (1991: 42) opined that "the main additional element (in explaining the growth of TFP) is the quality of labor," that is, human capital accumulation.

Total factor productivity gives us an idea about how efficient a country is as it progresses along its path of economic growth and industrialization. For example, imagine that the GDP

FOCUS 13.1   THE SALTER EFFECT: THE IMPORTANCE OF PHYSICAL CAPITAL INVESTMENT

Acquiring an independent technological learning capacity (ITLC) is not solely achieved via better education and augmentation of the human capital stock, though these are necessary. Knowing how to do technology requires experience gained primarily by actually producing. Best practice technological skills can only be acquired by using the most advanced manifestations of technology and of the ideas associated with them in production. This is the essence of learning-by-doing.

A significant proportion of new technological knowledge is *embedded* in the design of new physical capital equipment, such as computer-controlled arc welding devices, stamping machines, computer chips, and computer networks. Thus, the speed with which new capital replaces older capital will, to some extent, affect the pace at which best practice technological learning is integrated into local practice by becoming potentially appropriated knowledge possessed by local human capital and entrepreneurs.

This is another reason why export substitution industrialization strategies, discussed in Chapter 10, can contribute to more rapid economic growth. The faster the tempo of economic growth attributable to an expansion of manufactured exports and domestic production to accommodate such exports, the more new physical investment that will be required. Hence, to the extent that a more rapid pace of investment leads to the more rapid introduction of new physical capital embodying the latest technological knowledge, exporting can contribute positively to the domestic learning process.

On the other hand, slow-growing economies, such as those that have not graduated from easy import substitution industrialization to begin to export manufactured goods to the international market, do not introduce new capital with the latest embodied knowledge as quickly. Hence the speed at which technological knowledge is acquired and learned will be slower since any learning-by-doing effects in production will lag best practice technological knowledge as a result of the slower pace of physical capital accumulation.

The *Salter Effect* is the term applied to the speed at which new technological knowledge, embodied in new physical capital, is likely to be appropriated with higher levels of economic growth. The faster the rate of economic expansion, the more rapid is the potential rate of technological acquisition and hence future growth. The slower the pace of growth and investment, the slower the pace of technological learning and future growth is likely to be.

Thus exporting manufactured goods via an export substitution strategy, assuming the requisite human capital inputs have been created, can create a virtuous circle of technology learning, leading to altered path dependence.

Source: Salter 1969

per person of some country is growing at an average of 4.3 percent per year, but that it is discovered that the TFP = 0 for that country. What a TFP = 0 means is that there has been a *zero increase in efficiency* (i.e. no increase in the *productivity* of the inputs*)* involved in achieving that 4.3 percent increase in GDP per person.

How, then, was this economy able to grow at all, let alone an average of 4.3 percent per year, if there has been zero increase in the efficiency and productivity of the economy's inputs used in production?

The only way an economy's total output can increase if there is a zero increase in productivity (which is what TFP = 0 means) is if *more inputs* are added to production, inputs that are of the same quality as in the past. Typically, those inputs are physical capital and labor, but there could be other inputs as well (such as different types of workers, R&D, or any other input that might be identified).

Whenever GDP increases because there has been an increase in the inputs added to production, you will remember we call this *extensive economic growth*, i.e., economic growth resulting from adding more inputs to production. If TFP = 0, and a country has nonetheless experienced growing GDP, then *all* the increase in GDP has been due to the use of more labor and capital in production (and whatever other inputs there are), and all economic growth is extensive.

On the other hand, if a country has TFP > 0, then that means that *some part* of the country's economic growth is due to greater efficiency. When TFP > 0 that amount of growth is called *intensive* economic growth. TFP > 0 is a good thing, obviously, since this means that with the same quantity of inputs a country can produce more GDP than it could otherwise and at a faster rate than can be achieved by just adding new inputs to production. Having TFP > 0 is how countries can achieve even faster economic progress over the long term than would be possible otherwise. A good part of this increase in efficiency results from countries learning how "to do" technology.

Most of the time, if TFP > 0, there will have been *both* extensive and intensive growth, since nearly every economy is adding more inputs to production over time. So more inputs plus greater productivity of the inputs (a TFP > 0) adds up to both extensive and intensive growth at the same time.

Total factor productivity can be estimated by subtracting from the growth rate of total output the share of that total growth attributable to: (a) increases in the quantity of physical capital and (b) increases in the labor force, each weighted by their contribution to total production (of course, if there are more inputs, the concept for calculating TFP is the same). Any remainder can be interpreted as total factor productivity. In other words, TFP measures the synergistic effect of combining an economy's physical capital and its human capital, which can result in productivity increases beyond the contribution of of more physical quantities of the individual inputs. In the language of Chapter 3, TFP measures intensive economic growth (= total output growth − extensive growth).

For example, let's assume an economy with but two inputs to production, labor, L, and physical capital, K. If annual output growth was 2.5 percent; physical capital, K, grew by 3 percent per year and K's contribution to production was 30 percent; and the labor force, L, which contributed 70 percent to aggregate production, grew by 2 percent per year; then, TFP = total percentage change in output − (percentage change of K × contribution of K to production, as a decimal) − (percentage change of L × contribution of L to production, as a decimal) = 2.5 percent − (3 percent × 0.3) − (2 percent × 0.7) = 0.2 percent. (Note: the combined weights for the inputs must always add up to 1, regardless of the number of inputs. If there are more than two inputs to production, the weights must still sum to 1.) The 0.2 percent is the annual rate of TFP, that is, it is that part of total economic growth that cannot be explained by having added more inputs to the production process. It is the amount of intensive economic growth. And, yes, it can be zero or negative as well as a positive value as shown here.

In this example, of the 2.5 percent annual growth of total output, increases in K and L accounted for 2.3 percent growth per year and TFP (greater efficiency, better technology, better management techniques, better government regulations, etc.) resulted in additional growth of total output of 0.2 percent. In other words, 0.2 percent/2.5 percent = 8 percent of total output growth was due to TFP (intensive growth) and 92 percent was the result of adding more inputs to production (extensive growth).

TFP is an attempt to capture the impact of all the factors that contribute to the greater productivity of the inputs, K and L (or any broader definition of inputs used). Included in the TFP measure are: technological change and technological catch-up; improvements in the efficiency and learning capacity of the labor force due to human capital accumulation; the positive productivity effects of the structural transformation from agriculture to industry and other strategy switches; changes in state policy that contribute to greater efficiency, such as lower inflation rates or an improved tax structure; organizational and institutional altera-tions, such as better management practices and improved financial control mechanisms in the banking system, and so on.

In a general sense, all of the variables which might affect an economy's total factor productivity are related to an economy's acquisition of an ITLC and a national technological capacity to do technology and to be more effective users of resources.

Table 13.3 provides data on TFP estimates made by the World Bank for a crucial period of time. Part I shows annual rates of GDP growth, annual changes in the physical capital and labor inputs, and the resulting estimates of total factor productivity over the critical period 1960–87. Among the less-developed regions, East Asia's TFP growth rates were the highest, as one might expect from the larger number of scientists and the attention to R&D shown earlier in Table 13.1. It will also be noticed that East Asia's rate of capital accumulation was more rapid than in any other region and additions to the labor force were as high or higher than any other area. East Asia was thus not only experiencing intensive economic growth (TFP > 0) but also substantial extensive economic growth. No doubt the two sources of economic growth complemented one another.

All of these factors combined to give East Asia the highest rate of GDP growth among the regions and even relative to the industrial economies. Faster physical capital accumulation, particularly to the extent that it also embodied new knowledge, increased the pace of growth in the region (remember Focus 13.1 on the Salter Effect and the link between physical capital accumulation and the pace of technological change).

Table 13.3 Total Factor Productivity (TFP) estimates, 1960–1987 (percentages)

	GDP	Capital	Labor	TFP
Part I: Annual percentage changes				
Africa	3.3	6.3	2.2	0.0
East Asia	6.8	10.2	2.6	1.9
Latin America	3.6	6.3	2.6	0.0
South Asia	4.4	7.7	2.1	0.6
68 less-developed countries	4.2	7.2	2.3	0.6
Germany	3.9	4.8	−0.2	1.7
UK	2.4	3.1	−0.2	1.2
US	3.0	3.4	1.8	0.5
Part II: Total percentage of output growth as a result of changes in K, L and TFP				
Africa		73.0	28.0	0.0
East Asia		57.0	16.0	28.0
Latin America		67.0	30.0	0.0
South Asia		67.0	20.0	14.0
68 less-developed countries		65.0	23.0	14.0
Germany		23.0	−10.0	87.0
UK		27.0	−5.0	78.0
US		23.0	27.0	50.0

Source: World Bank 1991: 43, Table 2.2, 45, Table 2.3.

A higher growth rate of labor, the quality of which was increasing over time, also contributed to East Asia's rapid pace of growth. And all of the institutional, organizational and policy decisions made by the state and the private sector added, on balance, to positive improvements in the efficiency with which the K and L inputs to production were utilized, hence the relatively large increase in TFP.

In Africa and Latin America, by comparison, all the growth in output shown in Table 13.3 was the result of simply adding more physical capital and labor to production. The lack of complementary productivity-enhancing change, as registered by a zero TFP, is disconcerting. On average, there was no intensive economic growth, only extensive economic growth from adding more inputs to production. This evidence underscores the continuing need for economies in Latin America and Africa to undertake policies to improve their human capital resources and to stimulate a higher level of R&D that can speed up the acquisition of an ITLC if these economies are to more fully provide for a higher level of human development. Both regions clearly need more coherent policies that might contribute to national technological learning that would support the adoption and adaptation of the world supply of knowledge more effectively.[8]

Part II of Table 13.3 looks at the numbers in Part I in a slightly different way. According to the World Bank's estimates, East Asia's rate of TFP was double that of any other less-developed region. Over the period 1960–87, 28 percent of East Asia's total economic growth was due to increases in TFP and intensive growth, while 72 percent of economic growth was the result of adding more inputs, i.e., was due to extensive growth. For South Asia, which includes India and Pakistan, TFP over the same period was responsible for 14 percent of total economic growth and added inputs and extensive growth were responsible for 86 percent of economic growth.

In Africa and Latin America, on the other hand, we again see the zero TFP growth highlighted – that is, all the growth in output was due to extensive growth as more inputs, particularly physical capital, were added to the production process (World Bank 1991: 45, Table 2.3). For example, in Latin American 67 percent of all economic growth was due to adding more machines and tools and other capital goods to the production process.

In summary, East Asia and South Asia grew not only by being able to add more inputs to production, but by producing more intensively and more efficiently.[9] Africa and Latin America produced more output, but at a slower overall pace, and they did so solely by producing extensively, that is, by adding more of the same quality inputs to the production process, not by using those inputs in a more efficient manner or by augmenting the quality of the overall human capital stock. Recent research (Weiss and Jalilian 2004: 298–300) suggests that the gap in TFP rate between Latin America and East Asia continues, except perhaps for Mexico, which has increased its structural transformation toward export substitution policies.

The data in Table 13.3 suggest that the less-developed regions continue to experience a technology gap relative to the more-developed countries. There remains room for them to improve upon their national technological capacity. That this gap exists should not be too surprising. About 90 percent of all the world's R&D is done by the already-developed nations, where most of the ITCC capability ("know-why") currently exists. Until that balance shifts, there will remain opportunities for increased R&D and human capital augmentation in the less-developed countries to build and consolidate their technology learning capacities (ITLC), and thus the possibility of even more rapid growth is at least within the realm of possibility.

It is this catch-up gap which Gerschenkron (1962) believed would permit late-developers to advance rapidly. This, however, is true only if those economies make the required investments in their initial endowments – basically, the accumulation of human capital combined with the proper incentives for individuals to be able to succeed – which result in more technologically sophisticated *augmented endowments* that become the future's new initial endowments (Easterly 2001). In other words, there continues to be a need for better trained workers along with scientists, entrepreneurs, and other critical labor resources who are equipped to apply the ever-expanding knowledge constantly being added to the world supply of technological learning. Building a technological capacity, and the necessary human capital investment this requires, is what can alter the nature of past adverse path dependency.

Technology-centered development

To capture the full benefits of the world supply of technological knowledge requires the utilization of best practice production techniques. When technology is viewed not as an exogenous given or as a public good freely available to all but as an *endogenous process* to some extent dependent on indigenous factors specific to each economy, then education and the improvement of human skills in general and the creation of a core R&D cadre must become essential components of any development strategy aimed at real structural transformation.

Ideally, efforts along this path should begin in the earliest stages of industrialization, beginning with easy ISI, so as to continually add to the stock of human resources and to the skills of entrepreneurs who can learn in the process of producing. This is why we do not take the strong view of some economists that easy ISI failed or that other countries should not do import substitution in the future. Properly designed, as discussed in Chapter 9, import substitution industrialization is a vital training ground for creating technological competency and attaining an ITLC, with its potential long-run positive external effects. As Nobel Laureate economist Simon Kuznets (1968: 272) wrote:

> Far more important [than physical capital to economic growth] … are the economic and social characteristics that reside in the capacities and skills of an economy's population, determine the efficiency of the institutions that direct the use of accumulated physical capital, and guide the current production into proper channels of consumption and capital investment.

Technology exists as an intangible and accumulating body of knowledge *at the world level* capable of being utilized by any given country only *to the degree* it has developed a technologically sophisticated community, that is, an ITLC, which can use and adapt the existing supply of knowledge to employ the implements of production to advance economic progress. It is thus not possible for countries to effectively borrow the *manifestations of technology*, such as physical capital, tools, and machines which are so often the focus of the *technology transfer* literature, and expect to become developed if the human skills, culture, and institutions required to make effective use of this technological knowledge are absent or but poorly formed within the borrowing economy. As one study put it, people, not tools, "are the real agents of technology transfer and diffusion" (Radhakrishna 1980: 170). In most economies, the state will need to play an absolutely central role in pushing forward the technological acquisition process (see Focus 13.2 for some of the reasons that such intervention is necessary).

FOCUS 13.2 TRANSACTIONS COSTS, THE STATE, AND TECHNOLOGICAL ACQUISITION

Gerschenkron's (1962) historical study and those of East Asian scholars, like Amsden (1989) and Wade (1990) on Korea and Taiwan, found that developmental states were important in contributing positively to the pace of technological acquisition and, hence, the level and rate of economic growth over time. Building on the work of Nobel economist Douglass North and utilizing the concept of *transactions costs*, New Institutionalist Economics (NIE) researchers have argued that centralized state intervention was, in those instances, a lower cost means for achieving an independent technological learning capacity (ITLC) than a market-based approach would have been. In other words, the state contributed to economic efficiency rather than acting as a drag on the economy.

It appears that when political power is concentrated within a developmentalist state with a vision for achieving economic growth, rapid progress is possible. If, however, as in Pakistan in the 1960s, political power does not reside in the state, no matter how strong or centralized it may seem, but rather actually belongs to powerful private classes in agriculture and trade with no interest in fundamental change, the state's ability to contribute to technological acquisition will be severely compromised. In Pakistan, the higher transactions costs of coordinating decisions and of searching for compromises with these elite groups kept technological acquisition and an ITLC from being an attainable goal. The same is true of far too many other economies, even today.

While research in the transactions cost vein applied to development is quite new, it does highlight the importance of specific institutional structures, of power groups and classes, and of a number of supra-market considerations which can and do impinge upon economic development via their impact on the feasibility and the cost of technological acquisition.

Source: Harriss, Hunter, and Lewis 1995: especially Chapters 1, 2, 4, and 5

A technologically sophisticated community is composed not only of knowledge workers, like scientists, engineers, and researchers, but also of skilled workers on the shop floor who can utilize new ideas in the ways they are meant to be utilized, perhaps even improving upon them in their specific, local application. Just as importantly, there must exist or be created an *indigenous entrepreneurial nucleus* of determined agents capable of appreciating the potential of new ways of producing and who are able and willing to make use of new technology through constant innovation in the domestic production process.

The activities of this entrepreneurial nucleus will be concentrated predominantly in the private sector, but in some economies the state may be obliged to act as a collective entrepreneur to complement or substitute for missing private entrepreneurs. It is here especially that the state's macroeconomic policies, discussed more fully in Chapter 15, can either inhibit or contribute to rapid development through their effects on human capital formation, on R&D, and on the decisions made by the private sector to invest in creating the capacity to innovate.

The state may also be involved in the actual production process in some countries via *para-statals*, which are publicly owned enterprises, in key industries where "backward linkages" or positive externalities to the private sector are expected to be substantial, for example electricity, communications, ports, water, transportation, and even some heavy industries. Para-statals in the steel industry in Brazil and Mexico are examples of state firms that generated positive externalities for the economy as a whole, as were South Korea's and Taiwan's and Chile's publicly owned banking systems.

Technological diffusion via multinational corporations

At one time, it was a common dogma that *technological diffusion* from the more developed nations to the less-developed economies could help poorer countries skip over stages of domestic technological development. In this way, they would be permitted to enter directly into the intensive stage of technology utilization without needing to "reinvent the wheel." It was believed that such diffusion could materially contribute to a more rapid narrowing of the income gap between the developed and less-developed worlds. Some countries attempted to follow this diffusion path by hosting multinational corporations (MNCs) within their economies, yet most failed to become more developed. In fact, it might be argued that some economies, such as the larger Latin American countries, depended too much on MNCs and that their level of progress was adversely affected as a consequence.

The failure of countries to become more developed by depending upon technological diffusion from MNCs is not the result of any generalized conspiratorial plot by MNCs to keep the less-developed countries backward, as some commentators have argued. The problem is that many less-developed economies to which MNCs have brought, sold, or licensed technology have yet to create the requisite initial domestic technological culture and the domestic capacity for an ITLC that would permit them to capture the benefits of tool and machine diffusion through learning and spread effects at the point of production. In other words, the requisite human capital is not in place that would allow the country to learn the technological knowledge the MNC utilize.

If technological borrowing were simply dependent upon the arrival of MNCs in an economy and nothing else, then the domestic environment of an economy and the idea of national technologies would be significantly less important, if not wholly irrelevant, for understanding the process of development. In that case the issue of how to develop would dissolve into one of increasing physical capital accumulation and technology transfers via foreign direct investment and MNCs characteristic of the simple-minded foreign aid approach and the early neoclassical economic growth models.

Albert Hirschman long ago warned, however, of the inherent dangers of pursuing technological borrowing as the path to technological autonomy, particularly when technological knowledge is mediated by multinational corporate direct investment, as much of it has been in some countries. This has been a major issue in Latin America, where the large-scale promotion of MNC investment was fundamental for the (premature) introduction of the difficult ISI strategy (from Chapter 10). Hirschman cautioned that attempting to acquire technology through foreign direct investment may do more to "harm the quality of local factors of production" than to act as a spur to the expansion of the missing local inputs, such as innovating entrepreneurs and skilled workers which such investment might be hoped to encourage (Hirschman 1971: 227–9).

Rather than serving as a *complement* to local technological development and as a boost to locally controlled and locally directed production and to the establishment of a dynamic national technology, foreign inputs can become *substitutes* for the local factors of production and for the building of a domestic technological capacity. This is especially likely to occur in those countries where the necessary components of a technological autonomy strategy have not been implemented, and particularly where general education levels and technical education levels are low. How can the sophisticated knowledge imbedded in the MNCs be appropriated by a local economy lacking in skilled workers, professionals, scientists, and others who might be able to interpret what the MNC "knows"? In such conditions, the overwhelming influence and knowledge of the MNCs can stunt the development of the institutions and individuals capable of, and necessary for, learning from the tool, machine, and applied knowledge components of technology developed and used by MNCs.

When MNCs and their structures substitute for local entrepreneurs, skilled workers, managers, professionals, scientists, technicians, and other workers, we say that *factor substitution* or *factor displacement* has taken place. This is not caused by the MNCs so much as it is permitted and even desired by some elements of the local ruling elites in many less-developed countries, elites who often are uninterested in seeing technological autonomy achieved in their countries.

> The dominant classes know that technological development cannot be introduced merely as an isolated input to production; but is part of a global process, which once started is very difficult to stop, and which endangers the stability of the social structure on which their privileges are based.
>
> (Herrera 1971: 35)

As Herrera (1973: 33) argued, then, it is not actually an *absence* of policies toward science and technology and human capital creation which characterizes far too many countries and which manifests itself in the relatively small number of R&D scientists in Table 13.1. Rather, it is the existence of an "implicit science policy" that is actually hostile to broader applications of science and technology that is the source of the problem. It is an antagonistic attitude toward science and technology which inclines at least a segment of the dominant classes in many less-developed countries toward technological dependency, precisely because more rapid economic and social change might threaten the existing class structure. The position and privileges of elites often thrive on maintaining the prevailing configuration of inequality; for example, powerful agricultural interests who view fundamental structural transformation and industrialization as a threat to their wealth.

External interests such as MNCs certainly have a stake in preserving control over their own technological knowledge, which is often expensive for them to produce. It is not correct, however, to argue that technological dependency can be blamed exclusively or even primarily upon MNCs or any other outside force. *Technological dependency* and the absence of genuine efforts aimed at creating an ITLC is something that the policies of a country create and perpetuate. And it is policy made in the interests of a narrow, albeit powerful, elite and against the interests of the majority who lack access to power and to the state where overall development policy is made and where the spending priorities of the state are executed.

What is hopeful for change is that technological dependency is not in the interests of all members of the dominant elite. Many emerging industrialists in the infant ISI sector may be favorably predisposed toward a policy of technological autonomy and an ITLC. They increasingly require such technological knowledge if they aspire to be competitive on the world market and to export. Where the influence of this modernizing fragment of the elite has been strong and growing, as it has been in Brazil, Nigeria, Chile, and other less-developed nations, the changeover in state policies toward technology-creating institutions has been remarkable (Adler 1987).

The role of the MNCs

MNCs do not arrive one morning and begin producing in an economy. There is a long, sometimes too long, process of negotiation that takes place between MNCs and the national government on taxes, subsidies, regulations, property rights, labor laws, and a whole range of issues. It is at this stage that a government with a developmental vision can bargain with MNCs to encourage them to hire and train local workers, professionals, managers, engineers, scientists, and others who can, through on-the-job learning-by-doing, contribute to the diffusion of the knowledge imbedded in the MNCs to the local economy through spin-off companies and new industries.

To the extent that the knowledge gained while working for MNCs is generalized knowledge, workers, managers, entrepreneurs, scientists, technicians, accountants, and other professionals can carry that training and apply it to other firms and in other settings. This is how diffusion of technology truly takes place, as learned knowledge is applied to the domestic economy by those whose skills have been upgraded while working for the MNCs.

Vigorous state promotion of technological progress, from education, to science policy and research, to support for R&D, to favorable treatment in the production process of local science and technology efforts, to the conscious effort to use MNCs as a learning platform are *essential* to the success of the pursuit of technological autonomy and an ITLC. Domestically-controlled and adapted technological progress has substantial public goods characteristics and significant positive externalities over the longer term. As Sachs (2005: 41) puts it: "The beauty of ideas is that they can be used over and over again, without being depleted." However, the problem of market and institutional failure obliges the state to take action to avoid sub-optimal outcomes by making certain that the human capital and institutional structure is appropriate for adopting technological knowledge from the world supply, including that imbedded in MNCs (Adler 1988).

American economist Alice Amsden (1989: 9, 21, 76) noted that Korea "has entertained almost no direct foreign investment outside the labor-intensive sectors" and that "industrialization has occurred almost exclusively on the basis of nationally owned rather than foreign-owned enterprise." Direct foreign investment was viewed as another policy instrument to be selectively utilized in an effort to the meet the growth and technological objectives of the developmentalist regimes in all the East Asian economies, and in Japan as well before them.

Foreign investment was used to gain access to technological knowledge which foreign MNCs had created. MNCs also were a fulcrum around which domestic production linkages could be forged. But it was national capitalists and domestic finance which provided the base for the successful East Asian experience with both growth and shared development. This situation contrasts sharply with the experience of the major Latin American economies which have had *more than twice* the level of foreign direct investment as a share of total output, and substantially less success since initiating difficult ISI (see Focus 13.3 on how Korea learned foreign technology).

These differences, and Hirschman's observations above on the threat of factor displacement, suggest that foreign investment is not a perfectly substitutable factor input for domestic inputs in the development process. National development must be built upon national capital and national expertise (Evenson and Westphal 1995: 2237). In the next chapter, the possible benefits and costs of foreign direct investment are considered more carefully and thoroughly.

On one criterion, that of the acquisition of a national technological capacity and an ITLC, countries must be very careful and selective in their approach to multinational corporations. Too much foreign investment can prevent the creation of the technological autonomy and an ITLC that every country needs to sustain economic growth over the future. MNCs provide no shortcuts to such autonomy unless a country has created the entrepreneurial core, the skilled workers and the scientists and engineers who can assimilate the knowledge potentially

FOCUS 13.3 INDIGENOUS LEARNING AND KOREA'S STEEL INDUSTRY

Korea was quite adept at learning foreign technology along its industrialization path. This did not happen by chance. There was a conscious policy to appropriate the technological knowledge that foreign companies, workers and professionals held.

For example, when it was determined that the economy needed a steel industry, foreign engineers were brought in to construct the earliest mills. Korean engineers served as observers. What were they doing? They were learning how to build and then run these mills. During the second and third stage of steel mill construction, Korean engineers assumed greater responsibilities relative to foreign consultants. By the time that the fourth generation of steel mills was built, Korean engineers were able to oversee construction without foreign engineers or consultants. They had internalized the knowledge that foreign companies and experts held and made it their own. Interestingly, there was an increase in the efficiency of operation of each successive vintage of steel mill constructed.

This is a further example of the learning-by-doing effects and the positive externalities that arise with the ever greater application of technological knowledge to the production process. It also is an illustration of the importance to economies of the need to be focused on building an indigenous cadre of scientists, engineers, and technicians who become increasingly capable over time of performing closer to international best practice.

This can be accomplished through better education, including the training of students abroad at the world's best universities, students who then return home to adapt new knowledge to the domestic economy. But it is also possible to learn technology from MNCs via the direct training of workers at all levels of the firm if the state has put in place policies that encourage and reward MNCs who contribute to the formation of an ITLC.

After all, MNCs typically get special incentives, like tax breaks to subsidize buildings, when they begin operations in an LDC. Isn't it simply prudent for the LDC to ask that the MNC provide critical training for workers, managers, accountants, financial analysts and other professionals over a period of time as the quid pro quo for receiving state-funded incentives? This was the Korean approach, and it is one from which other economies could still learn.

Sources: Enos and Park 1988; UNCTAD 1996

available from the MNCs or the state imposes policies on MNCs to create such a base. Proper state policies *vis-à-vis* the MNCs must be in place, as discussed in the next chapter, if such learning is to be facilitated.

Industrial innovation: continuing technological progress

Grossman and Helpman (1994: 24) have referred to "industrial innovation as the engine of growth" for the expansion of a national technological capacity. Research and development is a purposive activity. It is one in which private firms will engage if they are: (a) encouraged to do so, for example by tax policies that treat R&D expenditures as tax credits or extend some other favorable treatment for such expenditures; (b) if they are compelled to invest to be more competitive, for example, as a result of the opening of the economy to foreign competition with reduced tariff barriers or when technological competency is necessary to increase a firm's exports as a condition of receiving loans or other rewards in contests for scarce state or private resources (as discussed in Chapter 10); or (c) if expected monopoly profits accruing to a firm are predicted to cover research and development costs *ex ante*.

To illustrate how the development of technology can be understood as part of an industrial innovation process, and one that requires continual investment and nurturing, rather than as a thing that can be appropriated easily or costlessly from other countries or firms, consider Grossman and Helpman's (1991) concept of a "quality ladder" faced by a firm. Each input to production has its own potential for improved productivity, or its own quality ladder, which is virtually unlimited.

What firms do by engaging in R&D is to search for ways to move up the quality ladder for one or more of their inputs. When such investments yield results, the discovering firm gains economic or monopoly profits over its rivals who have not discovered how to improve the productivity of their inputs so as to lower production costs. And this is where the importance of the size of the stock of human capital, particularly of R&D workers, becomes most important. Profit-maximizing firms will have an incentive to search for input quality improvements by investing in new R&D, assuming that any expected monopoly profits can be received. As new industries emerge, firms will form research and development centers, assuming a modicum of competition *and* the availability of a critical mass of R&D scientists and technicians capable of adapting knowledge to the domestic production process.

> [A]n increase in the magnitude of the typical quality improvement attracts additional resources into R&D. Then the growth rate [of the economy] accelerates, not only because the quality steps are larger, but also because advances come more rapidly.
>
> Grossman and Helpman 1994: 34

These are the positive externalities to R&D which begin to accrue beyond some critical threshold of R&D expenditure and given appropriate previous human capital accumulation. More innovations become possible, and more technological innovation, including greater technical efficiency change and higher rates of TFP, will be the result of passing this threshold. But that critical threshold must be in place before such gains can begin to be appropriated.

Interestingly, the structural transformation as presented in Chapters 9 to 11 have important consequences for the pace of technological progress. Some products and some sectors of production are likely to be better candidates for higher levels of technological change than are others. For example, the production of computers or other electronics products would seem to offer greater opportunities for new product innovation and improvements in factor productivity along a quality ladder than, say, the production of wheat or footwear. Then, assuming the requisite stock of human capital has been or is being accumulated, a country that has moved in the direction of more complex products and more capital- and knowledge-intensive production techniques would be expected both to do more R&D and to have a higher return to such investments compared to a country specializing in primary products or simpler manufactured goods predominantly destined for the domestic economy.

For primary products or the most basic easy ISI products, cutting-edge technology may not be required or be important, especially if tariffs have remained high to protect ISI industries. And even if they have not, there may be a limit to the productivity of the inputs in these labor-intensive areas of production. This is why strategy shifts along the lines explained in Chapter 10 that lead to the exporting of manufactured goods of ever greater complexity are so important to contributing to the long-run growth of an economy.

Industrial policies to promote an ITLC

State industrial strategies which target the promotion of knowledge- and technology-intensive industries as loci of dynamic comparative advantage quite naturally become a part of an

ITLC policy. This is because the returns to R&D and economic growth would be expected to be high and cumulative in precisely these sectors. Such promotion by government may include not only temporary infant industry protection measures but also special subsidies or contests for loans or other critical resources designed solely for firms in these sectors. As discussed in Chapters 7 and 10, any such targeting of specific industries for special treatment must be *performance based* if it is to have the desired effects.

Firms should receive special treatment that reduces their costs and increases profits *only* on condition that they meet certain objective standards which help the economy reach its development objectives. Such targeting has been most successful when the quid pro quo performance standard has been based on the firm's ability to increase its exports, particularly manufactured good exports, over time.

Why is exporting an effective performance standard for determining which firms are worthy of special treatment? Because it is a criterion that is implicitly based on the level of a firm's technological capacities. Firms which are able to export manufactured goods to the international market must be able to produce a product that at a minimum meets international quality and price standards, and even factoring in state subsidies, this must mean that the firm is producing with, or very near, international "best practice" technology.[10] In simple terms, such production must be efficiently produced and be of similar quality and price to close substitutes if the output is to be sold in the export market.

This is especially true as manufacturing production goes beyond simple non-durable consumer goods, such as textiles, clothing, and toys, and moves up the product ladder to more complex goods, such as electronics. It is a bonus, perhaps, that exporting can contribute to domestic economic growth, but a fundamental motivation for encouraging firms to export and for rewarding such behavior is the contribution to the essential technological transformation that the ability to export imparts to the economy. As noted in Chapter 10, openness to the international economy, which can be measured by either the share of total exports to GDP or by the share of manufactured exports to total exports, tends to be positively correlated with economic growth. No doubt the effect of additional exports on total income directly contributes something to this positive relation through the income multiplier acting on increased demand. But just as important as the direct export-income link is the domestic technological learning capacity that the ability to export enforces on producers and which is then transmitted to other sectors of the economy via positive spillover effects that extend the efficiency gains economy-wide (Edwards 1992; also see Easterly 2001).

It is this positive effect on national technology acquisition which makes manufactured good exporting so important. A strategy switch toward some kind of export substitution policy by the state will, if it is to be successful, compel state policy to carefully evaluate its spending priorities. Greater attention must be paid to human capital accumulation, to the monitoring of macroeconomic policies, to improvements in the operation of state decision-making and the civil service, to evaluation of the legal framework, including intellectual property rights, to the appropriateness of policies to foster private sector initiative, and so on.

In other words, an import substitution-cum-export substitution strategy along the general lines followed by the East Asian economies (Chapter 10) tends to oblige decision-makers to continually upgrade the national technological capacity if economic progress is to be sustained. Of course, government policies may be poorly conceived and the human capital endowments and incentives may be insufficient for success, so the outcome of setting out on such a path is not certain. However, for a government to choose export substitution following an import substitution phase would seem to imply recognition of the need for firms in the country to have the capacity to export and be efficient. Since that will require managerial, financial, and technological competence, the future path-dependent direction of the economy dictated by such a decision is likely to enforce upon the state a greater degree of commitment to provide the complementary inputs and policies to make such a strategy switch viable.

Macropolicies and technological change

Policies of the state as they affect the economy have an important impact on the level of total factor productivity (TFP). Policies which create an environment in which private firms are enabled and encouraged to produce and invest in technological acquisition and to be efficient are likely to have a greater positive impact on output growth than policies that are less facilitating. In particular, macroeconomic policies can either encourage or discourage private entrepreneurs to innovate and change. For example, policies such as easy export substitution that tend to encourage the hiring of relatively cheap labor, increased expenditures aimed at expanding access to education and better health care all tend to result in the sharing of the benefits of industrialization among more members of society, thus increasing the internal market and domestic sales and growth potential. Other policies that help to keep inflation rates and the balance of payments in check also would be expected to contribute to growth, national technological change, and development.

Table 13.4 presents some evidence on how macroeconomic policies relative to exchange rates, discussed fully in Chapter 15, affect growth and technological progress. The table shows that when exchange rates are over-valued ("high distortion"), then this tends to reduce the returns to education as seen in a lower level of GDP growth and, especially, in lower TFP rates. "Bad policy" (high distortion) thus reduces the efficiency of the economy's inputs, while "good policy" ("low distortion") raises efficiency all around. In fact, bad policy as measured by over-valued exchange rates, led to zero or negative TFP, regardless of the level of human capital accumulation.

The table highlights not only the importance of the level of education but also that increases in the level of education, particularly in an environment of "good policy," add significantly to national technological capacity, as measured by total factor productivity. This accents an important issue; though human capital investment is necessary, it is not sufficient for higher

Table 13.4 State policy, growth, and TFP

	Average annual GDP growth	Average annual TFP growth
Low distortion/high education level	5.5	1.40
Low distortion/low education level	3.8	0.25
High distortion/high education level	3.8	0.00
High distortion/low education level	3.1	−0.40
Low distortion/high change in education	5.3	1.30
Low distortion/low change in education	4.0	0.40
High distortion/high change in education	3.5	−0.16
High distortion/low change in education	3.4	−0.19

Source: World Bank 1991: 47, Table 2.4.

Note
High distortion refers to an exchange rate over-valued by more than 30 percent; *low distortion* refers to an exchange rate over-valued by less than 30 percent. *High education* means an average of more than 3.5 years; *low education* is 3.5 years average education or less. TFP is "total factor productivity" which measures the increased efficiency with which the labor and capital inputs to production are able to be utilized.

rates of economic growth. Likewise, good macroeconomic policies are, by themselves, insufficient to guarantee progress.

Summary and conclusions

Less-developed countries face the demands not only of initiating the fundamental structural transformation from agriculture to industry. They also must confront the challenge of creating a "national technological capacity" and an "independent technological learning capacity" (ITLC) as requisites for sustained progress. Much of the difference in incomes per capita among nations can be explained by the existence of technology gaps as a result of distinct capacities of different economies to do technology. Closing these gaps often compels an economy to completely shift its development strategy, to implement new policies at the macroeconomic level, to re-order spending priorities of the central government, and so on, all with the purpose of moving the country to a different path over the future.

What happens in an economy today, this month, and this year is path dependent, being the result of past decisions and particular historical circumstances that affect macroeconomic policies, spending on education, research and development expenditures, the level of tariffs, the efficiency of domestic entrepreneurs and workers, and so on. This list of contributing factors could easily be extended, but the point is that past actions condition outcomes today. To change the rate of economic growth and the level of development in the future, it is necessary that countries make choices *now* that will shift the economy's path dependency to a higher efficiency, higher income track. This requires that greater attention be afforded those factors which can improve the acquisition and adaptation of the world pool of knowledge to domestic production processes. An emphasis on technical education and science and mathematics should increase as the level of development increases. Better state economic policies can contribute in a complementary fashion to raising both private sector and public sector efficiency by rewarding technological competency, rather than connections or power.

In the effort to close the technology gap, decision-makers need to keep firmly in mind that this can be done only by creating a *national* technology and a *national* technological learning capacity. This requires that there be substantial *local control over* the production and learning processes. There must be an emphasis on forging genuine indigenous technological autonomy in which it is domestic scientists, domestic entrepreneurs, and domestic skilled workers who become the carriers and agents of technological knowledge. This knowledge can then be passed on to the next generation of workers who will become the future R&D scientists and technicians, the future entrepreneurs, and the future skilled workers and professionals.

This does not mean that each country must be independent of the rest of the world. Just the opposite is true. There is much to be gained by integrating with the world economy. Each economy must, however, develop the productive independence that comes with creating a domestic technological learning capacity that can permit it to utilize the world supply of knowledge for local development needs. Complete technological independence, in the sense of not making use of knowledge already created in the other countries and available from the world supply of technology, would be a foolish and unattainable goal for a less-developed economy hoping to make genuine progress. A genuine independent technological learning capacity requires domestic inputs and an effort by the state and private firms to attain such a degree of competence so as to be able to make use of the knowledge created elsewhere, which can then be applied in ways that suit local conditions, needs, and abilities.

Questions and exercises

1 If technology is not a computer, or computer software, or a new machine, what is it? Are people part of technology? If so, in what sense? In what ways are technological knowledge and a nation's human capital inputs complementary to one another?

2 What does it mean to say there is not technology but only "national technologies?" Why doesn't the same manifestation of technology, say a computer, have an identical productivity effect in every economy and every setting?

3 If there were not "national technologies" specific to each country, but rather an international supply of technology available freely and equally to all countries, would you expect to find per capita income differences among nations persisting over time? Why, or why not?

4 Some earlier development economists, like Alexander Gerschenkron, thought "late-developers" would have an advantage compared to early developers in increasing their levels of per capita income since they would be able to use the most advanced technology without having to re-invent such knowledge themselves.

   a Under what conditions would such an optimistic perspective on "international technological diffusion" have validity for a late-developing economy?

   b What role does government policy play in creating these conditions and in augmenting an economy's initial endowments that might make technological acquisition and its use more productive for an economy?

5 Distinguish between an ITLC and an ITCC. What is required for an economy to have an ITCC?

6 At what *stage of industrialization* did the East Asian economies achieve an ITLC? Why do you think this?

7 At what *stage of industrialization* did the Latin American economies achieve an ITLC? Why do you believe this?

8 Why are domestic entrepreneurs, domestic capitalists, and domestic scientists and engineers so important to the development process? Why is it difficult, if not impossible, for foreign inputs to substitute for these domestic inputs without short-circuiting the development process?

9 Why might economically and politically powerful elites in some less-developed countries be opposed to national technological competence? In what sectors of an economy might one expect to find supporters of an ITLC?

10 What is "factor displacement?" How can MNCs cause "factor displacement"? Would this be more or less likely to occur if an economy had already created an ITLC?

11 Explain how "openness" to the international economy, especially a growing capacity for local firms to export manufactured goods, would be likely to contribute to helping an economy create a national technological capacity or ITLC.

12 Over the period 1980–2003, Lebanon averaged per capita GDP growth of 2.9 percent per year. Over that same period, total physical capital (K) grew by 8.1 percent per year and the employed labor force (L) by 2.4 percent. We also know that about 35 percent of Lebanon's GDP in value-added terms was contributed by physical capital and 65 percent by labor.

   a Calculate Lebanon's average TFP over this period.

   b Explain what the value you calculated means.

   c Has Lebanon had extensive and/or intensive economic growth? If there has been both types of growth, how much of each kind of growth has there been?

13 In Malawi, total gross domestic product has increased at an average annual rate of 2.6 percent over the last decade. The annual growth of the labor force has averaged 2.2 percent and the increase in the physical stock of capital has increased an average of 4.5 percent per year. Labor's contribution to total output has averaged 30 percent over the period. Given these figures, calculate the annual rate of total factor productivity (TFP) for the Malawi economy.

14 Choose a country in which you are interested or one you are assigned. This problem will give you more practice in calculating TFP. Go to http://www.worldbank.org, click on "Data" at the top of the page and then choose "Data by Country" and then choose "AAGs." Find your country in the drop-down menu.

   a   Calculate the TFP for your country for most recent year using: percentage change in GDP per capita (next to last line in the yellow section), percentage change in gross capital formation (this is for the *K* variable; it's the next to last line on the first page and it is a percentage, too) and the percentage change in labor force (it won't be for just one year; rather it is shown as an average); this is your *L* variable (you'll find it near the top of page 1 of the data). Use 28 percent as the weight for the contribution of the physical capital input to production.

   b   How much of economic growth has been intensive and how much extensive?

   c   What does the TFP value you have calculated mean?

Notes

1 In the neoclassical growth model (Chapter 4), technology is modeled as if it is a public good available to all economies freely and with the same impact on productivity. In effect, the neoclassical model makes the not very likely assumption that all economies, rich and poor, have *exactly the same aggregate production function*. They do not differ in the technology they have available to them, since technology is a public good. Nor do they differ, apparently, in their innate capacity to use technological knowledge. In other words, technology is defined as a "thing" that any society can appropriate without any preconditions. Economies differ as to income per capita, then, only in their level of saving and investment and in their population growth rates, not in the availability of technology or the specific ability of any country to make use of that technology to its fullest.

In the endogenous growth models (Chapter 8), technology is not viewed as a public good or a "thing" appropriable by any economy without preconditions. Technology (the *A(K)* in equation 8.3) differs among economies, even though all potentially can tap into the same world supply of knowledge. The level and pace of technology differ in diverse economies because of dissimilarities in human capital accumulation and the stock of human capital, because of economic policies of the state (for example, on inflation or on income distribution), because of different levels of management and financial skills of enterprises, and because of a whole gamut of other variables that constitute the "path" a country has been following to any point in time. In this view, there are only *national technologies*, and the level and effectiveness of technology in each economy is dependent upon the resources each has devoted to technological appropriation.

2 This is not entirely true, as Fagerberg (1994: 1150 ff.) notes. Denison's (1967) early work had measured a "technological gap" that at least suggested the importance of country-specific efforts. The theoretical work on endogenous technical progress by Kenneth Arrow, H. Uzawa, Edmund Phelps, and Solow himself, among others, predates the current empirical work on the "embeddedness" of technological processes within a specific context in each economy. The major early articles on these themes are conveniently collected in Stiglitz and Uzawa (1969), a reading of which suggests that economists seem to rediscover old truths from time to time.

3 The pace of technological change is also related to the structural transformations discussed in Chapters 9–11. As a country begins to shift labor from agriculture and other rural production to urban, industrial pursuits, this typically results in higher productivity because of the higher level of physical capital and knowledge in use in industry. Thus the *structural transformation* from

agriculture to industry, often beginning with easy import substitution industrialization, is important precisely because it sets the stage for the *technological transformation* that can contribute to the transition to higher levels of development.

However, the speed at which this technological transformation will be able to progress depends upon the attention paid to human capital accumulation, to state policies on research and development, to the macroeconomic environment, to the skills of managers and entrepreneurs, and to a range of institutional factors that can either support or retard the technological transformation.

4 ITLC involves both "know-*how*" and increasing progress on the path of "know-*why*," or "deep technological learning," to use Lall's distinction (Lall 1984: 116–17) for what are here called an ITLC and an ITCC. A schematic representation of the relations might look like the following:

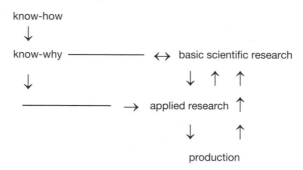

5 Remember that the numbers are the number of R&D researchers per 1,000,000 population for the most recent year during the period specified. To find the *total* number of R&D researchers, it is necessary to know the population of each country. For example, if we use Argentina's 1990 population of 32.6 million, the total number of R&D researchers can be estimated as 23,472. China had a smaller number of R&D researchers per million population than Argentina (663 versus 720), but since China's total population in 1990 was 1,135.2 million, the total number of R&D researchers was more than 750,000.

6 Both Level 1 and Level 2 economies were further sub-divided into three sub-categories, making for six levels of technological capacity in the less-developed countries. This sub-division is due to the interesting work of Weiss 1990.

7 We first encountered the concept of total factor productivity (TFP) in Chapter 8. It is the name now given to what was called the Solow residual in earlier growth accounting exercises. Calling the unknown factors that affect economic growth "TFP" certainly sounds more scientific than referring to them as a residual, but that does not change the fact that TFP is measuring all the non-identified determinants of economic growth other than changes in the quantity of the inputs.

8 These are not the only changes that countries in these lagging regions need to undertake. We shall see in the following chapters that there are other policy failures that can derail progress. However, building a technological capacity via human capital accumulation and judicious R&D expenditures is necessary for progress over time. Overcoming other policy lapses will be ineffective in accelerating economic growth and contributing to human development without having put in place the necessary augmented human capital, R&D, and scientific endowments that contribute to the achievement of an ITLC.

9 In an interesting study, Grier (2003) argues that only Hong Kong and Taiwan are "over-achievers" in terms of their economic growth. The other economies, at best, perform as expected if the standard is how developed economies perform. In other words, TFP values in the region are not as large as most studies argue. This is a controversial conclusion, but it is worth considering.

10 As pointed out in Chapter 10, there actually exists a quality-price continuum, not just one price/quality standard for any particular good. If a firm produces a good with low quality by international standards, it must be priced accordingly low if it is to compete in the international market. If quality is high relative to international standards for that good, then price could be above the average price. The point is that there exist a number of price/quality combinations that could make a product competitive in the world market when sold against similar goods (think Kias, Hondas, BMWs, for an example of but one price/quality continuum).

References

Adler, Emanuel. 1987. *The Power of Ideology: The Quest for Technological Autonomy in Argentina and Brazil*. Berkeley: University of California Press.

Amsden, Alice. 1989. *Asia's Next Giant: South Korea and Late Industrialization*. New York: Oxford University Press.

Bhalla, Ajit S. and Dilmus D. James. 1986. "Technological Blending: Frontier Technology in Traditional Economic Sectors," *Journal of Economic Issues* 20 (June): 453–62.

Denison, Edward. 1967. *Why Growth Rates Differ. Postwar Experience in Nine Western Countries*. Washington, D.C.: The Brookings Institution.

Dore, Ronald. 1984. "Technological Self-reliance: Sturdy Ideal or Self-serving Rhetoric," pp. 65–80 in Martin Fransman and Kenneth King (eds.), *Technological Capability in the Third World*. Basingstoke: Macmillan.

Easterly, William. 2001. *The Elusive Quest for Growth: Economists' Adventures and Misadventures in the Tropics*. Cambridge, MA: MIT Press.

Edwards, Sebastian. 1992. "Trade Orientation, Distortions and Growth in Developing Countries," *Journal of Development Economics* 39: 31–57.

Enos, John L. and Woo-Hee Park. 1988. *The Adoption and Diffusion of Technology: The Case of Korea*. London: Croom Helm.

Evenson, Robert E. and Larry E. Westphal. 1995. "Technological Change and Technology Strategy," Chapter 37 in Jere Behrman and T.N. Srinivasan (eds.), *Handbook of Development Economics*, vol. 3A. Amsterdam: Elsevier Science.

Gerschenkron, Alexander. 1962. *Economic Backwardness in Historical Perspective*. Cambridge, MA: Harvard University Press.

Grier, Robin. 2003. "Toothless Tigers? East Asian Economic Growth from 1960–1990," *Review of Development Economics* 7(3): 392–405.

Grossman, Gene M. and Elhanan Helpman. 1991. *Innovation and Growth in the Global Economy*. Cambridge, MA: MIT Press.

——. 1994. "Endogenous Innovation in the Theory of Growth," *Journal of Economic Perspectives* 8 (Winter): 23–44.

Harriss, John, Janet Hunter and Colin M. Lewis (eds.). 1995. *The New Institutional Economics and Third World Development*. London: Routledge.

Herrera, Amilcar. 1973. "Social Determinants of Science Policy in Latin America: Explicit Science Policy and Implicit Science Policy," pp. 19–37 in Charles Cooper (ed.), *Science, Technology and Development*. London: Frank Cass.

Hirschman, Albert O. 1971. "How to Divest in Latin America and Why," pp. 225–52 in A.O. Hirschman, *A Bias for Hope*. New Haven, CT: Yale University Press.

Kuznets, Simon. 1966. *Modern Economic Growth: Rate, Structure, and Spread*. New Haven, CT: Yale University Press.

——. 1968. "Trends in Capital Formation," in UNESCO, *Readings in the Economics of Education*. Paris: UNESCO.

Lall, Sanjaya (ed). 1984. Special Issue on "Exports of Technology by Newly-Industrializing Countries," *World Development* 12 (May–June).

Radhakrishna, K. (ed.). 1980. *Science, Technology and Global Problems: Views from the Developing World*. Oxford: Pergamon Press.

Sachs, Jeffrey D. 2005. *The End of Poverty*. London: Penguin Books.

Salter, W.E.G. 1969. *Productivity and Technical Change*. Cambridge: Cambridge University Press.

Solow, Robert. 1988. "Growth Theory and After," *American Economic Review* 78 (June): 307–17.

Stiglitz, Joseph E. and Hirofumi Uzawa. 1969. *Readings in the Modern Theory of Economic Growth*. Cambridge, MA: MIT Press.

UNCTAD (United Nations Conference on Trade and Development). 1996. *Fostering Technological Dynamism: Technology Capacity-Building and Competitiveness*. Geneva: UNCTAD.

UNDP (United Nations Development Programme). 1994. *Human Development Report 1994*. Oxford: Oxford University Press.

——. 1999. *Human Development Report 1999*. Oxford: Oxford University Press.

——. 2006. *Human Development Report 2006*. Oxford: Oxford University Press.

Wade, Robert. 1990. *Governing the Market*. Princeton: Princeton University Press.

Weiss, C. 1990. "Scientific and Technological Constraints to Economic Growth and Equity," in Robert E. Evenson and Gustav Ranis (eds.), *Science and Technology: Lessons for Development Policy*. Boulder, CO: Westview.

World Bank. 1991. *World Development Report 1991*. Oxford: Oxford University Press.

——. 1993. *The East Asian Miracle*. Oxford: Oxford University Press.

——. 2007. *World Development Indicators*. Oxford: Oxford University Press.

Part 4

Problems and issues

14 Transnational corporations and economic development

After reading and studying this chapter, you should better understand:

- the variations in the types of transnational corporations (TNCs): resource-dependent TNCs, commodity-trade controlling TNCs, "stand-alone" branch plants of TNCs operating under ISI programs, and integrated global production TNCs operating within core-subcontracting interfirm webs and commodity chains;
- the quantitative impact of TNCs on capital formation in poor nations;
- the qualitative impact of TNCs on capital formation, technology spillovers and the organization of production;
- the costs of hosting TNCs in terms of transfer pricing, net long-term resource transfers, and diversion effects of TNCs;
- how "thin" globalization and weak backward linkages often result from hosting TNC activities;
- the reasons why hosting TNCs involves poor nations in monitoring environmentally risky and complex production processes;
- the potential for successful bargaining with TNCs, and the reasons why most host nations fail to reap the potential benefits of TNC investment;
- the role of export processing zones (EPZs), and their limited potential for contributing to successful strategies of development;
- the impact of EPZs on women workers;
- why and how the impact of TNC activity has varied in Asia and Latin America.

Introduction

Transnational corporations (TNCs) are companies operating in two or more nations (with a significant equity investment of at least 10 percent in a foreign branch plant, subsidiary, or affiliate). Transnationals are far from being a new or recent element of the structure of economic relationships which define the less-developed world. In the early colonial period (Chapter 3), TNCs such as the Dutch East Indies Company and the British East India Company played a major role in the economic life of Java, India, Holland, and England. Even prior to the Industrial Revolution, these early trading corporations were determined to reap profits from their near-monopolistic control of certain trade routes and commodities. However, most of these early TNCs were involved in trade, not in the direct production of goods. With the onset of the second industrial revolution (1870–1910), giant vertically integrated corporations emerged in many branches of primary production, such as mining, and tropical commodities, such as bananas and rubber, and oil. Many of these vertically integrated companies established production and processing sites in the colonial areas, or in independent but poorer nations, such as in Latin America. These resource-specific transnationals often established a strong political presence, both within their nation of origin and within the host nation or territory.[1]

As noted in our earlier discussion of agriculture (Chapter 11), many nations in the less-developed world, particularly some of the poorest, remain virtual agricultural mono-exporters, depending for the bulk of their foreign exchange earnings on one or just a few export crops. Other nations are mono-exporters by virtue of their dependence on the marketing of one or just a few minerals or oil. In the international market for these commodities, huge buying TNCs, such as the grain transnational Cargill, or the oil transnationals such as Shell (with $131 billion in foreign assets and $203 billion in foreign sales in 2004, and 53,000 foreign employees) or manufacturing transnationals such as G.E. (with $449 billion in foreign assets and $56 billion in foreign sales, and 142,000 foreign employees) can exert strong pressure on the producing nations, particularly when they are among a handful of firms that dominate the buying, transportation, and distribution of these products.

John Cavanagh and Frederick Clairmonte analyzed the state of the global commodities markets in the early 1980s.

> [I]n the last two decades the domination of primary commodity markets has passed from single commodity traders (e.g., the former United Fruit Company) to firms paramount in several global commodity markets. The trade in three commodities, by no means exceptional, illustrates the dimension of marketing leverage: the trade in bananas, where three conglomerates dominate 70–75 percent of global markets; the cocoa trade, of which six corporations account for over 70 percent; and the trade in tea and tobacco, where 85–90 percent is under the direct control of six transnational leaf buyers.
>
> The market power of the multi-commodity traders stems from their self-reinforcing modes of conduct that contribute to enhance their bargaining stance vis-à-vis developing countries. Most multi-commodity traders are private and largely non-accountable, not only in developing but also in developed market economy countries. Many are integrated backward into plantations and forward into processing, and hence are in an even stronger bargaining position vis-à-vis national marketing institutions with which they deal.
>
> (Cavanagh and Clairmonte 1982: 16)

Table 14.1 details the pervasiveness of the near monopoly and oligopoly structures in the global trade in primary commodities, much of which is controlled by transnationals.

Import substitution industrialization and the TNCs

After the Second World War, a third round of transnational activity began. In their search for viable development policies, many less-developed nations adopted, as we know, easy import substitution industrialization (ISI) strategies as the means to initiate the structural transformation (Chapter 9). The ISI approach effectively locked out of the domestic market the products of many manufacturing companies of the advanced industrial nations, which, because ISI relied upon protective tariffs to encourage domestic manufacturing, found it more difficult to export to less-developed countries as a result. In response, many large manufacturing TNCs,

Table 14.1 Transnational control of global commodity trade, 1980

Commodity	Total exports (billions $)	Percent marketed by top 15 TNCs[a]
Food		
Wheat	16.6	85–90
Sugar	14.4	60
Coffee	12.6	85–90
Corn	11.8	85–90
Rice	5.0	70
Cocoa	3.0	85
Tea	1.9	80
Bananas	1.2	70–75
Pineapples	0.4	90
Agricultural raw materials		
Forest products	54.5	90
Cotton	7.9	85–90
Natural rubber	4.4	70–75
Tobacco	3.9	85–90
Hides and skins	2.7	25
Jute	0.2	85–90
Ores, minerals, and metals		
Crude petroleum	306.0	75
Copper	10.7	80–85
Iron ore	6.9	90–95
Tin	3.6	75–80
Phosphates	1.6	50–60
Bauxite	1.0	80–85

Source: Cavanagh and Clairmonte 1982: 17.

Note

a In most cases, 3–6 traders dominate the bulk of these markets.

particularly those domiciled in the United States, reacted, where they could, by "jumping the tariff walls" and setting up "stand-alone" branch plants in less-developed nations with reasonably large domestic markets.

It is conventional to associate easy ISI with nationalist policies adopted by governments in less-developed economies. And, indeed, during the peak ISI era, from roughly 1946 to the late 1970s, many nations sought to wrest control from TNCs. Nationalizations, in which foreign TNCs were taken over and converted to domestic ownership, were widespread from 1960 to 1980, with 587 recorded in various countries. These nationalizations were, however, largely concentrated in the areas of ore, minerals, and metals, and in food and raw materials production, that is, they were largely directed at foreign investments which had for the most part been established during the colonial era in resource-specific or resource-dependent production. Furthermore, 76 percent of these nationalizations took place between 1966 and 1976, a decade when North–South tensions reached a zenith. Not only were the bulk of the nationalizations concentrated in time, they were also concentrated in place. A study of seventy-nine nations during the 1960–85 period reveals a total of over 300 political regimes or governments, but a mere twenty-eight accounted for nearly two-thirds of all the expropriations of foreign transnationals (Kennedy 1992: 68–9).

Thus, during the time when ISI policies were being implemented, some less-developed nations did engage in "hostile" acts of expropriation. However, at the same time, the presence of other TNCs, particularly US TNCs in the manufacturing sector of the less-developed nations, was growing rapidly. As recent research has demonstrated, the growth of branch plant TNCs in manufacturing and the spread of easy ISI policies coincided for good reason. The largest US manufacturing corporations were not, in fact, in opposition to ISI, and the major less-developed nations were not hostile to *manufacturing* TNCs, even as they adopted and strengthened their ISI policies, at least partly to help create a domestic industrialist class.

During and particularly after the Second World War, the leaders of the largest corporations, and many policy-makers, were deeply focused on the difficulties of constructing a postwar international economic environment which would not degenerate into the fractious global struggle that had erupted prior to the Great Depression. Hanging over them was the realization that industrial capacity had leaped forward in the United States during the war. Policy-makers believed that a reinvigorated global system would be a necessity, and they accepted that the larger less-developed countries, as they adopted programs aimed at rapid industrialization, could help utilize the industrial capacity built up in the United States. As a result of such concerns, the United States, under President Truman, had promulgated the Point Four program (see Chapter 3) "not simply as an aid program but an effort to specify planning goals for Third World development. The numerous economic missions sponsored under the policy cost the U.S. little, but they had a substantial impact on the direction of less-developed world economic policy" (Maxfield and Nolt 1990: 58). During the Truman and Eisenhower administrations,

> U.S. technical aid missions were sent to most underdeveloped countries to help draft and implement ISI development plans. These plans specified the tariff, tax, and other incentives that would channel private investment into the targeted industries. They also became the basis for allocating U.S. and multilateral aid, and often local development resources, as well. This effort was an autonomous U.S. initiative; it was not simply a concession to less-developed world nationalists.
>
> (Ibid.: 49–50)

By 1960, US TNCs owned 49 percent of all of the direct foreign investment (FDI) spread around the globe (see Table 14.2). After the Second World War, some of the new-found strength of the United States arose as a result of its willingness to champion domestic ISI industrialization strategies, while simultaneously obtaining a preferred niche in many less-developed nations for US-based TNCs. Thus, even as the old-style mineral, food, and raw material TNCs confronted nationalization in the aftermath of often difficult transitions from colonialism to independence, US manufacturing TNCs were blazing a trail into new economic territory.

Table 14.2 Share of the stock of world FDI (percentage of world total)

Country	1914	1960	1978	1992	2000	2005
France	12.2	6.1	3.8	8.3	8.3	8.0
Germany	10.5	1.2	7.3	9.2	7.4	9.1
Japan	0.1	0.7	6.8	13.0	4.7	3.6
United Kingdom	45.5	16.2	12.9	11.4	15.0	11.6
United States	18.5	49.5	41.4	25.3	20.8	19.2

Source: UNCTAD 1994: 131; 2001: 307; 2006b 303.

Even though many of the new industrial plants were small, and therefore lacked economies of scale, they were profitable, because they were able to push prices upward in protected markets. Competing foreign-made goods often could be obtained only through imports, which frequently faced tariffs well above 100 percent, so there was plenty of room for increasing prices. While these new TNCs were frequently the subject of bitter controversy, they were rarely targets for nationalization. They tended to bring a new and more flexible corporate culture, adaptable to some degree to the development aspirations of the developing nations. In contrast, many of the older food, mineral, and raw material producers exuded an intransigent attitude which had usually served them well in an earlier era, but which failed them in the 1960s and early 1970s.

The globally integrated production system

Beginning in the late 1960s, accelerating throughout the 1990s, and continuing in the twenty-first century, a fourth form of transnational economic activity could be noted. Global factories began to emerge, sparked by revolutions in communications, transportation, and information-processing technologies. Here the motivation for investment was not the domestic market, nor were the economic activities of these new TNCs resource- or location-specific. Rather, new manufacturing activities spread in less-developed economies based upon their cheap labor, the near-absence of environmental restrictions relating to production activities, the absence of effective unions and labor laws, or other factors which essentially served to lower the costs of production. In the late 1960s and early 1970s, tariff barriers moved steadily downward, particularly in the developed nations. This helped facilitate the growth of truly global factories and shifted much of the emphasis in policy-making circles toward export-led industrialization and away from an over-emphasis on ISI.

As the so-called East Asian "tigers" developed during this period, and as new possibilities for foreign investors and for expanding export activities opened up, ISI strategies came under attack from economists (as we saw in Chapters 9 and 10). The institutions and technological processes needed to support the global factory system had not existed in the 1940s and the early 1950s, nor could they be quickly created. Thus the ISI era has been eclipsed by the era of **globally integrated production** as the nature of TNCs has evolved with advances in technology, from cellular communications to far-flung computer and data entry services. Without doubt, the age of the computer has accelerated the pace of change and the possibilities at the same time. Peter Evans describes the new era:

> The "new Internationalization" which has taken shape between 1973 and the present represents a different paradigm [from ISI]. Its production strategies are defined by global markets rather than local ones. Global production networks are typically constructed around a series of "strategic alliances" among TNCs but occasionally include Third World entrepreneurial groups. Manufactured exports from the Third World back to rich country markets are central to the new paradigm, while flows from the advanced countries to the Third World increasingly take the form of services and intangibles. The new internationalization pervades all regions of the Third World but East Asia, not Latin America, is the archetypal site.
>
> (Evans 1998: 197)

Why did the global factory system arise? Theorists have debated this point thoroughly.

Some have emphasized "indivisibilities" of management and technologies, patents, and trademarks which can best be exploited by siting production and/or distribution facilities in more than one nation. Richard Caves has suggested that the motivation to "go global" often arises from the fact that firms own or control specific production processes, designs, styles, and other types of know-how. These "intangibles" are difficult to price, to divide up, and are difficult to sell or license to other firms. Usually there is no orderly market, worldwide, for such in-house assets. Consequently, if these assets are not fully utilized within the domestic market, and/or if they can be adapted to higher production levels without incurring prohibitively rising unit costs, these firms can often increase their profits by operating additional production facilities abroad. Such firms might prefer to sell to foreigners these intangible assets to earn profits, but normally they cannot. Thus, their deeper utilization via foreign investment is one option; the alternative may be to completely forgo economic rents arising from the exploitation of the intangible assets they have created (Caves 1991).

Other theorists have emphasized the changing global conditions external to the individual firm, which have encouraged global production. For example, the average cost of ocean freight plus port fees dropped by more than 50 percent between the late 1940s and 1990. The price of an international call from New York to London fell tenfold between 1970 and 1990. Airline fees per passenger mile decreased even faster and further than did ocean freight costs from the late 1940s to 1990. And satellite utilization charges had declined to one-tenth their 1970 cost by 1990 (World Bank 1995: 51). Moreover, the firm-specific theory of Richard Caves and the perspective which emphasizes what might be called the global infrastructure approach are not mutually exclusive. Both contribute to our understanding of recent trends in expanding TNC production.

A third group of theorists emphasize mega-changes in production systems, such as the "factory-of-the-future," where modern machinery can perform complex tasks previously necessitating skilled and experienced shop-floor technicians and workers. Deskilling of the labor force as a result of new production machinery and techniques has allowed many firms to retain a core group of technicians and managers in the industrial countries, while outsourcing other production to less-skilled workers in the less-developed nations.

For example, Nike, a US-based TNC with annual sales of $4 billion in 1993, directly employed 9,000 highly skilled workers involved in product design, data processing, sales, administration, product development, production design, marketing, and distribution. Nike also employed 75,000 workers via independent subcontracting (offshore outsourcing) arrangements in China, South Korea, Taiwan, Indonesia, Malaysia, and Thailand, where labor-intensive production and assembly processes actually produce the final Nike product (UNCTAD 1994: 193). By 2007 Nike's subcontractors employed more than *800,000* workers in more than 700 plants, with nearly 60 percent of all these workers in East Asia, above all China (see Focus 14.1).

The activities encompassing FDI are distinct from offshore outsourcing, which is growing rapidly, particularly in the area of services. Outsourcing is also distinct from foreign trade, yet it is not as embedded in the developing nation's productive structure as is FDI. It is therefore a separate category, yet closely tied to profit-maximizing international strategies of the large corporations in the advanced industrial nations. Offshore outsourcing has important impacts on developing nations, but these effects are largely defined in terms of employment and working conditions. Outsourcing often occurs in Free Trade Zones (FTZs), alternatively known as Export Processing Zones (EPZs). These zones are examined later in this chapter.

How does the globally integrated production system function? Since the early 1980s, but with increasing emphasis, TNCs have turned to new forms of production, sometimes called

FOCUS 14.1   SUBCONTRACTING IN INDONESIA

Subcontracting (offshore outsourcing) has become an important strategy increasingly adopted by transnational corporations in the 1980s and 1990s. As labor costs have risen in Korea, Taiwan, and Singapore, many East Asian subcontractors have become small transnationals themselves, shifting their production and assembly operations away from nations such as Korea, to new low-wage havens, such as Indonesia.

Depending on market demand, Nike Corporation contracts with four to six Indonesia-based Korean subcontractors who employ roughly 5,000 Indonesian workers. According to the Nike Corporation, the advantage of locating in Indonesia is that a pair of shoes selling for $80 in the United States will involve direct labor costs in Indonesia of only $2.60. Thus there is greater opportunity for more profit.

Although the subcontractors who sell their output to Nike are pressured to pay a minimum wage of $52.50 per month, they often do not. For example, one twenty-two-year-old worker and his nineteen-year-old wife, both employees of a Nike subcontractor, earned a total of $82 per month. They rented one room for $23 per month. This housing, actually a six-foot-by-six-foot space, is described as follows:

> A single bare bulb dangles from the ceiling, its dim glare revealing a plain bed, a single gas burner, and a small plastic cabinet. Their room, one of a dozen in a long cement building, is provided with one container of water daily. If they want more water, each jug costs about 5 cents.

Attempts by the workers to raise their pay above the current average of $2.62 per day have met with harsh treatment from the government. Independent unions and the right to strike are not recognized by the government.

Source: Gargan 1996

flexible manufacturing, or "Japanese management techniques". While no two firms operate in an identical manner, many theorists of industrial organization believe that a blending of "just-in-time" inventory controls, total quality management techniques (JIT/TQM), and small-batch flexible production based on computer-aided designs and computer-aided manufacturing techniques (CAD/CAM), and, generally, "lean" production techniques capture the recent tendencies in worldwide best-practice production technology. In a study examining the growth of new production forms in the less-developed world, John Humphrey defined "lean" production as having the following attributes:

> Lean production involves three related transformations – the reorganization of production along JIT/TQM lines, the transformation of design, and the development of new relations with suppliers. It focuses not only on the factory, but also factors outside of the plant such as the design function and other firms. These interrelated changes are held to create a new production system, based on principles which contrast with [early twentieth-century assembly-line] mass production. ...
>
> The core of reorganization within the firm along the lines of JIT/TQM can be captured in the term "minimum factory." ... The aim of manufacturing production is to produce goods which satisfy the customer at the minimum possible cost. The ideal factory should have every stage of production oriented toward this overall aim, and all activities in the plant should contribute to transforming inputs into finished products which attend customers' needs. Any other activities are, in principle, a waste of resources. Such waste includes holding stocks, moving products around unnecessarily, producing items which

are defective and reworking products. The ideal factory responds rapidly to customer demands, producing rapidly a range of products which satisfies customers' needs with the minimum possible inputs of energy, materials, capital and labor.

(Humphrey 1995: 150, 152)

JIT/TQM techniques are now being adopted widely, particularly in the newly industrializing countries (NICs) and above all in Asia, but also in countries such as Zimbabwe and the Dominican Republic. Unfortunately, it presently appears that successful adaptation to the new techniques seems to be the exception. Most countries, including some of the first-tier NICs, such as Brazil and Mexico, are not able to compete effectively on the basis of their emerging production systems. Clearly, cases of relatively successful adaptation are to be found, such as the TNC automobile plants in Mexico, but the likelihood of most nations being passed over by such technology is quite high. For, unlike the early ISI stage, the demands for JIT/TQM global factory production systems extend much deeper into the economic fabric of a less-developed nation. Early ISI branch plants were to a large degree "stand-alone" operations, importing some of their inputs, and relying on the parent company for design and production techniques, but largely operating independently from the parent on day-to-day production decisions.

Under the emerging system of "globally integrated production," there is a greater reliance on a web, or network, of sophisticated suppliers which must be close at hand or "just-in-time." This means that FDI intended to meet the standards of JIT/TQM production must be embedded in a network of sophisticated supplier firms offering a full range of inputs, as well as upstream services such as delivery, marketing, and transportation. As the list of items that must be provided outside of the factory grows, the likelihood that a given less-developed nation has the deep, complex, and quickly adjustable production support system to meet the expectation of the TNCs declines. In fact, some case-studies in the early twenty-first century show that TNCs are being supplied more and more by other TNCs as the demand for sophisticated parts escalates (Ivarsson and Alvtam 2005). Thus, it is feared that these new production systems will be adapted by a small number of NICs which are already relatively developed, leaving the rest of the less-developed world at risk of being further marginalized from "deep integration" and advanced production techniques. Hence, JIT/TQM techniques may tend to reinforce the tendency toward "cumulative causation" and "backwash effects" discussed in Chapter 6.

This, too, is the tentative conclusion of the United Nations, which examined TNCs as "engines" of growth. Clearly, it is too soon to draw definitive conclusions regarding the new production systems. But just as clearly, the developing nations now face new and quite formidable challenges if they seek to attract and manage FDI and foreign capital in an ever more technological age. Evidence from the auto sector in Brazil and Argentina suggests that as integrated production systems expand, the role of local suppliers contracts and foreign-owned supplier firms arrive to service the high value-added supply needs of the TNCs: "[D]omestic firms in developing countries supplying to affiliates that are part of integrated production systems typically belong to a lower tier and provide relatively simple inputs – cardboard focuses, plastic and foam rubber packaging materials, metal stamping, die-making and simple assembly" (UNCTAD 2001: 137).

As a result of a complex process involving either the search to maximize the return on intangible assets, or the opportunity to take advantage of a global infrastructure, or to reap the advantages of labor deskilling and the potential gains by offshore outsourcing of production, by 1998, the transnationals of the advanced industrial nations were employing 19 million workers (a 58 percent increase since 1992!) in the less-developed world, most of whom were working in global factories. Overall employment by transnationals (including in the advanced industrial nations) has grown from 19.5 million in 1982 to 62 million in 2005. From 2004 to 2005 employment jumped by 2.5 million. Employment by the transnationals in developing nations in 2005 produced more that $500 billion in value-added (UNCTAD 2006b: 9–10). However, these figures do not include offshore outsourcing activities, such as those conducted by Nike described in Focus 14.1. Including subcontracting, the World Bank estimated that the direct employment effect of TNCs could be 100 percent higher (World Bank 1995: 62).

If these estimates are valid, it may be that in the early twenty-first century through direct employment in transnational subsidiaries or affiliates and through offshore subcontracting the TNCs are now employing approximately 40 million. Assuming job multiplier effects wherein for every job created one other job is indirectly created, this would bring the total effect to (very roughly) ± 80 *million* jobs created by the TNCs in the developing nations. Even after making allowances for the fact that many of these workers will be better paid than the average employee in a developing nation the impact of TNCs on the employment problem in developing nations has to be very modest. The International Labour Organization's estimate of the economically active population in developing nations in 2007 was 2.53 *billion* people. In this context, it is clear that transnational production, whatever its collateral effects (discussed below), *is not significant in addressing employment problems* in developing nations.

Today, transnationals are to be found in most less-developed nations, their presence being felt under the four broad categories of transnational activity:

1   trading companies controlling the marketing process;
2   resource-intensive vertically integrated transnationals;
3   branch manufacturing plants; and
4   global factory production sites.

In any given nation, it is likely that more than one of the above forms of transnational activity will be present.

Foreign direct investment

Foreign direct investment (FDI) entails the ownership of productive assets by a parent corporation in another nation. Such ownership should be distinguished from the purchase of foreign stock or the lending of funds to foreign companies and governments. These latter forms of investment are known as portfolio investments.

The *World Investment Report 2006* recorded that the advanced industrial nations operated some **55,500** transnational corporations and there were approximately **773,000** foreign affiliates spread throughout the world, almost half of them in developing nations (UNCTAD 2006b: 271). Within these same industrial nations there was an accumulated *stock* of $7.1 trillion of foreign capital in 2005. (The *stock* is a measure of the current market value of all previous foreign direct investments.) The developing nations had accumulated a *stock* of $2.8 trillion of FDI: $1.55 trillion in East and South Asia, $937 billion in Latin America, and $151 billion in Africa. Overall, the stock of FDI has grown at an impressive rate: in 1990 the FDI stock/World GDP ratio was 8.5, leaping to 22.7 by 2005 (UNCTAD 2006b: 307).

While nearly 28 percent of the total stock of FDI of the developed nations was invested in the less-developed world, in recent years the *flow*, that is, the annual change in the stock, of FDI has increasingly been directed to the less-developed world. In the three-year periods 1978–80, 1988–90, and 1998–2000 nearly one of every five dollars of FDI went to developing nations. In the 2003–6 period, marked by unprecedented cross-border mergers and acquisitions among the developed nations, an estimated 34 percent of these flows went to the developing nations (UNCTAD 2006b: 7).

A much more meaningful method to measure the trend of FDI *flows* is the ratio of FDI flows to GDP in the developing nations: this ratio has risen from 0.79 percent of GDP in 1975 to 2.34 percent in 2000 for a broad sample of fifty-nine representative developing nations (Ghose 2004: 38). For *all* developing nations in 1990 the *stock* of FDI equaled 9.8 percent of GDP, while in 2006 the stock of FDI had risen to 27 percent of GDP (UNCTAD 2006b: 308). In short, FDI is a *leading variable* and has been for more than one-quarter of a century.

In any given year, a relative handful of the developing nations receive the vast bulk of the FDI. In the period 1982–92, for example, the top ten nations in a given year received over 70 percent of all the direct capital flows to the less-developed world. While there was some variation in the top ten nations over the ten-year period, eighteen nations have accounted for over 80 percent of such investment. With few exceptions, these eighteen nations were not the poorest; in Africa, where per capita income is extremely low, only Egypt, Nigeria, and Tunisia were among the top eighteen recipients of FDI. In 2000 the top ten recipient nations – four in Asia – received 76.7 percent of all FDI going to developing nations (UNCTAD 2001: 52). In 2005 the top five (nearly a constant group since 1996) received 48 percent of total flows. International investments tended to flow to countries where economic growth already was taking place.[2]

Of the 55,500 TNCs with parent companies based in the developed nations, the top 100 firms accounted in any given year for roughly two-thirds of new FDI. In terms of asset size, the most important foreign productive activity of the top 100 firms is in the electronics sector, followed by mining and petroleum, motor vehicles, and chemicals and pharmaceuticals (UNCTAD 1994: 10).

While US-based TNCs continue to dominate global production patterns, their relative significance has changed rapidly in recent years. Table 14.2 shows that while in 1960 US TNCs accounted for 49 percent of the total stock of FDI, by 1992, this share had shrunk to just 25 percent, falling yet again by 2005 to 19 percent. For a while, most of the relative gain was made by Japan, whose share increased from merely 0.7 percent in 1960 to 13 percent in 1992 – but then stagnation pushed Japan by 2005 to a relative level not seen since the 1970s.

The European Union in 2005 held 51.3 percent of the accumulated stock of FDI (up from 45.2 percent in 2000). This increasing national diversity of FDI sources tends to strengthen the relative bargaining position of host nations *vis-à-vis* the TNCs, since they are likely to have to deal with more than one potential group of national investors for a given project and that is, as we shall see, critical to the host country if it is to reap the potential benefits of TNC investment.

While trade between countries has historically received a great deal of attention in development economics (see Chapter 16), it is important to keep in mind the fact that the sales of foreign affiliates of the TNCs now *exceed* the total value of all exports of goods and services for the entire world (UNCTAD 1994: 20). In 2005, TNCs had sales from their foreign affiliates of $22.2 trillion, while the total value of world exports of goods and services stood at $12.6 trillion (UCTAD 2006b: 9). Considering that global exports have grown rapidly in recent years, it is remarkable that while in 1982 sales of foreign affiliates were roughly equal to exports of goods and services and now the relationship is approaching a 2:1 ratio. About one-third of all TNC sales were intra-firm trades, a fact of some importance in our discussion of transfer pricing later in this chapter (UNCTAD 1994: xxi).

In the view of many specialists, the role of the TNC has now eclipsed that of foreign trade as a factor determining the overall evolution of the global economic system. When UN researchers combined the domestic production of TNCs with their international production and sales, they arrived at the estimate that one-third of all global output is now under the direct governance of the TNCs (UNCTAD 1994: 135). Never, they stated, had the influence of the TNCs been greater. Surely, it is much more so today.

Who in the less-developed countries gains from FDI?

In neoclassical economic thinking, as characterized by the Solow, savings-centered theory, developing nations are viewed as deficient in physical capital investment. Consequently, it would appear that inflows of FDI could only have a positive effect on the growth rate of a poorer nation. On average, however, new FDI amounted to less than 3 percent of total investment throughout the less-developed world in the period 1980–92.

There are important exceptions, of course; Hong Kong received more than 10 percent of its investment from foreign sources during this period, Singapore over 20 percent, and Malaysia over 6 percent. From 1993–9 reliance on FDI as a source of capital formation increased: In Asia it averaged 8.5 percent, in Africa 7.5 percent, and in Latin America 14.1 percent (UNCTAD 2001: 19, 24, 29).

The higher level achieved in the 1990s suggests that FDI can make a contribution to the overall investment level in many developing nations. For the years 2003–5 the average level of FDI expressed as a percentage of new capital formation (machinery and equipment, residential and non-residential construction) was 10.9 percent. Still, since this investment flow is concentrated among a few nations, most developing nations will receive only modest economic stimulus from FDI.

Furthermore, even when a nation is receiving large amounts of FDI, such flows do not always result in new capital formation. *Existing* plant and equipment are quite often the target of TNC investments through mergers and acquisitions, reducing the ownership and control of domestic capitalists. This effect has been referred to as denationalization, that is, the transfer of ownership of local capital to foreign capital owners (Gereffi and Evans 1981). While Mexico was considered one of the top receivers of FDI in 2001 71 percent of such investment was devoted to the purchase of already existing Mexican companies (Gazcón 2002: 15). More generally, according to United Nations data, 20 percent of the FDI flows to developing nations were used to buy out existing companies in 2004.

Even if a so-called "Greenfield" facility, that is, a new plant, is built by an TNC, this need not necessarily increase the total level of investment of a less-developed nation on a one-to-one basis. Ajit Ghose's study of fifty-nine representative developing nations in the 1975–2000 period demonstrated significant "crowding out" as foreign investors raised the price for inputs (and/or caused currencies to appreciate) or rapidly captured significant market share. This adversely affected nationally owned businesses that then cut back on their investments (Ghose 2004: 22)

Still, Ghose found that FDI *did* raise investment levels, but that it would be wrong to assume that this occurred on a one-to-one basis. That is, the negative effect on domestic producers (crowding out) was not so large as to negate all the impact of FDI, so that *net* investment went up moderately. In such cases, foreign FDI does not completely act as a *complement* to local investment, promising to increase the rate of growth, but rather, in part, as a *substitute* for local capital ownership, local control, and perhaps for local learning.

In a large study over the 1971–2000 period, Manuel Agosin and Roberto Machado found evidence of crowding out in some sub-periods in some developing regions (Africa and Latin America) and a "neutral" effect in Asia. FDI failed to stimulate "crowding in" of domestic investment, but then again it did not crowd out investment in Asia (Agosin and Machado 2005). The authors speculate that the reason why crowding out did not occur was that the Asian nations as a group were more aggressive in selecting foreign investors and more prone to impose conditions on these investors that would guard against adverse affects.

How important is it, then, if a developing nation receives an average injection of investment (equal to 10 percent of its investment level) from foreign investors? In the best-case situation, where the impact of FDI is *neutral*, it is likely that the overall impact of FDI on GDP growth will be small, as can be demonstrated using some concepts of early growth theorists.

In Chapter 4, the ideas of Roy Harrod and Evsey Domar were introduced. Harrod and Domar's simple Keynesian growth model can be shown to arrive at the following set of relationships: a nation's growth rate is the result of two key ratios – the investment/GDP ratio (I/Q) and the capital–output ratio (K/Q). K/Q shows how much output is generated in a year from a given stock of capital (K).

K/Q varies from country to country and over time, but a workable ratio for many developing nations would be within the range of 3 to 4. K/Q measures the "productivity" of capital and the "capital-intensity" of production. Ghose's data for the fifty-nine representative developing nations suggests that the I/Q ratio averages approximately 22 percent, but varies widely from year to year.

Combining all of the above with the Harrod-Domar formula for economic growth we have the following:

$$\Delta Q/Q = I/Q \times Q/K \qquad (14.1)$$

This simple formulation assumes that the higher the rate of investment and the *lower* capital–output ratio, the higher the growth rate ($\Delta Q/Q$). An investment rate of 22 percent and a capital–output ratio of 3.5 will, according to the H-D equilibrium conditions, generate a growth rate of ($.22 \times 1/3.5 = 6.3$ percent growth in GDP).

But how much difference does FDI make? FDI *adds* perhaps 10 percent to the level of funds invested, but then "crowding out" perhaps subtracts away one-half of this. In other words, had there been *no* FDI the investment rate would have stood at 95 percent of what it actually turned out to be. Or ($.22 \times .95 = .209 \times 1/3.5 = 5.97$ percent growth in GDP).

From this simple, but not distorted, example it can be readily granted that FDI, taking into account a reasonable "crowding out" effect, will have a modest positive *quantitative* effect on growth – but it is hardly the panacea that it is sometimes represented as being. Two final points must be taken into account: First is the fact that a significant portion of FDI will likely not add to the *growth-generating capabilities* of a developing nation, because luxury housing, the construction of sumptuous hotels and apartment buildings and palatial shopping centers all can be registered as FDI if they are financed abroad. A second twist is that all retained earnings by foreign corporations (profits not shipped abroad to the parent corporation) are registered as FDI. Yet it is common for TNCs to place these funds in the financial markets of the developing nation, where it is virtually certain such funds will not be used for capital formation.

If, with few exceptions, new FDI constitutes only a modest portion of total physical capital formation in any given year in less-developed economies, why has the role of the TNCs been so central to much of the recent development literature? The answer, clearly, must turn on considerations of the *qualitative* effects of FDI, rather than on considerations of quantitative relationships.

Collateral effects of TNCs: the modernization perspective

It has been suggested that TNCs, at least those associated with the ISI era and those that form part of the globally integrated system of production, can generate potential resource transfer effects through their activities in the forms of new capital, new product and process technologies, and management/labor-training and other organizational innovations. Proponents of this modernization perspective believe it is largely a fruitless exercise to attempt to "unbundle" the multiple interactive stimuli that accompany FDI.

But the modernization perspective rarely focuses on the important linkages between FDI flows and flows from stock and bond purchases (portfolio investment), bank and corporate lending (private loans), bilateral aid institutions (such as the United States Agency for International Development), and multilateral institutions (such as the World Bank or the regional development banks) which make official loans and grants. It is important to be aware of such linkages, however, since nations that maintain a so-called good investment climate toward FDI, that is, a pro-business environment, will often reap substantial indirect resource transfers via such inflows of capital. In this section, we explore some of the research findings of those who analyze FDI from the modernization perspective, a view which focuses on the potential growth-stimulating role which TNCs may play through capital formation, technology transfers, and superior organizational production structures.

To begin, Table 14.3 summarizes the distribution of capital and other financial flows in the 1991–2005 period. In observing this data it should be stressed that FDI amounted to only 26 percent of the net long-term flows to developing nations in the 1986–90 period. Note that, in the last row of the table, FDI's share of total flows jumped upward all through the 1990s, reaching a truly remarkable level of 83 percent of total flows in 2001, after which as a result of surging portfolio investments it fell back to 53.5 percent of all flows. Heretofore

Table 14.3 Net long-term resource flows into developing regions[a] (billions of dollars)

Type of flow	1991	1997	1999	2001	2003	2005[b]
Foreign Direct Investment	**35.7**	**168.7**	**183.3**	**176.9**	**161.6**	**237.5**
Portfolio investment[c]	21.5	71.7	41.7	11.1	45.7	116.4
Bank loans	5.0	44.0	−7.1	−10.8	9.8	67.4
Official flows	62.6	34.9	40.2	35.8	29.0	22.3
Total	124.2	319.3	258.1	213.0	246.1	443.6
FDI/total (%)	**28.7**	**52.8**	**71.0**	**83.1**	**65.7**	**53.5**

Source: World Bank, *Global Development Finance, 2002*: 3 (www.worldbank.org/prospects/gdf2002/; 2006).

Notes
a Excludes International Monetary Fund financing on account of its short-term nature.
b World Bank estimate.
c Includes net purchases of securities by foreigners in domestic stock markets and bond financing as well as "other" debt flows.

developing nations relied heavily on (a) "official loans" from the World Bank and the regional development banks (such as the Asian Development Bank), (b) grants, and (c) bank lending. But in the 1990s these sources of funding atrophied and have fallen ever since ("official" forms of lending are analyzed in Chapter 17).

Portfolio investment soared until the Asia crisis of 1997, while FDI increased more than fourfold in the period 1991–9, and has increased 30 percent in the period 1999–2005. Nearly 70 percent of FDI went to either East Asia (32 percent) or Latin America (35 percent – largely thanks to massive privatizations), with the Middle East attracting only 3 percent and Sub-Saharan Africa receiving only 6 percent in the 1990s.

Table 14.3 demonstrates the rising importance of private sector flows, particularly those of transnational corporations, from an upward spiral in investment projects driven by their new enthusiasm for globally integrated production systems. Yet the poorest nations rarely received any FDI – in 2000 the forty-nine least-developed nations obtained a mere 0.3 percent of total FDI (UNCTAD 2001: 1).

Capital formation

While the absolute amount of capital formation provided by TNCs, in relation to total investment in a developing nation, is likely to be small, probably below 10 percent, the qualitative significance of such investment can be much higher than one might assume. Such investment is often directed to a narrow range of industries that are important for economic growth, precisely because they are concentrated in manufacturing and services where new investment is associated with significant increases in productivity and production. Aggregate data can distort or even hide the role played by TNCs, a point well illustrated through the following summary of research on TNCs in India.

> In India, a study of 28 manufacturing industries in 1977–78 found that in nine industries, including motor vehicles, electrical machinery, metal products, plastics, chemicals and pharmaceutical, the foreign ownership share was greater than 20 percent. A second study of TNCs in India found that foreign-owned firms accounted for more than 30 percent of sales in manufacturing in 1975–76 and 1980–81. Foreign direct investment as a share of gross domestic investment has been very small in India, at 0.1 percent in the period 1976–80 and only slightly higher – 0.2 percent – in the late 1980s.
>
> (UN Transnational Corporations and Management Division 1992: 119)

Furthermore, aggregate FDI data fail to reveal non-equity arrangements within the host nation which can have a substantial impact on productivity and output. Among such deals, often numerous, one finds franchising agreements, licensing, long-term subcontracting, and non-equity joint ventures with local capital. Any of these production linkages with TNCs may form a conduit for the diffusion of product and/or process technologies and management/labor-skills, as well as providing opportunities for learning about more advanced organizational structures in marketing, advertising, finance, or research and development. It is often the case that indigenous business owners lack, as a group characteristic, an export culture, whereas manufacturing TNCs are likely to be quite proficient and dynamic in foreign marketing, almost by definition. To the degree that such skills are "spun off" to the host nation through joint ventures and/or the turnover of management personnel working for TNCs or other transmission mechanisms, TNCs can be an important mechanism for augmenting and enhancing the proficiency of domestic managers, professionals, and perhaps skilled workers.

Since the scarcity of foreign exchange is likely to form a crucial bottleneck for many less-developed nations, curbing their development potential, the ability to expand into foreign markets can be of paramount importance to the nation. The domestic market is too small in many developing nations as a result both of the highly unequal distribution of income and the size of the population. Thus, foreign sales can be important in "widening" the market and in allowing firms to realize greater economies of scale in production. Such effects, when they do occur, can further assist the development process by lowering production costs, possibly further expanding the market as lower-income consumers could be brought into the market if lower costs translate into lower prices. Thus, to the extent that TNCs transmit export skills to domestic producers, this is another potential benefit to the host country of such investment.

Table 14.4 reflects the new emphasis on global production, as well as the success of some Asian nations in building their own complex production facilities. Developing nations' exports as a share of world exports have grown at a tremendous pace, reaching 39.8 percent in 2006 (UNCTAD 2006–7: 10). Notice the dramatic drop in primary commodities exports, from over one-half of the non-fuel exports in 1980 to a mere 19 percent in 1998. Since then primary commodities have risen rapidly, reflecting the "resource boom" that accelerated in the 2003–7 period, partly because of high commodities demand by China and India.

The generalization that many developing nations find much of their economy dependent upon commodities exports should not be abandoned. We also see that relative to the overall level of world trade in 1998 (19 versus 14.8 percent) developing nations as a whole are much more reliant on commodity exports than were developed nations in 1998. Low-end labor-intensive production processes (assembly operations occurring commonly in Export Processing Zones) and resource-based manufacturing processes account for slightly less of total developing nations' exports in 2003 than in 1998 and 1980.

Note the dramatic rise in exports for medium- and high-skill production processes. Medium-skill exports more than doubled their share of total developing nations' exports in only eighteen years (1980–98), while a surprising 34 percent of all developing nations'

Table 14.4 Developing nations' exports: skill level, capital intensity (percentage share)

	Share of exports from developing nations			Share of world exports		
	1980	*1998*	*2003*	*1980*	*1998*	*2006*
Developing nations' exports[a]	–	–	–	15.4	24.3	39.8
Primary commodities	50.8	19.0	23.9	25.7	14.8	–
Resource-based and labor-intensive manufactures	21.8	23.2	20.7	14.7	15.0	–
Low-skill and technology-intensive manufactures	5.8	7.3	5.6	10.1	7.6	–
Medium-skill and technology-intensive manufactures	8.2	16.8	15.6	26.4	29.6	–
High-skill and technology-intensive[b] manufactures	11.6	31.0	34.2	20.2	30.2	–

Source: UNCTAD 2002: 55, 68; 2005: 150.

Notes
a Included are 225 production categories including raw materials, excluding fuels.
b Included are electronics products, parts and components – 80 percent of this category in 2003.

exports were accounted for by complex production systems that produce semiconductors, telecommunications and electronic equipment, and so on in 2003. And it is in these areas, typically not associated with developing nations, where the TNC-driven integrated production process is making its greatest gains in terms of the share of world exports. Yet it should be emphasized that much of the technologically intensive production, and the underlying R&D, occur in the advanced industrial nations, with developing nations often adding little more than cheap labor to the globally integrated process.

Are there spillover effects from FDI?

As we have seen in the above sections, when developing nations host transnational corporations they cannot reasonably anticipate that direct foreign investment will substantially help resolve the massive problems of underemployment, disguised unemployment, and unemployment. Nor can a nation expect that, except in the rarest of short-term circumstances, the rate of investment will significantly rise, thereby boosting the growth rate of the economy. Greatly debated in research sources is the role played by FDI in spawning technological learning (know-how) and innovative capacity (know-why). Backward linkages to national suppliers, sometimes promoted through local content requirements either directly or indirectly (e.g. granting a subsidy or tax break to a company that buys locally) can promote learning as national firms rise to meet the standards of a top international manufacturer who shares some production know-how.

Many times parent TNCs operate within relatively tight "vertically integrated" systems where the backward linkages are performed "in-house" by the firm or its subsidiary. Here there is likely to be little call for local content, and broad possibilities for the sharing of some "know-how" are few. But some learning can occur as the TNC firm advances the skills of the national workforce to meet the high "supplier" quality demands of the core firm. In this "second-best" situation, some workers with enhanced skills will eventually leave the firm and the new knowledge may be diffused to important portions of the national economy.

However, this process can be negated if the parent company does not use much local production, but rather imports a high portion of its inputs. Hence, few or no backward linkages of importance are created, a situation common when a developing nation hosts a Japanese TNC (Belderbos, Capannelli, and Fukao 2001). If spillover effects are to occur a host nation must have a strong, deep, and modern infrastructure and a base of capable national suppliers, otherwise parent firms will prefer imported inputs or the setting up of vertically linked suppliers.

Surprisingly, a large number of the empirical studies that attempt to find and calibrate possible spillover effects *combine* advanced industrial nations and developing nations in their sample of host nations, making their results difficult for understanding how FDI impacts developing nations. Yet one interesting result of such a combined study showed that when the parent company was primarily targeting the national market, instead of setting up an export platform, backward linkages were substantially higher (ibid.: 202). Meeting the needs of the local market tended to make the parent company more prone to using local knowledge adapted to existing consumer product expectations.

This runs counter to the hypothesis that as a result of export-oriented FDI significant learning will take place, but not if production is geared to the national (home) market. This same study of Japanese TNCs in twenty-four nations found that the higher the degree of research and development embodied in the product the less likely that local firms would be brought into the production chain. Hosting high-tech operations, other things remaining the same, would mean that a developing nation would find very few spillovers. Of course, this would tend not to hold true if a nation, on its own, had achieved substantial advances in R&D-related production – an exceptional situation that would tend to prove the rule, such as in some sectors of India's economy and in Korea and especially Taiwan.

China is the largest single recipient of FDI as a result of a policy initiative premised on opening the economy to acquire spillover effects. In a study of over 2,500 large and medium-sized textile and electronics firms in China in the 1995–9 period, Albert Hu and Gary Jefferson found that in the short run the impact on domestic electronics firms was negative – they were crowded out, losing market share and experiencing decline in productivity. However, national firm survivors did show some capacity to close the gap with foreign firms over a longer period, and the authors suggested that learning had occurred. It is interesting to note that the national firms were *more* R&D-intensive than were the TNCs, which may explain how some were able to survive and flourish.

This, however, raises important issues: the survivor national firms could have later improved their productivity in many ways that would not arise from direct or indirect impacts stemming from TNCs. This underlines a broader problem, which is that most of the attempts to find spillovers use productivity of domestic firms as a proxy for spillovers in econometric tests. If they find correlation with FDI and productivity it is *assumed* that the cause of the productivity increase was FDI. But the assumed causal relationship needs to be proven by direct case-studies that econometricians rarely undertake. In the case of China's national textile producers FDI did impose a negative impact through the entry of foreign firms, in that market share for national firms declined but productivity for the national firms did not decline (Hu and Jefferson 2002: 1073).

A major 1999 study by Brian Aitken and Ann Harrison that showed a *negative* relationship between an increase in FDI and productivity in national firms in Venezuela was the catalyst for a flurry of studies that attempted to find positive spillover effects for FDI (Aitken and Harrison 1999). Since this critical study appeared a deluge of attempted refutations have appeared in print, but these studies have not produced vigorous results. In other words, while results have varied to some degree, overall subsequent studies have revealed that economists' research on the relationship is inconclusive.

In a recent important book devoted to the study of the effects of externalities and spillovers from FDI it was once again confirmed that economists are unable to show definitive evidence of spillover effects. Summing up five new studies in this book, Gordon Hanson states:

> As international economists, what can we tell policymakers in developing countries about how they should treat multinational firms? Based on empirical work to date, the answer, unfortunately, is "not much." The literature is just beginning to seriously consider empirical evidence issues about FDI's effect on domestic firms ... Given the developing state of the field, it is important that policymakers realize that we do not know how [transnational] firms affect their economies. ... an abundance of evidence that FDI generates positive spillover effects does not exist. So far, researchers have yet to uncover robust empirical support for the kinds of subsidies that many countries have begun to offer multinational enterprises.
>
> (Hanson 2005: 178)

In the same collection of research, Maria Carkovic and Ross Levine studied a sample of seventy-two countries in the 1960–95 period to see if there was evidence that nations that receive FDI experience general macroeconomic improvements in their overall level of productivity. Thus their study looked at economies in their entirety instead of "firm-level" studies. While the authors note that some macroeconomic studies of FDI have shown positive effects regarding growth, these studies should be viewed with skepticism, they argue, because they have not adequately controlled for a number of factors that suggest flawed methods of investigation (Carkovic and Levine 2005: 196). In contrast, in their search for a *qualitative* impact from FDI, their study concludes that:

> After resolving many of the statistical problems plaguing past macroeconomic studies ... we find that FDI inflows do not exert an independent influence on economic growth. ... [Our] results are inconsistent with the view that FDI exerts a positive impact on growth.
>
> (Carkovic and Levine 2005: 219)

While not uniform in their results, it does seem that the bulk of the studies conducted on the spillover dispute have come to the conclusion that FDI has either a negative impact on domestic productivity, or – in the most positive versions – a very slight positive effect. This takes us far from the optimistic scenario projected in Chapter 8, where endogenous growth would occur as externality and spillover effects proliferate. It is worth stepping back for a moment from the complexities and vagaries of the many studies conducted on spillovers to remember some basic propositions that seem to have been lost in the search for spillovers.

First, transnational corporations are the premier private sector owners and creators of technological learning and capacity. This is their strongest asset. As such, they are going to combat wherever and whenever they can the loss of their competitive edge, guarding against "reverse engineering," imitation of their products, and the possibility that subcontractors can abscond with their hard-won technical knowledge (Nambiar 2001).

Second, when such firms decide to part with some of their power base, they will do so only grudgingly, when they find that the benefit of some loss of this knowledge base is outweighed by some cost-cutting advantage through the use of domestic suppliers. At this stage sharing of some capability is normally partial and therefore does not threaten the dominance of the transnational. What firms tend to part with is technical capacity that is fairly common, rather than forms of knowledge and technical capacity that are key to the firm's ability to exercise monopoly power. So it is helpful to envisage a *spectrum of capacities* used by the multinationals, divided into *low*, *intermediate*, and *high*. TNCs will part with the low-level capabilities if they find a net advantage in doing so, but this will not normally give national supplier firms a sizeable boost in their level of efficiency, because the TNC is able to combine the low-level capabilities with intermediate and highly valued, unique, and very costly forms of specialized know-how and know-why.

Third, in rare instances, TNCs can find it advantageous to part with some of their intermediate capacities. Under these conditions significant spillover effects can occur. But they will occur only if developing nations have *absorptive capacity*. That is, the developing nation has to be in a position to absorb transfers of knowledge, and this entails reasonably deep knowhow capacities that are the outcome of development policies in education, science, management, labor skills training, and engineering.

If we take these considerations into account it is not surprising that development economists have not been able to easily confirm the idea that TNC investments create spillover effects. The fact that some studies show modest positive effects, some no effect, and some negative effects would seem to be a logical outcome of the fact that TNCs will, in the first instance, be unwilling to part with any of their knowledge and capability. No passive knowledge transfers will occur. Only when nations are active in selecting foreign firms, only when nations have built the capacity to absorb lower levels of knowledge transfers, and only when such transfers appear to be advantageous to the TNCs – a fairly demanding string of conditions – will we be able to locate spillover effects from FDI.

Potential costs of TNCs to a host country

While there is evidence of situations where TNCs have enhanced productivity and economic growth in developing nations, the role of the TNCs has created a storm of controversy precisely because other research highlights the possible costs of TNCs to the host nations. In this section, we briefly consider how TNCs and FDI might deepen underdevelopment or facilitate a process of biased economic growth wherein the bulk of the economic benefits are retained by the TNCs.

Transfer pricing

TNCs buy many of their inputs from and sell much of their output to other branches or affiliates of the same TNC, though these often are located in different countries. The extent of such transactions varies from firm to firm and from industry to industry. Nonetheless, virtually all the research conducted on such TNC intra-firm transactions indicates that they are significant. Furthermore, since such transactions are not of an "arm's-length" character between two independent economic agents who have agreed on the terms at which to buy and sell, the TNCs are in a position to set favorable intra-firm transfer prices when it is to their advantage to do so.

A transfer price is simply an accounting price that all firms use for intra-firm transactions of inputs and semi-finished final goods, particularly as these are shipped between different branches of the same firms or different divisions for either reprocessing or sale. In the normal course of business, transfer prices are necessary to allow firms to keep track of costs within divisions or branches of the firm and to measure the profitability and productivity of different divisions or branches.

However, there exists the possibility, particularly in the intra-firm movement of inputs and semi-processed goods between countries, for TNCs to use transfer prices as a mechanism for avoiding taxes in one country or another and for avoiding any profit repatriation or other restrictions placed by any country within the company's global operations. Or a firm might simply want to disguise the extent of its profits as a matter of public relations or in order to avoid adverse repercussions, which could range from labor tensions to nationalization. Then it is likely the company will have two sets of books; one for "real" transfer prices so the TNC can monitor the effectiveness of production globally, and another to "cook the books" so as to increase and move global profits of the TNC to the most advantageous location. In the age of computer operations, the movement of such financial capital is only a keystroke away.

Not all TNCs are engaged in devious transfer pricing schemes, of course. But in one important study of the pharmaceutical industry in Colombia, Constantine Vaistos found that 82 percent of the companies' actual profits were hidden in transfer pricing schemes. Another study of such practices in Kenya by the International Labour Organization found that the actual outflow of profits and dividends was understated by perhaps 100 percent as a result of the over-pricing of inputs (these studies were from the 1970s, as cited by Crow and Thorpe (1988: 275–6)).

In the latter case, it is easy to see how such over-pricing makes TNC profitability in Kenya seem lower than it really is; the TNC, however, increases its global profitability. Usually, such strategies are utilized to extract profits from a country where removing profits now or later might be difficult or subject to restrictions. With such transfer over-pricing, however, it is easy to see how profits and income actually created in Kenya are withdrawn in the form of higher costs. Since most less-developed nations have extremely weak tax-collecting agencies, porous tax laws, and lax enforcement practices anyway, any loss of tax revenues from the TNCs through such transfer pricing arrangements can be extremely serious. (For a detailed treatment of the issue see Plasschaert 1994.) Further, such practices tend to reduce the pool of potential domestic investment funds.

Income transfers via TNCs

While TNCs can contribute to net resource inflows to a developing nation, they can also contribute to net resource outflows in other ways beside transfer pricing. First, parent corporations in the developed countries commonly make loans to their subsidiaries in less-developed economies. In time, such loans will be repaid as interest and amortization, constituting a potential drain on the balance of payments and foreign exchange earnings of the less-developed economy.

Unless the subsidiary is earning foreign exchange via exports or saving foreign exchange by contributing to import substitution in the host country, the outflows of interest and principal can exceed the original inflow of financial capital, thus creating a net outflow over time. Likewise, declared profits often are repatriated to the parent corporation, though profits from the subsidiary may remain within the host nation either to be lent out or reinvested in the operations of the subsidiary.

TNCs often find that their relative strength is in the mastery and control of intangibles, such as organization and information technologies and product technologies. As unique owners of such technologies, they are in a position, should they choose to do so, to sell or lease such technologies and other intangibles via joint ventures, franchises, and other interactions where there is no market for the product sold or leased, it being unique. It is presumed, therefore, that the price charged in such transactions does not represent only the cost to the TNCs of creating such unique information, but that the TNC also derives some degree of monopoly rent from such transactions. This, too, contributes to an outflow of income earned in the less-developed nation flowing to the TNC, presumably headquartered in a developed economy.

Diversion effects

Some evidence suggests that when TNCs enter an economy, indigenous research and development is curbed and redirected toward adaptive inquiry which merely follows the lead of the TNCs, rather than participating in the creation of knowledge. When such effects are present, there is a presumption that the indigenous technological base is narrowed and weakened. Thus the total effect of a strong presence of TNCs in an economy may be either to make no net addition to the R&D process or to divert that process away from appropriate domestic technologies, with an adverse impact on future growth possibilities (UN 1992: 148).

It has long been the claim of the structuralist economists that the TNCs employ capital-intensive production systems which are inappropriate in poorer nations where labor is both abundant and relatively cheap, and where the real rate of unemployment and underemployment may be alarmingly high, even if disguised by informal sector activities. Thus with more capital-intensive production techniques in use, TNCs contribute to urban unemployment and underemployment. Another diversion effect of the TNC may be an internal brain drain, whereby some of the top managers and best university graduates seek employment in the TNCs, leaving the indigenous industrial and agricultural firms with a relatively narrow cadre of managerial talent, and perhaps not always the best trained.

Increasing industrial concentration

The presence of TNCs is generally associated with increasing industrial concentration. Thus, according to standard static microeconomic analysis, resources are more likely to be used sub-optimally as monopoly power is enhanced and the degree of control of oligopolies is expanded. As economic concentration increases, the distribution of income is further tilted toward those at the top. Enhanced TNC activity can thus be associated with a greater polarization of incomes and a tendency to divorce economic growth from enhancement of economic well-being for the vast majority of the population (Newfarmer and Frischtak 1994). In a test of the hypothesis that FDI tends to worsen the distribution of income, Pan-Long Tsai reviewed the available research and concluded that virtually every study conducted on the subject had reached the conclusion that higher levels of FDI *were* associated with a worsening of the income distribution.

> The most striking result ... is the unambiguous positive partial correlation between (the stock of direct foreign investment) and the Gini coefficient.
> ... Our results thus confirm previous findings and support the assertion of the dependency proponents. That is, continuing inflows of foreign capital into the LDCs is very likely to be harmful to the income distributions of the host economies.
>
> (Tsai 1995: 475)

Weak linkages, thin globalization

Much recent data, some of it recorded in Table 14.4 above, suggests that developing nations are making great strides in terms of rapidly attaining efficient production systems that allow for a major surge in exports from developing nations. This perception, however, needs to be understood in a broader context that includes the new systems of global production financed by TNCs.

For national development the most telling indicator of successful incorporation of skill and technology transfers relates to the magnitude of the national linkages between the TNCs and the host economy. Since Mexico has regularly been one of the top ten nations in terms of FDI inflows in recent years it is instructive to note that current research does not suggest that Mexico's *national* industrial base has either grown, or diversified, or deepened its capital and knowledge/skill levels to any serious extent (Cypher 2001). Rather than articulating a new dynamized industrial sector to the national economy, Mexico exhibits the characteristics of a "disarticulated" economy with a dynamic export sector, overwhelmingly dominated by TNCs and largely unlinked to the broader domestic economy (Delgado Wise and Cypher 2007).

Kathy Kopinak refers to the huge *maquiladora* sector (employing well over a million workers in assembly operations) as an example of **thin globalization** (Kopinak 2003). By this it is meant that, while foreign capital has increasingly moved across borders and into Mexico, the degree of connectedness between the export sector and the national economy is very low.

This is an important generalization because it allows us to move beyond the stale "yes or no" debate as to whether "globalization" has been achieved. The modifier "thin" permits a critical understanding of the shallow level of spin-off and assimilation of technology transfers that dominates the processes entailed in the integrated global production system.

Thus TNCs and their joint-venture or strategic alliance partners may well achieve "thick" integration of their proprietary processes across national borders, while only loosely linking to subcontractors and domestic suppliers. The end result of the weak linkages scenario is to retain most of the value-added in manufacturing within the structure of the TNCs. (Value-added refers to the difference between the cost of all inputs into the manufacturing process, and the value of total output. High value-added activities normally are those where high skills and complex technologies are utilized in production.)

As we have seen in our discussion of Hirschman's concept of "backward linkages" (Chapter 5), major investments can create complex, interactive, virtuous circles of forces that will push an economy to a higher level of development. Recent research has centered on Hirschman's concept in great detail. The 2001 *World Investment Report* encapsulated the meaning of Hirschman's concept in the following quotation:

> [Backward linkages] are defined as transactions that go beyond arm's length, one-off relations and involve long-term relations between firms. In fact, a very large proportion of intra-industry transactions in every country involves linkages in this sense, marked by sustained exchanges of information, technology, skills and other assets. Linkages are of particular significance to developing host economies, because they provide a means of diffusing valuable knowledge throughout the economy – through direct flows to the linked firms as well as spillovers to and from the latter. The benefits provided through linkages with foreign affiliates tend to be of greater competitive significance than those among domestic firms because of the stronger knowledge and skills base of many foreign affiliates.
>
> (UNCTAD 2001: 127)

In the instances where these researchers find integral connections to the local production base two possibilities arise:

1   Core suppliers to the large transnationals are increasingly foreign-owned. These firms often exhibit the characteristics of cutting-edge suppliers sought by the TNCs – mastery of quality control, capacity for flexible "just in time" delivery, ability to independently design components and supplies at the level of original equipment standards, and, perhaps most important, the capacity to *jointly* address production problems with the contracting TNCs. Clearly, in this instance neither learning nor technology transfers occur with heightened FDI, and the domestic economy remains disarticulated from the accumulation process driven by the TNCs.
2   Deep linkages and dynamic technology and learning transfers occur normally when host nations intervene and set up their own "linkages promotion programs." As discussed in Chapter 7, the state can play a crucial role in tying together the forces of the TNCs and the national needs for rapid development. Not surprisingly, most successful linkage promotion programs have occurred in East Asia. Rather than passively receiving FDI, nations in East Asia have struggled to upgrade existing linkages, create new domestic sourcing possibilities, and force TNCs to reorient their production toward linkages to higher value-added activities. Six key processes have been encouraged by the state:

a   **Create** public/private sector forums to open a dialogue between the TNCs and unions, regional planners, national development agencies, business associations, supplier industry associations, and financial sector firms.

b   **Disseminate** to all parties information regarding successful examples of linkages.

c   **Limit and target** specific sectors or industries, bypassing areas where internationally integrated production systems are already dominant.

d   **Choose** to host foreign affiliates on the basis of their commitment to interact with and their potential to spin off crucial learning/technology to local suppliers.

e   **Select** suppliers based on their capability of meeting production standards, quality requirements, workforce skill requirements, and the commitment of local entrepreneurs to restructuring their operations to meet continually evolving standards set by the contracting TNC.

f   **Monitor** and evaluate local suppliers, rewarding those that meet the above goals.

Nations with **developmental states**, such as many East Asian nations, have been able to build strong backward linkages. Elsewhere, the lack of such states – particularly in Latin America – has led to a passive approach to hosting TNCs, and the results have been that these nations are now enmeshed in a process of "thin" globalization. In this situation the national economy is largely disarticulated and a new "global" dualism has emerged – ultramodern TNCs operating in a nearly autonomous transnationalized sphere and a domestic economy mired in low productivity, poverty, social decomposition, capital flight, and massive unemployment exhibited by a burgeoning "informal" sector of "self-employed" day laborers who are, in reality the "disguised unemployed."

Table 14.5 documents the trends to be noted in the new integrated global production system. Many nations have dramatically increased their manufacturing exports, but most are not increasing their share of manufacturing value-added. Rather, as their exports rise so too do their imports of machinery, equipment, technology, and intermediate supplies. In these nations it is common to note a process of deindustrialization as the export sector grows while the local manufacturing base shrinks and ownership shifts even more to the TNCs.

Table 14.5 Exports of manufactured products from developing nations (percentage)

	Share of world exports		Share of world manufacturing value-added	
	1980	*1997*	*1980*	*1997*
Developing nations	10.5	26.5	16.6	23.8
Developed nations	82.3	70.9	64.5	73.3
Latin America	1.5	3.5	7.1	6.7
(Mexico)	(0.2)	(2.2)	(1.9)	(1.2)
Newly industrialized Asian[a]	5.1	8.9	1.7	4.5
(Korea)	(1.4)	(2.9)	(0.7)	(2.3)
ASEAN-4[b]	0.6	3.6	1.2	2.6
China	1.1[c]	3.8	3.3	5.8

Source: UNCTAD 2002: 81.

Notes
a Hong Kong, Korea, Singapore, Taiwan.
b Indonesia, Malaysia, Philippines, Thailand.
c 1984.

The result of these processes is that value-added at the local level actually declines, meaning that there are few or no indirect or multiplier effects to be captured or enjoyed as FDI rises. But this is not the whole story: In Asia the ability to insert a national strategy into the process demonstrates that there is no inevitable fate for host nations. As active participants they can increasingly experience the positive effects of FDI. Thus note the dramatically different patterns exhibited by the top Latin American exporters and the eight Asian nations that have actively pursued national linkage strategies. Note the standout position of Mexico, commonly hailed as *the* success story of free trade: "between 1980 and 1997 Mexico's share in world manufacturing exports rose tenfold, while its share in world manufacturing value added fell by more than one-third, and its share in world income by about thirteen percent" (UNCTAD 2002: 80). In Asia only Hong Kong has been losing ground in terms of value-added, and this may be the result of its leanings toward the neoclassical free trade model and away from the developmental state approach.

Export promotion and the fallacy of composition

Critics of the TNCs have maintained that while the TNCs may well be in a position to expand exports, if a strategy of promoting FDI is employed at one time in a large number of nations, it must fail for all or many of these nations. The argument is straightforward. If the less-developed world, as a group, suddenly floods global markets with new manufacturing exports, prices could fall, and it is presumed that what is lost as prices fall might not be made up through the increasing volume of sales. In any case, price trends (falling or slowly rising) for exports would not be matched by equal price trends for imports from the industrial nations. In other words, the terms of trade for labor-intensive low-technology manufactured goods exports from the less-developed world would deteriorate, leaving the developing countries, as a group, worse-off.

There is evidence that this has been occurring. International Monetary Fund data show that the terms of trade for less-developed country manufactured goods exports fell by -0.88 percent per year between 1967 and 1987 (IMF 1988). This is a disturbing trend, which appears to have continued from 1990 to 2001 according to recent research. In a study of eighteen developing nations (including China and India) Arslan Razmi and Robert Blecker found evidence that developing nations heavily involved in the export of manufactured products are now competing with each other in low-technology production (Razmi and Blecker 2008). To gain market share nations will have to devalue against other nations and/or suppress their wage levels, which will lead to reciprocal actions generating "race to the bottom" strategies. Thus, not only do most low-income countries suffer from declining terms of trade for their primary products, but it appears that the tendency for the terms of trade to decline extends to the low-technology manufactured goods of the less-developed countries, according to recent research by the United Nations:

> The empirical evidence strongly suggests that global competition for labor-intensive manufacturing activities has risen over the past few years. This coincides with the shift in the mid-1980s of several highly populated, low income economies towards more export-oriented strategies. The countries with the lowest proportion of technology-intensive manufactures and the greatest proportion of low-skill labor-intensive products in their manufactured exports have faced declining terms of trade in manufactures.
>
> (UNCTAD 2002: 119–20)

Long-term costs of TNCs: the potential for environmental degradation

The overall impact of TNCs on the environment is difficult to determine, because research in this area is relatively recent and incomplete. Drawing inferences from the logic of transnational production is also somewhat problematic. On the one hand, it is very often true that TNCs have leverage with host governments which may allow them to engage in environmentally unsound activities which would be prohibited at home. From a cost-minimizing standpoint, they often have a strong incentive to function as environmental predators if permitted to do so. On the other hand, however, the TNCs are visible targets, and they have become deeply involved in presenting themselves as "environmentally conscious" producers in the advanced nations. As such they can be harmed by evidence of environmental insensitivity, both in their "home" market and in the less-developed nations.

Furthermore, TNCs, particularly TNCs which operate stand-alone production facilities dating from the early days of ISI policies, operate a full range of technologically diverse industries which tend to create most of the industrial pollutants found worldwide. For example, TNCs play a major role in the production of substances which account for approximately 80 percent of anthropomorphic greenhouse-gas generation (UN 1992: 226).

- TNCs are the primary producers and consumers of chlorofluorocarbons, the principal cause of stratospheric ozone depletion;
- TNCs account for at least 15 percent of greenhouse gas emissions;
- the twenty largest TNCs producing pesticides accounted for 94 percent of agrochemical sales in 1990 (UNCTAD 1994: 226);[3]
- TNCs have extensive involvement in the most highly polluting industrial activities, such as the production of industrial chemicals, synthetic resins and plastic products, non-ferrous metal products, iron and steel, petroleum production and refining, and paper manufacturing. The portion of FDI involved in pollution-intensive industries ranges between 20 and 50 percent (UN 1992: 231);
- several studies conducted in Asian nations indicate that TNCs maintain lower environmental standards in developing countries than these same companies uphold in developed nations, but that these lower standards are nevertheless higher than those of locally owned firms (UN 1992: 233–4).

Host nations generally have strong laws and regulations governing environmentally damaging forms of production, but do not always have the versatile scientific capacity to actually monitor and enforce the laws which already exist. Depth of scientific know-how, particularly at the level of monitoring officials needed to supervise the TNCs and local firms which are, in fact, much more numerous, is in short supply. Governing the environmental behavior of producers, including TNCs, is one of the most immediate and pressing problems facing developing nations today. Fortunately, consciousness of environmental degradation is spreading rapidly throughout the developing world (see Focus 14.2).

Export processing zones and the problems of small nations

Critics of TNCs have highlighted the role of export processing zones (EPZs), for they tend to illustrate the most undesirable consequences which may arise when a less-developed nation uncritically turns to FDI hoping for the potential benefits (see Focus 14.3). EPZs are special

FOCUS 14.2   TNCS IN THE LOGGING BUSINESS

Tropical forests are of two types. First, there are tropical rainforests which currently cover more than 1.5 billion hectares. Two-thirds of the rainforests are in Latin America, principally Brazil. Second, there are tropical dry forests, principally in Africa. They also occupy approximately 1.5 billion hectares of land.

In both types of forests, extensive ecological change is taking place. Current estimates suggest that 20 million hectares per year are being deforested, for a variety of reasons. Approximately 60 percent of the annual deforestation is due to conversion to agricultural uses. Access to this land often occurs as a result of logging operations. Land is frequently claimed by giant agribusiness TNCs or companies which contract with these TNCs. Another 20 percent of annual deforestation is the direct result of the logging industry. The logging industry encroaches, directly or indirectly, on the forests at a rate of roughly 4 million hectares per year.

About 15 percent of the world's commercial lumber comes from the rainforests. The tropical dry forests are the main source of industrial wood products. Thus the activities of the logging industry are particularly important to understanding the destruction of large regions of Africa.

The available research indicates that US TNCs had withdrawn from nearly all direct timber-cutting operations in the tropical forests by the early 1980s. In contrast, European TNCs remain extensively involved in much of the logging that is conducted throughout the developing world. This is particularly the case in Africa, where European corporations control 90 percent of the timber-cutting in Gabon, 77 percent of these operations in the Congo, nearly 100 percent of such activities in Liberia, and 88 percent of logging in Cameroon. The Japanese are extensively involved in logging operations throughout South-East Asia.

Aside from depletion of the forests, logging quite often leads to climatic changes which give rise to desertification or reduced rainfall. Silting of streams reduces or eliminates stream aquatic life, and could reduce fishing in oceans or lakes.

Sources: UN 1992: 228; World Bank 1992: 57–8

geographic areas, usually at or near ports or borders, where the normal "rules of the game" regarding foreign investors are relaxed by host governments. As a general rule, products entering and leaving EPZs are exempt from all import and export taxes, corporate and other taxes, license fees are waived for firms operating in the zones, labor unions are excluded, and even existing labor laws are not enforced, including, sometimes, minimum wage laws (see Focus 14.4). EPZs often attract foreign companies by offering a "tax holiday," suspending all corporate taxes for a multi-year period.

Furthermore, physical structures often are erected and leased at modest, typically below-market, rates in industrial parks in the EPZs. Good infrastructure, such as roads, is often offered at no cost or at highly subsidized rates. Such benefits can include below-market prices for electricity, gas, water, and waste disposal not available to firms outside the zones. Sometimes labor training and housing for workers is provided and/or subsidized.

The incentive for nations to establish EPZs is that they gain often badly needed foreign exchange, though this typically is limited to labor's value-added, that is, wage income, in production. Most of the employment is in labor-intensive manufacturing and assembly processes, thereby creating new jobs which can be very important to host nations. Unfortunately, EPZs generally fail to create either forward or backward linkages to local production; in fact, in most countries, firms located within EPZs are prohibited from having any but minimal sales to the internal market, so forward linkages are typically impossible. But neither do the firms locating in the EPZs form many backward linkages to potential supplying firms in the

FOCUS 14.3   WOMEN WORKERS IN EXPORT PROCESSING ZONES

Between 70 and 80 percent of the workers in EPZs are women. They tend to be young, inexperienced, poorly educated and poorly trained, and single. Their employment condition is insecure, with extremely high turnover rates, sometimes 200 percent per year. Unions are usually non-existent, and those that exist are dominated by the employers in the zones.

The plants tend to be modern, clean, well-ventilated and well-lit. Nevertheless, researchers have noted a wide range of employment-related problems, suggesting widespread hazardous working conditions. Some of the difficulties include exposure to radiation and toxic substances, chemicals used without adequate training or warnings, and inadequate safety equipment. Other research mentions common occurrence of eyesight deterioration, ulcers and other nervous disorders, puncture wounds, chemical burns, and electric shocks. The pace of work is demanding; workers sometimes repeat the same operations every five seconds, 7,200 times per day. Pay rates tend to be quite low by global standards, from approximately 45 cents (US) per hour to a few dollars per hour. But wages can also be much lower, with the National Labor Committee finding wages in the late 1990s at 9–20 cents per hour in Bangaladesh, 25 cents per hour in Pakistan and ten cents per hour in Indonesia. With benefits, which can include one or two meals, transportation to and from work, and some medical care, the employee cost to the firm may, however, be closer to double the wage.

Employers have often mentioned factors such as "a pliant nature," "non-union," "nimble-fingered" and "docile" in stating their preference for women workers. One study of electronics TNCs operating in Mexico's EPZ found that women workers constituted above 70 percent of the labor force, with the average age ranging between eighteen and twenty-four years. Average education received was six years, the average experience level was three years, and direct wages were 85 cents per hour.

In comparison to employment outside the EPZs, the work day tends to be 25 percent longer, with wages as much as 50 percent less than the industrial wage paid in similar operations. Within the EPZs, women tend to do the direct assembly work, while men operate and maintain complex equipment. Some EPZs now operate high-tech plants where men are increasingly being employed in direct production in preference to women workers.

Sources: Barry 1992: 144; Shaiken 1990: 91;
Sklair 1989: 172; UNCTAD 1994: 203

local economy. In one of the largest EPZ countries, Mexico, indigenous products other than labor constitute less than 5 percent of the value-added of the production in the EPZs. Often the national contribution over and above direct labor consists of little more than janitorial services.

There were nearly 551 EPZs in 1998, employing nearly 27 million workers. Some of these workers were in developed nations in North America and Europe or in transition economies in Eastern Europe, but the vast majority were in developing nations (ILO 1998a). Nearly one-third of the total number of workers employed by TNCs in the less-developed world were employed in TNC operations in an EPZ. In 1998, seventy-four nations had one or more EPZs, or were planning on adding such zones. While TNCs have played a crucial role in the establishment of the EPZs, in some of the older EPZs in Asia national businesses now play a vital role. Thus not all of the workers in the zones are employees of the TNCs, their subcontractors, or their subsidiaries. The EPZs continue to grow, sometimes very rapidly.

For example, by 1995, over 600,000 workers were employed in such zones in Mexico, but by early 2001 there were 1,300,000 such workers. Malaysia had 99,000 EPZ workers

FOCUS 14.4   UNIONS UNDER INTEGRATED PRODUCTION SYSTEMS

Unions can be effective agents for reducing economic discrimination against women workers and for enhancing the health and safety conditions in the workplace. One study of Mexican workers showed that in the non-union sector, women with identical skill and experience levels were paid 18 percent less than male workers. But in the unionized sector, there was no difference in pay between men and women workers. Labor unions have demonstrated that they can play an active and forceful role in enforcing health regulations and work standards.

Unions, however, play a smaller role in developing nations because 40 to 80 percent of production takes place outside the formal economy. In both agriculture and the informal sector, labor contracts are non-existent. Within the formal economy, unions have often become well established in nations with TNCs within their industrial sectors. Research indicates that the stand-alone subsidiaries of manufacturing TNCs typical of the ISI era generally paid manufacturing workers substantially more than did local employers.

However, the recent rise of the globally integrated system of production raises deep questions regarding the relationship between TNCs and unions. Integral to the new system is widespread subcontracting, often in export processing zones. Subcontractors are small, formally independent firms, operating in a dense web of intra-firm production relations organized by large transnationals, particularly in electronics and textile production and assembly. Employing perhaps 12 million low-wage workers, subcontractors are not the visible nationalist targets which TNCs constitute. As small manufacturers, they rarely operate within a sector where laborers' interests are independently represented by a union, however. There is evidence suggesting that subcontractors, the instruments of the giant TNCs, tend to sidestep unions, ignore workplace health and safety standards, often pay sub-minimum wages, and often fail to follow labor standards.

A few large garment-making TNCs have voluntarily imposed corporate codes of conduct to try to insure fair labor standards practices are adhered to by their subcontractors operating at the lower end of global commodity chains of production. Even consumer groups are getting involved, refusing to purchase products of major retailers whose suppliers refuse to conform to reasonable labor standards for their workers.

Sources: UNCTAD 1994: 193–4, 198–9, 201, 325–7;
World Bank 1995: 76, 81

in 1990, and 200,000 in 1997. Sri Lanka's EPZ employment soared from 71,000 in 1990 to 280,000 in 1998.

Outpacing all nations, China added 1,100,000 EPZ workers just between 1990 and 1992! In 1990 the number of EPZ workers was estimated at roughly 4 million (UNCTAD 1994: 190). Another sample covering only "large" programs with data drawn from the 1992–4 period, detailing employment in only thirty-one nations found employment totals of 5.5 million (ILO 1998b: 27–9).

We can see just how rapidly the EPZs are proliferating by noting that in the late 1990s the estimate of total employment had risen above 20 million – more than five times the level estimated in 1990 (ILO 1998c: 1). EPZs are scattered around the world, with the largest cluster in Asia, and a second, much smaller cluster in Mexico, Central America, and the Caribbean. In 1997 Mexico had 107 EPZs, Central America and the Caribbean 92, South America 41, the Middle East 39, Asia 225, and Africa 47.

EPZs in small nations as a special case

EPZs have often been envisioned as the "starter" for the export engine of growth of an indigenous manufacturing sector. For this to occur, however, the TNCs operating in the EPZs must be embedded in a production structure which forges ever-more profound linkages to the national economy of the host nation. Only in Korea and Taiwan has such a "virtuous circle" been created with export-oriented TNCs. Furthermore, in these nations, the EPZs became important sites for national capitalists to produce and export from, not simply for TNCs.

What is most notable is the emphasis in South Korea and Taiwan on increasing the degree of local sourcing of inputs as a condition for firms remaining in the EPZs and reaping the benefits of the exclusions from taxes and tariffs. However, this reward structure should no longer surprise. Korea's and Taiwan's industrial policies have been noted (see Chapter 10) for their monitoring of the effects of their policies and for the successful use of performance-based subsidy structures that reward results, in particular greater efficiency, while penalizing rent-seeking, unproductive behavior. Furthermore, as wages have increased in East Asia, these nations have proved adept at creating new forms of specialization to supplant the locational advantage of cheap labor which allowed them to attract FDI in those areas where FDI was desired.

When nations fail to force production linkages to the broader economy onto firms in the EPZs, as has most often been the case, then the EPZ becomes little more than an "export platform," and TNC investment will remain an enclave, disarticulated from other sectors of the local economy. What the local economy provides in such cases is limited to cheap labor power and an attractive investment climate, both of which contribute to a higher level of profit for the TNC, but without substantially improving the probability that a locally directed growth process will be initiated in the poor nation. This situation is particularly acute in small nations.

The vertically integrated manufacturing TNCs that small economies are able to attract maintain established, risk-reducing worldwide sourcing and distribution networks. These networks involve the transfer and sale of inputs, semi-processed goods, and final products among far-flung subsidiaries of the parent corporation. Existing networks are quite difficult to penetrate, particularly for new or potential firms in a less-developed economy with limited experience in dealing with the immense corporate structures characteristic of the TNCs.

Even when there is sufficient know-how, the TNC is not always ready to admit linkages with its subsidiaries, particularly when doing so increases the exposure of the TNC to local instability, or, more likely, because in small economies the difficulty of attaining scale economies may raise the cost of locally produced inputs above those which the TNC can provide via its existing external supply network. Furthermore, the deficiency of a production culture among domestic entrepreneurs accustomed to a protected ISI climate will often be apparent by a low level of quality control and/or an inability to maintain production and delivery schedules, though these transitional inefficiencies can be overcome.

The indigenous infrastructural system may make it all but impossible to offer reliable deliveries, as roads, rail, and waterway carriers can be extremely ineffective. In any case, the TNC often will resist local purchases under purely market-driven conditions, since to do so would be to reduce the profitability of a portion of their own productive apparatus. Such linkages were once forged through domestic content requirements or domestic hiring quotas in those areas for which the country feels it can provide inputs and from which the greatest possibility for positive external learning effects exist. Creation of the World Trade Organization in 1994 has made it difficult for nations to utilize domestic content restrictions, but the

WTO's strictures do not prevent nations from creating conditions wherein the local content occurs.

Nations need to encourage foreign affiliates of TNCs to (1) provide managerial and labor training to local supplier firms, (2) build an environment wherein foreign affiliates will be rewarded for sharing production information, (3) assist local suppliers by furnishing financial support, perhaps through advance payment for production and/or prompt payment on delivery, (4) transferring technology and know-how to supplier firms.

While this may sound utopian, case-studies involving Malaysia, Thailand, China, and Singapore in the late 1990s demonstrate that a committed, active state can engineer vital changes that lead to deep linkage effects in spite of the new barriers to local content legislation erected by the WTO (UNCTAD 2001: 149–214). Thus in the 1990s local sourcing of electronics inputs were only 28 percent in Mexico, but were 62 percent in Malaysia and 40 percent in Thailand – the difference accounted for by the existence of policies to stimulate linkages in Malaysia and Thailand (UNCTAD 2001: 135). The gap between those nations who have built linkage programs and the bottom-end EPZ nations is growing, with most nations able to supply only 5–10 percent from local content. Only nations with a broad development strategy are able to build linkage programs. More generally:

> Many MNCs have supplier development programmes in host developing countries ... The intensity of knowledge and information exchange in buyer-supplier relationships tends to increase with the level of economic development of host countries, particularly in complex activities, and where technological and managerial gaps with suppliers are not too wide.
>
> (UNCTAD 2001: xxii)

Vertically integrated TNCs and development prospects

The multiplier effects of backward linkages from TNC investments can be expected to be quite small unless a country is extremely diligent in helping local businesses to forge links with the TNCs. The International Labour Organization's research suggests that, generally, for every five EPZ jobs only one new (additional) job is created in the domestic economy – an extremely low job multiplier (ILO 1998b: 8). To the extent that export-platform promotion is a major component of a nation's overall development strategy, even wages paid will have a reduced multiplier effect when a significant quantity of consumption goods, including agricultural goods, are imported. To visualize this process, Figure 14.1 presents a stylized circuit of capital for a typical manufacturing TNC attracted to an EPZ in a small nation.

The production process is initiated outside the country in which the export subsidiary is located. Money capital (M) is used to purchase produced means of production and raw materials (MP) and labor (L), for the first stage of production (P_1). From this comes a partially transformed output or new means of production (C') with a value as yet unsold or "unrealized" greater than the initial outlay, M. With the completion of the first stage of production, C' is shipped by the TNC to its export subsidiary in the small, export-platform economy. There the semi-processed product is combined in the local production process (P_2) with unskilled, cheap labor.[4] Now, the subsidiary of the TNC produces final or partially assembled commodities, C'', which are then re-exported. Their value is realized, and the profit from production is accumulated not in the country where the EPZ is located, but elsewhere within the international structure of the TNC. Production ($P = P_1 + P_2$) and realization take place only on an international scale, in which many individual subsidiaries of a TNC in widely

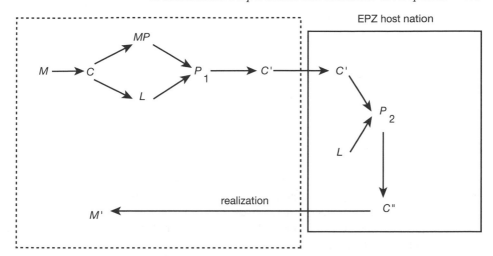

Figure 14.1 An EPZ circuit of capital.

scattered locations ultimately may participate. $C'' > C' > C$ and $M' > M$, where the difference $M' - M = S$, is the level of gross profit.

Structurally articulated *internally* with its own subsidiaries and already linked to established sourcing and distribution networks, the TNC's subsidiary (or affiliate) in a small nation is sectorally and structurally disarticulated from the local economic structure. The local economy is but a production point, and then for only a fragment, P_2, of the complete production process within the TNC. The manufacturing export-platform economy provides no more than a convenient physical location, albeit one that is frequently quite profitable. It is the non-specific locational bias of the purely export-oriented TNC, as opposed to the locationally specific food, raw material, mineral, and ISI manufacturing corporations of the past, which results in small host governments having reduced leverage when attempting to pressure the TNCs in EPZs to create or permit backward and forward linkages when they do not emerge spontaneously.

EPZs can create the appearance of industrialization and development in a country, without the substance. The location of the P_2 phase of production in a poor nation will almost always contribute to a higher GDP, though the *net* contribution of such production will be less than the gross effect to the degree that local production is adversely affected, especially in agriculture or other sectors which lose labor to urban areas near the EPZs where people migrate in hopes of finding employment. Moreover, the contribution of the TNC to the country's GNI will be less than its contribution to GDP by the level of repatriated profits, interest, and dividends. Even after taking such effects fully into account, the net contribution of the TNC will be overstated in a static analysis.

Given that the P_2 process is not location-specific, it can usually be transferred rather easily by the "footloose" export-only manufacturing TNCs. And, to the degree that the new host nation provides a greater array of incentives to locate in its EPZs, the relocation costs to the TNC are correspondingly reduced. Furthermore, EPZs are unlikely to contribute to the breakdown of stultifying social structures which continue to thwart movement away from the low-productivity trap of the "plantation economies" still characteristic of many small nations. Enclave EPZs do not spontaneously contribute to the expansion of the "industrial arts" in a dynamic process of creative destruction that breaks down restraining internal barriers to progress. This is partly so because the TNCs seek to maintain the low-wage sector that, with reasonable levels of productivity, contributes strongly to their global profits.

Bargaining with the TNCs

There are, however, nations which have made substantial economic and social progress while selectively and constructively interacting with TNCs. In *bargaining* with TNCs, particularly TNCs of the "stand-alone" type which desire to enter a nation in order to sell in that nation's home market, the host nation can exert some leverage. This is particularly the case for a host nation which has achieved embedded autonomy, as demonstrated by their successful pursuit of not only ISI but export substitution strategies (see Chapters 7, 9 and 10).

At the same time, some host nations have increasingly been able to exercise some bargaining strength because there has been a rapid dispersion of the power formerly exercised by US TNCs. A quick glance back to Table 14.2 will demonstrate that, while US TNCs controlled approximately half of the stock of FDI in 1960, their share of this capital fell dramatically to one-quarter of the total in 1992. As a consequence of this shift, some host nations have been able to improve the terms of engagement with TNCs because, more and more, when foreign firms seek to become involved in these nations it is likely that TNCs from other nations will also be interested. This competition among TNCs to locate in any country can work in favor of the host country.

In 1992, the United Nation's Transnational Corporations and Management Division published a benchmark work subtitled "Transnational Corporations as Engines of Growth" (UN 1992). This study drew together literally hundreds of research documents in order to address the crucial question of the links between FDI and economic development. Notice that the conclusions to this study, summarized below, do not address a number of thorny issues, such as the impact of TNCs on the environment (see Focus 14.5), or the intermediate-term effects of FDI on the balance of payments discussed above under the heading "Income Transfers via TNCs," or transfer pricing issues. Some of their key conclusions are worth careful scrutiny, for there are major lessons to be learned. The following quotation and the subsequent summary deal only with the quantity and quality of physical capital formation:

> The evidence indicates that FDI (foreign direct investment) inflows make a positive contribution to the quantity of new physical capital in developing countries, and that this quantitative contribution appears more significant in industries that are crucial to growth and development, such as manufacturing. Local purchasing by MNCs has, in many host developing nations, provided a stimulant to local investment. Evidence of the qualitative contribution of MNCs to host country investment is less clear cut. ... MNC management practices provide a model for efficient organization of production that can be learned by host country producers.
>
> The evidence on MNCs and host countries suggests that the benefits from the presence of MNCs may depend as much on host country conditions as upon the assets brought by foreign firms. ... When MNCs produce largely in export processing zones, their ability to stimulate domestic production is reduced.
>
> The general conclusion is that MNCs have had a positive influence on domestic capital formation in host developing countries ... the evidence for such a conclusion is drawn from a small number of developing countries, most of which are large and have had some success in stimulating growth.
>
> (UN 1992: 124–5)

FOCUS 14.5   ENVIRONMENTAL PROBLEMS IN MEXICO'S EPZS

With more than one million employees (in 2002) working in over 3,000 foreign-owned plants along the nearly 2,000-mile US–Mexican border, the environmental effects of Mexico's EPZs have received considerable attention.

Mexico has a body of laws and an environmental ministry, SEDESOL, which attempt to regulate the environmental effect of production in the EPZs. At best, SEDESOL is able to inspect one-third of the assembly plants in a given year, and enforcement is lax. Some of the effects noted by researchers are as follows.

- The city of Tijuana, just below San Diego, California, has experienced a 119 percent population increase as workers have flocked to the more than 550 EPZ firms. Industrial waste from the plants and household waste from the population are beyond the sewage treatment capacities of the city. As a result, 12 million gallons of untreated waste flow daily into the Tijuana River and then into the Pacific Ocean.
- In Nogales, Mexico, seventy-five assembly plants, along with the supporting population, daily discharge 18 million gallons of untreated waste. The Nogales Wash contains mercury, lead, and a variety of industrial solvents utilized by furniture assembly companies. Carcinogenic chemicals found in underground aquifers have forced water-well closings 10 miles north of the border.
- In Matamoros, one plant was found to be releasing xylene, an industrial solvent, at levels 6,000 times above that thought to be safe in drinking water. Another plant registered concentrations 53,000 times above the safe level. Releases of toxic hydrofluoric acid at one plant led to a ban on future worker settlements within 1.5 miles of the plant. Yet workers who already lived within this perimeter were permitted to remain there.

Passage of the North American Free Trade Agreement (NAFTA) in 1993 created new hope for an environmental clean-up of Mexico's EPZ plants. However, fraud and deception continue to overcome the attempt to control the disposal of toxic substances, with only 20 percent of the 12,500 tons of toxic solid wastes inspected for proper disposal.

Sources: Russell 1994: 254–60; Scheeres 1996

These summary conclusions are derived from several substantive findings.

- Manufacturing matters; attracting manufacturing TNCs can raise the total stock of capital available for production.
- Local sourcing of inputs matters; attracting foreign manufacturing capital is neither a necessary nor a sufficient condition for economic growth. The creation of backward linkages to the local production process is central to the benefits to be gained from TNCs. TNC capital must be compelled to link with local production sources.
- Host country conditions matter and are fundamental; host nations must be active participants in defining and revising the conditions under which foreign capital is permitted to operate in the domestic economy; market-driven passivity is inadequate if the potential gains from foreign capital investment are to have a chance of being realized.
- EPZs matter, but in a negative way; they have not been a viable basis for physical or human capital accumulation and for sustained growth.
- Host country size matters; relatively large nations have, as a rule, been most successful in controlling the interactive process of foreign investment and in being able to reap more of the potential benefits of FDI; there are exceptions, however. The Latin American countries have been less successful in this regard, partly because of a more *laissez-faire* approach to FDI, rather than a more activist and cooperative approach.

- History matters; successful, or relatively successful, nations in dealing with TNCs have had a history of fostering development through ISI.

FDI in Asia and Latin America: A Historical Case Study

As we have noted in earlier chapters, a great deal of comparative research has been conducted on the East Asian "miracle" economies and the largest Latin American nations. Another contrast to be noted is the manner in which the Asian nations have addressed the issue of the role of foreign capital. To begin to survey some of this research, it is useful to note the relative insignificance of TNCs at the top of the production pyramid in both Korea and Taiwan in the 1980s. In contrast to the large Latin American nations, private nationally owned firms clearly dominate the most important sectors of production, with state-owned firms holding a rather distant second-place position (see Table 14.6). In Latin America, by contrast, the TNCs have a very strong position among the leading corporations, while nationally owned firms hold a relatively small share of production compared to Korea and Taiwan.

In an attempt to account for the relatively strong performance of two of the Asian miracles, South Korea and Taiwan, in relation to the two largest Latin American nations, Brazil and Mexico, Barbara Stallings scrutinized the differing approaches to, and experiences with, foreign capital. She reached the conclusion that "the issue at stake is whether the State's choice of development strategy determines the role of foreign capital or whether foreign capital determines development strategy" (Stallings 1990: 80). Stallings found that:

- in South Korea and Taiwan the overall importance of foreign capital had declined over time; FDI had continued, but at a moderate rate;
- in Latin America, the importance of foreign capital increased from the 1960s, with the implementation of secondary ISI, until the 1980s, when the debt crisis virtually halted such inflows;

Table 14.6 Relative share of TNCs among the largest firms (percentage of total in each category, 1987)

Country	State-owned	National	TNCs
South Korea			
top 10	10	90	–
top 25	n.d.	n.d.	n.d.
Taiwan			
top 10	40	60	–
top 25	32	56	12
Brazil			
top 10	60	10	30
top 25	40	20	32
Mexico			
top 10	40	20	40
top 25	28	44	28

Source: Gereffi 1990: 92–5.

Note
n.d. = no data.

- the East Asian nations have had a relatively lower reliance on FDI for capital and technology;
- the East Asian nations have favored borrowing from foreign governments, with relatively easy repayment requirements, to having FDI;
- the East Asian nations have been able to maneuver between Japan and the United States, thereby improving their bargaining position in determining the conditions under which FDI has taken place;
- the East Asian nations had "strong" and cohesive states which were willing to operate strategically and plan strategically in pursuit of national development;
- the East Asian nations continued to weigh the relative merits of FDI against bank loans and other forms of credit, maintaining a balance between these in their favor;
- the Latin American nations tended to adopt one strategy regarding FDI, and foreign capital, to the exclusion of dynamic combinations regarding, first, openness to FDI versus protection and closure of certain key industries, and second, FDI versus bank loans.

Some of the creative and versatile strategies adopted by South Korea and Taiwan in their search to gain maximum advantage from FDI and foreign capital in general are summarized by Stallings:

[F]oreign capital took two main forms. One was direct investment, often in export processing zones that provided tax incentives and exemptions on import duties as long as output was exported. The other was marketing, typically through subcontracting arrangements with international retail chains.

Both the South Korean and Taiwanese governments were strong, centralized institutions, which used a combination of incentives and regulations to deal with foreign capital. The South Koreans had a more top-down approach and privileged loans over FDI since loans gave them greater control. The Foreign Capital Inducement Law of 1960 and its subsequent amendments set out procedures and guarantees for attracting foreign loans. Direct investors were also offered tax incentives, but they were never really encouraged during this period. In addition, the South Koreans were especially sensitive to the issue of dependency on the United States, and the normalization of relations with Japan in 1965 provided an opportunity to play off South Korea's two most important allies. ... Taiwan was more willing to let foreigners acquire equity participation in the economy. Much of this was initially carried out through EPZs. ... Nevertheless, the government maintained substantial control by ownership of upstream industries, including banking, and by targeting chosen sectors for investment. In both countries, the governments used their power to protect the interests of local firms as well as to regulate foreign participation.

(Stallings 1990: 77)

Analyzing the period from the mid-1950s to the late 1980s, Stallings noted that the reliance on foreign capital increased in the Latin American nations, while domestic savings rose in South Korea and Taiwan, thereby lessening the need for foreign capital flows (see Focus 14.6). In the 1950s and 1960s, the Latin American nations relied heavily on FDI, but they paid a price in terms of the loss of economic and political power by the central government and of a reduction in the importance of national capital. Meanwhile, the East Asian nations were able to access loans and aid funds which went directly to a clearly developmentalist

FOCUS 14.6   MANAGEMENT OF FDI: THE CASE OF TAIWAN

Taiwan's experience with foreign capital, particularly with FDI, is instructive. Taiwan constitutes an important case-study of the potential benefit from having well-designed foreign investment guidelines concerning the terms of entry, interaction, and exit of foreign capital in the host nation.

Like Japan and South Korea, Taiwan has imposed important conditions on foreign capital, but these conditions have been somewhat less restrictive than in other countries of the region. When Taiwan has considered the entry of foreign capital, the state attempts to ascertain the degree to which such capital will contribute to new exports, particularly to the penetration of new markets. Other important considerations are the degree to which the foreign capital will create forward and backward linkages or input–output links and the likelihood of significant transfers of needed technologies. Taiwan is concerned with how a given investment project will enhance its chances of attracting future FDI which will fit into its development strategy.

Local content requirements

As has been the case in many other nations which have sought to manage FDI, Taiwan has emphasized **local content legislation** which has forced TNCs, even those operating in EPZs, to make significant and growing use of locally produced inputs. Research from the 1980s indicated that local content in the EPZs was slowly raised to approximately 20 percent. In Mexico, in contrast, local content has been trivial in the EPZs, less than 5 percent. (Since the creation of the World Trade Organization in 1994 it has become very difficult to impose foreign content legislation, but many nations in Asia have found creative ways to circumvent the WTO requirements.)

Creating new comparative advantage

Taiwan has repeatedly revised its FDI conditions as the nation's economy has evolved. Thus in the 1970s it began to *discourage* labor-intensive FDI, while simultaneously working to provide a mass of well-trained engineers, scientists, and managers which could spearhead a drive into high-technology, capital-intensive industrial activities of the secondary ISI/secondary export substitution stage of industrialization.

Export requirements

Nations with sizeable, if not huge, populations may find that the key to development rests with the expansion of domestic demand. Intermediate and small nations will generally find that exports must play a vital role, but not necessarily the central role, in a viable development strategy. As Robert Wade points out, Taiwan has made constructive use of export requirements when considering the admission of foreign capital, while simultaneously inhibiting access to the domestic market, which has been largely reserved for national firms.

Taiwan has sometimes been portrayed as a free trader, but is nonetheless willing to use both assured access to the domestic market and protection against imports to attract the kind of FDI which will enhance its growth strategy.

> Import protection is important too, and here the subtlety of the approval mechanism is valuable. Firms which are highly sought after may be told that since Taiwan is a free-trading country it cannot offer sizeable tariffs or import bans; but that the government will ensure that the firm nevertheless gets an ample domestic market. What is being said, in effect, is that hidden protection via the approval mechanism will be given, while the outward appearance of little protection is maintained.
>
> (Wade 1990: 152)

In summary, Taiwan has, thus far, demonstrated how trade-related investment measures (known as TRIMS) and a dynamic adaptation to new forms of comparative advantage can be combined in a successful development strategy. This does not mean, of course, that the Taiwanese experience can or should be duplicated exactly in other nations. But it does point to the possibilities of constructive interaction with foreign capital, indicating that a cohesive cadre of state managers can, as Robert Wade points out, *govern* the market, rather than adapting to a strategy of merely following and being buffeted about by market signals, as they are transmitted through the impulse of foreign capital.

Sources: Grunwald and Flamm 1985: 230; Wade 1990

state, as we saw in Chapter 10, thereby permitting the state to channel resources first toward an easy ISI strategy and later to provide the incentives for a strategy switch toward export substitution. Reviewing the differing growth experiences of the Latin American nations and the East Asian economies, Stallings arrives at an incisive conclusion regarding the role of foreign capital in economic development.

[The] differing trends over time, toward a lesser need for foreign capital in East Asia and a greater ability to control it, add up to an objective set of reasons for East Asian specialists to be more positive than their Latin American counterparts about the role of foreign capital. The key to understanding the different experiences centers on the issue of host country autonomy, an issue that also links the two debates being considered. Regardless of its form – direct investment, private bank loans, or public sector credits – the purpose of foreign capital is to further the interests of those who provide it. Development of the host country is a fortuitous side effect at best, which will only come about if the host government maintains enough autonomy and control to guarantee that the benefits are shared between providers and recipients of foreign capital.

(Stallings 1990: 82)

Summary and conclusions

While FDI has expanded tremendously since the 1980s it is impossible to demonstrate one unique pattern between host developing nations and TNCs. Outcomes vary primarily in accordance with the strategies and tactics adopted by host nations. A passive strategy yields meager results, while nations that actively engage TNCs have demonstrated that dynamic policies to capture gains from FDI are possible. It would be impossible to offer a superior summary of the lessons that have been learned regarding FDI and development than that of the *World Investment Report*:

there is no ideal universal strategy on FDI. Any strategy has to suit the particular conditions of a country at a particular time, and evolve as its needs change and its competitive position in the world alters. ... Making effective strategy requires above all a development vision, coherence and coordination. It also requires the ability to decide on trade-offs between different objectives of development. In a typical structure of policy-making, this requires the strategy-making body to be placed near the head of government, so that a strategic view of national needs and priorities can be formed and enforced.

(UNCTAD 1999: 326)

Questions and exercises

1   Over the long period 1945–2007, global trade has generally grown much faster than the annual average rate of growth of global GDP. Proponents of an "export-led growth" strategy have argued that, with this growth of global trade, concerns over the "fallacy of composition" argument regarding trade as an engine of growth are exaggerated – that is, export growth has plenty of room for maneuver. Analyze this dispute, with particular reference to the possible duplications of the cases of Korea and Taiwan. What percentage of world exports is currently produced by less-developed countries? You can find this data at the UNCTAD website in the annual book of statistics.

2   Construct a chart listing the potential effects of inward direct foreign investment on developing nations. In one column, list the possible positive benefits of FDI; in a second column list the possible negative effects FDI can bring to a host nation. Some of these effects may be political, others economic, social, or environmental. Briefly explain each potential benefit and each potential cost.

3   You have been hired (at £500/day!) to advise on the establishment of an export processing zone in a Middle Eastern nation. Your task is to write a brief (500-word) outline entitled "Pitfalls to Avoid and Benefits to Capture in an EPZ."

4   A large TNC, heavily involved in subcontracting its production to various low-income nations, has become the target of an adverse publicity campaign which has centered on the low labor standards of its subcontractors. Your task is to compose a "Code of Conduct" which the TNC will impose on its subcontractors in the future. What rules would you include?

5   Summarize what is known about the potential for spillovers or technological transfers arising from FDI. Show that the degree of success a nation may have in this area with foreign investors is a function of national policies and capacities.

Notes

1   For example, more than any other factor, the political economy of oil has determined the modern economic history of the Middle East. At the epicenter of a vast and complex historical transformation, one finds the overwhelming influence of the huge oil-producing transnationals. John Blair's classic, *The Control of Oil*, continues to be the best introduction to the role of the oil industry in the Middle East, and to the nature of the largest single group of TNCs, the oil and chemical corporations (Blair 1978).

2   This shows, too, why international convergence of income, as discussed in Chapter 8, is perhaps not evident. Poorer countries are different from more developed nations; even among the less-developed nations themselves, there are differences. They do not have the same production functions, so the fact that they have less physical capital does not mean that the return to capital is higher, as the law of diminishing returns would suggest. Physical capital in the poorest countries is less effective, because the complementary inputs, like human capital, technology, government policies, and so on, that make such capital more productive are missing or but poorly formed.

3   Drawn to India by the market potential for fertilizers created by the Green Revolution, one pesticide manufacturer, Union Carbide, began production of chemicals and pesticides in Bhopal in 1970. In December 1984, Bhopal became an international symbol of environmental catastrophe when a pesticide product, methyl isocyanate (MIC), was released into the air in massive amounts. Safety conditions at the plant were totally inadequate, and 200,000 people in the city of 800,000 suffered from gas inhalation. Thousands died, and over 25,000 were treated by medical professionals. No one knows the long-term effects on the survivors, many of whom can no longer work (Gupta 1988: 55).

4   Wages in the EPZs tend to be one-tenth or less than average hourly wages in the advanced industrial nations for roughly similar work. Although productivity measured as output per hour is usually lower in the EPZs – often half that of the advanced nations and sometimes above 80 percent – the profitability of such production can be quite high.

References

Agosin, Manuel and Ricardo Machado. 2005. "Foreign Investment in Developing Countries: Does It Crowd-Out Domestic Investment?" *Oxford Development Studies* 33(2): 149–62.

Barry, Tom (ed.). 1992. *Mexico: A Country Guide*. Albuquerque, NM: The Inter-Hemispheric Education Resource Center.

Blair, John. 1978. *The Control of Oil*. New York: Vintage Books.

Belderbos, R. and G. Capannelli. 2001. "Backward Vertical Linkages of Foreign Manufacturing Affiliates," *World Development* 29 (January):189–208.

Carkovic, Maria and Ross Levine. 2005. "Does Foreign Direct Investment Accelerate Growth?," pp. 195–220 in Theodore Moran, Edward Graham, and Mangus Blomström (eds.), *Does Foreign Direct Investment Promote Development?* Washington, D.C.: Institute for International Economics.

Cavanagh, John and Frederick Clairmonte. 1982. *The Transnational Economy*. Washington, D.C.: The Institute for Policy Studies.

Caves, Richard. 1991. "The Multinational Enterprise as an Economic Organization," pp. 146–60 in Jeffrey Frieden and Anthony Lake (eds.), *International Political Economy*, 2nd edn. New York: St. Martin's Press.

Crow, Ben and Mary Thorpe *et al.* 1988. *Survival and Change in the Third World*. Oxford: Oxford University Press.

Cypher, James. 2001. "Developing Disarticulation within the Mexican Economy," *Latin American Perspectives* 28 (May): 11–37.

Delgado Wise, Raúl and James Cypher. 2007. "The Strategic Role of Mexican Labor under NAFTA: Critical Perspectives on Current Economic Integration," *Annals of the American Academy of Political and Social Science* 610 (March): 120–42.

Evans, Peter. 1998. "Transnational Corporations and Third World States: From the Old Internationalization to the New," pp. 195–224 in Ricard Kozul-Wright and Robert Rowthorn (eds.), *Transnational Corporations and the Global Economy*. London: Macmillan.

Gargan, Edward. 1996. "An Indonesian Asset is Also a Liability," *New York Times* (March 16): 17–18.

Gazcón, Felipe. 2002. "Para fusiones y adquisición de empresas, 71% de la IED," *El Financiero* (8 May): 15.

Gereffi, Gary, 1990. "Big Business and the State," pp. 90–109 in Gary Gereffi and Donald Wyman (eds.), *Manufacturing Miracles*. Princeton: Princeton University Press.

Gereffi, Gary and Peter Evans. 1981. "Transnational Corporations, Dependent Development, and State Policy in the Semiperiphery: A Comparison of Brazil and Mexico," *Latin American Research Review* 16: 31–64.

Ghose, Ajit. 2004. "Capital Inflows and Investment in Developing Countries," *Employment Strategy Papers* (November). Geneva: International Labour Organization. Online at http://www.ilo.org/public/english/employment/strat/download/esp.11.pdf

Grunwald, Joseph and Kenneth Flamm. 1985. *The Global Factory*. Washington, D.C.: The Brookings Institution.

Gupta, Avijit. 1988. *Ecology and Development in the Third World*. London: Routledge.

Hanson, Gordon. 2005. "Comment," pp. 175–8 in Theodore Moran, Edward Graham, and Mangus Blomström (eds.), *Does Foreign Direct Investment Promote Development?* Washington, D.C.: Institute for International Economics.

Hu, Albert and Gary Jefferson. 2002. "FDI Impact and Spillover: Evidence from China's Electronic and Textile Industries," *World Economy* 25 (August): 1063–76.

Humphrey, John. 1995. "Industrial Reorganization in Developing Countries," *World Development* 23 (January): 149–62.

ILO (International Labour Organization). 1998a. *Labor and Social Issues Relating to Export Processing Zones*. Geneva: International Labour Organization.

——. 1998b (Bureau of Multinational Enterprise Activities). "Export Processing Zones: Addressing the Social and Labor Issues," 1–31. Online at http://www.transnationale.org/pays/epz.htm

——. 1998c. "Export Processing Zones Growing Steadly," press release of ILO (September 28), 1–5. Online at www.ilo.org/public/english/bureau/Inf/pr/1998/34.htm

International Monetary Fund. 1988. *IFS Supplement on Trade Statistics*, no. 15.

Ivarrson, Inge and Clas Alvtam. 2005. "Technology Transfers to Local Suppliers in Developing Countries," *World Development* 33 (August): 1325–44.

Kennedy, Charles. 1992. "Relations between Transnational Corporations and Governments of Host Countries," *Transnational Corporations* 1 (February): 67–92.

Kopinak, Kathryn. 2003. "Maquiladora Industrialization of the Baja California Peninsula: The Coexistence of Thick and Thin Globalization," *International Journal of Urban and Regional Studies* (June): 319–36.

Lewis, Paul. 1996. "Cutting Back in West, Corporations Invest in 3rd World," *New York Times* (March 13): c4.

Maxfield, Sylvia and James Nolt. 1990. "Protectionism and the Internationalization of Capital," *International Studies Quarterly* 34: 49–81.

Nambir, Shankaran. 2001. "Knowledge, Technology Transfer and Multinational Corporations," pp. 136–53 in B.N. Ghosh (ed.), *Contemporary Issues in Development Economics*. London: Routledge.

Newfarmer, Richard and Claudio Frischtak (eds.). 1994. *Transnational Corporations, Market Structure and Performance*. London: Routledge.

Plasschaert, S. (ed.). 1994. *Transnational Corporations: Transfer Pricing and Taxation*. London: Routledge.

Razmi, Arslan and Robert Blecker. 2008. "Developing Country Exports of Manufactures," *Journal of Development Studies* 44: 21–48.

Russell, Philip. 1994. *Mexico under Salinas*. Austin, TX: Mexico Resource Center.

Scheeres, Julia. 1996. "Waste Repatriation to the US," *El Financiero International*, January 8–14: 5.

Shaiken, Harley. 1990. *Mexico in the Global Economy*. San Diego, CA: Center for US–Mexico Studies, University of California, San Diego.

Sklair, Leslie. 1989. *Assembling for Development*. Boston, MA: Unwin Hyman.

Stallings, Barbara. 1990. "The Role of Foreign Capital in Economic Development," pp. 55–89 in Gary Gereffi and Donald Wyman (eds.), *Manufacturing Miracles*. Princeton: Princeton University Press.

Tsai, Pan-Long. 1995. "Foreign Direct Investment and Income Inequality," *World Development* 23 (March): 469–84.

UN (United Nations Transnational Corporations and Management Division). 1992. *World Investment Report 1992*. Geneva: United Nations.

UNCTAD (United Nations Conference on Trade and Development). 1994. *World Investment Report 1994*. Geneva: United Nations.

——. 1999. *World Investment Report 1999*. Geneva: United Nations.

——. 2001. *World Investment Report 2001*. Geneva: United Nations.

——. 2002. *Trade and Development Report, 2002*. Geneva: United Nations.

——. 2006a. *Trade and Development Report, 2006*. Geneva: United Nations.

——. 2006b. *World Investment Report 2006*. Geneva: United Nations.

——. 2006–7. *Handbook of Statistics*. Geneva: United Nations.

Wade, Robert. 1990. *Governing the Market*. Princeton: Princeton University Press.

World Bank. 1992. *World Development Report 1992*. Oxford: Oxford University Press.

——. 1995. *World Development Report 1995*. Oxford: Oxford University Press.

15 Macroeconomic equilibrium

The external balance

After reading and studying this chapter, you should better understand:
- what the balance of payments is measuring and why it is so important to economic policy;
- the connections between internal macroeconomic disequilibriums and external macroeconomic disequilibriums;
- the components of the current and capital and financial accounts of the balance of payments;
- the importance of official foreign exchange reserves;
- what is meant by a "balance of payments problem";
- the difference between "good" and "bad" current account deficits;
- the importance of monitoring the balance of payments accounts so as to anticipate potential crises;
- bilateral exchange rates and currency appreciation and depreciation;
- how fixed, floating and managed-float exchange rate regimes function and the impact of changing economic conditions on each exchange rate regime;
- how exchange rates are affected by inflation;
- the interrelation between exchange rates and the balance of payments;
- the impact of over-valued and under-valued exchange rates on the balance of payments and economic progress.

Introduction

In an increasingly global economy, where barriers to trade and financial flows among nations have been lowered since the early 1970s, policy-makers must be ever vigilant in ensuring that their country's balance of payments and exchange rate evolve in ways that create the possibility of expanded and sustained economic growth and development. In modern economies linked by virtually instantaneous and twenty-four-hour flows among the world's financial markets in London, Paris, Frankfurt, Tokyo, Hong Kong, Seoul, Sydney, Mexico City, Buenos Aires, Toronto, and New York, disequilibrium situations that are not corrected can lead to severe crises over the longer term.

It is no exaggeration to suggest that in the current context of economic policy-making, it is the external equilibrium condition imposed by the balance of payments which is one of the most important values to be monitored by nearly every economy. If this constraint is not prudently respected, a balance of payments disequilibrium can thwart other positive steps policy-makers and society have taken on the road to becoming more developed. This is why an understanding of the workings of the balance of payments accounts is essential for coming to grips with the challenges facing many economies today.

This chapter considers the relation between a country's exchange rate, its balance of payments position, and the links between the macroeconomic *internal* balances, especially the rate of inflation, and these *external* balances. To understand how balance of payments difficulties may arise, it is necessary also to consider how exchange rates are determined under different possible exchange rate regimes – floating, fixed, and managed float – and the connection between a nation's exchange rate and its balance of payments position.

Let us begin by considering the balance of payments accounts.

The balance of payments

For most countries, disequilibrium in the balance of payments is often the ultimate binding constraint on policy-making. Good policy-makers learn to monitor their country's balance of payments accounts for signs of impending difficulties, and they take steps to modify their economic, social, fiscal, and monetary policies to correct problems before they erupt into full-blown crises. In effect, good policy-makers use the evolution of the balance of payments accounts as a *signaling device* for judging the effectiveness of their other interventions into the economy. The ability to adjust to disequilibrium situations in an agile fashion seems to have been one of the hallmarks of the success of the East Asian economies in a wide range of situations, and adjusting to balance of payments problems before they reach a crisis stage is another of those instances.

What, exactly, is the balance of payments all about?

Very simply, the *balance of payments* measures all the outflows and inflows of foreign currency across the national borders of a country in transactions with the rest of the world (ROW) over some period of time, usually a year, but often calculated quarterly or even monthly. Simplifying somewhat, the balance of payments measures what a country earns and "borrows" in foreign exchange terms from the ROW and what it spends in and "lends" to the ROW in foreign exchange. The balance of payments is focused on accounting for all these flows of *foreign exchange*, that is, foreign currency, that take place between one nation and the rest of the world.

Just as for individuals, families and firms, a nation's spending in the ROW will be exactly equal to what it earns from the ROW, plus any net borrowing (= borrowing − lending) that it does from the ROW. Nations thus ultimately can only import goods and services or travel or invest in other countries to the extent that other countries purchase their exports or travel or invest in their country. In the final analysis, spending in the ROW by any country is, over time, limited to the income earned from the ROW.

The balance of payments (B of P) is composed of three parts: the *current account balance*, the *capital and financial account balance*, and *net errors and omissions*. Because of double-entry accounting, the following statement is always true.

$$\text{B of P} = \text{current account balance} + \text{capital and financial account balance}$$
$$+ \text{ net errors and omissions} = 0 \qquad (15.1)$$

What this means is that all the inflows of foreign currency into a country are exactly matched by an equivalent outflow of foreign exchange from the economy. Always. The components of the balance of payments always sum to zero by definition.

What, then, can it possibly mean to say that a country has a balance of payments *problem* if there is always a zero balance no matter what policies a country may follow? Before answering that question, we shall quickly review the elements entering into the different parts of the balance of payments account, one-by-one.

The current account: foreign exchange earnings and spending

The *current account* of the balance of payments measures the outflows ("spending") and inflows ("income") of foreign exchange of a country *vis-à-vis* the rest of the world for current transactions, such as the purchase of cars or insurance, or contracting services, or payments on international loans. Throughout our discussion of the balance of payments, it will be helpful to keep in mind that all transactions creating *inflows* of foreign exchange to an economy will have a positive value. All transactions resulting in *outflow* of foreign exchange from an economy will be recorded with a negative value. What the balance of payments does is to sum all those transactions, some of which are positive values (inflows of foreign exchange) and some of which are recorded as negative values (outflows of foreign exchange).

Table 15.1 lists the major components of the current account.[1] In a rough-and-ready sense, the current account is simply a measure of an economy's spending and income balance with the ROW.

For most countries, the largest item in the current account is the *balance of trade*. The overall balance of trade measures the net trade of all goods and services of a country with the rest of the world (ROW); these are the sum of entries A to D shown in the last line of Section I of Table 15.1. Note that when these items are added, merchandise imports, item B, and service imports, item D, have a negative sign attached to their value, indicating that these items create an outflow of foreign exchange from an economy. Exports (items A and C) create an inflow of foreign exchange, so the value of those items have a positive sign attached to them, indicating there is an inflow of foreign currency generated by these transactions.

A *surplus in the balance of trade* means that the foreign exchange earned from all exports sold to the ROW exceeded the foreign exchange spent on imports from the ROW (trade surplus = + \$X − \$M > 0). When a country spends more foreign exchange on imports than it earns from its exports, the country will have a *deficit in the balance of trade* (= + \$X − \$M < 0). Again, the value of imports is given a negative sign, because imports result in an outflow of foreign currency from an economy.

It often is of some interest to disaggregate the balance of trade by separately determining the balance on *merchandise trade* and the balance on *service trade*. The balance on merchandise trade (A − B in Table 15.1) includes the export and import values of all real, tangible merchandise or goods, such as motor cars, oranges, rice, computers, computer programs, mattresses, golf clubs, wine, and so on.

The balance on service trade includes exports and imports of all services (C − D) that create flows of foreign exchange between countries, such as banking, insurance, advertising, film, television, video rentals, technology and product licensing, contracting and building services, and shipping plus all flows of foreign currency due to travel and tourism that takes place between a country and the ROW.[2]

Section II of the *current account* in Table 15.1 (items E and F) measures the income earned (a positive value) in foreign currency and the payments of foreign exchange (an

Table 15.1 The current account of the balance of payments

Item	Transactions creating an inflow of foreign exchange	Transactions creating an outflow of foreign exchange
	+	−
I Trade		
A Merchandise exports	X	
B Merchandise imports		X
Balance on merchandise trade = A − B		
C Service exports	X	
D Service imports		X
Balance on service trade = C − D		
Balance of trade = A − B + C − D		
II Factor income receipts and payments		
E Receipts from ROW of interest, profit and dividends, and employee compensation	X	
F Payments to ROW for interest, profit and dividends, and employee compensation		X
Balance of factor income = E − F		
III Current transfers		
G From ROW	X	
H To ROW		X
Balance of current transfers = G − H		
Balance on the current account = A − B + C − D + E − F + G − H		

outflow, hence a negative value) from flows of interest, profits and dividends, and employee compensation that are the result of loans and investments made in or by other countries. For example, borrowing by the Brazilian government from US and other foreign banks in the 1970s created an outflow of foreign currency on Brazil's current account as interest was paid to the United States and other lenders. At the same time, an identical transaction was recorded on the current account of the lending economies, albeit as a positive inflow of foreign exchange comparable to income earned from exporting a good or a service. It is just that these are flows of foreign exchange income and foreign exchange spending that result from prior investments and loans rather than from the current sale of goods or services.

In a similar way, countries which are hosts to foreign multinational firms or which have foreign investors involved in their domestic stock or bond markets are likely to experience an outflow of foreign exchange (an "expenditure," recorded as a negative value) on item F of the current account as foreign exchange payments flow to the foreign owners of those assets. These are income payments compensating for the *current value* of the services of past loans and investments. We shall see in Chapter 16 and Focus 16.2 that such movements of income payments can be quite important for some countries, especially those which incur large amounts of external debt.

Items G and H in Section III of the current account measure any *transfers* of foreign exchange that take place between nations. These are *unilateral* transactions, that is, one-way flows, of foreign exchange between economies. There is no corresponding equal and opposite flow of a good or service in the other direction, as is the case for all other items in the current account balance. For example, when Great Britain provides a package of aid worth £50 million to Kenya to build an electrical generating facility for the capital city of Nairobi, this would appear as a positive inflow of foreign exchange on Kenya's current transfers account and a negative entry of the same value on the UK's current transfers account.

Another example of a current unilateral transfer would be the remittances of income that Turkish immigrant workers earn in Germany or Mexican immigrants earn in the United States that are sent to family in their native countries. Such remittances create an outflow of foreign currency from the German and US economies that are recorded as negative values in the current transfer section of their current accounts while simultaneously creating a positive inflow of foreign exchange ("income") from the ROW for Turkey and Mexico in their current transfer balance.

Deficits and surpluses on the current account balance

The *current account balance* is equal to the sum of items A − B + C − D + E − F + G − H in Table 15.1.[3] Alternatively, we can equivalently say that the

> *Balance on the current account* = balance of trade + balance of factor incomes
> + balance of current transfers.

There is a *deficit on the current account* when the current account balance is less than zero, i.e. when "the balance of trade + balance of factor incomes + balance of current transfers < 0." In a very rough but reasonable sense, we can say that an economy with a current account deficit has spent more foreign exchange in the ROW than it has earned from the ROW. When there is a current account deficit, foreign exchange outflows to the ROW exceed foreign exchange inflows from the ROW.

How can a country spend more foreign exchange in the ROW than it has received from the ROW? Just as for a family or business, foreign currency expenditures of a country in the ROW can only exceed foreign exchange income from the ROW if the difference (a) is borrowed, (b) is financed out of past savings, or (c) is financed by selling off some assets or wealth. In other words, a country that runs a current account deficit can only do so by going into debt or reducing its existing international foreign exchange assets to be able to spend more than its current foreign exchange income. There are no other alternatives. We shall examine more what such borrowing means and what the implications are of such borrowing in the next section.

In a similar fashion, a current account surplus means a country has earned more foreign exchange from the ROW than it has spent in the ROW. A *surplus on the current account* occurs when the sum of A − B + C − D + E − F + G − H > 0, which means that the "trade balance + the balance of factor incomes + the balance of current transfers > 0."

A country with a current account surplus will find that it has accumulated foreign exchange savings (= foreign exchange income from the ROW not spent in the ROW), some of which may even be lent to other countries needing to finance current account deficits. Countries running a current account surplus will be accumulating international assets *vis-à-vis* the rest of the world (see Focus 15.1 on the evolution of the current accounts of various regions). They will have foreign exchange income earned from the ROW that was not spent on goods and services, transfers or factor services in the ROW.

FOCUS 15.1   EXPLORING CURRENT ACCOUNT BALANCES

While aggregation can hide what is happening to individual countries, it is still useful to consider the evolution of the balance of payments by region to see if there are any obvious tendencies. The top row for each region shows the current account balances for select years. The emboldened row shows net factor income payments (i.e., E–F from Table 15.1). All values are in billions of US dollars.

	1987	1990	1995	2000	2005
East Asian economies[a]	32.8	17.0	12.1	40.1	92.2
	–0.6	**4.1**	**6.0**	**4.1**	**14.9**
Africa	–4.4	–3.0	–17.3	6.5	6.5
	–14.2	**–17.3**	**–14.6**	**–23.4**	**–40.2**
Latin America and the Caribbean	–11.1	–2.0	–31.2	–47.8	3.8
	–31.9	**–38.4**	**–45.2**	**–53.0**	**–69.6**

Note
a Hong Kong, Singapore, South Korea and Taiwan.

Africa and Latin America incurred persistent current account deficits until very recently, while the four East Asian countries (Hong Kong, Singapore, Taiwan, and South Korea) have run current account surpluses for decades. One important contributing factor to current account deficits in Latin America and Africa has been interest payments on external debt (discussed more fully in Chapter 16).

The figures in bold type show the *net or balance of factor income* for each region, which include the sum of payments (an outflow of foreign exchange) and receipts (an inflow of foreign exchange) of *interest, profits*, and *dividends* (and small amounts for labor services). The largest component of income payments is for interest on *external debt* which was accumulated to finance past current account deficits. These factor income payments would be recorded as a negative value for item F in Table 15.1. For Africa and Latin America, this net outflow of income payments has been consistently negative and increasing.

For example, even though Africa had a positive *trade* surplus of $18.3 billion in 2000 (not shown in the table), much of this net inflow of foreign exchange earned from the ROW (plus net current transfers from the ROW of $11.6 billion, also not shown) was used to pay the $23.4 billion in net factor income payments to the ROW, resulting in an overall current account surplus of only $6.5 billion (= $18.3 billion trade balance –$23.4 billion balance of factor income + $11.6 billion current transfers balance). Most of the $29.9 billion positive inflow of foreign exchange due to trade and transfers ended up being used to pay for the negative outflow of foreign exchange required to repay the $23.4 billion in interest and profits on past debt obligations in the ROW.

The situation in Latin America and the Caribbean in 2005 was even more severe. Finally, the region was running a current account surplus (actually beginning in 2003). But how was it able to do so? Look at the $69.6 billion dollar outflow of foreign exchange needed to pay income to the ROW for interest on past external debt and for profits and dividends. This completely swamped the positive trade balance of $32.4 billion (not shown), and if it had not been for a positive inflow of foreign exchange equal to $41.0 billion from current transfers in 2005, the current account could easily have been in deficit. The current account balance was positive, but only because the sum of the trade surplus plus net current transfers (= $73.4 billion) generated an inflow of foreign exchange large enough to fund the outflow of $69.6 billion paid as net factor income to the ROW.

For some countries current account deficits which resulted in borrowing from abroad over a series of years can contribute to future current account deficits, requiring further borrowing or other financing. On the other hand, the East Asian economies have had positive net inflows of income payments (except for 1997 when there was a brief crisis), even though they too, especially Korea, incurred external debt obligations in the past. It is somewhat disturbing that economies like those in Latin America that are success-fully expanding their exports and actually are generating significant trade surpluses, as economists have been recommending that they do, are not able to benefit from their efforts. Instead, a significant proportion of net foreign exchange earnings from trade end up flowing to the already-developed nations as income payments on past debt.

The differences in the evolution of the current account balances and net income payments between Africa and Latin America and the Caribbean, on one side, and the East Asian economies on the other, highlight the importance of past decisions on structural transformation, industrialization, human capital accumulation, technology acquisition and a good policy environment for successful development. One does not have to go back too far in time to find the East Asian economies with persistently large current account deficits too. We will be considering what they did and what other economies might do to improve their balance of payments situation so that trade earnings are available for the purchase of exports and not just the servicing of debt.

Sources: IMF 1995: 159–60; 2002: 195–8; 2005: 237, Table 25, 240, Table 27, 243–4, Table 29

The capital and financial account: foreign exchange borrowing and lending

From statement 15.1 above, the second major component of the balance of payments is the capital and financial account. You will remember we said that in a very simplified sense we can think of the *current account* as a way to measure an economy's spending in and income from the ROW. It is useful to think of the capital and financial account in a similar simplified manner as measuring an economy's borrowing from and lending to the ROW.

Before we consider the details of the capital and financial account, let's consider the relation-ship between the current account and the capital and financial account using a simple numer-ical example. Assume a country's balance of payments accounts look like the following:

  I   current account balance = −$11.5 billion
 II   capital and financial account balance = + $8.5 billion
III   net errors and omissions = + $3.0 billion.

From statement 15.1, we know that the three parts of the balance of payments must sum to zero, as they do in this example. What does the current account balance of −$11.5 billion mean? If you said it means there is a current account deficit, good; but what does that mean? A current account deficit means that this economy spent more foreign exchange in the ROW than it earned from the ROW for all the types of transactions shown in Table 15.1. Outflows of foreign exchange exceeded inflows of foreign exchange, so that overall the current account had a negative value, indicating a net outflow of foreign currency from the economy to the ROW.

How can an economy spend more foreign exchange than it has earned? If you answered "borrow," you are right again. What must be borrowed, remember, is foreign exchange and that means borrowing foreign currency from another country, a foreign bank or some other entity which creates an inflow of foreign exchange into the economy. This borrowing of foreign exchange is what is being measured in the capital and financial account.

From this simple example, you can see that this economy "borrowed" more foreign exchange from the ROW than it "lent" to the ROW, since the sign of the capital and financial account balance is positive, indicating a net inflow of foreign exchange into the economy.[4] There also was a net inflow of foreign exchange into the economy from net errors and omissions (what this is all about will be explained below). The current account deficit of − $11.5 billion, which means this economy spent more foreign exchange than it earned, would not have been possible without the net positive inflows of foreign exchange from borrowing and errors and omissions that "financed" the excess of spending above income by generating a net inflow of foreign exchange equal to + $11.5 billion.

We thus often find that economies that run current account deficits and are spending more foreign exchange than they are earning will have positive capital and financial account balances that reflect the necessary "borrowing" to finance the current account deficit. Similarly, economies that have positive current account balances, meaning they are earning more foreign exchange than they are spending, typically may be expected to have negative capital and financial account balances which indicate that they are "lenders" of foreign exchange to the ROW (remember: "negative" here does not necessarily have a "bad" connotation; in the balance of payments it simply means an outflow of foreign exchange).

Table 15.2 summarizes the items included in the capital and financial account.

While the capital account is important, it is in the financial account that some of the most important long-term flows of assets across national borders are recorded, and it is on those items we will focus.

Table 15.2 The capital and financial account of the balance of payments

Item	Transactions creating an inflow of foreign exchange		Transactions creating an outflow of foreign exchange
	+		−
IV Capital account			
I Net capital transfers[a]	X	or	X
V Financial account			
J Loans from ROW	X		
K Loans to ROW			X
L Investments from ROW[b]	X		
M Investments in ROW[b]			X
N Sale of official foreign exchange reserve assets[c]	X		
O Purchase of official foreign exchange reserve assets[c]			X

Balance on the capital and financial account = I + J − K + L − M + N − O

Notes

a This includes debt forgiveness and other types of capital movements not included in the financial account. This item is not one we will focus on, and it is typically small for most economies.

b Investments include both foreign direct investment (FDI) and portfolio investment.

c These are purchases and sales by the central bank of foreign currencies, gold, and IMF special drawing rights (SDRs), a kind of international currency created by the International Monetary Fund and allocated to nations for use in settling transactions between countries.

Items J and K measure the inflows and outflows of foreign currency resulting from international loans. When one nation receives a foreign currency loan from another nation or when an individual, business or government acquires a loan from a bank or other financial intermediary or even another individual located in a foreign country, a positive inflow of foreign exchange is recorded on Item J of the financial account of the borrowing economy. For the lending country, there is an outflow (a negative value) on item K of the financial account identically equal to the amount of that lending. For example, when Japanese citizens buy US$1 billion of US Treasury bonds in the US bond market, Japan is making a loan to the United States that creates a foreign currency inflow (= + US$1 billion) to the United States and an equivalent outflow (= −US$1 billion) from Japan.

Similarly, items L and M measure investment transactions that create inflows or outflows of foreign currency as the result of financial investments or foreign direct investment (FDI) in productive facilities. An inflow of investment can be considered a type of loan as the inflow of foreign exchange contributes to total investment in the country, increases income and thus, potentially, permits an expansion of current consumption and investment. It also must be "paid" for in the sense that if profits are earned or dividends paid, there will be an outflow of foreign exchange from the borrowing economy. Thus when a country has a positive inflow on items J or L in the financial account, this inflow of foreign exchange due to borrowing will contribute to a future outflow of foreign currency in the "Factor incomes" portion of the **current account** as these loans and investments are repaid or earn profits and dividends.

If the sum of $J - K + L - M > 0$, this means that there is a *net inflow* of foreign currency from the ROW and that the country is a *net borrower* from the ROW. If the value of this part of the financial account is < 0, then this means that there is a *net outflow* of foreign currency to the ROW and that the country is a *net lender* to the ROW.

Official foreign exchange reserve assets

One especially important part of the capital and financial account is an economy's *use* of its total official foreign exchange reserve assets, items N and O. *Total official foreign exchange reserves* are holdings by the central bank of foreign currencies plus gold and SDRs.[5] It is useful to think of an economy's *total* official foreign exchange reserves as a form of "savings" in the form of foreign currencies.

Why does a country hold on to foreign currency reserves? These are retained to pay for needed imports or other foreign currency needs a country might have in periods when, for one reason or another, there is a short-fall of foreign exchange earnings. For example, export income might be hurt by a down-turn in prices or bad weather, making it difficult to pay for imported goods. Countries thus always desire to hold some quantity of foreign exchange reserves, often the equivalent of at least five to six months of import expenditures, as a cushion or buffer in case of unexpected events.

Official foreign currency reserves – which are held by the government and are not circulating in the economy, that is, they are *outside* the economy – can be used to finance foreign exchange outflows when the government makes these available to the economy by running down its total official reserves and injecting these into the economy's spending stream. Foreign exchange "savings" can be used along with any net borrowing from the ROW to pay for foreign exchange expenditures that exceed foreign exchange earnings on the current account, just as an individual's or a family's savings and borrowing can be used to pay for the purchase of things above and beyond what their current income would permit.

Item N in Table 15.2 records the sale of official foreign exchange reserves by the government from existing holdings of foreign currencies and/or gold and SDRs. Such sales create an *inflow* of foreign currency into the economy as some of the government's official foreign reserves are traded on the foreign exchange market. This means a country is injecting some of its own previously accumulated foreign exchange assets into the economy to be used to pay for imports or to finance some other expenditure that is not being met by current foreign exchange income or borrowing of foreign exchange.

The injection of foreign exchange into the economy from the government's reserves is recorded as a positive (+) value on item N in the capital and financial account, since it is an inflow of foreign exchange *into* the economy. Prior to that, this foreign exchange was *out*side of the economy in the sense that it was not available for spending, since it was held as "savings" as part of the government's official foreign exchange reserves. This positive inflow of foreign exchange reserves into the economy, however, means that the country's total official exchange reserves have *decreased*, since this inflow of foreign exchange came from the total foreign exchange savings of the central bank. This interpretation can often be a source of confusion, so re-read this paragraph carefully to be sure you understand. An inflow of foreign exchange that comes from official foreign exchange reserve assets is recorded as a positive value on item M, and it means that *total* official reserve assets have decreased by that amount since these reserves were drawn down to make this injection of foreign exchange into the economy.

Item O in Table 16.3 has the opposite interpretation to item N. When there is a purchase of official foreign exchange reserves, that is recorded with a negative (−) value in the capital and financial account. This means there has been an outflow of foreign exchange from the economy in the sense that it is leaving the economy's spending stream and is unavailable for use, but this foreign exchange is being added to the central bank's *total official foreign exchange reserves*. There thus will be an *increase* in total official foreign exchange reserve holdings of a country due to this transaction.

Countries via their central bank and the normal channels where foreign exchange deals are transacted are continually both selling from and adding to their foreign exchange reserves. What is most important is the change in the *net* position on official foreign exchange holdings over time, that is, the difference between the value of N and O. When $N - O > 0$ – meaning the sales of foreign exchange from official reserves exceed the purchases of foreign exchange added to official reserves – the country will suffer a net *decrease* in its *total* official foreign exchange assets. Perhaps this seems counterintuitive, but a net positive value for $N - O$ means that foreign exchange has entered the economy. And since this foreign exchange "entered" from the government's official foreign exchange reserves, this must mean that those reserves are smaller than they were before. A decrease in official foreign exchange reserves is equivalent to dissaving by the country and thus occurs when $N - O > 0$.

When $N - O < 0$, a country experiences a net *increase* in its total official foreign exchange reserves. A net negative value for the change in official foreign exchange reserves means that foreign exchange is leaving the economy, and in this case it is "leaving" to be added to the government's total official foreign exchange reserves. An increase in official foreign exchange reserves represents a form of national saving since it is foreign exchange that has been taken out of circulation of the local economy in the sense that it is not available for spending but rather has been added to total official foreign exchange reserves.

What happens to an economy's total official foreign exchange reserves is extremely important, and we shall see that changes in official reserves are a gauge of the "health" of the balance of payments, so be sure you understand this section!

Net errors and omissions

The third and last major component of the balance of payments is "net errors and omissions." This could just as easily be called the "statistical discrepancy," because the value of net errors and omissions is whatever it needs to be to make statement 15.1 sum to zero, that is, so that "the current account balance + capital and financial account balance + net errors and omissions = 0."

To illustrate using our simple example from the previous section, the net errors and omissions value of + $3.0 billion was determined as a residual. How? When the current account balance (− $11.5 billion) and the capital and financial account balance (+ $8.5 billion) were added together, the sum equaled −$3.0 billion. Since by definition 15.1 and the principles of double-entry bookkeeping we know that the inflow of foreign exchange must equal the outflow of foreign exchange and that the sum of the current account, the capital account and the net error and omissions must equal zero, then the value of net errors and omissions must be +$3.0 billion for that to be true. In this way, the balance of payments "balances" in the sense that inflows and outflows of foreign exchange are made equal and the sum of the components of the balance of payments is zero, as it must *always* be.

Nonetheless, net errors and omissions is an important component of the balance of payments accounts. It does "measure" some very important transactions. It is not just a "spillover" category. First, it is a measure of all those legal transactions that get missed in some way in the normal collection of statistics due to errors of bookkeeping, misreporting, human error, and a whole host of other possible reasons. With millions of individual transactions taking place between a country and the ROW every year, even the best designed accounting and reporting systems will not be completely accurate. So, first of all, the net errors and omissions portion of the balance of payments recognizes that there inevitably will be inaccuracies in the records that must be accounted for so that all inflows and outflows of foreign exchange are equal, as they must be.

Secondly, however, the net errors and omissions portion of the balance of payments is one way to capture a whole range of transactions between one country and the rest of the world, mostly if not always illegal, that no official statistics will ever be able to capture: the marketing of illegal drugs and narcotics, gun-running, money-laundering operations, and capital flight. For example, Pakistan has a thriving trade in opium and heroin, all of it illegal. This "trade" creates a substantial inflow of foreign exchange into the economy. This inflow of foreign currency is not recorded in the current account under exports, of course, since it is illegal.

So, how does this inflow of foreign exchange that is available to pay for imports, to make loans to other countries, to be used for foreign investments, and for other financing other outflow of foreign currency get accounted for? Since there are outflows of foreign currency that are taking place that do not have a corresponding and balancing inflow of foreign currency elsewhere in the balance of payments, those inflows are imputed to "net errors and omission." In fact, variations over time in the size of the net errors and omission portion of the balance of payment are one means by which governments and international agencies can track the illegal drug trade, illegal arms movements, and illegal flows of financial funds to and from economies. This part of the balance of payments is thus measuring something quite real but which is not counted directly in any of the other accounts of the balance of payments.

What does it mean to say that a country has a balance of payments problem?

Now that we have looked at the various components of the balance of payments, what does it mean to say a country has a balance of payments problem? If the sum of the current account balance + capital and financial account balance + net errors and omissions always sum to zero, how can we know if a country has a problem?

Let's think about this. If a country is running a current account deficit it means that the country will be obliged to *borrow* foreign exchange from the ROW or reduce its own official foreign exchange reserves to finance the excess of foreign exchange spending over foreign exchange income. Whether the borrowing takes the form of loans from foreign governments, banks, multinational corporations, individuals, or some other institution, the loan is denominated in a foreign currency and must be repaid in that same foreign currency in the future. If the borrowing takes the form of portfolio or direct foreign investment, there is still a foreign exchange obligation in the future to pay profits and dividends to the foreign investor.

If a country *cannot* borrow foreign exchange from the usual sources in the international market or its foreign exchange reserves become dangerously depleted, then the country will be unable to run a current account deficit. Why would a country be unable to borrow foreign exchange from the ROW? The inability to borrow would likely be due to concerns by international lenders that the country was accumulating "too much" foreign exchange debt and was becoming a greater risk for default. While it is not correct to claim that *every* current account deficit is a problem, any country with persistent and large current account deficits may be *signaling* to international lenders possible future problems and underlying weaknesses in the economy that continue to result in such deficits.

Once a country cannot borrow any more foreign exchange, the possibility of continuing to run current account deficits will be limited by the size of its official foreign exchange reserve assets, which are obviously finite. Official reserve assets cannot be a source of continued spending of foreign exchange above what is earned. In fact, *declining* official foreign exchange reserves over some period of time is a pretty good indication that an economy has a balance of payments problem, especially as those reserves drop below a couple of months of import spending.

Thus, when the possibility of borrowing and of using foreign exchange reserves to finance a current account deficit are both exhausted, a country will no longer be able to run a current account deficit, and this typically marks a full-blown balance of payments crisis. Costly adjustments to the economy will need to occur when borrowing options are exhausted and foreign exchange reserves are tapped out, as will be discussed in the last two chapters.

Current account deficits that persist over time, then, may be signals of future difficulties in the balance of payments *if* the borrowing burden becomes excessive. Rapidly declining official foreign exchange reserves, however, are a *sure* sign that there is a balance of payments crisis in the works or looming.

On the other hand, countries that manage to run current account surpluses are unlikely to have future balance of payments problems (though not every current account surplus is a good thing, as we shall see). So, even though the accounts in the balance of payments always sum to zero, the specific values in each account are important and why they are what they are remains important to examine if we are to grasp when there may be potential problems and when there are not. More will be said on this below in considering "good" and "bad" current account deficits. Hopefully, as you gain more experience in looking at the balance of payments accounts by doing the exercises at the end of the chapter, your understanding of some of these subtleties will be enhanced. Let us now turn to understanding exchange rates.

Exchange rates

A country's *bilateral exchange rate* is the number of units of a foreign currency that can be obtained for each unit of the domestic currency or, alternatively, the number of units of the domestic currency required to buy one unit of some foreign currency.[6] Table 15.3 shows the bilateral exchange rates for a number of different currencies with the US. The values shown are the number of units of each national currency received for one US dollar or, alternatively, the number of units of the national currency that must be paid to buy one US dollar. These values are exclusive of any exchange rate conversion charges.

The table tells us, for example, that 1 US dollar exchanged for 4,026 Cambodian rieles on February 4 2002 and 4,142.8 rieles on May 14 2007. Or, vice versa, the table tells us it took 4,026 rieles on February 4 2002 to buy 1 US dollar and 4,142.8 rieles to buy one US dollar on May 14 2007.

Each country has many bilateral exchange rates, one for each country with which it trades, has financial transactions, or to which its citizens travel or from which visitors arrive. The table lists only a few of the more than 160 bilateral exchange rates between various countries and the United States stated in terms of the number of units of currency exchanged for 1 US dollar. You also can calculate from the table the bilateral exchange rate for 1 unit of any of the currencies listed in terms of the number of units of a US dollar that would be received. For example, the exchange rate on May 14 2007 for 1 Mexican peso was US$0.09278 (= $1 ÷ 10.77804 pesos).

Currency appreciation and depreciation

Let's consider what happened to the value of Ghana's cedi between 2002 and 2007. From Table 15.3, the bilateral exchange rate in 2002 meant that to buy 1 US dollar, 7,797.9 cedis had to be paid. In 2007, the cost of buying 1 US dollar had risen to 9,594.2 cedis. What had

Table 15.3 Bilateral exchange rates, selected countries

	Units of foreign currency received for US$1, Feb. 4 2002	*Units of foreign currency received for US$1, May 14 2007*
Argentina (peso)	2.025	3.0844
Bangladesh (taka)	59.478	71.035
Brazil (real)	2.5029	2.0214
Cambodia (riel)	4,026.00	4,142.80
China (renminbi yuan)	8.2866	7.6866
Ethiopia (birr)	8.8109	9.2404
Ghana (cedi)	7,797.90	9,594.20
India (rupee)	48.41	41.29
Kenya (shilling)	79.05	67.4639
Malaysia (ringgit)	3.805	3.54356
Mexico (peso)	9.153	10.77804
Pakistan (rupee)	63.023	60.49
South Korea (won)	1,318.00	964.413

Source: http://www.oanda.com/convert/classic. Local currency names in parentheses.

happened to the value of the cedi? Had it gone up (*appreciated*) or had it gone down (*depreciated*) in value?

The correct response is that the cedi had *depreciated* between 2002 and 2007, as it took more cedis to buy 1 US dollar. Each cedi had less buying power in exchange for US dollars in 2007 than it had in 2002. At the same time, the US dollar had appreciated relative to the Ghanaian cedi, as 1 US dollar was able to purchase a larger quantity of cedis in 2007 than in 2002. Each dollar was worth more in terms of its buying power in purchasing cedis.

In Table 15.3, six of the thirteen currencies depreciated in value and seven appreciated in value relative to the US dollar. You should be able to correctly identify these. We will be using the idea of appreciation and depreciation of currencies throughout the remainder of the chapter. And we shall see that currency appreciation and depreciation have very direct effects on a country's balance of payments and the flows of foreign exchange between nations. But before we look at these connections, let's consider how exchange rate values are established.

Types of exchange rate regimes

Exchange rate values are determined in different ways in different countries. Exchange rates can be regulated solely by the free market and the forces of supply and demand, called a floating exchange rate, or determined by a government at a set value (or range of values) relative to other currencies, a fixed exchange rate, or the exchange rate value can be determined by an intermediate mix of government regulation and the forces of supply and demand in the market. The way in which exchange rate values are determined for a particular country is referred to as its *exchange rate regime*.

Freely floating exchange rates

If a country chooses to operate with a freely floating exchange rate regime, the nominal value of the exchange rate relative to other currencies will depend solely upon the demand for and the supply of the domestic currency on the foreign exchange market. This can be illustrated in Figure 15.1, which shows the market demand curve, $D_\$$, and the market supply curve, $S_\$$, for US dollars in Sri Lanka, assuming Sri Lanka has a freely floating exchange rate regime. The vertical axis tells us the "price" (the exchange rate) in terms of the number of Sri Lankan rupees that must be given up to buy 1 US dollar.

Who demands US dollars in this foreign exchange market? In other words, who might wish to exchange their Sri Lankan rupees so as to be able to buy US dollars?[7]

1   Importers of goods into Sri Lanka who need to pay their suppliers in dollars.
2   Sri Lankans or others holding rupees who wish to invest in the US stock or bond markets, to make deposits in US banks, or to otherwise invest in the US or any location in the world where US dollars might be accepted.
3   Sri Lankans or others holding rupees travelling abroad who will need US dollars for their expenses.
4   Anyone currently holding Sri Lankan rupees who wishes, for whatever reason, to hold dollars rather than rupees, e.g., for speculation reasons.

As for most demand curves, it is reasonable to presume that as the price of dollars decreases then the quantity demanded of dollars will rise. Why? When it requires fewer rupees to buy

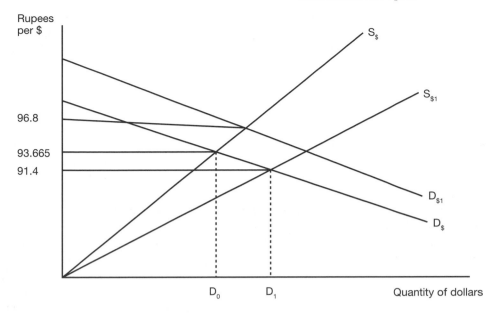

Figure 15.1 Exchange rate determination: floating rates.

each dollar, buying a dollar is easier and cheaper. This means that travel to US for those holding rupees will then be cheaper, goods imported from the US will cost less in terms of rupees given up, and so on, and it is reasonable to presume that more dollars will be desired. Thus the demand curve for dollars, $D_\$$, is drawn sloping downward to the right.

What determines the supply of dollars entering the foreign exchange market to buy Sri Lankan rupees? It is more or less the obverse of the factors influencing the demand for dollars.

1   The desire of importers in, say, the United States holding dollars who need rupees to pay for goods bought from Sri Lankan producers.
2   US citizens (or anyone with US dollars) wishing to travel in Sri Lanka who need to exchange dollars for rupees for spending while in the country.
3   Investors in the United States, or anyone holding dollars, wishing to make a deposit in a Sri Lankan bank or to otherwise invest in the economy who needs rupees to do so and who thus supply their dollars to the foreign exchange market in exchange for rupees.

As for other normally shaped supply curves, it seems reasonable to presume that as the number of rupees that can be obtained for each dollar given up increases, the quantity supplied of dollars will be larger. Thus the supply curve for exchanging rupees for US dollars, $S_\$$, is drawn with an upward slope.

Equilibrium with a freely floating exchange rate

The equilibrium exchange rate between the United States dollar and the rupee when there is a freely floating, or independently floating, rate is determined by the intersection of the demand and supply curves, $D_\$$ and $S_\$$. To buy ("demand") one dollar the price paid at equilibrium is 93.665 rupees. Alternatively, selling ("supplying") one dollar resulted in the receipt of 93.665 rupees in exchange.[8]

This is the equilibrium exchange rate toward which the foreign exchange market will tend if there are no barriers to such adjustments given the demand curve, $D_\$$, and the supply curve, $S_\$$. The equilibrium price of 93.665 Sri Lankan rupees for one US dollar will prevail as long as the demand and supply curves remain constant. What happens, however, if one or the other, or both, of the curves change?

An increase in the supply of dollars, shown by $S_{\$1}$, results when those holding dollars wish to trade more of them for rupees at all possible exchange rates. This might happen because those living in the US wish to purchase more Sri Lankan goods as their incomes rise or because investment opportunities have improved in Sri Lanka. Or a tourism push by the Sri Lankan government could make the country seem trendy and attract more visitors from the US who wish to exchange additional dollars for rupees to pay for their hotels, meals, and other expenditures. Whatever the reason, the shift to the right of the supply curve of dollars means that there are more dollars entering the Sri Lankan foreign exchange market in search of rupees than before at all possible exchange rates.

The shift in the supply of dollars will, with freely floating exchange rates, result in a new equilibrium value of the exchange rate at the intersection of the demand curve, $D_\$$, and the new supply curve, $S_{\$1}$. With the increased supply of dollars and the demand for dollars unchanged, the exchange rate value of the dollar will *depreciate* as the number of rupees that can be obtained in exchange for US\$1 declines from 93.665 to 91.4 rupees. Thus, someone trading 100 dollars after the increase in the supply would receive only 9,140 rupees compared to 9,366.5 before the shift in supply. The same quantity of US dollars, 100, is worth less than previously in terms of the number of rupees that can be bought. In this case, the value of the dollar has fallen or depreciated, because the supply of dollars increased given a constant demand.

At the same time that the US dollar's value depreciated, the value of the Sri Lankan rupee of course must have *appreciated*. Each rupee now is worth *more* than before the shift in the supply of dollars. This is because it now takes fewer rupees to purchase one US dollar: 91.4 versus 93.665 before the increase in the supply of dollars. With a higher-valued rupee, the rupee cost of purchasing anything priced in dollars will now be less in terms of the number of rupees that must be given up, even when the dollar price of what might be purchased remains unchanged. Each rupee is worth more than before in terms of its US dollar buying power.

For example, a T-shirt from the US costing US\$5 or a music download from the internet costing US\$5 will require the sacrifice of only 457 rupees after the increase in supply of US dollars compared to 468.325 rupees at the original equilibrium exchange rate, a decrease in the rupee price of 2.4 percent.

Thus, when the rupee appreciates in value relative to the dollar, it encourages Sri Lankans to import more US goods and services, to travel more to the US, and to increase their investments in the United States, because the price of those things, valued in rupees, will be lower. A higher valued rupee encourages an outflow of foreign exchange from Sri Lanka. This means that the items in Tables 15.1 and 15.2 that register an outflow of foreign exchange in the current account and in the capital and financial account will tend to increase in Sri Lanka as the value of the rupee rises relative to the US dollar, while those that register an inflow will tend to be reduced.

Herein lies an important connection between the balance of payments and a country's exchange rate. When the value of the bilateral exchange rate changes, it has an impact on inflows and outflows of foreign exchange as spending decisions are affected in the current account and in the capital and financial account.

Let's return to our original equilibrium of $D_\$$ and $S_\$$ where the exchange rate was 93.665

rupees for one US dollar and consider a different scenario. Now let the demand for dollars in the Sri Lankan foreign exchange market rise (what factors might cause such an increase in demand?) from $D_\$$ to $D_{\$1}$ with $S_\$$ now remaining the same. The dollar would now *appreciate* in value from 93.665 rupees per dollar to 96.8 rupees per dollar, as more rupees could be obtained in exchange for each dollar in the foreign exchange market. Of course, the other side of this appreciation in the value of the dollar is the *depreciation* in the value of the Sri Lankan rupee, as it now takes more rupees to buy each dollar at the new higher equilibrium value.

This depreciation in the value of the rupee will have the effect of:

a discouraging imports from the United States to Sri Lanka, or any import priced in US dollars, since these will now require more rupees in exchange for any given dollar price;

b encouraging the purchase of Sri Lankan exports by those who pay in US dollars since it now is easier to obtain rupees than before;

c decreasing travel from Sri Lanka to the United States and encouraging travel in the reverse direction; and

d discouraging Sri Lankans from converting rupees to dollars for investments outside the country, while encouraging those with dollar holdings to bring dollars to Sri Lanka where more rupees can be obtained in exchange for any desired investment purpose.

In other words, depreciation in the value of the rupee will tend to encourage an inflow of foreign exchange from the rest of the world into the Sri Lankan economy and discourage foreign exchange expenditures from Sri Lanka flowing to the ROW. On both the current account and the capital and financial account of the balance of payments, the depreciation of the rupee will tend to increase the values of the positive entries and decrease the values of the negative entries so that, overall, there is a net effect of encouraging the inflow of foreign exchange.

Fully floating exchange rates are strictly market-determined rates. For an economy with this type of foreign exchange regime, the movements of supply and demand for that country's currency relative to other currencies determine the "value" of the bilateral exchange rate. A floating exchange rate is one extreme on the exchange rate regime continuum. It represents a policy of complete *laissez-faire* with respect to the exchange rate value.

Fixed exchange rates

At the other end of the spectrum from a fully floating exchange rate regime is a *fixed or pegged exchange rate* regime. Until the early 1970s, most countries operated with fixed exchange rates set in cooperation with the International Monetary Fund (IMF) as part of the Bretton Woods institutional arrangements for international trade and finances established at the end of the Second World War (see Chapter 17 for a fuller discussion of these matters). Following a series of crises, first in the United States and then with the oil price hikes of 1973, many countries elected to adopt floating or some intermediate exchange rate regime, leaving the fixed exchange rate era behind.

Many less-developed nations continue, however, to operate with fixed, or quasi-fixed, exchange rate systems, so they are not fully a remnant of the past. Typically, the exchange rate is fixed relative to the currency of the largest trade partner(s), often a former colonial power, so as to facilitate trade flows. How do fixed exchange rates work, and what is their impact?

When exchange rates are fixed, the adjustment to a new equilibrium exchange rate value shown in Figure 15.1 *cannot* take place, since the exchange rate value is locked in at some pre-determined level. Let us assume that the exchange rate of the Sri Lankan rupee is set by the government at 93.665 rupees per dollar, as shown in Figure 15.2, a value which coincides with the current equilibrium at the intersection of the demand and supply curves.

What happens when the demand or supply (or both) of dollars changes, or if the current nominal exchange rate does not, by chance, correspond with the intersection of the supply and demand curves?

For example, if the demand for dollars increases to D_{S1} and the supply curve of dollars remains unchanged at S_S, there will be an unmet demand for dollars in the Sri Lankan foreign exchange market. This is because the quantity of dollars brought to market at the fixed price of 93.665 rupees by those wishing to trade dollars for rupees, Q_S, is less than the quantity of dollars demanded, Q_D, by those who wish to exchange their rupees for dollars at the prevailing fixed exchange rate. As a result, dollars are "cheaper" to buy than they should be, and rupees are more "expensive" than they should be compared to what the market equilibrium value would be at the intersection of the two curves. As a result, not enough dollars are being made available by those exchanging dollars to meet the demand for dollars of those wishing to sell rupees in the Sri Lankan foreign currency market. A shortage of dollars equal to $Q_S - Q_D$ and a simultaneous surplus of rupees at the current fixed exchange rate is the result.

What happens to the excess supply of rupees? Where does it go? Alternatively, how is the problem of the shortage of dollars handled?

The shortage of dollars can be fully met and the surplus of rupees absorbed only if the Sri Lankan government *sells* some of its US dollar *official foreign exchange reserves* equal to the $Q_D - Q_S$ gap. Those foreign exchange reserves, accumulated in the past by exporting more than importing or as a result of other net dollar flows into Sri Lanka, are a part of the Sri Lankan government's official foreign exchange reserve savings. When, as in Figure 15.2,

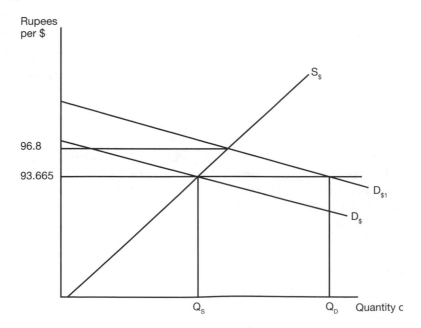

Figure 15.2 Exchange rate determination: fixed rates.

the quantity demanded of dollars exceeds the quantity supplied at the fixed exchange rate, the Sri Lankan government *must*, if the exchange rate is to remain fixed, buy the excess supply of rupees, and it can do so only by selling off some of its official foreign exchange reserves of US dollars.

If insufficient dollars are held as official foreign exchange reserves by the Sri Lankan government to trade for the excess supply of rupees that Sri Lankans wish to exchange for dollars, or if the Sri Lankan government refuses to supply the quantity needed to cover the shortage for whatever reason, dollars somehow will have to be *rationed* to those wishing to exchange rupees for the limited supply, Q_S, of dollars being made available on the market at the fixed price.

For example, requiring *import licenses* as a prerequisite for obtaining dollars is one way to allocate the limited supply of dollars relative to the larger quantity demanded at the fixed exchange rate value. Limits on the quantity of rupees that can be exchanged per transaction is another way to restrict the quantity demanded so that it is closer to the quantity supplied on the market. These are all examples of *administrative means* devised to ration a limited quantity of dollars among those demanding them.

Other administrative mechanisms for allocating the limited supply of dollars in the foreign exchange market might include giving precedence in exchanging rupees for dollars to those importing essential goods from the United States, followed by: importers of non-essential goods getting secondary priority for buying foreign exchange; Sri Lankans travelling on business to the United States; and then regular tourists to the United States. Speculators interested in transferring some of their financial assets to the United States might be last in the queue for exchanging rupees for dollars. The government could utilize such a priority ranking to determine how to allocate the dollars traded on the Sri Lankan foreign exchange market and thus avoid having to dip so deeply into its official US dollar reserve holdings.

There is a risk in using such administrative means to control the exchange of currencies. Some who hold Sri Lankan rupees and wish to exchange them for dollars, but who find themselves unable to do so under the administrative rules, will look for alternative avenues to obtain the dollars they want. Likewise, those who have been able to buy dollars may find it profitable to re-sell them. Illegal and quasi-legal foreign exchange markets, so-called "black or gray or parallel markets," are likely to emerge. The greater the discrepancy between the fixed exchange rate value and its equilibrium value, the more likely that such markets will materialize and the greater will be the quantity of transactions taking place in these secondary markets (see Focus 15.2 on these secondary markets).

If the government does not use administrative means to limit the quantity demanded of dollars to the limited quantity supplied, the ability of the Sri Lankan government to maintain the fixed exchange rate of 93.665 rupees per dollar will be determined by the quantity of total official foreign exchange reserves and the willingness of the government to continue to support the fixed exchange rate out of these reserves. As foreign exchange reserves approach or are reduced below some acceptable level, the Sri Lankan government will be forced to *devalue* the rupee (i.e. to *increase* the number of rupees required to buy each dollar) to a new value closer to the equilibrium value where $D_{\$1}$ intersects with $S_\$$, thus eliminating or reducing the dollar shortage problem.[9]

For example, if the rupee is devalued to the equilibrium value of 96.8 rupees per dollar shown in Figure 15.2 at the intersection of the supply and demand curves, then the dollar shortage disappears as the quantity supplied of dollars (which is also the new quantity demanded of rupees) exactly matches the quantity of dollars demanded (which is also the supply of rupees).[10]

FOCUS 15.2   PARALLEL MARKETS

One way to gauge the misalignment of exchange rates relative to the equilibrium value is by examining the *parallel market* exchange rate. The parallel market includes an estimate of non-sanctioned or "black" market exchange rate values and exchange rates prevailing in non-official "gray," but legal, markets. In the following table, the values shown are the parallel market exchange rate premium, which is the percentage difference between the parallel market rate and the official exchange rate.

	1981–1986	*1990–1991*
Sub-Saharan Africa		
Gambia	13.8	21.3
Kenya	15.1	7.3
Mozambique	2,110.8	62.6
Nigeria	232.7	25.1
Tanzania	248.8	74.5
Zambia	46.3	149.7
Zimbabwe	81.3	23.5
Others		
Argentina	32.8	42.4
Bolivia	136.2	1.5
Indonesia	4.2	2.6
Mexico	13.9	6.8
Philippines	12.3	7.1
Thailand	–2.2	2.0
Venezuela	110.3	5.2

A positive percentage exchange rate premium indicates by how much the parallel market rate exceeded the official exchange rate and is an approximate measure of the extent of *overvaluation* of the official exchange rate. Over the period 1981–6, for example, Nigeria's official exchange rate was over-valued by more than 200 percent. In general, economies in Sub-Saharan Africa had somewhat higher levels of exchange rate overvaluation than countries in other less-developed regions. Note Thailand's *under-valued* exchange rate in the first period and the mild overvaluation in the later period.

With the exception of Gambia and Argentina, there was a tendency to reduce the degree of overvaluation of official exchange rates between the two periods. This has meant *depreciations and devaluations* of official rates closer to their equilibrium values, with all the effects on the balance of payments that such changes engender. *(What are those effects?)*

You will remember that an over-valued exchange rate makes exports of a country more expensive than they should be and imports less expensive. While maintaining over-valued exchange rates is not *a priori* bad policy, as discussed, extreme overvaluation can lead to stagnant, over-protected domestic production and a weak export sector that encourages outflows of foreign exchange and discourages inflows. That is the worst of all possible worlds.

In examining Sub-Saharan Africa, the World Bank found that for those countries that had depreciations of their real exchange rate of 40 percent or more, growth rates of per capita income averaged 2.9 percent. For countries with smaller depreciations, per capita growth rates averaged –0.4 percent. And for those countries where real exchange rates become more over-valued, per capita growth rates averaged –2.7 percent.

Large exchange rate overvaluation impacts negatively on the competitiveness of an economy and can dramatically slow economic growth. Exchange rate overvaluation is not, however, the only factor which can impede growth and adversely affect competitiveness, though it is important.

For example, in a detailed study of Mexico, UNCTAD found that from 1990 to 1994, the real exchange rate became severely over-valued by more than 50 percent. Not surprisingly, Mexico's international competitiveness in manufacturing decreased, with the index of competitiveness rising from 136.5 in 1990 to 197.4 in 1993. (The index measures the unit labor cost of production in constant US dollars. An increase in the index indicates a decrease in competitiveness.) At the same time as the exchange rate was becoming over-valued, real wage increases outstripped increases in labor productivity by nearly four times (+70 percent versus +18 percent).

Overvaluation of the exchange rate thus was not the only factor affecting Mexico's decreased international competitiveness. Internal structures and slow productivity growth relative to income growth contributed as well. The latter effects may reflect the inadequacy of Mexico's past human capital accumulation efforts and weak technological acquisition skills. Further, the failure of Mexico to pursue export substitution policies until very recently in the climb up the structural transformation ladder, and the premature initiation of capital-intensive, higher wage difficult import substitution contributed to the inability of Mexico to sustain economic growth and development, as was discussed in detail in Chapter 10.

Sources: UNCTAD 1995: 85; World Bank 1994: 228, 242

A managed float exchange rate regime

Somewhere between freely floating exchange rates and fixed exchange rates lies the *managed float*. With a managed float exchange rate regime, a government allows changes in the supply of and demand for its currency to have an effect on the spot market exchange rate value, but it may intervene to prevent full and complete adjustment of the exchange rate toward its equilibrium value to prevent abrupt changes in values or to maintain the value of the exchange rate within a "band" of values.

For example, in Figure 15.2, if Sri Lanka had a managed float exchange rate regime, then the shift in the demand for dollars to D_{S1} might result in a change in the exchange rate from the initial value of 93.665 rupees per dollar to an intermediate value of, say, 94.5 rupees per dollar between the initial value and that of the full adjustment to the market equilibrium value of 96.8 rupees. The rupee will have depreciated in value – it now takes more rupees than before to buy one dollar – but the depreciation is not as large as it would have been if the full adjustment to the equilibrium had taken place, as it would if exchange rates were freely floating. This reduces, but does not fully eliminate, the shortage of the quantity supplied of dollars in the foreign exchange market compared to what would prevail with a fixed exchange rate. At any exchange rate below 96.8 rupees per dollar, the Q_D will still be greater than the Q_S.

There thus remains a shortage of dollars supplied to the Sri Lankan foreign exchange market relative to the demand that will need to be filled through the depletion of official US dollar foreign exchange rate reserves or some queuing system. A managed float can reduce but does not necessarily eliminate the need for the Sri Lankan government to supply dollars from its official foreign exchange reserves or to impose rationing measures to sustain the exchange rate at a value below equilibrium.

With a managed float, a country exercises some degree of control over its exchange rate, not letting it simply be buffeted about by market forces as happens with a freely floating exchange rate. This is often done to foster greater stability in the value of the exchange rate over time so as to permit those involved in international trade and investment to project with less uncertainty the future value of the currency.

Other exchange rate regime types

Other possible exchange rate regimes are a *crawling peg* and a *band* exchange rate. With a crawling peg, which is a more transparent type of managed float, the government fixes, or "pegs," the currency's value *vis-à-vis* one or more foreign currencies, typically of the country's major trading partner(s). The pegged value is announced and is regularly adjusted toward its equilibrium value, which is the "crawl," but the value is fixed for some period of time. As we shall see in the next section, the crawling peg may help to keep the *real* value of a country's currency from becoming too over-valued, if the "crawl" downward of the pegged value is of the proper amount and is done in a timely manner.

A "band" exchange system is a kind of modified float/modified peg. The value of the currency is allowed to fluctuate freely according to market forces of supply and demand, but only *within* an agreed upon range of upper and lower values *vis-à-vis* another currency or currencies. The government commits to maintaining the value of the currency within that band, so there may be times when it will be necessary either to sell off official foreign exchange reserves or to accumulate such reserves to preserve the currency's value within the predetermined range.

Few governments have perfectly freely floating exchange rates at all times. Most economies with floating exchange rate regimes are not so committed to that policy as to forgo some form of a managed float policy depending on the circumstances. In today's electronically integrated world economy, where twenty-four-hour trading in currencies is not only possible but a reality, few countries are willing to let possible temporary disturbances in the foreign exchange markets completely dictate spot exchange rates because of the potentially adverse affects this can have on trade and financial flows and domestic income and production. Thus virtually all countries, developed and less-developed alike, are willing to utilize a managed float system to avoid wide and unproductive swings in the value of their exchange rates when it is necessary. Of course, the ability of a country to "defend" its exchange rate depends upon having sufficient reserves of foreign exchange to do so.

Real versus nominal exchange rates

The *nominal exchange rate* is the current value of a currency as stated on the foreign exchange market. In other words, it is the exchange rate that a government controls when it has a fixed or managed exchange rate, or it is the equilibrium value determined by the intersection of the supply and demand curves when exchange rates are freely floating.

What, then, is the *real exchange rate*? How and why would the nominal and real value of an exchange rate differ? You will remember from Chapter 2 when we compared nominal and real GDP that it was changes in prices that make nominal and real GDP values differ. The same is true for nominal and real exchange rates, but now it is the difference in changes in prices *between* economies that matters, that is difference in inflation rates between economies.

What happens to the real exchange rate, as opposed to the nominal exchange rate, for pesos versus dollars if there is a difference in inflation rates between the United States and Mexico?

The real exchange rate will be affected unless there is a freely floating exchange rate regime. For example, suppose that during the course of 2008, prices in Mexico rose by 10 percent while prices in the United States remained constant. If Mexico had a *fixed* exchange rate regime so that 10 pesos traded for US$1 throughout the year (this is the *nominal* rate), at the end of December 2008 the *real* exchange rate of the peso would be 9.091 pesos per dollar [(10 pesos/US$1) × (100/110)]. In other words, with a constant nominal exchange rate, the higher rate of inflation in Mexico meant that the *real value* of the peso appreciated. It was easier, in real terms, to buy US dollars with pesos at the end of the year than it was at the beginning of the year because of the inflation differential.

Even though the nominal exchange rate remained constant at 10 pesos for US$1, the higher rate of inflation in Mexico versus the US meant that the purchasing power of each peso *increased* in terms of its buying power of goods from the US. Of course, the appreciation in the real value of the peso meant that at the same time the real value of the US dollar fell, as the purchasing power of each US dollar in the Mexican economy fell.

For the exchange rate to have maintained its real value with inflation in Mexico 10 percent higher than in the United States over the year, the *nominal* bilateral rate should have risen by the end of the year to 11 pesos for US$1 (how was this determined? 10 pesos/US$1 = ? × (100/110)). The intuition behind this calculation is as follows. Since prices in Mexico rose by 10 percent while prices in the United States remained unchanged, the nominal exchange rate value would have to fall by 10 percent to maintain the real rate. If the real exchange rate value between the dollar and the peso is to be maintained, Mexicans should need to give up 10 percent more pesos to buy one dollar after the inflation as before. What is 10 percent of 10 pesos? It is 1 more peso, or a total of 11 pesos, that should be required to buy each dollar if the real value of the exchange rate is to be maintained.

Equivalently, holders of dollars should receive 10 percent more pesos per dollar after the inflation so that the same number of dollars can buy the same quantity of Mexican goods after the inflationary episode when prices are 10 percent higher. To pay for higher priced Mexican goods after 10 percent inflation, more pesos per dollar must be received in exchange. Again, the required nominal bilateral exchange rate needed to maintain a constant real exchange rate would be 11 pesos for US$1.

Consider the following example that may make this clearer. Assume that a US importer was buying handkerchiefs from a Mexican company and that the price of each handkerchief was 10 pesos on 1 January 2008. The US importer would have needed to exchange US$1 for each handkerchief imported to obtain the 10 pesos needed to pay the Mexican exporter at the 10 pesos for US$1 exchange rate. After the inflationary episode, and assuming that the price of handkerchiefs increased at the 10 percent rate of inflation, the Mexican exporter's price per unit would have risen to 11 pesos per handkerchief (10 pesos × 1.1). To maintain the real value of the exchange rate, the United States importer would now need to receive 11 pesos for each dollar exchanged. At this rate, US$1 continues to be able to buy one handkerchief just as before the inflation.

If the nominal exchange rate had remained at 10 pesos to US$1, each handkerchief would have required the United States importer to pay $1.10 to obtain the 11 pesos needed to pay for each handkerchief, an increase in the dollar price even though there had been no inflation episode in the US. The adjustment in the nominal value of the peso versus the dollar is necessary to maintain the real value of the two currencies in exchange for one another. If this adjustment does not happen, countries with high inflation rates relative to their trading partners will find it easier to spend and invest in the rest of the world, leading to an increased outflow of foreign exchange from those economies. Likewise, the inflow of foreign exchange to the higher inflation countries will be adversely affected as it will be increasingly more expensive for the rest of the world to spend and invest in those economies.

Changes in the real exchange rate value can have profound effects on a country's balance of payments as currencies become over- or under-valued.

Real exchange rates, over- and undervaluation and the balance of payments

If exchange rates are freely floating, the market will tend to automatically adjust to maintain the real exchange rate value of currencies so that any inflationary differentials between countries will be compensated for by movements of the nominal bilateral exchange rate in the proper direction.[11]

On the other hand, if a country has a *fixed* exchange rate and its domestic rate of inflation exceeds that of its trading partners, its real exchange rate relative to those of its trading partners will tend to appreciate. This means that the currency is becoming *over-valued*, that is, it is worth more than it *should be* at its equilibrium value. Looking back at Figure 15.2, if it only takes 93.665 rupees to buy one US dollar instead of the equilibrium value of 96.8 rupees, it is easier to buy US dollars than it should be at equilibrium. The rupee is worth more than it should be; we would say it is over-valued. An over-valued exchange rate tends to stimulate spending outside the country and encourages the outflow of foreign exchange at the same time that it deters spending from the rest of the world in the higher inflation economy and discourages the inflow of foreign exchange.

An over-valued exchange rate means it will be easier for Sri Lankans to import goods from the US and cheaper for them to travel in the US than it would be at the equilibrium exchange rate value. What does that mean for the balance of payments? There will be more spending in the US and a larger outflow of dollars on the current account of the balance of payments. Investments in the US also will be easier, so that will encourage an outflow of foreign exchange on the capital and financial account.

At the same time, Sri Lankan exports will be more expensive to buy for those in the US and travel to Sri Lanka will be more expensive than it "should be." This will reduce the inflow of foreign exchange on the current account of the balance of payments. Foreign investment in Sri Lanka will be more expensive, too, and that will reduce the inflow of foreign exchange on the capital and financial account.

The net effect of an over-valued exchange rate, then, is to encourage outflows of foreign exchange and discourage inflows, thus tending to push the current account and capital and financial account balances toward deficit or making them more negative if they already were in deficit. You will remember from our discussion earlier that the only way a current account deficit can be financed is either by borrowing foreign exchange from the rest of the world or through the drawing down of the country's own official foreign exchange reserve assets. When the exchange rate is over-valued, spending is encouraged and borrowing discouraged, so there is a tendency to increase the outflow of foreign exchange relative to the inflow overall in the balance of payments accounts. This puts more pressure, then, on the official foreign exchange reserves to make up any shortfall in foreign exchange.

Contrariwise, if a country has a fixed exchange rate and an inflation rate that is *lower than* its trading partners, the real exchange rate will *depreciate* and the domestic currency will be *under-valued*, i.e., it will be worth less than it should be at its equilibrium value. An under-valued exchange rate discourages the outflow of foreign exchange and encourages the inflow of foreign exchange. You should be able to think this through and realize that this can be very good for a country's balance of payments, since the tendency of an under-valued exchange rate is to promote a positive net inflow of foreign exchange into an economy by artificially making exports and foreign investment cheaper, while increasing the price of imports and investments outside the economy.

If a country has a managed float exchange rate regime and an inflation rate that exceeds that of those countries with which it has financial and trade relations, then it will be necessary to allow, or force, a depreciation of the nominal value of the exchange rate by the amount of the inflation differential to prevent an overvaluation of the exchange rate from occurring.

For those countries with *lower* inflation rates than their trade and financial partners, however, a decision as to whether to allow their currency to remain under-valued with a managed float will depend upon the nature of the trade and financial flows with their partners and, of course, the actions of the bilateral trade and financial partners to their now over-valued exchange rates.

If a high-inflation country is a major importer of goods from a country with lower inflation, an under-valued exchange rate in the low-inflation nation will encourage even further the purchase of its exports. A country with an under-valued exchange rate often has little incentive to make any adjustments if it is a major exporter (think of China, for example, which is often accused of maintaining an under-valued exchange rate). However, if the low inflation nation imports essential goods from a higher-inflation country, maintaining an under-valued exchange might be counter-productive to economic growth and/or economic welfare by making such imports artificially expensive relative to the equilibrium value. In such a circumstance, forcing an appreciation of the exchange rate might very well be the appropriate policy decision. For managed exchange rate regimes, the nominal value a country decides upon will depend on the importance of exports and imports to the economic structure of that particular economy relative to its trade and financial partners.

Countries with fixed exchange rates that have inflation rates that differ substantially from those of their trade and financial partners will be aware quite quickly that their bilateral exchange rates are either over- or under-valued. The greater the divergence in inflation among countries, the larger the likely disequilibrium in the external balance that is likely to emerge if exchange rates remain fixed (see Focus 15.2 on parallel markets). Countries that choose to have a fixed exchange rate system will be compelled to keep their own rate of infla-tion equal to, or even below, that of their most important trade and financial partners. If they fail to do so, the country can experience a continual drain on its official foreign exchange reserves as its currency becomes over-valued and there is a net foreign exchange drain on the balance of payments accounts. Alternatively, frequent devaluations or mini-devaluations may be required, thus in effect, creating something more like a managed float regime.

Some economists actually support fixed exchange rates for some countries precisely for the internal fiscal and monetary discipline they engender, specifically the need to restrain inflationary pressures that otherwise would disrupt the balance of payments and threaten official foreign exchange reserves. In reality, countries with fixed exchange rates do have other options besides exhausting their official foreign exchange reserves when inflation gets out of hand: rationing of foreign exchange; borrowing on the international market; and periodic devaluations, so the discipline of fixed rates is not absolute. For nations unable or unwilling to manage their economic affairs properly, there always seem to exist, for a time anyway, means to avoid the required adjustments that can facilitate growth and development. However, continued over-valued exchange rate disequilibrium is typically not sustainable.

Exchange rates and the balance of payments

There is a close relation between a nation's exchange rate, its exchange rate regime (fixed, floating or managed float), and the balance of payments accounts that we already have considered briefly. After all, the flows of foreign currencies that end up in a country's foreign exchange markets are transactions that are captured somewhere in a country's balance of payments accounts.

Balance of payments adjustment with floating rates

If a country's exchange rates are fully floating – that is, if their value is determined by the market forces of supply and demand – it is technically impossible to have a balance of payments problem. Why is this?

Imagine that Pakistan, at the current spot nominal exchange rate, is running a current account deficit. This may be due to the fact that Pakistanis wish to spend more on imports than is earned from Pakistani exports (or any reason that results in current expenditures in the ROW exceeding current income from the ROW). The quantity supplied of rupees to the foreign exchange market by those wishing to buy imports will then exceed the quantity demanded of rupees by those as payment for Pakistan's exports at the current exchange rate, as shown in Figure 15.3.

At the current exchange rate of $0.04 per rupee, there is a *surplus* of rupees (equal to *mn*) on the foreign exchange market as a consequence of the current account deficit. If exchange rates are freely floating, however, this surplus will be but a very temporary phenomenon. At the current exchange rate "too many" rupees are being offered for exchange relative to the quantity desired. This means that the current nominal exchange rate of rupees is too high. The result will be a depreciation of the rupee to its equilibrium value of $0.03 to 1 rupee. This is the typical textbook adjustment to the equilibrium price whenever there is a surplus of a good in a competitive market.

As the exchange rate of the rupee falls, i.e., depreciates, and the cost of purchasing a unit of foreign currency rises, two important effects will result.[12] The willingness of holders of rupees to buy imports from the US falls as it is now more difficult to buy dollars than before since it takes more rupees to buy US$1 at 1 rupee = $0.03 than when the exchange rate was 1 rupee = $0.04. Imports of goods become more expensive in terms of the rupees that must

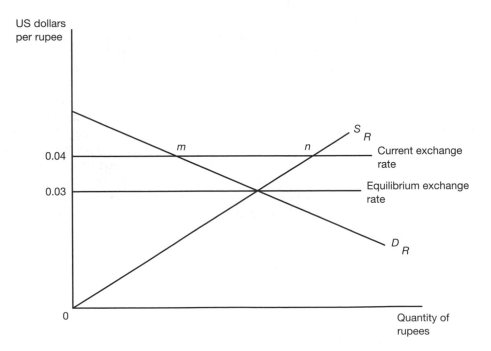

Figure 15.3 Floating exchange rates and the balance of payments.

be given up. As a result, the *quantity supplied* of rupees declines. On the other hand, the desire of foreigners to buy Pakistani exports increases as their prices in terms of foreign currency fall, and thus the quantity demanded of rupees rises. The exchange rate value tends to automatically adjust toward the equilibrium value at the intersection of the demand and supply curves in Figure 15.3.

Pakistan's exports will increase and its imports will decrease, and this will continue until the current account is brought into balance with the value of exports equal to the value of imports, or, more generally, until the outflows of foreign exchange are balanced by an equivalent inflow of foreign exchange.

Likewise, differences in the inflows and the outflows on the capital and financial accounts will result in similar equilibrating tendencies, so that the freely floating exchange rate will tend toward balance in all the parts of the balance of payments accounts. As a consequence of these exchange rate movements there will be no systematic tendency for a country's official foreign exchange reserves to either increase or decrease over time. There may, of course, be temporary changes in these balances, but these will be smoothed over time so that once a country has reached its desired level of foreign exchange reserves, a floating exchange rate regime will tend to maintain its foreign exchange reserves relatively intact over time.

Balance of payments adjustment with fixed exchange rates

If Pakistan operates with fixed exchange rates, then the imbalance between the supply of and demand for rupees in Figure 15.3 created by an exchange rate value which is "too high" and is reflected in a current account deficit is more problematic. At the nominal exchange rate of $0.04 per rupee, the rupee is over-valued relative to its equilibrium value, that is, more US dollars are received per rupee than should be. If the exchange rate and the supply and demand curves remain the same, there will be a persistent current account imbalance created as foreign exchange outflows are encouraged and foreign exchange inflows by foreigners are discouraged by the over-valued exchange rate. If the current account is now in deficit, the deficit will be worsened; if the current account is in surplus, the surplus will shrink over time and may turn into a deficit.

Let's assume that the current account is already in a deficit situation. Maintaining the exchange rate at the fixed value of Figure 15.3 likely will require a financial account surplus. Borrowing or inflows of direct foreign investment from the ROW will be required to compensate for the excess spending relative to foreign exchange income on the current account. In future periods, such borrowing and investment will exacerbate any current account deficit, as income payments for interest, dividends, and profits (item F in Table 15.1) are required to service loans. Alternatively, or most likely in conjunction with such financial inflows, the government will need to use some of its official foreign exchange reserve holdings to finance the excess supply of rupees, *mn*, brought to market as a result of the current account deficit.

Currency overvaluation and the possible impact on the balance of payments

From this brief description of the impact of an over-valued fixed exchange rate on the balance of payments accounts, one can see why policy-makers need to be very vigilant in monitoring the balance of payments. At least two alternative general scenarios with quite distinct effects can result from an over-valued exchange rate.

A beneficial current account deficit

A current account deficit caused by currency overvaluation can allow a country to import at a lower cost than otherwise critical goods and services that may be required for accelerating economic development. An exchange rate that is worth more than it should be makes it easier to pay for capital goods, new technologies, foreign technicians who train local experts, the training abroad of scientists, engineers and health professionals, and so on. An over-valued exchange rate can help a country purchase vital inputs relatively cheaply, since overvaluation reduces the price of imports in terms of the home currency.

If such a strategy is to be successful over time and is not to thwart progress, however, the exchange rate will need to be adjusted downward toward or even below its equilibrium value at some time in the future. The enhanced ability to produce created during the transition period of over-valued exchange rates must be translated into a capacity for the economy to export an expanding array of goods to foreign markets and to produce import substitutes competitively with foreign imports. In the best of all circumstances, this productive transformation will push the current account into surplus. At a minimum, a successful transitional overvaluation strategy will result in a stable or shrinking current account deficit.

In particular, during the stage of easy import substitution industrialization (ISI), overvaluation can be a means to cheapen the costs of production for new firms. It can have the same effect on costs as a subsidy by reducing direct costs of production by making it cheaper to purchase imported inputs, materials, and physical capital.[13] When accompanied by other measures discussed in Chapter 9, currency overvaluation can contribute to overcoming some of those transitional inefficiencies which make infant industry protection necessary during ISI. By lowering the costs of production and contributing to technology acquisition and learning, overvaluation can contribute to the desired goal of having new domestic enterprises reach levels of international competitiveness more quickly.

Policy-makers walk a thin line in following this policy. Timely mini-devaluations, carefully managed to guard against speculative attacks on the currency, can help to create the conditions for this strategy to be successful. Much like the programmed reduction in infant industry tariffs that we argued are necessary for ISI to contribute to future progress, overvaluation as an indirect subsidy to industries which buy imported inputs should have a time table for phase-out as well. Overvaluation cannot be a sustainable policy for very long; the risks are just too great.

A debilitating current account deficit

A current account deficit resulting from an over-valued exchange rate may result in eventual crisis rather than setting the stage for future progress. If protected industries do not become more efficient, the financial account borrowing required by any current account deficit will have been wasted. When funds borrowed from the ROW are not directed to productive investments that have the potential to *increase* exports or to *reduce* import expenditures, then such borrowing will, if sufficiently large, eventually lead to crisis. Sooner or later, increased payments of interest, dividends, and profits to pay for past borrowing will push the current account deficit to limits that are difficult or perhaps impossible to finance with new loans from abroad.

When that happens, more and more of the country's official foreign exchange reserves will need to be injected into the economy in an effort to maintain the over-valued fixed exchange rate. There is, of course, a limit to any government's official foreign exchange holdings, and when those are exhausted, or when the government finally appreciates the unsustainability of the over-valued exchange rate, action will need to be taken to bring the exchange rate and the balance of payments accounts into equilibrium. Far too many countries seek temporary and ill-advised means to try to increase foreign exchange inflows, choices that typically do little to improve the chances of long-term development (see Focus 15.3 on trade in toxic wastes).

When a country is forced to make a rapid and large devaluation of the currency once overvaluation becomes impossible to maintain, the result is almost always a slow-down and often a reversal of economic growth. Devaluation is required to stimulate export sales and encourage foreign exchange inflows and to simultaneously discourage import purchases and

---

FOCUS 15.3 TRADE IN TOXIC WASTE: ONE WAY TO ENCOURAGE FOREIGN EXCHANGE INFLOWS

Balance of payments problems have led some less-developed nations to engage in the trade of hazardous and toxic wastes. Burdened with large and difficult to finance current account deficits, some countries have begun to "export" environmental waste disposal services to the already-developed countries as a means of earning foreign exchange income.

In effect, in return for a foreign exchange inflow, countries agree to accept toxic waste materials from more developed countries which have encountered difficulties in disposing of such substances. "Hazardous waste is defined as waste which, if deposited in landfills, air or water in untreated form, will be detrimental to human health or the environment."

Where does such hazardous waste end up? Latin American countries, with their large current account deficits (look back at Focus 15.1), have recently been a key destination. Many African nations also have accepted substantial inflows of toxic materials.

- Guinea-Bissau received 15 million tonnes of waste from the UK, Switzerland, and the US over a period of five years.
- The Congo received more than 1 million tonnes of solvents and chemical wastes from the US and Europe in one year alone.
- Nigeria had nearly 4,000 tonnes of mixed chemicals and other waste from Europe dumped, illegally, in the country.
- Equatorial Guinea received 2 million tonnes of chemical wastes from Europe for a land-fill on Annoban Island.

Less-developed countries typically have fewer restrictions on the dumping of hazardous materials, at least partly because they have had less experience with them given their lower levels of development. And, given the foreign exchange that can be earned by countries finding it difficult to export with their lack of structural transformation and other failures of internal policy making, the temptation to accept trade in unsafe materials can be large. For example, Guinea-Bissau was offered by two British companies an amount per year equal to half of the country's total GNI for burying hazardous chemicals on its soil! One can see how attractive this might be to cash-strapped economies and, perhaps, to government officials willing to bend the rules.

The capacity of less-developed countries to monitor and control the effects of such toxic waste disposal is low, if it exists at all. In recognition of this, the Organization of African Unity (OAU) called for a ban on hazardous waste imports in 1988, but it has been ignored by many member states on the continent. Given their need for foreign exchange earnings, many less-developed nations with current account deficits continue to be tempted to provide relatively low-cost dump sites for developed world wastes. With better economic policies in the future, this Faustian choice would cease to be so attractive.

Source: Elliott 1994: 35–7

foreign exchange outflows. However, if a country has failed to invest in export industries, any growth in export income from devaluation will be less than it could have been if future export capacity had been strengthened. Often, to be able to achieve a current account balance or even a surplus sufficient to generate the foreign exchange earnings required to service past borrowing, imports will need to be repressed severely.

Import repression can be achieved via so-called *austerity measures* designed to provoke a domestic recession that reduces the propensity to import by reducing total national income. Besides currency devaluation, which makes imports more expensive and tends of itself to depress economic activity, other austerity measures that may be introduced, sometimes in consultation and at the urging of the multinational lending institutions, especially the International Monetary Fund (IMF) and the World Bank, are:

1   a reduction in the rate of inflation via greater control over both the fiscal deficit and the money supply that create and perpetuate inflation ("stabilization policies");
2   an increase in domestic interest rates and a reduction in trade barriers with the ROW ("adjustment policies");
3   limits on wage increases to less than the inflation rate;
4   lay-offs of government employees; and
5   privatization of state enterprises, to name a few.

Such "belt-tightening" or austerity policies are often instituted at the urging of the International Monetary Fund (IMF) when a country's balance of payments difficulties become so severe that outside intervention seems to be the only solution. Economic growth is typically adversely impacted by such measures, and economic development prospects are put on the back burner while correcting exchange rate misalignment and the replenishment of official exchange rate reserves take precedence. This adjustment creates severe hardships for the great bulk of the population, especially the poor. These issues will be touched upon again in the following two chapters.

"Good" external imbalances

The discussion in the previous section demonstrates something of great importance: at times, the correct external *im*balance can result in substantial positive economic growth dividends. A "good" external imbalance from, say, an over-valued exchange rate can contribute to a nation's progress where it counts, that is, in stimulating and increasing domestic employment, income and human development. However, some external imbalances can be harmful to the internal balances and may actually lead to a deterioration of aggregate economic welfare when, for example, over-valued exchange rates are allowed to persist for too long.

A current account deficit and an over-valued exchange rate (two external imbalances) can contribute to more rapid economic growth and development (improvement in the internal balances) *if* the borrowing from the ROW is used productively. However, this can only be a transitional strategy. Over time, a fixed or managed float exchange rate value will have to be adjusted downward toward and perhaps below its equilibrium value. As the net gains from an over-valued exchange rate strategy reach the point of diminishing returns, devaluation (or depreciation, in the case of a managed float) becomes necessary to preserve the gains of the disequilibrium development strategy.

This is an example of what MIT economist Alice Amsden (1989) has called "getting prices right by getting some prices wrong," that is, promoting more rapid growth and development via selective disequilibria, a strategy that harkens back to Albert Hirschman's "unbalancing" recommendation for initiating development (Chapter 5). However, the appropriate institutional structure and the other preconditions for successful structural transformation must be in place for this strategy of a *managed external disequilibrium* to have a chance to work. It is necessary to effectively monitor the external disequilibrium and know when the time has come to alter policies that can shift the external accounts towards a more balanced state, as the East Asian economies apparently have been successful in doing, even after the 1997 financial crisis (Wade 1990; World Bank 1993). The transition from easy ISI to easy export substitution followed by Korea and Taiwan and by other East Asian producers, considered in Chapter 10, was part of this broader strategy to "unbalance" and expand exports so as to gain the growth advantages of a good external imbalance over time. But as we discussed in that chapter, a whole range of policies, from human capital accumulation to government assistance, is necessary.

A second type of "good" external imbalance often supplants a prior "good" imbalance. Policy-makers may opt for an under-valued exchange rate after operating for some time with an over-valued exchange rate. They are especially likely to do so, or at a minimum to substantially reduce overvaluation of the exchange rate, when export substitution (remember back to Chapter 10) becomes an integral part of the overall industrialization strategy. Then two "good bads" can result in substantial positive gains.

Consider Figure 15.4. Given the supply, $S_\$$, and the demand, $D_\$$, for the United States dollar in the Korean foreign exchange market, the fixed (or managed float) value of 780 won to the dollar is "too low." The won is *under-valued* relative to the dollar, so that it takes more won to buy one dollar than it would at equilibrium. Of course the reverse side of this is that each dollar exchanged results in the receipt of 780 won rather than the 750 that would be received at equilibrium.

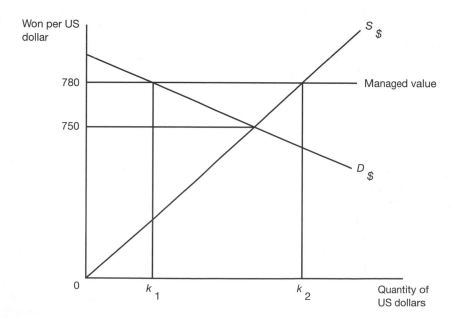

Figure 15.4 An under-valued exchange rate.

The undervaluation of the won relative to the dollar will encourage, by making them cheaper, the sale of Korean exports to the United States. At the same time, it will discourage, by making them relatively more expensive than they should be, imports into Korea from the United States market. Of course, the stimulation of exports and the discouragement of imports will tend, all else equal, to increase economic growth and employment in Korea. For a country wishing to push its new industrial exports into the international market, under-valuation of the exchange rate lowers prices and makes them more attractive to foreign consumers and can help to further spur economic growth.[14]

If undervaluation persists and is the norm with all, or the most important, of Korea's trading and financial partners, a current account surplus will, sooner or later, likely be the result. This means that Korea will be earning more from the ROW than Korea spends in the ROW on goods and services, unilateral transfers and on profits, dividends, and interest. The other side of the current account surplus would be a capital and financial account *deficit*, indicating that Korea would be accumulating net assets *vis-à-vis* the ROW through the extension of loans, through portfolio and foreign direct investment, or through the build-up of its offi-cial foreign exchange reserves. This accumulation can be seen in Figure 15.4 as the excess supply of dollars, $k_1 k_2$, which measures the additional quantity of US dollars supplied (k_2) to purchase Korean exports, for travel, and for investment in Korea relative to the smaller quantity demanded (k_1) of dollars to purchase goods and services and invest in the US.

Interestingly, a good disequilibrium brought on by a conscious undervaluation of a coun-try's exchange rate does *not* impose upon policy-makers the same binding economic need to eventually remove the source of disequilibrium. A current account surplus disequilibrium as a result of currency overvaluation is economically sustainable through time since the likeli-hood of external borrowing is reduced, while official foreign exchange reserves will most likely increase.

There thus is an *asymmetry* at work in the impact of exchange rate misalignment on the balance of payments. Economies with an over-valued exchange rate, beyond mild overvalu-ation, will *eventually* be forced to devalue, since it is impossible for less-developed countries to sustain a current deficit indefinitely through external borrowing or the running down of official foreign exchange reserves. An under-valued exchange rate and a current account surplus, however, may be economically feasible through time, though not *politically* sustain-able (see Focus 15.4 on China's experience with undervaluation).

Summary and conclusions: monitoring the external balances

Countries must carefully monitor what is happening to their balance of payments accounts and to exchange rates. There is no a priori means of determining if a current account deficit *per se* is "good" or "bad" or if exchange rate misalignment is harmful or not. It depends upon how the excess of spending financed by any capital and financial account surplus is being used. If international borrowing is dedicated to improving productivity via tech-nology development, research and development, funding new physical capital purchases for export producers, financing more human capital training, or other such expenditures, then a deficit and an over-valued exchange rate can be "good" in terms of their contribution to economic growth. A "good" current account deficit also will not result in the depletion, or at least will not contribute to any significant deterioration, of the central bank's official foreign exchange reserves. An early warning sign for any government that it has a balance of payments problem and severe currency overvaluation is any sustained deterioration in its official foreign exchange reserves.

FOCUS 15.4   IS CHINA'S CURRENCY UNDER-VALUED?

China is often accused of having an under-valued exchange rate. Can you think why some analysts might think this? Consider the following data (all in millions of US$).

	1985	1990	1995	2000	2005
Trade balance of goods	−13,123	9,165	18,050	34,474	134,189
Current account balance	−11,417	11,997	1,618	68,659	160,810
Total reserves (minus gold)	12,728	29,586	75,377	168,278	821,514

Since 1985, China's trade balance in merchandise and the current account balance have gone from a deficit to an increasingly large surplus (except 1995 for the current account) as more foreign exchange has been "earned" than has been "spent." From our discussions above, this is often the result when a currency is under-valued, that is, when it is easy for foreigners to buy the currency. Official foreign exchange reserves have grown rapidly too; total reserves in 2005 exceeded total import expenditures for that year, providing a very comfortable margin of "savings" for the economy. This supports the undervaluation argument.

There *would* seem to be an imbalance, or one would expect the trade balance or the current account to trend toward a lower surplus or small deficit over time if the exchange rate were near its equilibrium value. The problem with this way of looking at China's exchange rate is that the Chinese currency, the renminbi, is not fully convertible. Chinese citizens cannot freely exchange their own currency for euros, dollars, yen, or other foreign exchange.

Some analysts argue that if the renminbi were made fully convertible there would be a burst of spending by the Chinese on imports and a rush to make investments abroad that would rapidly undo the trade and current account surplus and put pressure on the government to inject official foreign exchange reserves into the economy. Either that or the exchange rate of the renminbi versus other major currencies would experience a rapid devaluation. What do you think?

Source: World Bank, *World Development Indicators Online*

Recurring and chronic current account deficits and over-valued exchange rates accompanied by decreasing official foreign exchange reserves most often reflect underlying problems in a nation's overall development strategy and the failure to promote the needed internal productive structural transformations we have been discussing since Chapter 1. It is true that there may be temporary *external* shocks to an economy that can create a balance of payments crisis. However, over a longer time frame of two to three years, the causes of the continuing crises are most likely to be found in *internal* failures of economic policy, in the design of such policies and in their implementation, as well as inattention to overvaluation of the exchange rate.

Countries have the option of following different paths and of making decisions about their future. The evolution of a country's balance of payments accounts and the exchange rate over time can be important indicators of whether the range of internal economic decisions, within the given external environment, are on the correct course or not. Those countries which successfully climb the structural transformation ladder discussed in Chapters 9–13 are more likely to avoid creating unsustainable current account imbalances and having badly misaligned exchange rates.

Questions and exercises

1   This exercise will give you practice in putting together the pieces of the current account of the balance of payments. Choose a less-developed country that interests you or which you have been assigned. Make a table with your country name at the top and include the numerical values for the requested items for the two years of data which are available. Refer back to Table 15.1 for help in how the current account is constructed. You can find the data at http://devdata.worldbank.org/wdi2006/contents/Section4.htm, Table 4.15 (if the link no longer works, go to http://www.worldbank.org and find World Development Indicators; the data will be in the Economics section).

   a   Record total goods and service exports and imports and *calculate* the *balance of trade* for the two years.
   b   Record your country's net factor payments ("net income") for those two years.
   c   Record your country's net transfers ("net current transfers") for those two years.
   d   *Calculate* your country's current account balance for the two years from the data you have collected and *compare* it to the value shown at the World Bank website. Are the two values the same? If not, have YOU made an error or is it them?
   e   Briefly *explain* what the current account balance value for your country means. Is your country spending more foreign exchange than it is earning or is it earning more than it is spending?
   f   From the current account balance, do you expect your country to be a net borrower of foreign exchange from the ROW? Explain.

2   Use the following information to determine (a) the current account balance, (b) the capital and financial account balance, (c) the change in official foreign currency reserves within the capital and financial account balance, and (d) the net errors and omissions of the balance of payments. Refer back to Tables 15.2 and 15.3 for details on which transactions go into the current account and which into the capital and financial account balance.

   Service imports, $14.1 billion; foreign investments from the ROW, $9.9 billion; service exports, $6.6 billion; total official foreign exchange reserves, beginning of the year, $42.2 billion; merchandise imports, $28.8 billion; net transfers, −$7.8 billion; profits, interest and dividend earnings from the ROW, $7.8 billion; foreign investments in the ROW, $3.2 billion; total official foreign exchange reserves, end of the year, $38.7 billion; foreign loans extended to ROW, $15.2 billion; foreign loans received from ROW, $9.4 billion; merchandise exports, $32.6 billion; profits, interest, and dividends paid to the ROW, $6.7 billion.

3   Carefully explain what it means to say that a country has a balance of payments problem. What part or parts of a country's balance of payments accounts might provide an "alert" that there is the potential for crisis? Explain.

4   Mozambique ran a current account balance of −$607 million in 2004, i.e., a deficit.

   a   Explain what could cause such a deficit on the current account.
   b   Explain what this deficit likely means about Mozambique's capital and financial account balance.
   c   What might be happening to official foreign exchange reserves? Explain.
   d   Discuss some steps Mozambique might take in the future to reduce the size of the

current account deficit. Be careful to explain how each policy proposal's specific impact in correcting the current account deficit.

e Does a current account deficit mean Mozambique has a balance of payments problem? Explain.

5 Peru's *total* official foreign exchange reserves on January 1 2008 were equal to US$18.1 billion. From its capital and financial account data for the balance of payments for 2008, we also know that item N in Table 15.2 was equal to + US$4.7 billion and item O was equal to −US$5.2 billion. What were Peru's total official foreign exchange reserves on December 31 2008? Show your work and explain.

6 Find the number of months of import coverage of your country's official foreign exchange reserves at http://devdata.worldbank.org/wdi2006/contents/Section4.htm, Table 4a (if that link no longer works, go to www.worldbank.org and look for World Development Indicators, and then go to the Economics section). How does your country compare to other countries? Is the coverage high or low by comparison? What does your country's coverage ratio compared to that of others tell you about your country's official foreign exchange reserves situation? Do you think the data suggests your country has a balance of payments problem? Explain.

7 Choose a less-developed country that interests you or which you are assigned. Using the exchange rate data located at http://www.oanda.com/converter/classic:

a list the *bilateral* exchange rate for today for 1 unit of your country's currency with the euro (write this as: 1 unit of (your country's currency) = x units of euro);

b list the *bilateral* exchange rate for today for 1 unit of your country's currency with the US dollar;

c now *calculate* the *implied* bilateral exchange rate between 1 US dollar and the euro from what you have found from the two bilateral exchange rates for your country above;

d now look up and list the *actual* bilateral exchange rate of 1 US dollar and the euro as found at the OANDA website. Is there any potential for "*arbitrage*" suggested by differences in the implied bilateral rate and the actual bilateral rate? In other words, is there enough difference between the implied rate and the actual rate that one could exchange dollars for euros (or vice versa) and make a known profit? Explain.

8 Looking back at Figure 15.1, what factors – economic and political – might cause a *decrease* in the demand for dollars and a downward shift of $D_\$$, assuming $S_\$$ constant? Assuming freely floating exchange rates, what effect does the decrease in the demand for dollars have on the exchange rate for *rupees*? Does it appreciate or depreciate with the decrease in demand for US dollars? What effects would you expect such a change in the exchange rate to have on Sri Lanka's exports? Its imports? Its total national output and total national income?

Now consider what factors – again economic and political – might cause the supply of rupees, $S_\$$, to decrease, now assuming $D_\$$ remains unchanged? What would happen to the exchange rate value of the rupee? To Sri Lankan exports? Imports? Travel in Sri Lanka? Foreign investment in Sri Lanka?

9 Choose a country that interests you or which you have been assigned. We are going to look at what was happening to that country's official foreign exchange reserves for the most recent two years available. You can find the data at http://devdata.worldbank. org/wdi2006/contents/Section4.htm, Tables 4a and 4.15 (the first year's data is in the

first table, the second in the other; if the link no longer works, go to http://www.world-bank.org and look for World Development Indicators; the data will be in the Economics section). Did your country's *total* official exchange rate reserves increase or decrease between the two years? Does that change tell you anything about whether your country's currency value is over- or under-valued? Explain. (Hint: think about the effect of over- or undervaluation on the balance of payments account, especially the effect on the current account balance.)

10   Choose a less-developed country that interests you or one you are assigned.

a   Go to http://www.imf.org/external/np/mfd/er/2004/eng/0604.htm and scroll down to near the bottom of that page. Find your country in the table. Is you country's *exchange rate regime* fixed, or floating, or a managed float, or pegged to some other currency? Try to make sense of what is there by reading what is in the left-hand column and along the top rows.

b   Does the exchange rate system for your country help to explain why your country's currency might be over- or under-valued or at equilibrium as you described it in the previous question? Explain.

11   Many less-developed countries suffer at times from "capital flight," as individuals with sufficient income, banks, and large companies convert their domestic assets into foreign currencies. They typically do this to invest or deposit these foreign currencies abroad, usually to escape high inflation, devaluations, and unstable domestic economic, political, and social conditions. What effect does the *return* of capital flight money to less-developed countries have on exchange rates? Show using a graph. What economic incentives might countries provide to encourage the return of flight capital money and why should they do so?

12   Assume that the current nominal exchange rate between the British pound and Belizean dollar is £1: $B2, and that this is the "correct" real equilibrium value. During the year, inflation in Britain is 10 percent, while in Belize it is 20 percent. What new nominal exchange rate will maintain the real exchange rate value of the two currencies constant? (Hint: What will the new rate of exchange be in terms of the number of Belize dollars exchanged for £1?)

13   Which term should be used – depreciation or devaluation – in referring to a falling exchange rate value when there are fully floating rates? Which term should be used – depreciation or devaluation – in referring to a falling exchange rate value when a currency's value is determined by a managed float? Which term should be used – appreciation or revaluation – in referring to rising exchange rate value when there is a fixed exchange rate?

14   What situations might cause a currency to depreciate in value? To appreciate in value? To be devalued? To be revalued?

15   What are the risks to a country's balance of payment from having an over-valued exchange rate? Are there any situations under which an over-valued exchange rate might be beneficial to economic growth? Explain.

16   What are the potential benefits to a country's balance of payments from having an under-valued exchange rate? Are there any situations when having an under-valued exchange rate might be harmful to economic growth? Explain.

17   Look at Focus 15.4 on China's supposed undervaluation. Is it still true that China has a large trade and current account surplus? Are official foreign exchange reserves still rising? If not, what has happened and, more importantly, why?

Notes

1 Our explanation and listing of the specific items in the current account and in the capital and financial account is a summary exposition. There are many more sub-categories and details for classifying transactions than are shown here. The details can be found in IMF (1993).

2 When a French resident travels to Spain on holiday and stays in hotels and eats in restaurants, this is the equivalent of Spain "exporting" a service to France, thus creating an inflow of foreign exchange for Spain on its current account. The French traveler injects foreign exchange into the Spanish economy for lodging, food, drinks, entertainment, and other expenditures. The same expenditure creates an outflow of foreign exchange, recorded as an import of tourism and travel, in the French balance of payments accounts of an exactly equivalent amount.

3 Again, it is important to remember that that we are summing the different items in the current account, some of which are signed positive (transactions creating inflows of foreign exchange) and some of which are signed negative (transactions creating outflows of foreign exchange).

4 Countries also can "borrow" from themselves by injecting foreign exchange into the economy from the government's holdings of official foreign exchange reserves. This will be discussed later in this section. Here we are simplifying only to make the point about the relation between the current and the capital and financial accounts.

5 SDRs are "special drawing rights," a kind of international asset created by the International Monetary Fund and used by countries only when they need to borrow from the IMF.

6 We will be concerned here only with the *spot exchange rate*, that is, with the rate of exchange for currencies in the market on a daily, or current, basis. There also are future values determined for many exchange rates, such that one can buy or sell many foreign currencies to be traded at some fixed time and a fixed value in the future. These exchange rates also are reported in the major financial papers, such as the *Wall Street Journal* or the *Financial Times*, on a daily basis, as well as in the business sections of all major newspapers. If you have access to the internet, current bilateral exchange rates can be found at http://www.oanda.com/convert/classic.

7 Sri Lankans and others holding rupees and who exchange them for dollars in the foreign exchange market are simultaneously supplying rupees and demanding US dollars. We could just have easily drawn Figure 15.1 showing the supply and demand for rupees rather than for US dollars.

8 We continue to ignore for simplicity the transactions costs involved in making foreign currency exchanges. As anyone who has travelled abroad knows, the "buy" and "sell" prices of currencies are never the same, the difference being a measure of the cost charged to make such exchanges.

9 Fixed exchange rates are thus not necessarily *constant* at some given value forever. A country that has fixed exchange rates may find it necessary to change the fixed value of its currency *vis-à-vis* other currencies from time to time when severe imbalances between the quantity supplied and the quantity demanded of currencies persist. Fixed exchange rates do not, however, respond automatically, as do floating rates, to changes in the supply of, and the demand for, foreign exchange. Fixed rates are determined by government fiat and can be maintained only by government intervention of one sort or another.

10 Devaluation is an administrative means to achieve the depreciation of the rupee that a freely floating exchange rate would more or less automatically attain through the change in the equilibrium value via the market. The effect of a devaluation of a currency on the balance of payments is exactly the same as that of depreciation. The term for the administrative increase in the value of a currency is re-valuation, the effect of which on the balance of payments accounts is identical to appreciation, the upward adjustment of a currency value with freely floating exchange rates.

11 Why does this adjustment take place automatically with floating exchange rates? Assume that the nominal exchange rate of the Mexican peso has not yet reached the 11 pesos to US$1 value, but that there are freely floating exchange rates. Let's suppose that the current market rate is at 10.5 pesos to US$1. This will mean that, given Mexico's inflation of 10 percent, the nominal exchange is worth more than it "should be" compared to its equilibrium value. This will make imports from the United States, travel to the United States, and Mexican investment in the United States cheaper than they were before the inflation. This will tend to increase the demand for dollars by Mexicans, and, assuming all else unchanged, this outward shift of the demand curve will continue until the *real* rate of 10 pesos to US$1 is restored at the *nominal* exchange rate of 11 pesos to US$1. In fact, the supply curve of dollars will also be decreasing at the same time, as holders of dollars are less willing to trade them for pesos on account of the higher real price of Mexican goods with inflation

(remember, for holders of dollars, until the real value of the exchange rate is restored, the dollar has *depreciated* in value), so the adjustment to any inflation differential between the two countries will be even more rapid.

This adjustment with floating exchange rates to conserve the real value of the exchange rate works to maintain *purchasing power parity*, so that the same traded goods in each country in terms of a common currency would sell at roughly the same price when prices are converted to a common currency. If the purchasing power parity condition is violated, the price of traded goods in one country will differ from that in another measured in terms of a common currency. In fact, when such differences in traded good prices are observed, this may be evidence of the absence of self-adjusting, fully floating exchange rates.

12 The rupee depreciates as the exchange rate goes from US$0.04 to US$0.03, since fewer units of the US dollar are being received per rupee. Each rupee has less purchasing power than before.

13 For example, imagine a metric ton of imported hot rolled steel for a toy factory costs US$750 on the world market. At the equilibrium exchange rate of US$0.03 per rupee, the imported cost of the steel would be 25,000 rupees. At the over-valued exchange rate of US$0.04 per rupee, the imported cost of the steel to the toy factory drops to 18,750 rupees, a saving of 25 percent. Clearly the cost savings can help to make such an ISI firm more competitive *vis-à-vis* imported toys by reducing average total costs.

14 By simple national income accounting,

$$Q = Y = C + I + G + (X - M),$$

where Q is the value of national output, Y is income, C is total consumption, I is gross investment, G is government spending, X is export value, and M is import value. Clearly, increasing X and decreasing M, as an under-valued exchange rate tends to do, will increase Q and Y, all else equal. Two of the important "all else equal" assumptions are (a) that any imports discouraged are not essential to the domestic production process (e.g., technology, new capital) or that compensating policies (e.g., subsidies) neutralize such effects, and (b) that the economy is not at full production, or else increases in X will simply subtract from domestic C or I.

References

Amsden, Alice. 1989. *Asia's Next Giant: South Korea and Late Industrialization.* New York: Oxford University Press.

Elliott, Jennifer A. 1994. *An Introduction to Sustainable Development.* London: Routledge.

IMF (International Monetary Fund). 1993. *Balance of Payments Manual.* Washington, D.C.: IMF.

——. 1994. *Annual Report 1994.* Washington, D.C.: IMF.

——. 1995. *World Economic Outlook* (May). Washington, D.C.: IMF.

——. 2002. *World Economic Outlook* (April). Washington, D.C.: IMF.

——. 2005. *World Economic Outlook* (April). Washington, D.C.: IMF.

UNCTAD (United Nations Conference on Trade and Development). 1995. *Trade and Development Report, 1995.* Geneva: UNCTAD.

Wade, Robert. 1990. *Governing the Market: Economic Theory and the Role of Government in East Asian Industrialization.* Princeton: Princeton University Press.

World Bank. 1993. *The East Asian Miracle.* Oxford: Oxford University Press.

——. 1994. *Adjustment in Africa.* Oxford: Oxford University Press.

16 The debt problem and development

After reading and studying this chapter, you should better understand:

- what external debt is and how it differs from internal debt;
- the origins of the external debt crisis;
- petrodollar recycling and OPEC's absorption problem;
- when it is prudent for a country to accumulate external debt either to finance a current account deficit or an investment project;
- how to measure the burden of the external debt and external debt-servicing costs;
- the impact of "debt overhang" on current and future growth possibilities;
- some possible solutions to the external debt problem.

Introduction

Throughout this book, we have examined fundamental action areas for countries wishing to accelerate economic growth and human development. We have considered the critical need for greater attention to education and human capital accumulation. Universal primary education and progress toward universal secondary education are important benchmarks for future advances in growth and development. Tertiary education must be geared to turning out a larger number of research scientists and technicians so that the needed focus on technology is facilitated.

The creation of an efficient and honest civil service is another goal of education and training policies. These efforts require that the central government take an active role in setting priorities, in mapping future projects carefully, in monitoring results, and in devoting sufficient public resources to all levels of education and professional training so that the goals which have been set have a reasonable chance of being achieved.

The importance of maintaining moderate or low rates of inflation, of carefully limiting central government budget deficits within sustainable boundaries, of avoiding severely over-valued exchange rates, of not running persistently large current account deficits in the balance of payments, and so on are fundamental policy areas for any economy interested in improving the pace of economic progress and human development.

Of course, all of these suggestions are premised on the assumption that key decision-makers truly are interested in achieving a higher level of economic welfare that promotes greater equity and human progress. It is presumed that leaders in the central government with such a vision will create the necessary mechanisms and will find the human talent to carry out their mission, even against the wishes of elites with a vested interest in maintaining the status quo. The *desire to develop* must be firmly a part of the vision of the central government and other leaders, or there can be little hope for sustained progress.[1]

However, even visionary leaders committed to setting a new path for the future and who seemingly follow all the rules and avoid the pitfalls of over-valued exchange rates, budget deficits, balance of payments problems, and so on, still may encounter an entrenched barrier that can make progress more difficult: excessive external debt accumulation inherited from the past.[2] This is especially true for newly democratic governments attempting to forge ahead on both the political and economic front.

This predicament has confronted many Latin American and Sub-Saharan African countries since the early 1980s, when an international debt crisis erupted (the 1997 Asian financial crisis was more locally contained and less pervasive). Accumulated external debt is not subject to the sorts of internal policy modifications that allow countries to correct for the exchange rate or balance of payments problems, or central government budget deficits, or even to choose an entirely new development path. Yet a large external debt burden may undo the best-laid plans of the most visionary country. External debt accumulated during previous, often non-democratic and military, regimes can thwart the efforts of newly democratic governments seriously interested in promoting economic growth and equity within their economies. External debt thus can constitute a serious *external barrier* to necessary structural transformation, but is one that is not particularly amenable to domestic manipulation. We will see that the international community has made efforts to reduce external debt, but there remains work to do.

Origins of the 1970s–1980s external debt dilemma

We know from the previous chapter that countries often borrow foreign exchange to be able to run a current account deficit when desired spending in the rest of the world exceeds the inflow of foreign exchange into the economy to pay for imports, payments on past borrowing, and for unilateral transfers. In the 1970s, many economies forgot, or overlooked, the importance of carefully managing their borrowing of foreign exchange and their external debt accumulation.

For many oil-importing economies, the decision in October 1973 of the Organisation of Petroleum Exporting Countries (OPEC) to raise the price charged for a barrel of crude oil marked the beginning of a prolonged crisis, though the actual crisis period was nearly a decade away.[3] The price per barrel of Saudi Arabian light crude oil, a benchmark for other prices, rose from $2.59 in January 1973 to $5.18 in November 1973 and then to $11.65 in January 1974. From 1973 to 1980, oil prices rose by about 500 percent after another spike in price in 1979–80 (Wee 1976: 133; Vernon 1987: 290).

OPEC had been in existence since 1960, but it had been unable to effectively function as a *cartel* with the goal of limiting production and setting monopoly prices until 1973. Given that about two-thirds of the world's known petroleum reserves were located in OPEC nations, as long as the cartel's restricted supply and higher prices remained in effect, every economy that required imported oil to generate electricity to run its factories and other industries and as industrial inputs – not to mention to fuel its motor cars, trucks, and trains – found their import expenditures on the balance of payments to be substantially greater *assuming* the same quantities of all imports continued to be purchased after the price hikes as were bought before.

For most less-developed oil-importing nations, the OPEC price hike resulted in a trade deficit as import expenditures ballooned beyond export revenues. This also typically meant growing current account deficits in their balance of payments. From the previous chapter, you will remember that a current account deficit must be financed by a corresponding surplus on the capital and financial account (ignoring the statistical discrepancy), including any decrease in official foreign exchange reserves of the central government. Thus a larger oil import bill as a result of higher petroleum prices forced oil-importing economies to face, at least in the short term, the need for increased external borrowing or the running-down of official foreign exchange reserves to finance their current account imbalance.[4]

It needs to be said that there did exist another option to running larger trade and current account deficits and undertaking external borrowing to finance a higher level of foreign exchange spending. Oil-importing economies *could have* reduced their oil or other import expenditures sufficiently to maintain their trade and current account balances at the level they had been prior to the OPEC price hike.

This decision, however, would have meant slower rates of economic growth as there would have been fewer imported inputs, and the effect would have been stronger the deeper the import cut-back required to keep import expenditures constant. Such *adjustment policies* were pursued voluntarily by only a very few economies in the 1970s. Perhaps not surprisingly, those economies that best adjusted to the oil crisis were East Asian economies like Korea and Taiwan that did not encounter a debilitating debt crisis, despite what seemed like high levels of debt accumulation. But we are getting ahead of our story.

With higher prices, oil-importing nations found themselves facing a difficult decision. They were forced to choose between reducing the overall volume of imports and thus a slower economic growth rate, or the reality of further accumulation of external debt to pay for more expensive oil and other desired imports.

However, given that OPEC was a classic, textbook cartel, economic theory suggested that it would falter and break down as members "cheated" on one another by producing more than their "quota" of output set by the cartel. After all, cartels can only raise prices by restricting total output. If members do not respect the supply restraints asked of them and "over"-produce, the cartel cannot keep the price as high as desired.

Economists expect such cheating from cartel members and thus many countries might reasonably have hypothesized that the price increases from the OPEC could be expected to be temporary, thus providing a justification for short-term external borrowing to smooth import consumption. And past experience of cartels, including OPEC, suggested this was a reasonable assumption.

However, once the price hikes had not only been maintained but increased over six months, a year, and then six years, the logic of borrowing for the short term could not be sustained any longer.

As we will explain more fully below, borrowing simply because imports suddenly cost more because of a price increase for a key product does not meet the standard for incurring external debt over the long term. Far too many countries ended up making decisions on their external debt that had adverse effects on their future development prospects. External debt accumulation, when not handled correctly, can set off a chain of events that result in adverse path dependence far into the future, and for many economies that is what happened.

Petrodollar recycling

Unfortunately, the OPEC price hikes seemed to offer their own solution for meeting the increased need for borrowing by petroleum-importing nations. Rapidly rising oil revenues from higher prices created an *absorption problem* in the OPEC economies. One of the motivations for raising prices in the first instance was to allow oil-exporting nations to share in the wealth of their own natural resources – rather than selling it cheaply to other countries to spur economic development elsewhere, particularly in the Western developed economies, as had been done for years – and to use the increased revenues for improving infrastructure, education, technology, and in a myriad of other uses. However, the increase in export revenues flowed in so quickly there simply were not enough projects to absorb the additional revenues fast enough. The OPEC economies faced a classic "absorption" problem.

OPEC nations thus deposited their excess export earnings in international banks in New York, London, Tokyo, and Frankfurt in so-called Euro-dollar or Euro-currency markets where they could earn interest until appropriate private or public uses for the funds could be initiated. This helped to solve the OPEC nations' need to make productive and profitable use of their large and growing oil export revenues. However, the large inflow of OPEC deposits represented a challenge to the private international banking system which needed to find sufficient additional borrowers for this large volume of loanable funds if they were to be able to pay the interest on these new deposits (see Focus 16.1). Though the increase in deposits would seem to be good news for the banks that received them, the shift in the

---

FOCUS 16.1   OPEC'S ABSORPTION PROBLEM

The increase in oil prices beginning in 1973 resulted in a huge financial transfer from oil-importing to oil-exporting economies. One measure of the size of this transfer can be seen in the evolution of the *current account balances* of importers and exporters of petroleum over the critical early years of the crisis shown below (figures are in billions of US dollars).

	1973	1974	1975–8	1979	1980	1981
Middle East oil exporters	6.5	55.9	33.8	61.9	99.6	56.3
Developing countries	−9.1	−21.0	−39.5	−51.7	−68.0	−105.1

For the Middle East oil exporters, current account surpluses grew dramatically following each oil price increase, first in 1974 and again in 1979–80. These current account surpluses occurred even though the Middle East oil exporters increased their own expenditures on imports from $3.5 billion in 1972 to more than $52 billion in 1982 and invested billions in infrastructure and other internal investments. These numbers give some idea of the magnitude of the flows of foreign exchange from oil importers to oil exporters the price increases set in motion.

The other side of the current account surpluses of the Middle East oil exporters was the growing financial transfer from the oil-importing developing countries, as measured by the evolution of their current account deficits shown in the second line above, which grew from small negative to large negative balances over the period.

The OPEC oil exporters could not absorb in productive uses, including expanded import expenditures, all the new foreign exchange income being earned. There was a need to look for alternative investment alternatives. In 1974, 51 percent of the $56.2 billion invested internationally by OPEC nations found its way to private international banks, particularly in Europe (other uses of these funds were in direct foreign investments, bonds, real estate in Europe, and so on). When oil prices were increased again in 1979, international bank deposits absorbed 65.2 percent of the $62.1 billion invested internationally by the OPEC economies. In 1980, $100.2 billion was placed internationally, 44.2 percent of which went to private international banks. The size of these new loanable funds flowing to the international banks gives some idea of the dilemma the banks faced in finding borrowers for those funds without interest rates plummeting.

Sources: World Bank 1985: 33, 89; Zanoyan 1995

supply of funds entering the banking system was so large it threatened to reduce interest rates and profits as the spread between bank lending and borrowing rates shrank.

What the private banking system did to resolve this potential dilemma was to create a new class of borrower, the so-called *sovereign borrower*, which expanded the demand for loanable funds. This helped to keep interest rates and earnings high (you should be able to see the dynamics of these changes in a simple supply and demand graph with loanable funds on the horizontal axis and interest rates on the vertical). These new sovereign borrowers were none other than many of the petroleum-importing countries themselves who became the recipients of aggressive efforts to provide them with the needed foreign exchange to finance their growing current account deficits as the price of oil increased over the 1970s.[5] In effect, a portion of the earnings of the OPEC oil exporters deposited in private international banks was loaned back – *recycled* – to the petroleum-importing countries from which the increased bank funds had been derived in the first place!

Petrodollar recycling was the name given to this circulation and recirculation of petroleum revenues from the oil-importing nations to the OPEC economies to the private international banks and then back again to the oil-importing nations in the form of loans, only to make the round again and again (Devlin 1989 is an excellent source for the full story of the private international banking system's aggressive marketing of loans to sovereign borrowers). The loans made by the private international banks to petroleum-importing nations permitted them to continue to purchase oil and other goods and services at roughly the same levels as prior to the OPEC price increases.

Over the years, additional funds were lent to oil importers not just for import purchases but also to repay the interest and principal coming due on past debt obligations. New external debt was added just to be able to make interest and principal obligations on prior external debt, without having to reduce import expenditures to do so. And so began the cycle of external debt accumulation.

Dimensions of the debt crisis

Table 16.1 shows the growth of external debt accumulation after 1970 for a few nations. Debt rose rapidly for some countries, particularly those in Latin America and especially for Mexico, Brazil, and Argentina. But external debt also increased quite dramatically in the 1970s and into the early 1980s for Korea as well.[6]

As the table shows, the first major episode of external debt accumulation occurred during the 1970s and the early 1980s (see Focus 16.2 for data on aggregate external debt accumulation prior to the 1970s). After 1985, debt continued to rise for many countries, especially Argentina, Brazil, India, Mexico, and Korea. In some heavily indebted Sub-Saharan African countries, and for very special reasons discussed later, external debt showed a tendency to fall. Korea's debt rose more than three times between 1993 and the 1997, as the so-called Asian financial crisis struck hard, but the Korean economy managed to avoid the crises that other countries have experienced (Amsden 2001: 254–5).

Over the 1970s, private international banks provided the bulk of the loans to cover the foreign currency shortfalls of oil importers in Latin America and Asia. For example, nearly two-thirds of all new financing in Latin America over the period 1977–81, and an even larger percentage of total borrowed funds, was provided by the private banking system (Ffrench-Davis and Griffith-Jones 1995: 240). Sub-Saharan Africa, on the other hand, borrowed mainly from other governments or multilateral lending institutions, and their problems have been quite different, as we shall consider below.

Table 16.1 Total external debt, 1970–2005 (millions of US$)

	1970[a]	1980	1985	1990	2000	2005
Argentina	1,878	27,157	44,444	62,233	146,172	114,335
Brazil	3,236	71,012	106,730	119,964	237,953	187,994
Chile	2,060	12,081	20,221	19,226	36,978	45,154
Congo	135	1,526	1,760[a]	4,934	4,887	5,936
Côte d'Ivoire	256	7,445	8,446	17,251	12,138	10,735
Ghana	489	1,407	1,170[a]	3,734	6,657	6,739
India	7,940	20,582	35,460	83,628	100,367	123,123
Kenya	313	3,394	4,219	7,055	6,295	6,169
Korea	1,797	29,480	47,996	–	134,417	152,800
Malaysia	390	6,611	13,384[a]	15,328	41,797	50,981
Mexico	3,206	57,379	97,429	104,442	150,288	167,228
Pakistan	3,059	9,936	12,965	20,663	32,091	33,675
Sudan	319	5,163	5,086[a]	14,672	15,741	18,455
Tanzania	248	2,476	9,105	6,454	7,445	7,763
Zimbabwe	233	786	2,143	3,279	4,002	4,257

Sources: World Bank 1983: 178–9, Table 16; 1987: 232–3, Table 16; 1995: 200–1, Table 20; 2002: 264–6, Table 4.16; *World Development Indicators 2007*, Table 4.16.

Note
a Includes only *public* external debt. Other years include both public and private external debt.

Bank loans were extended at market and variable rates of interest as risk was transferred to sovereign borrowers whose repayment obligations varied with the level of world inflation.[7] On the other hand, most Sub-Saharan African countries, being quite poor and higher-risk borrowers, tended to receive the bulk of their external debt in the form of *concessional* loans from non-private lenders. These loans often came with below-market interest rates and with extended periods for repayment, often thirty years or more. Concessional loans were provided by governments or bilateral lending institutions, such as the African Development Bank (AfDB), or multilateral institutions, like the World Bank and the International Monetary Fund, and not by the private international banking system (see Chapter 17 for more details of the lending activities of the multilateral institutions).

When to borrow externally

When is it economically justified for a country to borrow externally, that is, when is it appropriate to incur debt denominated in foreign currencies?

External borrowing will be necessary to finance any part of a current account deficit not covered by foreign investment inflows, aid inflows, or a reduction in a country's official foreign exchange reserves.[8] In fact, a country cannot incur a current account deficit without having the ability either to borrow foreign currency or without having accumulated sufficient official foreign exchange reserves to cover any spending greater than export and other income earnings.

One acceptable reason to borrow externally can be to finance what is expected to be a *short-term* current account deficit. This may occur as a result of some temporary imbalance in which expenditures for imports exceed export earnings, perhaps because of an unexpected drop in export prices caused by, say, bad weather, or any other unforeseen but transitory situation in which import expenditures exceed export earnings and results in a current account deficit. A temporary increase in the prices of critical imports, say oil, could be one such contingency.

FOCUS 16.2   THE EVOLUTION OF EXTERNAL DEBT ACCUMULATION AND THE DEBT BURDEN

In 1970, the entire external debt of the less-developed countries totalled $68.4 billion. By 1980, external debt had multiplied by nearly ten times, reaching a total of $635.8 billion. Debt rose less rapidly in the 1980s, but the total nearly doubled again by 1990, reaching $1,298.7 billion.

By 2000, estimated external debt for the low and middle-income nations totalled $2,492.0 billion, nearly forty times larger than in 1970 and in 2005, total external debt for the low- and middle-income countries had grown an additional 10 percent to $2,742.4 billion.

Debt burden ratios (don't confuse these with debt *service* ratios later in the chapter), calculated as total external debt divided by total export income, showed a tendency to fall over the 1990s for all regions except Sub-Saharan Africa. Still, in all regions, the total external debt-to-exports ratio was higher in 1999 than it had been in 1980 prior to the outbreak of the debt crisis.

What were the costs of the very high debt burdens of the 1990s? The opportunity cost of using foreign exchange earnings for debt repayments must be considered. What might such funds have been used for if they had not been earmarked to repay previously incurred external debt? To give just one example, Zambia found itself spending in 1994 *thirty times more* to make its debt payments than it spent on education! Think about what that might mean for future development in an era of rapidly changing knowledge and technology.

By 2005, debt burden ratios had declined significantly everywhere, as debt relief reduced total debt, and as many economies, especially in Latin America and South Asia, began to shift their development strategies more toward export substitution. This increased foreign exchange income inflows as more valuable manufactured goods exports began to replace the lower-value primary export base that had existed since colonial times. As the growth rate of total debt declined (the numerator of the debt/export debt burden ratio) and as export income grew more rapidly (the denominator of the debt burden ratio), the average debt burden ratio fell dramatically, being everywhere lower than they had been in 1980 (though only marginally so in Sub-Saharan Africa), (see below).

Since the debt burden ratio measures total external debt as a percentage of the total foreign exchange income earned from exports available to repay external debt or to be used for other purchases from the rest of the world, these declining ratios signal that export income had been rising faster than total debt since 1990, a seemingly positive indicator for the future, at least when looking at regional averages. What happened to individual countries is another issue, and one we ask you to consider in an exercise at the end of the chapter.

	1980	1990	2000	2005
East Asia	81.8	114.3	81.8	44.1
Latin America	201.8	279.7	178.5	101.7
South Asia	160.5	380.8	181.9	84.3
Sub-Saharan Africa	91.7	219.3	186.6	89.0

Sources: World Bank 1997: 247, Table 17; 2001: 250–3, Table 4.15; 2002: 266, Table 4.16; *World Development Indicators 2007*, Table 4.16

External borrowing in such circumstances can help a country avoid unnecessary disruptions to production and employment and can smooth the consumption of imports over the short term. Once export revenues recover or import expenditures return to normal levels, then the need for such external borrowing will have ended. Under such circumstances, external borrowing can help to maintain the level of import purchases and stabilize the economy over time, thus contributing to greater social welfare.[9]

For example, if the OPEC petroleum price increases in 1973 had been expected to be temporary (and since OPEC was a cartel, that might have been a reasonable hypothesis), then external borrowing to get past that short-term disruption might reasonably have been justified. However, after a few months had passed and the price of petroleum remained at its higher level and then was increased again by OPEC in 1974, this justification for external borrowing to pay for roughly the same physical quantity of imports could no longer be sustained. Clearly the price increase had become something beyond a temporary disturbance that was going to go away quickly. OPEC, as a cartel, had not imploded. Any short-term justification for incurring external debt was no longer tenable.

When the need for external borrowing to finance a current account is expected to be a *recurring long-term* likelihood given current or expected levels of imports and exports and the magnitude of other capital and financial account inflows and outflows, then the decision to borrow externally needs to be appraised very carefully.

Long-term external debt accumulation must contribute either to foreign exchange *savings* or to foreign exchange *earnings* in the future. In other words, borrowed funds must either be dedicated to expanding *import substitution* industries which, in the future, can reduce future import expenditures, or such borrowing needs to be targeted to the expansion of *export production* which increases future foreign exchange earnings.

If external borrowing is to take place, it should be directed only toward those productive investments that expand the output of *tradable goods and services* that can generate the foreign exchange required for repaying the borrowed funds. Obviously export goods are tradables, but so too are all import substitution commodities. If the output of import substitute industries were not being produced domestically, it would be imported, that is, traded. Thus investing foreign exchange borrowing in projects to replace imports is a way to save on foreign exchange needs in the future and to contribute to foreign exchange savings that can be dedicated to repaying external debt.

Borrowing to finance infrastructure that can contribute to greater export earnings or import substitution production by lowering costs also could be acceptable. Investments in roads, communications systems, electricity, water, and perhaps even the legal system might qualify as means to generate foreign exchange earnings or foreign exchange saving investments and thus justify external debt accumulation.

The key issue in deciding on the wisdom of external borrowing over the long-term is determining whether such borrowing is being dedicated to investments that are expected to generate foreign exchange earnings or foreign exchange savings sufficient to pay down the external debt undertaken. The issue is not whether external debt accumulation contributes to the overall economic growth of an economy; that is an insufficient criterion. The question is whether such external borrowing contributes sufficiently to the growth of the tradable goods sector to be self-liquidating. If it does, external debt may be advisable; if not, external debt accumulation is not recommended, since the so-called "transformation problem" of generating sufficient foreign exchange to repay the debt will not be met, as foreign exchange borrowing will not be "transformed" into foreign exchange earnings or savings in the future (World Bank 1985: 48).

External borrowing to finance the expansion of production in non-tradable output – for example, the construction of new homes, shopping malls, and hospitals – may be important to the well-being of the population. However, investing in these kinds of goods and services does not contribute to the ability to repay external debt, since the output created does not generate foreign exchange earnings or savings. These are goods and services sold and traded in the internal market only, and they generate funds only in the domestic currency. Therefore, external borrowing to finance such investments cannot be justified. Neither can many other types of possible expenditures, such as national defense.

Both import substitution and expanding exports can help to close a trade gap and contribute to a smaller current account deficit. There may be, nonetheless, some preference for using external debt to finance export expansion projects over import substitution purposes, since there is a natural limit to the foreign exchange savings that can be expected over time from the latter. Not all imports can be replaced by domestic production, so the potential savings of foreign exchange from import substitution ultimately is finite.

The expected earnings from export expansion, however, can continue to grow over the future, with no rigid upper-boundary, though there is no absolute guarantee that investing in export growth will pay off, either. Market conditions can change, new exporters can enter the same market thus reducing each country's effective demand, and so on (Focus 16.3 illustrates the riskiness of the decision to borrow externally, using the case of Mexico as an example). Still, investing in export expansion, particularly of manufactured goods, is more likely contribute to the ability to generate the needed foreign exchange to repay the debt, as well as contributing further to the transformation of the overall economic structure.

FOCUS 16.3   THE MEXICAN DILEMMA

When OPEC raised the price of petroleum in 1973, Mexico was an oil importer despite having significant domestic oil reserves controlled by the public corporation, PEMEX. One group within government argued that higher petroleum prices created an opportunity for Mexico to begin to export oil and generate revenues that could help to finance economic and social development over the future. Their argument was that external financing was needed to fund the modernization of the petroleum industry. Then, with increased productive capacity, petroleum exports and the foreign exchange revenues they generated could be used to pay back the external debt, while still leaving a surplus to fund economic and social needs within Mexico.

Others in Mexico feared that this rosy scenario hinged on continued high oil prices. If the price of petroleum were to decrease significantly in the future, export revenues would be less than anticipated, cutting into planned projects for social and economic development. If the price decrease were to be sharp enough, external debt repayment might require Mexico to export an ever-larger quantity of petroleum (since export income equals the price of oil multiplied by the quantity of oil exported) in order to be able to earn the needed foreign exchange to meet the external debt obligations. If this concern sounds reminiscent of the declining terms of trade debate from back in Chapter 3, it shows you have been paying attention!

This anti-debt group within and outside of government argued against any expansion of oil production that needed to be financed by external debt accumulation to be paid from uncertain future petroleum export income. The fear was that since petroleum is a non-renewable commodity, that is, non-producible, Mexico would be unable to regulate the pace at which its oil was used up if the country's oil reserves were "pledged" to repay external debt obligations. Falling oil prices could trigger a more rapid rate of oil depletion, as a larger physical quantity of oil would need to be exported at a lower price of oil to earn the necessary foreign exchange to service the debt, thus threatening future economic growth and increasing Mexican dependency on others.

Continued

The pro-debt forces prevailed, however, and external debt accumulation to renovate the petroleum sector took place at a rapid pace. Public spending financed by external debt jumped from 30 percent of GDP in 1978 to nearly 50 percent in 1982. The government's fiscal deficit more than doubled from 8 percent of GDP in 1980 to 18 percent in 1982.

Mexico's exports came to be dominated by oil. By 1981, oil exports accounted for 69 percent of all exports. And when the price of oil collapsed in the 1980s, the need to expand the quantity of petroleum exports to service the country's external debt obligations increased, as more cautionary voices had foreseen.

Mexico's oil "patrimony" was in danger of being depleted just to repay past external debt, without leaving much to fuel the social and economic development that had motivated the expansion of oil production in the first instance. It was only as a result of a change in economic strategy that fueled the growth of manufactured exports as export substitution finally began that the oil gamble did not result in a more serious crisis.

In recent years, Mexico's manufactured exports have averaged around 80 percent of total exports, as the overall importance of petroleum exports has waned with the economy's shift to export substitution industrialization. But the dangers of thinking that current conditions will remain the same when making the decision to borrow externally could not be clearer than in Mexico's costly venture into expanding its petroleum production.

Sources: World Bank 1985: 63; World Bank Trade Data online

Whether external borrowing is dedicated to expanding export earnings or to creating import savings, the *expected* increase in foreign exchange should be sufficient to cover repayment of the principal (*amortization*) and interest on the external debt incurred over the life of the loan. For this to occur, the annual rate of increase in foreign exchange earnings from "growing" exports plus the rate of foreign exchange savings from reducing imports must be greater than the average rate of interest charged on a country's external loans.

As Focus 16.3 suggests, external borrowing should be approached extremely cautiously, and any guesses about future export prices and future import prices should err on the side of understating them in attempting to determine the wisdom of accumulating higher levels of external debt. Countries that find themselves with "too much" external debt relative to their ability to repay may find their future growth and development prospects seriously compromised. Thus, in considering whether to borrow to expand exports, the estimation of future expected export earnings should be based on a presumption that the future prices of exports will be *lower*, perhaps significantly lower, than they are in the present, especially for primary commodities.

Likewise, in estimating expected future import expenditures in valuing the worth of investing in import substitution, it should be assumed that future import prices also will be lower than current import prices. Such *discounting* will tend to make the standard for borrowing externally to finance export expansion or import substitution more rigorous, such that the incentive to borrow is reduced and not based on transitory elements.

There is one further consideration. Even when countries do borrow for the right reasons, such borrowing may be less than effective because of changes in the capital intensity of production or inefficiency, as Focus 16.4 points out.

External borrowing, adjustment policies, and savings

The foregoing caveats concerning external loans refer to decisions to borrow to finance persistent current account deficits. Such disequilibria may arise from external events, such as

FOCUS 16.4   INEFFECTIVE USE OF EXTERNAL DEBT

Even when borrowing is done for the right reasons – export expansion or import substitution – investments funded by external debt still can be inefficiently utilized. In a study of the Philippines, Argentina, and Morocco, the World Bank found that incremental capital–output ratios (ICORs) in all three countries rose substantially during the period in which external borrowing was taking place.

For example, Argentina's ICOR increased from 4.4 in 1963–72 to 11 over the period 1973–81 when there was a rapid build-up of external debt. What a higher ICOR means is that to generate an additional unit of output, the required quantity of physical investment rose from 4.4 to 11 units between the two time periods. Thus, new capital investment was *less effective* in generating output as a result of an increase in more capital-intensive production that required more physical capital to create one more unit of GDP, or because of the less effective use of this physical capital as a result of negligible or even negative total factor productivity (TFP) rates. Even worse, virtually none of the $35 billion Argentina borrowed externally between 1976 and 1982 resulted in a *net* addition to investment, i.e., it substituted for investment that likely would have occurred anyway.

The same tendencies were noted in the Philippines, where the ICOR doubled, and in Morocco, where the ICOR rose from 2.6 in 1965–72 to 6.7 in 1979–82 as external debt rose

By comparison, Korea's ICOR remained at about 3 as its external debt grew, indicating sustained efficiency in generating new output from new investment, a reflection of the region's positive TFP rates considered in Chapter 13. The structural transformations on the path to expanded industrialization pursued by Korea examined in previous chapters, combined with good state policy, helped to avoid severe and lingering debt problems from decreasing returns to physical investment in creating one unit of GDP.

Source: World Bank 1985: 52, 68

the petroleum price increase. But they also may be a reflection of underlying, and often quite severe, problems and failures of internal economic policy. Policy errors that result in high levels of inflation and over-valued exchange rates can create situations in which the current account of the balance of payments is in deficit, requiring a compensating inflow of external financial resources on the capital and financial account, some of which may be in the form of external debt owed to private banks or to bilateral or multilateral lending institutions.

At a more fundamental level, a persistent imbalance in the current account may reflect the failure of an economy to successfully negotiate the series of "strategy switches" in economic policy that contribute to the necessary structural transformations on the path toward greater industrialization and diversification of production discussed in Chapters 9–11. It is in those instances, where external financing is used to attempt to *maintain* the status quo and to avoid the costs of better economic policy-making, that external debt is economically inadvisable, though it may well be the preferred political choice.

The Latin American debtor countries followed this path of least resistance, using external debt to finance current consumption, or military expenditures, or to repay past external debt obligations. Too little was ploughed into investments that expanded the foreign exchange earnings or savings needed to service the external debt responsibilities. This had the effect of perpetuating existing backward economic structures and policies that badly needed to be changed. In particular, external debt accumulation permitted the continuation and deepening of import substitution industrialization and the region's inward orientation and the *skipping* of the crucial export substitution stage of industrialization that moved the East Asian economies forward so quickly, as discussed in Chapter 10. The failure to develop the capacity to export manufactured goods to the world market was reflected in inefficiencies in production, as measured by both low aggregate economic growth rates and non-existent rates of total factor productivity, which stifled progress in Latin America after the 1960s.[10]

The twin deficit and productive borrowing

If external borrowing to finance a current account deficit is properly used to expand the production of export tradables, then such borrowing may be an important contributor in the attempt to transform the economic structure. In these cases, external borrowing is not only justifiable, but such debt, being self-liquidating, can be integral in creating an economy that is more efficient and more technologically focused by financing needed investments, both public and private.

Even if a country does not have a current account imbalance requiring inflows of foreign exchange, external borrowing could still be warranted if used productively. That is, even a country with a current account surplus may choose to borrow externally to fund warranted investments.

Using the concept of the twin deficit and assuming there is no central government deficit, the following basic relation must hold assuming, for now, no external debt accumulation:[11]

$$S - I = X - M = 0 \tag{16.1}$$

Statement 16.1 shows that if savings (S) equals investment (I) then there will be no trade gap (i.e., no deficit or surplus) and no need for external financing (since exports, X, will equal imports, M). In a country without access to external sources of financing, the domestic level of investment will be constrained by domestic savings.

On the reasonable and usual assumption that $S = s(Y/L)L$, s, the savings rate, is likely to be smaller the lower per capita income, Y/L, is so low-income countries are likely to generate low levels of total domestic savings.[12] Low levels of domestic saving mean that the bulk of an economy's production goes to consumption, leaving little left over for investment. Low levels of investment, including financing for investment in human capital like education, health care and technology, result in low levels of income per person in the future. Thus, a vicious cycle of poverty is reinforced, with poor countries remaining poor because they begin poor, as they are lacking in sufficient capital of all types for expanding productive investments over the future due to the low level of savings taking place.

However, if domestic savings, S_d, can be supplemented by foreign savings, S_f, via external borrowing, then total investment can be pushed above what would be achieved from domestic resources alone ($I = S_d + S_f$). When this occurs, statement 16.1 becomes:

$$S_d - I = X - M < 0 \tag{16.2}$$

since $S_d - I = -S_f$, which is negative for all $S_f > 0$.

Statement 16.2 shows that for domestic investment to be greater than domestic saving, the equivalent value of additional (investment) goods must be imported, resulting in an excess of import expenditures over export earnings.

In other words, foreign borrowing can finance the twin deficit by boosting the level of domestic investment and simultaneously financing the import of investment goods and other inputs to production. This creates the possibility of a *virtuous* cycle of foreign borrowing, domestic investment, and increases in domestic production. Of course, our admonition that such borrowing *should* be channeled toward tradables, be they export production or import substitution goods, still applies. If this condition holds, external borrowing can contribute to higher economic growth rates and to structural transformation in the production process along the lines suggested in Chapter 10, permitting poorer nations to supplement domestic resources in short supply with foreign resources.[13]

The debt service obligation: the real cost of debt repayment

Given that external debt must be repaid using foreign exchange earned from exporting, it is often convenient to use the ratio of total debt divided by total exports (D/X) as a measure of the *debt burden*. We briefly considered the evolution of the debt burden by region in Focus 16.2.

However, the *debt service ratio* is another measure of the severity of total external debt that is more often used for assessing the current cost of external debt. This is calculated as the share of total export income used for repaying principal and interest on the debt. In other words, it compares total foreign exchange obligations to repay external debt as a percentage of total foreign exchange earnings from exports. Table 16.2 shows the debt service ratio for a number of years for the same countries as in the previous table. The 2005 debt *burden* ratio is also shown.

Let us first consider Mexico's debt service ratios to see what these mean. In 1980, the equivalent of nearly half of Mexico's foreign exchange export revenues was required to pay amortization and interest on the external debt. That left only a bit more than half of export earnings available for purchasing imports or for other foreign exchange purposes. The debt service ratio had decreased by 1990 to about a fifth of export income, only to rise again by 2000 to a bit over 30 percent. By 2004, Mexico's debt service ratio had once again fallen to about 23 percent of foreign exchange export earnings.

The contrast between the years in terms of the actual cost to the Mexican economy of external debt servicing is striking, however. In 1980, prior to the debt crisis of mid-1982 (discussed in the next section), Mexico was able to borrow foreign exchange from the private

Table 16.2 Debt service ratios and the debt burden

	1970	*1980*	*1990*	*2000*	*2004*	*D/X*
Argentina	18.2	37.3	37.0	70.7	28.5	225.0
Brazil	31.9	63.1	22.2	93.6	46.8	134.2
Chile	27.2	43.1	25.9	24.8	24.2	90.5
Congo	9.2	10.6	35.3	1.6	4.0	119.2
Côte d'Ivoire	6.8	38.7	35.4	22.6	6.9	126.6
Ghana	9.1	13.1	36.9	15.6	6.6	168.9
India	20.9	9.3	32.7	14.5	18.9	104.4
Kenya	17.1	21.0	35.4	20.9	8.6	114.3
Korea	13.1	19.7	10.8	24.6	10.2	70.1
Malaysia	3.1	6.3	12.6	5.6	7.9	30.6
Mexico	28.2	48.1	20.7	30.4	22.9	65.3
Pakistan	23.6	17.9	23.0	25.2	21.2	140.4
Sudan	5.0	25.5	7.5	9.7	6.0	307.8
Tanzania	7.2	25.9	32.9	12.8	5.3	260.8
Zimbabwe	4.4	3.8	23.1	–	4.7	240.3

Sources: World Bank 1983: 178–9, Table 16; 1987: 236–7, Table 18; 1995b: 178–9, Table 9, 206–7, Table 23; 2001: 258–60, Table 4.17; *World Development Indicators 2005*; *World Development Indicators 2007*, Table 4.16.

Note

Debt service ratio = ($ amortization + $interest)/$ exports.

banking system not only to pay for its imports but also to pay for its debt servicing obligations. So even though the equivalent of half of Mexico's export income apparently was absorbed by debt service in 1980, much of the actual payment on the debt was done by simply "rolling over" old debt by incurring new debt. This meant that debt servicing in 1980 did not have a particularly adverse effect on Mexico's ability to import goods and services, since very little of its export income was used to pay amortization and interest payments. Most of the country's foreign exchange earnings were available to purchase desired imports or for other purposes.

After the debt crisis began in 1982, however, the ability to borrow to repay debt virtually ended, so that each country's debt service ratio more accurately reflected the real cost of debt as measured by the use of foreign exchange earnings and, hence, forgone import or other expenditures. Thus in 1990, something closer to 20 percent of foreign exchange income from exports was being used by Mexico to service existing external debt. This meant that something real, in opportunity cost terms, was being given up to service the external debt.

The last column of Table 16.2 shows the total debt-to-export ratio, or the debt burden, that we considered by regions in Focus 16.2. For Mexico in 2005, the debt burden was 65.3, meaning total external debt was equivalent to 65.3 percent of Mexico's total foreign exchange earnings from exports. This is a lower debt burden than in 1999, when the D/X ratio was 108, and almost a third of the 1993 debt burden, when total external debt was 1.75 times total exports (these values are not shown in the table).

Mexico's debt burden has shown a tendency to fall as special attention has been given to debt reduction measures and, more importantly, as Mexico's exports have risen faster than new debt has been incurred as export substitution polices have taken hold. By contrast, Brazil's and Argentina's debt burdens are quite high and were larger than in the early 1990s, at least partly a reflection of the low level and growth of their export income. This reflects more fundamental underlying failures to make the necessary structural transformations in these two large Latin American debtors, including the formation of human capital and technology acquisition capabilities discussed in previous chapters that could expand export substitution possibilities. This has handicapped two promising economies in their ability to make sustained progress.

In contrast to Mexico, which among the Latin American economies has done reasonably well, consider Korea's debt experience. Between 1980 and 1990, Korea's debt service ratio fell dramatically, amounting to but slightly more than 10 percent of export income. Then it rose sharply by 1999 as total accumulated external debt increased rapidly (Table 16.1), at least partly as a result of the Asian financial crisis of the late 1990s. But by 2004, the debt service ratio was comfortably back in the 10 percent range. The reasonable level of debt servicing has been primarily due to Korea's rapid expansion of exports (at the rate of 12.1 percent annually compared to the growth of external debt of 7.5 percent, 1984–2004), which made external debt repayment easier over time, even following episodes of sudden borrowing when there was a crisis.

Because of the faster growth of export earnings compared to debt accumulation, Korea's debt burden is on the decrease, as the adverse short-term impact of the financial crisis of the late 1990s passes. In 1993, the ratio had been only 46.2 percent, the second-lowest debt burden among all countries at that time. Still, being able to repay, theoretically at any rate, all external debt out of one year's foreign exchange export revenues suggests that Korea (and Malaysia) have managed to avoid the excessive build-up of external debt that plagues other debtor nations, especially in Latin America, but also in Africa.

Sudan's, Tanzania's, and Zimbabwe's debt burdens are a matter of grave concern, even though their debt service ratios are quite low because of extraordinary efforts by the international community to delay current repayments. The potential future income from exports to pay for such a level of total external debt is just not there (see Focus 16.5 on debt relief measures).

The 1980s debt crisis

The accumulation of external debt at the pace of the 1970s certainly should have been seen as unsustainable. It was based on the availability of funds from OPEC being deposited in the international banks that were then used to finance the current account deficits of the oil importers. At some point, this variation of a Ponzi scheme had to come crashing down. The onset of the international debt crisis is usually dated as beginning when Mexico announced its decision to suspend scheduled payments on its debt in August 1982. Other countries soon followed suit. What set off this moratorium on debt obligations that for a time threatened the stability of the world financial markets?

By mid-1982, the private international banks had begun to dramatically reduce their petro-dollar recycling to sovereign borrowers as a consequence of a slow-down in the rate of growth of the international economy. Stringent monetarist policies to reduce inflation introduced by the United States and British central banks under pressure from Presidents Carter and Reagan in the United States and from the Conservative government in Great Britain had resulted in sharp recessions that spread quickly through the global economy.[14] As income in the developed countries like the US and the UK declined so too did their import purchases, including imports from the less-developed economies.

With a decline in export earnings for the oil-importing nations, the private international banks suddenly decided that sovereign borrowers were no longer the desirable borrowers they had been judged to be since 1973. After all, everyone knew that the only way external debt ultimately could be repaid was via foreign exchange earnings obtained from exporting that exceeded importing. The commercial banks thus quickly acted to reduce their lending exposure to the debtor economies, as the perceived riskiness of further lending increased. Since many borrowing nations already had been using new loans to pay their debt-service obligations and import expenditures, and had dedicated relatively little of the borrowed funds

---

FOCUS 16.5   THE FIRST DEBT-FOR-NATURE SWAP

The first debt-for-nature swap took place in 1987 and involved Bolivia and a non-governmental organization (NGO) called Conservation International. Conservation International purchased $650,000 of Bolivia's external debt on the secondary market for $100,000, a discount of 85 percent. This was swapped for the equivalent of $250,000 of Bolivia's currency to be used in setting up and operating the Beni Biosphere Reserve to protect forest land from logging and other destructive practices. Bolivia reduced its external debt obligation by $650,000 in hard currency terms, but without using foreign exchange to do so. Instead, via the swap, external debt was retired using domestic currency.

Other countries also have done such swaps. Brazil had $100 million of debt-for-nature swaps in 1991. Mexico and Costa Rica also have been parties to such transactions. These swaps have been no panacea for either developing country debt reduction or for protecting the environment, as the totals were small relative to the total debt of any country. On the other hand, such swaps are innovative means to try to combine efforts to increase the level of development and to protect threatened natural resources simultaneously.

Source: Elliott 1994: 55–6

to productive uses in tradables that would have saved or earned foreign exchange in future, when the so-called loan window of the private banks closed, debtor nations faced a daunting foreign exchange crisis, given the current account deficits being run by so many of them.[15]

Without access to new loans to finance current account deficits and with finite official foreign exchange reserves to draw upon, many countries were soon confronted with difficult decisions. With the global recession rapidly reducing their own export earnings, it was impossible to both service past debt *and* continue to import at the same level, given the sudden loss of access to external funds.

When external borrowing was still an option, it was possible for an economy to have import expenditures (M) that exceeded export earnings (X) (i.e., $X < M$). However, when it became impossible to borrow foreign exchange in the early 1980s, then a country's import spending was limited to its export earnings, that is, $X \geq M$. How was the switch from spending more foreign exchange than was earned to be turned into a situation of earning at least as much or more foreign exchange than was spent? This transformation occurred primarily by repressing import spending in the debtor economies, since exports could not be expanded rapidly.

However, any reduction in imports to save on foreign exchange meant a lower current living standard and lower GDP, particularly when critical inputs to domestic industries were affected by any cutback. Making matters worse, all foreign exchange to pay debt servicing now had to be derived from current export earnings or official foreign exchange reserves, as external borrowing was impossible.

Mexico's announcement of a moratorium on its debt service had the effect of immediately reducing the size of the current account deficit that required financing by an amount equal to the sum of the deferred debt servicing. This meant that without having to dedicate any of its export earnings to debt repayment more goods and services could be imported than if Mexico's debt service obligations had been met on time. Deferred debt servicing thus saved on foreign exchange, leaving more for other purposes. Soon, other indebted nations followed suit, declaring a debt servicing holiday to conserve on their scarce foreign exchange earned from exporting, choosing to use them for import purchases.

The debt servicing moratorium had the immediate effect of mobilizing the private international banks and their governments to attempt to find the means to get Mexico and other nations to resume their debt service payments. This was necessary to minimize the volume of loans that would be declared "bad," or non-performing, a situation that threatened many of the large international private banks with bankruptcy as a result of the excessive lending levels to some sovereign borrowers. A fundamental defining feature of the 1970s lending frenzy, as already noted, was the exceptionally high level of private bank debt held by the largest borrowing nations.[16]

While it might have been *individually* rational for each private bank to have ceased lending as the riskiness of new loans increased with the onset of the global recession at the beginning of the 1980s, it was *socially irrational* for them *all* to suspend lending simultaneously. In fact, it was this *lack* of coordination of international financial flows – combined with a healthy dose of greed on the part of the banks – that led the private banks to *over*-lend before the outbreak of the crisis and then to *under*-lend when the United States- and United Kingdom-administered global recession resulted in the sharp decrease in world trade after 1980.

In at least partial recognition of this divergence between private and social benefits and costs, and the seriousness of the market failure problem, an important part of the effort of the international community was to minimize the damage to the private banking system and the global economy after the moratorium was declared (Pastor 1987). There thus emerged a concerted effort by the International Monetary Fund and the United States Treasury to force the large private banks to initiate so-called *involuntary lending* to the major debtor countries, i.e., to open the channels of lending yet again as a way to avoid collapse of the international financial system. In effect, as a condition of being repaid and avoiding bankruptcy, the banks would provide new loans to meet the debt servicing requirements of the debtor economies.

In making such loans and in providing other concessions to the debtor nations – such as lower interest rates and longer repayment schedules, albeit without much enthusiasm – the larger private banks avoided the worst effects that a full-scale default would have implied. The banks provided "bridge loans" that made continued repayment to the large private lenders possible, and they thus avoided technical defaults by the debtor economies. Many smaller banks were, however, left out of the international reorganization deals, and quite a few collapsed when their loans went unpaid.

Longer-term efforts to overcome the debt crisis[17]

The initial efforts of the international community to overcome the 1982 debt crisis focused on measures that might enable potentially defaulting countries to continue to service their debt obligations without unduly affecting long-term economic growth. These measures included the involuntary lending by the banks discussed above. There were also numerous initiatives to lengthen the maturities of commercial loans, to reduce interest rates charged and to capitalize overdue payments by adding them to the principal value of the loans. Some write-downs, or cancellations, of private bank loans occurred, but these have not been particularly significant. Turning loans into long-term bonds, even perpetual bonds never requiring the repayment of the principal, was an early proposal still worthy of more widespread application, especially for the most deeply indebted economies (World Bank 1985: 29). As we saw from Table 16.1, for many countries, external debt has continued to increase.

Multilateral (e.g., World Bank and IMF loans) and bilateral (e.g., government-to-government) debt has been somewhat easier to reschedule or even cancel. Various rounds of negotiations of the so-called Paris Club had some success in reducing non-commercial debt of the twenty-five to thirty poorest of the most indebted nations (having GDP of less than $500 or debt burden ratios exceeding 350 percent), most of which have been in Sub-Saharan Africa.

Under the 1994 Naples terms of the Paris Club discussion, for example, up to 67 percent of non-commercial public external debt was potentially eligible for long-term rescheduling and even, in some instances, cancellation (UNCTAD 1995: 36–9). The goal has been to reduce the debt service ratios of the poorest debtors to below 20 percent. However, debt reduction or extensive stretching-out of maturities is not enough. It is also necessary to correct whatever it is that resulted in excessive debt accumulation, and for most countries that begins with a failure to have properly initiated and carried through the required structural transformations discussed in Chapters 9–11.

Another type of debt reduction measure that was popular for a time was the *debt swap*. In a debt swap, an indebted country trades something of value to a holder of its debt in return for a reduction or even cancellation of some of the country's external debt. For example, a *debt-for-equity swap* might involve the holder of Mexican debt with a value of, say, $1 million exchanging that debt with the Mexican government for ownership in a newly privatized, formerly state-owned, company. The holder of the Mexican debt might receive, for example, an equity value in the company equivalent to $1.2 million, though that equity would now be denominated in pesos, not in dollars. It is clear that there were potential gains to both parties in such transactions. The holder of Mexican debt with a face value of $1 million would "buy" $1.2 million worth of equity in a Mexican company at a discount (maybe substantially less than the face value of the debt). The Mexican government is able to retire $1 million worth of external debt that had been denominated in dollars, thus reducing its future debt servicing requirements and the outflow of foreign exchange.

Other kinds of swaps also were completed. Debt-for-nature swaps were used to encourage countries to set aside rainforests or other land areas as protected reserves. In these swaps, the holder of external debt might be an organization like the World Wildlife Fund (WWF) or some other non-governmental organization (NGO) with an interest in preserving the natural environment. How would such a group come to be a holder of, say, Costa Rican debt that could be swapped for rainforest preservation? They most likely purchased this debt on the *secondary debt market*. The secondary debt market is a "discount" market for sovereign debt instruments. Banks or any institution holding sovereign external debt can trade their debt to others willing to purchase it.

Chase Manhattan Bank, for example, could decide that it wishes to remove external debt with a face value of $20 million from its portfolio of loans because of concern over the likelihood of repayment or to reduce its exposure in the external debt market or any other reason. In the secondary market in 1989, for example, the discount on such Brazilian debt was in the neighborhood of 70 percent, so the WWF could have purchased $20 million worth of Brazilian debt instruments for about $6 million. Then, the WWF could "swap" this debt with the Brazilian government for an agreement that sets aside the equivalent of, say, $10 million worth of Brazilian rainforest from future economic development by transferring ownership to a trust, to a government agency, or even to the WWF. In this way, the WWF is able to protect $10 million worth of Amazonian rainforest from overuse at a cost to its members of $6 million. The Brazilian government reduces its external indebtedness at a 50 percent discount (by giving up the equivalent of $10 million of Brazilian forest to retire $20 million of external debt), though the actual cost may be significantly less than this, since there is no outflow of foreign exchange associated with this swap (see Focus 16.5 on the first such debt for nature swap).

There was even some hope, for a time, that approaches such as the Brady Plan, proposed in 1989, might actually lead to a voluntary reduction of the external debt burden of the most deeply indebted nations as commercial banks and other institutions were encouraged to write down their debt holdings. That did not happen to any great extent, however, and many countries continue to be saddled with large debt burdens that make the structural transformations required for further development even more difficult to achieve.

Debt overhang and future economic growth

For many countries in Latin America and Sub-Saharan Africa, poor economic policy decision-making in the past led to further bad decisions in the 1970s to accumulate large external debts so as to finance unsustainable current account deficits. All too often, external debt was not used to promote the adjustment of the economy to a more productive economic structure but was used to maintain the status quo and inequitable structures and supporting policies. Further, much of the accumulation of 1970s external debt was undertaken by non-democratic governments that overspent and wasted public monies during their tenure in power.

In many of the indebted countries, particularly in Latin America, democratic governments emerged in the mid- to late 1980s with reformist and more democratic agendas, as totalitarian regimes collapsed across the region and around the world. These were governments, often at the urging and with the assistance of the IMF and the World Bank, interested in fundamentally altering the structure of their economies by making them more efficient, more technologically-based, and more independent. However, the *debt overhang* of accumulated external debt and its repayment acted as a brake on efforts at transformation, making economic growth substantially more difficult and costly to attain and more protracted than it needed to have been (Sachs 1989).

Debt overhang can adversely affect investment decisions of potential investors, both domestic and foreign. They may fear higher taxes or periodic domestic economic recessions will be necessary to find the funds required to repay the external debt obligations. Such fears may discourage productive investment from taking place, thus reducing economic growth rates (on debt overhang, see Chowdhury (1994); Cohen (1995)). Table 16.3 provides some indirect evidence of the impact of external debt accumulation and debt overhang on investment levels after 1980 for various economies.

In Argentina, Brazil, Mexico, and a number of African economies, the decrease in gross investment from 1980 to 1990 is evident and indicative of the costs arising from the effects of the debt crisis. Argentina in 2005, for example, had an investment rate below the level that had been reached in 1970. Korea, Chile, and India have managed to increase their investment rates, thus fueling higher economic growth rates, though the effects of the 1997 Asian financial crisis was still being felt in Korea and Malaysia in 2005. As seen in Table 16.2, the burden of debt (*D/X*) in those countries is now not so severe.

Also apparent from the data for many of the African countries is the instability of investment rates. In some years, investment rates have been respectable, but they seem not to be sustainable. The recovery in investment in the Congo is probably due at least partly to the fact that, as for Mexico, the Congo is now an oil exporter. For the severely indebted economies, particularly those which remain primary product exporters, like Argentina and Côte d'Ivoire at more than 70 percent, debt overhang continues to make any desire by government and the private sector to initiate the desirable structural transformations toward a more sustainable, productive, and efficient economy more difficult as valuable foreign exchange is drained to pay external debt obligations.

In one comprehensive study, the effect of debt overhang on economic growth was estimated to become negative, on average, when the debt burden exceeded 160–170 percent of exports and 35–40 percent of GDP (Pattillo, Poirson, and Ricci 2002). From Table 16.2, that

Table 16.3 Gross capital formation (as percentage of GDP)

	1965	1970	1980	1985	1990	2000	2005
Argentina	19	24	25	18	14	16	21.5
Brazil	25	21	23	19	20	21	20.6
Chile	15	19	21	17	25	23	23.0
Congo	22	24	36	30	16	24	24.1
Côte d'Ivoire	22	22	27	13	7	12	10.7
Ghana	18	14	6	10	14	24	29.0
India	18	17	21	24	25	24	33.4
Kenya	14	24	25	22	20	13	16.8
Korea	15	25	32	30	38	29	30.1
Malaysia	20	20	27	25	32	26	19.9
Mexico	22	23	27	21	23	23	21.8
Pakistan	21	16	18	18	19	16	16.8
Sudan	10	13	15	9	7	14	23.3
Tanzania	15	23	22	–	17	13	18.9

Sources: World Bank 1982: 118–19, Table 5; *World Development Indicators 2002* and *2007*.

would include Argentina, Ghana, Sudan, Tanzania, and Zimbabwe, with Brazil and Pakistan very close to having a *D/X* ratio in that range. However, the marginal negative effects of debt overhang were manifest at *D/X* ratios equal to half the average, meaning in the 80–85 percent range. By that measure, all the economies in Table 16.2, with the exceptions of Korea, Malaysia, and Mexico, had some predicted negative impact on the economy from debt overhang. The authors also found that debt overhang affected not just investment rates but also total factor productivity (TFP) rates, i.e., intensive economic growth, thus slowing economic progress.

Looking at the almost forty so-called "heavily indebted poor countries" (HIPCs), their investment rates in 2005 averaged 20.9 percent compared to 28.6 for all low-income economies and 27.1 percent for all low- and middle-income economies (WDI online 2007). However, as some economists have pointed out, there are likely other structural factors – bad policy decisions, poor infrastructure, a lack of fundamental structural transformation – besides debt overhang that more likely explain the low investment rates for many of the HIPCs. Still, high debt burdens do not help, even if they are not the major factor in slowing economic and productivity growth.

The social effects of servicing debt also can be quite severe. A 1996 Oxfam report found that:

> For less than is currently being spent on debt, it would be possible by the year 2000 to make social investments which would save the lives of around 21 million African children, and provide 90 million girls with access to primary education.

The amount spent by governments in Sub-Saharan Africa to service debt amounts to *four times* what is spent on health care and *exceeds* the total amount spent on primary education and primary health care combined. It is the poorest debtors, particularly those in Africa, such as Mozambique and Zambia, which find that their debt payments greatly exceed spending on social infrastructure.[18]

Some way must be found to relieve the pressure of debt overhang, perhaps through new forms of lending that convert old debt into perpetual bonds never requiring repayment of the principal. This will at least open the possibility that such economies will not be bound by poor policy decisions from the past. This step is all the more urgent, because many of these loans were undertaken by non-democratic governments under which few in the population benefited.

Summary and conclusions

Far too many economies accumulated external debt during the 1970s for the wrong reasons. Mostly, the rapid build-up of debt was a response to OPEC's increases in oil prices, which resulted in the demand for borrowing to finance larger current account deficits. Too often, this external debt was not used productively, a reflection of the fact that many of the major borrowers, especially in Latin America, had failed to transform their economies in the ways we considered in earlier chapters. In particular, economies with inefficient industrial production and disappointing progress in shifting from a primary product export base to a secondary export structure were more likely to accumulate "too much" external debt and find repayment difficult and costly for economic growth. The fact that much of the external debt was owed to private commercial banks who clearly over-lent complicated matters when the debt crisis began in 1982.

Taking a longer-term view, the debt crisis had some positive effects. Because of pressures from the international community to change the way their economies operated, not all of which were viewed at the time as helpful, many non-democratic governments disappeared and were replaced by the return, or the beginning, of democratic political processes. With such political openings and the continued pressure to reduce barriers to trade in international agreements (discussed in the next chapter), more economies, especially in Latin America, but also in Asia, experienced important structural changes imposed by international competition. One consequence of this has been the growth in manufactured goods exports in many economies, as export substitution policies took hold. This has helped to decrease the importance of primary product exports and made it easier for countries to service their external debts, as export income tends to grow faster with the shift toward secondary and other non-traditional exports.

Many economies continue to suffer from some degree of debt overhang. Whether it reduces investment or productivity or cuts into social or other spending, there is some measurable adverse effect on these economies. Given the circumstances under which much external debt was accumulated, in particular by non-democratic regimes, there continues to be a pressing economic and moral need to minimize the adverse impact of debt on current governments intent on fomenting positive transformations of their economic structures.

Questions and exercises

1   Carefully define external debt. How is it different from the internal debt of an economy?
2   Why do countries incur external debt?
3   For what purposes can the accumulation of external debt be justified?
4   What are two or three "bad" reasons for incurring external debt *other than* those listed in the chapter?
5   How is external debt repaid, i.e., where do the funds come from to repay external debt?
6   Table 16.1 shows the total external debt for a few nations. However, in comparing total debt among nations, such a gross comparison may be a bit deceptive. Countries with larger populations may be better able to repay a given amount of debt than a country with a smaller population. First, using the total debt values from Table 16.1, rank the countries from 1 to 14, using 1 for the country with the highest total debt and 14 for the country with the lowest total debt.

Per capita external debt, 2005

	Total external debt ranking	*Population*	*Debt per person*	*Ranking*
Argentina				
Brazil				
Chile				
Congo				
Côte d'Ivoire				
Ghana				
India				
Kenya				
Malaysia				
Mexico				
Pakistan				
Sudan				
Tanzania				
Zimbabwe				

Then, find the total population for each country from www.worldbank.org or some other source and calculate per capita external debt. Then rank the countries by debt per person, using 1 for the country with the highest debt per person and 14 for the country with the lowest debt per capita. How do the rankings for total debt differ from the rankings for debt per capita?

7   Imagine a country with total external debt of $22,000 million, on which an average rate of interest of 8.7 percent is charged. Its exports are currently equal to $31,000 million and are growing at a rate of 4.5 percent per year. Calculate the current debt/export ratio and, assuming no new external debt accumulation, the debt/export ratio in five years' time.

8   What effect does a deterioration in a country's terms of trade have on its ability to service its external debt obligations? What effect does a devaluation or depreciation of a country's currency have on its ability to service its external debt obligations? If you can, use some simple numerical calculations to show these effects. (For example, when the value of the Mexican peso fell from roughly 3 pesos:US $1 to 6 pesos:US $1 in early 1995, did this depreciation make repayment of Mexico's debt easier or more difficult? Were more or fewer exports, in physical terms, required for a fixed amount of debt service?)

9   For a country that interests you and for the region in which the country you chose is located and for the low- and middle-income countries, use the table below to input the requested information for two years, using data for, say, 1990 and the most current year. You can find the data for parts a–c (below) at http://www.worldbank.org. Click on "Data," then "Data by Topic" and then choose "Debt." For d go to http://hdr.undp.org/reports and then in the left-hand column click on "HDR," then click on "Chapters" and then choose "Tables" (you will have to do a search on "debt service" to find exactly where the data is located). Find and record the following for two years:

a   total external debt;
b   long-term debt as a share (i.e., percentage) of total debt (you will have to calculate this!);
c   by what percentage the total external debt of *the low- and middle-income* countries has increased between the two years;
d   debt service ratio (*using exports as the base, not GDP*) for the two years. Has your country's situation improved?

For each of these items, briefly (in a sentence or two) explain what these specific values for your country mean and how your country measures up to the region to which your country belongs and compared to all low- and middle-income economies.

	1990	
Low- and middle-income countries		

10   Last year, Indonesia had to repay $3.45 billion in interest on its total external debt of $66.7 billion. It also had to repay principal (amortization) of $2.81 billion. Indonesia's total imports last year were $45.13 billion and its exports were $46.67 billion. From this data, calculate Indonesia's debt service ratio. Show your work.

11 What are some of the opportunity costs countries might face when repaying external debt, particularly when debt was accumulated for the wrong reasons?

Notes

1 This is a political precondition that we have, admittedly, not specifically addressed, not because we think it unimportant, but because it would take us too far afield from our current inquiry. Unfortunately, it would appear that in many circumstances governing elites are not truly concerned with improving economic and social conditions for a broad range of the population. They often seem to be more interested in consolidating specific gains for a narrow segment of a ruling elite of which they are a part. Under such conditions, the economic know-how about development will be less immediately important than are the necessary political changes which can strengthen democracy and participation in the decision-making process of the country.

In some instances, political change will need to be quite revolutionary, certainly in the sense of displacing former centres of political and economic power, if not also literally in the sense of overthrowing corrupt and non-democratic regimes. Such fundamental political changes preceded the rapid progress observed in South Korea and Taiwan after the 1950s. In other countries with entrenched ruling classes wielding economic and political power, the nullification of powerful interests may be as important for the future as are the proper exchange rate and human capital accumulation.

2 *External debt* is borrowing denominated in a foreign currency, typically a *hard* or stable international currency like the US dollar or the euro. We discussed such external borrowing in the previous chapter in the context of economies that borrow to finance a current account deficit in their balance of payments.

3 Currently, the membership of OPEC includes: Algeria (1969), Angola (2007), Indonesia (1962), Iran (1960), Iraq (1960), Kuwait (1960), Libya (1962), Nigeria (1971), Qatar (1961), Saudi Arabia (1960), the United Arab Emirates (1967), and Venezuela (1960). The date of membership is shown in parentheses. Ecuador was a member of OPEC from 1973 to 1992 and Gabon from 1975 to 1994. OPEC itself was founded in 1960 at the Baghdad Conference by the five founding members whose membership year is 1960. See http://www.opec.org/aboutus/ for more details, including current prices of oil.

4 US dollars were the key currency for external debt. Anywhere from 65 percent to more than 75 percent of external public debt was denominated in dollars over the period 1974 to 1983 (World Bank 1985: 22). External debt is incurred when governments or businesses borrow from foreign governments, from foreign private banks, from foreign businesses, from individuals in other countries, or from a multilateral lending agency, such as the World Bank or the International Monetary Fund. External debt can be repaid only by earning the necessary foreign exchange, that is, by exporting goods and services.

By contrast, *internal debt* arising, for example, from the central government's need to borrow to cover a budget deficit, is most often denominated in the country's own currency. While the possibility, and the danger, of simply printing money to repay an internal debt exists, thus making repayment assured, such a possibility is not available for servicing external debt payments. External debt repayment requires that foreign exchange in excess of expenditures be earned from the rest of the world; printing money to repay external debt is not an option.

5 Sovereign borrowers were thought to be better risks than other borrowers. The thinking of the private banking community was that, as independent and sovereign countries, the oil-importing borrowers would always be able to repay, on the assumption that countries "do not go bankrupt." Of course sovereign borrowers were different from other borrowers in another significant sense, too. They did not provide any collateral to the private banks when they borrowed as other borrowers, like businesses or households, do.

As we shall see, the banks made a logical error. While it may be true that sovereign nations do not go bankrupt in the usual sense of the term, they certainly can decide to not make on-time payments on loans (a *moratorium*) or even at all (a *default*). The international banking system's thinking also demonstrates its lack of "memory." Very similar banking crises had erupted in the 1890s and in the 1930s with almost the same cast of bad debtors, particularly the larger Latin American countries (see Stallings 1988). It might be worth remembering a dictum, appropriately updated, attributed to economist John Maynard Keynes, a warning the international banks apparently forgot: if you owe the bank $100,000, you have a problem. If you owe the bank $100 million, the bank has a problem.

6 Just prior to the outbreak of the debt crisis, in 1982, South Korea was the third-largest debtor nation, at least in terms of total external debt, after Brazil and Mexico.

7 In 1974, 18.4 percent of all public external debt was in floating interest rate loans; by 1982, 51.2 percent of public external debt had been contracted at variable rates of interest (World Bank 1985: 21, Table 2.4).

8 We are here concerned with the *practical* arguments for incurring external debt, as opposed to the *theoretical* rationales often found in the economics literature, particularly those concerned with the free flow of capital between nations. (We are also concerned with the issue of capital inflows resulting from borrowing, as distinct from capital inflows that result from foreign aid or from multinational direct foreign investments discussed in Chapters 14 and 17.)

For example, it is often argued that when financial and physical capital flow to less-developed nations from more-developed nations, these contribute to an increase in the level of world efficiency, as capital moves from regions with lower rates of return, that is, more-developed economies with relatively large stocks of capital, to regions with higher rates of return, that is, the less-developed nations with smaller stocks of capital. In this way, it is argued, external sources of savings can add to internal savings, thus permitting lower-income countries to grow more rapidly.

These efficiency and mobilization-of-savings arguments are often put forward as compelling reasons for countries to rapidly open the capital and financial account of their balances of payments accounts, that is, to allow the free flow of financial capital within the international economy without government interference with such flows. However, as Stiglitz (1993) has argued, the flow of financial capital is not at all like the flow of goods, and any market imperfections can result in too much or too little movement of capital. In fact, Stiglitz makes the case that when financial markets are imperfect, government oversight of capital flows can increase economic efficiency. Recognizing, then, the complexities of external capital flows, we are considering the rationale for such borrowing, assuming an imperfect world with imperfect information, that is, a Stiglitz-type world.

9 Alternatively, it might well be argued that one of the reasons countries hold foreign exchange reserves is to have the ability to undertake precisely such import consumption smoothing.

Borrowing for consumption smoothing is a situation when a short-term need to borrow externally should be roughly matched on the other side of the business cycle by an excess of foreign exchange earnings over foreign exchange spending such that a surplus on the current account permits repayment of previously accumulated external debt obligations.

10 The political economy of the problem of external debt accumulation is even more complex than shown here. At least a part of the reason for the twin deficit discussed in the next section and for a persistent current account imbalance in many less-developed nations, and certainly many Latin American economies, is related to income inequality. A narrow but wealthy stratum of the population has a high propensity to import. The demand of this elite for imported consumer goods and, indirectly, for imported inputs of domestic capital-intensive industries, adds to the import bill and reduces the share of any export earnings that might be dedicated to other uses.

One possibility for dealing with recurrent current account deficits might, then, involve a tax on high-income families, which will reduce import demand and the external borrowing requirement. Such tax revenues could provide a source of funds for financing the structural transformation and the expansion of export substitution production, further reducing external borrowing requirements.

11 This result can be derived from a simple rearrangement of the basic macroeconomic identity where $Y = C + I + (G - T) + (X - M)$. If $G - T = 0$, i.e., there is no central government deficit, then we can rewrite the equation as $Y - C - I = X - M$. Since saving $S = Y - C$, we can further simplify to $S - I = X - M$, which is statement 16.1 in the text.

12 S is total savings, Y is total national income (say, GDP), L is total population, Y/L is per capita income, and s, which is the proportion of income saved ("the savings rate"), has a value of $0 < s < 1$.

Thus this equation states that domestic savings is equal to (determined by) the percent of income saved times the income per person times the number of persons in the economy. Obviously if $s = 0$ or is close to zero, the total level of savings will be zero (or close to it). This means there can be no domestic investment (since $S = 0 = I$) and no expected economic growth in the most simple economic model, as there will be no new physical capital being created.

13 The full twin deficit equation, $(S - I) + (T - G) = X - M$, demonstrates another possible cause of the need to borrow externally. If the central government runs a budget deficit such that $T - G < 0$, then, assuming $S - I = 0$ or $S - I < 0$, an external borrowing requirement is also created by the internal, domestic fiscal deficit.

This reinforces the need for prudent government finance and oversight of internal macroeconomic policy. Internal debt can lead to external debt accumulation. On the other hand, government may find it wise to borrow externally when loanable funds are short at home, but only if such borrowing meets the same requirements of expanding tradables in the future. Such state spending may be directed to a broader range of investments which can have such an effect: education, research and development, international marketing research, and so on.

14 Basically, by reducing growth in the money supply, interest rates were pushed upward dramatically, thus discouraging borrowing and investment. This induced a slow-down in economic activity which resulted in a slower pace of inflation as aggregate demand fell.

15 In 1981, all of the countries listed in Tables 16.1 and 16.2 had substantially larger current account deficits than had prevailed in 1970 prior to the OPEC price increase. For example, Mexico's current account deficit had risen from $1,068 million in 1970 to $12,933 million in 1981; Chile's from $91 million to $4,814 million; Kenya's from $49 million to $736 million (World Bank 1983: 74–5, Table 14). Part of this was due to higher oil costs. Part, however, was the consequence of the larger external debt service obligations to repay interest and principal that created an added outflow of foreign exchange on the current account.

External debt incurred to finance current account deficits thus added to future current account deficit financing needs as a result of the outflow of interest and principal repayment required for debt servicing. In many countries, particularly in Latin America, with weak or non-existent restrictions on movements of financial assets, capital flight also seriously exacerbated the need for external borrowing beyond that reflected in the current account imbalance alone, as investors converted their domestic currency to dollars and moved them off-shore.

16 This was particularly true for the Latin American debtor nations and in East Asia. For most African economies and South Asian borrowers, the bulk of their external debt had been provided by multilateral agencies such as the World Bank or the International Monetary Fund, or by other governments at concessional rates of interest and with easier repayment schedules. In 1980, 74.4 percent of South Asia's external debt was concessional; 27.0 percent of Sub-Saharan Africa's was concessional, but only 4.4 percent of external debt in Latin America was concessional (World Bank 1995b: 206–7, Table 23).

The world recession adversely affected the African and South Asian countries' ability to repay as well. However, the effect of any default on multinational lending agencies or on other governments that had extended concessional loans was quite different from a default impacting on *private* banking institutions' balance sheets and accounting rules. The debt crisis set off by Mexico's and other debtors' moratorium was a real crisis for the international financial system, since it threatened the stability and even the possibility of survival of several major private banks. If this crisis had not been solved quickly, the impact on the world economy could have been quite severe (see Felix (1987) for a historical perspective on earlier debt crises affecting Latin America).

17 For a readable and informative early overview on external debt reduction, see "Symposium" \(1990).

18 For example, between 1990 and 1993, Mozambique was able to meet only about 10 percent of its scheduled debt repayments, equal to about $70 million per year. Yet this amount alone would have been sufficient to pay for ten times the number of textbooks required for all the country's primary schools.

References

Amsden, Alice H. 2001. *The Rise of "the Rest": Challenges to the West from Late-Industrializing Economies.* Oxford: Oxford University Press.

Chowdhury, Khorshed. 1994. "A Structural Analysis of External Debt and Economic Growth: Some Evidence from Selected Countries in Asia and the Pacific," *Applied Economics* 26 (December): 1121–31.

Cohen, Daniel. 1995. "Large External Debt and (Slow) Domestic Growth: A Theoretical Analysis," *Journal of Economic Dynamics and Control* 19 (July): 1141–63.

Devlin, Robert. 1989. *Debt and Crisis in Latin America: The Supply Side of the Story*. Princeton: Princeton University Press.

Elliott, Jennifer A. 1994. *An Introduction to Sustainable Development*. London: Routledge.

Felix, David. 1987. "Alternative Outcomes of the Latin American Debt Crisis: Lessons from the Past," *Latin American Research Review* 22(2): 3–46.

Ffrench-Davis, Ricardo and Stephany Griffith-Jones (eds.). 1995. *Coping with Capital Surges: The Return of Finance to Latin America*. Boulder, CO, and London: Lynne Rienner Publishers.

IMF (International Monetary Fund). 1995. *World Economic Outlook*. Washington, D.C.: IMF.

Pastor, Robert A. (ed.) 1987. *Latin America's Debt Crisis: Adjusting to the Past or Planning for the Future*. Boulder, CO, and London: Lynne Rienner Publishers.

Pattillo, Catherine, Hélène Poirson and Luca Ricci. 2002. "External Debt and Growth," *Finance and Development* 39 (June): 35–8.

Sachs, Jeffrey. 1989. "The Debt Overhang of Developing Countries," pp. 80–102 in G.A. Calvo *et al.* (eds.), *Debt Stabilization and Development*. Oxford: Oxford University Press.

Stallings, Barbara. 1988. *Banker to the Third World: U.S. Portfolio Investment in Latin America, 1900–1986*. Berkeley: University of California Press.

Stiglitz, Joseph. 1993. "The Role of the State in Financial Markets," *Proceedings of the World Bank Annual Conference on Development Economics*, vol. 2. Washington, D.C.: World Bank.

"Symposium: New Institutions for Developing Country Debt." 1990. *The Journal of Economic Perspectives* 4 (Winter): 3–56.

UNCTAD (United Nations Conference on Trade and Development). 1995. *Trade and Development Report 1995*. Paris: UNCTAD.

Vernon, Raymond (ed.). 1987. *The Oil Crisis*. New York: W.W. Norton & Co.

Wee, Herman van der. 1976. *Prosperity and Upheaval: The World Economy, 1945–1980*. Berkeley: University of California Press.

World Bank. 1982. *World Development Report 1982*. Oxford: Oxford University Press.

——. 1983. *World Development Report 1983*. Oxford: Oxford University Press.

——. 1985. *World Development Report 1985*. Oxford: Oxford University Press.

——. 1987. *World Development Report 1987*. Oxford: Oxford University Press.

——. 1995a. *Annual Report 1995*. Washington, D.C.: World Bank.

——. 1995b. *World Development Report 1995*. Oxford: Oxford University Press.

——. 1997. *World Development Report 1997*. Oxford: Oxford University Press.

——. 2001. *World Development Indicators 2001*. Washington, D.C.: World Bank.

——. 2002. *World Development Indicators 2002*. Washington, D.C.: World Bank.

Zanoyan, Vaban. 1995. "After the Oil Boom," *Foreign Affairs* 74 (November/December): 2–7.

17 International institutional linkages

The International Monetary Fund, the World Bank, and foreign aid

After reading and studying this chapter you should better understand:
- the functions and evolution of the International Monetary Fund and the World Bank and their lending programs;
- what an IMF stand-by loan is and its purpose;
- the theory supporting, and the purpose of, IMF austerity and adjustment programs;
- the effectiveness of IMF austerity and adjustment programs;
- the difference between World Bank project loans and structural adjustment loans
- (SALs);
- Poverty Reduction Strategy Papers (PRSPs) and pro-poor growth
- the focus and limitations of foreign aid;
- the nature of donor bias in aid giving.

Introduction

As we have seen in the previous chapters, developing nations have to make a wide range of choices regarding their development strategies. For sustainable development, we have seen that, in the final analysis, countries must draw primarily upon their own resources and capabilities. However, since virtually all less-developed nations are members of the IMF and the World Bank (IBRD, the International Bank for Reconstruction and Development), and since almost all of the poorest and some of the not-so-poor nations draw significant supplements to their savings and production capabilities from foreign aid, it is necessary for every student of economic development to acquire a basic understanding of the role of these institutions in the development process.[1]

When sovereign nations turn to the multilateral institutions such as the IMF and the World Bank, or when they accept foreign aid, they then are able to extend their production capabilities by supplementing domestic savings and investment (or consumption) with foreign resources. But while such access creates an opportunity, it also presents a challenge to the developing nations, since the international institutions never lend or grant funds without also attempting to influence the course of events and the economic dynamics of the less-developed nations. When international institutional linkages improve on the overall developmental potential of the recipient nation, there is little reason for concern. Unfortunately, in the opinion of virtually all observers of aid, including the lending institutions themselves, this fortuitous outcome has too rarely been achieved. Consequently, the role and effects of international institutional linkages have long been a subject of much debate and sometimes confusion.

It is often difficult to penetrate to the core of this debate, because the recipient nation may find it convenient to exaggerate the impact of the international institutions on their development trajectory in order to avert criticism of its own policies. Meanwhile, the lending and donor agencies have operated with varying degrees of secrecy, making it extremely difficult for development economists to evaluate objectively the impact of these international institutional linkages. Of all the various international institutions involved in development issues, the IMF is by far the most opaque in its operations. We will turn to this entity first, then to the World Bank, and finally to bilateral foreign aid. Little specific attention will be paid to the regional development banks, the main ones being the InterAmerican Development Bank (IDB), the Asian Development Bank (ADB), and the African Development Bank (AfDB). These regional banks are important, and they function much as does the World Bank, but with a mandate limiting their activity to a geographic region.

The IMF

Both the IMF (or "the Fund") and the World Bank were conceived at the Bretton Woods conference held at the Mount Washington Hotel in Bretton Woods, New Hampshire, in 1944. This conference brought together representatives of forty-four nations in an attempt to think through and plan out a new international financial and trade system. The new system needed to be both stable enough to maintain confidence and able to avoid the international economic chaos of the 1920s and 1930s, and yet be flexible enough to accommodate changing circumstances. It is somewhat ironic that John Maynard Keynes dominated the conference, because in most respects the two main progeny of the conference, the IMF and the World Bank, have never demonstrated a strong affinity for Keynesian-type approaches to economic issues. Most of the proceedings of the Bretton Woods conference were devoted to the creation of the IMF, with the World Bank idea left semi-defined and much in the background.[2]

The IMF officially came into existence in late 1945, whereupon thirty-nine countries pledged quotas totaling $7.4 billion. According to the Articles of Agreement of the Fund, voting power was directly related to a nation's quota, expressed as a percentage of the total subscribed quotas, with each country's individual quota being determined jointly by its level of economic income and population size. (The World Bank also shares this structural characteristic.) Powerful and economically advanced nations, particularly the United States and Britain, pledged the largest amounts to the Fund, and consequently received a proportionately larger vote, usually enough to veto any actions that might be proposed by the Fund which the United States and Britain strongly opposed. The majority of the nations joining the Fund were poor and developing, and they lacked the level of economic development and the hard currency reserves or gold necessary to create a strong position in the IMF's voting structure. Fund membership has grown steadily, reaching 185 members as of September 2007 (see Figure 17.1). The IMF's capital stock grew to $325 billion in 2007, with slightly more than $200 billion uncommitted and available to the member countries.

In 2007, the United States continued to be the Fund's largest participant, holding 16.8 percent of the voting power. Yet US influence in the Fund has steadily diminished, as other nations vie for world economic dominance. In 1982, for example, the United States held 19.6

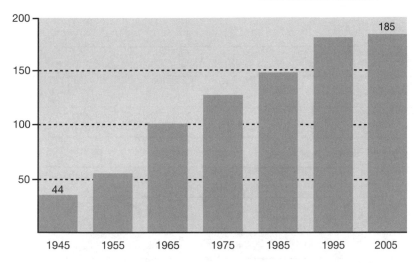

Figure 17.1 Growth in membership of the IMF.

percent of the voting power. As the United States' influence within the Fund has declined over the years, so Japan's share (among others) has advanced. Nonetheless, the United States' role is extremely important, since major changes in Fund policy can only occur when there is 85 percent of the voting power in favor of such changes. Thus, though relative US dominance in the Fund has been reduced, the United States retains ultimate veto power over any major decision it might wish to block.

History of the IMF

From 1946 to 1955 the Fund lent virtually nothing to its members, restricting its actions largely to technical assistance to European member nations which were in the process of achieving full convertibility of their currencies (see Figure 17.2). Technical assistance is quite important as the Fund, like the Bank, exercises great influence through its consultations and advice to its member nations. During this early period, the Fund was attempting to reach agreement in interpreting its charter and mandate, much of which was not fully defined until 1952. Of note at this juncture was the creation of the **stand-by arrangement**, which articulates the policies and procedures to be utilized when a nation seeks access to the Fund's resources in excess of 25 percent of its quota (or first credit tranche). Borrowing *below* the 25 percent limit is freely allowed without approval or condition, since this amount represents the hard currency reserves and gold each country pays into the IMF.

A nation goes to the IMF to borrow to cover a current account deficit or because of exchange rate problems requiring foreign exchange reserves. Typically, resort to IMF financing reflects an inability on the part of a country to access more normal channels of international financing. In other words, going to the IMF is tacit recognition of currently unsustainable economic policies, due either to internal policy failures or to external changes in the international economy that adversely affect an economy – such as a sudden shift in the terms of trade or collapse of a major export commodity. In theory, the Fund's loans are short term and were conceived as "bridges" for resolving short-term balance of payments and exchange rate difficulties.

Billions of US $

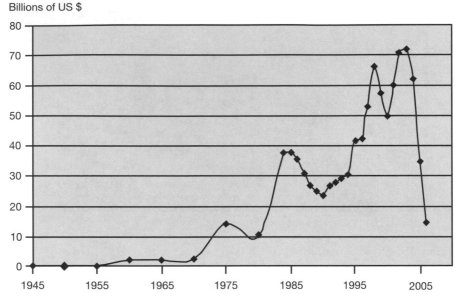

Figure 17.2 IMF lending.

Note
a   In billions of SDRs (1 SDR = 1.55 US dollars, September 2007).
     Data for 2007 through September.

Stand-by arrangements

A "stand-by arrangement" is a two-part process, whereby a member nation can draw from its quota over a period of twelve to eighteen months.[3] The first part of the stand-by arrangement consists of a process whereby a *letter of intent* is signed by both the borrowing nation and the representatives of the Fund. In order to prepare for such an agreement, a nation desiring Fund resources must first accept the visit of an IMF delegation, which makes its own assessment of the conditions of the borrowing nation and the macroeconomic difficulties which have led to the need for a request for international assistance.

At this stage of negotiation, both the potential borrower and the Fund will engage in extensive bargaining, with each side seeking to guide and control the borrowing process. The Fund will demand "conditions" for its willingness to make a loan, thus the term **conditionality** for such requirements, while the borrowing nation will attempt to ensure that conditionality is as mild as possible (see Focus 17.1). How draconian the stand-by loan conditions are depends on many factors, of which the negotiating skill of the borrowing nation is of particular importance.[4]

Once a **letter of intent** has been signed, "drawing" of the quota can begin. In this second stage, the Fund reviews the progress the borrowing nation has made on meeting the agreement's conditions every six months, with subsequent drawings dependent upon meeting the conditions imposed. Failure to meet the conditions may, and sometimes does, result in suspension of a stand-by arrangement. A "drawing" from the Fund consists of a transaction whereby the Fund sells "hard" currency, like the United States dollar or the euro, to the borrowing country in exchange for its own currency, which is deposited at the Fund in the country's account. To repay the loan, the borrowing country must "buy back" its own currency by using hard currencies to repurchase what it deposited, thus replenishing the Fund's supply of hard currencies.[5] Under a stand-by arrangement, the more a nation borrows, the greater the scope of the conditionality and the greater the restrictiveness.

In the early years of the Fund, borrowing was never extensive. In the period 1947–67, half of the borrowing actually was done by the advanced nations. It was not until the late 1960s, and particularly the early 1970s as a result of the first oil shock, that the Fund became oriented toward lending to the developing nations. To be sure, the Fund continues to wrestle with issues of currency stability and financial balance on a global scale – its original mission – but increasingly the Fund has become an institution specializing in the problems of the developing nations. In mid-1995, the IMF had active stand-by arrangements (or similar loans, to be discussed below) with sixty-two nations (see Figure 17.2).

During the period 1979–93, the Fund financed 353 separate programs, suggesting that relatively few less-developed nations were exempt from the Fund's direct influence in recent years (Killick 1995: 60). The Fund appeared invigorated by its vastly expanded role, envisioning much larger programs for the twenty-first century. These anticipations, however, were steadily undermined by a wave of crises in the late 1990s. The Asian crisis (1997) and

FOCUS 17.1   WHAT IS CONDITIONALITY?

For a country to make use of IMF financial resources, it first must meet, or at least agree to, certain macroeconomic policy conditions. These **conditionality** requirements range from rather general commitments to cooperate with the IMF in setting policies to formulating a specific, quantified plan for financial and fiscal policies.

Conditionality seeks to ensure that members using IMF resources will adopt the policy measures the IMF believes are needed to improve the balance of payments positions and to resolve their exchange rate difficulties. It is also important that the country be able to repay the IMF in a timely manner. For "high-conditionality" arrangements, that is for upper credit tranche* stand-by and extended arrangements, four conditions are generally included:

- a letter of intent, which outlines the government's policy intentions during the program period;
- policy changes, known as "prior actions," that must be taken before approval of the arrangement;
- performance criteria, which are quantitative targets for certain policies, such as limits on the budget deficit or on the money supply, that must be met on a quarterly or semiannual basis for drawings to be made and which serve as a monitoring device; and
- periodic reviews during the life of the lending arrangement, another device through which the Executive Board of the IMF assesses the consistency of policies with the objectives of the adjustment program.

As befits the unsettled nature of Fund policies in recent years, the IMF has decided that its policies on conditionality have often *contributed* to further economic turmoil. The Fund in 2002 openly discussed the "growing intrusiveness of conditionality" stressing that recipient countries should "own" any restructuring program. The new conditionality guidelines mandate that the Fund will work in "more of a cooperative venture" with borrowing nations, reduce the number of conditions and work more closely with the World Bank on structural changes imposed as conditions for loans. (These changes were part of a grand initiative known as the **Poverty Reduction Strategy Papers** discussed later in this chapter.)

* A "tranche" is a credit "slice" equal to 25 percent of a nation's quota, with upper tranches being defined as borrowing above 25 percent of the quota.

Sources: IMF 1995d: 234; 2002: 390; 2007a

the Russian crisis (1998) pushed lending to new heights – by 2002 lending amounted to nearly twice the peak level achieved in 1985–6 (Figure 17.2).

The Fund turned defensive as critiques of its policies and program abounded – from the far right of the political spectrum through the middle ranks and on to the left. The Fund's new role, providing mega bail-outs with surprising frequency, raised the visibility of an institution that had long been comfortable with a very low public profile. In November 1998, for example, the Fund pledged a $41.5 billion loan to Brazil for release in 1998 and 1999. Then, in August 2002, the Fund approved another loan to Brazil in the amount of $30 billion. An unprecedented 1995 mega-loan to Mexico (discussed below) had unleashed a firestorm of criticism and commentary. The August 2002 loan to Brazil caused little notice and even less dissent (outside Brazil).

In this new environment the Fund grappled with the stresses of a new era burdened with the sudden and unanticipated economic breakdowns that befell some of the largest and most important developing nations. The confidence of the early 1990s had been replaced by a guarded wariness as the Fund sought to revise many strategies and programs. But suddenly, in the 2002/2003 period, conditions for the Fund were once again rapidly changed: the **commodities boom**, enduring through 2007, brought an avalanche of foreign exchange to almost all developing nations. As prices for "hard" commodities such as gold, copper, lead, oil, etc. reached record levels, and as "soft" commodities such as soy and wheat generally followed a strong upward trend (with some important exceptions such as coffee), borrowing from the Fund collapsed. From a peak of 72 billion SDRs in credits and loans outstanding in 2003 borrowing fell to only 14 billion SDRs in 2006. Lending activity was on a par with that of the late 1970s before the debt crisis of the 1980s that had made the IMF infamous.

Other lending facilities of the IMF

In 1963, the Fund created a new lending source, the Compensatory Financing Facility, which would supplement resources borrowed under stand-by arrangements. This new Facility signaled both a change in the direction of the Fund's concerns toward the developing nations and the fact that the Fund would continue to reinterpret and amend its original mandate under its Articles of Agreement. The new Facility became one of eight to be created in the period 1963–93, with three new lending facilities created during the turbulent years 1974–5, designed to increase the amounts that could be lent to borrowing nations above the original quota amount.

The **Compensatory Financing Facility** allows member nations to borrow for the specific purpose of coping with external shocks to export earnings and/or food imports. In effect, the Fund acknowledged that a broad range of developing nations, which remained primary commodity exporters to the international market, often faced sudden and uncontrollable movements in export earnings due to the intrinsic instability of global markets for primary commodities and their terms of trade, particularly agricultural goods.[6] Such concerns also were echoed by the creation of the **Buffer Stock Facility** in 1969, which was designed to help stabilize the prices of raw materials from the cyclical volatility so characteristic of many primary products.

Further, as a result of the spike in oil prices in the early 1970s, many poor nations which were totally bereft of petroleum resources were particularly impacted, with fuel import costs soaring, as we saw in Chapter 16. The Fund reacted quickly by creating two other lending sources to facilitate borrowing due to petroleum price changes: the **Oil Facility** and the

Extended Fund Facility (1974). The Extended Fund Facility allowed countries that had used all of their regular quota drawing rights to continue to receive supplementary funding from the Fund.

These four new Facilities were all addressed to the particular problems of the less-developed nations and, taken together, demonstrated the new orientation of the Fund as an entity which was primarily involved with the problems of the poorer countries. Through the 1980s and into the 1990s, the Fund continued on this trajectory. It has created three new **Structural Adjustment Facilities**, which lent over a multi-year period in order to change the productive and institutional structures of the poor nations. (Structural adjustment lending actually was originated by, and continues at, the World Bank, as is discussed later in the chapter.) In early 1995, the Fund once again demonstrated its ability to innovate and evolve when it signed an unprecedented $17.8 billion stand-by arrangement with Mexico, following the massive devaluation of the peso at the end of 1994. This huge loan was 50 percent larger than all other current stand-by loans combined, and ten times greater than Mexico's quota! The Fund justified this loan as necessary to stabilize the fragile emerging financial markets of the less-developed nations, not only in Latin America, but in Asia as well, which reacted quickly and adversely to the Mexican peso crisis. In doing so, the IMF widened its scope of authority and influence, once again.

Yet the deepening difficulties the Fund faced from 1997 onward forced further adaptations – thus in 1997 a **Supplemental Reserve Facility** was created to deal with "financial contagion" problems. Loans of this nature – beginning with a $13.1 billion loan to Korea in 1997 and a $5.3 billion loan to Russia in 1998, are included in stand-by arrangements. *Anticipatory lending*, a new and unusual concept, was created through the **Contingent Credit Lines** program in 1999.

Breaking new ground, the IMF is now willing, in principle, to provide loans to nations without any balance of payments or foreign reserves problems if either the nation or the Fund felt they could *anticipate* a forthcoming crisis. This is an important threshold step for the Fund, which will allow member nations to borrow up to 500 percent of their quota to deal with a "contagion" threat. Also in 1999 the **Enhanced Structural Adjustment Facility** was rechristened the **Poverty Reduction and Growth Facility** (PRGF). Access to this fund is restricted to "low income" members with loans lasting up to ten years. In 2007 sixty-three nations, many African, had PRGF approved credits – the total of which was 3.9 billion SDRs, or 35 percent of all loans outstanding (IMF 2007b).

While stand-by arrangements continue to be the primary focus of Fund lending, it is important to recognize that increasingly the IMF has become concerned with lending for periods well beyond the twelve- to eighteen-month focus of the typical stand-by arrangement. Indeed, in the 1991–5 period, stand-by arrangements accounted for only 45 percent of Fund loans, while longer-term loans of up to approximately five years accounted for the remainder of all approved loans, demonstrating the importance of the expanded lending facilities. Table 17.1 records the IMF's lending activities in recent years. Note that in 2006 new loans all but evaporated, while through September 2007 the fund had lent only 1.2 billion SDRs!

Fund surveillance

While the Fund is most active with a nation when it seeks, accepts and draws a loan, the Fund exercises its influence in other ways, notably through what is termed *country surveillance*. Each year, every member country must undergo an annual surveillance consultation which,

Table 17.1 New IMF loans, calendar year (billions of SDRs)[a]

	1985	1990	1995	2000	2002	2006
Total new loans	4.0	4.8	18.3	7.7	26.6	2.9
Stand-by (+ other General Resources Account)	4.0	4.27	17.0	7.18	25.24	2.4
Structure adjustment facilities (+ PRGF funds)	0.0	0.53	1.3	0.52	1.36	0.5

Source: IMF, "Past Disbursements and Payments"; http://www.imf.org/external/np/tre/tad/extrepl.cfm.

Note
a One SDR = $1.55 USD in September 2007; $1.37 in March 2003; $1.28 in August 2001: $1.32 in January 1997.

according to a 1977 amendment to the Articles of Agreement of the Fund, is to include "a comprehensive analysis of the general economic situation and economic policy strategy of the member" (IMF 1995c: 154). Surveillance is a process which can allow the Fund to exert leverage over economic policy-making, even when a nation is not seeking a loan from the Fund. Of course, a country may largely sidestep the recommendations of the Fund at this stage, but this may lead to more difficult negotiations, and more stringent limits, on any loans which are sought from the Fund at a later date.

Objectives of the IMF

When the Fund lends to a less-developed nation, what does it hope to achieve? In the view of the IMF, borrowing nations are largely responsible for their own economic duress. Consequently, the Fund loans and intervenes so as to impose conditions which it believes will lead to greater economic stability. Thus, except for the periods of the oil spikes of the early and late 1970s, the Fund's basic position is and has been that it is fundamentally *endogenous*, rather than *exogenous*, factors which explain the need for Fund intervention.

From the perspective of the IMF, nations are forced to make appeals to the Fund because they have mismanaged their resources. In particular, the Fund concentrates on a nation's exchange rate and its balance of payments position. Nations which seek out the Fund's assistance have virtually exhausted their official hard currency reserves to finance a trade or other current account deficit. But why do nations run a trade or current account deficit? Largely ignoring exogenous factors such as the terms of trade, the Fund argues that troubled nations have deliberately over-valued their currency, in effect, pricing themselves out of the market for exports, while drawing in too many products from the international economy via imports. Nations which are in financial trouble with unsustainable external macroeconomic imbalances, then, are essentially living beyond their means. Excess aggregate demand is the underlying macroeconomic cause leading nations to seek loans from the Fund in this way of looking at the situation.

To begin to solve the problem of such an imbalance, in the Fund's perspective, a **stabilization program** must be introduced that typically results in **compression** of the economy. Excess demand and spending by consumers and government must be wrung out of the system, and therefore a short-term economic downturn must be imposed. Once the so-called fundamentals of the economy, that is, the key economic variables, are stabilized and brought into equilibrium, the Fund believes that the economy will bounce back, but with a stronger foundation for economic expansion, especially if stabilization is followed by a fundamental adjustment process in the way the economy functions so that disequilibrium situations are less likely in future. In the Fund's view, adjusting the "fundamentals" requires several steps:

1   a devaluation of the currency to its sustainable, equilibrium value to stimulate exports and discourage imports;

2   control of the rate of growth of the money supply in order to stem inflationary pressures which lead to overvaluation of the currency and excess aggregate demand in the economy;

3   a reduction of government spending, especially to control the *fiscal deficit*, to restore the balance between the public and private sector's roles in the economy and to reduce inflationary pressures;

4   a reduction in real wages (that is, of inflation-adjusted wage payments) in order to make exports more attractive on the world market and to mitigate internal aggregate demand at the same time. By reducing real wages, the profit share of industry is expected to rise, as will the profit rate. A higher profit rate will attract more direct foreign investment, which will provide a net addition to the capital stock, thereby strengthening the export capability of the economy and reducing the external borrowing requirements.

While the relative emphasis on the above four components varies somewhat from nation to nation, they constitute the essence of what is generally known as an IMF **austerity package**. It is worth briefly reviewing each of these components of an austerity program.

Devaluation

Unquestionably, the Fund's view that exchange rate overvaluation is a significant underlying factor contributing to current account deficits and economic crisis often has a solid basis, as was argued in Chapter 15. Poor nations far too often do have a tendency to over-value their currencies. Why? Necessary imports of machinery and equipment and intermediate products can be acquired relatively cheaply via overvaluation, and this may speed the development process, particularly during the import substitution phase of industrialization (see Chapter 9).

Unfortunately, however, superfluous luxury consumer good imports and foreign travel also are made cheaper for domestic elites with overvaluation. A politically weak government may appeal to the middle class, proffering travel and imported luxuries at low prices in exchange for their political support. Thus there are tempting political and economic reasons for currency overvaluation, particularly in countries lacking a strong democratic tradition.

In the Fund's view, devaluation of the currency will accomplish two desired objectives: imports will decline, while exports will increase, closing the trade gap and reducing the current account deficit. While this is true in theory, as we saw in Chapter 15, in real time exports may not respond strongly to a devaluation as a result of a low price elasticity of demand, particularly if such exports are primary products.[7]

Thus, the bulk of the austerity package's effect from devaluation tends to fall heaviest on import compression via higher import prices. The foreign trade account may well come into balance with time, but often only by under-cutting the productive base of the economy as a result of the increased cost of importing needed capital and intermediate goods for industry. In the longer term, the effect of a devaluation may well be to reduce the capacity to export to the extent that imported inputs enter into the production of export industries, thus creating precisely the opposite result from that sought by the Fund.

We are not arguing, let it be clear, against devaluation *per se*, or in favor of maintaining import substitution industrialization beyond the time period when ISI can usefully be sustained, as the discussions in Chapters 9 and 10 made abundantly manifest. Nor are we arguing in favor of over-valued exchange rates, as Chapter 15 hopefully made clear. We are suggesting that, at times, a devaluation, particularly a sharp and large devaluation, actually may interfere with a nation's trajectory of structural transformation, rather than supporting it. By asymmetrically and adversely affecting import substitution industries more rapidly and more severely than contributing to export expansion, a devaluation, if not carefully considered, and perhaps bolstered with compensatory programs, such as public investment, may actually inhibit the desired adjustment process that the IMF would wish to encourage, aimed at altering the productive structure of the less-developed country. Thus, current research shows, in repeated cases, that one of the consequences of acceptance of a Fund program is a *decline* in investment. Another effect, to be expected when investment declines, is that GDP growth turns *significantly negative* during the period when nations are under Fund programs (Bird 2001: 1851–2). Adam Przeworski and James Vreeland found in a recent study covering a wide number of cases or "observations" that GDP growth was lowered by an average amount of 1.5 percent per year while nations were participating in IMF programs (Przeworski and Vreeland 2000). This is no small matter when we consider that many nations have been under some form of IMF program for extended periods of time. For example, in the period 1971–2000 the Philippines were under IMF programs for 24.7 years, Haiti for 21 years, Panama for 20.8 years, Uganda for 18.4 years, El Salvador for 11.5 years (Bird 2004: 34). As Graham Bird notes, "On the positive side IMF programs do seem to be associated with a statistically significant and enduring depreciation in the real exchange rate. Perhaps connected with this, they also appear to be associated with some significant strengthening in the balance of payments" (Bird 2001: 1852).

Inflation

According to the IMF, domestic inflation is a major cause of currency overvaluation. The Fund anticipates that a country with an over-valued currency is simultaneously one wherein the domestic rate of inflation has been so high, relative to the world average, as to create overvaluation, particularly if exchange rates are not freely floating. Inflation is viewed by the IMF as a monetary problem, one of "too much money chasing too few goods." This excess demand arises from many sources, but two are considered primary: first, the governments of less-developed nations attempt to expand spending too rapidly relative to the effective tax base, providing social services and engaging in poorly thought-out spending programs. The resulting "fiscal deficit" is believed to crowd out the private sector, by pushing up interest rates as government borrows to finance expenditures above revenues, thus absorbing the limited amount of investment funds. Second, workers, particularly unionized workers and government employees, who also may be unionized, push up wages beyond justified productivity increases in an economy that already suffers from excess demand conditions.

So, behind the balance-of-payments crisis, the IMF finds overvaluation of the currency; behind overvaluation lie excessive inflationary pressures; and behind high inflation is profligate government spending on development and social projects, without proper regard for the limited resources of the developing nation. Given this interpretation, the Fund imposes limits on the growth of the domestic money supply, requires a tightening of bank credit, and imposes a ceiling on wage increases, typically well below the rate of inflation. This is part of the IMF's overall view of the need for reining in excessive state involvement in the economic activity of less-developed economies.

Government spending

Less-developed nations often run central government budgets that are in deficit, contributing to the inflation process. The Fund views the government's deficit as *prima facie* evidence of excess demand and therefore imposes strong cuts on government spending as a condition of receiving loans. Governments in the developing world often provide subsidies on basic goods such as food staples, milk and meat products, fuels, and pharmaceutical products. The Fund generally will impose a "get prices right doctrine" and call for the elimination of such subsidies, letting market-determined prices prevail.

As a consequence, austerity programs often impose an inordinate burden on those in society who can least afford the effects of income and spending compression. (Ironically, by deregulating the prices of basic goods, inflation often surges.) Other targets for government cutbacks can vary widely from nation to nation, but governments often reduce their educational budgets and/or physical infrastructural outlays, which will, unfortunately, reduce the supply capacity of the developing nation in the future. Nonetheless, in searching for ways to reduce state spending and the government deficit, these are often where cuts are made, rather than in military spending, because of political pressures from domestic elites and the military itself.

The Fund requires cuts in central government spending as a condition for its loans, given its competitive equilibrium approach, which leads it to argue that resources released, that is, not spent, by the public sector will be more productively employed by the private sector.[8] This assumption, however, is often unwarranted when the private sector is structurally weak and competition, in the economic sense, is absent. As a result, the institutions of society, from banks to private businesses operating in the private sector are not well developed and do not respond well or quickly to investment resources freed up by the public sector.

Business interests may react to the general downturn in the economy brought on by reduced government expenditure, in fact, by reducing production and investment. Or, as is sometimes the case, these business interests may have drained much of their liquid funds from their own nation in anticipation of the devaluation which the Fund will surely impose. *Capital flight* often may be more appealing to business interests than higher levels of investment or the expansion of domestic productive capacity and the social capacity to do technology.

Again, we do not wish to invite misunderstanding. There is no denying the culpability of many governments in running unsustainable fiscal deficits, in poor project design, and in unnecessary and wasteful spending. But IMF demands to simply cut state spending, without some fundamental analysis of the structural and institutional transformations desired for that particular society, can inhibit further progress. No doubt many blanket subsidy programs for staple foods or for utilities are wasteful, providing benefits not only to the poor, but also to non-poor who could afford to pay more. Targeted subsidy programs by government would retain the spirit of such spending measures by helping those who needed them most, thus reducing the cost of such programs without eliminating them.

Cutting back indiscriminately on central government, educational, health, and certain infrastructural expenditures would not seem to be advised, certainly not on the basis of the new growth theory evidence examined in Chapters 8 and 12. What we are suggesting is that the IMF's condition requiring a cut in government spending so as to reduce the fiscal deficit and hence inflationary pressures has been too often a terribly blunt instrument, cutting into areas of social investment with substantial positive external effects. More attention also could be placed on better and more effective tax collection measures. Reducing the fiscal deficit is a two-sided objective, and it can be achieved by reducing government expenditures and/or raising tax revenues.

Wage repression

Wage cuts have their counterpart in a reduction in total consumption and that tends to reduce total national income. Thus it becomes problematic to argue that an increase in the profit rate alone, created by wage cuts, will be sufficient to stimulate additional production, since reduced demand is likely to follow lower wages. If additional production can be easily exported, however, wage repression may result in a net increase in output, but it may not if the export sector is weak.[9] It is also difficult to determine how foreign investors may respond to lower wage costs, as there are many other factors that enter into a decision to commit to an investment abroad besides the cost of labor.

The Fund posits that a nation that is in the process of stabilizing its economy and which is serious about adjusting its economic structure will attract foreign capital. But if the domestic economy is in a shambles, and export markets show weak growth, foreign capital may choose to stay on the sidelines. James Vreeland conducted a massive study involving 110 countries that underwent IMF programs from 1961–93. He concluded that IMF programs have a negative effect on manufacturing labor and therefore shift the distribution of income from labor to capital. On average, controlling for many factors, Vreeland shows that labor's share of income in the manufacturing sector under IMF programs falls from 39.8 percent to only 36.4 percent – and this is found within the context of a falling GDP (Vreeland 2002: 121–30). One of Vreeland's most interesting findings, long argued by opponents of IMF austerity programs with little evidence, is that the degree of income redistribution toward capital is so great that industrialists are actually better off under the IMF programs than they would have been had economic growth been satisfactory. Table 17.2 summarizes Vreeland's startling findings in three cases.

Compression effects versus expansionary effects of IMF programs

Having now traced out some of the possible effects of an IMF austerity package, it is important to add a significant qualification regarding the compression effects of the Fund's program. While the Fund's approach, in and of itself, would seem to point to an induced economic downturn for the borrowing nation, the Fund also injects hard currencies into the economy when it lends, and this should act as a stimulus to economic expansion, moderating the various dampening effects of the components of the austerity program. Furthermore, and this is a very important point, nations which consummate a loan arrangement with the Fund are able, by virtue of now being under the guidance of the Fund, to essentially alter their country risk status in the eyes of international lenders and often gain access to new credits from abroad. This is a second possible stimulus working to counteract the adverse affects of a domestic austerity program. A third stimulus will almost surely come from the World

Table 17.2 The impact of IMF austerity programs: capital's share and labor's share

Country	Years	GDP (%)	Δ Capital's income[a] (%)	Δ Labor's share[a] (%)
Congo	1985/1986	−2.99	+9.5	−8.5
Uruguay	1989/1990	−1.03	+2.0	−2.7
Ecuador	1982/1983	−5.7	+36.0	−18.0

Source: Vreeland 2002.

Note
a Manufacturing sector income.

Bank (discussed below) which will lend because the Fund has lent, as usually will the relevant regional development bank for that country, such as the African Development Bank for African countries and the InterAmerican Development Bank in Latin America. In addition to this threefold injection of hard currencies from the Fund, from the international financial markets, and from the World Bank and/or the regional development bank, if the borrowing nation is quite poor, it is likely to receive some financial grants from bilateral foreign aid entities such as the United States Agency for International Development (AID). However, in a significant study Graham Bird's evidence demonstrates that IMF programs *generally do not* serve as a catalyst to attract either private or bilateral or other forms of multilateral financial flows (Bird 2001: 1856–62).

If equity investments (DFI) are arriving, and a variety of new loans and grants are extended, the stimulus effects may well outweigh the compression effects of the austerity program. However, new DFI may introduce other problems for a less-developed nation (Chapter 14), grants may come at the price of other concessions to a powerful and wealthy neighbor, and new loans will surely cause a poor nation to exchange short-term liquidity for longer-term financial obligations which create an outflow on the current account. Only if the nation actually becomes a better producer, that is, only if the inflows of financing contribute to structural transformation and a fundamental adjustment of the economy along the lines set out in Chapters 9–13, will the loans, grants, and investments make any long-term developmental sense, as was argued in the previous chapter concerning external debt.

These positive effects *can* materialize, but these newfound sources of liquidity may merely be utilized by the borrowing nation as a short-term expedient, while the structural problems of the nation remain unaddressed, again as occurred during the debt crisis. Consequently, even if, under the best of circumstances, GDP growth is quickly resumed in the aftermath of the imposition of an IMF austerity package, it is also necessary to analyze the post-compression debt levels, and to take account of the manner in which DFI and new foreign aid grants impact the productive capacity of an economy.

In any given year, the IMF does not loan immense sums of money, certainly in comparison to the problems the Fund hopes to address. As we have seen in Table 17.1 in 2000 the Fund made loans in the amount of 7.7 billion SDRs (approximately $10 billion US$), but received repayments in that year of 15.8 billion SDRs. Thus, the net effect of the Fund's lending in that year was to *contract* global liquidity by about $10.5 billion US$. In 2002, by contrast, the Fund was a net contributor to global liquidity (IMF 2003b). But, then again in 2006 it contracted global liquidity by an impressive $28.8 billion US$ (IMF 2007b). What the Fund really has to offer to a nation in difficult straits is its *imprimatur*, the Fund's stamp of approval to the international financial community, from which other loans, grants, and DFI will flow, in varying proportions, to the beleaguered nation, or so it is argued. And, the Fund strongly believes, good technical economic advice, particularly concerning macroeconomic policy, will be another major benefit arising from an IMF program.

Do IMF programs work?

The answer to this question depends on how we interpret it. If we take it to mean that, once the less-developed nation reaches an agreement with the IMF, follows IMF conditionality to the letter, and undergoes a "successful" stabilization and adjustment of the economy whereby inflation is thereafter controlled, the currency is thereafter realistically valued in terms of hard currencies, the trade account remains in balance, investment remains high, and the economy grows and prospers, the answer (in most instances) is assuredly "no."

The IMF has been very interested in posing and answering this question. In their most recent attempt at self-evaluation, the Fund's research economists studied forty-five stand-by and Extended Fund Facility arrangements which the Fund approved between mid-1988 and mid-1991 in thirty-six countries. According to the Fund, the results were as follows.

- Improvement was most notable on a pre-loan, post-loan comparison basis for exports. With the imposition of a Fund agreement, exports improved strongly, but over time export strength weakened.
- Only approximately half of the countries benefitted from additional capital inflows.
- Regarding inflation, "a few countries achieved dramatic reductions from very high initial rates, but many continued to experience moderately high inflation; a few even recorded upward trends."
- Regarding growth, "few if any countries shift[ed] to a distinctly more rapid pace of growth backed by higher savings ratios."
- Regarding investment, "few countries saw any increase in overall investment ratios, although private investment rates rose as public investment rates fell" (IMF 1995b: 234).

Clearly, the results of the Fund's study, which largely parallels numerous studies made previously both by the Fund and independent researchers, portray the IMF's impact in a less than flattering light. Hostile critics of the Fund would have a difficult time mounting a more severe critique than the Fund has made of the consequences of its own policies. But the Fund seems unburdened by these findings.

Undismayed and undeterred by this latest report indicating that the IMF's model has failed to come to grips with the persistent problems of the less-developed nations, the Fund's Executive Directors drew two inferences from this study: first, that the Fund should warn nations which undergo adjustment that they cannot expect improvement on both the external balance of payments account and in short-term improvement in growth and investment; second, that the Fund should lend for a longer period of time, that is, the Fund should continue to shift its programs away from stand-by arrangements, lasting twelve to eighteen months, toward intermediate adjustment program loans with a duration of three to five years.

Of the many studies conducted on the effectiveness of the Fund by independent researchers, a 1992 study headed by Tony Killick broadly confirms the IMF's inhouse study cited above, while adding new dimensions worth noting. Killick and his associates analyzed the effects of 266 Fund programs in the 1980s, 220 of which were stand-by arrangements. Forty-eight percent of the stand-bys were never completed, indicating that the recipient nation was unwilling or unable to comply with the conditionality demands of the Fund.[10] Thirty-three percent of the discontinued programs broke down almost immediately. And, in the 1988–90 period, the non-completion rate on stand-by loans reached 88 percent.

Why? According to Killick, easier credit conditions allowed the less-developed nations to go elsewhere for loans, and thereby to avoid IMF oversight and conditionality. Another important finding is the prevalence of recidivism: "no less than nineteen countries had six or more programs approved by the Fund, encompassing 131 programs or 44 percent of the total for the period" (Killick *et al.* 1992: 590). On a somewhat more positive note, Killick and his research associates *did* find in a study of IMF arrangements in the 1979–85 period that Fund adjustment programs led to improvements in the balance of payments, without any long-term "strangulation" of imports. But the study of the 266 Fund programs, referred to above, found that, over time, net capital inflows did not improve as "Fund credits were often used to repay other creditors." Killick argues that, although countries under a Fund program may, and probably will, attract new financing from the World Bank, the regional development banks, and foreign aid donors, "there appears to be no general catalytic effect on private flows" (Killick 1995: 179). Meanwhile, 40 percent of the completed programs were associated with *increased* rates of inflation. And, most important for considerations of economic development, "the brunt [of adjustment] falls on the fixed investment ratio, which declines substantially and significantly over the whole period. Overall, the programs appear unable to exert any appreciable squeeze on private and public consumption" (Killick *et al.* 1992: 593–5). Since Killick completed this important study many econometric analyses have been conducted pointing out that IMF programs reduce growth rates, such as Axel Dreher's examination of ninety-eight countries in the 1970–2000 period, and James Butkiewicz and Halit Yanikkaya's review of 100 nations in the 1970–97 period (Dreher 2006; Butkiewicz and Yanikkaya 2005).

In summing up the complex state of the evaluative literature on the IMF a number of conclusions appear to be accepted by both critics and supporters of the Fund.[11]

- Short-term improvements in the balance of payments are significant, even for countries which abandon the IMF programs (Killick 1995: 68).
- IMF compression and austerity are most often associated with compression of wage income, compression of social services and compression of investment, but without any compression of overall consumption, which implies that upward income redistribution occurs.
- One of the strongest effects of IMF programs, as Manuel Pastor's research on Latin America clearly demonstrated, is a decline in the wage share of GDP (Pastor 1987). Pastor's results are particularly applicable to workers in the state sector and wage workers in the formal sector, who feel the brunt of wage compression in a standard IMF program. Peasant producers, on the other hand, *may* find that the emphasis on devaluation and export promotion increases their earnings.
- While in the short term some countries do find that the rate of growth of GDP rises modestly, in relation to the situation immediately preceding the crisis which precipitated the IMF program, over a somewhat longer period of time the basic capacity to sustain growth often appears to be *undermined* by reductions in public- and private-sector investment. This, apparently, helps to explain why many nations which have either completed or abandoned IMF programs subsequently enter into new programs with the IMF.

Some critics and observers of the Fund, citing studies such as the two summarized here, argue that the IMF is an inept institution which should either cease to do business or radically recast its approach. Others maintain that the IMF does, in fact, serve its purpose and meet its objectives. To these observers, the Fund's objectives are not really tied to the improvement of the performance of the less-developed nations, but to the long-term improvement of conditions which allow major participants in the international economy, such as the transnational corporations, relatively free access to the widest possible range of production and sales sites in the global economy (Pauly 1994: 204–15; Crow *et al.* 1988: 310–30). In this view, the IMF is a "mechanism of integration," bringing the less-developed nations into a new international division of labor and ensuring the repayment of international bank loans which soared in the 1970s. If this, indeed, is the criterion by which the Fund should be evaluated, high marks are surely to be awarded. Certainly the Fund has been consistent in its hostility to import substitution industrialization, at least since the early 1970s. And it has unquestionably advocated a more open trading regime around the world.

Prior to the Asian crisis of 1997 the Fund was a supremely confident, even swaggering, institution. But, in the early years of the twenty-first century the IMF found itself the target of some very influential sources – among them Joseph Stiglitz, whose *Globalization and Its Discontents* opened with a blistering two-chapter critique of the IMF informed by Stiglitz's years as chief economist of the World Bank (Stiglitz 2002: 3–52). Also breaking ranks, the United Nations' *Human Development Report 2002* focused on the "democratic deficit" of the Fund (and the World Bank along with the World Trade Organization), noting that only seven of the 184 nations in the IMF controlled 48 percent of the voting power of the institution. While the Fund urged "transparency" and "good government" and "participation" on the member nations during IMF austerity programs, the United Nations noted in some detail the lack of these crucial elements *within* the organizational structure of the IMF (United Nations 2002: 112–17). Stung and seemingly confused by these critiques, high-level Fund officials who rose to prominence in the 1980s and 1990s were less than convincing in their statements that critics really did not understand the complexities and intricacies of high-level economic theory, and that time had proved IMF policies correct, or at least or would do so (Boorman 2002: 241, 245–8). While widely disparaged, the Fund continues to exert *tremendous* influence – at the close of 2002 the IMF held vital influence over the lives of hundreds of millions of citizens of fifty-three developing nations through the IMF's programs. Even in 2007, after five years of the **commodity boom**, some sixty-three nations were beholden to some extent to the Fund because they were participating in **Poverty Reduction Strategy Programs** operated by both the IMF and the World Bank, as will be discussed below. A global superpower in itself (functioning with over 2,700 employees in 2007), the Fund's pivotal role in development issues is beyond dispute.

The World Bank

Like its twin Bretton Woods institution, the IMF, the World Bank was created in late 1945 and commenced lending on a very modest scale in 1947. The International Bank for Reconstruction and Development (as the Bank was originally, and still officially is, known) loaned an average of slightly more than half a billion dollars per year from 1947 to 1967, a relatively meager sum when spread over the many nations that sought to receive Bank support. Until the 1970s, one distinguishing characteristic of the Bank was that it loaned "long," that is, for a multiyear period, while the Fund loaned "short," for periods of twelve to eighteen months.[12]

Another distinction between the Fund and the Bank in the early years was that the Bank offered project loans and technical expertise to promote large-scale capital-intensive mega-investment projects in less-developed nations. Highest on the list for loans was water projects such as dams, irrigation systems, flood control, and hydropower installations for promoting agricultural development and electricity generation for industry. Until 1968, when Robert McNamara became World Bank president, the most notable change at the World Bank was the creation of the International Development Association (IDA) as a new component of the World Bank Group. The IDA was assigned to be the entity to make long-term loans to nations which otherwise could never receive funding in adequate amounts from the Bank, as a result of their general financial weakness. IDA loans are concessional, meaning that a significant portion (more than 25 percent) of the interest cost of the loan is waived and other easier terms, such as grace periods for the repayment of interest, can be built into the loan. Under its charter, the Bank may lend only to governments.

With the exception of the IDA loans, it expects to, and does, make a respectable profit. It is not, therefore, in the strict sense of the word, an aid institution. Still, the Bank is not just another financial institution, because it does lend to nations for the long term on unproven projects, often with substantial externalities, and for which private sources are usually reluctant to make loans. Even after the IDA came into existence, the World Bank attracted little attention. Lending from the IDA amounted only to a modest average of one quarter of a billion US dollars per year up to 1967 (see Focus 17.2).

FOCUS 17.2   THE WORLD BANK GROUP

The International Bank for Reconstruction and Development: Until the 1980s, the IBRD, known popularly as simply the World Bank or "the Bank," lent for specific development projects, usually with a seven-year cycle from planning to completion. In its early years, the IBRD definitely reflected an "engineering" orientation. From 1947 to 2006, the Bank made cumulative loans of $420 billion to ninety-four nations. Loans normally have a five-year initial grace period, after which they are to be repaid over a period of fifteen to twenty years, at the market rate of interest. The Bank does not reschedule or cancel its loans. Borrowing governments have an outstanding record of paying off these loans, since failure to repay the Bank would virtually destroy the credit rating of a developing nation. The IBRD has always achieved a substantial rate of profit on these loans. Loans are heavily concentrated: in 2006, 52 percent went to Brazil, China, India, Mexico, and Turkey.

The International Development Association (IDA): Established in 1960 to forestall the creation of a similar agency at the UN, the IDA lends to nations which cannot qualify for IBRD loans under the usual lending rules. Only the poorest nations are eligible for IDA loans, in 2008 the qualifying limit was below a national per capita income level of $1,065. In 2007 the IDA had 80 nations (2.5 billion people) as potential candidates for its "credits." Over 41 percent of the $135 billion in IDA loans issued from 1961 to 2002 went to India, China, Bangladesh, and Pakistan. In 2007 39 percent of all loans went to India, Pakistan, Nigeria and Vietnam. Formally the IDA does not issue loans, but rather "credits." These "credits" have a nominal interest rate of 0.75 percent, a grace period of ten years, and repayment over the following forty years. In 2007 IDA lending reached a record level of $11.9 billion (49 percent for Africa).

The International Finance Corporation (IFC): Created in 1956, the IFC supports private-sector development, functioning as a co-investor and assisting the private sector to obtain debt and equity financing in the international financial markets. In 2006, for example, the IFC created 284 new projects in sixty-six nations – up from fifty-one nations in 1992. With an emphasis on small- and medium-sized businesses, the IFC has become more significant since the 1970s as a result of changes in policy orientation at the World Bank. Nonetheless, the IFC is much smaller than the IBRD and the IDA; its total outstanding loans amount to $21.6 billion. The World Bank has continued to prioritize the IFC with growth in annual lending more than doubling from 1992 to 2002. IFC loan commitments reached an all-time record of $8.2 billion in 2007 – 64 percent of the level of IBRD lending. The IFC's rapid growth reflects the heavy emphasis on private-sector development originating with the US from the 1980s onward. The IFC has a distinct culture, functioning more like a venture capital bank than an aid institution. It expanded the reach of its lending by 42 percent in 2006 through co-financing from other lenders who partially funded new IFC projects.

The Multilateral Investment Guarantee Agency (MIGA): Since 1988, the MIGA has functioned to guarantee direct foreign investments against non-commercial risks, such as nationalization, and has given policy advice, particularly to potential foreign investors. The MIGA organizes international conferences to promote investment opportunities in developing nations and also trains nationals in poor nations on methods of investment promotion. In 2007 the MIGA guaranteed $1.4billion – up from $313 million in guarantees in 1992. Cumulative investment guarantees amounted to $16 billion in 2006.

US influence at the Bank

Since its inception, the Bank has had only US citizens for its presidents. (In a mirror image of this tradition, and reflecting international power relations which prevailed when these institutions were created, only Europeans have headed the IMF.) As in the IMF, the United States has been the dominant shareholder in the World Bank. Yet, its sway over the Bank has diminished somewhat over the years, as its share of the Bank's capital subscriptions, and consequently its share of the voting power within the IBRD, has fallen from 35 percent in 1947 to 21 percent in 1981, and then 16.4 percent in 2003. Once again, it has been Japan which has gained the largest relative share of influence in the Bank in recent years, though it held only 7.9 percent of the voting share in 2003. Much of the money lent by the Bank to less-developed nations also has served to stimulate production in the United States economy and in the other advanced nations. On average, roughly 60 percent of all loans and credits consist of orders for equipment and supplies furnished by the economies of the advanced nations. The US has used its voting power to significantly influence concessionary lending patterns at the IDA, according to an analysis conducted for the years 1993–2000 (Barnebeck, Hanson, and Markussen 2006).

The McNamara era and the basic human needs approach

As an institution, the Bank rapidly changed under the leadership of Robert McNamara (1968–81). With McNamara the Bank moved to center stage in the development dialog. It built up a vast cadre of highly trained economists, reaching 6,100 full-time staff in 1994, with 1,375 consultants or temporary staff. By 2004 the bank had a full-time staff of 10,000. McNamara changed the Bank in practically every way imaginable. Its funding vastly expanded, its orientation changed radically, and its "mission" was completely and dramatically redefined. Heretofore, the Bank had modest goals. But McNamara accepted a new approach to development, known as the **basic human needs** approach, first advocated by the International Labour Organization in the late 1960s. Now, the central focus of the Bank would be to put an end to world hunger, poverty, and misery. Thus, the Bank leaped from its modest objectives of placing a few selected loans in the developing nations to attacking the most intractable and broadest of developmental objectives. McNamara and his close associates became advocates of the basic human needs approach which sought to channel development funding to programs in less-developed nations that would directly benefit the poor, particularly the poorest 40 percent of the population. This meant a vast new role for the IDA, and a new emphasis on housing projects, water sanitation, the Green Revolution, schooling, and related matters (see Focus 17.3).

Between 1967 and 1993, the IBRD lent $224 billion on over 3,000 separate loans, while the IDA lent an additional $76 billion. Just as important, however, was the fact that co-financing allowed the Bank to vastly increase its importance, because other entities, particularly international banks, lent funds for Bank-approved loans. Co-financing can expand the reach of the Bank by 80 percent or more; in 1992, for example, the Bank loaned $16.4 billion, but also generated $13.3 billion in co-financing. Thus, in terms of its importance in generating long-term capital flows into the less-developed nations, the Bank can be nearly twice as significant as its annual lending numbers would suggest.

In the 2002–6 period the roles of the IBRD and the IDA were reversed: in each of those years the IBRD had a negative net lending position, while IDA lending steadily increased. In 2003 and 2004, the IBRD's net withdrawal of funding was very strong – loans amounted to

FOCUS 17.3 THE WORLD BANK AND THE ENVIRONMENT

Beginning in the late 1970s, prominent environmental groups began to carefully examine the lending policies of the World Bank. Their mounting critique helped push the Bank into issuing an official statement in 1984 mandating that the Bank would no longer finance projects which "cause severe or irreversible environmental degradation."

In 1987, with criticism of the Bank's environmental commitment mounting, Bank president Barber Conable announced that he would create an Environmental Department and increase the Bank's research on environmental degradation, desertification, and environmentally threatening forestry practices. By 1989, Conable had introduced the Bank's first environmental review process to screen some loans and projects for their potential environmental impact. From 1989 to 1993, 300 projects were evaluated for their environmental impact. Critics charged that the majority of loans and projects, however, were not subject to adequate environmental review. But by 1992 the Bank was employing 279 full-time analysts to work on environmental issues.

In 1993, the Bank indicated that its commitment to environmental concerns was deepening. A new role of Vice-President for Environmentally Sustainable Development was created with the objective of helping "Bank operational staff better understand the linkages between poverty and the environment and to view social, environmental, cultural, and agricultural concerns as more interrelated." Between 1992 and early 1995, the Bank devoted nearly 10 percent of its funding to projects with environmental objectives.

The Bank is also the implementing agency for the Global Environmental Facility (GEF), created in 1991 and restructured in 1994. The GEF is a financial mechanism under the combined trusteeship of the World Bank, the United Nations Environmental Program, and the United Nations Development Program. By mid-1995, the GEF had funded projects with a combined worth of $558 million, while committing to lend $2 billion from 1994 to 1997. These project loans address a range of broad environmental issues, such as climatic change, depletion of the ozone layer, and land degradation.

Does all this constitute a "Greening" of the Bank? Critics are not sure, but they do acknowledge that the Bank has made serious steps toward addressing environmental issues which it long ignored or down-played. Some critics are less sure:

> The environmental movement has won some project-by-project skirmishes but it has been strategically and ideologically outflanked. Through a combination of reassuring rhetoric and some genuine improvements, the Bank has distanced itself from outright hostilities with the opposite camp.
>
> Sources: George and Sabelli 1994: 183; World Bank 1984: 4; 1995a: 26, 28

$11.9 billion in 2003, but repayments on past loans came to $19.9 billion. In 2004 the figures were $10.1 billion and $18.5 billion for loans and repayments, respectively.

Table 17.3 records total Bank lending and co-financing for recent years. Note that these figures are in current, rather than inflation adjusted, dollars. Adjusting for inflation, and after soaring in 1999, Bank lending actually fell somewhat from 1990 to 2002.

The rise of structural adjustment lending: 1979–2007

By the late 1970s, McNamara's vision had gone beyond that of meeting basic human needs. He now believed that successful economic development would require that the Bank itself provide much of the guidance and implementation of a development program to less-developed nations. In this view, these countries would have to share, if not relinquish, decision-making powers over a vast array of economic policy matters which heretofore

Table 17.3 World Bank lending and co-financing (billions of US dollars, fiscal years)

	1990	1993	1995	2000	2002	2007
Gross disbursements						
IBRD	13.9	12.9	10.4	10.9	11.5	12.8
IDA	3.9	4.9	5.7	4.4	8.1	11.9
Total	**17.5**	**17.8**	**18.4**	**15.3**	**19.6**	**24.7**
Co-financing	n.a.	11.6	8.2	7.0	4.7	4.9[a]

Source: World Bank, *World Bank Annual Report* (Washington, D.C.: World Bank, various years); www.worldbank.org./annualreport/.

Note
a 2006.

had been considered strictly the sovereign province of independent nations. With these new loans, which McNamara never completely defined prior to stepping down in 1981, the World Bank once again recast its "mission"; now, it would guide the economic trajectory of entire nations in their quest for development. The new-style comprehensive loans were termed **structural adjustment loans** and **sectoral adjustment loans**. These loans have continued to be a prime focus of the World Bank's activities.

The global economic crisis of the late 1970s had altered McNamara's perspective. In his view, as he expressed it in his annual presidential address to the World Bank in 1980, the debt crisis, the rise in oil prices, and the slow growth in aggregate demand in the advanced nations were all working to undermine the development prospects of the less-developed nations. Consequently, the basic human needs approach was not enough; it was not possible to rely on the less-developed nations to define their paths to development, while the Bank attempted to care, through its lending, for those who had been left out of the process of economic growth. Rather, now it was necessary to help build, adjust, and remold the economic foundations of the developing nations. A wide range of issues which, previously, the World Bank had left to the determination of the borrowing nation would now be uppermost in the Bank's analysis when it considered which countries were eligible for loans and credits.

From the late 1970s, when the first structural adjustment loans, called SALs, were made, through to 1986, the role of SALs within overall Bank lending grew to the point where approximately one out of every three dollars in lending was for the purpose of structural adjustment. In 2002 *total adjustment loans* accounted for *64 percent* of all lending, with 48 percent of loans going either to restructuring the public sector or the financial sector! In essence, a SAL is granted not to build anything in particular, but to change national economic policies in some desired direction. Consequently, the borrowing nation has some discretion on where and how it will spend the SAL funds, unlike project loan funds from the Bank which are very much under the control of the Bank for a specific undertaking.

Depending on circumstances and the nation involved, SALs attempted to address a broad range of macroeconomic problems. Once a SAL has been arranged, funds are disbursed over time in a conditional manner, much as for the IMF, being dependent on the success of the economy in making fundamental changes in pre-selected policy areas. Between 1980 and 1986, the average SAL had conditions in ten of the nineteen policy areas which the Bank wished countries to address. The most frequent conditions were to "improve export incentives" (76 percent of all SALs incorporated this as a condition), to "reform the government's budget or taxes" (70 percent), to "improve financial performance of public enterprises" (73 percent), "to revise agricultural prices" (73 percent), and to "strengthen capacity to formulate and implement public investment programs" (86 percent) (Mosley *et al.* 1991: vol. 1, 44).

Adjusting the state sector

It is clear from this brief summary of the most common conditions for SAL loans that the role of the state was at the epicenter of the Bank's analysis regarding what most needed to be "adjusted" in the poor nations. This orientation reflected the so-called "new political economy" perspective of Anne Krueger, who was for a period in the 1980s the Chief Economist of the World Bank, as well as reflecting the views of many other influential economists within the Bank. As will be recalled from our earlier discussion in Chapter 7, the focus of neoliberal economists has been upon what they believe has been the excessive role of the state in the economy which, they argued, constituted a serious impediment to economic development. Thus, it comes as less than a surprise to find that the central thrust of the SALs was largely concentrated on paring back the role of the state intervention, particularly through the sell-off, or privatization, of state-owned firms via programs often financed and directed by the Bank.

The ultimate aim of the Bank was to achieve a new form of macroeconomic management which would successfully integrate the borrowing nation into the global system of trade, finance, and investment. Any nation which sought to hold on to the vestiges of import substitution industrialization did not receive much assistance from the Bank; dismantling ISI and instituting export production became a virtual *sine qua non* for obtaining Bank assistance. In striving for a complete reorientation of the economies of many nations, the World Bank ventured into territory which had long been the sole domain of borrowing governments, such as the size of the public administration apparatus, the organization of the civil service, and the general structure of the public sector, labor regulations, and public investments. In every instance, the Bank sought to remold the society and economy to create an environment it believed would be more encouraging to the private business sector, including international corporations.

By 1987, the Bank was ready to formalize its shift to structural adjustment lending via what it termed its "integration policy," which sought to coordinate all Bank programs within a nation in order to obtain consistency under the umbrella concept of structural adjustment. In effect, then, even though loans formally defined as SALs remained at the level of roughly one-third of annual outlays, in nations where "integration" was adopted, all loans, including project loans, were intended to be coordinated within the framework of the SAL concept. Furthermore, under **cross-conditionality**, nations could only receive SALs if they had stand-by arrangements with the IMF. And, they could only receive stand-by support from the IMF *if* they accepted SALs from the Bank. (Meanwhile the IMF itself began to enter into SAL lending with the creation of the Structural Adjustment Facility in 1986 and the Enhanced Structural Adjustment Facility in 1987.)

Did SALs speed the development process?

One survey of the effectiveness of World Bank SALs was conducted on 241 such loans conferred upon thirty-three African nations between 1980 and 1989. The results were that average per capita income fell on average 1.1 percent per year in these nations, while per capita food production declined overall. The purchasing power of the minimum wage fell by an average of 25 percent. Government expenditures for education declined by 36 percent, and the total number of elementary school students decreased by 14 percent. Not surprisingly, the numbers of the poor increased steadily (George and Sabelli 1994:141). These are not particularly encouraging outcomes, though one might argue that the special problems of the poor African nations makes this an unfair measure of success or failure of SALs, as other adverse forces also were at work. On the other hand, the Bank never suggested that some countries, in Africa or anywhere, might find a deterioration of economic progress to be the outcome of accepting SALs. An independent research team composed of Paul Mosley, Jane Harrigan, and John Toye attempted to evaluate the effects of SALs via a detailed study of nine nations from countries in Africa, Asia, and Latin America. They buttressed this sample with a broader comparison of twenty countries that had received SALs between 1980 and 1987 with twenty similar nations which had no SAL loans over the period. Their findings were largely similar to the study conducted on Africa, cited above. Their four main conclusions were:

1   SALs had a positive impact on exports and on the balance of payments;
2   overall investment declined under the SALs;
3   SALs failed to increase the economic growth rate and the flow of international capital, but they did not decrease either growth or international capital flows over the period prior to the SALs;
4   living standards for the poor, however, declined under SALs (see Focus 17.4).

Their overall evaluation of SALs was little short of devastating:

> By contrast with the Bank's generally acknowledged success in project lending (e.g., an average ex post rate of return of 17 percent across all projects between 1960 and 1980), it is not even clear whether the net return, in terms of growth of gross national product, on the $25 billion which the Bank has so far invested in policy-based ending is positive or negative.
>
> (Mosley *et al.* 1991: vol. 1, 302)

FOCUS 17.4   WOMEN AND "INVISIBLE ADJUSTMENT"

Women have proven to be more vulnerable than men to the loss of household income following the implementation of structural adjustment loans (SALs). To compensate, women have adopted new survival strategies increasing their workload and engaging in prolonged periods of greater self-sacrifice. This process has been termed "invisible adjustment," since such strategies are normally not included in the evaluation of the effects of SALs.

The process of "invisible adjustment" is complex. One aspect concerns the need for adaptive strategies in the face of sizeable reductions in public spending, which normally are required as a condition for receiving an SAL. When public health spending is reduced, for example, women must attempt to adapt by increasing the time they spend as informal medical aides, nurturing and nursing sick children and other family members who, prior to the SAL, might have been treated at rural health clinics or urban hospitals. With food subsidies eliminated or reduced, women often must spend more time shopping and preparing food, and the food they have available after an SAL may have a significantly reduced protein content. Even relatively poor women in many less-developed countries sometimes employ "servants," usually young girls, to help with the labor-intensive tasks of food preparation and washing-up. But when household income falls, this "luxury" is quickly eliminated, and women and girls in the family perform these tasks.

This helps set up a vicious circle, since a restricted diet for children often means increased vulnerability to illness and longer periods of recovery. Furthermore, a reduced diet means that family workers will have much less energy to devote to remunerative labor, thereby risking dismissal because of lower productivity or increased absenteeism.

SALs often include restrictive monetary policies designed to create higher unemployment and thus reduce real wages. In the formal sector, women are more vulnerable to such unemployment effects, and they often are forced into the informal sector where compensation is lower and the effort to survive is typically greater. In an attempt to compensate, women often increase their hours of work. For those women working outside of the home, their increased absence often necessitates that older children care for younger siblings. Under such circumstances, it is usually older girls who lose the advantage of an education in order to provide child-care at home. One study of a major urban area of Ecuador found that during a period of structural adjustment, the share of women working in the informal sector jumped from 3 percent in 1988 to 21 percent in 1992.

SALs appear to impose a three-fold burden on women: time devoted to market activities (in either the formal or informal sectors) increases; household labor increases; and nurturing labor (helping with sick children and relatives) increases.

Sources: Henshall Momsen 1991: 97–9; World Bank 1995b: 106–8

Critiques of World Bank and IMF SALs

Criticism of the SAL strategy has fallen into two distinct categories. First, some observers, including many from the developing nations, have felt that the World Bank and the Fund have abused their vast powers by overstepping their proper boundaries and usurping a considerable share of national sovereignty at a time when the developing nations were particularly vulnerable to pressure, due to the decline in primary commodity prices and the ravages of the debt crisis. Second, other observers have argued that the Bank and the Fund have operated from false premises and assumptions derived from the neoliberal school, which maintains that by "freeing-up" resources from the public sector and orienting the economy toward the export sector, the economy will expand at a much higher rate. With the Bank seemingly impervious to the early critical work on SALs, and with the focus on SALs increasing through 2002, the Bank – under considerable pressure from citizens' groups and non-governmental organizations – consented to a joint World Bank–Civil Society review of SALs with their participation. The report of the Structural Adjustment Participatory Review group – which examined the impacts of SALs on Bangladesh, Ecuador, Ghana, Hungary, Mexico, the Philippines, and Zimbabwe – was sufficiently devastating that the Bank reached the following key conclusions regarding structural adjustment lending:

- trade liberalization has been pushed through indiscriminately, allowing import growth to surpass that of exports, destroying domestic firms;
- lack of meaningful participation of national stakeholders in the design and implementation of trade policies have rendered these measures technically inefficient;
- financial assets have become more concentrated;
- [financial] reforms have promoted short-term speculation and investment in non-productive activities;
- employment levels have worsened and real wages have deteriorated and income distribution is less equitable today;
- women have suffered the most as a result of labor-market reforms;
- employment has become more precarious;

- the elimination of universally provided subsidies for essential goods has negatively affected the poorest (SAPRIN 2002).

Regarding the first of these propositions, while it is true that the World Bank and IMF SAL programs have effectively sought to usurp a portion of national sovereignty, it would be a mistake to view the borrowing nations as passively accepting the various conditions of the SALs. Rather, as the research of Mosley, Harrigan, and Toye has shown, the borrowing nations have used the new SAL format as a basis for carrying on sophisticated bargaining with the World Bank and the IMF. Most recipient nations have not fully complied with the intent of the SALs, and they have sought to bend the conditionality of the SALs to their best advantage (whether this advantage accrues to a narrow elite or to the nation as a whole is debatable and, ultimately, the real issue). Desiring influence, the World Bank, at least, has reluctantly accepted the fact that the issue of governance of a nation will not be willingly handed over to a group of World Bank economists. Failing to find the leverage which they sought, the World Bank has been forced to settle for some influence, rather than maximum influence. At the same time, non-compliance by countries has left advocates of SALs, as effective instruments of change, a convenient escape route when SALs have failed to demonstrably improve the overall macroeconomic environment in borrowing nations; they have argued that, had the borrowing countries followed World Bank and IMF advice to the letter, matters would have turned out differently.

Sustainable development, comprehensive development framework, and a knowledge bank?

In 1991, when the World Bank selected its eighth president, Lewis Preston, the evidence regarding the weaknesses of the SAL approach had mounted, and there was a growing chorus of voices decrying the Bank's apparent abandonment of the world's poor. Some of those voices came from within the World Bank itself, where many of the top research economists simply did not share the ideological fervor of the neoliberal economists who had proposed and advanced the SAL agenda so rigidly, and often with little regard for the particular history of individual nations. Troubled by signs of weakness in many aspects of the Bank's past accomplishments, Preston called for a full evaluation of the Bank's lending practices to be headed by the then Bank vice-president, Willi Wapenhans. In 1992 the "Wapenhans Report," entitled "Effective Implementation: Key to Development Impact," was presented. Its results exerted a strong, perhaps unprecedented, influence on the Bank, at least up until 1995. The main conclusion of the report was that, compared to the early 1980s, the Bank's loan portfolio had suffered a rapid decline in performance. Wapenhans found that in the early 1980s, the Bank had classified only 11 percent of its loans as "troubled," but by 1991, 37.5 percent fitted that category. In only 22 percent of the cases had borrowers fulfilled all of the agreements of a loan. Preston reacted rather quickly by bringing the concept of "sustainability" to the foreground, much as McNamara had emphasized the basic human needs approach throughout most of his tenure.

Sustainability shares with the basic human needs approach an emphasis on the poor, but in addition the Bank was to seek to insure that its loans were consistent with environmental concerns (for details, see Chapter 2 on "sustainable development"). A third pillar of the Bank's sustainability concept is population control. Preston reoriented the Bank toward sustainability, so defined. The dual track approach of the Bank's thrust (SALs + *sustainability*) became a complex mix of SALs + *sustainability* + *comprehensive development framework* + *social capital* + *good government* + *a knowledge bank* under James Wolfensohn, who took over the Bank's presidency from 1995 to 2005. While the above terms will not be detailed here, suffice it to say that one critic charged that under Wolfensohn the Bank has suffered from "a burgeoning agenda … and a concomitant overload of objectives and conditionalities" (Kapur 2002: 69). Others find evidence of "loss of control over its agenda," an "operational loss of focus," and the embrace of "mission creep and accelerating goal proliferation" as the Bank has continued to deepen its commitment to SALs while simultaneously attempting to focus on sustainability, transparency, accountability, participation based on country "ownership" of programs, and "institution building," most under the heading of the **comprehensive development framework** (Pincus and Winter 2002: 20).

Much of this approach – critics label it a diversion – is closely tied to the sustainability concept in the Bank's annual *World Development Report 2003*, devoted to "Sustainable Development in a Dynamic World" (World Bank 2003). Here readers can follow the Bank's text as vague issues such as "interpersonal networks, share values and trust" are entertained (ibid.: 19). Many critics have argued that the Bank, beset by the same barrage of criticism as the IMF, has sought to partially commit to a plethora of goals to deflect the criticisms (largely well documented) leveled against the Bank from the early 1990s onward. One informal group of trained observers has called for a return of the Bank to its earliest role as a *Development Bank* (see Focus 9.3), dropping the structural and sectoral loans, stepping back from the comprehensive development framework, because the Bank lacks the operational framework and resources to pursue the plethora of goals it has now set forth (Pincus and Winter 2002). It would probably be an overstatement to argue that the Bank is currently in a "crisis," but the institution is challenged as never before by its constituents, its observers/critics, and its funders.

The Poverty Reduction Strategy approach

The widespread critique of World Bank structural adjustment policy led to one major innovation which subsumed policy-based lending (such as the SALs and the sectoral adjustment loans) under the heading of the Poverty Reduction Strategy Papers (PRSPs). The PRSPs program – sometimes labeled the "new aid model" – came into effect in 2000 and rapidly expanded to become the centerpiece initiative regarding poor nations for the International Monetary Fund, the World Bank, bilateral aid agencies, and non-governmental organizations (NGOs) that are involved with development policy. By 2003 twenty-two nations had completed PRSPs, in 2005 there were forty-nine, and in 2007 the number had risen to sixty-four out of seventy nations, containing 2 *billion* people, originally identified as potential candidates (Malaluan and Guttal 2003: 2; World Bank and IMF 2005: 1; IMF 2007c: 1). The program involves not only the World Bank, but also the IMF, essentially bringing them together in a policy-based lending operation over a minimum of three years (but the time frame is generally projected to be considerably longer). Not only are the two Bretton Woods lenders involved; the Poverty Reduction Strategy approach is further complicated because it asserts that the borrowing nation will be brought into the program as the first among equals, "owning" the new policy-based loan. Moreover, the program is not merely tripartite, since it is designed to offer the framework under which "Development Assistance" (more commonly known as foreign aid – discussed in the following section) is to be applied. This is important, particularly since in 2005 the advanced industrial nations committed to an increase of $50 billion in Development Assistance by 2010 – effectively doubling foreign aid for Africa. The PRS Approach is designed to totally integrate Development Assistance into a long-term framework that is consistent with the capabilities and objectives of the borrowing nation – a conceptual break from prior foreign aid practices that have generally been vertical in nature, uncoordinated with the Bretton Woods institutions and often of an essentially *ad hoc* nature.

Coordinating the process was, at the official level, to be handled by the three major participants – the borrowing nation, the IMF, and the World Bank. Yet, at the level of operation the World Bank has been the dominant element. The idea of combining the IMF and the World Bank in a given project is novel because it is an attempt to wed two very distinct institutions. The IMF is an essentially "vertical" and homogeneous organization that centers its analysis on a static macroeconomic adjustment model focused on the balance of payments. The World Bank has a distinct underlying model, based essentially on the dynamic Harrod-Domar growth theory (see Chapter 4) which assumes that the levels of savings and therefore investment are the determining variable in defining the level of growth of the economy (Bergeron 2005: 111–12). The World Bank also has a somewhat heterogeneous focus, with large units devoted to a broad range of issues such as agriculture, basic needs, and women and development. In other words, absent balance of payments problems there are no "defining restraints" for developing nations according to the IMF. But for the World Bank, in theory there can be a great variety of restraints, chief of which is the now quite out-dated idea that with sufficient capital formation poor nations can rise from underdevelopment. Little introspection would be needed to predict that the IMF and the World Bank would find it impossible to work together on a project designed to potentially reach all nations eligible for IDA support – the 2.5 *billion* people in nations below the threshold level of $1,000 in annual average per capita income.

Key elements of the Poverty Reduction Strategy Program

The PRSPs are extremely complex and the entire project is the most ambitious ever undertaken by the Bretton Woods institutions. In essence, PRSPs are national development programs, based on the hypothesis that foreign trade and investment are the engines of growth, and that economic growth is the best, and nearly the only, way to address poverty. Under the PRS approach there are four essential elements to be pursued:

1   stabilization of the macroeconomy through the application of IMF conditionality using a minimum of targets with funding from the IMF's **Poverty Reduction and Growth Facility**;
2   implementation of structural adjustment concepts in accordance with the Washington Consensus, emphasizing privatization, reduction in government, opening to international trade and investment, and prioritization of private-sector development consistent with IFC objectives; providing concessional funding from the World Bank's International Development Agency via its **Poverty Reduction Support Credit** (PRSC) program designed to alter policy and institutions in recipient nations;
3   focus on economic growth as the underlying means to reduce poverty on the assumption that the rate of growth of income for those who are poor will be *higher* than the rate of growth of incomes for those above the poverty line. Failing the *automatic* appearance of "**pro-poor growth**" there should be minor emphasis on social safety nets designed to target poverty reduction coupled with other strategic outlays, as needed, to enhance the participation of the poor in the growing economy – such as agricultural infrastructure investments that target poor farmers, or schooling for youth, particularly girls (Ravillion 2004: 20);
4   domestic "participation" in the formulation, and eventual "ownership," of the PRS program.

An analysis of the four essential elements of the PRSP

Taking these elements as listed, the first has largely been the province of the IMF. However, in the context of the PRS program the IMF is unable to act with the autonomy to which it has long been accustomed. Any stabilization package will be viewed not only in terms of its short-term impacts on the balance of payments, but in addition – in the first instance – by the World Bank in terms of the likely inconsistencies between IMF conditionality leading to the compression of aggregate demand (reducing or eliminating growth) and the under-lying objective of achieving intermediate to long-term growth. Joining in the PRS program has thrust the IMF into unknown territory. Its ability to combine the opposing forces of conditioned stabilization with a viable growth strategy as envisioned by the World Bank is presumably far beyond its "core" competency.

Moving to the second element, a sense of *déjà vu* is overwhelming. Although now out of fashion, and explicitly rejected by some high-ranking World Bank officials in the Bank's 2005 book *Learning from a Decade of Reform*, it is hard to escape the conclusion that the World Bank's operational arm continues to apply the Washington Consensus approach with the PRS framework (Rodrik 2006: 977). Here the World Bank's low-income lender, the IDA extends long-term PRSC loans to achieve the goal of altering the structure of the national policy-making process while "building institutions for markets." In short, viewing the PRS approach from the perspective of the operational arm of the World Bank, the new program would seem to be reducible to "SAL +," the + being the three other elements.

In terms of the third element, **pro-poor growth** is initially assumed to be growth of the economy wherein the rate of growth of income for those who are perhaps in the bottom third or one-half of the distribution of income is higher than the rate of growth of those who are in the upper two-thirds or one-half of the income distribution. This directly contrasts with the **Kuznets curve** analysis introduced in Chapter 1 wherein Simon Kuznets found an inverse relationship between economic growth and reduction of income inequality until per capita income rose to an intermediate level. It is worth recalling from Chapter 5 that the most widely accepted model of the initiation of the development process – as constructed by Arthur Lewis – is premised on the argument that growth will be biased against workers and subsistence farmers. There seems to be no acceptable basis in development economics for assuming that in a *laissez-faire* economy such a process as pro-poor growth should occur in a poor nation – particularly one wherein the IMF and the World Bank are determined to reduce government programs and forms of regulation that have been constructed to help those who are disad-vantaged or weak in an unregulated economy. Should growth not show a bias in favor of the poor, the strategy would be to introduce very limited, targeted programs designed to create safety nets or "social protection measures." But such interventions remain vaguely defined, and subordinated to the goal of growth. While there has been little or no independent review of the PRS approach, the Bretton Woods institutions have nonetheless presented an awkward attempt to demonstrate that PRSPs are tilting toward pro-poor policies: In their 2005 review of the PRSPs the IMF and the World Bank found for a sample of 27 countries that the level of "poverty reducing expenditures" expressed as a percentage of government revenue rose from 41 percent in 1999 to 49 percent in 2004 (IMF and World Bank 2005: 22). They like-wise found that these outlays in relation to GDP rose from 6.4 to 8.3 percent. However, in a footnote the same document states that the category "poverty reducing expenditures" "is not always based on a good understanding of the appropriate public interventions necessary to reduce poverty" with programs often "skewed towards better-off households" (World Bank and IMF 2005: 22). The reader is left to wonder what exactly might be a "poverty reducing expenditure" and how it could be the case that such outlays are skewed to the better-off and if that is true how any of this might necessarily connect to the goal of expanding programs designed to reduce poverty! One is also left with a sense of wonderment: could one-half of all public outlays in a poor nation undergoing the PRS program be allocated to poverty reduction? What is it that the IMF-Bank have decided to label as "poverty reduction" public expenditures?

Finally, we come to the last element, considered the key one by many, country "owner-ship" of the program. To begin to understand this concept within the framework of the PRS program, it is important to recognize that national "ownership" of the program does not mean that the borrowing nation will have any say whatsoever in the manner in which the IMF implements its stabilization program, nor will this nation be able to bargain or influ-ence the structural adjustment program financed and implemented by the World Bank. The Bangkok-based research center Focus on the Global South critiqued the Bank–Fund concept of "ownership" in the following manner:

> When advising governments on how to prepare a PRSP, Bank-Fund missions have come prepared with *their* perspectives on the country's poverty situation, *their* analysis of the country's obstacles to growth, *their* menu of policy options, and *their* views on how to mobilize resources for the PRSP, including external donor assistance. Their perspec-tives form the basis of all discussion between Bank-Fund missions and borrowing governments about the structure and content of PRSPs. And despite claims that "causes and solution of poverty are country-specific," all PRSPs are expected to contain "core elements" that the Bank and the Fund consider essential to poverty reduction.

PRSP processes have been extremely narrow in both their substance and participation. Participation has by and large been limited to inviting prominent and well-resourced NGOs to offer their perspectives on pre-prepared documents. Unions, workers' organizations, farmer and fisher groups, women's groups, indigenous peoples, medical associations, and even academics have not been included in the process. Most PRSP consultations have yet to involve local populations in devising strategies for nationally meaningful development plans, or in monitoring the impacts of past policy reforms and programs.

> In a number of countries, initial drafts of the ... PRSP were not translated into local languages until the final stages thus excluding local input into the formulation process.
> (Malauan and Guttal 2003: 7, 9, 10)

At the outset of the implementation of the first PRSPs in 2000, critics of structural adjust-ment polices were enticed by the allure of the concept of "ownership." But by 2003, it was claimed that they are a new "technology of control" that suggested empowerment and there-fore served to mystify the fact that PRSPs are a new and deeper way to discipline the national economies of poor nations than anything previously constructed by the Bretton Woods insti-tutions (Fraser 2005). PRSPs are viewed as a means to "engineer consent" because they have managed to incorporate some of the most articulate and capable NGOs into the PRS process – along with wealthy-to-poor nations' aid programs – while reducing the visibility of any one external agent. Thus they have served to camouflage, in particular, the IMF while shrouding World Bank leverage in a fog of "participatory" rhetoric. In effect, critics view the PRSP as a new form of *dependency* where there is a superficial appearance of "willing participation" on the part of governments caught in the complex web of the PRS approach.

The PRS approach has escaped greater scrutiny not merely because it is both exceedingly complex in its structure and intentionally subtle in terms of mystifying the power relationships of the process. In addition, since 2002/2003 the rapid spread of PRSPs has taken place within the context of a commodities boom unprecedented at least since the Second World War. With few exceptions, throughout the world the nations of the South have experienced five years of relatively rapid economic growth – growth which the Bretton Woods institutions are not hesitant to claim as the outcome of the PRS approach. Nonetheless, the future of the PRSPs was thrown into doubt with the arrival of the "Malan Report" delivered by an external review committee on Bank–Fund collaboration in the PRSPs (IMF 2007). Noting that there had been a drastic cut in IMF outlays to the **Poverty Reduction Growth Facility** in 2005 and 2006, the committee recommended that this fund be closed and that the IMF withdraw from long-term financing, effectively taking the IMF out of the complex PRS equation (IMF 2007d: 44). In effect, the "Malan Report" is a recognition that the conditioned stabilization model employed by the IMF is designed to force an adjustment in the balance of payments through repression of aggregate demand. The IMF's institutional structure can only work at cross-purposes to policies designed to engender growth. Should the IMF withdraw from the PRS program this will not necessarily limit the Bank's financial capacities, but it could mean that the Bank will eventually become a much more visible target for critics – particularly when commodity prices stop rising or fall.

Foreign aid

The term **foreign aid** is often loosely and incorrectly applied to programs that are *not* concessionary, such as loans from the IBRD or the IMF (excluding the **PRGF**), or to bilateral programs that are essentially military or strategic in nature. *All foreign aid is concessionary*; it comes either in the form of concessionary loans or outright grants. The major source of foreign aid is bilateral assistance from the advanced nations to a selected number of poorer nations. Nearly all foreign aid is intended for the purpose of economic development; relatively little (10–15 percent) in a given year will be for the purpose of "emergency assistance," such as food, clothing, and emergency medical care for victims of disasters, war, and famine. Food aid is normally less than 10 percent of all aid. Multilateral organizations such as the United Nations certainly play a role in the decisions made and funds expended for foreign aid, but their programs are smaller than the sum of the bilateral programs of developed countries.

Among the many misconceptions regarding foreign aid, one in particular tends to stand out above all: contrary to popular conception, the really poor and destitute nations do not receive much of the foreign aid in any given year. This fact is brought to light in a summary of some of the known research regarding the recipients of foreign aid presented in the United Nations Development Program's (UNDP) *Human Development Report 1993*. In discussing the unique role played by the NGOs in transferring aid to the poor nations, the UNDP stated some of the more disturbing characteristics of foreign aid programs: "If government and official aid programmes usually fail to reach the poorest 20% of income groups, most NGO interventions probably miss the poorest 5–10% … On the whole it is easier for NGOs to reach the not-so-poor than the very poorest" (UNDP 1993: 96). Why is this so? Because aid programs tend to be designed for those that already have some assets, such as small farmers, rather than, say, landless farm laborers or informal service workers. Even a self-help housing program designed for the poorest of the poor may put aid officials in an awkward position, since these destitute families often will be "squatters" on land owned by others.

Providing assistance to such families would place the aid-giving group in direct opposition to the guardians of the property laws in the aid-receiving nation, and they thus shy away from such projects and controversy.

In 2005 total "official" foreign aid, or Official Development Assistance (ODA), from the advanced nations and OPEC and other nations came to roughly $110 billion (UN 2007: 153, Table A.19). About 23 percent of this total was transferred to multilateral institutions such as the World Bank, the remainder being spent as bilateral aid, about three-quarters of which was devoted to grants. In addition perhaps as much as $20 to $30 billion was raised by NGOs along with foundations such as the Global Fund which anticipates annual grants reaching the $10 billion level by 2010, and the Gates Foundation with assets of $34.6 billion in 2006. NGOs (and foundations) come in all sizes, with highly varied focuses. Some are supported by religious organizations, others are secular. Some are extremely specialized, such as Doctors without Borders, and highly effective.

Many do not have a humanitarian rather than developmental perspective. And many bring highly honed skills in language and culture to facilitate social movements with organizational knowledge that results in empowerment. If all the various forms of concessional aid were added together, and if these funds were distributed broadly to all developing nations, foreign aid would allow for about 5 cents (US) per person per day of external support in the poorest nations of the world. Targeted directly to the best projects in a few of the poorest nations, ODA can make a difference, helping to set a society on a new path. But this can only happen when programs actually reach the poor, when programs are well designed and crafted to meet the very specific needs of a recipient country, *and* when overall ODA outflows rise to the growing challenge of global poverty.

None of this appeared to be happening until recently. ODA, adjusted for inflation, reached a peak in 1992, and by 1997 aid flows had fallen 23.7 percent in relation to 1992 (Hjertholm and White 2000: 85–6). In 2000 – estimating the effects of inflation – official aid was well below the 1992 level, and on a rough par with that of 1997. But by 2006 it had recovered to the relative level achieved in 1992 – 0.33 percent of the combined national income of the Development Assistance Committees countries (UN 2007, x). Commentators explained the serious drop in relative aid contributions from 1992 through 2003 as a result of the end of the Cold War. During the Cold War poorer nations had some leverage with the superpowers of the era. Furthermore, it was asserted that "*aid fatigue*" – arising from unexplained causes but thought to be based in the intractable nature of many of the most pressing problems in poor nations – explained the twenty year downturn. In 1998 the World Bank published a highly influential study *Assessing Aid* which essentially argued that aid did not help poor nations in many instances, and that in the future donors should direct their aid funds to nations that had "good" government and "good" policies – which essentially seemed to mean market-friendly neoliberal governments and policies (World Bank 1998). Aid fatigue was encouraged by the study's findings that only 29 cents of every US dollar intended for aid expenditures actually went to such ends (World Bank 1998: 19, 21). Aid, then was *fungible*, suggesting that the remaining 71 cents of each dollar intended for aid was wasted or misspent or misappropriated. This conclusion, however was not demonstrated in the study. In many cases, perhaps, recipient nations used the additional funds to support high priority projects that yielded a satisfactory social return. Serious study of this issue remains to be conducted: one recent polemical follow-on attempt failed to make a compelling case in support of the "aid has failed" hypothesis (Easterly 2006; Radelet 2006). In the US strident criticism has come from the right of the political spectrum, particularly through the Metzler Commission formed by the US Congress in 1998 to analyze the role of international financial institutions – especially the

World Bank and the IMF (Sanford 2002: 747–51). The Commission was hostile to the international financial institutions seeking either major reductions or the elimination of both the IMF and the World Bank. The Commission was also hostile to aid, buttressed in its views by the very critical analysis presented in *Assessing Aid*. As a result, the US government, adopting many of the Metzler Commission's views, had called for the conversion of 50 percent of the IDA's funding from loans to grants. This, of course, would eventually end the IDA, as it currently relies for much of its ongoing financing from the repayment of loans (twenty to forty years after the loans have been issued). On the other side of the aid debate, Jeffery Sachs has been extremely influential with both governments and multilateral institutions. Sachs is the able director of the UN's Millennium Project. His work with corporations and corporate-sponsored, aid-oriented foundations illustrates his impressive abilities as a fund raiser. His eloquent recent book *The End of Poverty* has been widely read (Sachs 2006). Particularly valuable are his many ideas on how to address debilitating poverty in Africa with targeted aid programs. Sachs has no "magic bullet" theory. His goal is not the end of poverty, but rather the end of *extreme* poverty. Lifting people above an arbitrary line of $1 or $2 a day in per capita income, however, will hardly end "poverty" – except in some statistical sense. Nor will having $2.01 per day (putting an individual over one of the "lines") obliterate the need to continue to devise strategies that will result in meaningful and adequate economic development.

Aid, which had not been much discussed in development economics, became a major area of dispute after 1997. The *Journal of Development Studies* devoted an entire issue to the controversies stirred by *Assessing Aid*, finding weaknesses in the key econometric studies that the report was based on. Researchers urged that aid not be restricted to nations that had embraced neoliberal policies. Rather, aid should be used to build good policies, instead of restricting aid to nations that had already adjusted their institutions and policies to the neoliberal model (Hermes and Lesink 2000: 1–15). But, as suddenly as aid was disparaged in many powerful quarters it was aggressively re-embraced by the World Bank and even the US government after the UN sponsored the Millennium Summit in 2000. The UN, pushed into a background position on aid issues, has steadily regained prestige and momentum after it began publishing the *Human Development Index* (see Chapter 2) in the early 1990s. Under Kofi Annan's leadership as Secretary General of the UN, the industrialized nations signed on to the Millennium Development Goals in September 2000. To meet the goals – which include (1) the eradication of extreme poverty and hunger, (2) the achievement of universal primary education, and (3) reduction of child mortality rates by two-thirds, *all by 2015* – ODA would have to roughly triple from its 2000 level to $175 billion a year (in current dollars). Given the context set by *Assessing Aid* and the Metzler Commission, the abrupt *volte-face* regarding aid policy issues was extreme. Observers attributed the success of the Millennial Conference to the underlying weakness in the global economy first exhibited with the Asian crisis of 1997 and to the polarizing effects of globalization. The Millennial Conference was subsequently supported by the 2002 Monterrey (Mexico) Conference sponsored by the UNDP – where the US Administration announced that it would raise ODA spending by 50 percent in the next three years! On the way to the Monterrey Conference, the World Bank issued a staunch defense of its role as an institution involved in aid assistance, thereby distancing itself from the paradigm suggested in *Assessing Aid*.

This dizzying chain of events seems to suggest three things: first, the UN has gained a new voice, new legitimacy, and new urgency in leading with the Millennium Development Goals project. Second, the World Bank is now officially supporting the program, claiming that the "goals have been commonly accepted as a framework for realizing development progress" (World Bank 2003: 1). Third, the US's position in favor of converting IDA to grants as an indirect way to end development aid has undermined its own legitimacy, creating a new political space for Europe and Japan in the debate over aid (Sanford 2002: 754–7). *Aid fatigue is no more*, and the United Nations suggested in 2007 that the rate of growth in aid outlays (through 2006) indicates that the 2010 target level of ODA of $130 billion will be reached.

Table 17.4 presents a range of data regarding ODA flows of some of the major donor nations comparing outlays in 1970 with those of 1991, 2000 and 2005 as a share of gross national product (GNP). Note that while the United States is the second largest donor nation in absolute size, it is by far the *smallest* contributor among the wealthy nations when viewed from the standpoint of the share of ODA to GNP. The UN has set a target of 0.7 percent of GNP as a goal to be achieved by the donor nations for their aid contributions; all donor nations fall well below that UN benchmark, as Table 17.4 demonstrates. Indeed, by 2000 the "aid commitment" level had fallen to only 0.22 percent of GNP – 33 percent below the level of 1991, the lowest registered since 1973 (IMF 1996: 1, 7).

When aid is directed to the poorest nations and to the poor in the less-developed nations, serious difficulties often arise with the process of delivery. This is most painfully obvious in the case of emergency assistance. Press reports of food piled up at docks in the midst of a famine are common. Road and rail transport is too often in insufficient supply; the food may have come from thousands of kilometers, while the distance between the starving and the food supply on arrival may be only a few kilometers, but it might as well be ten thousand. Maybe it is a case of roads being destroyed, of bridges gone, or of the government or a tribal leader pilfering the food for individual profit. Whatever the reason, failure to deliver the aid is the outcome.

In other instances the same problem of an inhibiting institutional structure arises, but in a more subtle form. Agricultural aid is a good example of this situation, where new technologies, such as the Green Revolution discussed in Chapter 11, cannot be diffused because the recipient nation lacks the necessary technically trained cadre of farm advisers who can communicate with the peasantry and overcome their doubts. Indeed, studies of agricultural aid in India have shown strongly positive results, only because of a relatively large number of technically literate individuals who were able to fill the gap between the technology and knowledge and those who would *use* the technology. India's success has rarely been duplicated elsewhere, particularly in Africa. Consequently, it is necessary to recognize, once again, that a vicious circle of poverty is hard to overcome merely by providing one or only a few of the necessary ingredients for development. Aid programs that are not well integrated into the

Table 17.4 ODA flows of selected advanced nations

	2005 outlays	Percentage GNP				Per capita		
	(billions of US dollars)	1970	1991	2000	2005	1991	2000	2004
Japan	13.1	0.23	0.32	0.28	0.28	77	102	70
US	27.5	0.31	0.17	0.1	0.22	44	35	67
Germany	9.9	0.33	0.41	0.27	0.36	92	71	91
UK	10.8	0.42	0.32	0.32	0.48	99	79	131
France	10.0	0.46	0.54	0.32	0.47	115	80	137
Total or average ODA	**106.4**	–	**0.33**	**0.22**	**0.26***	**75**	**67**	**91**

Sources: UNDP 1993: 203; 2002: 202; 2006: 343; UN 2006: 343.

* 2004 data.

wider complex of social institutions within the less-developed nation may succeed in spite of the odds against them, but the probability of success is typically low. This lack of an *absorptive capacity* for aid is perhaps obvious enough to students of economic development, but it is too often overlooked in the broad, politically charged, debates surrounding aid giving.

Donor bias

Most aid is disbursed via bilateral programs – 77 percent of all Development Assistance from the OECD nations, or $82 billion in 2005. Much bilateral aid reflects the biases of the donor nation. Donor bias arises from the following considerations.

Commercial interests

Most foreign aid is **tied**, meaning that a proportion of the aid funds must be spent in the donor nation. For loans and grants this means that up to 75 percent of the inputs for the project (machinery and equipment, materials and supplies) are to be purchased from suppliers in the donor nation. This often results in more capital-intensive projects than necessary.

In the area of technical assistance it is common to require 100 percent from the donor nation. Tied aid has been found to raise the cost of projects in recipient nations by 15–30 percent above an identical project wherein the inputs and technical assistance were acquired from the most competitive suppliers. Sometimes the pressure to accept tied aid is more subtle, amounting to *strategic non-lending* for nations which have previously received aid, but failed to buy their inputs primarily from the donor nation. In other instances, commercial interests shift the focus from product sales to the maintenance of prices and production; this is particularly the case with food aid, which pushes surplus agricultural commodities off the domestic and global market into non-market aid channels, thus helping to keep market prices higher in the donor nation than they might otherwise be. Unfortunately, food aid can undermine production by local producers of competing commodities in the aid-receiving nation by diverting local demand to the "dumped" food-aid imports. No one can compete against food products which are either given away or sold below their cost of production. This process can force many local producers from the market, perhaps contributing to a dependence on imported food staples from the developed countries.

Figure 17.3 illustrates one attempt to take into account the quality of foreign aid. The index reduces the contribution of nations which require that aid be tied. It also expresses foreign aid as an annual net expenditure, reducing gross aid outlays by the amount a nation receives in repayment on previous aid loans. Further, donor nations that lend to well-off nations or corrupt regimes have their aid contribution adjusted downward.[13] In effect, the index asserts that $US 1 of aid from Denmark or Sweden is worth roughly $5 from Japan. Not only are these nations (along with Norway and the Netherlands) able to deliver high-quality aid, they are also much more committed to high levels of aid: their average aid outlay as a percentage of GNP in 2005 was 0.87 – more than 80 percent higher than the UK, the most generous nation of the "big five" presented in Table 17.4.

Spheres of influence

Most of the large donor nations distribute their aid with a high emphasis on maintaining positive relationships with former colonial regions and/or regions where they have historically maintained a degree of political and economic hegemony. Another consideration may be

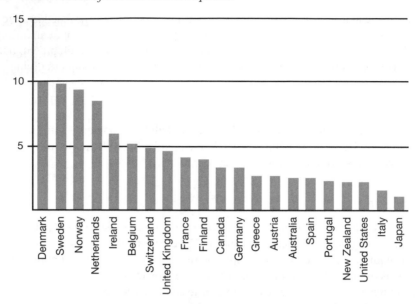

Figure 17.3 A bilateral aid quality index, 2006.
Source: Center for Global Development 2007.

national strategic leverage in a region. Such considerations largely explain why Egypt was the number one US aid recipient in 1991; the United States has based much of its Middle East strategy on maintaining Egypt as a friendly Arab nation, leading it to contribute most of the $4.6 billion in ODA funds received by this nation. This also served to explain why Iraq and Afghanistan were the number one and number two aid recipients in 2004.

Procedural imperatives

In many instances, aid programs are allocated for one or only a few years. Yet in order to foster development, a multi-year aid commitment would be necessary. It may be procedurally necessary to limit aid programs as a result of budgetary considerations, or changes in political rule in the donor nation, leaving the recipient nation without the follow-through to make a project viable.

Ideological imperatives

When ideology drives the aid process, as it often does, the neediest nations and the best projects may be overlooked, or under-funded. Since the late 1970s, aid agencies have, for the most part, emphasized the desirability of private-sector development, a reflection of the dominance of neoliberal thinking. Nations which have resisted this orientation have often found that aid funds are difficult to obtain.

Aid and the multilaterals

While most aid is bilateral (77 percent in 2005), the largest donor nations generally work closely with the IMF and the World Bank. This has been even more the case since the Poverty

Reduction Strategy Papers have become the centerpiece for concessional lending since 2002. Nations that are deemed to be unwilling to cooperate with the Fund and the World Bank are often considered to be unworthy of bilateral aid. Thus, in the1980s when the Bank and then the Fund placed such emphasis on structural adjustment and neoliberal economic doctrine, the aid agencies and governments generally followed the lead of the multilaterals. This new tendency toward a three-way interlocking of the IMF, the World Bank, and bilateral aid is explained by IMF Deputy Director Mark Allen:

> ODA is increasingly channeled to countries with IMF- and Bank-supported adjustment programs. The donor community finds that the existence of such programs gives an assurance that aid will be invested more productively. If we compare 1990–3 with the previous three years, nominal ODA to countries with IMF-supported programs increased by 35 percent, while that for countries without such programs rose by only 6 percent. Thus, continued financing from the IMF and the Bank is a catalyst for considerably large ODA flows to these countries.
>
> (IMF 1995a: 339)

Since neoliberal economic advice often resulted in a reduction of programs and expenditure which were most likely to reach the neediest, aid often became a supplement to structural adjustment, attempting to fill in some of the gaps in the social fabric created by the SALs. The UN Economic Commission for Latin America and the Caribbean conducted a study of income distribution changes in the course of the 1980s when structural adjustment lending was first introduced; all but one of the eight nations studied experienced strong shifts toward greater income inequality. Only two countries stood out as exceptions; Uruguay's income distribution was essentially unchanged, while Colombia's improved (ECLAC 1994: 1). Absent from the study was Mexico, the nation with the second-largest population in Latin America. It too experienced a dramatic shift toward even greater income inequality. Mexico, it will be remembered, was the World Bank's largest single experiment with SAL programs. With Mexico's recovery after the peso crisis of 1995 that nation was held up as a shining example of the new era of the 1990s: "Trade, not Aid!" Yet, predictably, the World Bank/IMF/US "Washington Consensus" view on Mexico crumbled along with the Mexican economy in late 2000. The Mexican case had been taken as proof of the benefits of unrestrained opening to trade and investment. But this shallow perspective was not really based in the realities of the Mexican economy which had long exhibited deep pathological traits before the export-led boom evaporated in late 2000 (Cypher 2001: 11–37).

Conclusion

Enjoying the benefits of the commodities boom from 2003 through 2007, many developing nations actively sought to repay their debts to the IMF and the World Bank. IMF credits and loans outstanding are at levels not seen since the early 1970s (with nearly one-half extended to one nation). The World Bank's gross lending through the IBRD was lower in 2007 than it was in the early 1990s. For the Bretton Woods institutions combined net lending was negative. Most activity for the multilateral institutions has been focused on the Poverty Reduction Strategy approach which has attempted to combine the short-term stabilization focus of the IMF with the "capital for growth" approach of the World Bank through the IDA. The Poverty Reduction Strategy approach has also brought bilateral lenders and NGOs into a new policy initiative which has quietly deepened and broadened the reach of "Washington Consensus," structural adjustment programs in nearly seventy poor nations. These programs, for the most part, address poverty in their titles, but not in the content of their policy-based lending. The Poverty Reduction Strategy approach is one that highlights high economic growth. Growth *per se* will reduce poverty. But this will occur as a by-product, not as the central thrust of growth. Most importantly, growth *per se* will leave those who are isolated from the accelerated economic processes of a rapidly expanding economy with little or no benefit. Landless and subsistence farmers, the aged, poor children, the sick, and the disabled will not be direct beneficiaries of the growth process. Public goods are not automatically funded nor are externalities necessarily addressed when an economy expands. The Poverty Reduction Strategy approach is based on the novel idea of pro-poor growth as the probable outcome of high economic growth in poor nations. Growth biased toward the lower third or fifty percent of the income distribution is an exotic idea with little to no empirical support. Failing this, the Poverty Reduction Strategy approach is to be amended with targeted safety-net programs. There has been no independent assessment of the massive Poverty Reduction Strategy loans from the IDA, the IMF, the bilateral lenders, and the NGOs. Nor is there evidence of the creation of adequate safety-net programs – an idea that works at cross-purpose with a central thrust of the Poverty Reduction Strategy approach which is to reduce the role of the state to a minimum. Yet by 2003 the situation regarding aid and the multilaterals had changed fundamentally – the World Bank was touting aid as the chief force behind the twenty-year increase in life expectancy in poor nations since 1960, while cutting their illiteracy rate by 50 percent (Kahn 2002: W1, 7). At this level the "Washington Consensus" was widely disparaged, the critical thrust of *Assessing Aid* was no longer a touchstone for a radical policy shift, and the Millennium Development Goals suggested the possibility that the UN's "Sustainable Human Development approach" could move into a position of dominance in development policy. By 2007 bilateral ODA aid had reached the record level of $106.4 billion. In 2006 the EU was expected to have 0.43 percent of its gross national income devoted to aid. The United Nations anticipates that the Development Assistance Countries of the OECD will reach their goal of raising development assistance to $130 billion per year in 2010 – a step largely consistent with the ambitious demands of the Millennium Development Goals. These are positive steps that should be respected. Nonetheless, it is well to recall that this chapter began with an attempt to contextualize aid: nations must, in the final analysis, rely upon their own capabilities to mount a process of sustainable development. Aid may help push a nation over crucial thresholds, if it is used strategically to meet the objectives of the developing nation.

Thus, at one and the same time, the Washington Consensus approach seems to be gaining ground and losing ground. But, much more threatening to the neoliberal Washington Consensus approach is the possible rise of what Charles Gore termed the "Southern Consensus." Gore envisioned a possible new development paradigm based on the understanding of the process of development as experienced in East Asia and upon the critical analytical work of the UN's research centers such as CEPAL (ECLAC) and UNCTAD. This *neostructural* consensus would call for the strategic integration of developing nations with the world economy based on a carefully sequenced opening of the trade sector. Strategic integration would call for limited capital account liberalization and safeguards against "hot money" flight from developing nations leading to massive currency devaluations. Under this approach inbound FDI would be constrained to activities that actually contribute to building the productive base of the developing nation. Dynamic comparative advantage would form the basis of integration, while trade policy would emphasize improvements in supply capacity, education and training of the labor force, and independent technological capabilities. Policy-making would be embedded, while capable policy-makers would formulate dynamic policy incentives based on performance criteria for national firms (Gore 2000: 789–804). Which way will development economics go now? Toward (1) an entrenched neoliberalism, (2) a "growth with equity" approach based in Sustainable Human Development, meeting the Millennium Development Goals, or (3) toward a new "Southern Consensus"? Will the nations of the South seize the golden opportunity of the commodities boom of the twenty-first century to redirect their economic surplus toward an aggressive project of national development? Unfortunately, there are very few signs that such a bold initiative is under way. Perhaps the near future will hold a bit of each approach – and the debates over development economics will continue.

Questions and exercises

1   You have been selected as the chief negotiator to represent your country, which is facing an economic crisis and must seek assistance from the IMF. You must draw up a draft version of a letter of intent and a secret document which will represent the bargaining position of your nation as negotiations open with the IMF. First, describe the economic conditions which have created a crisis for your nation. Second, explain the "policy actions" which will be undertaken by government to improve the functioning of the economy during the program period. Third, what "prior actions" is your government willing to undertake in order to obtain an IMF stand-by loan? How does your position differ from that which the IMF will probably present? How will you attempt to bargain with the IMF in order that your nation is adequately represented?

2   "The Fund and the World Bank tend to assume that endogenous, policy-related errors lie at the base of a nation's difficulties. In fact, exogenous difficulties are usually more of a factor. Consequently, adjustment programs fail to address the causes of an economic crisis. Such problems are invariably brought on by structural problems." Discuss this statement. Do you agree? Why, or why not?

3   Based on your reading of this chapter, identify five major public misconceptions regarding foreign aid.

4   How might a typical IMF stand-by program, or a typical World Bank structural adjustment loan, contradict some or all of the basic objectives of "sustainability"? Imagine that this SAL is applied to a nation which has little industrial or manufacturing capability. How might a structural adjustment loan lead to new burdens being placed upon the environment of the nation?

5   "Governments often achieve objectives they have long held, but have been unable to achieve, while operating under an IMF or a World Bank adjustment program." Why might this be so?

6   Go to the World Bank's website and select a nation undergoing a PRSP. After reading the nation's PRSP, evaluate it in terms of the critique offered by those who are convinced that the PRSP is an inadequate strategy for the development of poor nations. Do you find reasons to dissent from the view of the critics?

7   "Aid has been a failure, a naïve dream." Evaluate this assertion in light of the material presented in this chapter. Can you make a convincing case in support of this statement?

8   Why are small northern European nations the largest aid contributors with the highest ratings in terms of the quality of their aid programs?

9   Find an NGO involved with aid on the web. To what degree do the policies and programs of this NGO conform to the material presented in this chapter?

10   Can you find evidence of "pro-poor growth" in a nation undertaking a PRSP, or in any other nation? If so, what conditions were necessary to produce this outcome?

11   Has the Washington Consensus gone "underground" or has it been essentially repudiated?

Notes

1   Foreign aid is defined as the receipt of concessional lending and grant funds, as well as technical assistance. "Concessional lending" involves loans that are received at a discount of 25 percent or more below the normal market rate of interest. Normally, a concessional loan will also have a longer-than-average repayment period, with a "grace" period of several years when no payment of interest or principal is required. A "grant" is aid received which never requires repayment. "Technical assistance" constitutes advice and guidance, as well as training, offered by a donor and received by a developing nation. Most foreign aid is bilateral, that is, direct donor-to-recipient assistance. But some foreign aid comes via the World Bank and the regional multilateral development banks, such as the InterAmerican Development Bank. A third source of foreign aid funds comes from the non-governmental organizations (NGOs), such as Oxfam and others. The NGOs are of growing importance in the distribution of aid; in 1990, they channeled $7.2 billion into the less-developing nations, of which $2.2 billion came from donor governments, and the rest came from funds directly raised by the NGOs.

2   A third pillar of the Bretton Woods conference, the World Trade Organization (WTO), designed to mediate trade disputes and to eliminate trade wars and reduce tariffs among nations, was not ultimately approved. Instead, a looser organization, known as the General Agreement on Tariffs and Trade (GATT), became the means by which trade and tariff disputes were resolved and through which freer trade has been achieved since 1945. Only in 1995 was the WTO finally reborn as a vehicle for managing international trade disputes, following a period in which the world economy had passed through more than a decade of crisis from the debt debacle of the 1980s to the global slow-down of the early 1990s.

3   When members borrow hard currencies under stand-by arrangements, they can have access to 100 percent of their quotas. In addition, such members may be able to access other so-called "Facilities" of the Fund, such that during a three-year period, they could, at a maximum, have access to an amount equivalent to 600 percent of their subscribed quota, through stand-by drawings and special facility loans.

4   It may not, however, be a simple task for a less-developed nation with limited resources and few trained professionals to successfully bargain with the Fund; the IMF has vast resources, which include a staff of 2,600 highly trained professionals, who endeavor to impose the Fund's preferred package of conditions, if possible.

5   "Hard" currencies are those that are readily convertible into other currencies and which are relatively stable in value over time. As a rule, the US dollar and the pound sterling meet these general conditions, but preference for the strongest, or hardest, currencies is subject to change, with the Japanese yen and the German mark being held in high regard in the early 1990s. "Soft" currencies are more volatile in value and are potentially more difficult to convert into hard currencies; in other words, with soft currencies, there is a risk of devaluation which is carried by the holder of such currencies.

6   The continued importance of primary product exports reflects the difficulty, or unwillingness, of less-developed nations to transform their productive and export structures more toward secondary and tertiary commodities. You will remember from Chapter 6 the terms of trade problems that being a primary product exporter and a manufactured good importer can impose on less-developed nations.

7   This is part of the so-called J-curve phenomenon. With devaluation, export income may not grow by much for a time, as a result of the slower response of export sales to the lower unit price of exports, in real terms, that a devaluation implies. Thus total export income may not rise by much very quickly. On the other hand, total expenditure on imports can actually increase after a devaluation, depending on the price elasticities of demand. With higher import prices, if the quantity of imports purchased does not fall by more, in percentage terms, than the price has risen, the import bill will grow. Thus, it is quite possible that a devaluation, in the short term at least, will result in a deterioration of both the trade deficit *and* the current account deficit.

8 The theoretical assumptions and the model employed by the Fund to analyze the difficulties of the borrowing nation are important to explore in any serious assessment of the Fund's activities. Basically, the Fund assumes away the problem of economic development by treating the potential poor borrowing nation *as if* it already had a fully articulated and developed market economy. There is no place for economic dualism in the Fund's analysis; all factors of production are assumed to be fully employed, and there is complete mobility of factors of production within the economy. Lewis's dualism and the reservations of Prebisch and Singer and other developmentalist economists (Chapters 5 and 6) have no role to play in the model employed by the Fund. The Fund's approach largely derives from the large body of work of a little-known Fund economist, Jacques J. Polack, who, in 1943, developed an analysis known as the "Polack Model," which we have described above, albeit in a non-rigorous manner. Readers wishing to have access to Polack's highly influential work (spread over fifty years!) should consult the two-volume work by Polack (1994).

9 In a completely closed economy with no trade, wage repression that leads to an increase in the share of total income going to profits would unambiguously reduce the overall level of output and income, as long as the usual assumption holds that the marginal propensity to consume out of profits (MPC_p) is less than the marginal propensity to consume out of wages (MPC_W).

10 Updating this research through 1993, Killick has determined that of 305 programs examined between 1979 and 1993, 53 percent were never completed (Killick 1995: 60–1).

11 Studies of IMF programs often do not clearly indicate why a given sample of nations has been chosen, or why particular dates have been utilized. Many studies do not adjust for size of the nations involved, or other variables which would permit the results to achieve greater reliability. Furthermore, although the Fund prefers to present its programs as being guided by the principle of "uniformity of treatment," it has often bent the rules regarding conditionality in order to lend to governments which either the Fund or the major donor nations support as a result of their ideological stance or because of their strategic influence. The most recent example of the role which ideology, and even personal ties, can play in determining how the Fund will react to a nation in economic difficulties is that of the $17.8 billion Mexican loan in early 1995. The Fund's managing director, Michael Camdessus, acknowledged that he had become a personal friend of some of the top economic policy-makers in Mexico, particularly Mexico's influential finance minister, and that as a result his professional objectivity regarding Mexico's looming economic disaster had been compromised. Camdessus admitted that the inconsistencies revealed in the Mexican situation were not unique and that the Fund's unwillingness to impose adequate surveillance on Mexico in 1994 pointed to "a global problem with the culture of the Fund" (Gerth and Sciolini 1996: A6).

Given this "political element," quantitative tests of the "effectiveness" of the Fund's programs become more problematic. If uniformity of treatment is violated because of special relationships the IMF forges with some countries, it becomes very difficult to determine on the basis of comparative empirical studies of Fund programs what the general effect of a program may be.

12 This distinction, however, has increasingly been blurred, because the Fund has drawn the conclusion that its stabilization programs have performed badly as a result of their short-term orientation. The Bank has, since the late 1970s, increasingly shared the theoretical perspective of the Fund and has sought to link short-term stabilization programs of the Fund to long-term lending programs at the Bank. When this linkage occurs, it is known as a cross-conditional program.

13 The index makes several other smaller adjustments.

References

Bird, Graham. 2001. "IMF Programs: Do They Work?," *World Development* 29(1): 1849–65.

——. 2004. "The IMF Forever: An Analysis of the Prolonged Use of Fund Resources," *Journal of Development Studies* 40(6): 30–58.

Barneback, Thomas, Anderson Henrik Hasen and Thomas Markussen. 2006. "US Politics and World Bank IDA-Lending," *Journal of Development Studies* 42(5): 772–94.

Bergeron, Suzanne. 2005. *Fragments of Development.* Ann Arbor, Michigan: University of Michigan Press.

Boorman, Jack. 2002. "Interview with Jack Boorman," *IMF Survey* (August 5): 241, 245–8.

Butkiewicz, James and Halit Yanikkaya. 2005. "The Effects of IMF and World Bank Lending on Long-Run Growth," *World Development* 33(3): 371–91.

Center for Global Development. 2007. "Aid." Online at http://cgdev.org/section/initiatives/_active/cdi_components/aid/

Cypher, James. 2001. "Developing Disarticulation within the Mexican Economy," *Latin American Perspectives* 25(6): 11–37.

Dreher, Axel. 2006. "IMF and Economic Growth: The Effect of Programs, Loans and Compliance with Conditionality," *World Development* 34(5): 769–88.

Easterly, William. 2006. *The White Man's Burden*. New York: Penguin Books.

ECLAC. 1994. "Social Panorama of Latin America," *CEPAL News* (July): 1–3.

Fraser, Alastair. 2005. "Poverty Reduction Strategy Papers," *Review of African Political Economy* 32(104/105): 317–40.

George, Susan and Fabrizio Sabelli. 1994. *Faith and Credit: The World Bank's Secular Empire*. London: Westview Press.

Gerth, Jeff and Elaine Sciolini. 1996. "IMF Head: He Speaks and Money Talks," *New York Times* (April 2):1, A6.

Gore, Charles. 2000. "The Rise and Fall of the Washington Consensus as a Paradigm for Developing Countries," *World Development* 28(5): 789–804.

Henshall Momsen, Janet. 1991. *Women and Development in the Third World*. London: Routledge.

Hermes, Niels and Robert Lesink. 2000. "Changing the Conditions for Development Aid: A New Paradigm?," *Journal of Development Studies* 37 (August): 1–16.

Hjertholm, Peter and Howard White. 2000. "Foreign Aid in Historical Perspective," pp. 80–102 in Finn Tarp and Peter Hjertholm (eds.), *Foreign Aid and Development*. London: Routledge.

IMF. 1995a. "Coordinated Approach to Multilateral Debt," *IMF Survey* (October 23): 338–9.

——. 1995b. "Record IMF-Supported Adjustment Programmes Assessed," *IMF Survey* (July 31): 233–6.

——. 1995c. "Strengthening IMF Surveillance," *IMF Survey* (May 22): 153–6.

——. 1995d. *IMF Survey* (July 31).

——. 1995e. "IMF Provides Financing for Macroeconomic and Structural Adjustment," *IMF Survey* (September Supplement): 10–14.

——. 1996. "Official Financing Fell in 1994," *IMF Survey* (January 8): 1, 7–8.

——. 2001. "IMF Financial Facilities," *IMF Survey* (September Supplement): 12–13.

——. 2002. "New Conditionality Guidelines," *IMF Survey* (December 16): 390–1.

——. 2003b. "Past IMF Disbursements and Repayments," IMF (March): file:///D:/Input/2000a4cf/www.imf.org/external/tre/tad/extrepl.cfm.

——. 2007a. *Final Report of the External Review Committee on Bank-Fund Collaboration* (February): http://www.imf.org/external/np/pp/eng/2007/022307. pdf

——. 2007b. *IMF Financial Activities September 20, 2007*. Online at http://www.imf.org/external/np/tre/activity/2007/092007.htm

——. 2007c. *Poverty Reduction Strategy Papers* (September). Online at http://www.imf.org/external/np/exr/facts/prsp/htm

——. 2007d. *Final Report of the External Review Committee on Bank Fund Collaboration*. Washington: IMF, 1–58. Online at http://www.imf.org/external/np/pp/eng/2007/022307.pdf

IMF and World Bank. 2005. *2005 Review of the Poverty Reduction Strategy Approach*. Washington: IMF, 1–114.Online at http://www.imf.org/external/np/pp/eng/2005/091905p.pdf

Kahn, Joseph. 2002. "World Bank in Report Defends the Use of Aid," *New York Times* (March 12): W1, W7.

Kapur, Devesh. 2002. "The Changing Anatomy of Governance," pp. 54–75 in Jonathan Pincus and Jeffery Winters (eds.), *Reinventing the World Bank*. Ithaca: Cornell University Press.

Killick, Tony. 1995. *IMF Programmes in Developing Countries*. London: Routledge.

Killick, Tony, Moazzam Malik, and Marcus Manuel. 1992. "What Can We Know about the Effects of IMF Programmes?," *World Economy* 20 (September): 575–97.

Malaluan, Jenia Joy Chavez and Shalmali Guttal. 2003. "Poverty Reduction Strategy Papers." Bangkok, Thailand: Focus on the Global South. Online at http://focusweb.org/publications/2003/PRSP_2003.pdf

Mosley, Paul, Jane Harrigan, and John Toye. 1991. *Aid and Power: The World Bank and Policy-Based Lending*, 2 vols. London: Routledge.

Pastor, Manuel. 1987. "The Effects of IMF Programmes in the Third World," *World Development* 15 (February): 249–62.

Pauly, Louis W. 1994. "Promoting a Global Economy: The Normative Role of the International Monetary Fund," pp. 204–15 in Richard Stubbs and Geoffrey Underhill (eds.), *Political Economy and the Changing Global Order*. New York: St. Martin's Press.

Pincus, Jonathan and Jeffery Winters. 2002. "Reinventing the World Bank," pp. 1–25 in Jonathan Pincus and Jeffery Winters (eds.), *Reinventing the World Bank*. Ithaca: Cornell University Press.

Polack, Jacques J. 1994. *Economic Theory and Financial Policy*. Aldershot: Edward Elgar.

Preworski, Adam and James Vreeland. 2000. "The Effect of IMF Programs on Economic Growth," *Journal of Development Economics* 62: 385–421.

Radelet, Steve. 2006. "Reply to Easterly: Evidence beats Rhetoric every Time." Online at http://www.cato-unbound.org/2006/04/09/steve-radlet/evidence-beats-rhetoric/

Ravallion, Martin. 2004. "Pro-Poor Growth." Washington: World Bank, 1–36. Online at http://siteresources.worldbank.org/INTPGI/Resources/15174_Ravallion_PPG_Primer.pdf

Rodrik, Dani. 2006. "Goodbye Washington Consensus, Hello Washington Confusion," *Journal of Economic Literature*, XLIV (December): 973–87.

Sachs, Jeffery. 2006. *The End of Poverty*. New York: Penguin Books.

Sanford, Jonathan. 2002. "World Bank: IDA Loans or IDA Grants?," *World Development* 30(5): 741–62.

SAPRIN (Structural Adjustment Participatory Review International Network). 2002. "The Policy Roots of Economic Crisis and Poverty." (April) SAPRIN. Online at http://www.saprin.org/ SAPRI_Findings.pdf

Sheehy, Thomas. 1994. "The Index of Economic Freedom: A Tool for Real Reform of Foreign Aid," *The Heritage Foundation Backgrounder* No. 986 (May 6): 1–18.

Stiglitz, Joseph. 2002. *Globalization and Its Discontents*. New York: W.W. Norton & Co.

UN (United Nations). 2007. *World Economic Situation and Prospect 2007*. New York: United Nations.

UNDP (United Nations Development Programme). 1993. *Human Development Report 1993*. New York: Oxford University Press.

——. 2002. *Human Development Report 2002*. Oxford: Oxford University Press.

——. 2006. *Human Development Report 2006*. Oxford: Oxford University Press.

Vreeland, James. 2002. "The Effect of IMF Programs on Labor," *World Development* 30(1): 121–39.

World Bank 1993. *World Development Report 1993*. New York: Oxford University Press.

——. 1984. (Office of Environmental and Health Affairs). *Environmental Policies and Procedures of the World Bank*. Washington, D.C: World Bank.

——. 1995a. *The World Bank Annual Report 1995*. Washington, D.C: World Bank.

——. 1995b. *World Development Report 1995*. New York: Oxford University Press.

——. 1998. *Assessing Aid*. Washington, D.C: World Bank.

——. 2003. *World Development Report, 2003*. Washington, D.C: World Bank.

World Bank and the International Monetary Fund. 2005. *Synthesis, 2005. Review of the PRS Approach*. Online at http://siteresources.worldbank.org/INTPRS1/Resources/PRSP-Review/Synthesis_2005_PRS_Review.pdf

Index

Focus boxes are marked with a capital F after the page number: e.g. BNDES 286–7F. Tables (t), figures (f) and notes (n) are marked after the locator: e.g. children, mortality rates 403t12.4; floating exchange rates 516f15.3; current account deficits, 552n10. Equations are noted in brackets after the locator: e.g. aggregate demand function 250(8.3).

The Development Economics Reader

Edited by **Giorgio Secondi,** Occidental College, USA

This book collects the most recent and authoritative contributions to the field of development economics and provides a wealth of pedagogical materials that make it ideal for classroom use. As countries such as China and India are experiencing tremendous economic growth, other parts of the world such as sub-Saharan Africa remain mired in poverty and unable to raise standards of living. This volume helps readers understand why poor countries are poor and why designing policies to reduce poverty is such a challenging task.

Contemporary and highly accessible, *The Development Economics Reader* is an invaluable resource for all students of the discipline.

Contents: 1. Introduction: Economic Growth, Economic Development and Human Development 2. Geography, Institutions and Governance 3. Beyond Growth: Inequality and Poverty 4. People in Development: Population Growth, Health, Education, and Child Labor 5. Agriculture, the Environment, and Sustainable Development 6. Financial Markets and Microcredit 7. Globalization and Financial Crises 8. Foreign Aid and Debt Relief

April 2008: 246x174: 584pp
Hb: 978-0-415-77156-6: **£85.00 $170.00**
Pb: 978-0-415-77157-3: **£30.99 $61.95**

Routledge books are available from all good bookshops, or may be ordered by calling Taylor and Francis Direct Sales on +44(0)1235 400524 (credit card orders) For more information please contact Gemma Anderson on +44 (0) 207 017 6192 or email gemma.anderson@tandf.co.uk

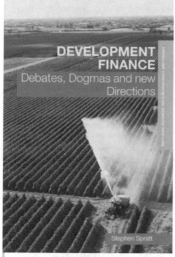

CL

338. 9 CYP